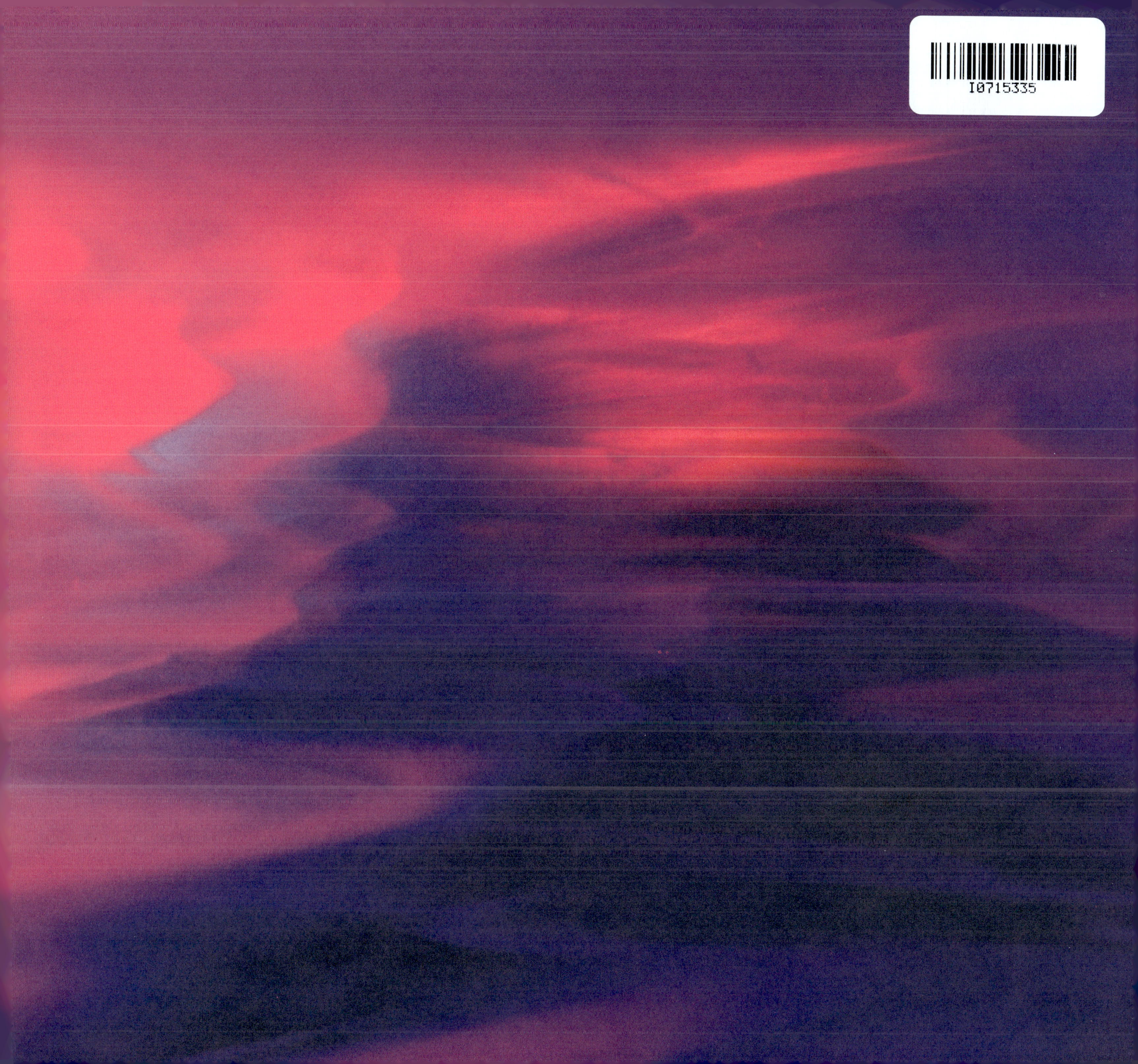
I0715335

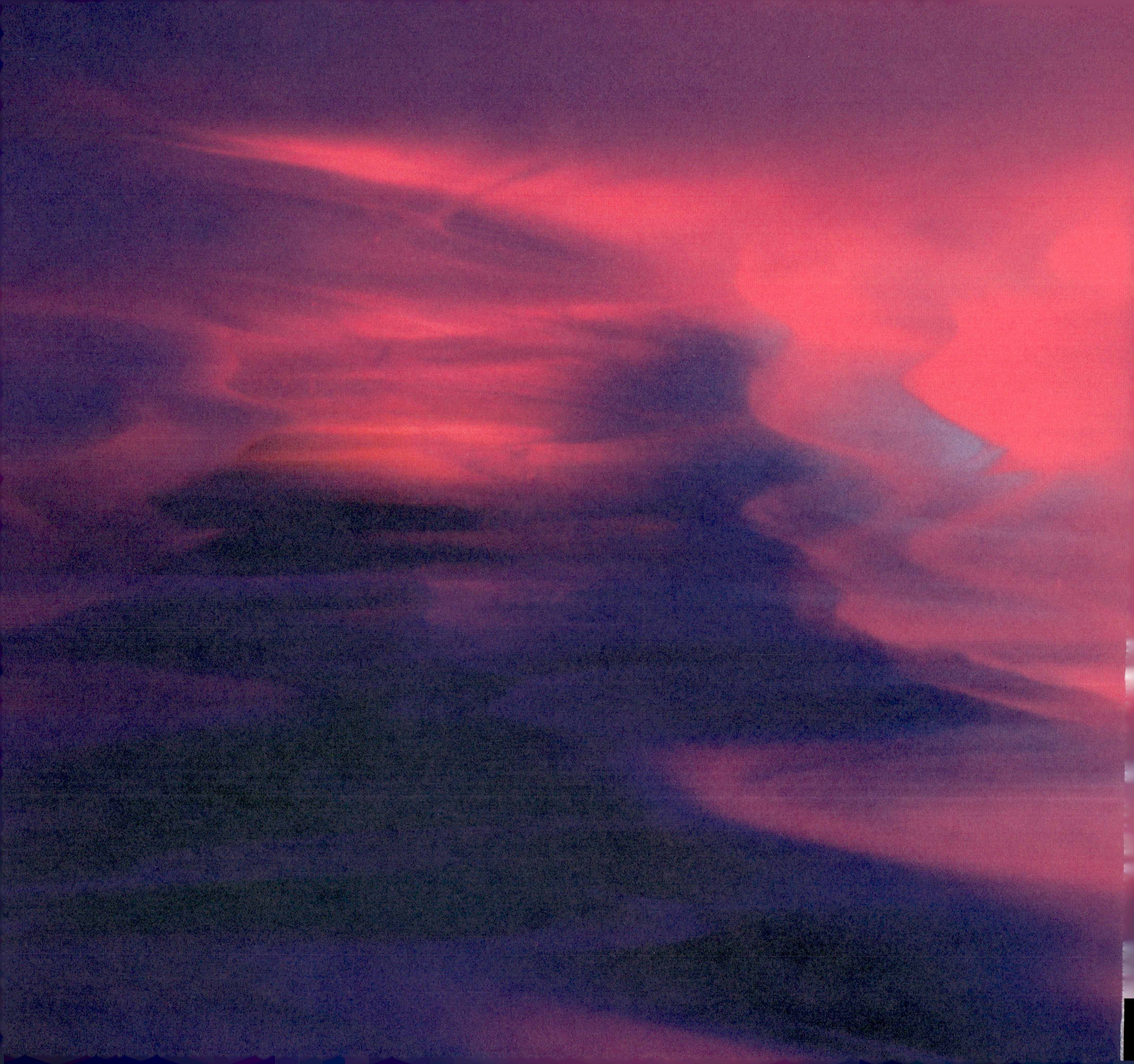

STAR TREK II™

THE WRATH OF KHAN

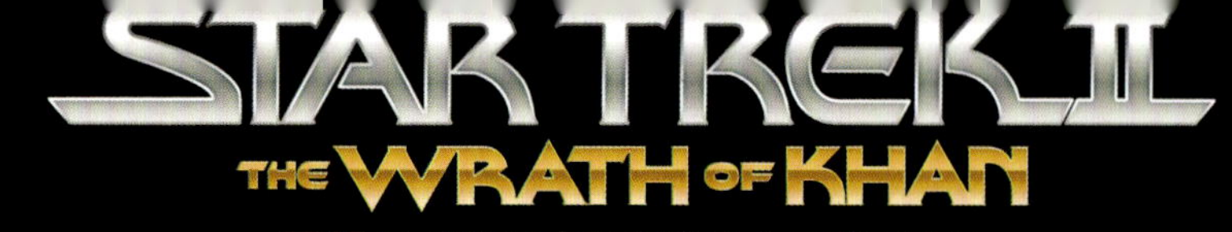

ISBN: 9781789099751
E-BOOK ISBN: 9781803360775

Published by

Titan Books

A division of Titan Publishing Group Ltd

144 Southwark St

London

SE1 0UP

www.titanbooks.com

First edition: September 2023

10 9 8 7 6 5 4 3 2

Page 70: Costume Sketch of William Shatner as Admiral Kirk in the Paramount Pictures Production of '*Star Trek II: The Wrath of Khan*', 1982, by Robert Fletcher 2023©Photo Scala, Florence. Digital Image Museum Associates/LACMA/Art Resource NY/Scala, Florence

All material from the Papers of Nicholas Meyer – The University of Iowa Libraries used with permission.

Every effort has been made to contact the copyright holders of all photographs used.

Did you enjoy this book? We love to hear from our readers.
Please e-mail us at: readerfeedback@titanemail.com or
write to Reader Feedback at the above address.

To receive advance information, news, competitions, and exclusive offers online, please sign up for the Titan newsletter on our website: www.titanbooks.com

THANKS

Titan Books would like to thank a few individuals, in addition to those people included in the authors' Acknowledgments, for their help in sourcing visual material for this book: Bailey Adolph, Chris Hawkinson (ILM), Cristina D'Alessandro (Scala Group Spa), Frank Ordaz, Mary Haegert (Houghton Library, Harvard University), Peter Balestrieri (University of Iowa Libraries), Steve Lansdale (Heritage Auctions)

STAR TREK II

THE WRATH OF KHAN

THE MAKING OF THE CLASSIC FILM

JOHN TENUTO & MARIA JOSE TENUTO

TITANBOOKS

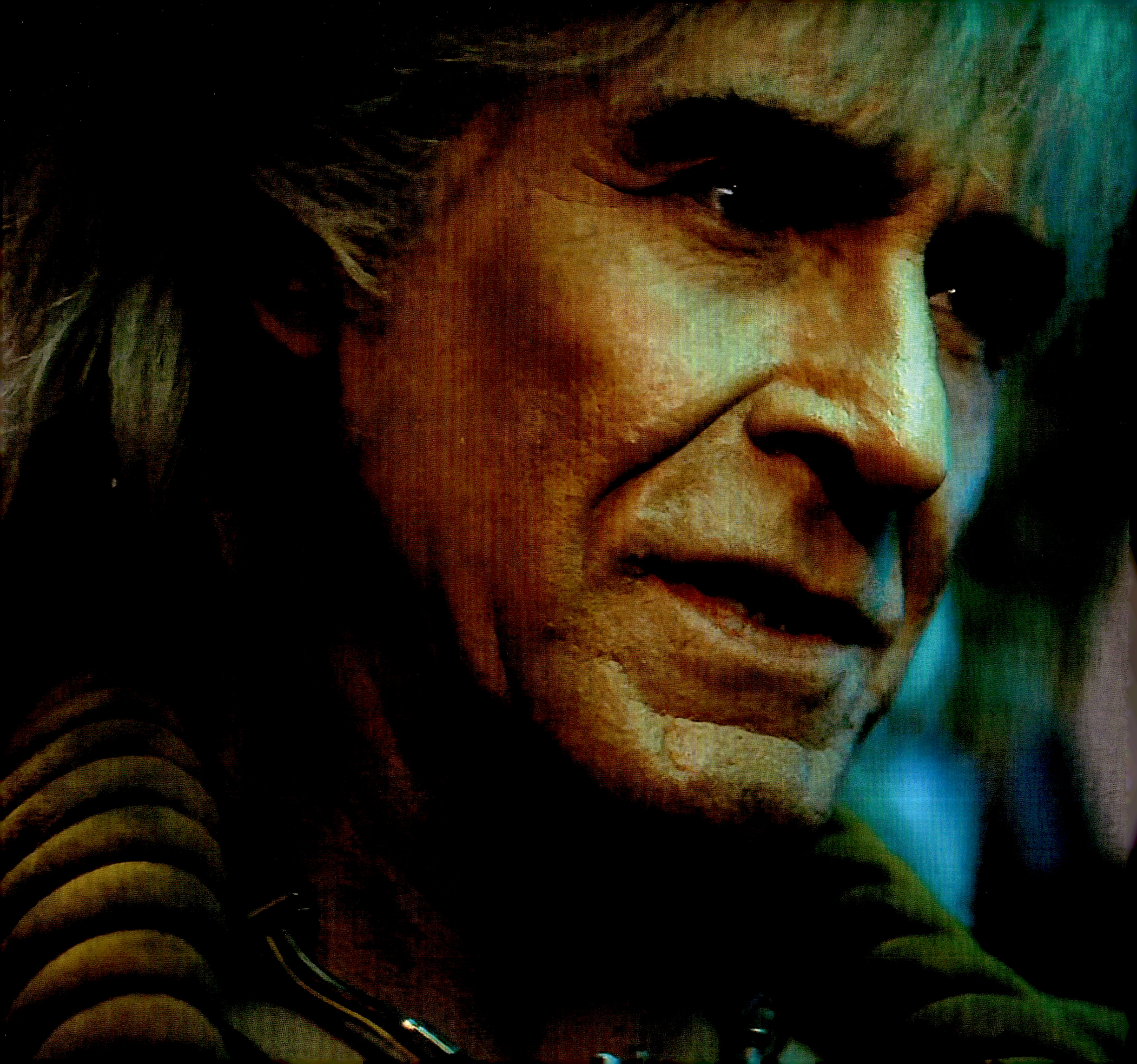

CONTENTS

FOREWORD

As the daughter of the late Leonard Nimoy, I had many opportunities to watch my dad perform throughout his life. Seeing him on television, film, and stage was one of my greatest joys growing up. I realized very early on in childhood that my dad was a busy man, and if I wanted to spend more time with him, I'd have to join him on his life's journey in the entertainment world. I admired his undeniable talent and his ability to capture different characters. His performances were strong and engaging and his capacity to memorize entire musicals seemed effortless. Needless to say, I enjoyed every moment being a part of his adventure.

When John Tenuto, a college sociology professor, writer, and *Star Trek* aficionado, reached out asking if I'd be willing to write the foreword for this book, I was honored and thrilled. John, along with his wife, Maria Jose Tenuto, have created a time capsule filled with memories and photos that are near and dear to my heart. I was on set during production of *Star Trek II: The Wrath of Khan*, and most importantly, I witnessed my dad play out one of the most unforgettable scenes in *Star Trek* history.

The persona of the beloved Vulcan, Mr. Spock, was adored throughout time, beginning with the original *Star Trek* TV series in the late sixties, through the *Star Trek* franchised films, starting with *Star Trek: The Motion Picture*. After the first film received mixed reviews from both critics and the fans, my dad, who was involved in other projects at the time, decided he would not participate in

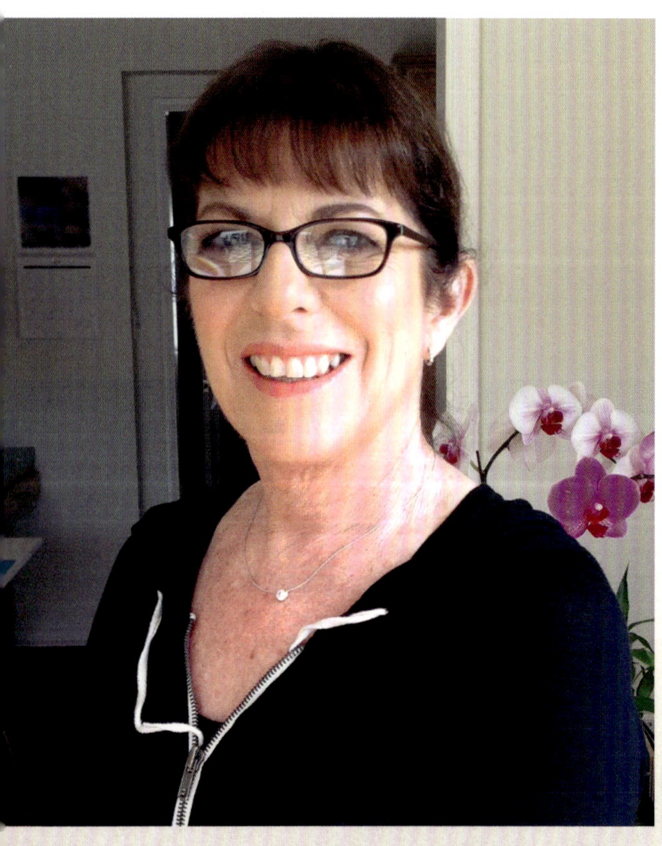

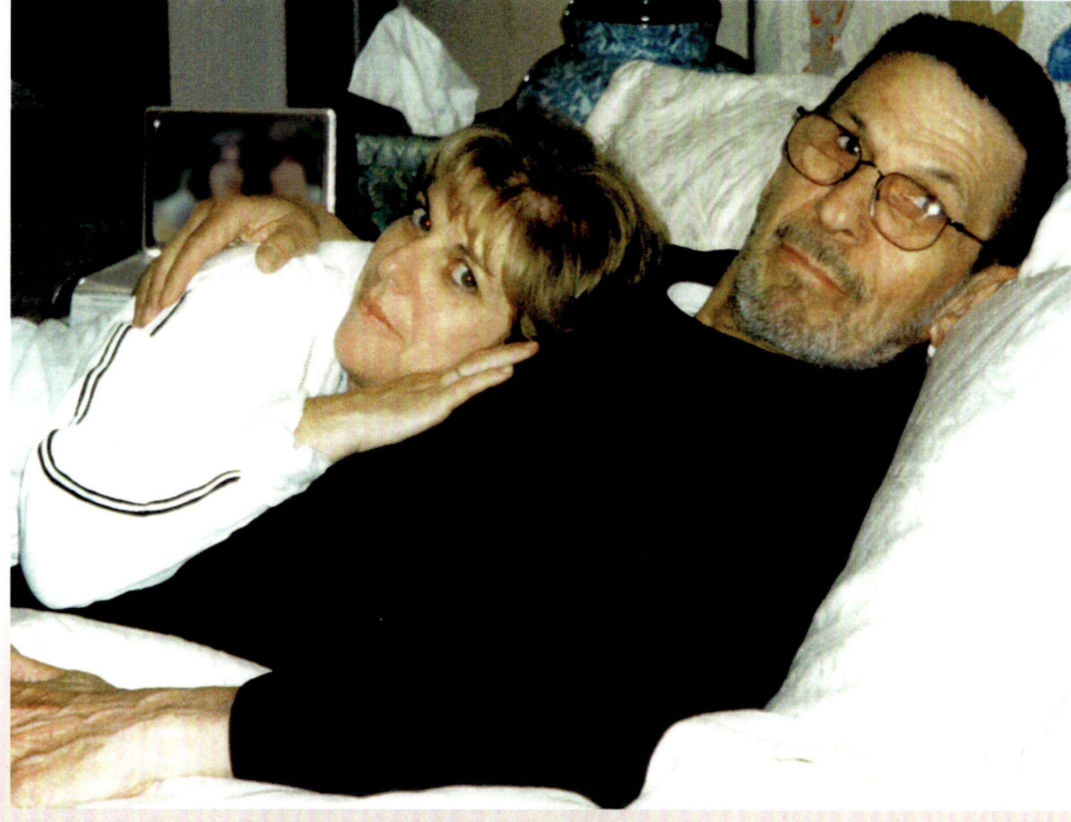

LEFT AND FAR LEFT: Julie Nimoy now and with her father, Leonard, in the late nineties. Images courtesy of Julie Nimoy and David Knight.

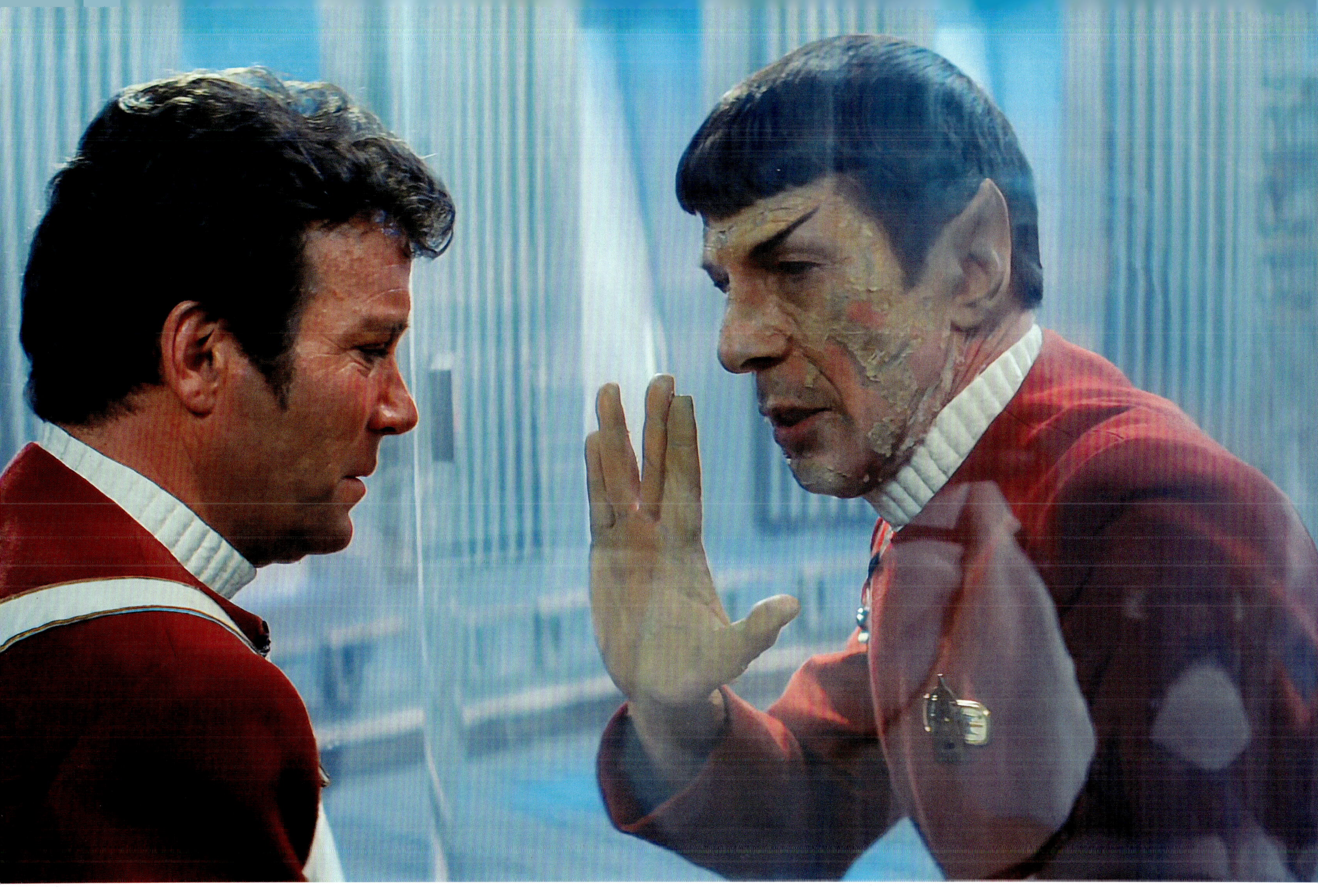

any more *Star Trek* movies. It wasn't until he was persuaded by Paramount Pictures, who promised him that Spock's character would end up having a dramatic death scene, that he agreed to appear in *Star Trek II: The Wrath of Khan*.

On the day of Spock's death scene, I was aware that dad was deep in thought during our drive to the studio. We didn't speak the entire way, as I knew how difficult it would be for him to finally let go of the character he loved. I was sitting with the crew and cast members while Spock played out the scene with Kirk. I felt a combination of pride and sadness as I watched Spock perform a selfless act of humanity by saving the *Enterprise* and its crew. My dad put his heart and soul into the film. The cast and crew were so in awe of his powerful scene that there wasn't a dry eye on the sound stage.

LLAP.

Julie Nimoy
Executive Producer, *Remembering Leonard Nimoy*
January 2023

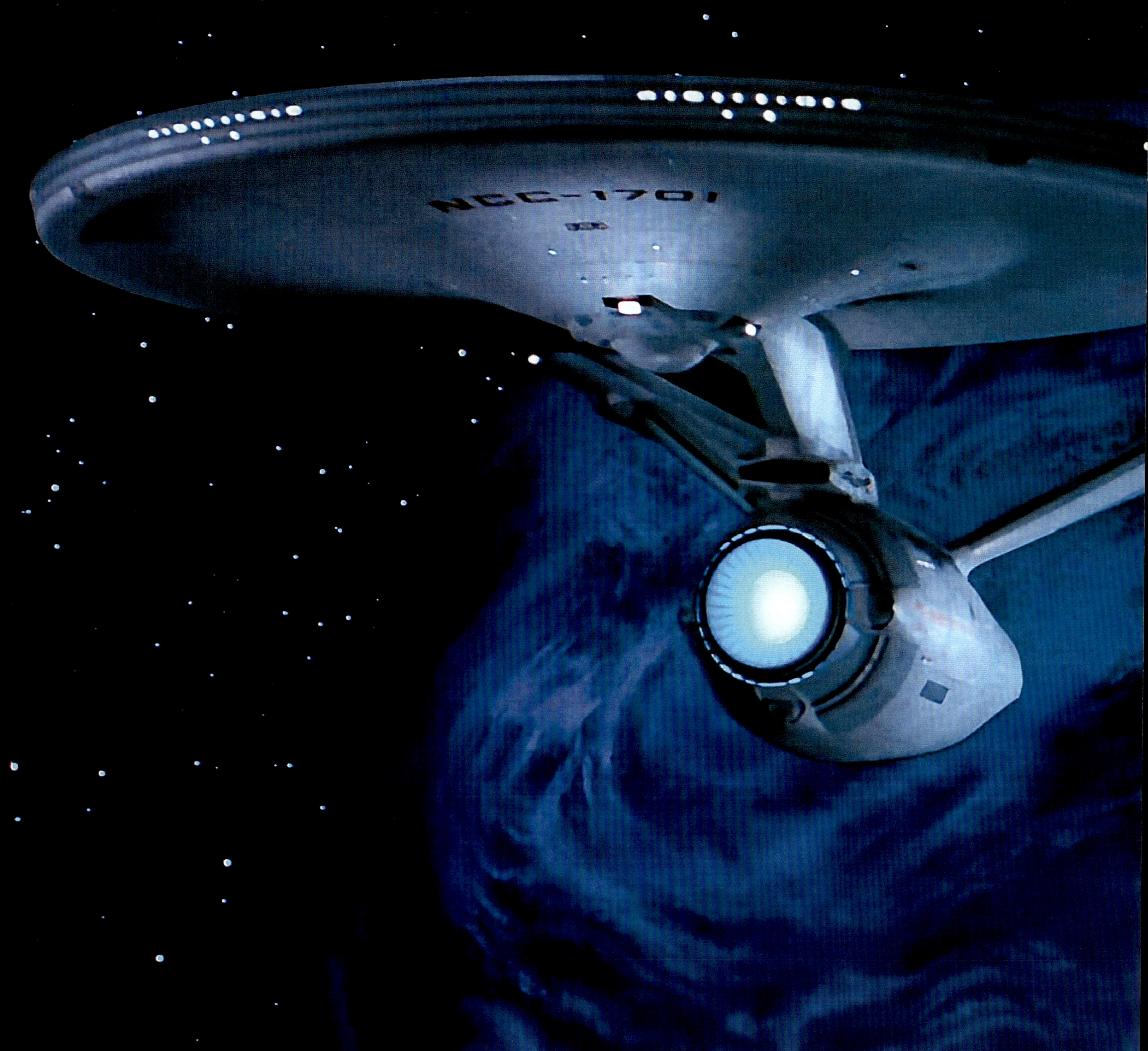
NCC-1701

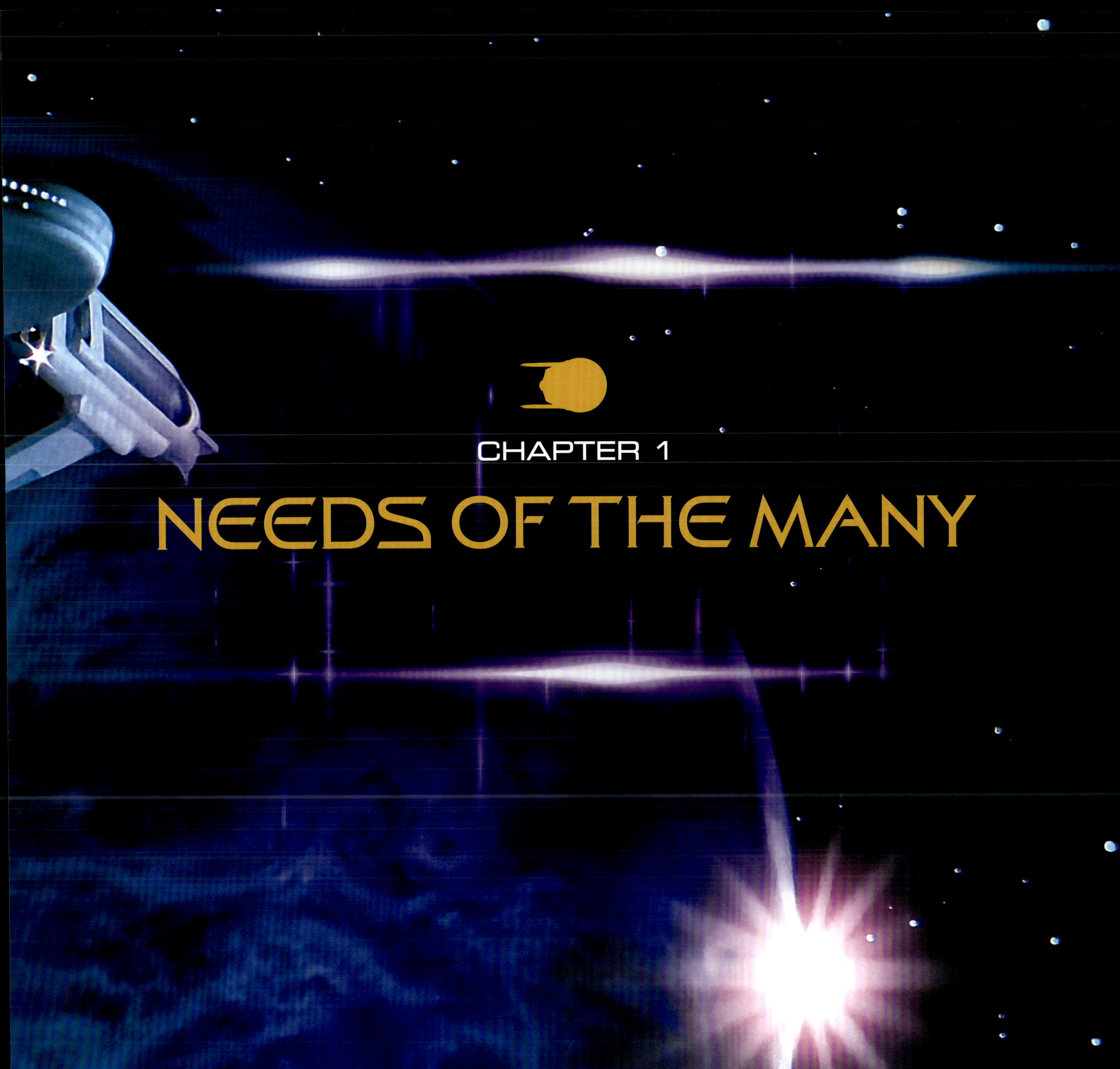

CHAPTER 1
NEEDS OF THE MANY

HARVE BENNETT, EXECUTIVE PRODUCER

In the summer of 1969, as producer of the television show *The Mod Squad*, Harve Bennett had beaten *Star Trek* in the ratings. By the fall of 1980, he was being asked to save it.

When Bennett was invited to a meeting at the office of Barry Diller, Chairman and Chief Executive Officer of Paramount Pictures Corporation, he presumed it was to discuss ideas for developing new dramatic series. It was a safe presumption. Only two weeks before, Bennett had signed a contract with Paramount Television to create exactly that kind of programming. That the meeting was actually to determine the future direction needed for *Star Trek* was the first of many surprises for Bennett.

Another surprise was who was at the meeting. Diller and Bennett were being joined by no less than Charles G. Bluhdorn, Chairman of Gulf and Western Industries, Inc., the parent company of Paramount, and the owner of the *Star Trek* franchise. There was no one more powerful at Paramount, and few more powerful in Hollywood. Also participating

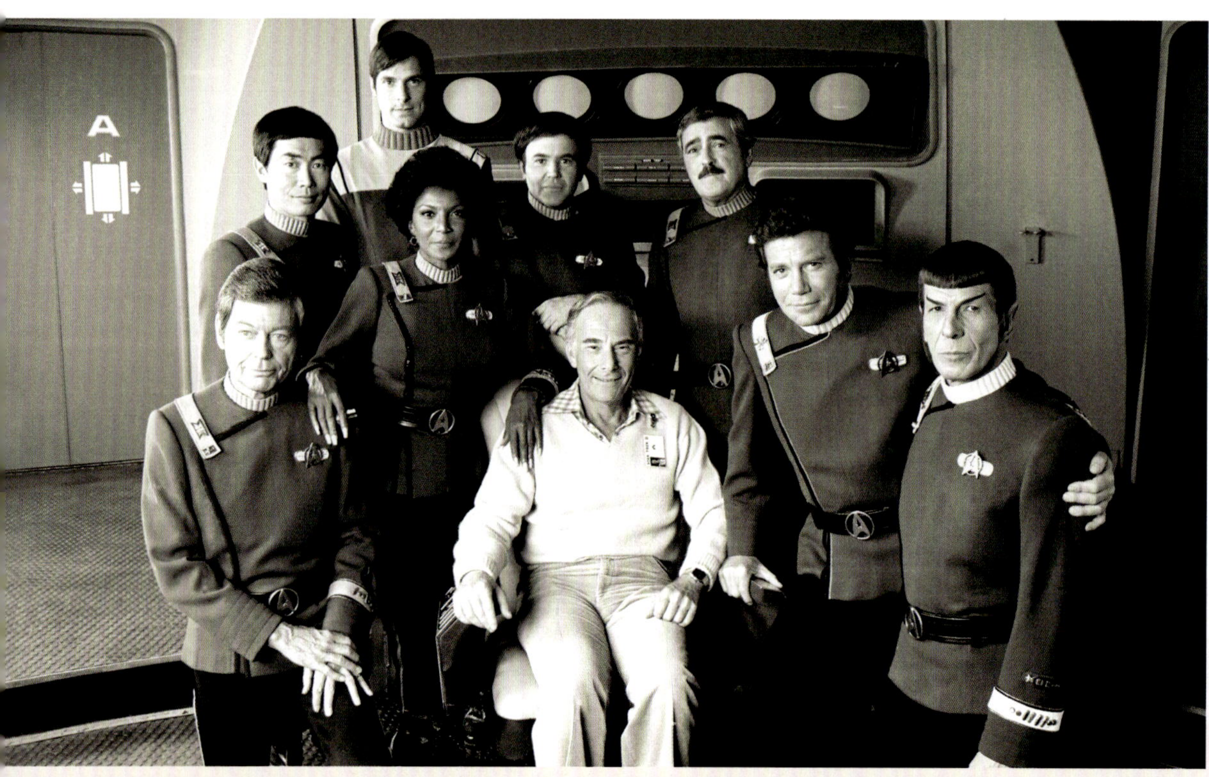

ABOVE: As difficult as the road was from the original series to *Star Trek: The Motion Picture*, the production of *Star Trek II: The Wrath of Khan* was equally challenging. Script problems, technology limitations, fan protests, and time and budget constraints were so constant that Bennett (front & center) described "this entire eighteen months as a series of minefields. Nothing was easy."[11]

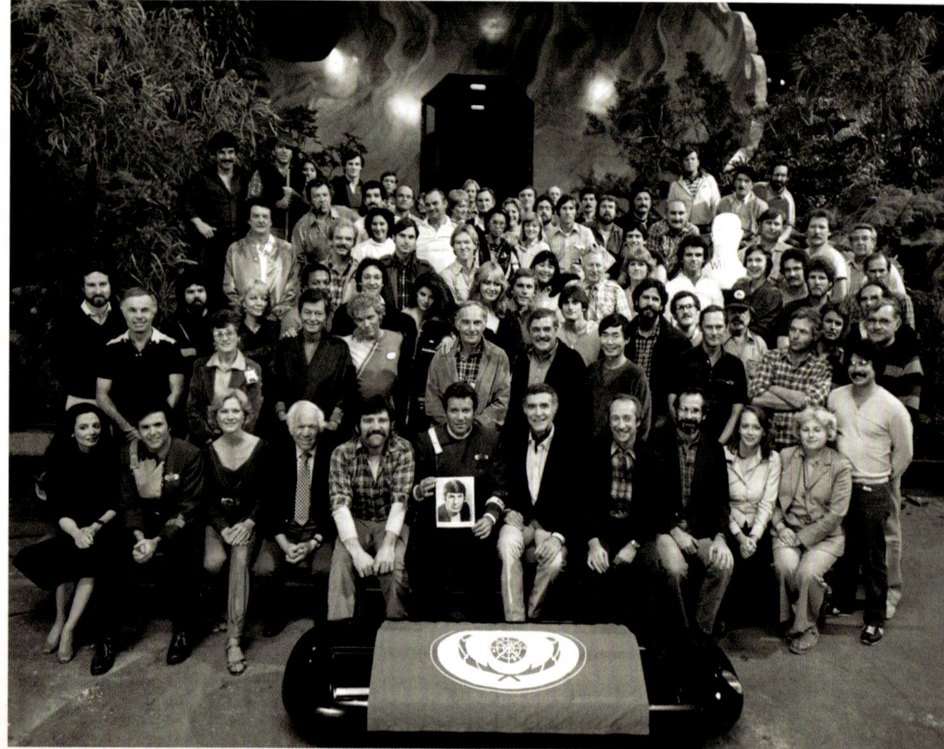

ABOVE & OPPOSITE: As a sly wink of the eye, Spock's photon torpedo tube is placed center stage in honor of Nimoy's character. These cast and crew photographs are the only known images of Shatner and Montalban together on set as the two actors never acted directly with each other during filming.

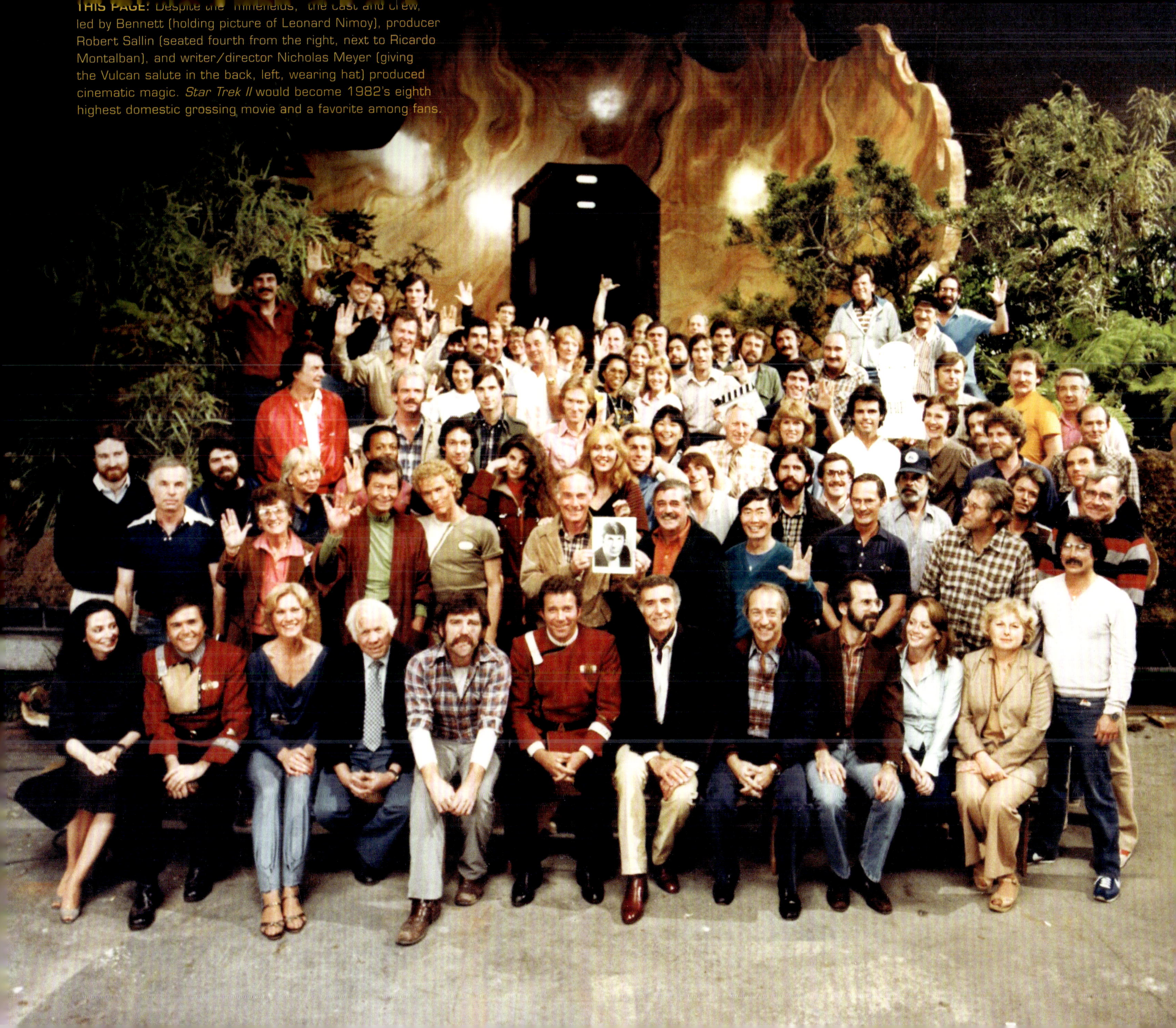

THIS PAGE: Despite the "minefields," the cast and crew,
led by Bennett (holding picture of Leonard Nimoy), producer
Robert Sallin (seated fourth from the right, next to Ricardo
Montalban), and writer/director Nicholas Meyer (giving
the Vulcan salute in the back, left, wearing hat) produced
cinematic magic. *Star Trek II* would become 1982's eighth
highest domestic grossing movie and a favorite among fans.

⭐ HARVE BENNETT

Born Harve Bennett Fischman in Chicago on August 17, 1930, Bennett got his start in show business as one of the five kid panelists on the popular game show *Quiz Kids*. With a reported IQ of 175, his love of history made him one of the most popular stars on the program. Bennett began his enthusiasm for storytelling because *Quiz Kids* enabled him to meet many celebrities and to find a productive use for the 16mm camera his uncle had given him for his birthday. "Everywhere I went, I took my movie camera and shot scenarios and different events and famous people. I got stuff of Franklin Roosevelt shaking hands with us as well as many other greats and near greats of the time. That's the way I really got my first camera experience."[10]

After service in the United States Army, Bennett graduated from the University of California, Los Angeles film school and began his television production career at CBS, working with television legend Johnny Carson. He would go on to produce some of the biggest television shows of the 1960s and '70s, including *The Mod Squad*, *The Six Million Dollar Man*, and *The Bionic Woman*. It is Bennett's voice that begins the famous opening credits of *The Six Million Dollar Man*, "Steve Austin, astronaut, a man barely alive," before actor Richard Anderson (who played Oscar Goldman) takes over the narration. In 1976, Bennett would help pioneer the television miniseries format with his production of *Rich Man, Poor Man*.

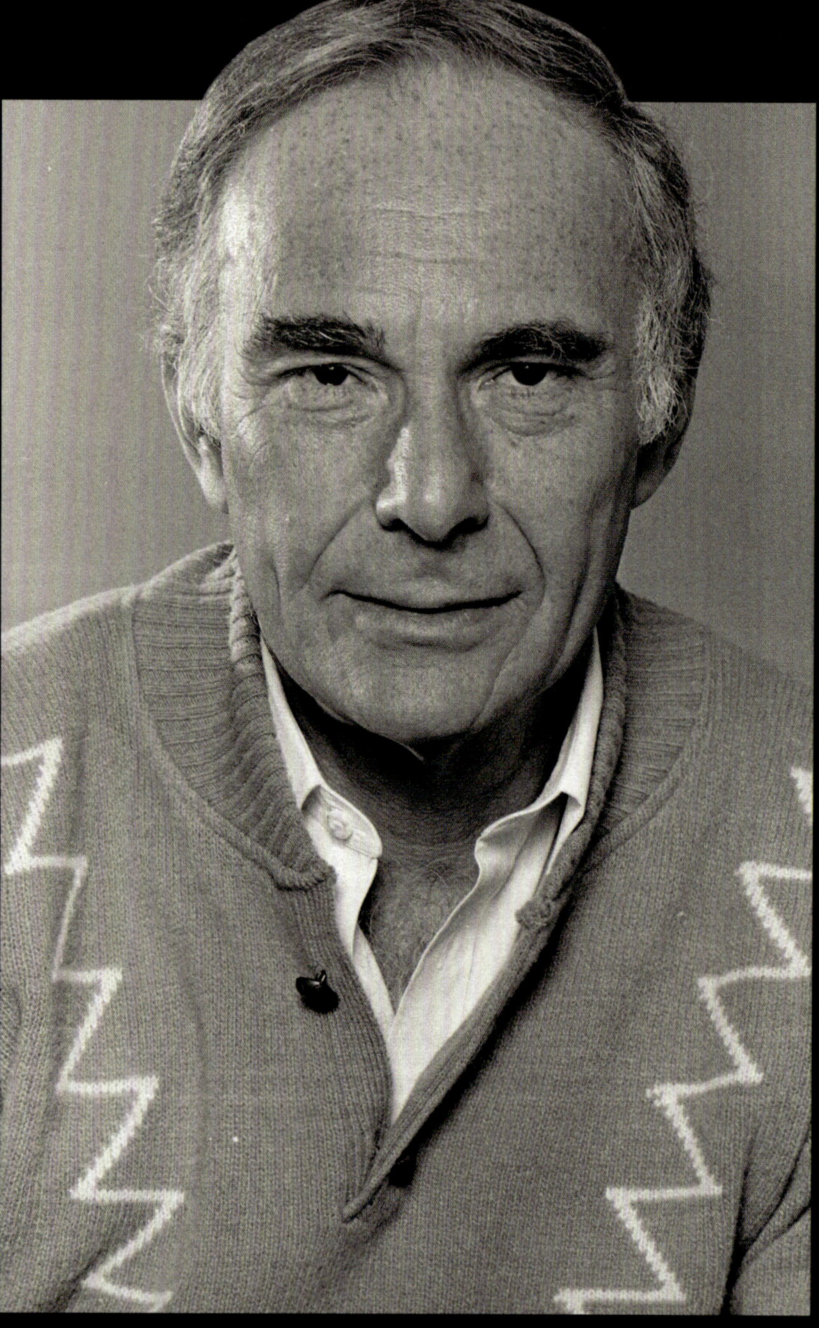

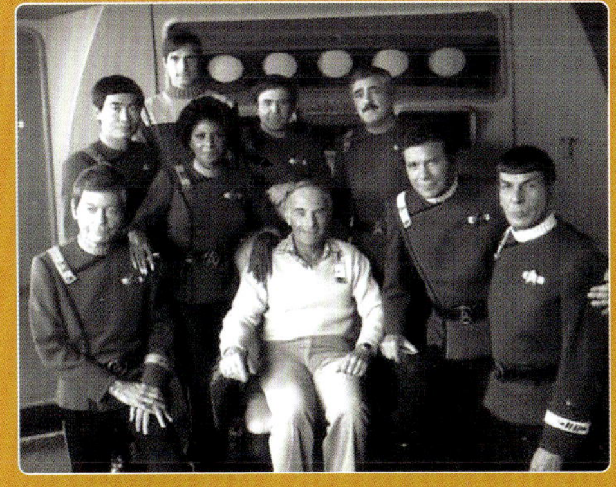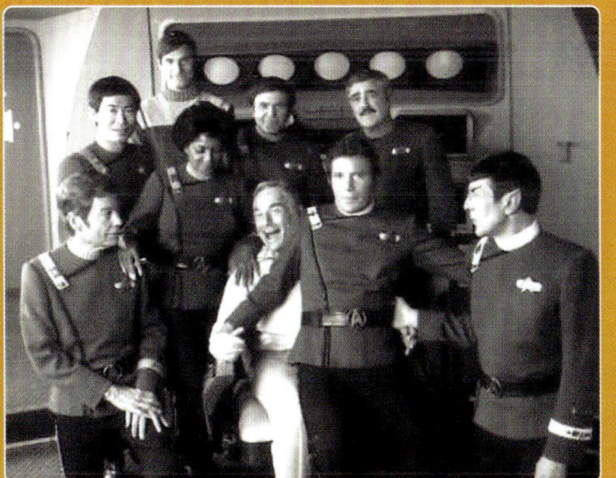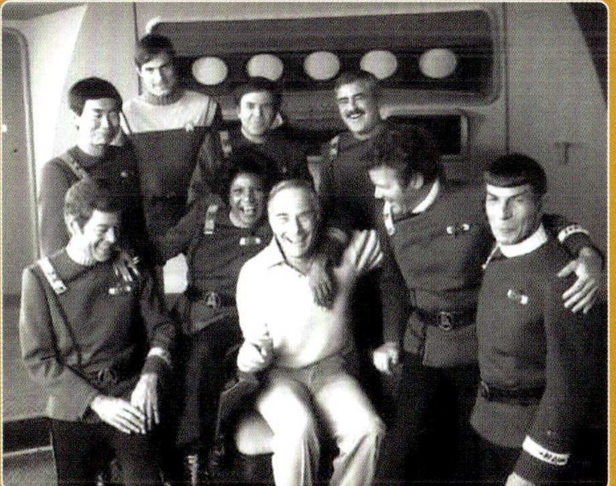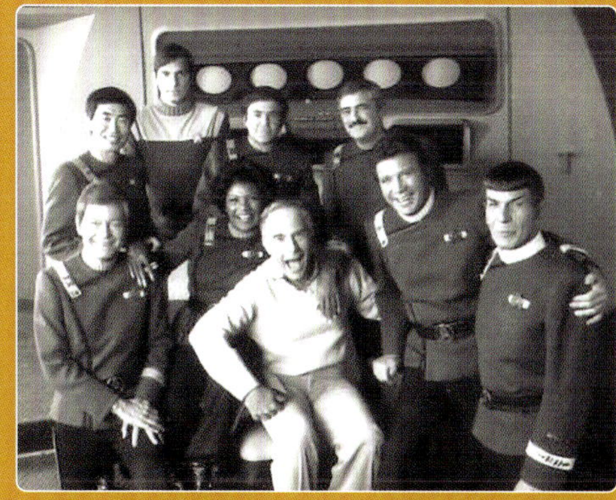
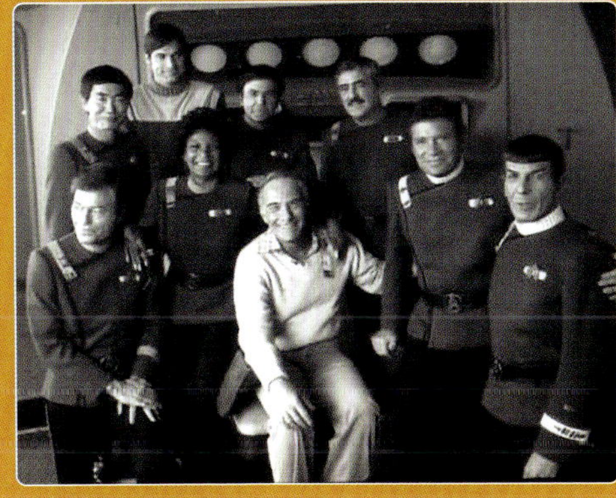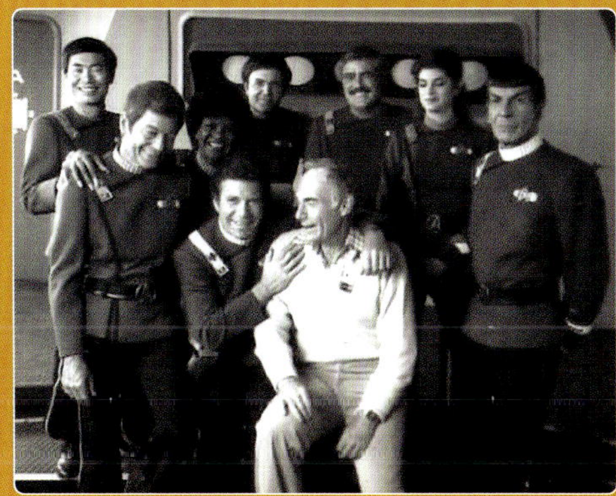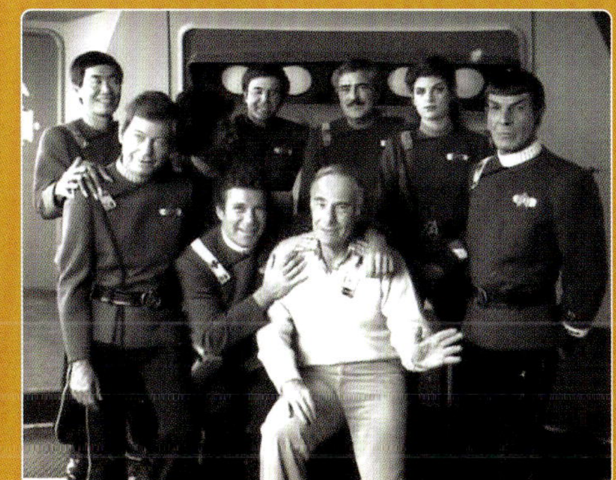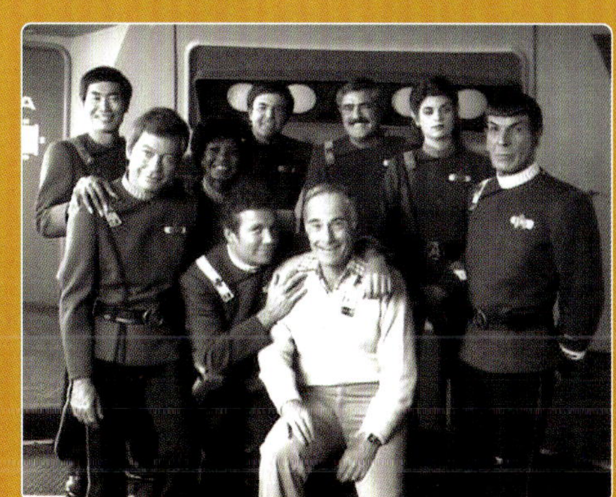

were Chief Operations Officer Michael Eisner and President of Production Jeffrey Katzenberg, the team that had been responsible for 1979's *Star Trek: The Motion Picture*.

Deserved or not, the general feeling at the studio was that the first *Star Trek* movie had been a successful failure. In the success category were the domestic box office returns of $82 million, international grosses totaling another $57 million, lucrative licensing fees, and the pre-sale of the film to ABC for eventual network television broadcast. It had been an unprecedented, herculean accomplishment to resurrect a decade-old cancelled TV show as a major motion picture. In the failure category were the troubled production and budget overruns that eventually cost the studio nearly $45 million. *Star Trek: The Motion Picture* had the dubious distinction of being listed as the highest over budgeted film by the *Guinness Book of Records* (acknowledging at the time, however, that *Superman: The Movie* may have actually cost more[1]). Never mind reality, the displeasing reputation had already been established. Adding insult to injury, many journalists had been critical. Derek Malcolm, reviewer for the British newspaper *The Guardian*, called it "*Star Trek*, the motionless picture,"[2] referring to a perceived overemphasis on special effects.

While ultimately profitable and a certified box office champion, *Star Trek: The Motion Picture* had failed to ignite the enthusiasm thought necessary for *Star Trek* to become an ongoing winner for the studio.

Bluhdorn's instinct was to want a sequel despite protestations from others at Paramount, but he wanted it made under certain conditions, including the proviso that the production be more cost efficient. Whatever form it was going to eventually take, the sequel would be produced under the Paramount Television banner, rather than the motion picture unit, to control costs. Hence, the inclusion of Bennett. Bluhdorn's instincts usually proved correct. After emigrating to the United States in 1942 from Austria, Bluhdorn went from a $60-a-week employee at an import-export company to a millionaire by the age of thirty. Under his ownership, Paramount thrived, producing such critical and commercial achievements as *The Godfather* (1972), *Chinatown* (1974), and *Grease* (1978). He had watched closely during the 1970s as fans generated an unparalleled enthusiasm for *Star Trek* after its cancellation, with sold-out conventions numbering in the thousands, brisk sales of

---

1. For all footnotes, see pages 190-191.

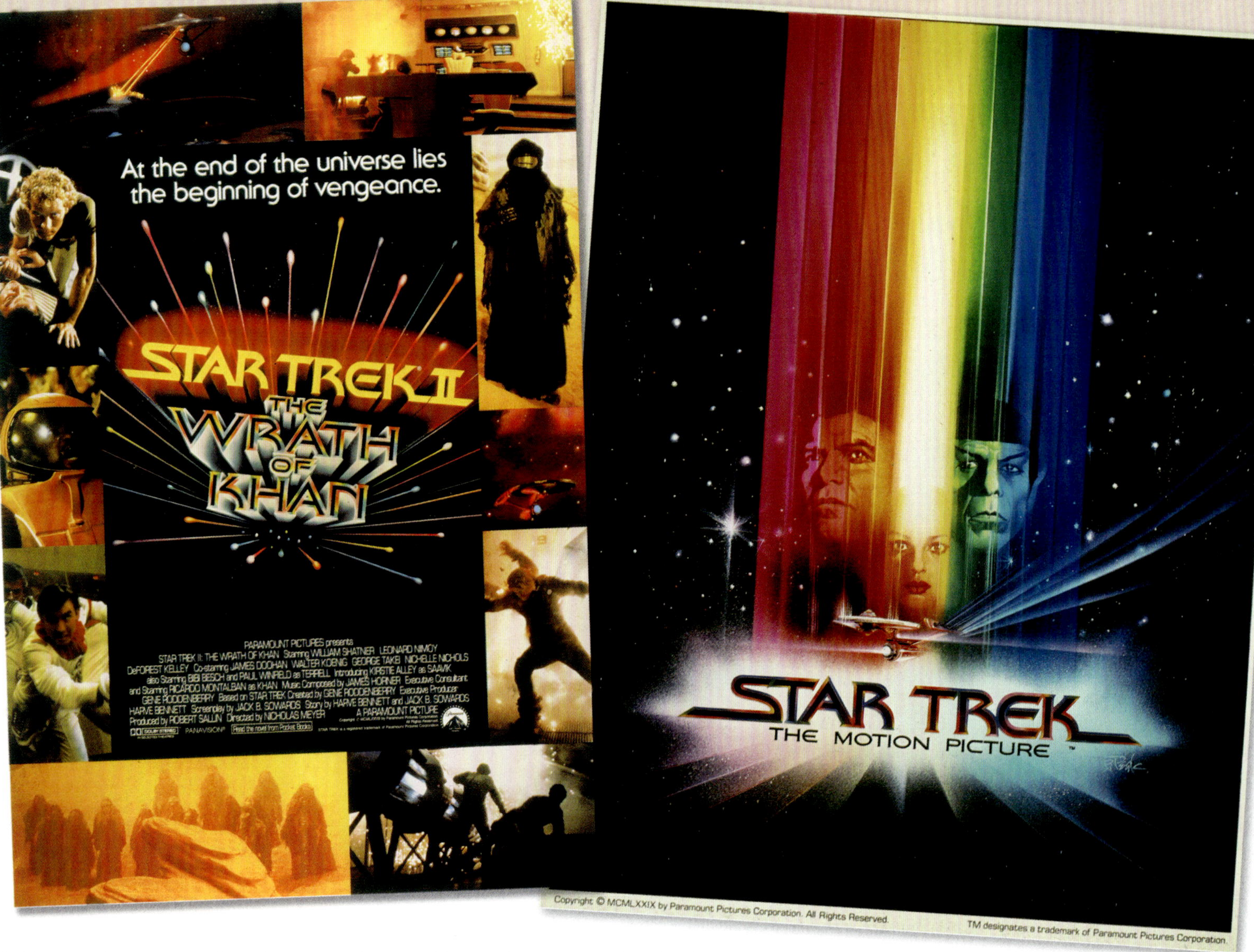

books and merchandise, and high ratings for the show in syndicated markets, sometimes beating new network programming.

The no-nonsense Bluhdorn got right to the point as the meeting started. Asking Bennett, "Did you see *Star Trek: The Motion Picture*?"

"Yes," answered Bennett.

"What did you think of it?"

"I thought it was boring."

Bluhdorn then turned to Eisner, and with his notorious candor, joked, "See? By you, bald is sexy!" referencing the character of Ilia from *Star Trek: The Motion Picture*.

Turning again to Bennett, Bluhdorn queried, "Can you make a better picture?"

"Yes."

"Can you make it for less than $45 *bleeping* million?"

"Where I come from, I could make three or four pictures for that."

"Then do it."[3]

Star Trek would be given one more chance, but without its creator, Gene Roddenberry, in his customary role. Until the spring of 1980, Roddenberry had been generating ideas for a possible sequel, but by the time of the Bennett/Bluhdorn meeting, Roddenberry had been given an executive consultant role and removed from active production responsibilities. The marching orders to Bennett were that Roddenberry's opinions should be considered, but that he was not beholden to them. It would be upon Bennett's decisions that the future of *Star Trek* turned. This would become the first of many challenges that Bennett and his crew would face during the production of the sequel. "It's hard to do another man's legend," Bennett admitted, "and there's no question about what Gene Roddenberry has done to make this a legend."[4]

The Bionic Woman and *The Six Million Dollar Man* had given Bennett experience producing popular science fiction on a cost-effective budget, something of a mantra for *Star Trek II*. Additionally, Bennett had another valuable skill: he was comfortable producing new stories from someone else's template. "The body of my work has been literally adaptive," Bennett said at the time. "Most of the things that I have successfully done well have not been my own creations but adaptations of other people's original material. *Mod Squad*, of course, was someone else's idea that I fleshed out with Aaron [Spelling]. The 'bionics' shows were both based on Martin Caiden's novel. *Rich Man, Poor Man* was an Irwin

Shaw novel, which I adapted with the hand of Dean Reisner writing it, and so on. Adaptation is a medium in which I feel very comfortable."[5]

What Bennett did not have was an intimate knowledge of *Star Trek* itself. His career had brushed near *Star Trek*, but he had no direct connection to the show. Although *Mod Squad* filmed next door to *Star Trek* at the studio, he recalled, "I had never seen *Star Trek*. Oh, an occasional rerun. I knew who Kirk was, who Spock was… I'd never seen the original series as it ran."[6]

Now what was required was for Bennett to attend his own version of Starfleet Academy. "I had to become a Trekkie."[7] He sought out fan opinions by reading popular resources such as Bjo Trimble's *Star Trek Concordance*, Teri Meyer's *Interstat* fanzine, which focused on fan opinions shared via letters, and Vel Jaeger's *Trekism*, a special interest group fanzine geared towards members of Mensa International, the high IQ society. Bennett corresponded with fans and spoke with actors such as DeForest Kelley (McCoy) about their perspectives. All this helped familiarize Bennett with the characters, premises, and the qualities that made *Star Trek* unique.

Whatever *Star Trek II* was going to be, it was not going to be a direct sequel to *The Motion Picture*. There could be no V'Ger, no evolved Ilia and Willard Decker. What it could be was a sequel to one of the episodes. That is, of course, if one was worthy enough for a big screen adventure. Bennett spent three months screening every episode of the original series on what he described as "faded 16 millimeter prints in the back projection rooms of Paramount."[8]

The episodes he liked best were the ones that focused on the family of characters whose charisma was more compelling than any special effect. "I found that one third of the episodes were brilliant, one third were okay, and one third were uh-uh. That's a pretty good average for someone who has done series television, believe me, and I also found out that there was a name on the third I loved most… Gene L. Coon. I had known Gene very briefly at Universal. Gene epitomized what we now call the showrunner…. Every time his name appeared on the screen, the story was essential and the characters came to life."[9]

Star Trek producer Gene L. Coon contributed much to the show's legacy. His teleplay for "Arena" demonstrated the compassion of humanity as Kirk struggles with the Gorn Captain. He wrote "The Devil in the Dark" after seeing a Janos Prohaska-produced costume for the Horta, crafting a timeless story about the dangers of prejudice and presumption and the healing powers of empathy. With "Errand of Mercy," Coon defined the Klingons for generations of writers to follow. But it was one script in particular, written by Coon and Carey Wilber, that caught Bennett's interest because of a comment by Spock at episode's end: "It would be interesting, Captain, to return to that world in one hundred years and learn what crop had sprung from the seed you planted today." Upon seeing this moment, Bennett stood up in the projection room at Paramount and elatedly instructed, "Stop the projector. I got it!" Nearly thirteen years after the episodes had originally premiered, Bennett had found the foundation upon which to build *Star Trek II*.

That episode: "Space Seed." The antagonist: Khan Noonien Singh.

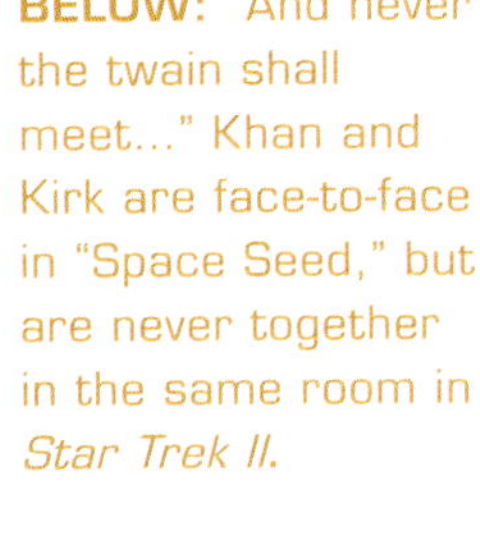

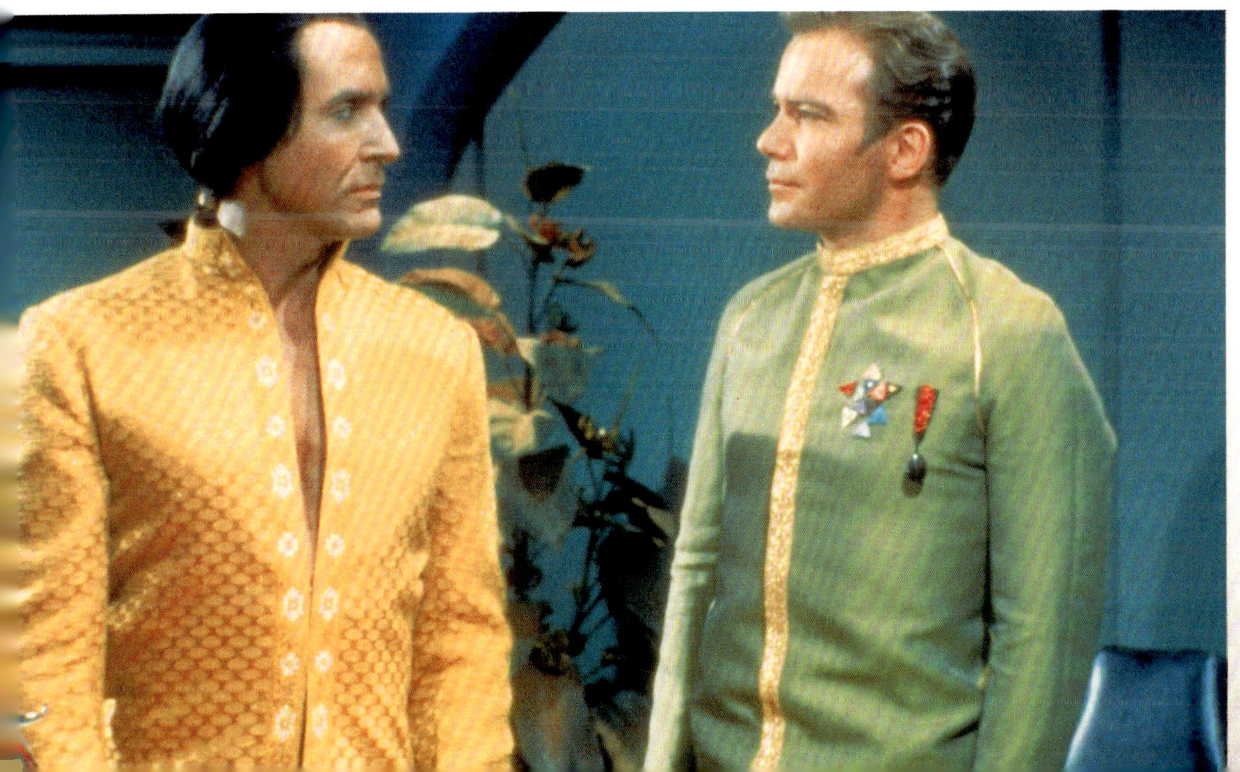

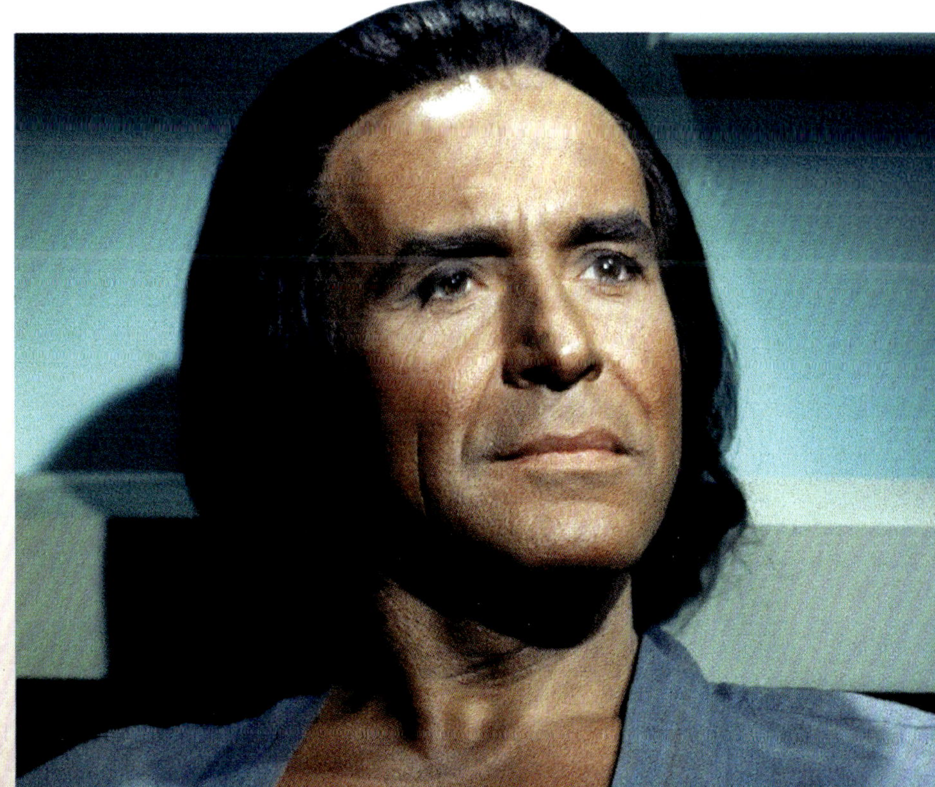

THE WRATH OF RAGNAR

The character Khan Noonien Singh was born from a question asked in an August 29, 1966 eighteen-page outline submitted by writer Carey Wilber a week before *Star Trek* ever premiered: "What would happen if a man of our age could be transported five hundred years into the future?"

In that outline, the character was named Harald Ericsson, a criminal with a "magnificent" body. During the early weeks of September 1966, producer Gene Coon sent memos to Wilber with suggestions on improving the story. "I want to rather do more with him than you have indicated in the story outline," Coon writes, wanting Erickson to be "in fact very similar to James Kirk, our captain, except that our captain has made an adjustment to this world and this culture." Then, Coon offers a challenge: "In other words, Carey, build us a giant of a man."

Wilber's October 26, 1966 script transforms Erickson into a former criminal whose followers call him The King—his criminal empire long ago controlling a large portion of the Earth. Coon rewrote Wilber's script and his December 7, 1966 teleplay has many of the familiar elements the "Space Seed" audiences know, except now the man from the past is renamed John Ericcson, eventually revealed to be an alias used by the infamous Ragnar Thorwald, former leader of the First World Tyranny and himself a genetically engineered human of Nordic heritage.

Imagine an alternative universe where Admiral Kirk yells "Ragnaaarrr!" instead of "Khaaan!" in a film titled *Star Trek II: The Wrath of Ragnar*. It is amongst handwritten notes as the script neared production that Ragnar becomes Khan. The change was necessitated by casting director Joseph D'Agosta's suggestion that Ricardo Montalban be offered the role. Montalban had everything that the character was meant to display: strength, intelligence, charisma, and leadership. Khan would still undergo a few more name changes. He was initially Sibahl Khan Noonien—the version of the name that appears in the episode's 1968 book adaptation by James Blish. *Star Trek*'s primary script researcher and fact-checker, Kellam de Forest, suggested yet another change, to Govin Bahadur Singh, the reason being to closer approximate Sikhism traditions. Roddenberry and Coon ultimately changed the name to its final form, keeping Noonien because Roddenberry hoped the name would be recognized by a World War II friend who he wished to reconnect with. After three months of rewrites, Khan Noonien Singh had arrived.

LEFT: Montalban poses for the camera between takes.

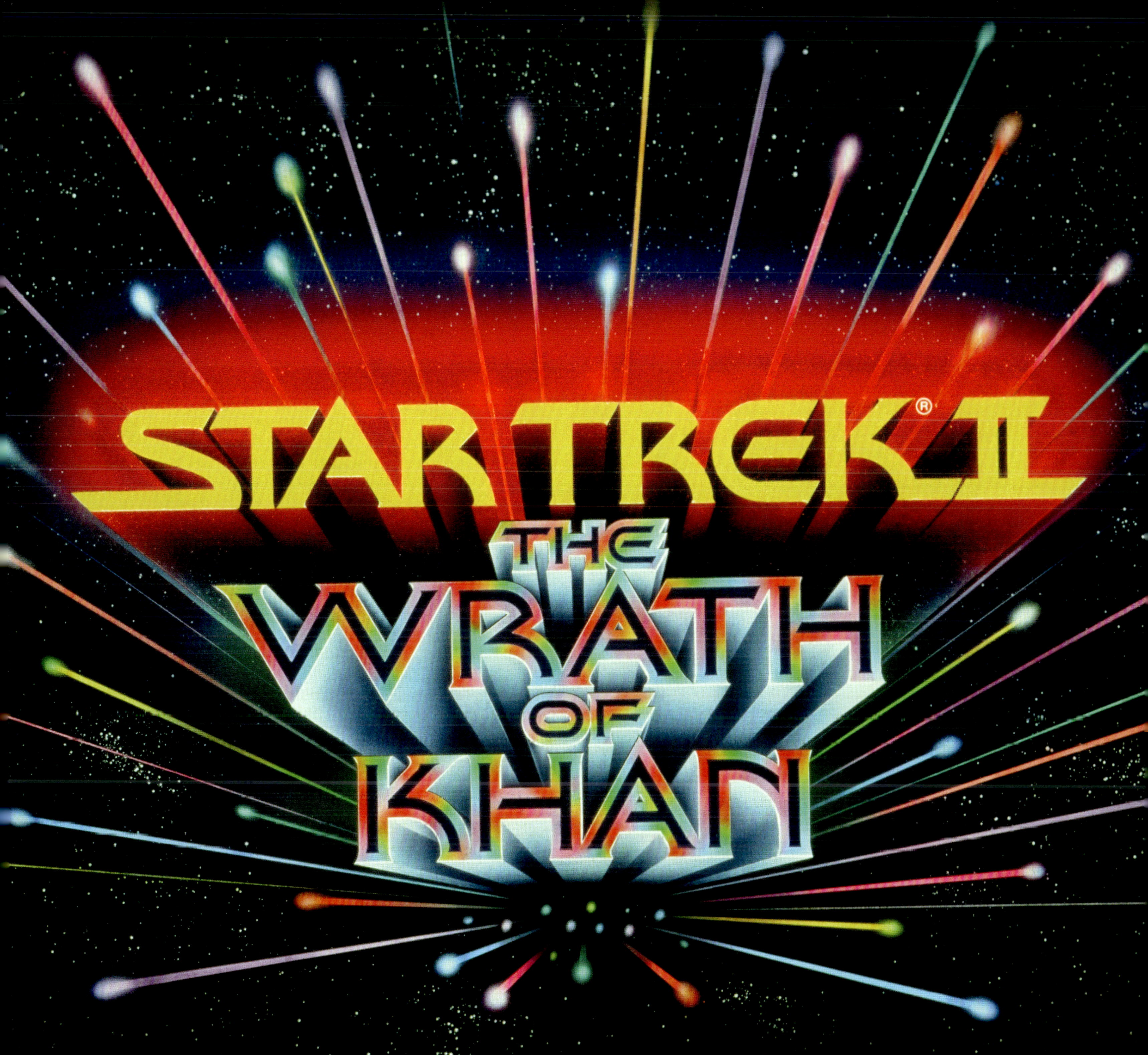

STAR TREK II
THE WRATH OF KHAN

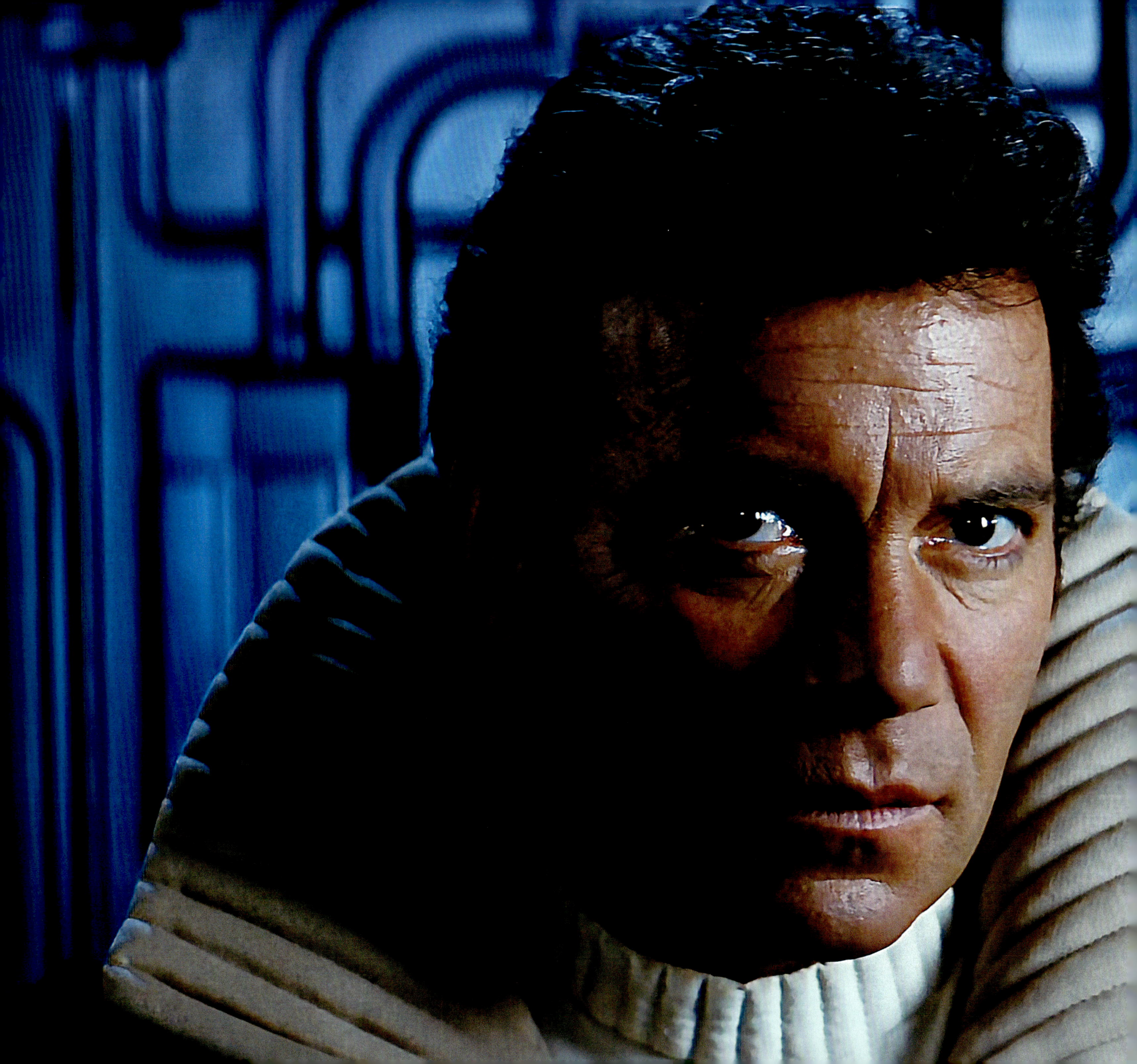

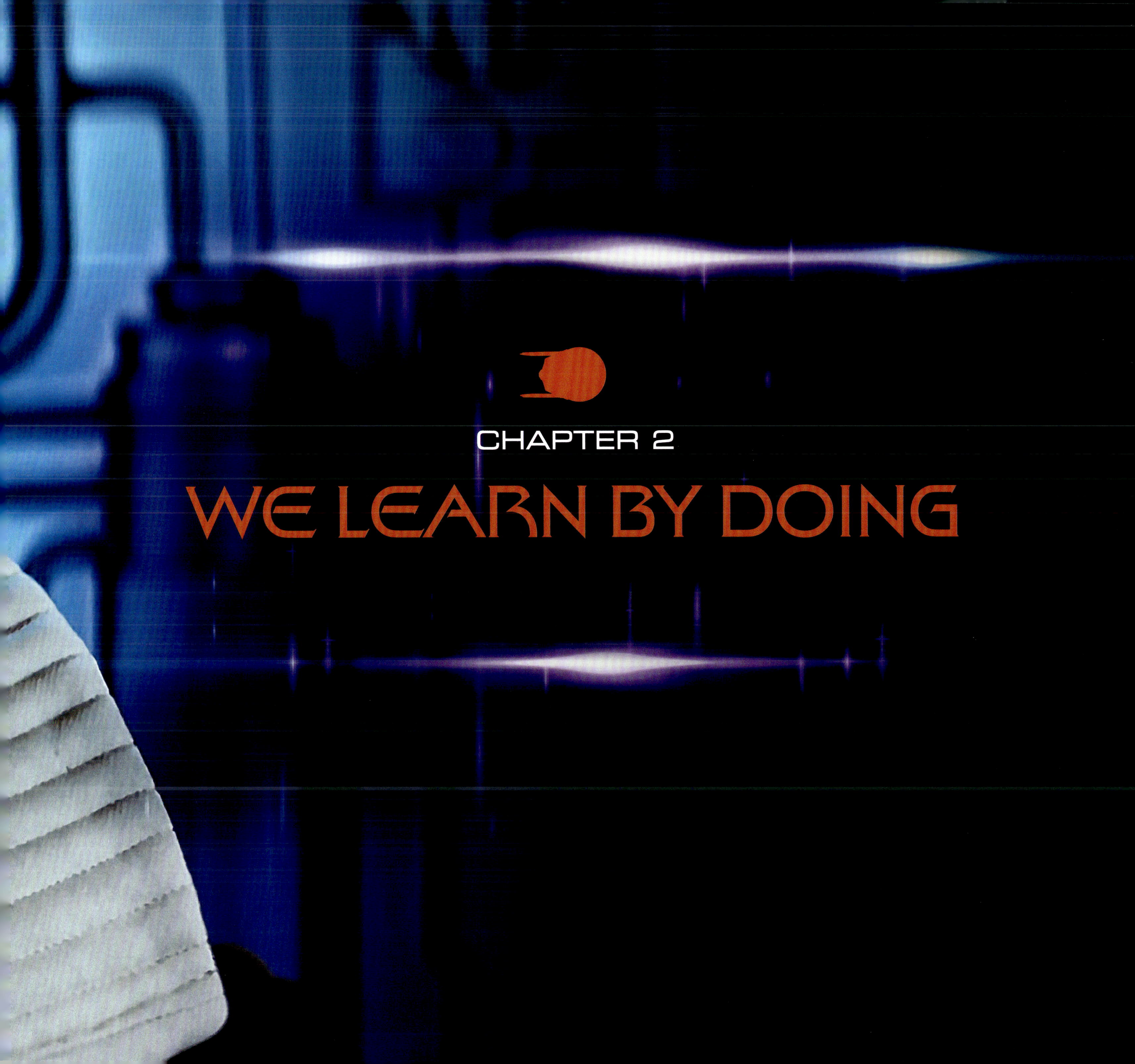

CHAPTER 2
WE LEARN BY DOING

EARLY SCRIPTS

"**I** sat alone at an empty desk in an empty office on the Paramount lot, a man in total despair," Harve Bennett recalled of when he began assembling the elements that would form *Star Trek II* and the foundation upon which all movies depend—a workable script. "I had accepted the responsibility for re-igniting the *Star Trek* torch. And I didn't have a clue about what to do next."[1]

Bennett's immersion into *Star Trek* had involved screening episodes, consulting with fans, and drawing on his own comprehensive experience as a producer. Further help was sought when Bennett asked Robert Sallin to join the production. One of the first challenges facing Bennett and Sallin was the writing of a workable script, a journey that would prove as tortuous as the sands of Ceti Alpha V itself.

On November 13, 1980, Bennett submitted a one page Kirk-focused outline that he had begun writing by hand on yellow legal paper. It would become the

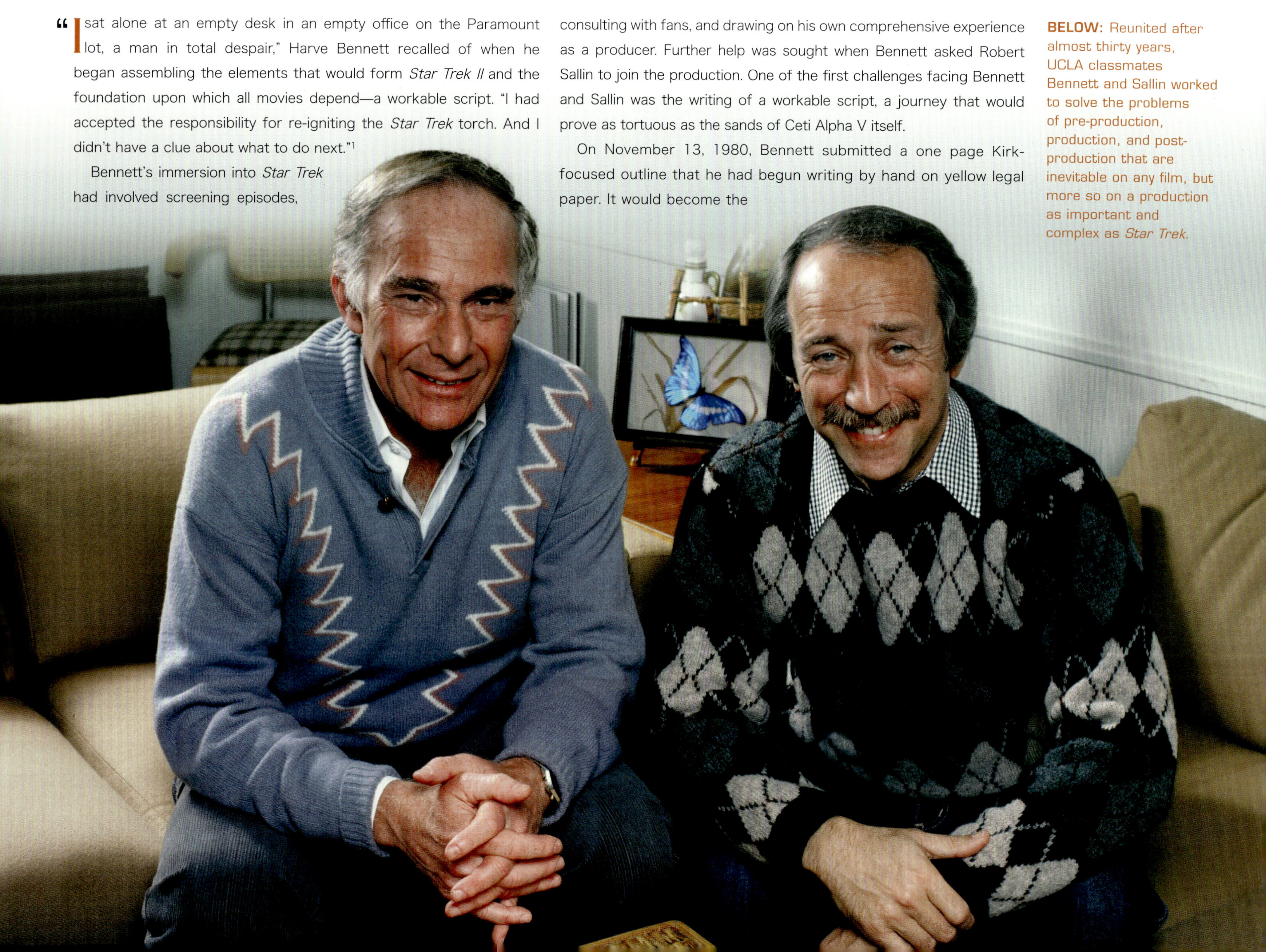

BELOW: Reunited after almost thirty years, UCLA classmates Bennett and Sallin worked to solve the problems of pre-production, production, and post-production that are inevitable on any film, but more so on a production as important and complex as *Star Trek*.

⍟ ROBERT SALLIN

Born in 1931, Sallin was a UCLA classmate of Harve Bennett. The two had collaborated on the 1952 Varsity Show "It's Time You Knew" and would subsequently reunite for various projects over the years. Sallin brought with him both creative and practical skills after years of producing and directing television commercials. That experience helped the *Star Trek II* production find solutions to the ever-present production "minefields." Sallin would solve problems with scripts, costuming, design, hiring, and even imagined the memorable entrance scene of Admiral Kirk during the *Kobayashi Maru* scene. Meyer told Trekmovie.com, "He also had a more sophisticated visual sense than I did after having only made one movie. I remember that Kirk's entrance was reshot. He was backlit like a rock star when he comes out. This was at Bob's instigation. And throughout the movie he made many contributions along similar lines. And then at the end when I—for reasons which may or may not have been proved sound—was very upset at the notion of filming the coffin on the planet, Bob went up to San Francisco at the Botanical Gardens and he shot it. So, his contributions are significant."[2]

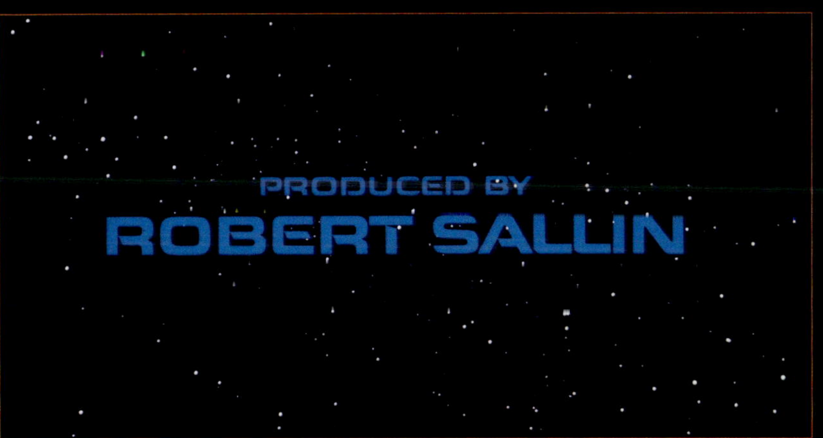

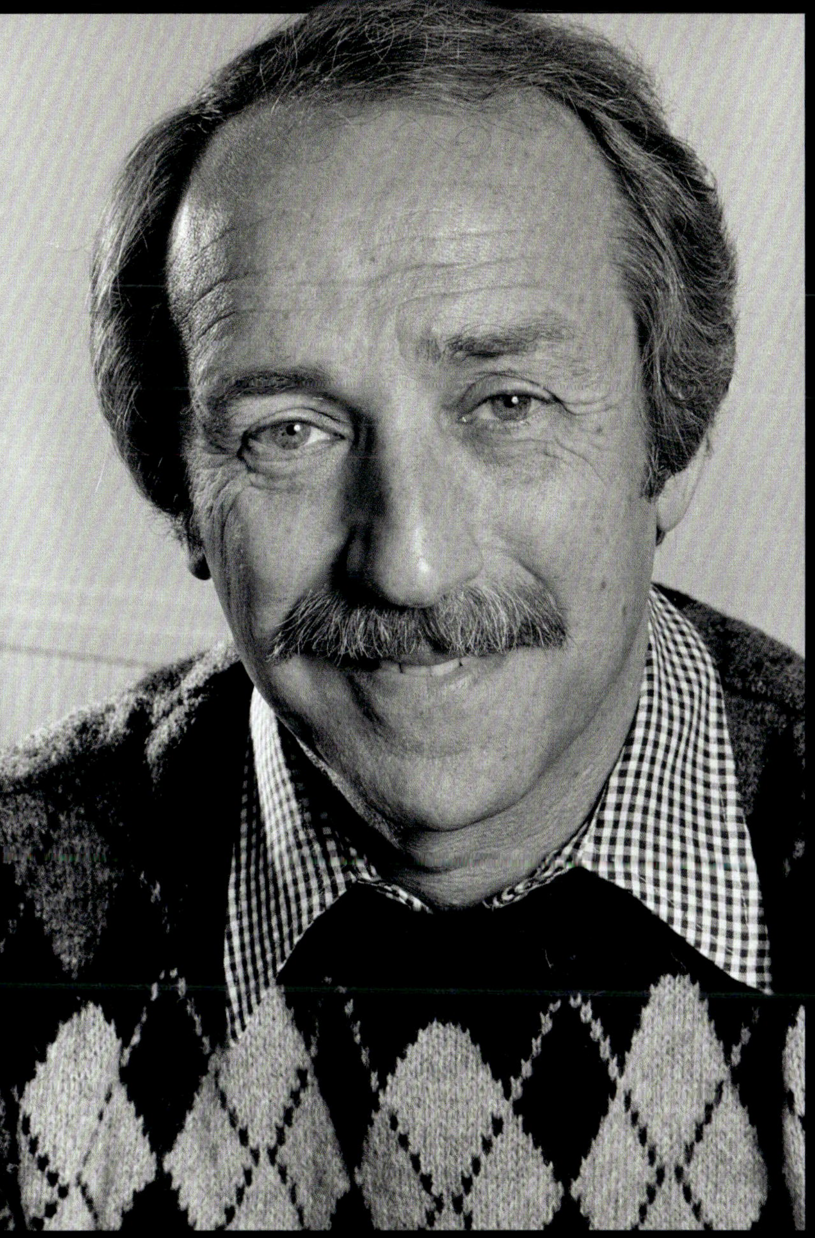

JACK B. SOWARDS

A prolific TV writer, with Writers Guild of America Award and Hugo Award nominations, Sowards created scripts for shows as diverse as *Bonanza*, *The Bold Ones: The Lawyers*, and *The Streets of San Francisco*. Sowards would eventually return to the *Star Trek* universe, writing the *Star Trek: The Next Generation* second season episode, "Where Silence Has Lease." Among his many contributions to *Star Trek*, it would be Sowards who would create the *Kobayashi Maru* simulator sequence, naming it for his former neighbors when he lived in the Hancock Park area of Los Angeles.[3]

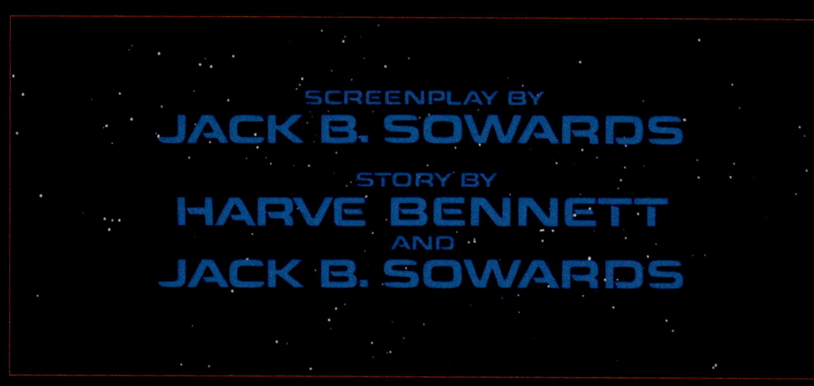

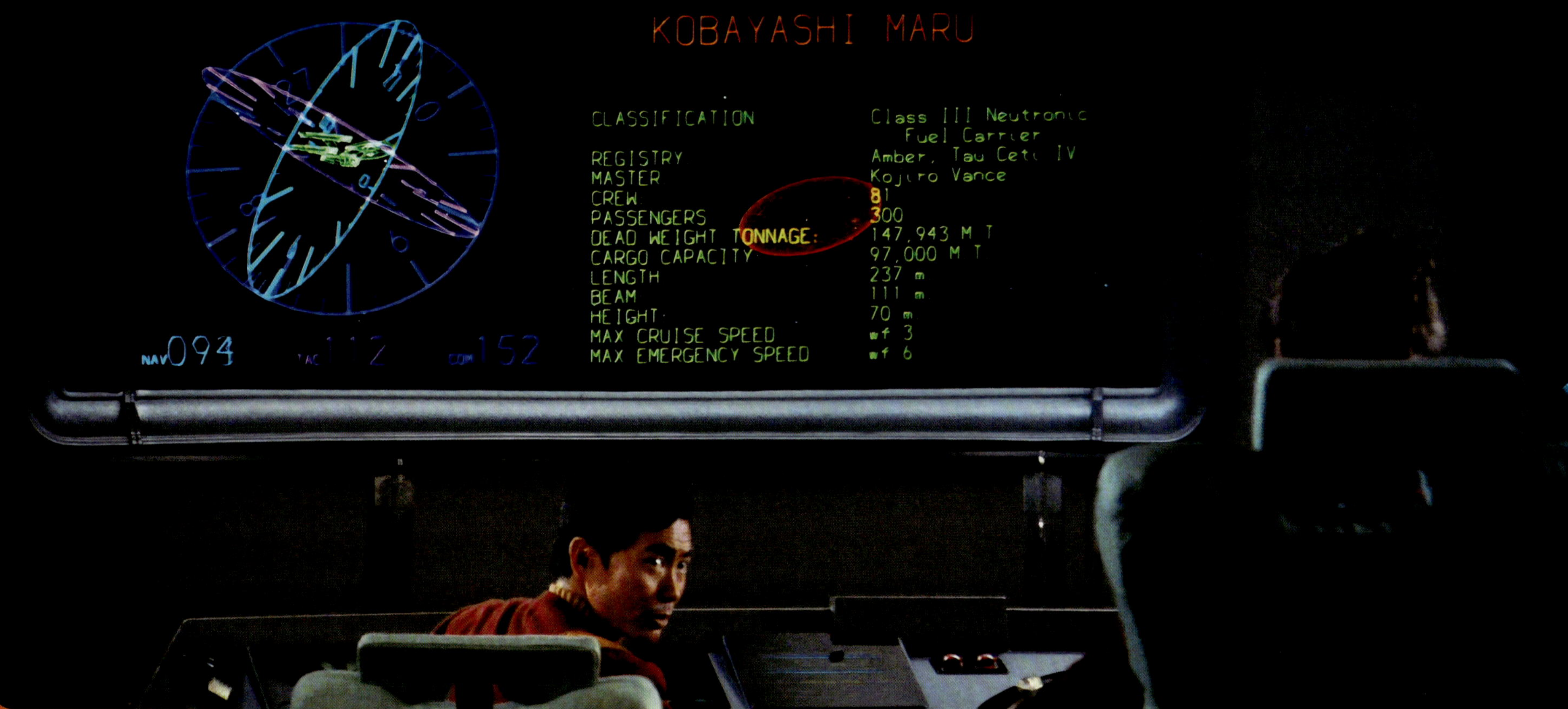

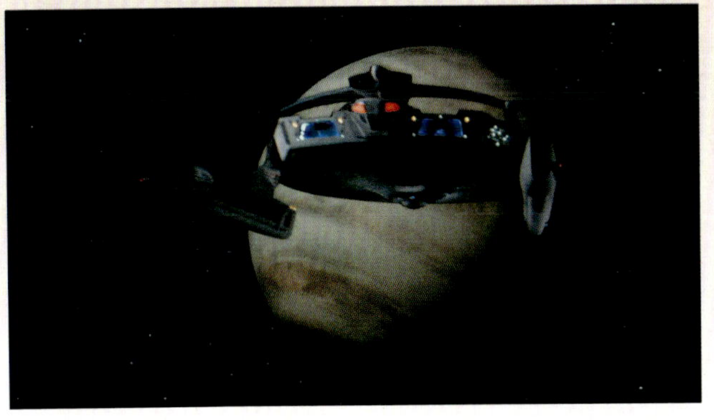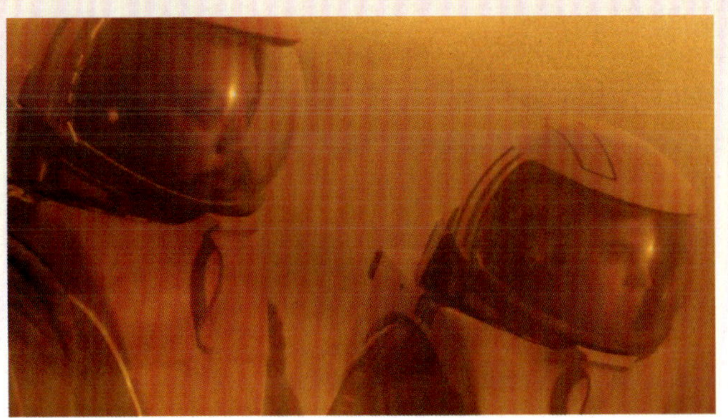

first story idea for *Star Trek II*. The outline's sole focus on Kirk reveals a story approach that was partly the result of the studio's uncertainty at the time about which actors would or would not be returning for the sequel. Despite its brevity, there are elements of "War of the Generations"—as it was titled—that would permeate all other drafts: aging, the mistake of accepting a promotion, a former love, a revelatory son, and the threat of Khan.

To expand on the outline, Bennett met with scriptwriter Jack B. Sowards on December 4, 1980. Given the "War of the Generations" outline, Sowards was to develop the idea into a longer treatment, and once approved, into a first draft script. On February 20, 1981, after several treatments, Sowards delivered his first draft script, running 113 pages, titled "The Omega System."

Opening with a view of a star-field, the script begins with a series of fake-outs. First, "Nothing moves for a long beat, then one of the points of light can be seen to move. It APPROACHES, and we see it is a Federation Star Ship. It is the *S.S. Reliant*. A ship of the Enterprise Class." For the audience expecting to see the *Enterprise*, having the familiar *Constitution* outline be revealed to be the *Reliant*

would have been quite the surprise. Even more, as the ship passes, the voice of Captain James T. Kirk recording a log report is heard, making the audience think he is the *Reliant*'s captain. In reality, what is occurring is Pavel Chekov, first officer of the *Reliant*, is playing an old recording (reviewing the events of the episode "Space Seed") as he prepares for a mission. During the review, it is established that Khan was exiled to planet Ceti Alpha V twelve years before—a time frame that would be expanded to the more accurate fourteen years in subsequent versions of the script—and that the planet had been under constant monitoring by Starfleet ever since. Then, four years before, all life signs had ceased.

Clark Terrell, who in this version is both the captain of the *Reliant* and the commander of the nearby Gamma Regula IV Starfleet planetary base, is planning a test of a devastating new Starfleet weapon, code named Project Omega. A single omega device can destroy everything within a nine hundred-mile radius. Several of the devices could destroy a planet. Ceti Alpha V has been selected as a proving ground. As a team of five from the *Reliant* beam down, including Terrell and Chekov, to confirm no life exists on the

ABOVE LEFT: The *Reliant.*

ABOVE RIGHT: Terrell and Chekov on Ceti Alpha V.

BELOW: Chekov observes Ceti Alpha V from the *Reliant.*

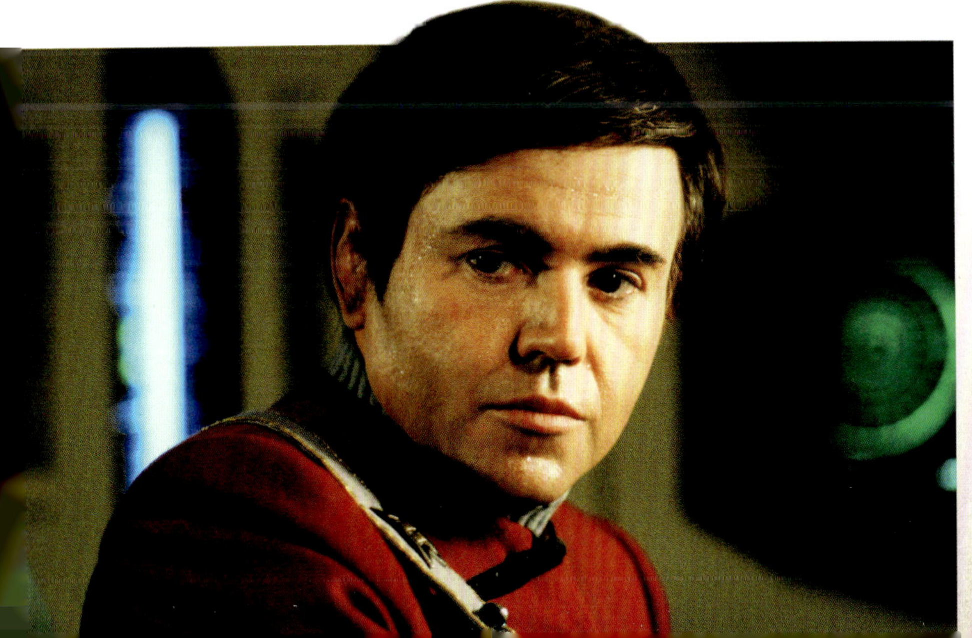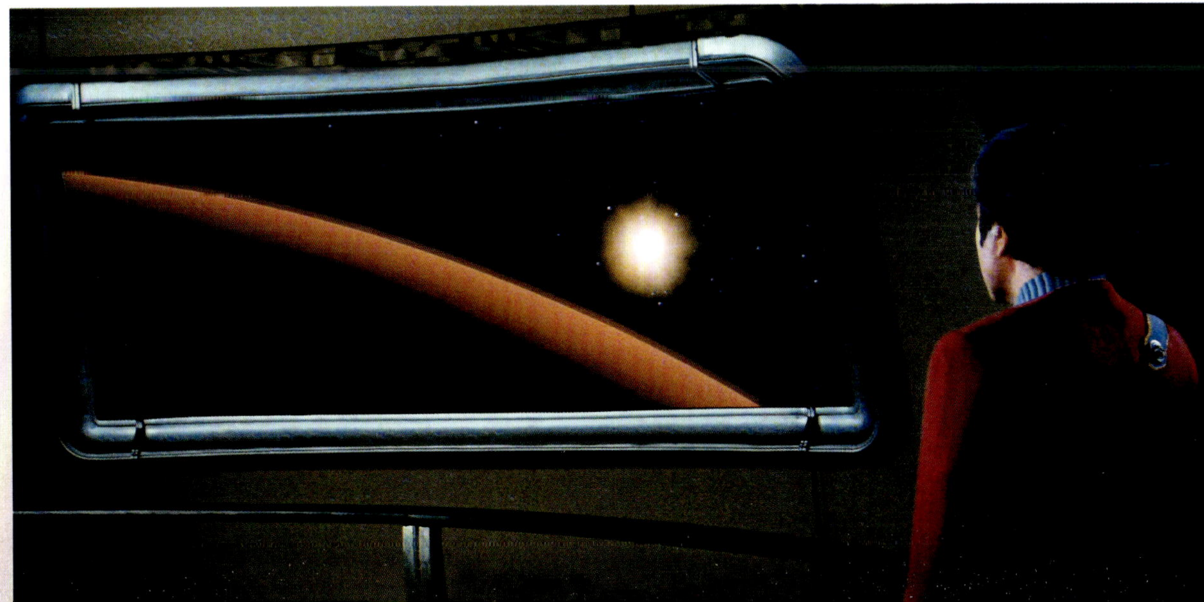

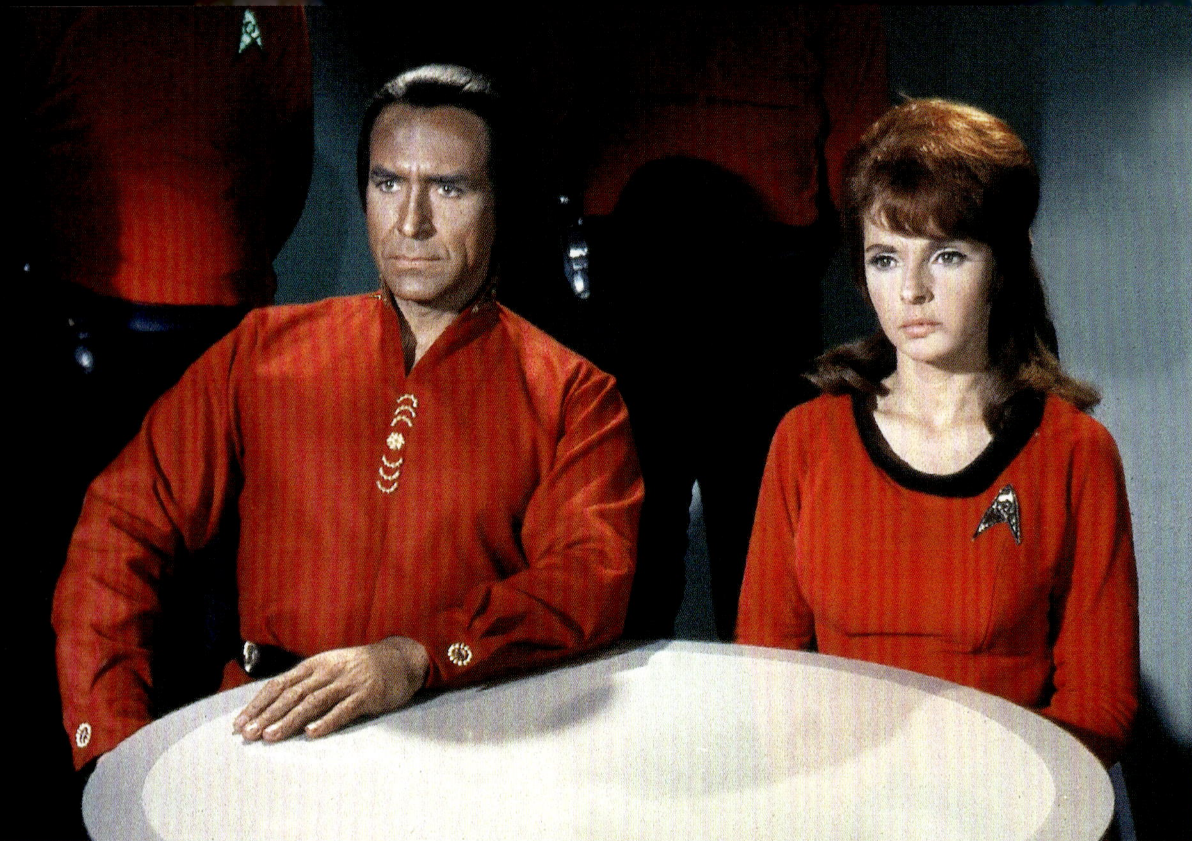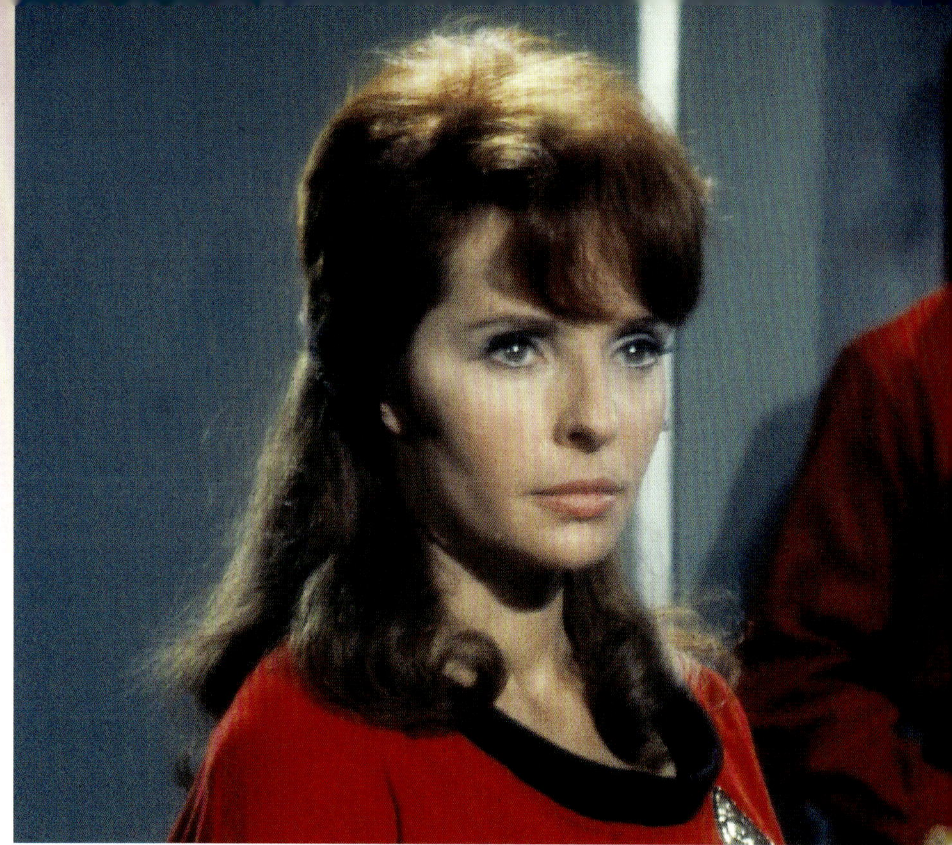

planet anymore, a series of illusions begin, changing the perceived environment from a sand planet to a grassy valley. As Chekov reaches for his communicator, the device turns into a rat. Again the scenery changes and the *Reliant* crew find themselves face-to-face with Khan, his wife and former Starfleet historian Marla McGivers, and Khan's followers, in a stone chamber.

Khan reveals that he blames Kirk for his exile and that the only reason his people have survived the harsh conditions of the world was because of the mind powers that he had developed. Now, it is time for revenge. To gain their cooperation, and from which Khan will eventually learn about the existence of the Omega Project, the crew of the *Reliant* are exposed to what the script calls "wee beasties," creatures that resemble spiders or soft, slithery crabs who control the mind of those they inhabit (see Chapter 9).

Meanwhile, Admiral Kirk is beleaguered by the paperwork from his aide-de-camp Uhura. McCoy stops by to remind Kirk that it is time to wish the new captain of the *Enterprise* their best before the starship departs, but Kirk has no time. McCoy tells Kirk, "You didn't have the time then… You don't have the time now… There's just never going to be enough time," establishing a theme that permeates the script. As they speak, Kirk receives a message from Dr. Janet Wallace—played by Sarah Marshall in the original series episode "The Deadly Years"—who is now Deputy Chief of Project Omega. She asks Kirk

for his help, sharing vague worries. Kirk delays the request as he is too busy at the moment.

On board the *Enterprise*, Captain Spock, Sulu, Scott, and Dr. Chapel are joined by new characters: Lieutenant Charles Waters at security, Lieutenant Diane O'Rourke at communications, and Savik (note spelling), a male Vulcan who is described as having "a gleam in his eye" and "a sense of humor." During the departure farewell assembly, Kirk notes that Spock appears almost exultant and the two commiserate about Kirk's responsibilities. Spock reveals that he, too, was contacted by Dr. Wallace and speaks to Kirk about how time is a commodity he should not waste, helping to change Kirk's mind.

At Gamma Hydra IV, a mutiny has begun. Mostly younger Starfleet officers, led in part by Janet's son, Lieutenant David Wallace, are concerned about Captain Terrell's behavior since returning from his mission to Ceti Alpha V. They are unaware that Terrell, Chekov, and others are now controlled by Khan's wee beasties. When Terrell reveals his plans to bring the Project Omega weapons into the Neutral Zone, an act of provocation that will certainly result in war with the Klingons, David and his peers decide to act. The mutineers steal the thousand omega devices and the necessary triggering mechanism, hiding in caves after an elaborate phaser fight and escape.

As the *Enterprise* nears Gamma Regula IV, the *Reliant*, with Khan, McGivers, and Khan's followers on board, attacks, leaving

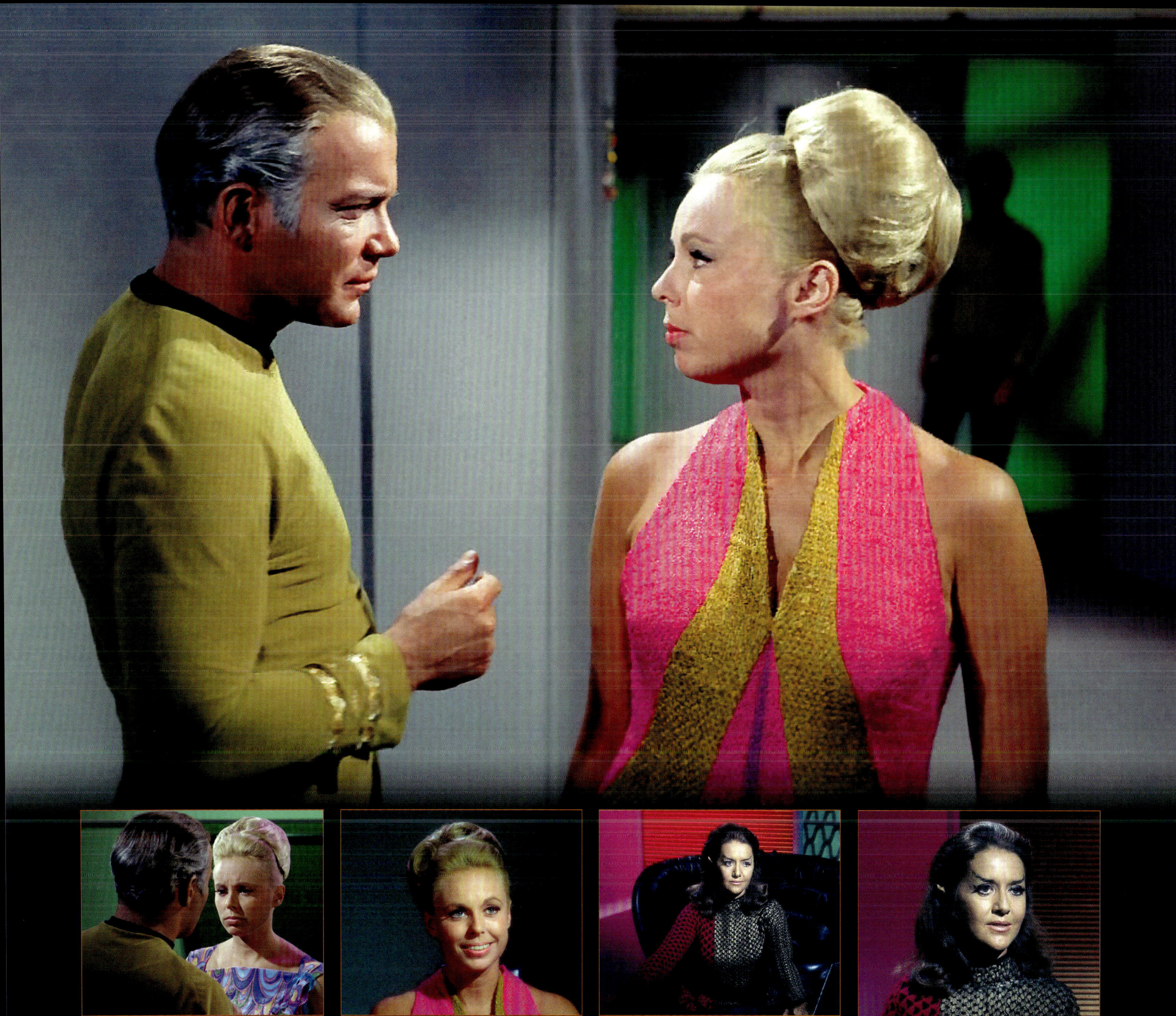

the *Enterprise* damaged. The starship loses power as radiation is flooding the engineering area. Spock goes to engineering, and against the protestations of Scotty, enters the radiation zone in order to reestablish power. The *Reliant* retreats because of the restored capabilities of the *Enterprise*. Kirk, McCoy, and Spock speak to each other as Spock dies (see Chapter 13).

While mourning in his cabin, Kirk is given a cassette recording by O'Rourke, left for him by Spock in the event of his death. Kirk plays the recording, learning that Spock was affected by the events with V'Ger, realizing that it was wrong to deny his emotions. Spock learned from V'Ger that there is more than mere logic. Spock warns that Kirk is having the same crisis as there is more than mere bureaucracy.

Upon arrival at Gamma Hydra IV, Kirk, Savik, and O'Rourke first meet with Terrell to learn details of the rebellion, and then go in search of the mutineers. Yet it is David who finds Kirk and Savik first. Kirk is suspicious of David, thinking he is behind the *Reliant* attack on the *Enterprise*. David is suspicious of Kirk, thinking he only wants the omega devices. Janet tries to bring a sense of trust to the two, neither of who yet know they have a special relationship. Kirk agrees to investigate more of David's claims and returns to confront Terrell.

Khan, however, has been watching through both surveillance technologies and via reports by those he controls. He takes the omega devices with him after surprising the mutineers, but because of the timing of the attack, David and the mutineers believe Kirk is behind the theft.

During their meeting, and under Khan's control, Terrell attacks Kirk, but Savik intervenes. Chekov then resists his wee beastie, which leaves his body.

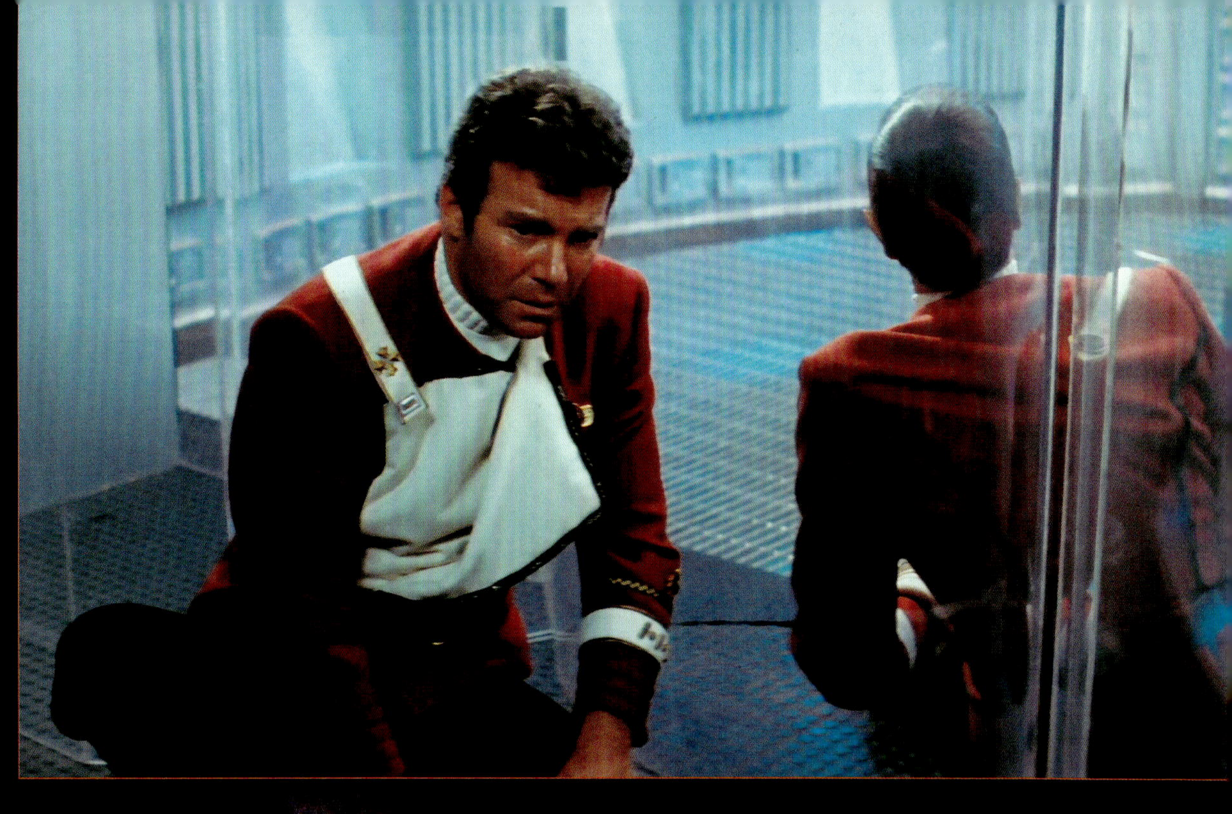

O'Rourke takes the creature back to the *Enterprise* for study. Kirk returns to David to share what he knows, but David and the mutineers arrest Kirk for the theft and he is scheduled for execution. Meanwhile, O'Rouke learns that the wee beasties are native to Ceti Alpha V, which triggers concerns that somehow Khan is involved with what has been occurring.

To sojourn the execution, Janet reveals that Kirk is David's father. Despite his now confused feelings, David does not think the other mutineers will change their minds. As the execution is about to begin, Khan attacks again. He wants the triggering mechanism, without which the omega devices are useless. Khan creates a series of illusions as he battles Kirk and David, but Kirk knows that illusions cannot hurt unless a person believes in them. Together, Kirk and David begin to defeat Khan, who produces the illusion of a wall of flame, steals the triggering mechanism, and retreats to the *Reliant*.

Kirk returns to the *Enterprise* and a space battle begins, with the *Reliant* firing torpedoes affixed with the omega device at the *Enterprise*. Savik realizes that shields are useless and that speed is the better strategy. The *Enterprise* lowers its shields during the battle to gain maneuverability, avoids the torpedoes, and keeps attacking the *Reliant* in volley after volley. The *Reliant* explodes, destroying both Khan and the remaining omega devices.

Sulu decides to join Chekov in rebuilding Gamma Hydra IV, while David leaves Janet to serve with Kirk on the *Enterprise*. As the film ends, O'Rourke lets Kirk know that she is interested in him romantically. Kirk initially refuses, saying he does not have the time. O'Rourke admonishes, "I think you have that backwards, sir. You don't have a personal life to have the time for." Kirk thinks about this, and perhaps reflecting on Spock's message and warning, he tells her that he would like to discuss the idea later. He promises, "I will make the time... borrow the time... or steal the time... but I will have the time." The script ends as Kirk says to his new navigator David, "You may cast off, Mr. Wallace."

While divergent, there are many elements of this script that would be transformed but present in the sequel as filmed. The wee beasties would become the Ceti eels. This first draft has a dry dock departure scene where Spock has Savik take the *Enterprise* out for the first time that is reminiscent of *Star Trek II: The Wrath of Khan*, albeit without the humorous exchange of a nervous Kirk and McCoy. Terrell and Chekov being ordered by Khan to assassinate Kirk plays similarly in both versions, although in the film Terrell acts heroically to kill himself to save Kirk. Most importantly, Spock dies by sacrificing himself to restore power during an attack by the *Reliant* in both versions.

There are, however, important differences. Gone are the characters of O'Rourke and McGivers in the film. With the death of McGivers prior to the events of *Star Trek II: The Wrath of Khan* providing Khan with an even more powerful motivation for his revenge. Savik—who began as a character named Wicks in one of the early treatments—was not yet female, nor half-Romulan. Most glaringly, the script's conceit that Starfleet would develop a planet-destroying weapon chafed against its peaceful mission.

Thanks to his education in *Trek* lore, Bennett wanted Omega rethought. Art director Michael Minor, who had contributed to both the original series and *The Motion Picture*, and who was himself a fan of the show, suggested that Omega become a terraforming device, more in line with the spirit of the scientific and exploratory nature of Starfleet.

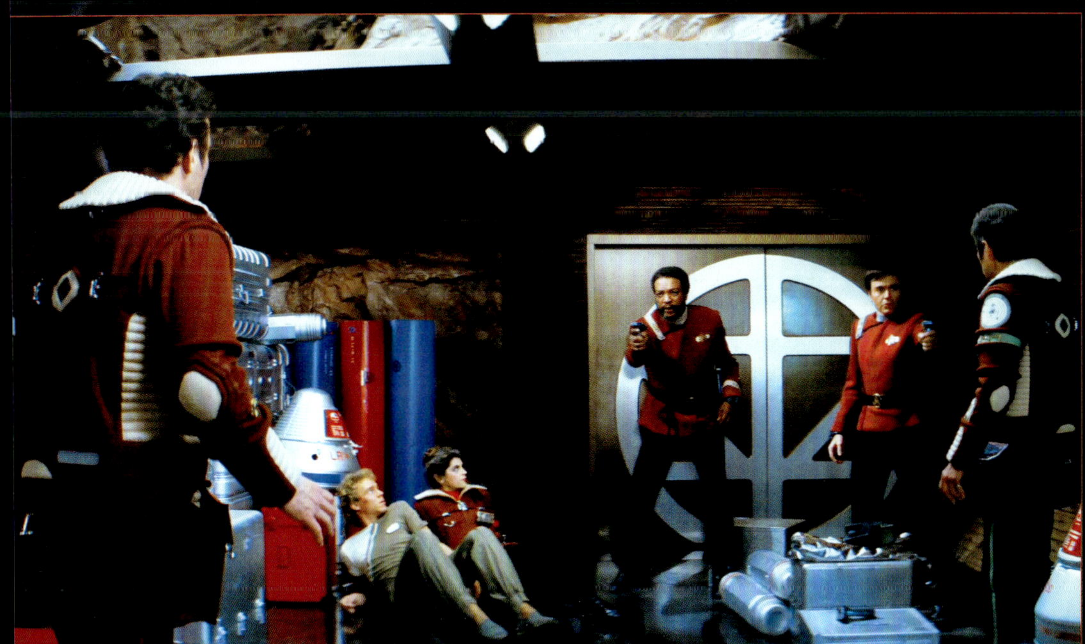

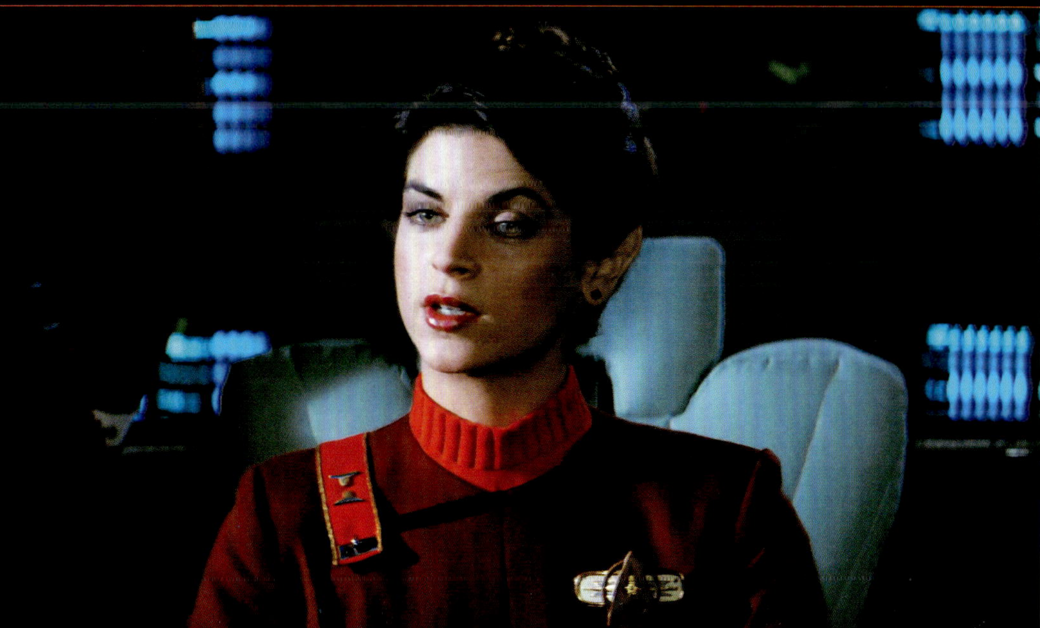

Sowards went to work on the next version of the script, but had a time limitation to deal with because of the impending possibility of a Writer's Guild of America strike occurring (a result of the then-burgeoning home video and pay-TV markets necessitating new contracts). The 130-page final draft of the now-named "The Genesis Project" script, with Sowards and Bennett credited as writers, was submitted on April 10, 1981, a mere day before the union called for action.

The script improves on the previous version, with some interesting changes. Janet and David Wallace have become new characters named Carol and David Baxter. Carol is described as the "leading microbiologist of the Federation." A running joke in the script is McCoy and Spock telling Kirk he should have married Carol when he had the chance. When they are reunited later in the script, Kirk asks Carol that same question. Gone are the mutinous young Starfleet officers. Rather, David will lead a team of scientists who worry about the militarization of the Genesis terraforming device at the Gamma Hydra IV planetary base in the act of rebellion. Terrell, dissembling and under the control of Khan via his Ceti eels, orders Starfleet to take possession of the Genesis System technology, claiming the Klingons want to use the device as a weapon and therefore the technology must be protected. (This element of the script would prove "prophetic," as the idea of Klingons seeking Genesis would form the threat of *Star Trek III: The Search for Spock*.) The scientists—now including Neela, David's lover, and Jedda, a Vulcan—hide the Genesis device and the molecular encoder necessary to activate it in a secret Cave of Eden on the planet's surface. The wee beasties have been replaced with the more familiar Ceti eels (see Chapter 9). Savik is now described as having mixed parentage.

A major addition to "The Genesis Project" script is the *Kobayashi Maru* scene. The simulation plays somewhat differently to the film version, because it is Kirk who is present on the bridge, not Spock. The adversaries of the program are not the Klingons, but the Romulons [sic]. McCoy plays a larger role in this sequence, highlighting the script's commitment to the trio of characters, and he is involved in the conversation Kirk has with Spock, who wishes to learn how his new crew performed on the test. It will be O'Rourke and Savik, at different times in the script, who wonder about how a test without a solution is considered fair, introducing the no-win scenario theme prominent in *Star Trek II: The Wrath of Khan*.

Much of the script follows the same edifice as its previous incarnations, including Spock sacrificing himself to restore power to the *Enterprise* during the *Reliant*'s first attack. A few interesting elements are that Khan (much like another famous science-fiction film villain a few years later) creates the illusion that a "bright blue flash of energy darts from his fingertips" during his fight with Kirk and David, and uses what is described as a Romulon [sic] Medusa Whip, which has live snakes at the end. This version of the script also has both Chekov and Terrell surviving.

The three-month writer's strike gave producers time to evaluate the scripts, and while there were elements to like, it was determined that a new approach was needed. Samuel A. Peeples was hired, writing an outline named "Worlds that Never Were" and subsequently submitting a script retitled to "The New Star Trek" on August 24, 1981. It made sense that producers turned to Peeples in their efforts to create a new *Star Trek*. He had served as a consultant on the original *Star Trek* pilot, "The Cage," and wrote the second pilot, "Where No Man Has Gone Before," returning in 1973 as the writer of "Beyond the Farthest Star," the pilot episode of *Star Trek: The Animated Series*.

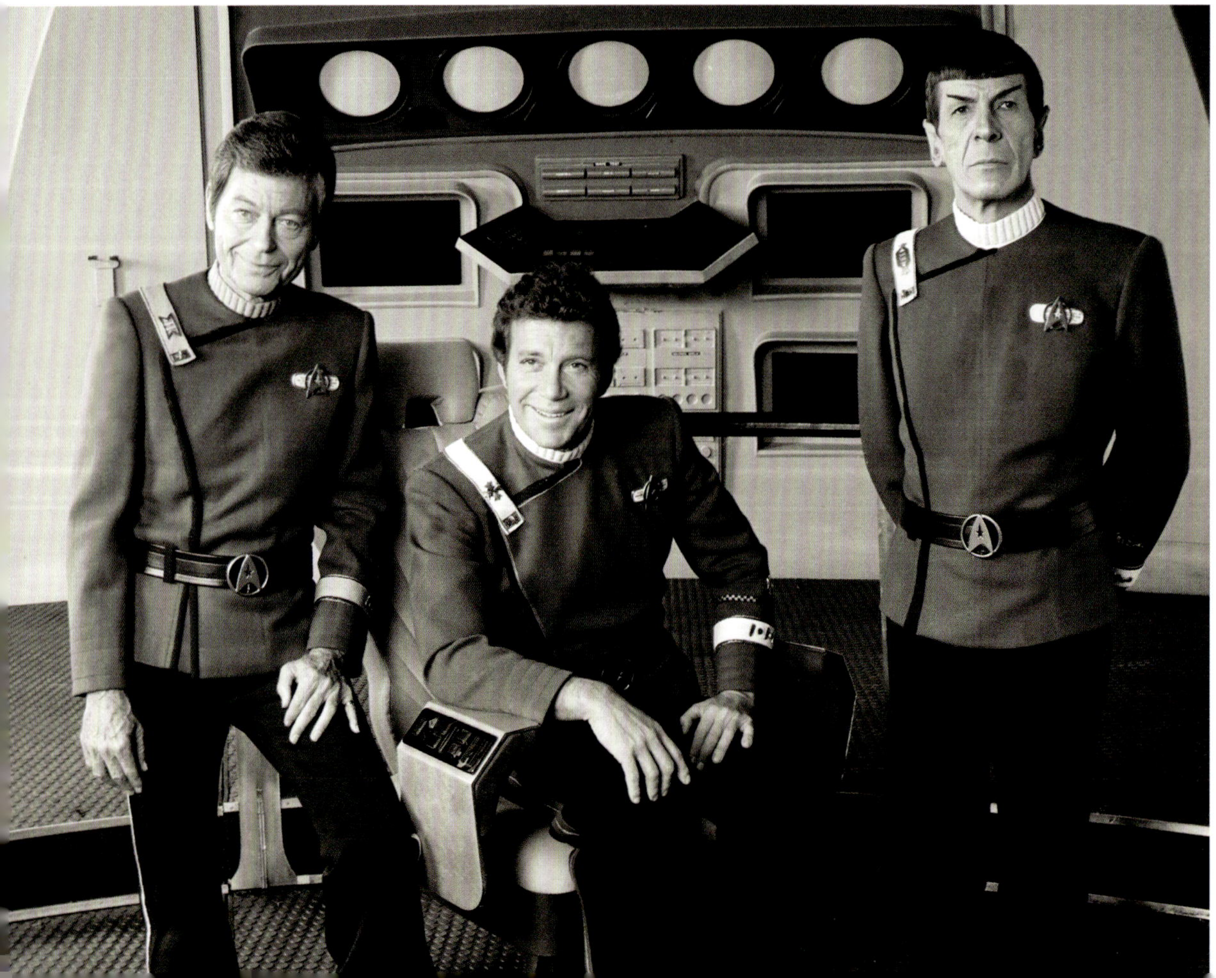

While Peeples hung his script on the frame of Sowards' previous endeavors, he contributed several important elements. Most especially, Peeples transformed Savik into the character fans are familiar with,

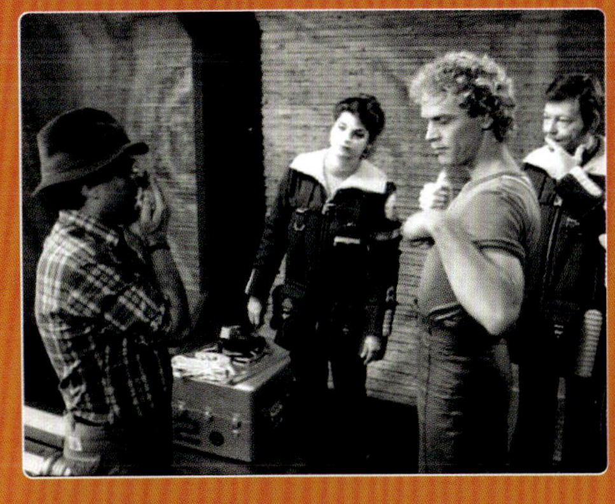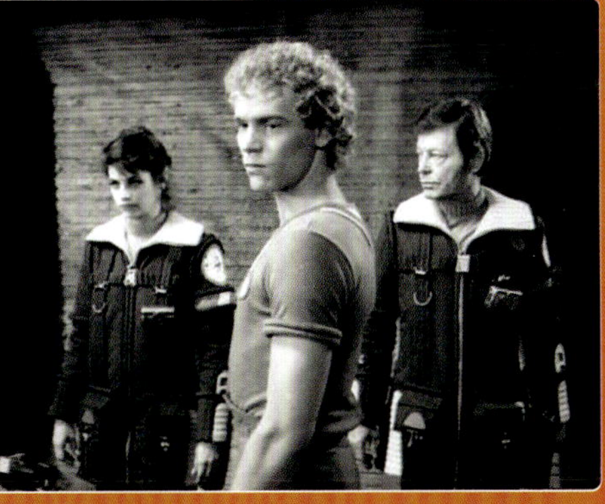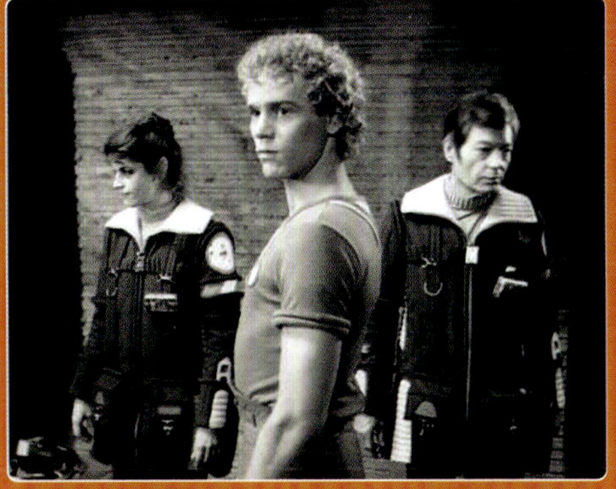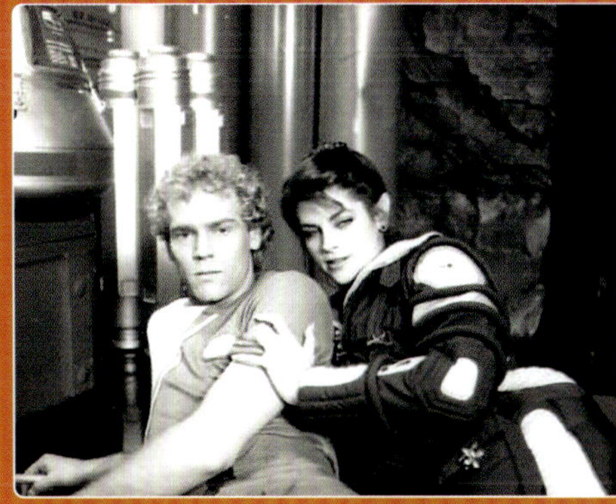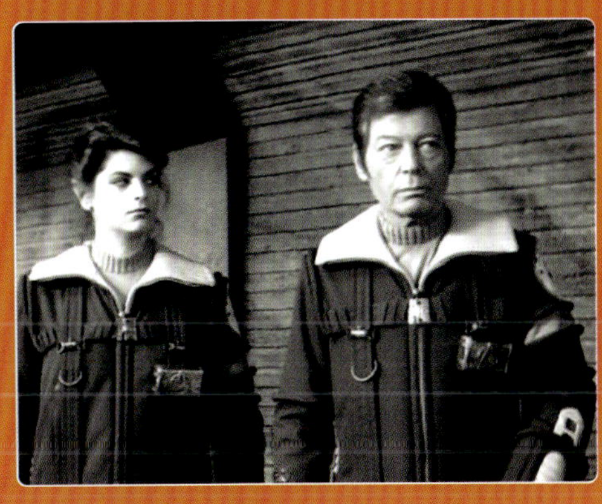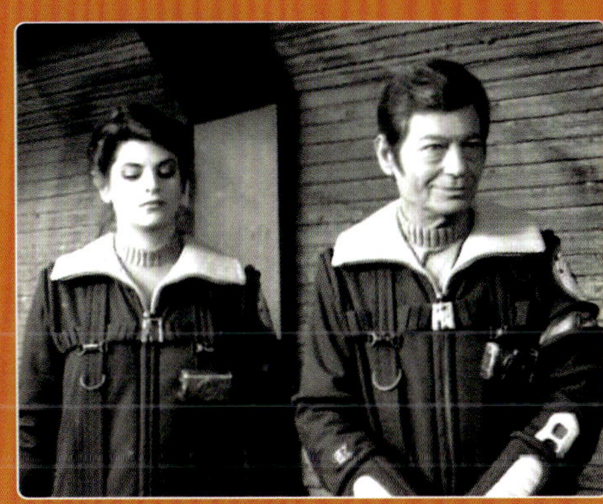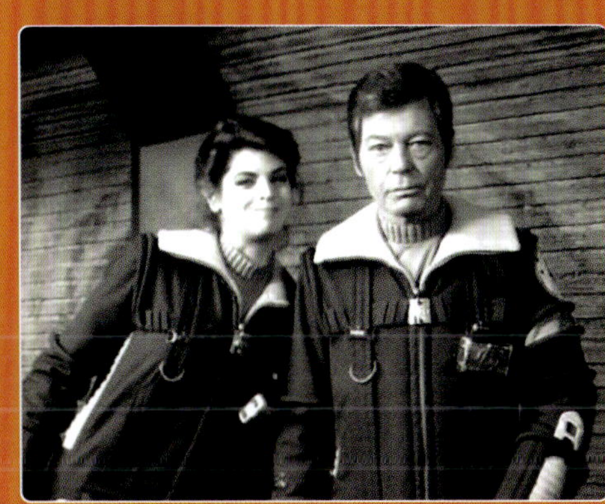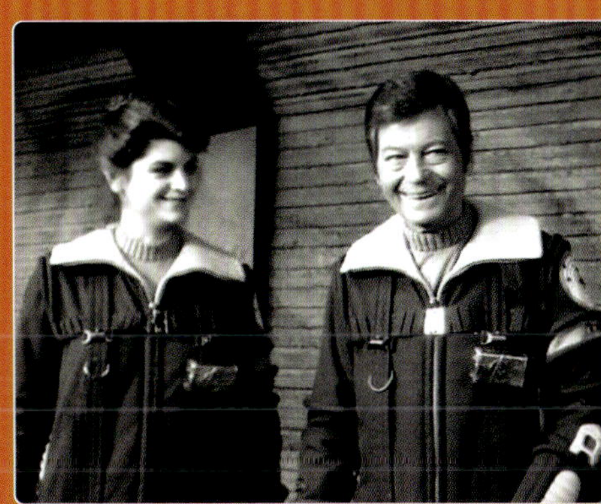

a half-Vulcan half-Romulan female. Fascinatingly, this version of Saavik (initially Ssavik) would have been the daughter of the Romulan Commander from the third season episode "The Enterprise Incident," played by Joanne Linville. The Commander used some of Spock's genetic material to produce Saavik, making the character not merely the protégée of Spock, but rather his actual progeny. Critically, Spock's sacrifice was retained, but moved to the end of the movie, where it would stay.

There were also some significant changes. Khan and Marla were not characters in the "The New Star Trek" script. Rather, they were replaced by powerful aliens named Sojin and Moray. The idea of celebrating a birthday is introduced by Peeples, but it would be Spock's, with the crew singing him the traditional birthday song in Vulcan. Peeples added more science fiction tropes, including a small robot companion to Carol and David named Ru-byk who helps defend against the seizure of Genesis by Starfleet. The *Enterprise* crew includes more aliens, such as Polar bear-like Thal Arctos. Sulu has taken the place of Terrell, teaming with Chekov.

The script had beneficial elements that would be incorporated into what eventually became *Star Trek II: The Wrath of Khan*. However, it was not met with enthusiasm by the producers, who faced notification of a serious, impending limitation: time. As pre-production began, the special effects artists at Industrial Light & Magic made it clear that without a workable script from which to begin model design and visual effect planning, the film would not be ready as promised by the summer of 1982.

A script was needed and it was needed now.

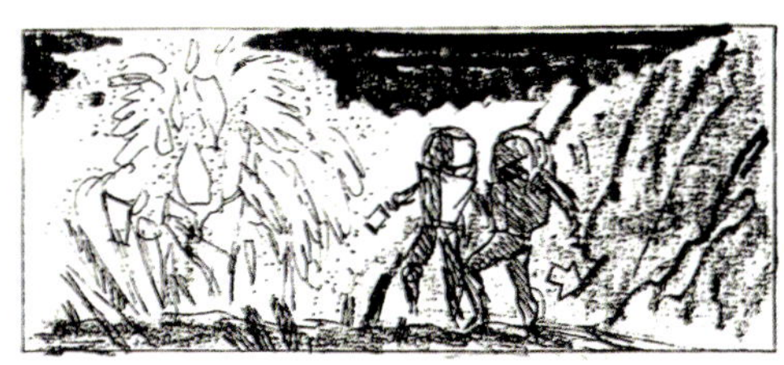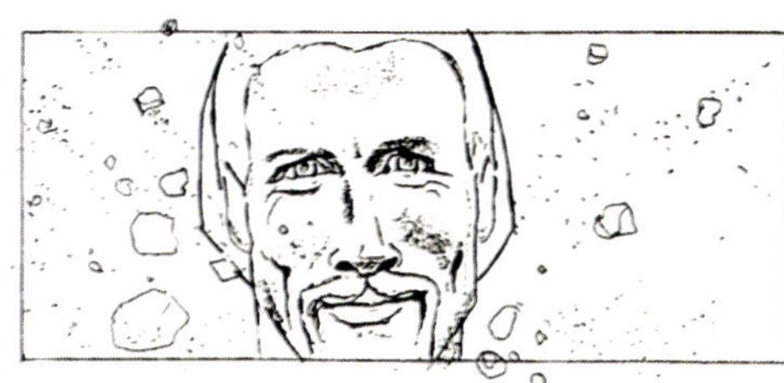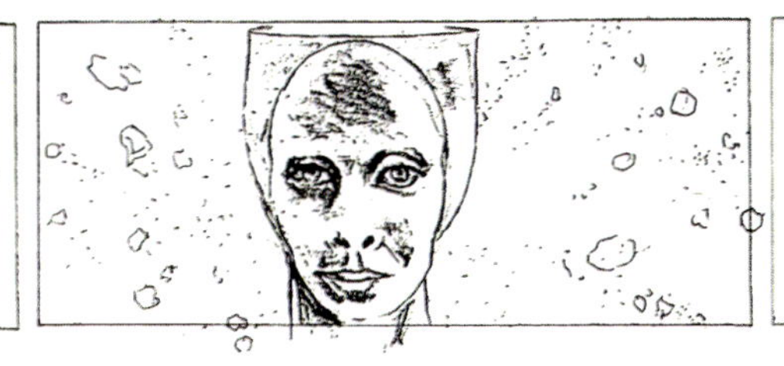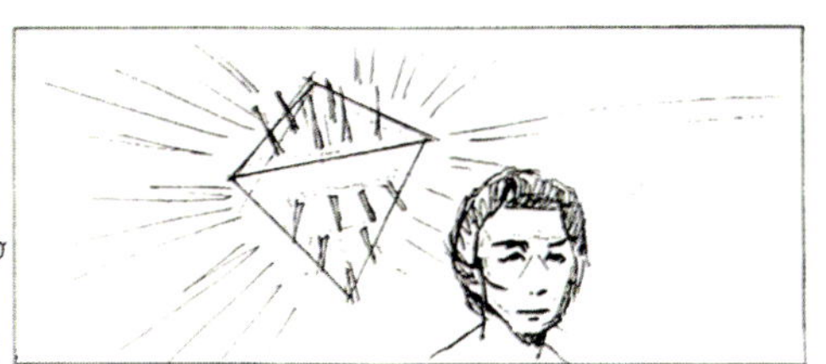

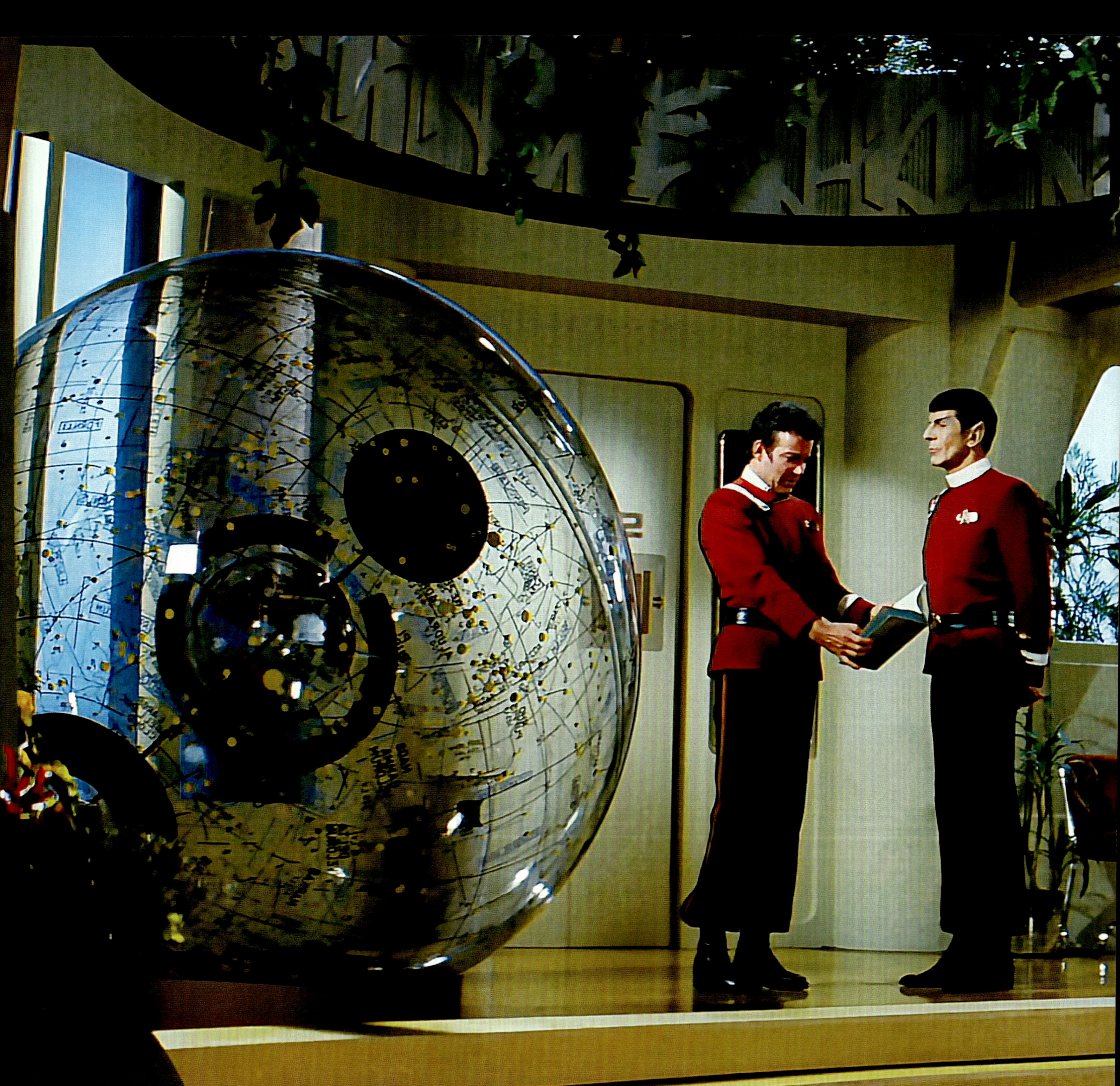

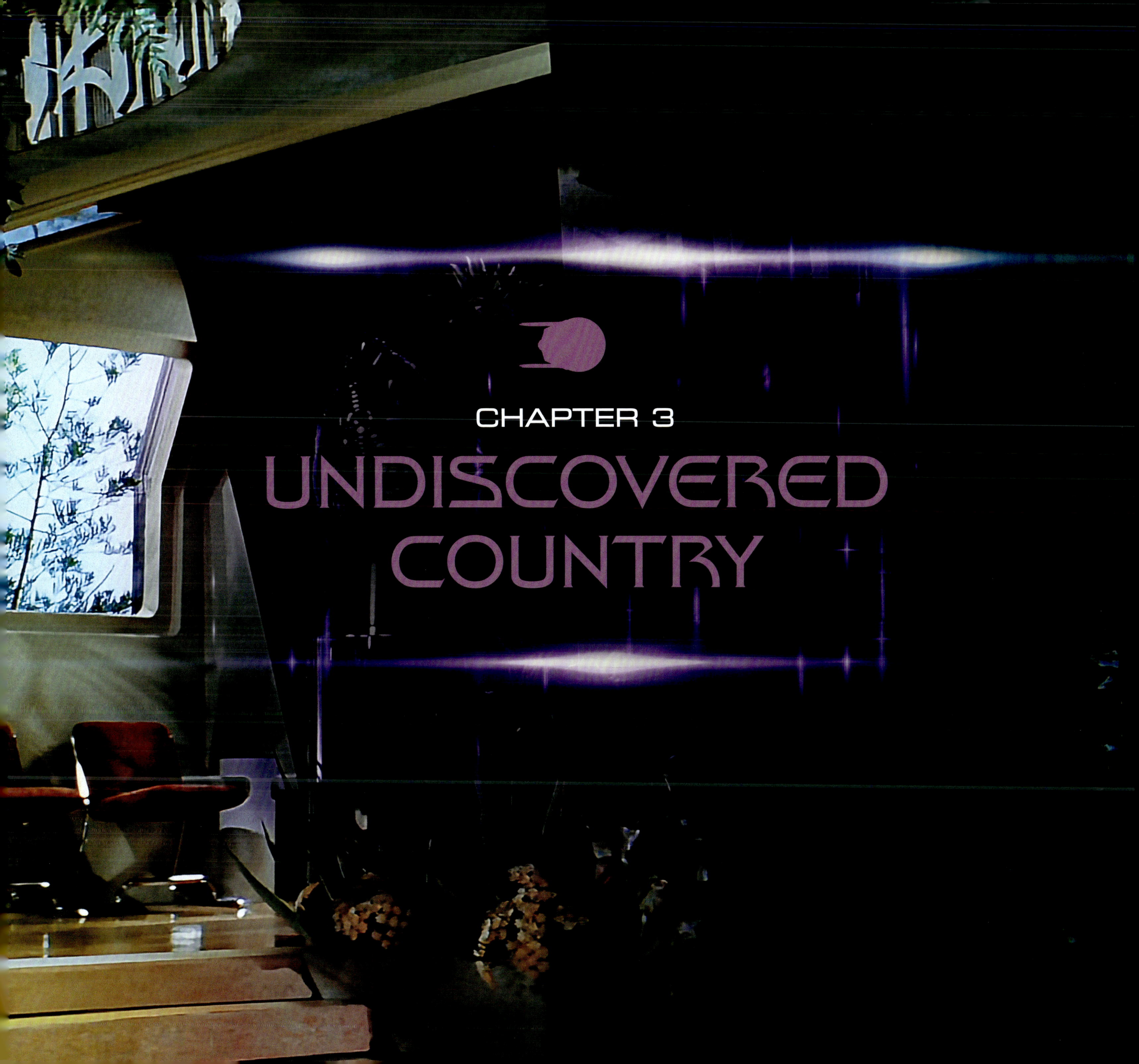

CHAPTER 3
UNDISCOVERED COUNTRY

NICHOLAS MEYER

A cinematic and literary heritage permeates *Star Trek II*, with on-screen nods to *Moby Dick* and *A Tale of Two Cities*, costuming influences from *The Prisoner of Zenda* (1937), and thematic debts to *The Enemy Below*. It is appropriate then that the person who would encircle *Star Trek II* with such film lore would be its director and scripter, Nicholas Meyer, who thinks and speaks frequently in the language of art, most especially film.

As Harve Bennett and Robert Sallin faced a looming problem of needing to give a workable script to ILM for special effects production in order to meet the June premiere date, Sallin was looking for a director after considering Ron Howard and Hugh Hudson as possibilities, among others. Meanwhile, Meyer was turning down offers to direct films as he was looking for what he considered a special project.

While barbequing—actually burning, according to Meyer—hamburgers at his Laurel Canyon home for friend and Paramount executive Karen Moore during summer 1981, Meyer got advice from Moore, telling him to stop procrastinating and do something creative with his time. She recommended that Meyer meet with Bennett. Having enjoyed *Star Wars*, Meyer began to be interested in the idea of making a space fantasy. It would be Meyer's chance to writ large the amateur science fiction film of his youth.

The meeting between Bennett, Sallin, and Meyer was productive, with Meyer agreeing to direct. He also offered the producers a lifeline solution to their script problems. Meyer had the idea of gathering together all the versions of the previous scripts by Bennett, Jack B. Sowards, and Samuel A. Peeples. They would choose what they liked, keep it, and Meyer would rework everything, adding original dialogue and scenes, restructuring existing sequences—all in a mere twelve days. Meyer recalls the writing process, "I didn't just write all the dialogue (as long as I am setting the record straight here), I took five different themes or plots from these five different movies and intertwined them. The dialogue was poured over the top like ketchup from start to finish, but the trickier part—because dialogue writing for me is easy—was intertwining: Kirk meets his son, Khan, the Genesis project, Lieutenant

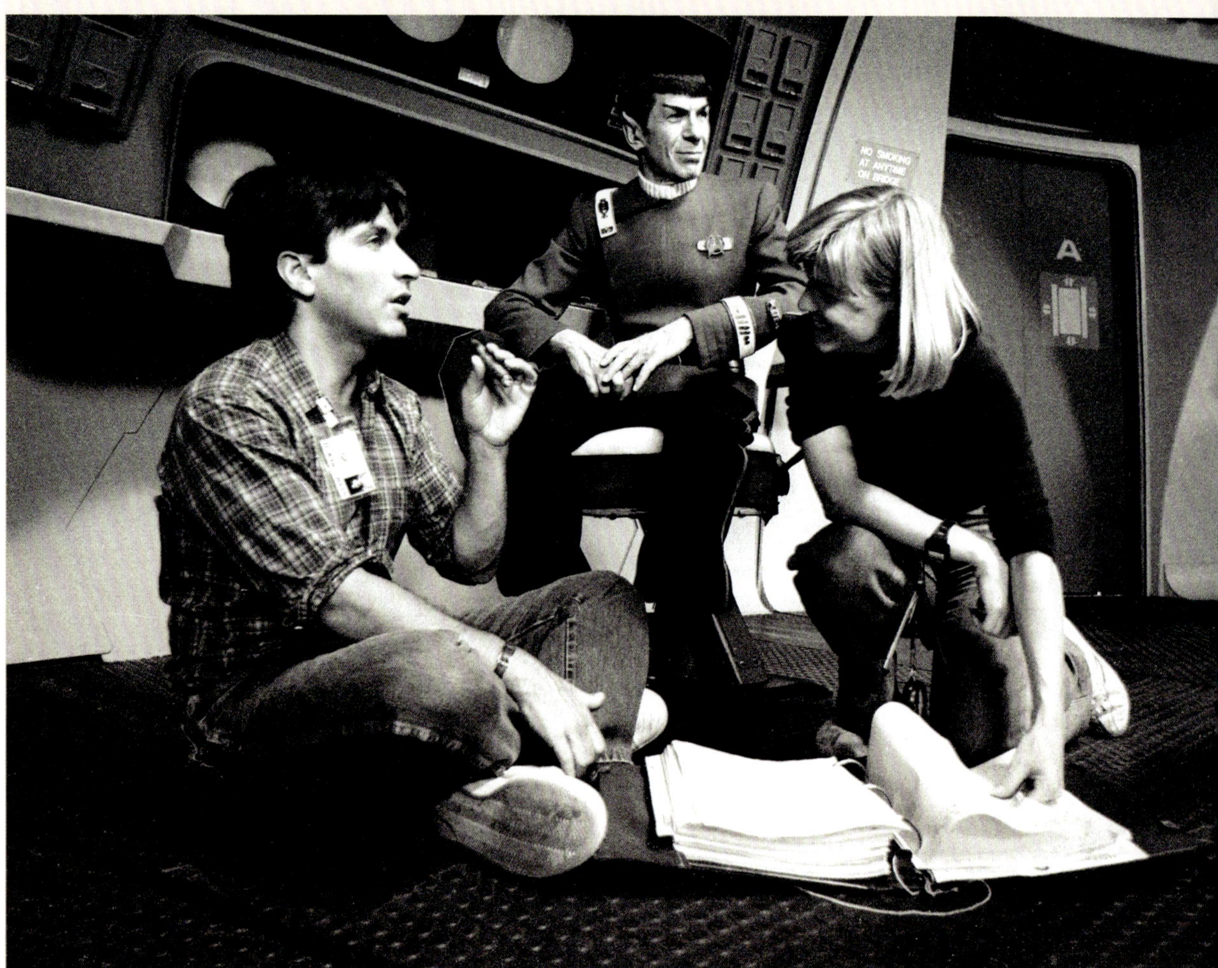

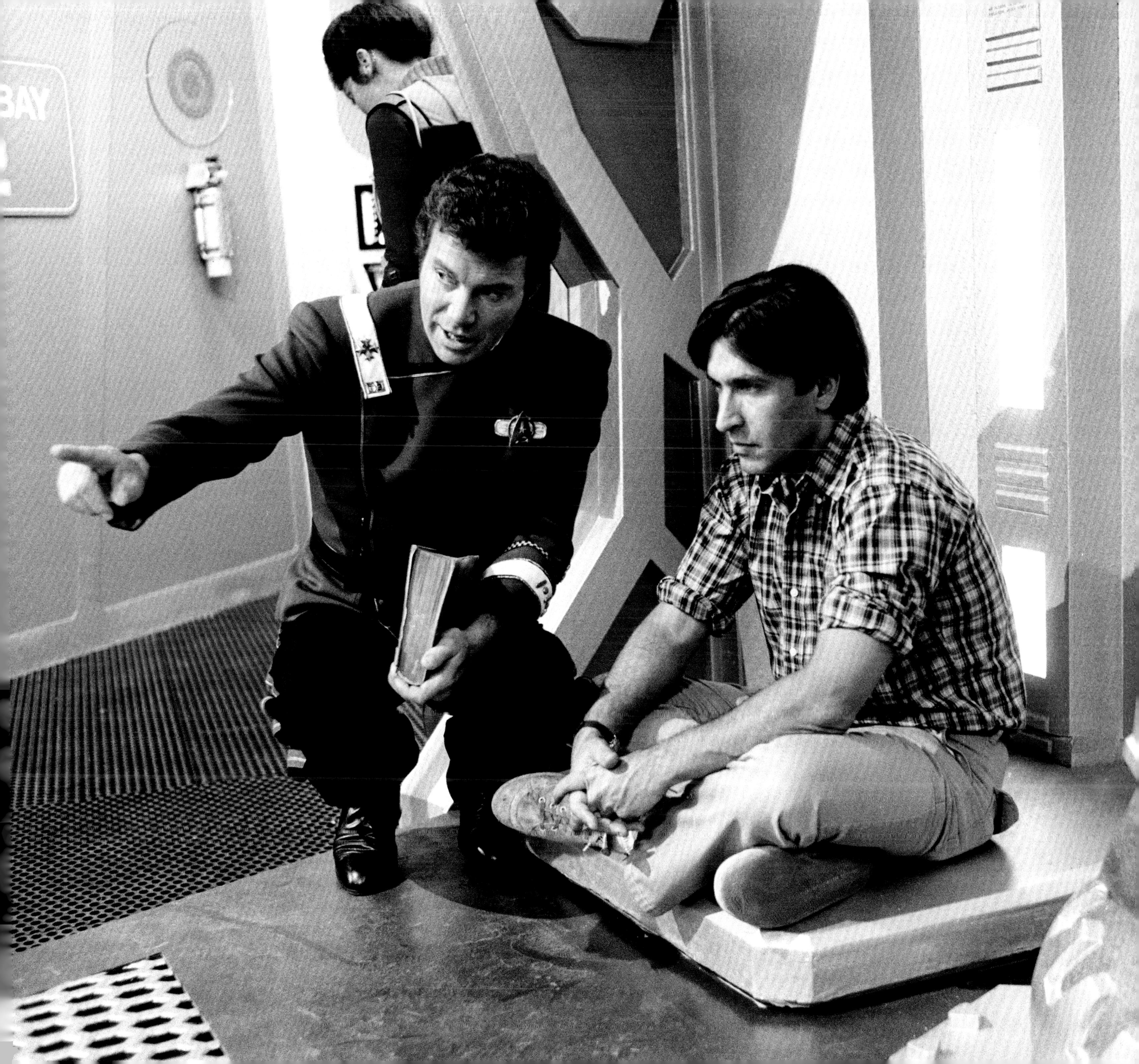

NICHOLAS MEYER

Born mere months after the end of World War II, on December 24, 1945, Nicholas Meyer grew up in a home that prized art and creativity. His mother Elly, born in Finland, was a concert pianist, his father Bernard a physician and psychoanalyst. Music, reading, and film were companions to Meyer, whose film tastes ran from the Marx Brothers to adventure fare such as *The African Queen*. He celebrated his birthday in 1956 with his parents by seeing *Around the World in 80 Days*, starring David Niven and Cantinflas. The film had a profound influence, inspiring Meyer to make his own, amateur version of the 1872 Jules Verne book. It would be a multi-year project for father and son, working together to produce what would become Meyer's first movie.

After the loss of his mother to cancer and graduating Fieldston High School—where he paraphrased a line from a John Dryden poem as his yearbook quote: "Happy the man who is able to say: Tomorrow do thy worst, for I have lived today."—Meyer went to the University of Iowa to study speech and the dramatic arts. For the school newspaper, the *Daily Iowan*, Meyer wrote film reviews, and during free time, his first screenplay. It was at UI that Meyer discovered not only his love of writing but of directing, when he directed weekly radio plays. At the school, one of his professors taught a lesson that would prove predictive. The teacher challenged students to watch an episode of *Star Trek* and *Mission: Impossible* without the sound on and again without the picture on. The idea was to demonstrate that *Star Trek* could be understood without the image, because it was a dialogue-heavy show, much like a radio drama, while it would be a near impossible mission to understand an episode of *Mission: Impossible* without the images.

Meyer would begin his career in the film industry as a publicist for Paramount Pictures. In 1974, Meyer combined his father's influence in the field of psychology and his own enthusiasm for the literary adventures of Sherlock Holmes and wrote the novel *The Seven-Percent Solution*, told from the perspective of John Watson, as his friend Holmes was helped with his cocaine addiction by Sigmund Freud. The book would become one of the best sellers of the year and Meyer wrote the Oscar®-nominated screenplay to the movie that followed. His first—and until *Star Trek II*—only Hollywood directing credit was *Time After Time*, the 1979 fantasy thriller that has H. G. Wells chasing Jack the Ripper through time. Meyer directed and wrote the screenplay, based on a story by Steve Hayes and an unpublished novel by Karl Alexander.

Meyer would return to the world of *Star Trek* as the cowriter of *Star Trek IV: The Voyage Home* and cowriter and director of *Star Trek VI: The Undiscovered Country*. He served as a consulting producer on the first season of *Star Trek: Discovery* and on September 8, 2022 confirmed that he is scripting *Star Trek: Khan: Ceti Alpha V*, a Khan-centric scripted podcast prequel to *Star Trek II*.

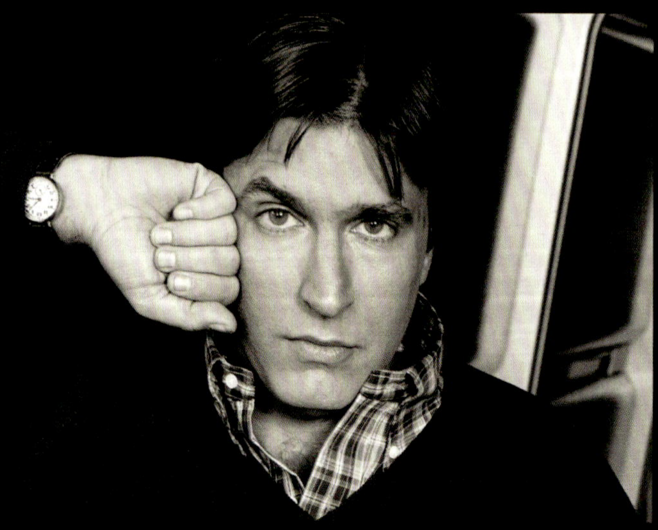

Saavik, Spock dies, the simulator sequence. That was sort of the more involved thing. Once I understood how they were going to link up, then it was fairly easy to write the dialogue."[1]

For Meyer, rooting *Star Trek* in something familiar was not only necessary from a story perspective, it was necessary for him to understand the world he would be writing and directing. Never a fan of the original television show, and only passingly familiar with it because of friends, Meyer needed a hook upon which to hang an emotional and intellectual understanding of the characters and situations that Roddenberry had created. For him, thinking of Starfleet as the future version of either the Navy or Coast Guard was something he could appreciate. "I had a sort of generic association not only with Horatio Hornblower but destroyers and battleships and submarines, absolutely when I was thinking about the Mutara Nebula. But I didn't recollect the very specific movie when I wrote my memoir [*The View from the Bridge*]. I did not recollect, at the time, the movie that had the biggest influence on me was a favorite of mine and it is called *The Enemy Below*. I didn't have a conscious recollection of that specific movie while we were doing ours. It was only later that I thought, 'Where did I get that idea for the destroyer versus the submarine and prowling about?' and that was it."[2]

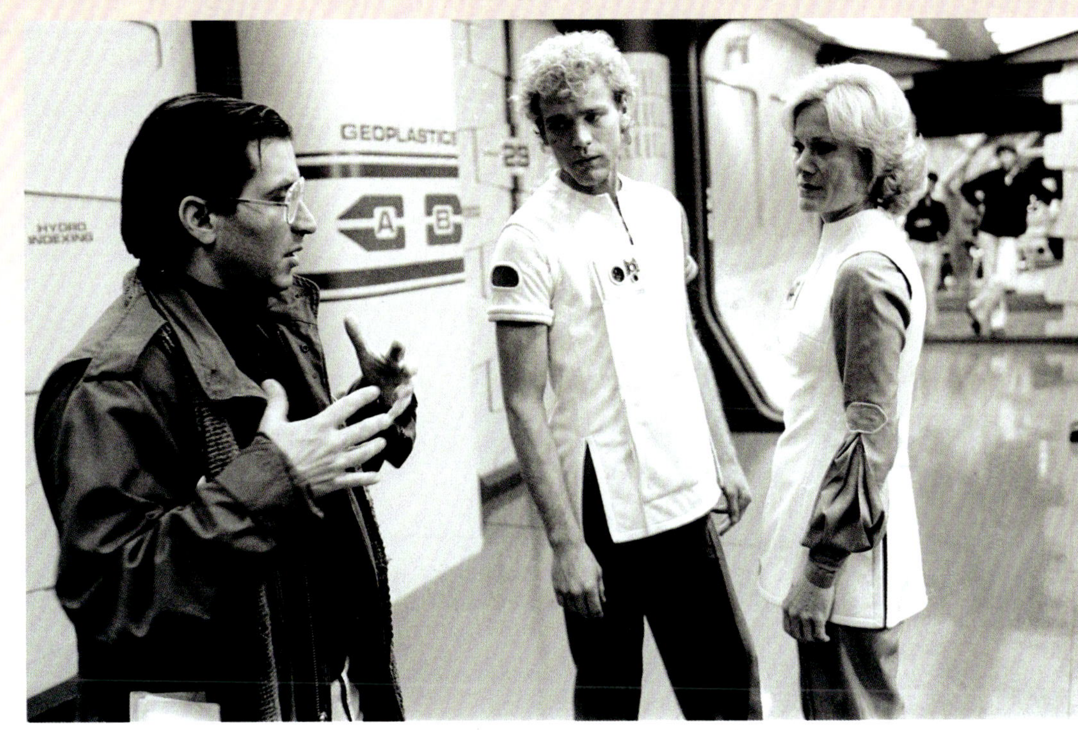

ABOVE: Meyer: "Bibi Besch (who later acted for me to great effect in my television movie *The Day After*) played former sweetheart of the libidinous Kirk, while a young actor named Merritt Butrick played their illegitimate son."[13]

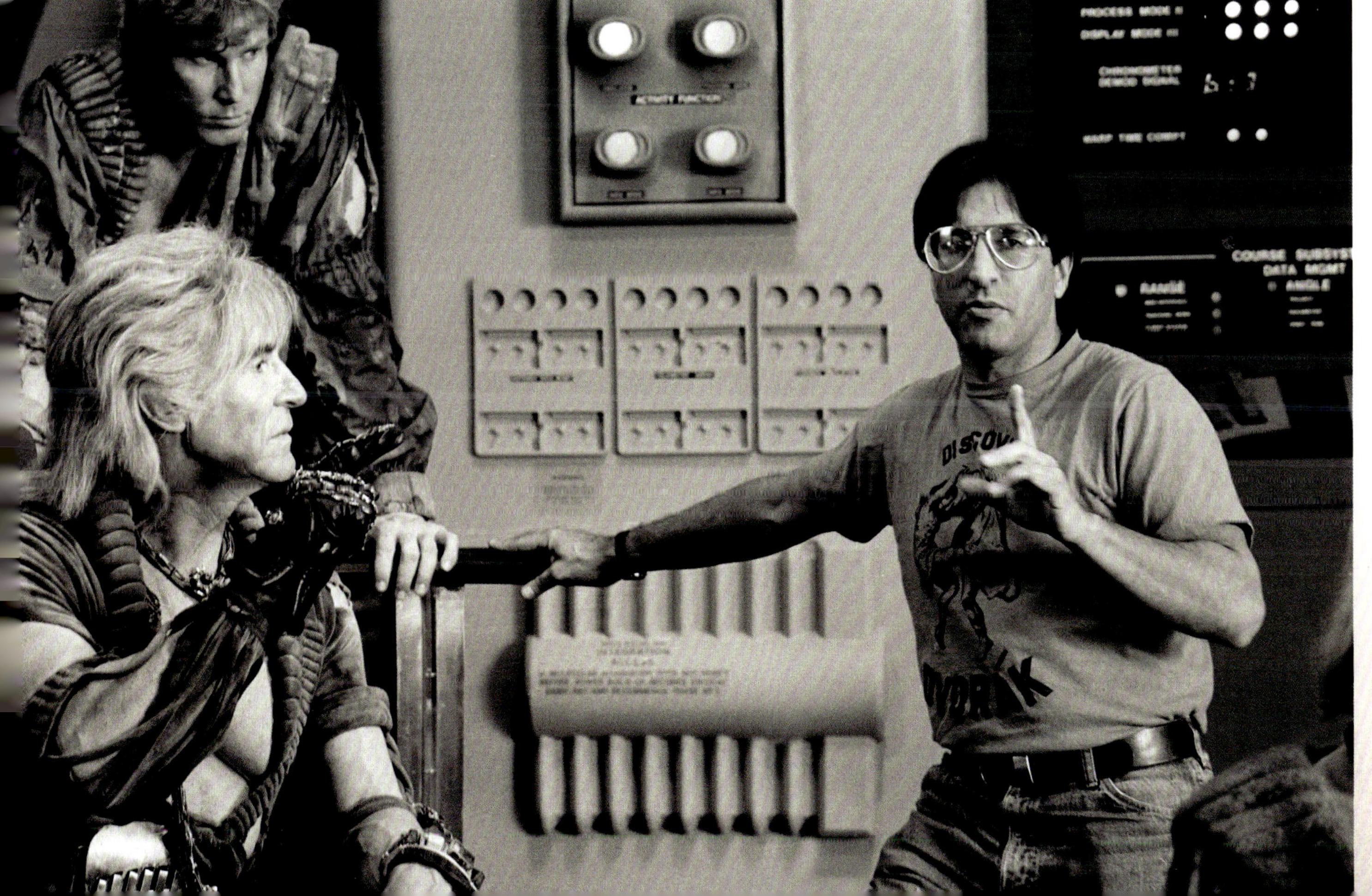

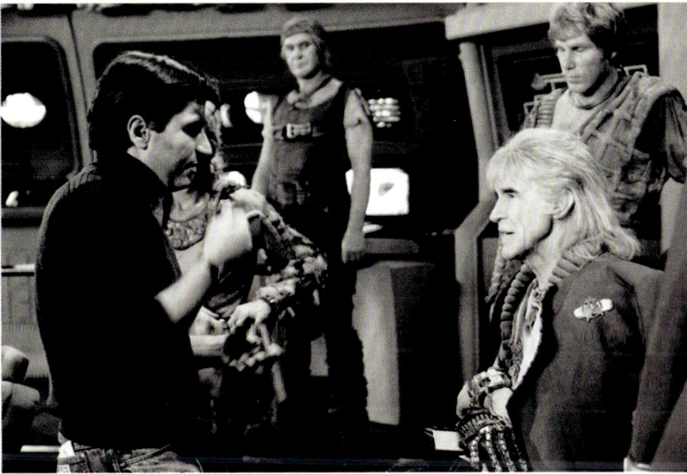

LEFT & ABOVE: Meyer and Montalban would become good friends during and after the filming of *Star Trek II*. Meyer was in awe of meeting one of Hollywood's iconic performers, and gave him a copy of *Moby Dick* when they met, telling Montalban everything he needed to know about Khan was in Herman Melville's writing.

Fans of *Star Trek II* will appreciate the cinematic inspiration that is *The Enemy Below*. The 1957 cat-and-mouse duel between a United States destroyer, led by Captain Murrell (Robert Mitchum), and German U-boat commander Von Stolberg (Curd Jürgens) was directed by Dick Powell. Although Powell was best known to audiences as a musical comedy performer and a dramatic actor, his gripping direction of the game of brinksmanship between Murrell's destroyer on the surface of the South Atlantic and Von Stolberg's submarine below the surface would greatly influence the Mutara Nebula battle scenes of *Star Trek II*.

It was an experience that Meyer had when he was eight or nine years old that would inspire a life-long fascination with submarines. "My father decided to take his family on a mid-winter vacation and we went to Puerto Rico and the Virgin Islands. In the Virgin Islands, we visited the island of St. Thomas and the town of Charlotte Amalie and the naval base. We got to go on board a submarine, which I recall was the USS *Tusk*." Meyer got separated from his parents, and found himself as a "kid on the loose in the Caribbean." The crew of the *Tusk* adopted him for the day and Meyer went on maneuvers with the submarine

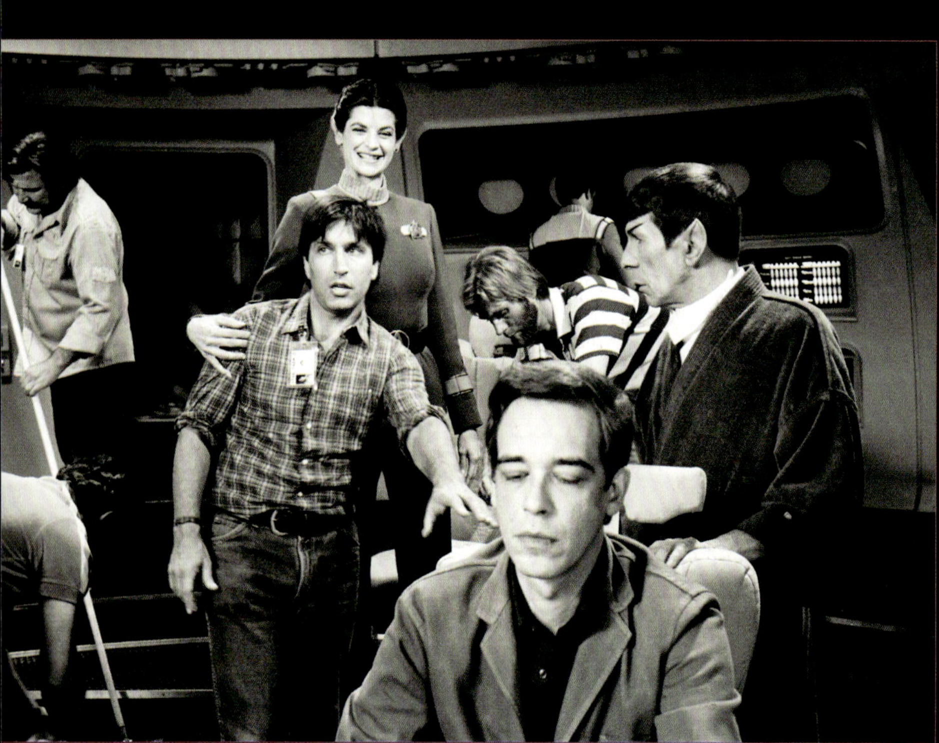

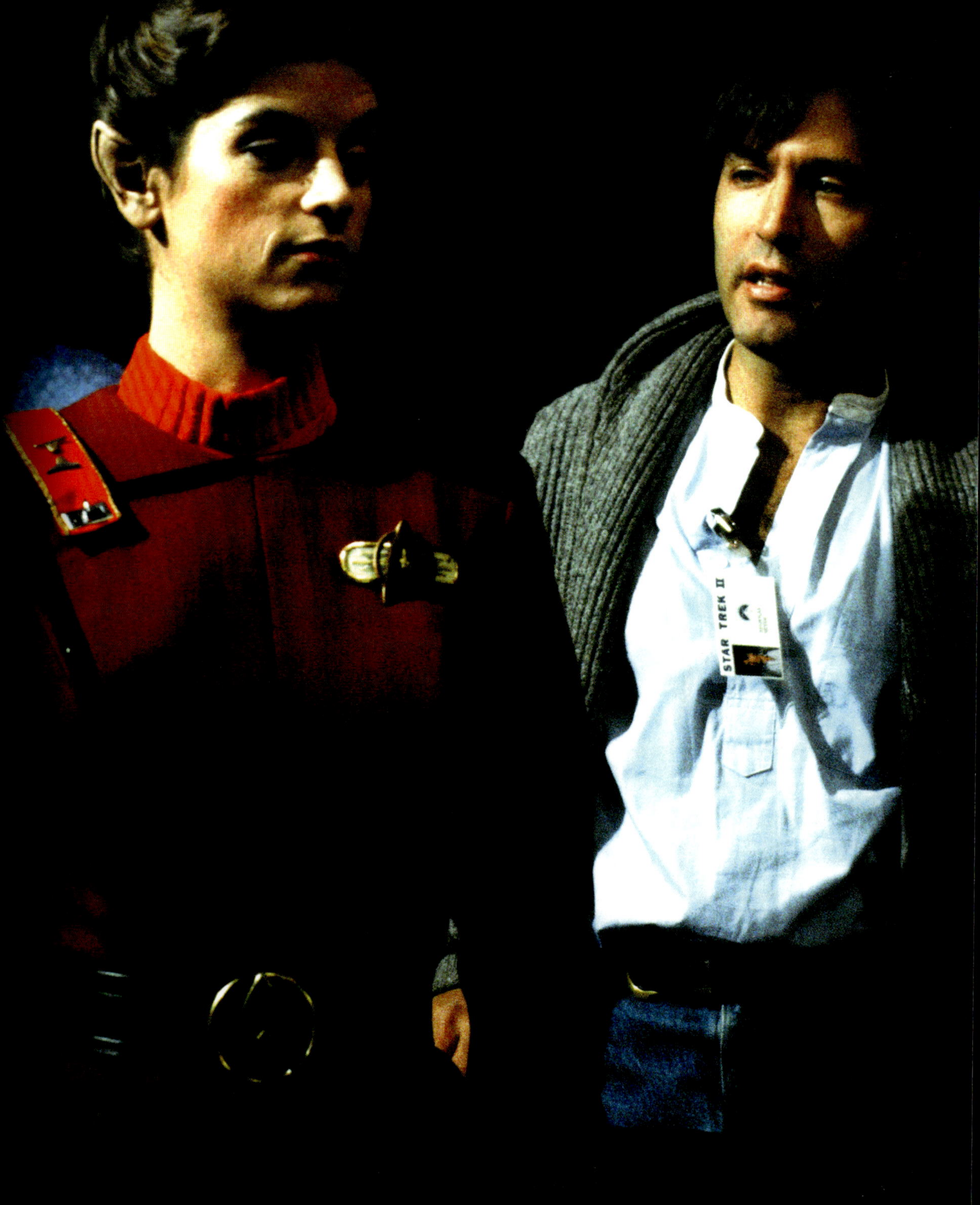

BIRTHDAYS

In *Star Trek II*, Spock and McCoy observe Kirk's birthday, an event that inspires an existential crisis for the admiral. On set, however, birthdays were much happier events. December 24, 1981, Meyer celebrated his 36th birthday, including a cake (far right) and a thank you card signed by the actors playing Khan's followers reading "Nice to have worked with you: KHANSMEN." January 20, 1982, DeForest Kelley celebrated his 62nd birthday with a cake that featured, appropriately, bones (below).

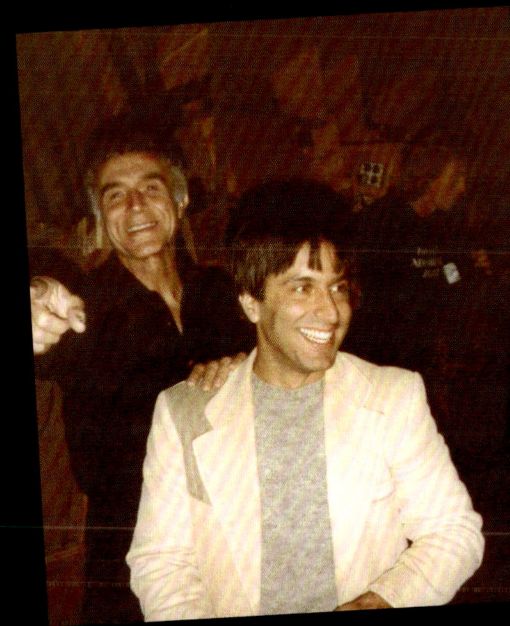

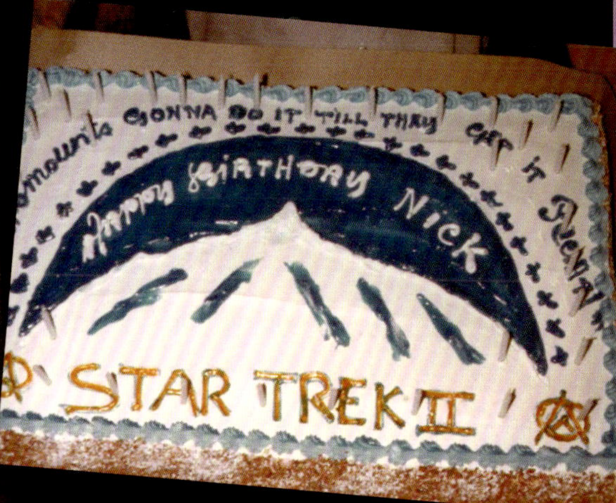

LEFT: Montalban helps Meyer celebrate his 36th birthday

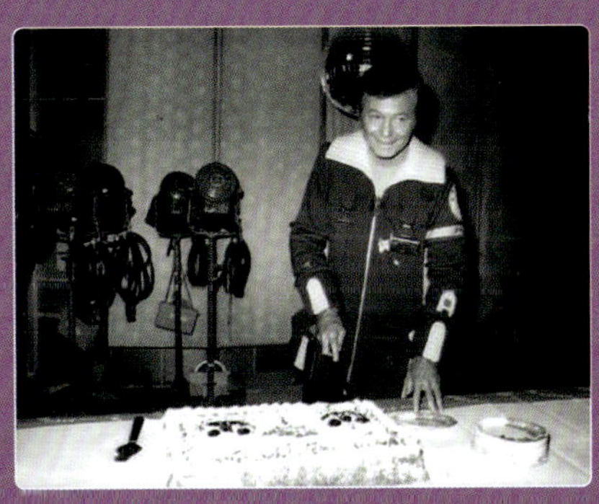

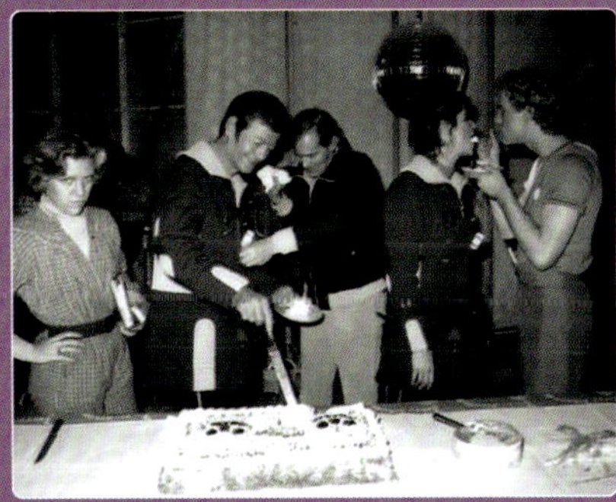

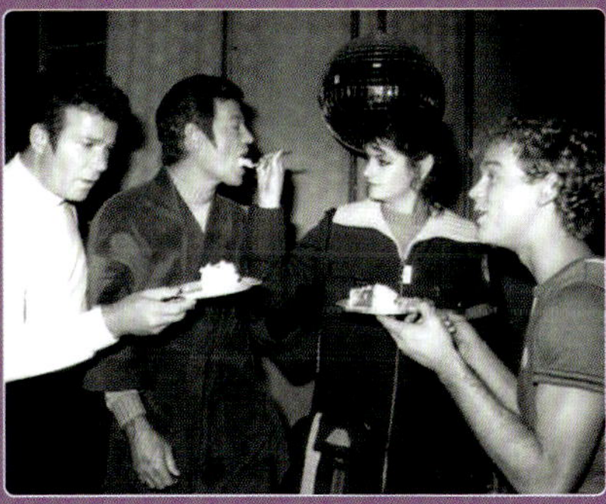

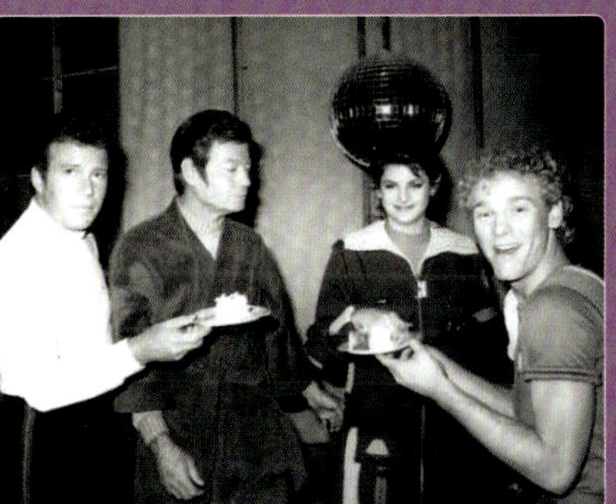

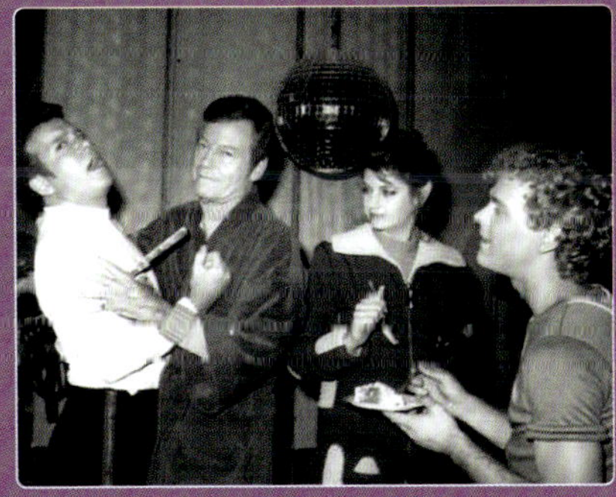

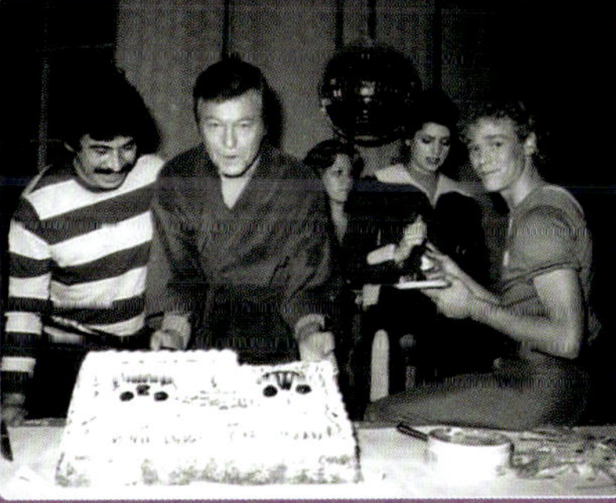

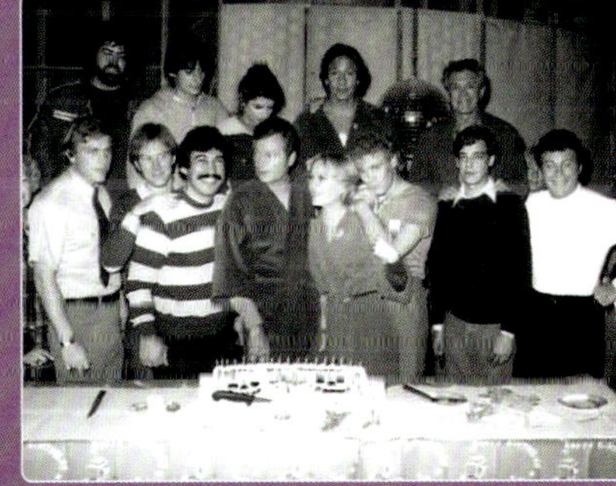

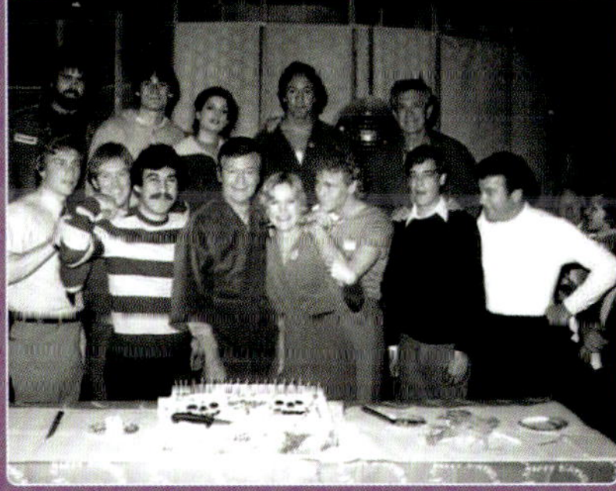

WAS *STAR TREK II* EVER A TV MOVIE?

The confusion began when fanzines and professional magazines like *Starlog* reported that the sequel was a television movie of the week. "*Star Trek* Back on the TV Track" proclaimed the May 1981 issue of *Starlog*. "Paramount Pictures is currently developing a two-hour *Trek* TV film with Harve Bennet [sic]—best known to SF fans for his work on *The Six Million Dollar Man* and *Salvage I*—as producer and Jack Soward [sic] as writer. The decision to make a television movie instead of a *Star Trek: The Motion Picture* sequel was obviously based on cost factors. (Actors' and crews' salaries are almost always much higher on a film made for cinematic release.) Yet Paramount has admitted that if the TV-movie is good enough, it could be released theatrically instead of being broadcast on the tube (as was done with Universal's *Buck Rogers* pilot). Even if the film is aired—either on network television or via syndication—it will inevitably be released overseas as a feature film. If the first telefeature is successful, Paramount will produce a series of *Star Trek* 'specials.'"[9]

The September 9, 1981, issue of *Weekly Variety* gave the same idea: "Paramount will release the project theatrically abroad, but has decided to take a 'wait and see posture' domestically. At one point, it had been planned as a two-hour telefilm and later anticipated as a feature. Word is creative personnel are receiving salaries 'commensurate with a feature film.'"[10]

Adding to the uncertainty, a September 18, 1981 press release by Paramount tried to clarify that *Star Trek II* had never been planned as anything except a full-length motion picture.

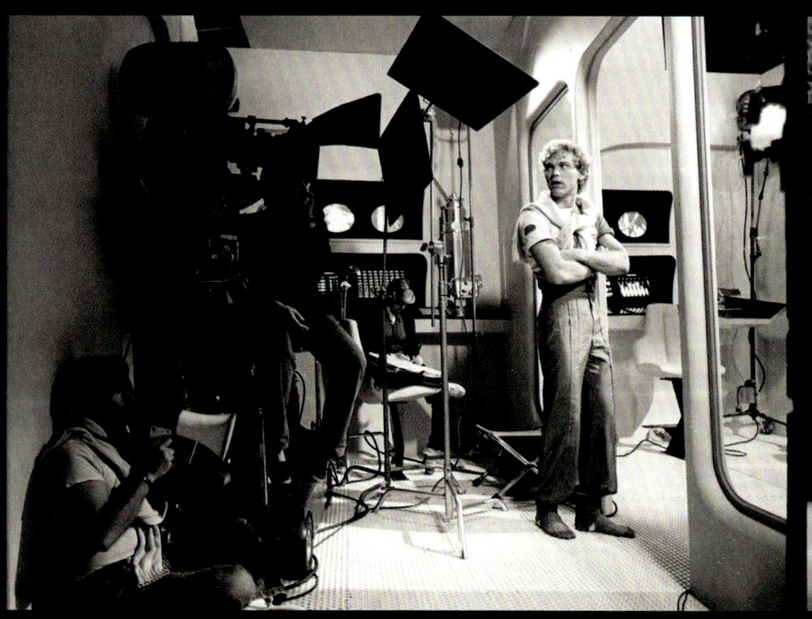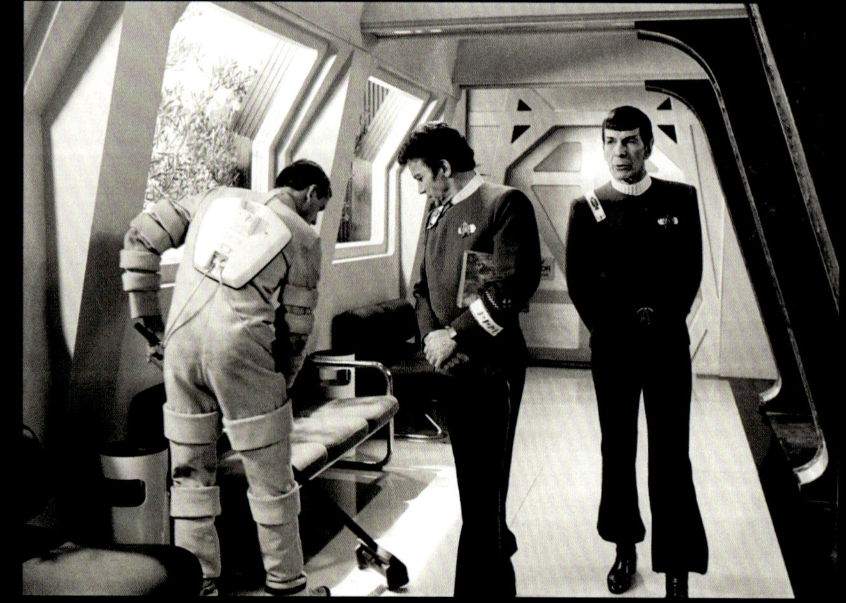

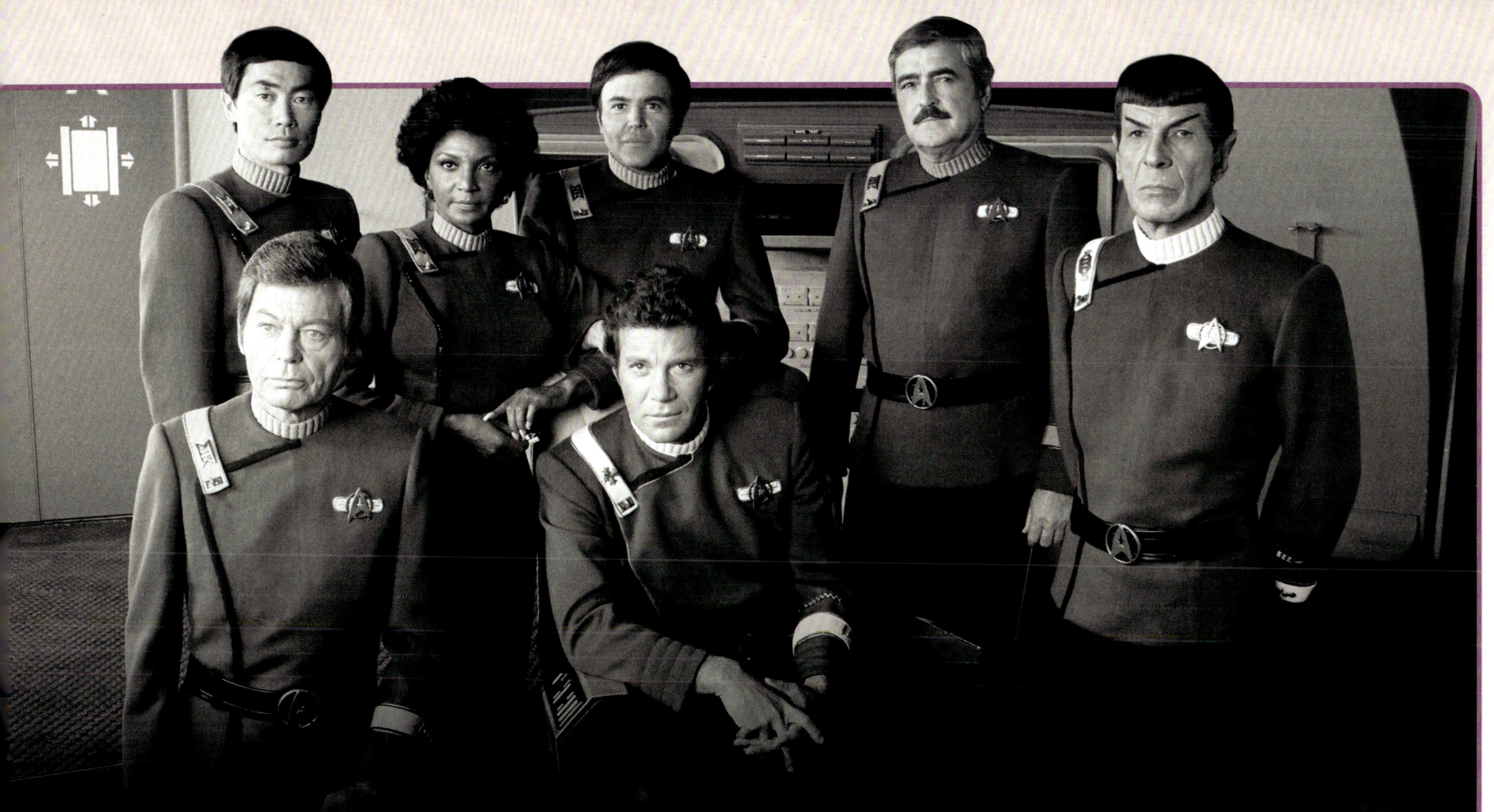

The reality is that *Star Trek II* was planned as a movie of the week from the start, but with the option to pivot to a theatrical film if merited. A September 29, 1981 memo by Bob Rosenbaum to Gary Nardino of Paramount Television presented a detailed summary of the situation. According to the memo, on June 9, 1981, Television Production had produced a budget for *Star Trek II*, using the April 10, 1981 script by Harve Bennett and Jack B. Sowards as the guide. It was budgeted as a two-hour movie of the week to be made in thirty-five days at a cost of $4,914,786 plus visual effects costs. However, sometime after June 9, the decision was made to go theatrical and anamorphic. Rosenbaum wrote, "To summarize, things have changed." Preliminary budget adjustments are detailed, for example, how wardrobe would now cost approximately $99,783 more if a feature film. The number of production days was anticipated to be more, about forty or fifty days, it was estimated.

Rosenbaum wrote, "Management's decision to go theatrical and anamorphic has changed some things. Detail on the large screen is much more obvious than were it to be on television. Set construction, set dressing, special effects, wardrobe and, of course, special optical effects have to be much more sophisticated. This along with crews to be hired knowing that this is now a major motion picture (as was so announced) and who will not work for less than feature money have made this first budget escalate."

Meyer does not recall ever conceiving of the project as anything except a theatrical film, which is another indication that the decision to make *Star Trek II* a film rather than a movie of the week was decided before his involvement began in August 1981. However, before that summer, and certainly at its inception, a movie of the week was the original plan.

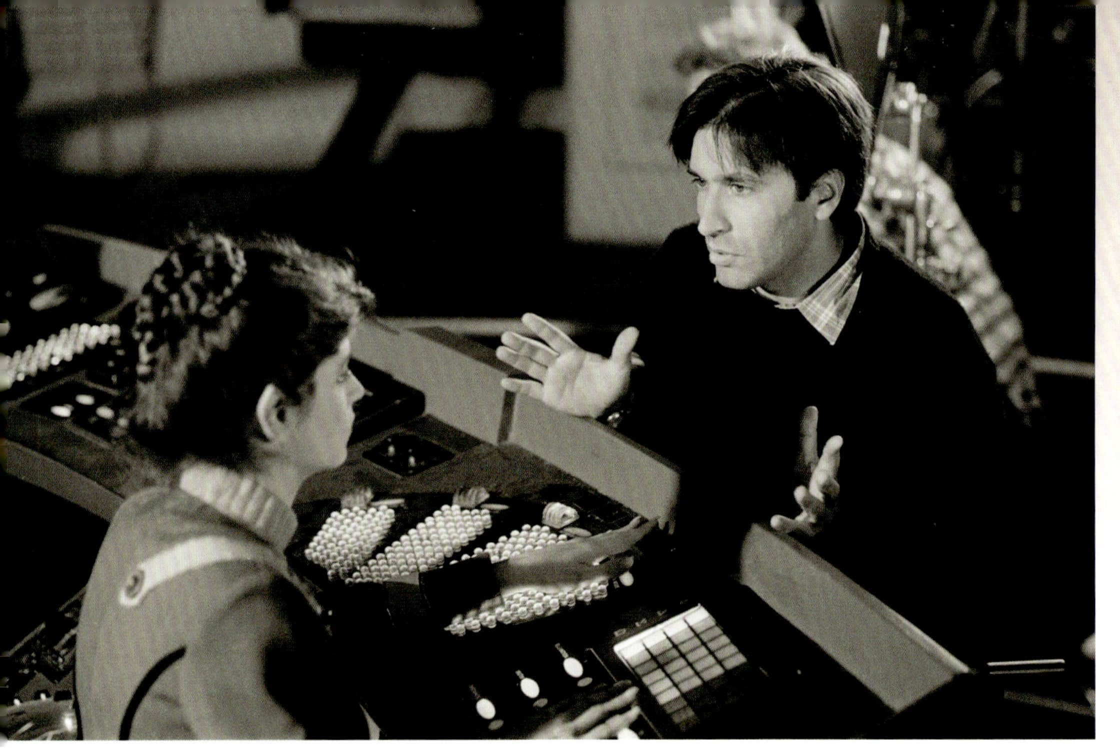
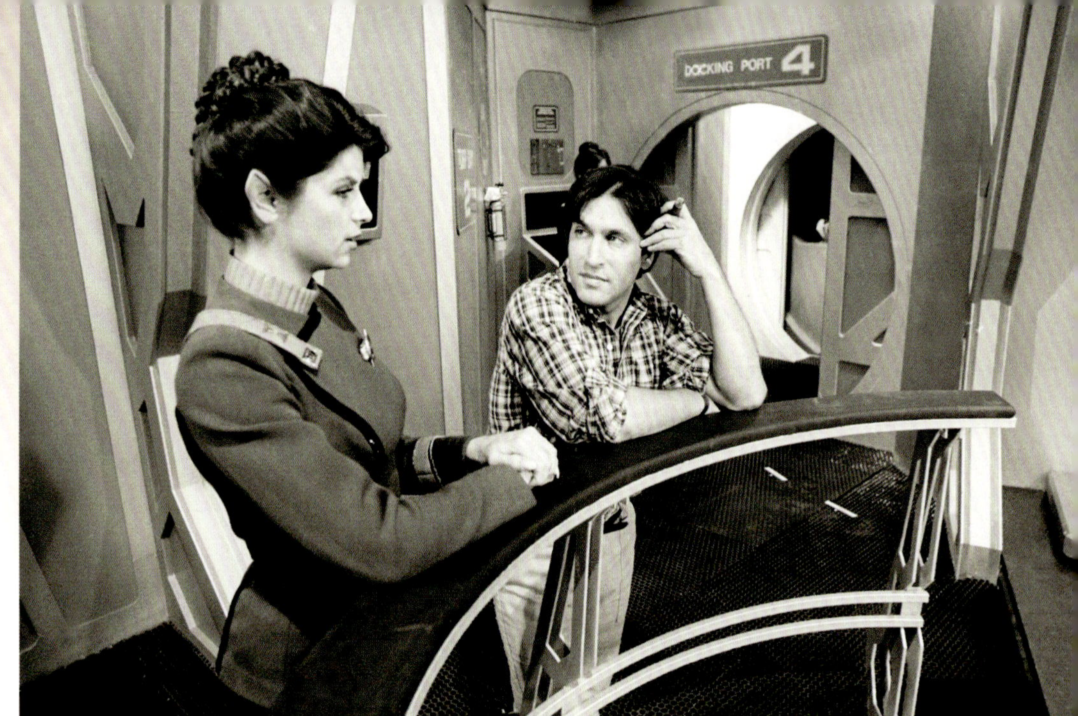

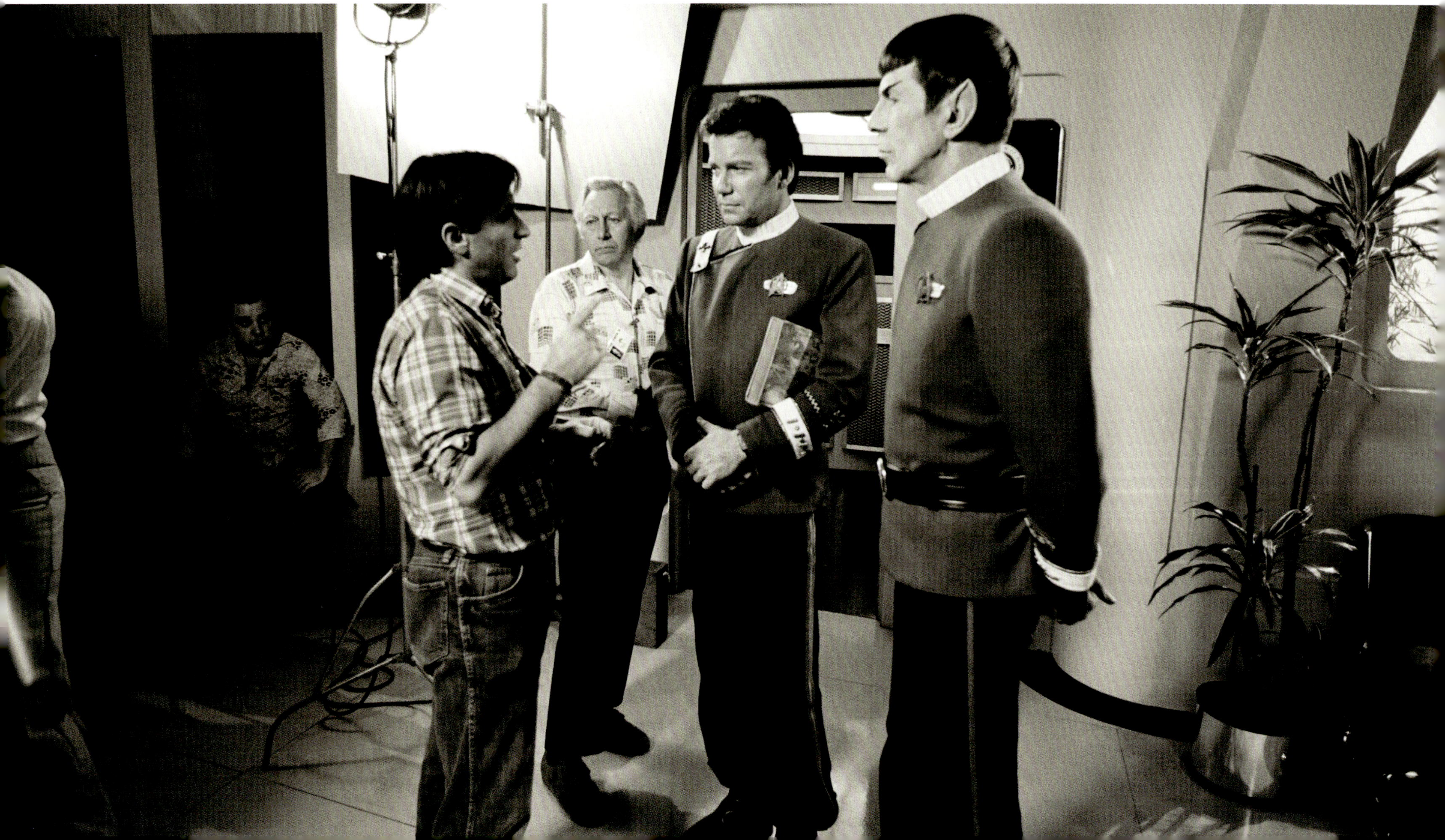

crew while his parents were located. "Once I sunk my teeth into the naval analogy, the Hornblower analogy or metaphor, I stuck with that. I just said, 'Okay this is about the Navy and this is the Navy in outer space.'"[3]

With his metaphor in place, Meyer wrote his first version of the script and delivered it on September 10, 1981, named "Star Trek: The New Frontier." While met with enthusiasm by most, there were changes requested, necessitating more reworking and versions. One change was eliminating the reference to Kirk's specific age of forty-nine and also the removal of a face-to-face Kirk and Khan fight.

Bennett also recommended some dialogue changes and additions. Meyer reveals, "There are a few lines of dialogue that are Harve's: 'Would you care for a tranquilizer?' 'Captain, this is the garden spot of Ceti Alpha V,' and there's a couple of others. At one point I had used the word patricide and Harve said, 'No, no, no. That's too Rococo for this show.' So, it became something like, 'You'll have killed your father.'"

By September 16, Meyer submitted another version, now named "Star Trek: The Undiscovered Country." In order to get the project rolling, Meyer forwent a writing credit, despite his significant contributions to story and dialogue.

As director, Meyer faced a personal minefield: *Star Trek II* was not the normal kind of film. It was part of a legacy, with actors who had played their characters for fifteen years, and with an enthusiastic, sometimes vociferous fan community. Yet, he had only directed one other film. The mood on a film set is very much a reflection of the personality and experience of the director. Not wanting to have the kind of stress that some had experienced on the *Motion Picture* set, Meyer would make a series of decisions about how to approach the film that would make the set a happy, creative one despite the challenges.

Drawing on his theater roots, Meyer understood the value of rehearsal in helping not only actors find their characters, but in building a company of artists comfortable with one another. Meyer reveals, "The thing about rehearsals is that studios don't want you doing them. Agents don't want you doing them, because from the agent's standpoint the actor isn't being paid to rehearse. From the studio, they don't want to budget for it. So it is only actors, out of professionalism, who are intent on or gratified to do some rehearsals. It is just by default. The film wasn't even mentioned. It was just, 'Where are we going to do this where no one is going to bother us?' And I said, 'Do it at my house.'"[4] Bibi Besch (Carol) and Merritt Butrick (David), new to *Star Trek*, found the rehearsals especially helpful in making them feel part of the family.

Planning was a strategy that Meyer knew would not only save time and money, but creative energy. Sallin, too, knew the value of proper prior planning. The use of storyboards, designed mostly by art director Michael Minor and Sallin, was one way to avoid problems. "The storyboards were essential for many reasons. One of which is if you are doing a movie with special effects, you really have to plan how you are going to achieve those effects and what you want those effects to look like on the screen. So storyboards were essential. Another fact—this was only the second movie I had ever directed and I needed all the help I could get in terms of planning what I was going to do,"[5] Meyer shared.

Meyer wanted a set where anyone could contribute an idea. Yes, the film would be his vision as director. Yet, he knew that he was surrounded by actors, artists, and technicians with decades more experience. A good idea was a good idea. "When I said what I wanted, these guys felt like they were let out of school. That I had turned them loose. I guess so much of this had been under the vision of Gene Roddenberry and so tightly controlled and I would say, 'Look, let's forget all that. I don't want to see them in the Dr. Denton [sleepers-style] outfits. I want the Navy and let's just start over.'"[6]

OPPOSITE: Meyer on set with Alley, Shatner and Nimoy.

BELOW: *Star Trek* newcomer Besch and veteran Kelley on set between takes.

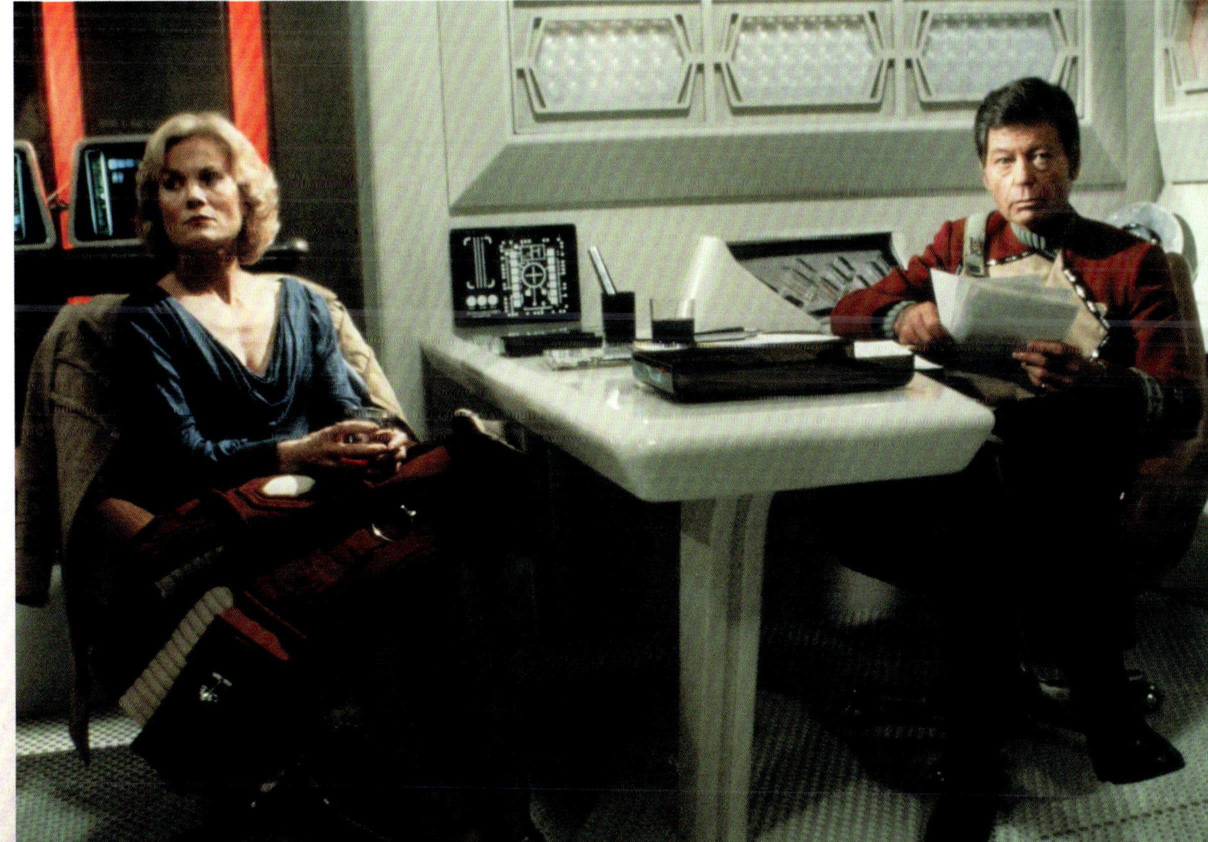

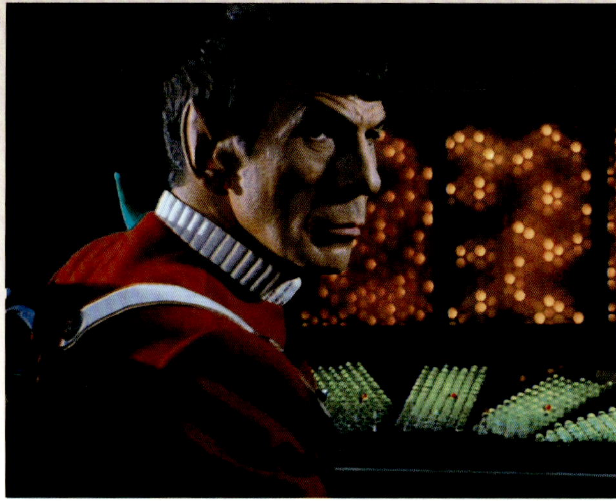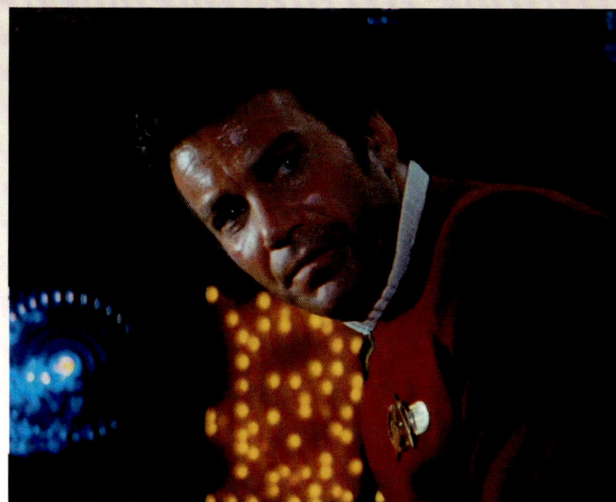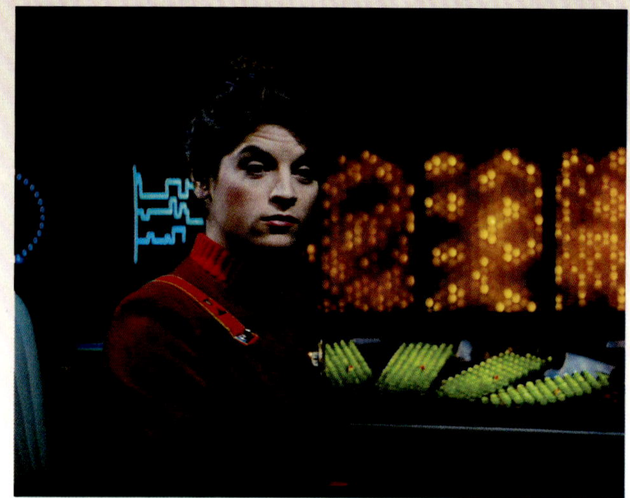

Nichelle Nichols agreed about the collaborative spirit, "With *Star Trek II* I think everyone had a sense that the show was going to be a return to the series. We felt that this movie would be the essence of *Star Trek*. We rehearsed prior to it, we met at Nick Meyer's home. We went through it and we talked about even the smallest things. We said to Nick, 'Those are our characters, who we were.' Even if it was one line or a huge scene. In other words we fed to him who we are so that when he went on that stage he would know about those characters."[7]

The result was a set where business got done, but without everyone forgetting to have a good time. Nichols describes one of the jokes that would be played on Meyer: "We had a running joke about the honeycomb panels on the bridge. It was called the honeycomb effect. On the first movie, Bob Wise and Doug Wise, who was the assistant director, didn't quite know what to do with this crazy cast (Laughter). Every time they needed it, the honeycomb lights would not go on or they would forget to turn it on. When the director would yell for the honeycomb, the entire cast would break out into the song "Honeycomb!" (Laughter)… On *Star Trek II*, my costumer and I got together and she got a tape of the original "Honeycomb" song by The Kingston Trio. We got with the special effects guys and the sound people and we waited all day long until they forgot to turn the honeycomb lights on. Sure enough, somebody yelled and they fell for it! (Laughter). He yelled for the honeycomb and we turned on this tape that went through the entire set of The Kingston Trio singing "Honeycomb" right in the middle of an important scene!"[8]

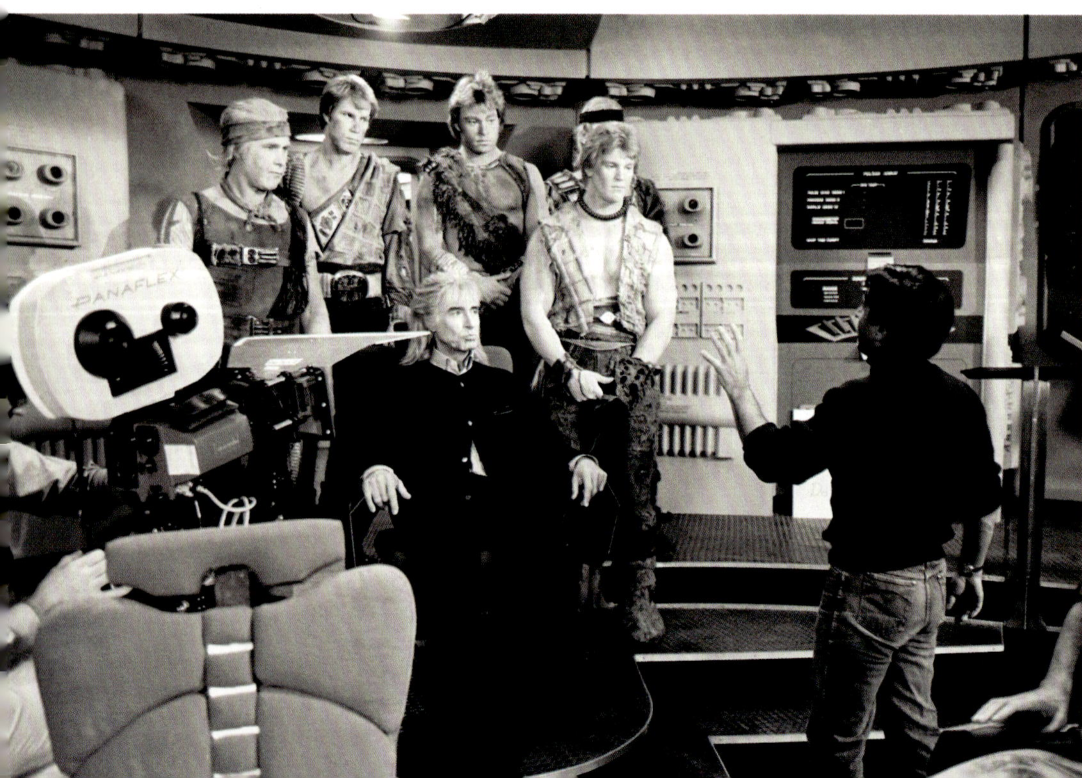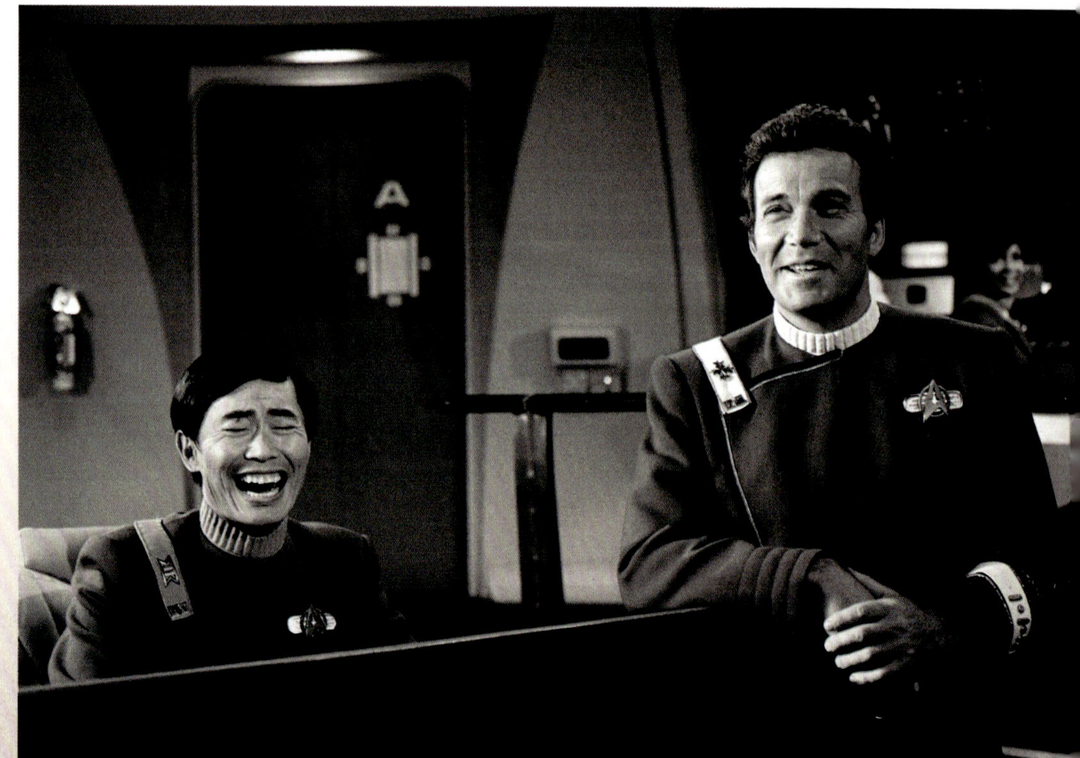

THE KHAN BABY

Perhaps the most intriguing character edited out of *Star Trek II* was its youngest: the Khan Baby. As originally scripted, Chekov first sees the Khan Baby through the porthole window of the *Botany Bay* cargo containers as he and Terrell first discover what would turn out to be Khan's encampment. Chekov screams, excitedly pronouncing, "A face! I saw—it was like a child…" As they search the cargo containers, Chekov again hears the child making noises and they discover the baby sitting on the floor right before Chekov sees the name Botany Bay on the safety belt and pieces together their situation. This scene was filmed and appears in the novelization to the movie by Vonda McIntyre.

As the script continues, when Khan captures Chekov and Terrell and recounts his experiences, he begins to cry, and thinking of his wife, says to his captives, "A plague upon you, murderers and traitors all.

Who will be a mother to my infant son?" Clearly, then, the Khan Baby was exactly as his mullet and costume hint at, Khan and Marla McGivers' son. However, by the November 6 script revision, the plague line stays, but the identification of the child as Khan and Marla's son is removed.

The Khan Baby would have made a second appearance in the movie. The original plan was to have the child, drawn by the bright lights of the Genesis Device, crawl towards the torpedo once it was armed. The implications are devastating, that the first victim of the Genesis explosion would have been the child closest to it. When the time to film the scene occurred, the actor playing the child was too scared by the bright helicopter lights that comprised the torpedo prop and the scene could not be filmed. First camera Craig DeNault and Meyer tried to acclimate the child to the environment, but to no avail.

According to Meyer, the idea of the Khan Baby scenes were to show that Khan and his people had a possible future, that they were surviving despite conditions, and that Khan was willing to sacrifice that future because of his obsession. However, the darkness of the implications of the second scene, if it had been included, could have overshadowed the film.

Being unable to film the second scene may be considered a fortunate happenstance and an example of how sometimes even production minefields can improve a movie.

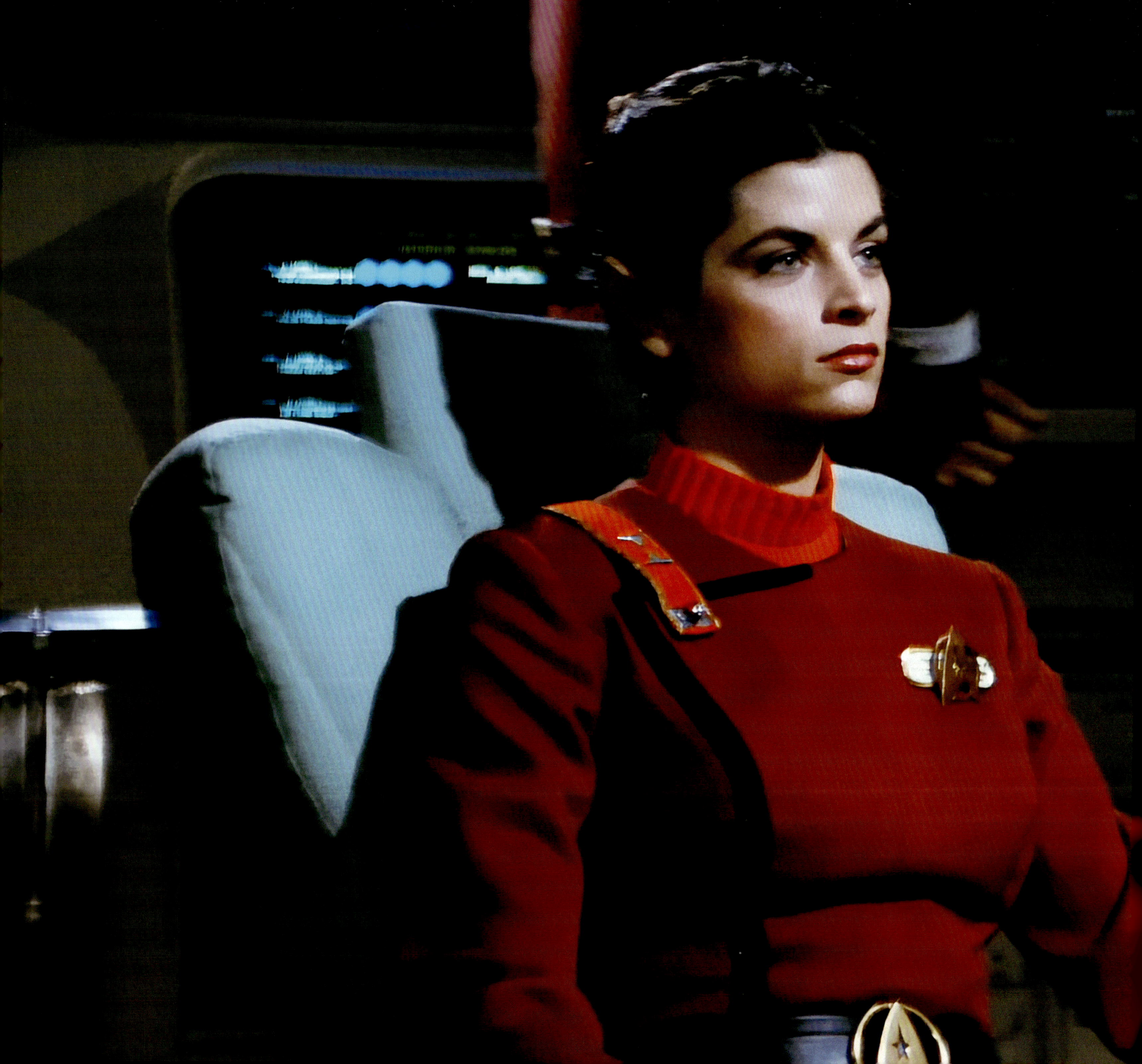

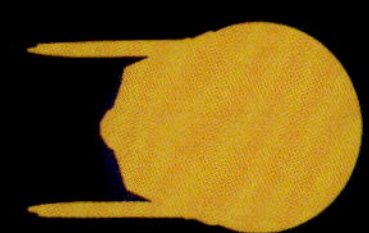

ENTERPRISE WELCOMES YOU

NEW AND RETURNING FACES

Star Trek is both absolute and variable. There are rules and conventions to *Star Trek* that have to be adhered to: the *Enterprise* is the *Enterprise*. Spock is Spock. Each new writer and director must balance the needs of their original contributions with established lore, or as the religiously inspired label refers to it, canon. Nicholas Meyer observed in his autobiography *The View from the Bridge*, "It is they who provide the new music to the *Star Trek* words, or, to switch metaphors, the wine may be new but the shape of the bottle is always the same. I was pouring my own brew into the bottle of *Star Trek II*, trying to fill it without breaking it." Choosing new guest stars to join the established actors adds a freshness, and if chosen correctly, a bold new flavor, to *Star Trek*'s appeal.

During October 1979, Kirstie Alley was a contestant on *Match Game*, where Robert Pine—father to future Kelvin Universe Captain James T. Kirk's Chris Pine—was one of the celebrities who helped her win the big money match. On the program, Alley identifies herself as an interior designer from Wichita, Kansas. Alley had moved to

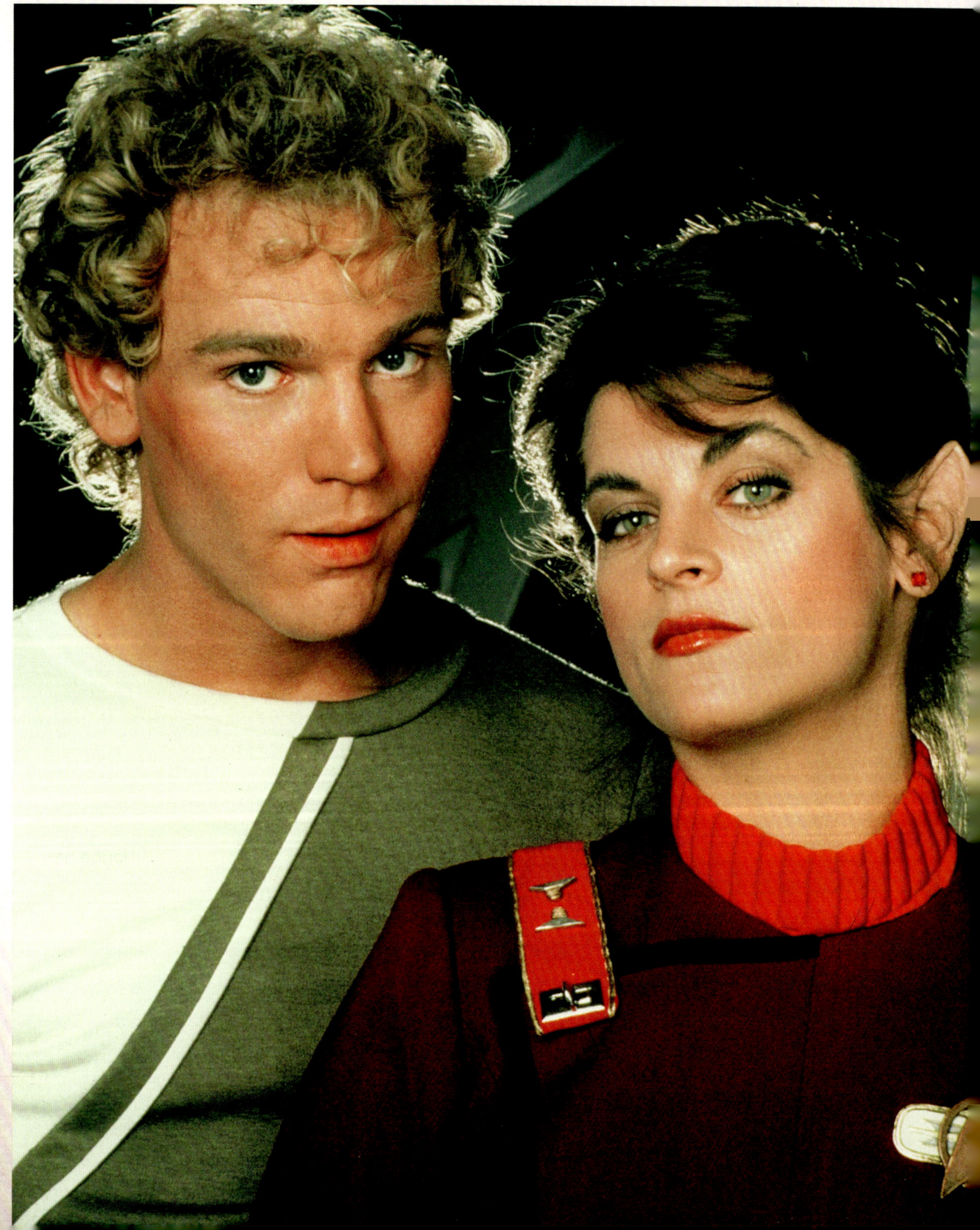

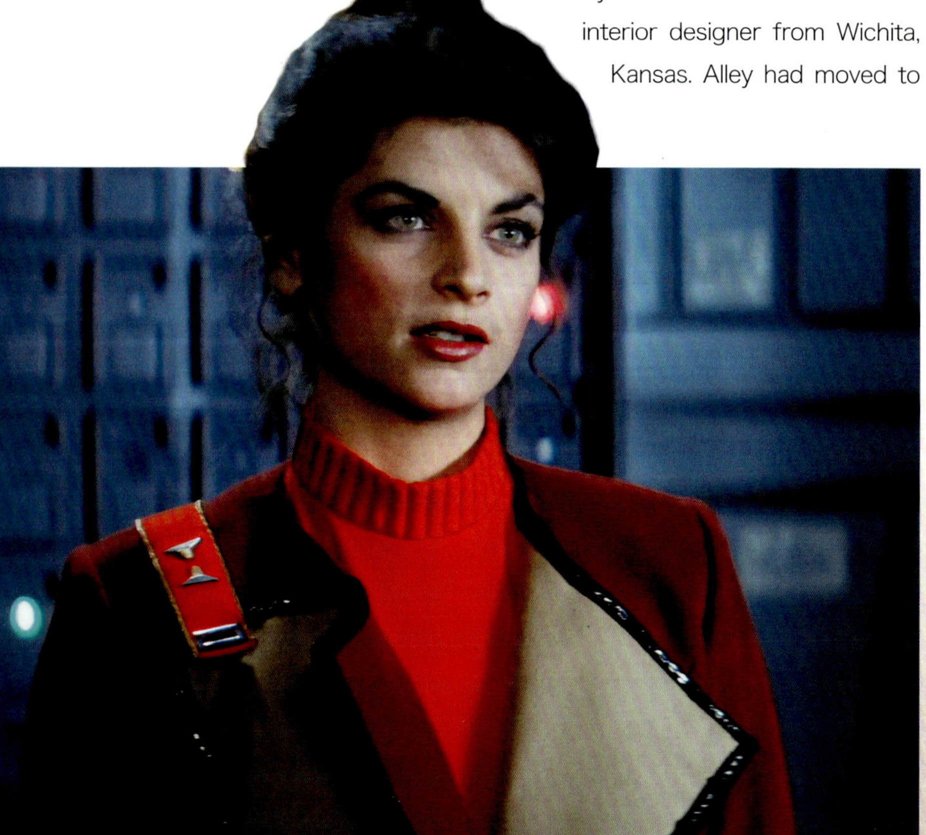

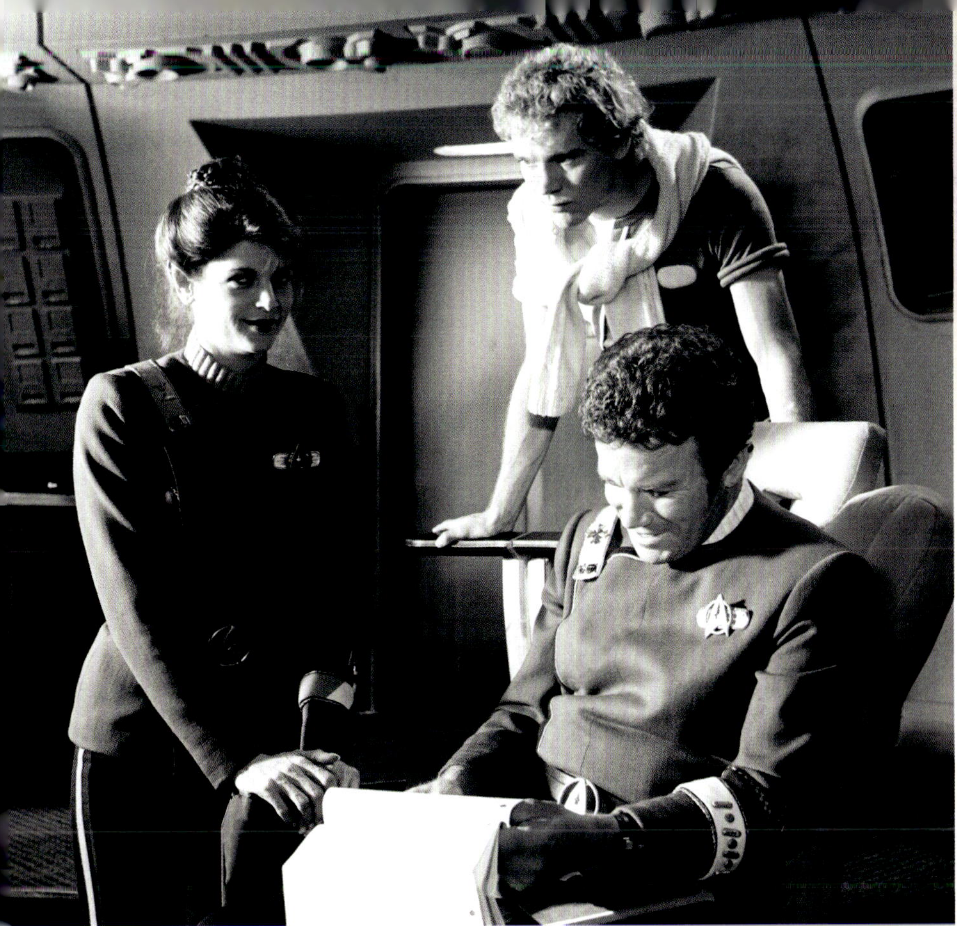

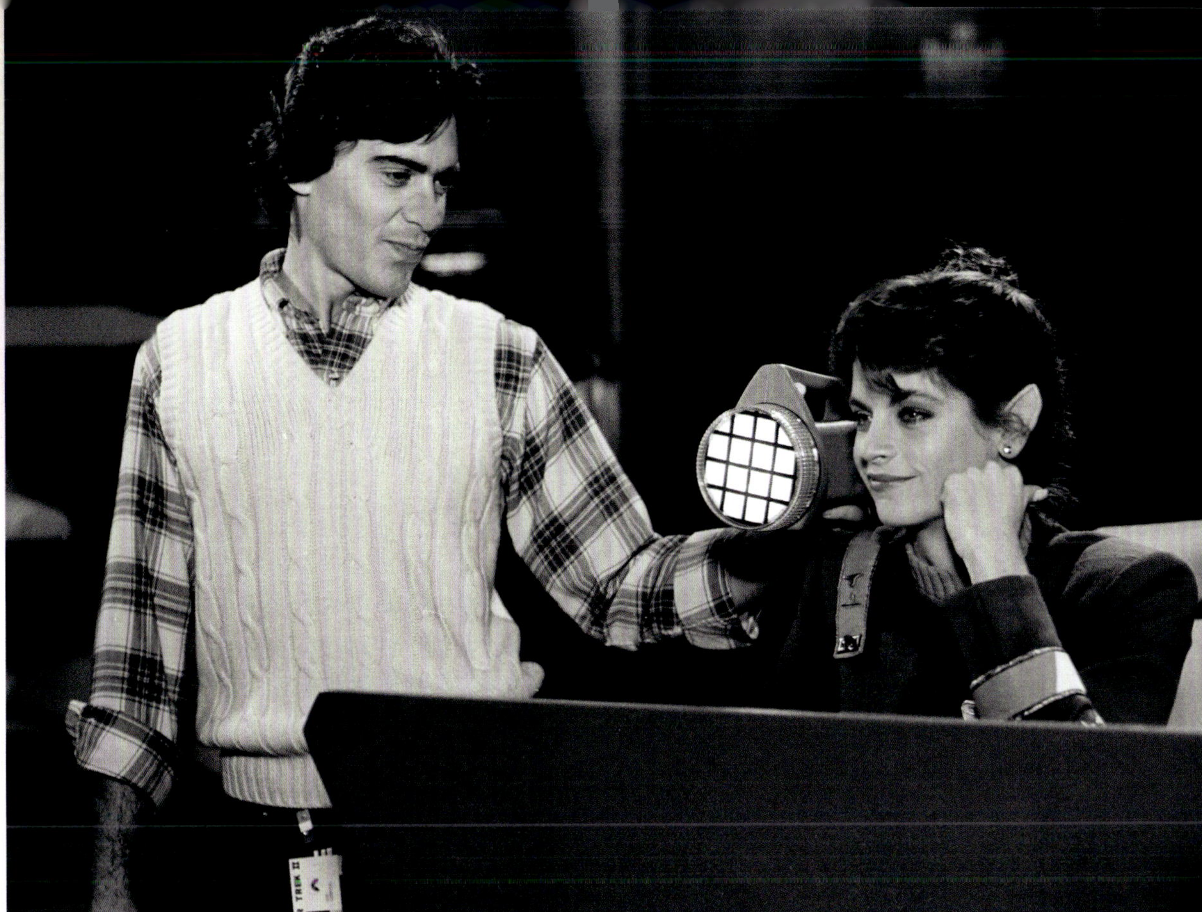

Los Angeles with dreams of becoming an actor. Sustaining herself as she secured an agent and tried to get her first acting jobs, Alley worked as a decorator and housekeeper. Her agent got her an audition for *Star Trek II*, where she returned three times for screen tests and interviews.

Alley shared her audition experience with editor Ian Spelling of StarTrek.com in 2016: "I was supposed to have a meeting on a Monday for my final audition for *Star Trek*, in front of Paramount and the studio guys. That weekend, my parents were in a car wreck and my mother was killed. That was on a Friday night. I flew back to Kansas. It killed my mother, and my Dad was in bad condition. So I called my agent and I said, 'I can't make this meeting Monday.'" Alley's agent informed her that this was an iffy situation, because at the time of her audition, she was not yet in the Screen Actors Guild and filming was beginning soon. Alley said, "I understand, but I'm not leaving my Dad. So you're gonna have to tell them that, and you're gonna have to tell them that I can come back into town when my Dad is out of danger. Out of intensive care."

Alley called the *Star Trek* team's willingness to wait for her to deal with her personal tragedy the single kindness she is most grateful for in her entire career. She continued, "I don't even think I'd told my parents I really wanted to be an actress. I go, 'And when you get out of here and you're doing well, I get to go audition for this.' That night—I'm not even making this up. This would seem so made-up, in a movie—but that night his doctor called me and said, 'Your Dad has pulled out all of his tubes, and we're going to see if he can make it on his own.' I was like, 'Okay.' Then, the next day when I went in, he said, 'So you're gonna be an actress. You're going to be in a movie.'"

Alley would play Saavik one more time after *Star Trek II*, albeit unofficially and on stage. On June 19 and 20, 1982, the Ultimate Fantasy convention was held at the Summit Auditorium and Shamrock Hilton Convention Center. William Shatner, DeForest Kelley, George Takei, Nichelle Nichols, Walter Koenig, Merritt Butrick, original series and *Star Trek: The Motion Picture* actor Mark Lenard, Harve Bennett, and Alley were guests. As part of the festivities, Koenig wrote a play called *The Machiavellian Principle* featuring the actors playing roles, using their real names yet functioning the same as their *Star Trek* characters, as the crew meets a new alien species named the Gonika.

After *Star Trek II*, Alley would star as Rebecca Howe in the iconic television sitcom *Cheers*, winning an Emmy for Outstanding Lead Actress in a Comedy Series and Golden Globe Award for Best Performance by an Actress in a Television Series Comedy or Musical. She was nominated for a Saturn Award for her performance as Saavik. Alley passed away in 2022 age seventy-one.

Bibiana Maria Köchert, known to *Star Trek II* fans as Bibi Besch, was born in Vienna in 1942. As a result of the influence of her mother, film star Gusti Huber, Besch had an early ambition to be a performer. Arriving at age four in the United States, she would eventually adopt the last name of her step-father, radio executive Joseph Besch, and begin acting. Her early experiences were on stage and in daytime soap operas, eventually earning guest starring roles on popular TV shows and films such as *Meteor* (1979). Besch stated that the road to playing Carol Marcus in *Star Trek II* was one of diligent work and dedication to the craft: "I have been acting for twenty years and this is the first hit that I have been associated with. *Star Trek [II]* is the first hit."[3]

It was a combination of recommendations by *Star Trek II* casting director Mary Buck, Paramount executive Karen Moore, and Bennett that helped Besch win the role of Dr. Marcus. As with many of those actors new to *Star Trek*, Besch found it a daunting experience. "Terrifying! It really was. I mean, there was Captain Kirk, and McCoy, and Sulu, and there was his chair! (Laughter). You know what I mean? (Laughter). I was a bit star struck with it myself. And in addition to that, you know the scene in the picture, at the very end, where they're standing by the rail looking out into space? That's the first scene I shot. The last scene of the picture."[4]

Although the character of Carol Marcus did not return in any of the remaining original series-inspired feature films, she almost did. Meyer and Denny Martin Flinn scripted a scene for the beginning of *Star Trek VI: The Undiscovered Country* that would have shown that Kirk and Marcus had continued their relationship. That scene and an entire prologue of the film were abandoned due to costs. However, Besch would reunite with director Meyer for his 1983 miniseries *The Day After*. Besch earned two Emmy nominations, one for her work in the TV movie *Doing Time on Maple Drive* and one for her guest starring role on *Northern Exposure*. Besch passed away in 1996 at age fifty-four.

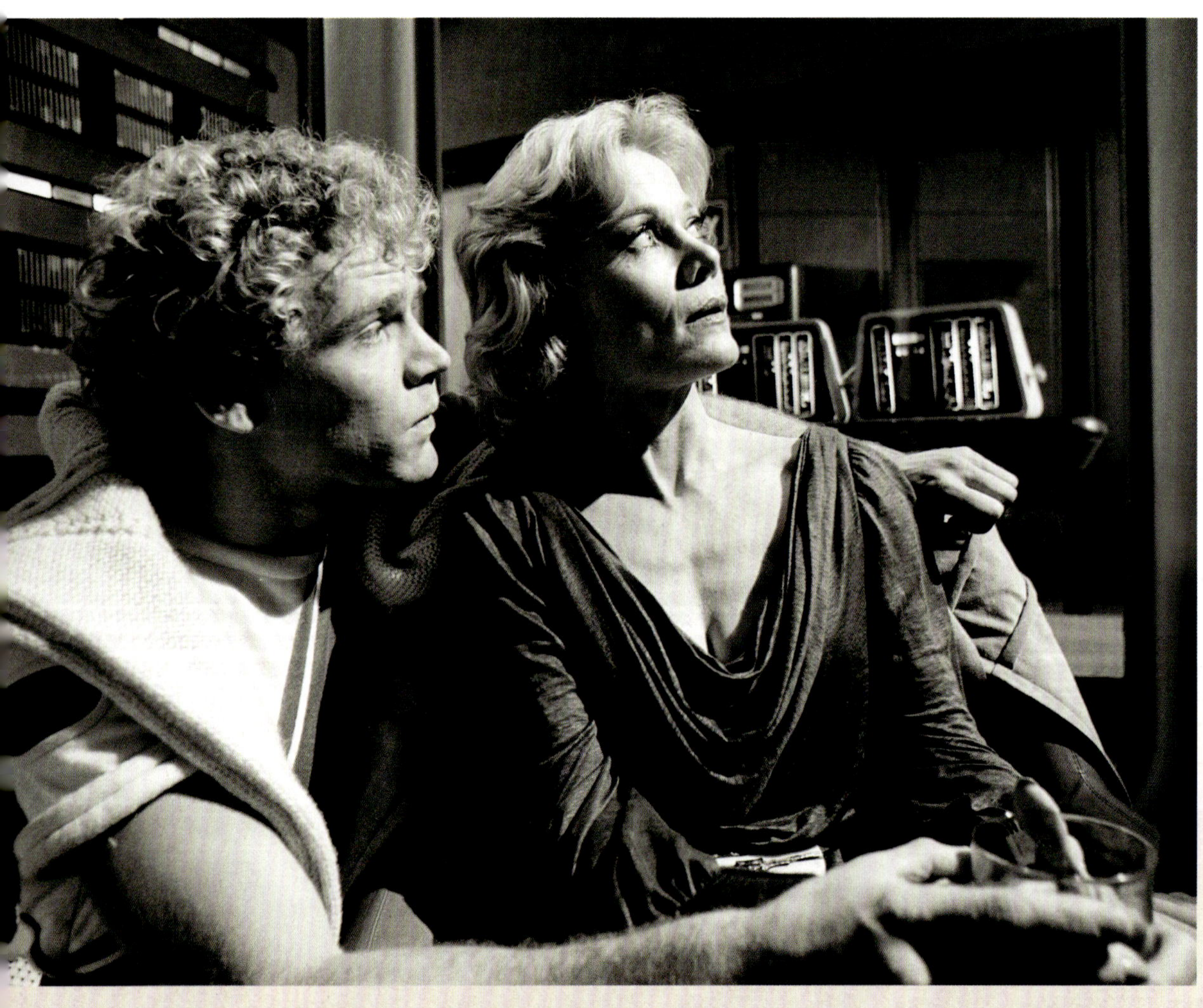

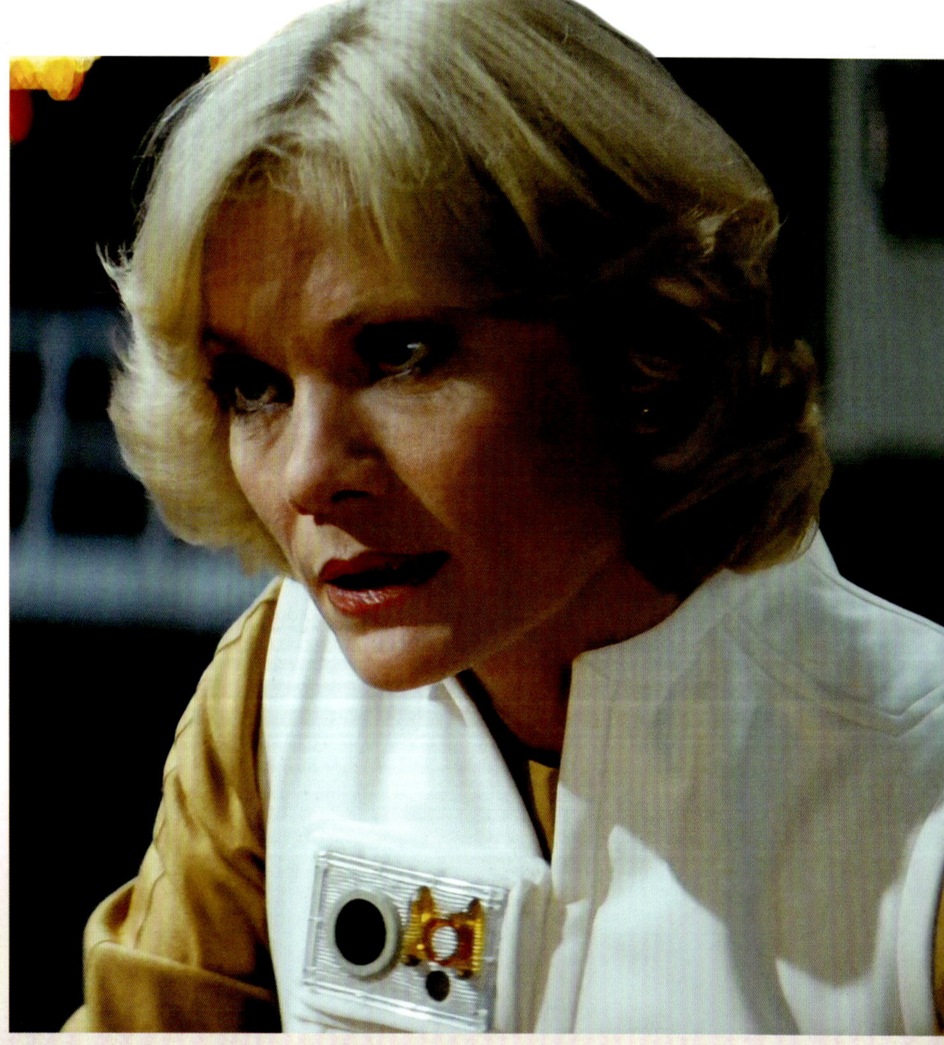

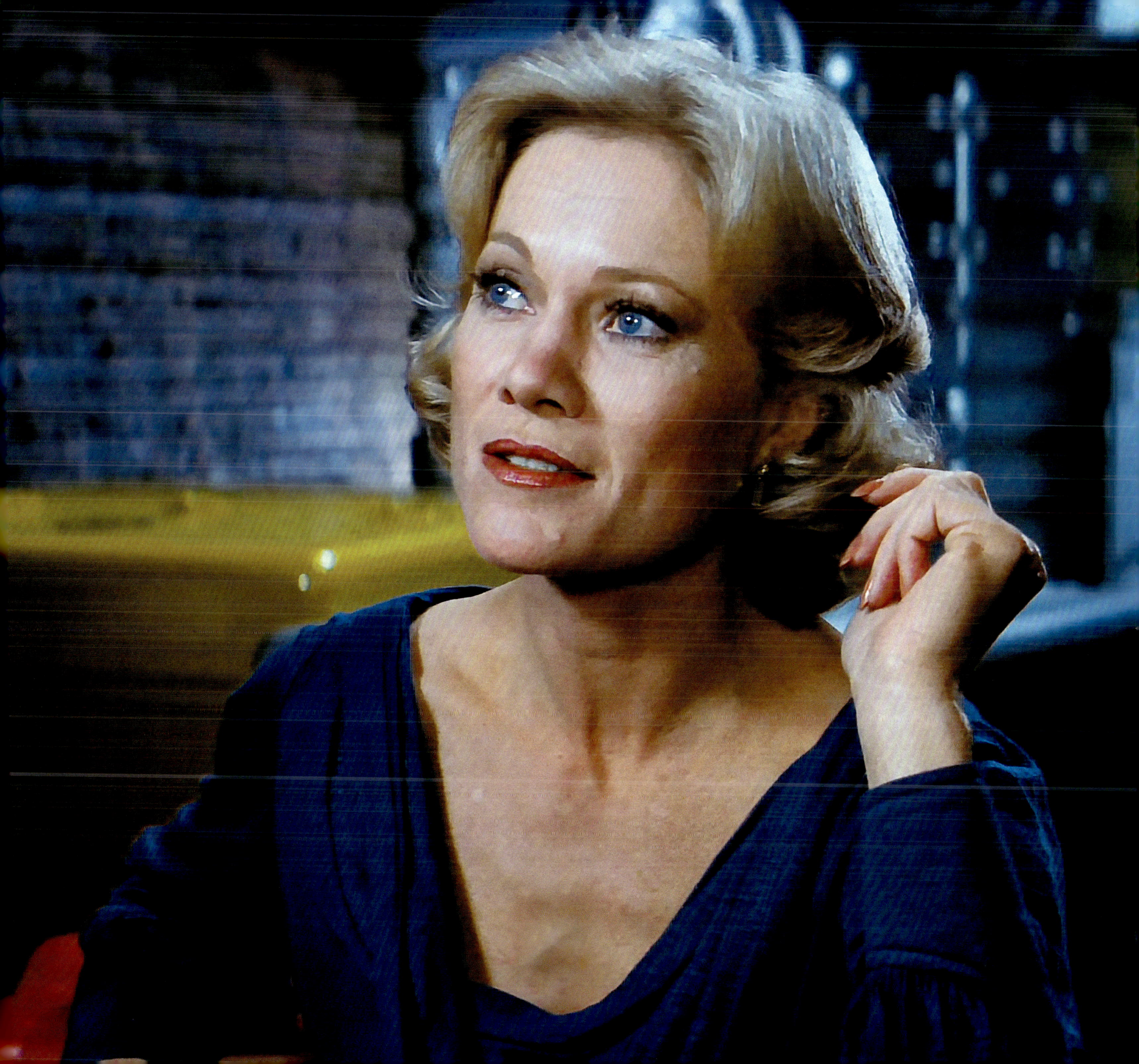

1982 was a busy year for twenty-two-year-old Florida-born actor Merritt Butrick. He had been cast as John "Johnny Slash" Ulasewicz on the school sitcom *Square Pegs*, starred as Gary Cooter in the teen comedy *Zapped!*, and earned the role of David Marcus in *Star Trek II*. For Butrick, it would be the role of David that would have the most immediate effect and teach him about the importance of acting professionally, with concern for the needs of other actors. "*Star Trek [II]* was really my big break. It was the first time I had ever had that much responsibility in a role."[5]

During his audition, Butrick was not told it was for the *Star Trek* sequel. He only knew he was trying out for the role of a scientist in a science fiction film. However, Butrick was a fan himself, and he realized that the script pages he was provided were similar to *Star Trek*. Finding the right actor who both looked like William Shatner and could play David sympathetically was no easy task for casting director Mary Buck. Butrick recalled, "I went in and read four times total and ended up having to do a screen test. It was between me and another actor at that point. I didn't convince them then that I was right for the part. I was very tired and frazzled. So, Nick Meyer had to convince them to screen test and they were finally convinced after that."[6]

Being a fan helped, because Butrick understood who Kirk was and could bring hints of the character into his performance. Being a fan could also be a hindrance. That was especially a challenge for Butrick during the rehearsal readings that were held at Meyer's house before filming began. Drawing on his background in live theater, Meyer appreciated how rehearsals could help actors form relationships and experiment. Butrick shared, "It was strange, because I was totally cool, calm, and collected until they started reading and it was Nichelle Nichols' voice that really set me back. You know, I'm of the age where I was raised listening to *Star Trek* at 6:00 every night… I felt like I had fallen through the TV and I was ten years old again."[7]

Butrick would form a bond with fellow newcomer Kirstie Alley, turning to her for support. Soon enough, Butrick became a *Star Trek* veteran, returning as David for *Star Trek III: The Search for Spock* and playing the role of T'Jon in the second season episode of *Star Trek: The Next Generation*, reuniting with fellow *Star Trek II* alumnus Judson Scott, who plays his nemesis Sobi. Butrick passed away in 1989 at age twenty-nine.

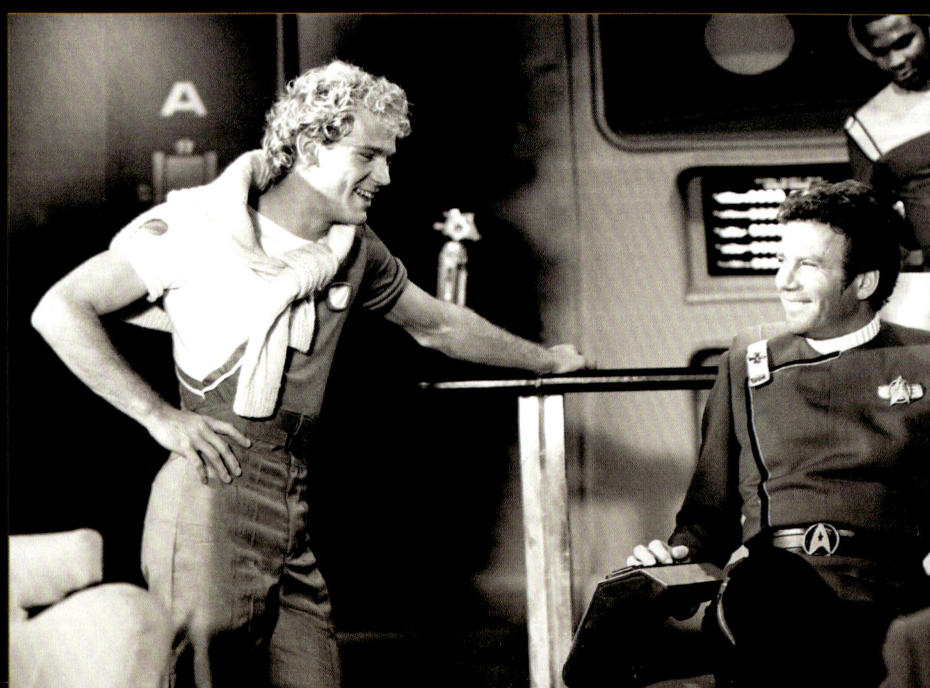

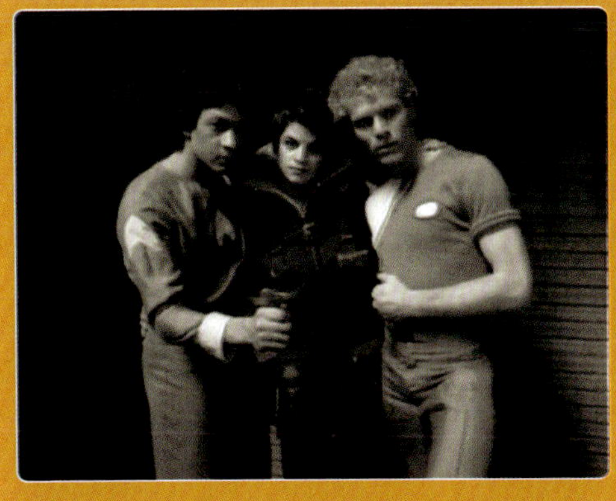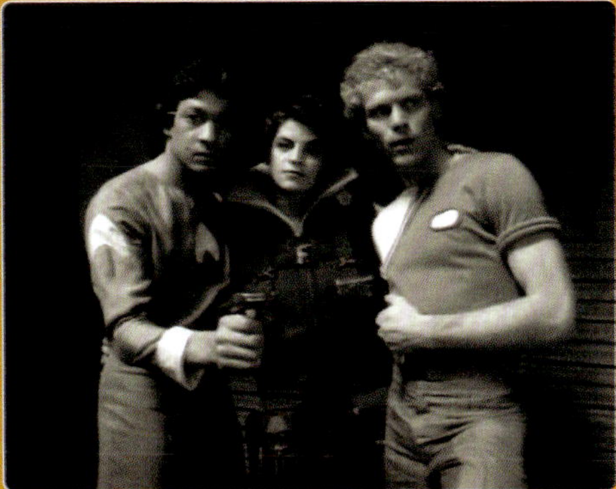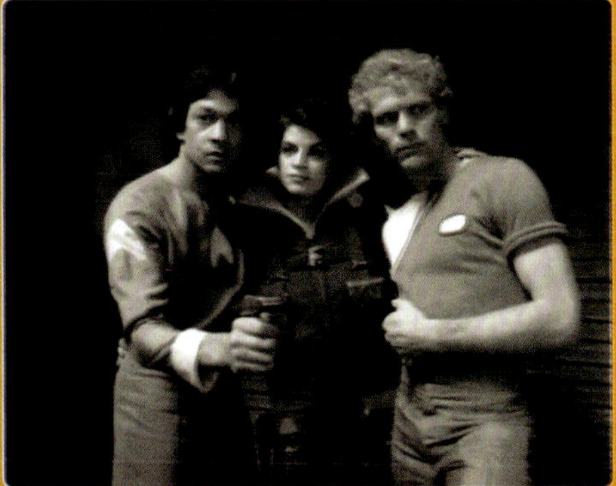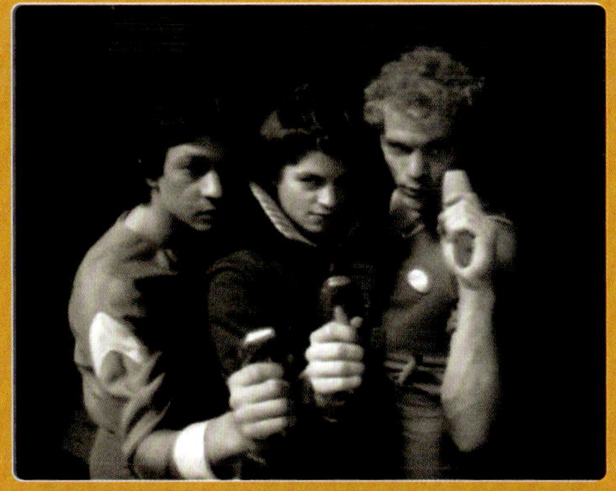
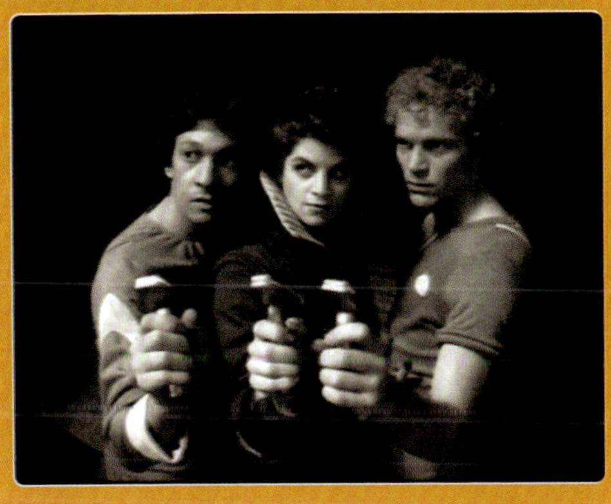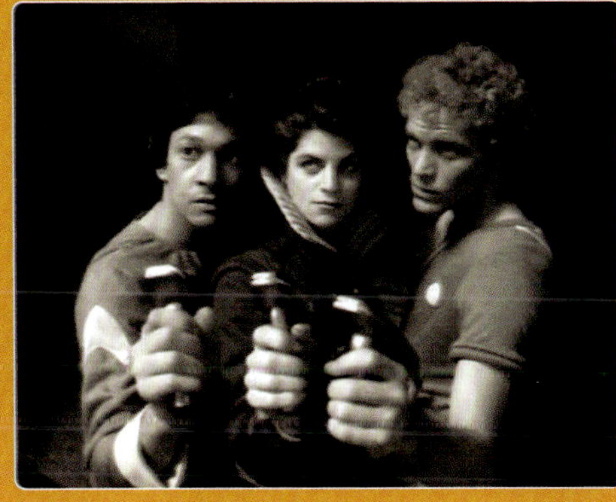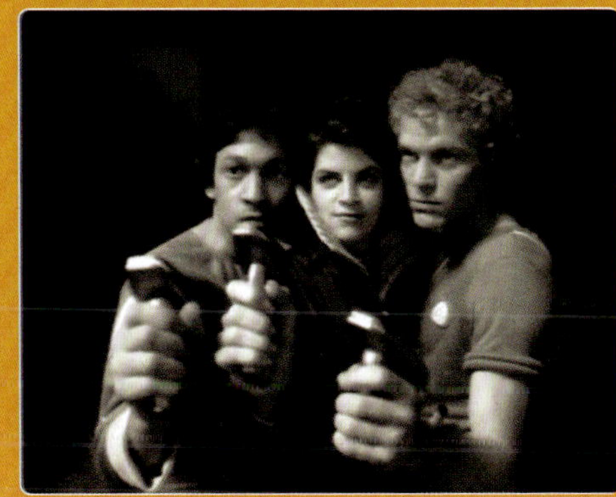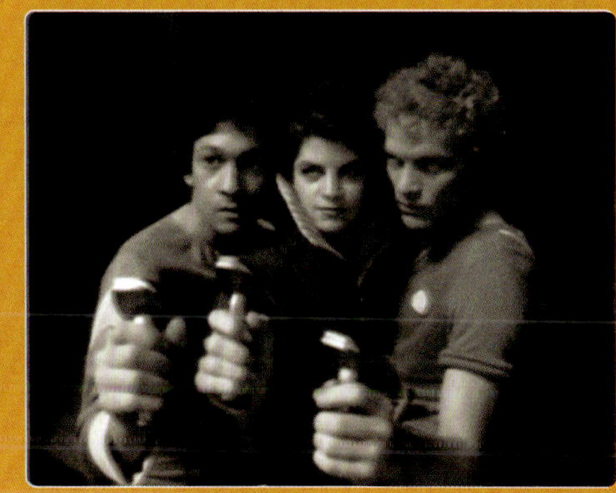

John Vargas was born in the Bronx, New York City, in 1958. After spending time in Puerto Rico during his youth, Vargas would return to the United States to study at the Carnegie Mellon University drama department, becoming a pioneer as the first Puerto Rican graduate of the program. He would have roles in *The Incredible Hulk* television program and the 1981 Neil Simon-scripted movie *Only When I Laugh*, before joining the cast of *Star Trek II* as Jedda.

Originally described as a Vulcan character in the April 10, 1981 script, Jedda would be transformed into a Deltan in the January 18, 1982 version of the script, one of the few references to *Star Trek: The Motion Picture* in the sequel. As with *Star Trek II* colleagues Butrick, Scott, and Paul Winfield, Vargas would return to *Star Trek*. He played Tau, a thief who steals technology from the *U.S.S. Voyager* in the "Concerning Flight" episode of *Star Trek: Voyager*.

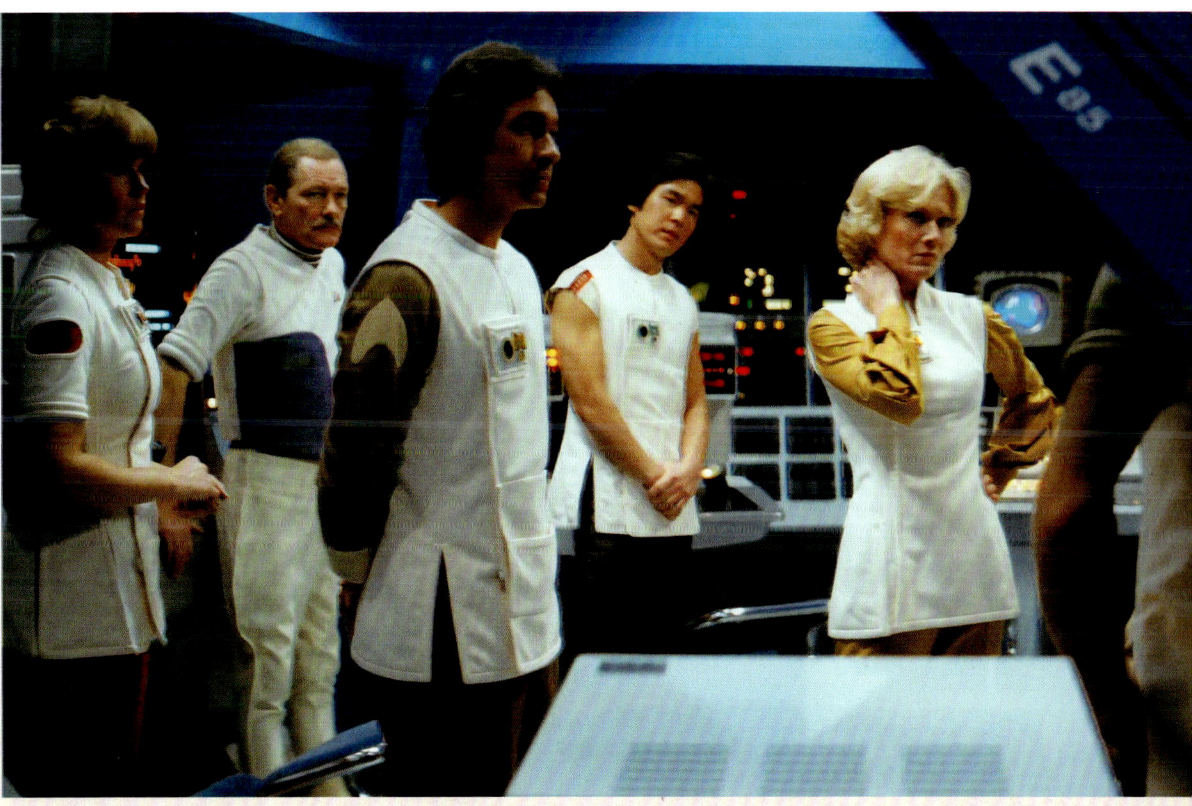

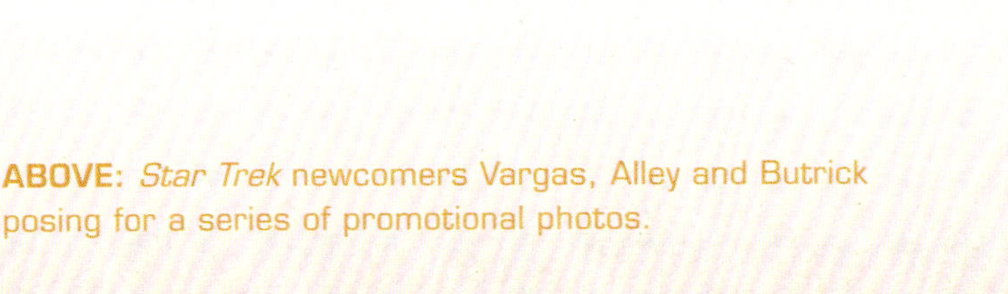

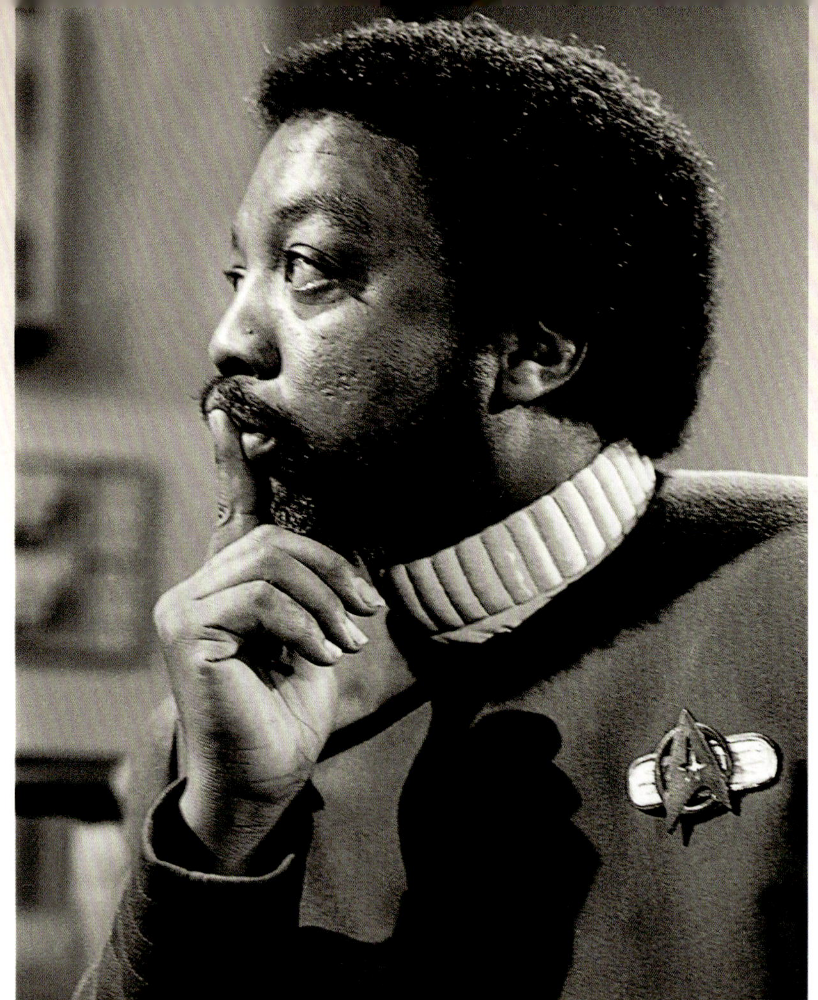

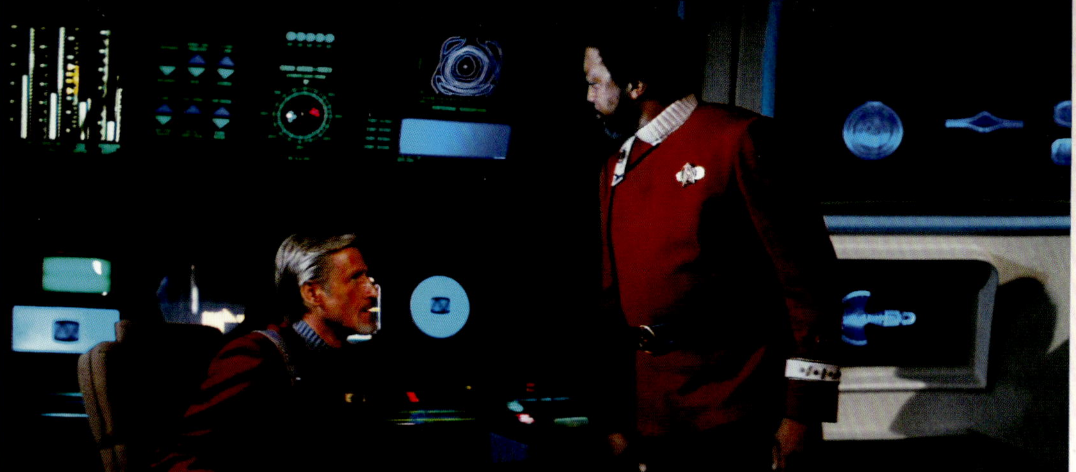

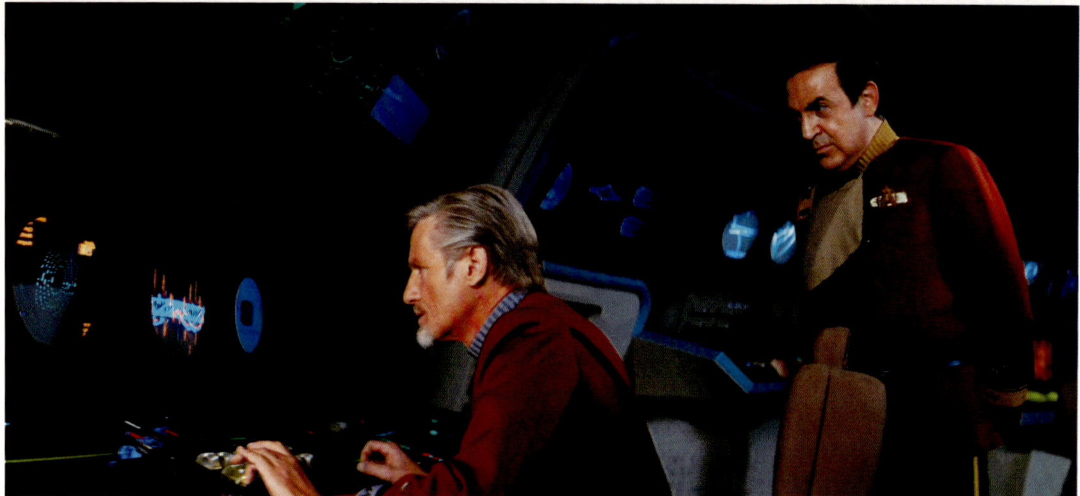

Although edited from the film, the January 18, 1982 revised final draft script confirms that Admiral Kirk did not know Captain Clark Terrell, but that McCoy had previously served with him. Upon discovery of Chekov and Terrell on the Regula I space station, McCoy announces, "That's Clark Terrell, Jim. I've served with him." Actor Paul Winfield proved the perfect choice for the role.

Born May 22, 1939, Winfield was a constant student of the arts and a life-long member of the Actor's Studio. He began acting in high school and then earned a Bachelor's degree at the University of California, Los Angeles, with classmate Walter Koenig. Before *Star Trek II*, Winfield had already had pioneering roles, earning a Best Actor in a Leading Role Academy Award® nomination for the film *Sounder* (1972) about the life of a sharecropper caring for his family while suffering through the Great Depression. Winfield would earn an Emmy Award nomination for his role as Rev. Martin Luther King Jr. in the 1978 biographical television miniseries *King*. It would be the first of three Prime Time Emmy Award nominations, with Winfield eventually winning for his 1994 guest starring role on the television show *Picket Fences*. Winfield would again play a pivotal role in *Star Trek* with his turn as Captain Dathon, the Tamarian who speaks only in metaphors, in *Star Trek: The Next Generation*'s season five episode "Darmok."

Winfield was a fan of *Star Trek* before joining the crew. "I liked *Star Trek*. I was a Trekkie, I guess! I liked the characters, and I love space things and imaginative stuff that shows you what other worlds may be."[8] As much as Winfield was a fan of science fiction, director Nicholas Meyer was a fan of Winfield. Meyer shared, "I had wanted to work with [him] since I saw *Sounder* and I thought, 'Wow, what a lovely actor.' There was no real reason for him to be the captain of the *Reliant*, other than my great desire to direct him in scenes! I knew he could do it, without any question."[9] Winfield passed away in 2004 at age sixty-four.

John Winston returned to the *Star Trek* crew as John Kyle in *The Wrath of Khan*. Formerly *Enterprise* transporter chief during eleven episodes of the original series, "City on the Edge of Forever," "Space Seed," and "Mirror, Mirror" among them, Kyle would get a promotion to commander, becoming communication officer of the *U.S.S. Reliant*. Serving alongside Winston in *Star Trek II* is actor Paul Kent as Commander Beach. Winston passed away at age ninety-one in 2019, and Kent at age eighty in 2011.

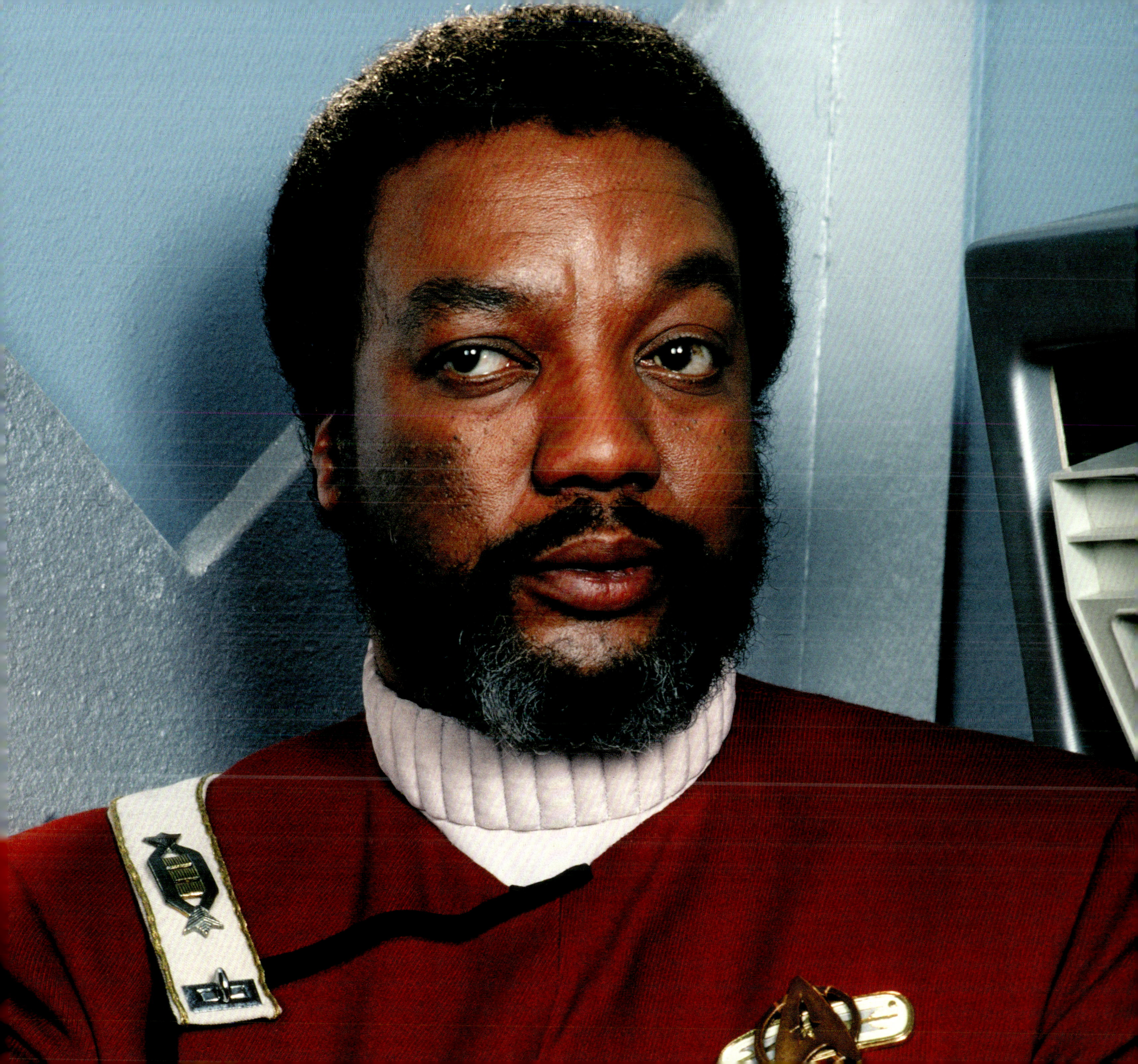

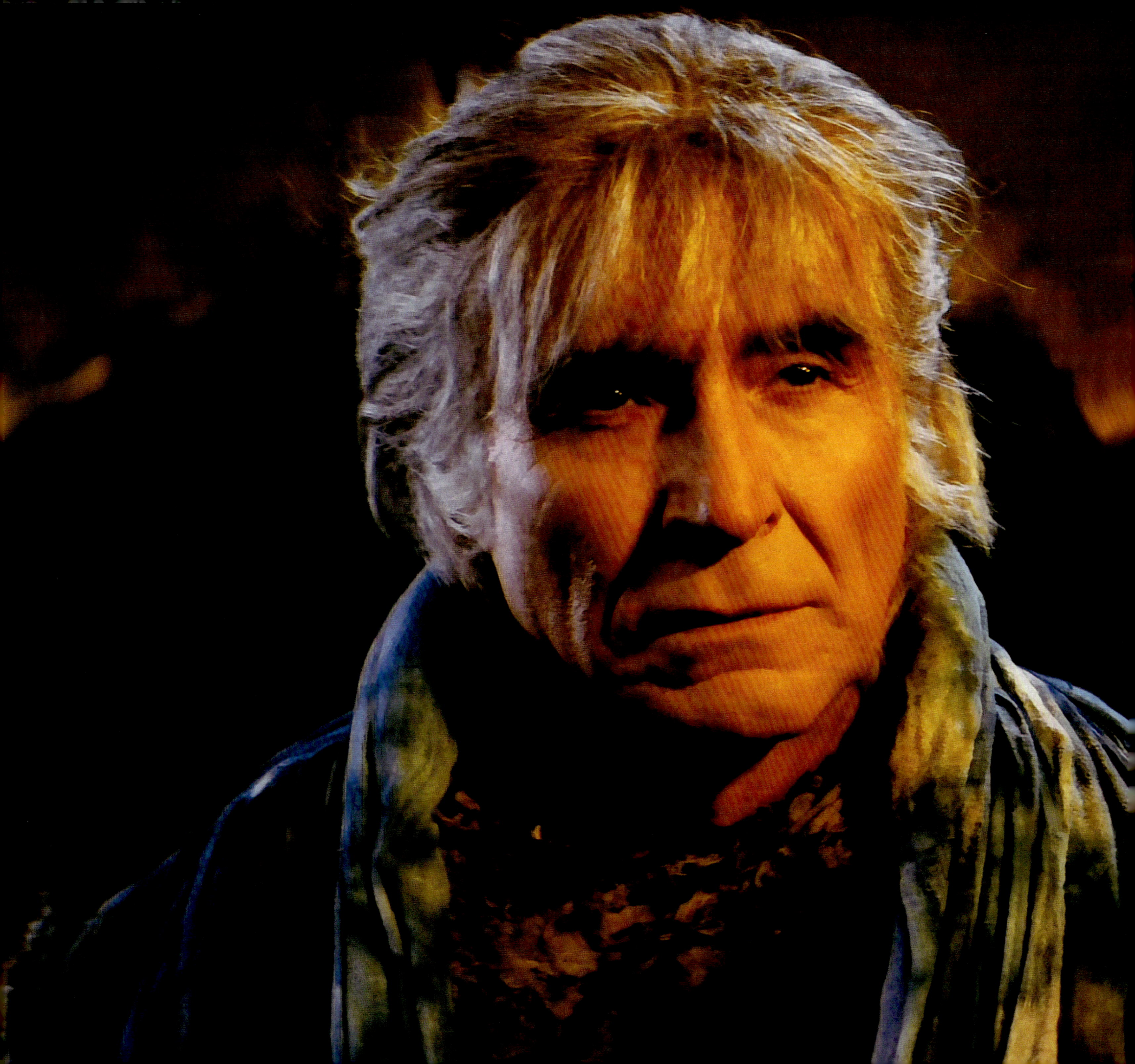

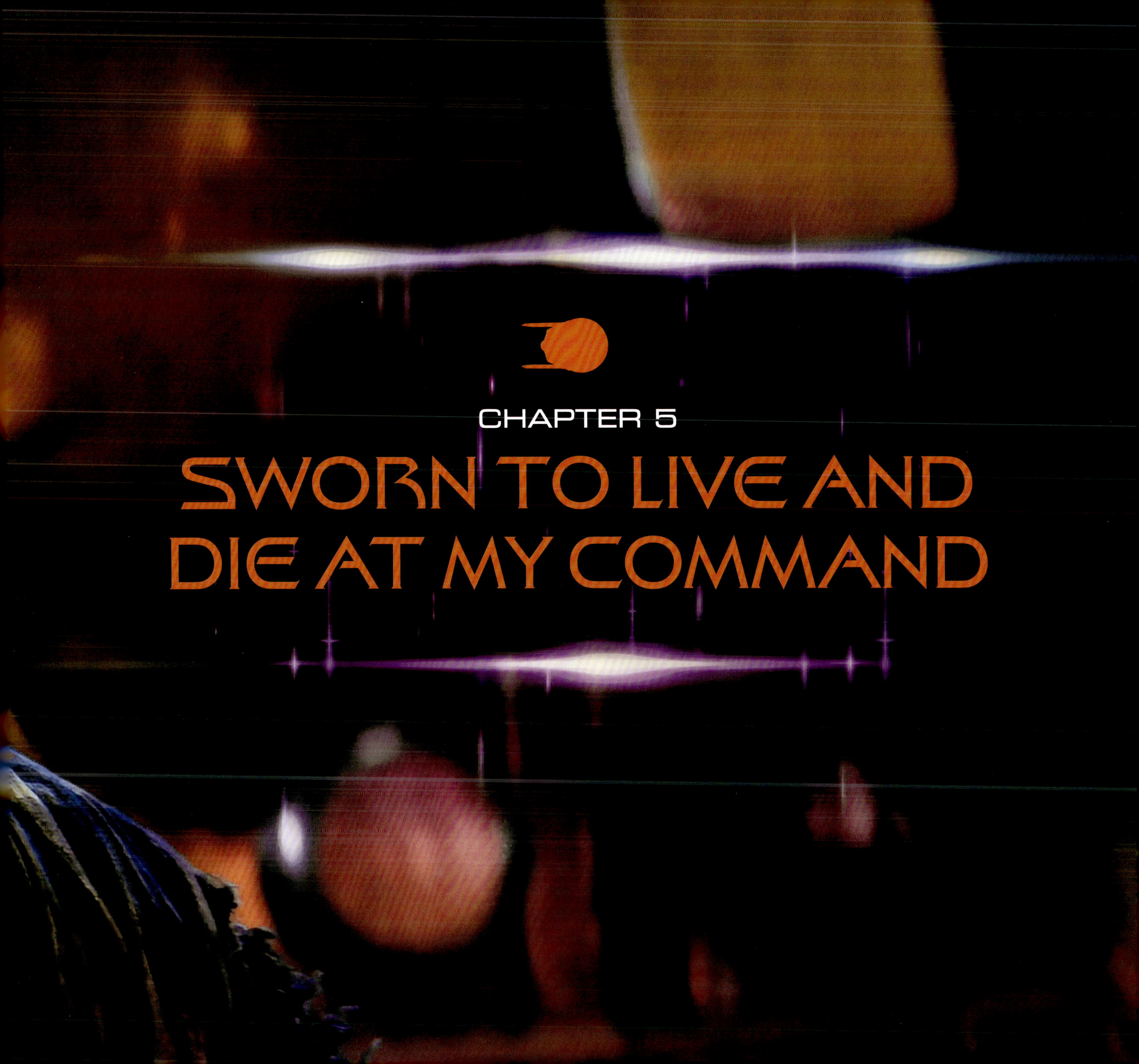

CHAPTER 5
SWORN TO LIVE AND
DIE AT MY COMMAND

COMPANY AND CREW OF THE *BOTANY BAY*

Ricardo Gonzalo Pedro Montalbán y Merino changed the world, both through his own artistic achievements, and because of his activism and inspiration. Born in Mexico City on November 25, 1920, Ricardo Montalban—the professional name he used from early in his acting career—would arrive in the United States on February 4, 1939, with ambitions of being an architect. But a teacher named Araxi Jamgochian at Fairfax High School told Montalban that the best way for him to learn to speak English was to perform it in front of an audience. Everything changed for Montalban while appearing in the school play *The Whole Town's Talking*, his first on-stage appearance. "I had a small role, but the experience of being on stage nevertheless overwhelmed me. I was still shy, especially in a land where I was unsure of the language. Yet onstage I discarded my identity and became someone else."[1]

With a newfound purpose, Montalban returned to his native Mexico, working to establish himself as a successful actor in the vibrant Mexican film industry, alongside icons such as Cantinflas. His first Hollywood picture was the 1947 film *Fiesta*, where he proved himself not only an accomplished actor, but a dancer, keeping pace with Cyd Charisse, who would become a frequent co-star. His range was dynamic, despite the limitations and stereotyping that permeated the media for Mexican actors. Montalban could play comedy or romance, drama or adventure, and as the studio system changed, he found himself an actor-for-hire, honing his craft on the Broadway stage, television, and films. In 1957, Montalban starred in *Jamaica* with Lena Horne, a noteworthy play because of the racially diverse cast and crew and the production featuring one of the first interracial kisses on a Broadway stage.

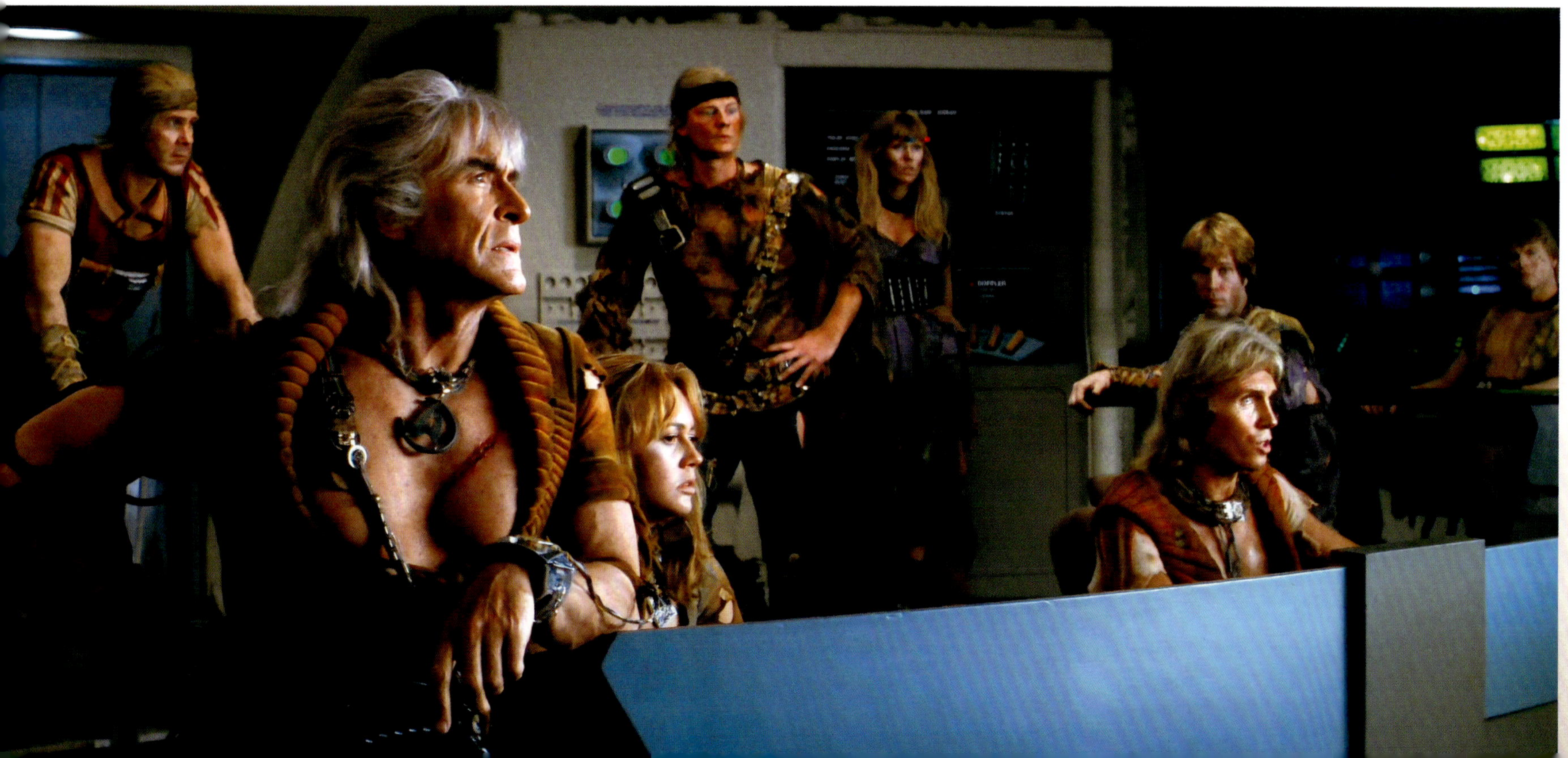

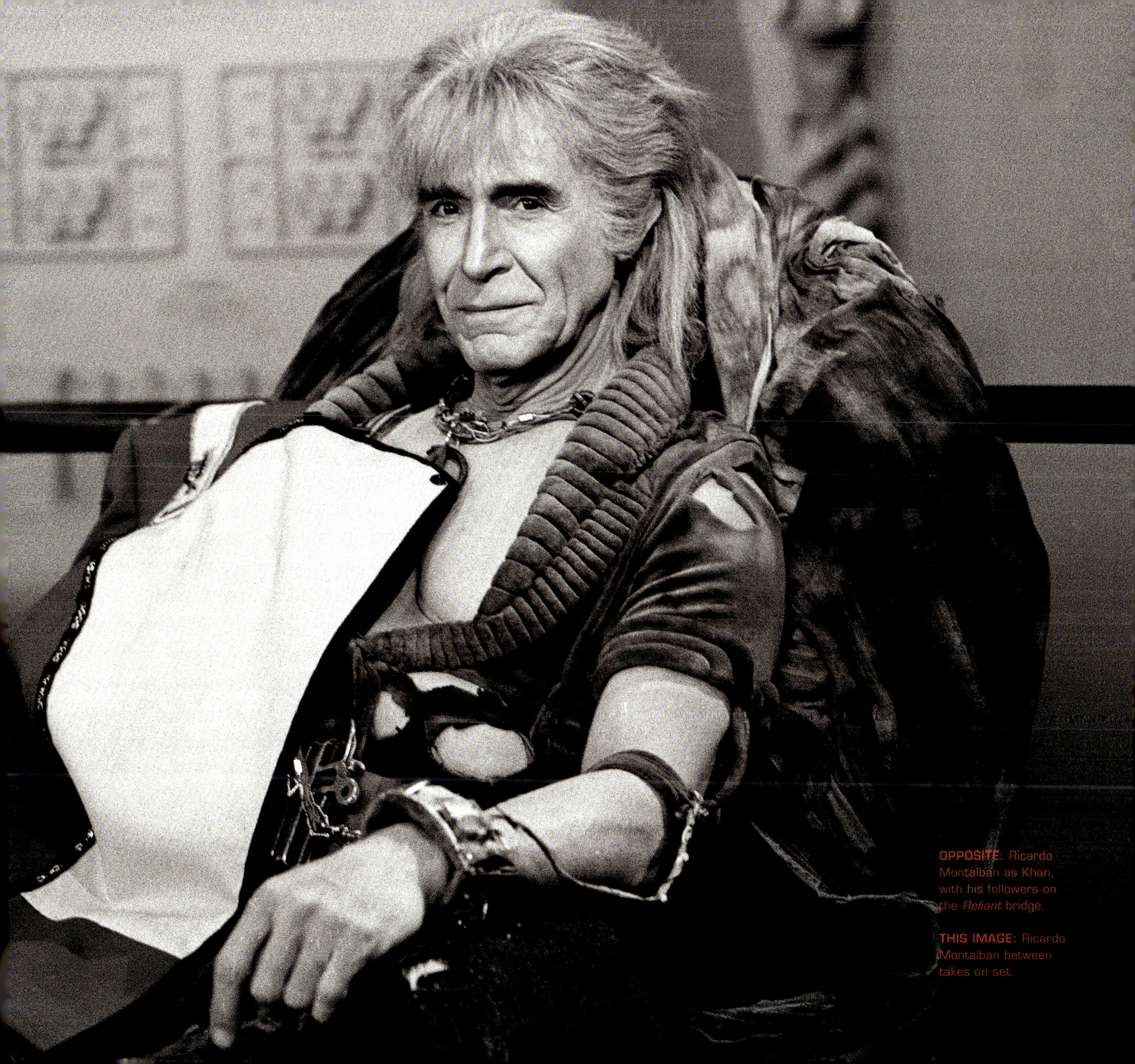

OPPOSITE: Ricardo
Montalban as Khan,
with his followers on
the *Reliant* bridge.

THIS IMAGE: Ricardo
Montalban between
takes on set.

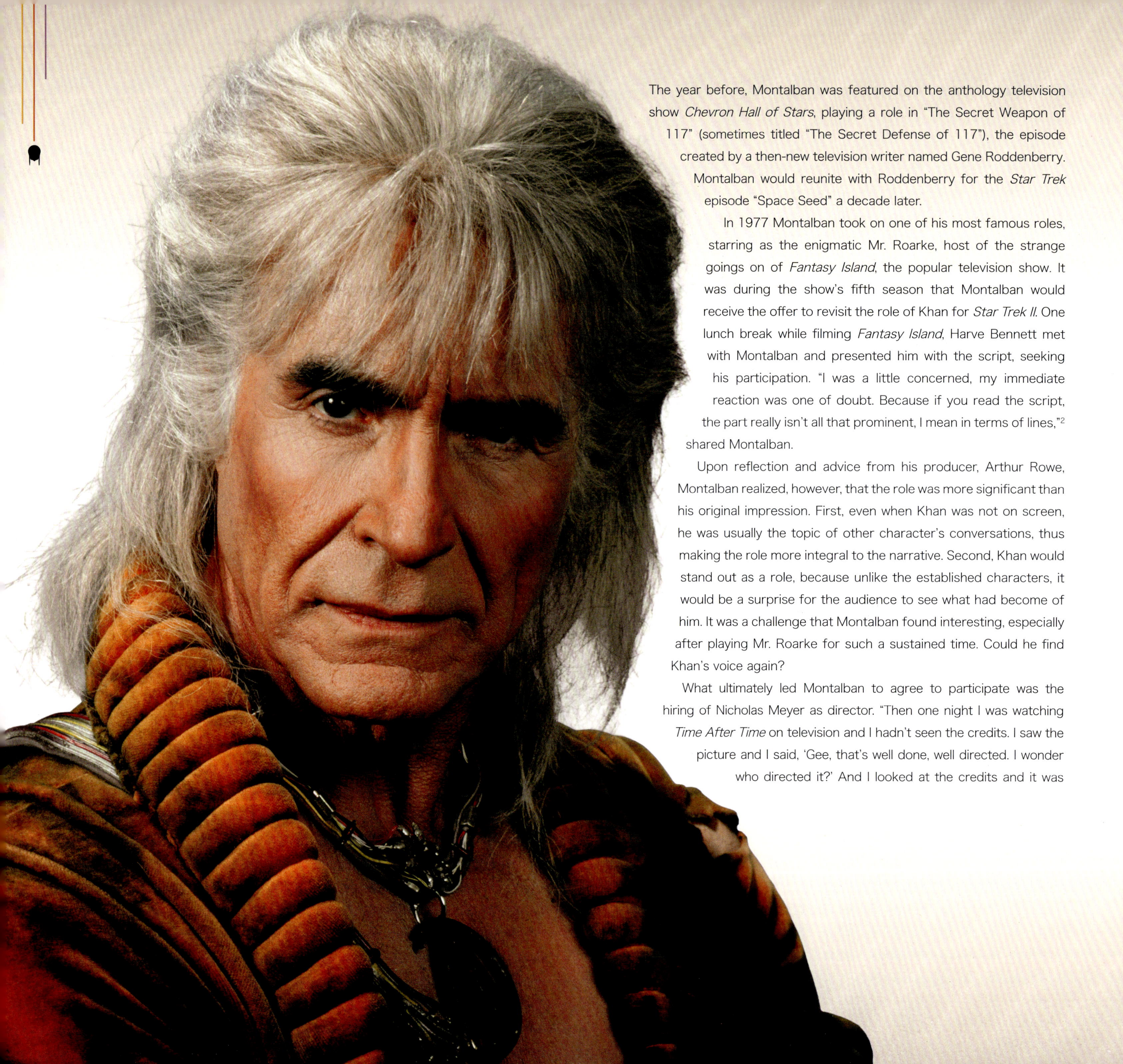

The year before, Montalban was featured on the anthology television show *Chevron Hall of Stars*, playing a role in "The Secret Weapon of 117" (sometimes titled "The Secret Defense of 117"), the episode created by a then-new television writer named Gene Roddenberry. Montalban would reunite with Roddenberry for the *Star Trek* episode "Space Seed" a decade later.

In 1977 Montalban took on one of his most famous roles, starring as the enigmatic Mr. Roarke, host of the strange goings on of *Fantasy Island*, the popular television show. It was during the show's fifth season that Montalban would receive the offer to revisit the role of Khan for *Star Trek II*. One lunch break while filming *Fantasy Island*, Harve Bennett met with Montalban and presented him with the script, seeking his participation. "I was a little concerned, my immediate reaction was one of doubt. Because if you read the script, the part really isn't all that prominent, I mean in terms of lines,"[2] shared Montalban.

Upon reflection and advice from his producer, Arthur Rowe, Montalban realized, however, that the role was more significant than his original impression. First, even when Khan was not on screen, he was usually the topic of other character's conversations, thus making the role more integral to the narrative. Second, Khan would stand out as a role, because unlike the established characters, it would be a surprise for the audience to see what had become of him. It was a challenge that Montalban found interesting, especially after playing Mr. Roarke for such a sustained time. Could he find Khan's voice again?

What ultimately led Montalban to agree to participate was the hiring of Nicholas Meyer as director. "Then one night I was watching *Time After Time* on television and I hadn't seen the credits. I saw the picture and I said, 'Gee, that's well done, well directed. I wonder who directed it?' And I looked at the credits and it was

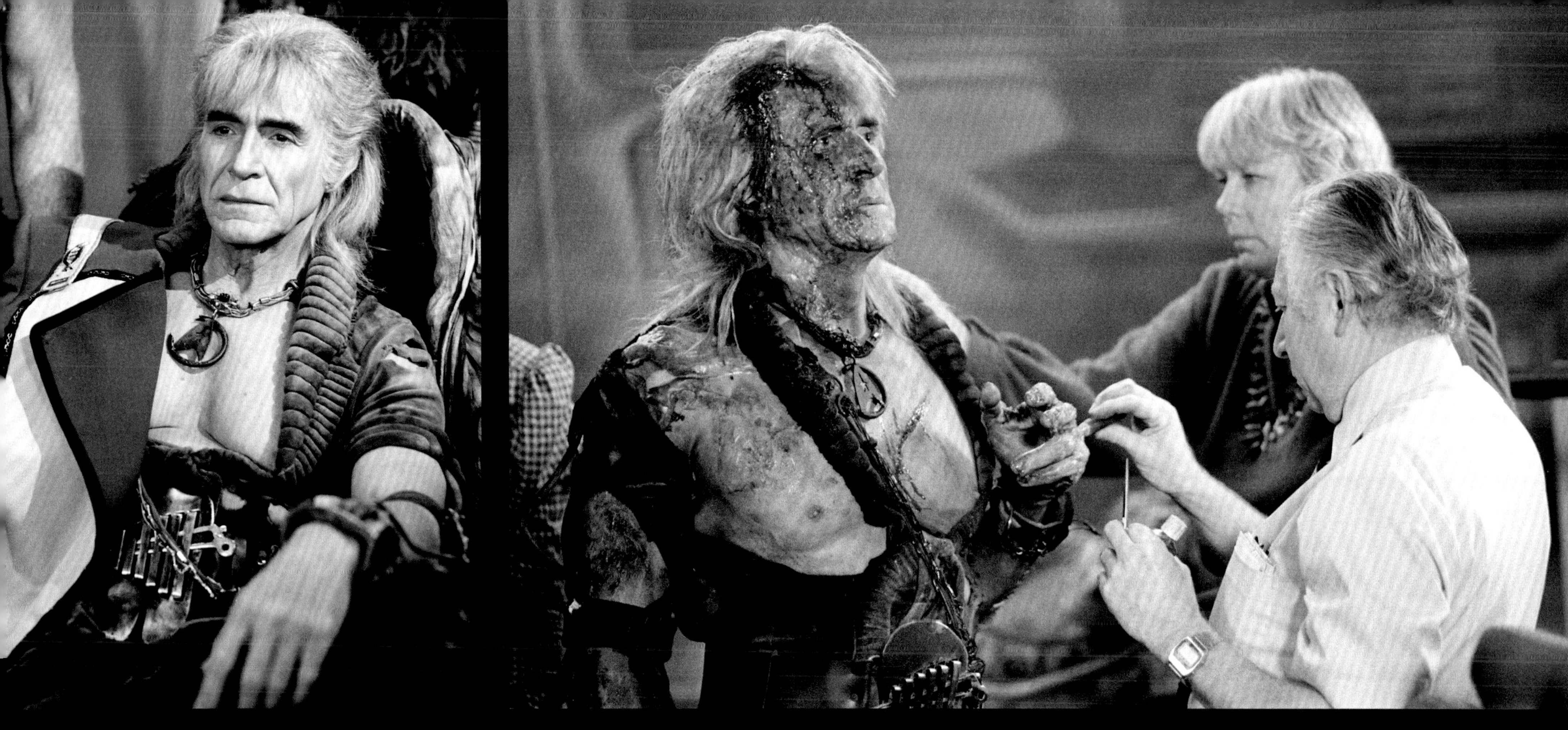

Nicholas Meyer! A very talented man! So then the next day I said, 'Now, who's going to direct this *Star Trek* picture?' And they said, 'Nicholas Meyer.' And I said, 'I'll do it.'"[3]

The contribution that Montalban would make in helping *Star Trek II* become successful cannot be exaggerated. In her review of the film, *The New York Times* film critic Janet Maslin wrote, "Most fun of all is Khan himself, played as the classiest of comic strip villains by Ricardo Montalban, who really is something to see."[4]

As a new actor, Laura Banks, who played Khan's Navigator, recalls being in awe of Montalban's work ethic and concentration. "When I would watch him rehearse and when we were in between takes, he'd stay in character. And sitting back the way he did in that character and watching his slow movements and watching his laser intensity, I think what I learned was to let the camera read you. Be transparent."[5]

Easily the most asked question about *Star Trek II* has been whether or not Montalban's chest in the film was really his own or the result of clever makeup prosthetics and costume design. Meyer addresses the subject in his autobiography, *The View from the Bridge*: "The question I am most often asked about the movie is whether the chiseled sculpture was indeed Ricardo Montalban's actual torso. For the umpteenth time

those pecs are his."[6] Costume designer Robert Fletcher also commented on showing Montalban's impressive musculature: "We wanted to show Ricardo Montalban's physique. He was rather proud of it, as he should have been. That was a theatrical gesture."[7] Fans looking for further confirmation might check out Montalban's beach scenes in the 1979 *Fantasy Island* episode "The Wedding."

Montalban passed away on January 14, 2009, at the age of eighty-eight. He left behind not only treasures of the stage, cinema, and television, but a world changed by his philanthropy and activism. He worked for decades to diminish the stereotyping too common in the media, and the organizations he led and helped to found, Nostoros and The Ricardo Montalban Foundation, have created opportunities for a diverse group of artists, writers, and directors to find their voice. His family continues to run the organizations in his honor and to continue his mission. For Montalban—in stark contrast to the personality of Khan—the answer to achieving social harmony was never wrath, but love: "You can love only that which you know. If people of other backgrounds would *really* get to know those of other colors, religions, and national origins, then the word *prejudice* would not exist in our vocabularies."[8]

A DAUGHTER REMEMBERS: ANITA MONTALBAN-SMITH ON HER FATHER, RICARDO

Anita Montalban was born in 1949, the third of four children born to Georgiana and Ricardo Montalban. After graduating high school, Anita became a model, leading shows for many of the era's best designers. Like her father before her, Anita was also a dancer, incorporating graceful moves into her runway performances. In 1983, Anita married photographer Gilbert Smith and they had a daughter Lydia. By 2005, the couple had joined with Ricardo to help run The Ricardo Montalbán Theatre, the first major venue of that size to be named for a Latino in the United States, and the Ricardo Montalban Foundation, whose mission is to create opportunities for Hispanic artists and entertainers. Anita passed away on November 5, 2021 after a courageous battle with cancer. Days before her passing, she shared thoughts about her father Ricardo for this book, with the help of her husband Gil and daughter Lydia.

Anita on Montalban's favorite roles:

"I don't believe that my father had one favorite role. He enjoyed learning Kabuki to play Nakamura in *Sayonara*. His performance in the film was considered by many to be one of the most complete transformations, with the immersion into the ancient Japanese art and performance. He was a wonderful dancer and enjoyed the sequences dancing opposite Cyd Charisse. Of course, playing in the role of Khan Noonian Singh in *The Wrath of Khan*. We were invited to a Paramount Studios private theater for the first cast and crew screening. As we were leaving to return home, my father asked me to guess how much screen time where he was active in the scene. I guessed forty-five minutes and he wryly responded with eighteen minutes. He said that it was a great illusion to have the characters search for or talk about him even when he was not in the scene. He also enjoyed working with Nicholas Meyer and with the entire crew. He had wonderful direction with Nicholas Meyer and their work together at the front end of the shooting schedule changed the tone of the story. In fact, the title of the film was changed based on everyone's reaction to his performance."

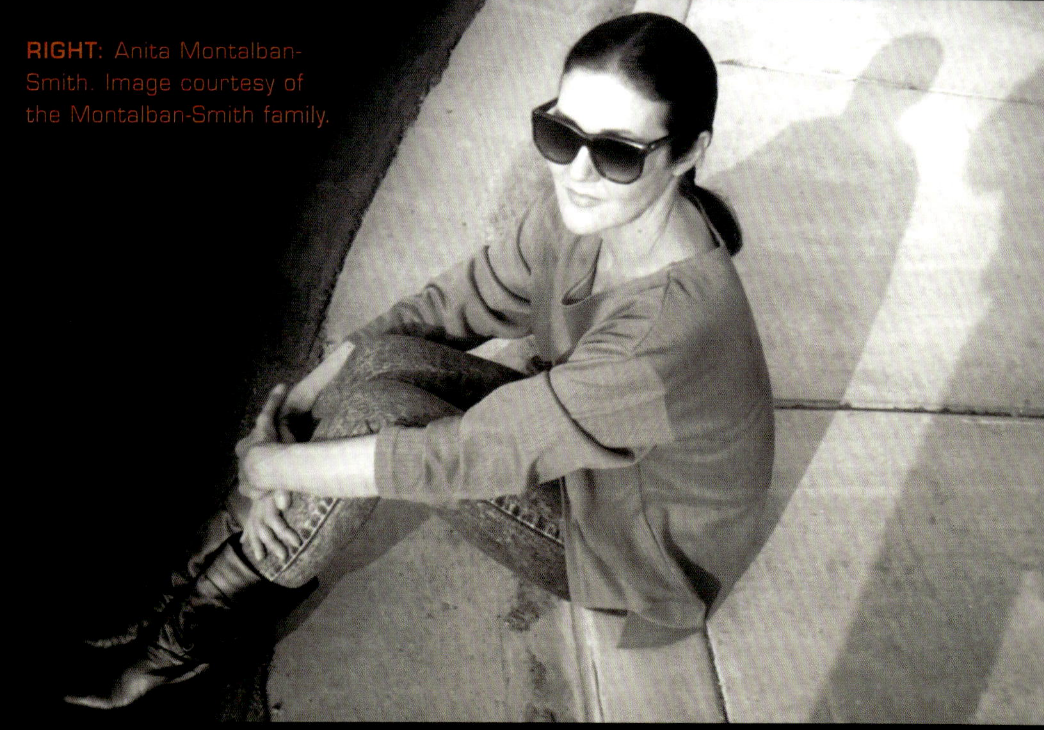

RIGHT: Anita Montalban-Smith. Image courtesy of the Montalban-Smith family.

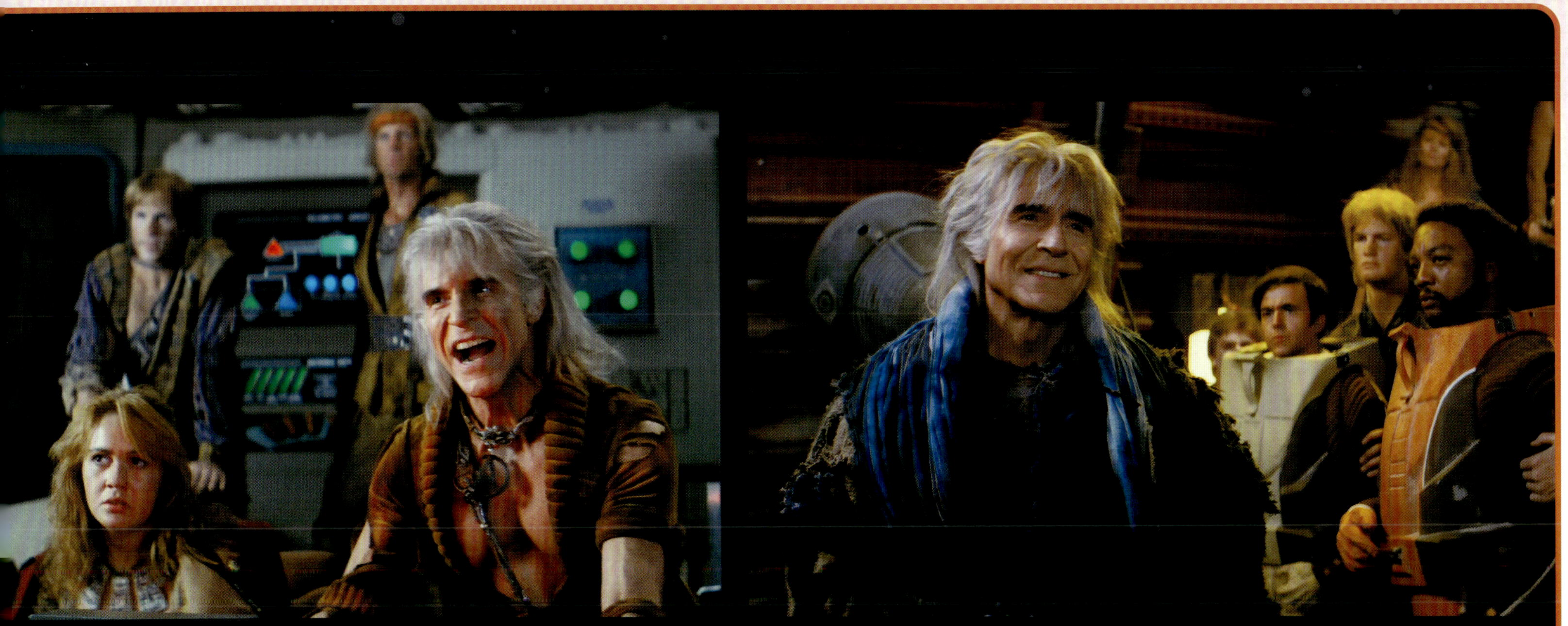

Anita on Montalban's commitment to Khan:

"He was challenged to get back into perfect shape both mentally and physically. After signing to reprise his earlier television role of Khan, he worked out for three hours daily from 3am to 6am prior to film and throughout his time with the production. He laughed about the fact that the production decided to shave him head to toe. He marveled at the never-ending flow of fan mail and demand for personal appearances where Trekkies gathered socially. He was pleased to see polls that rated his role as the greatest villain of all time."

Anita on Montalban's sense of social justice:

"He was asked to return to the New York Broadway stage to perform a leading romantic role in *Seventh Heaven*, playing opposite Gloria DeHaven. That role led to his being asked to join Lena Horne in *Jamaica*. He enjoyed challenging bigotry or racism. His kissing Lena Horne on stage as a mixed-race romantic couple caused controversy and made headlines that provoked change as we emerged from the Jim Crow era, when racial equality caught the spotlight to reshape our political stance, moral obligations, and religious lessons.

My father was always seeking ways to help, assist, and promote diversity. His dedication to elevating the perception of Latin culture was documented, but the credit for his activism was never front-page news. He followed his moral and religious education to apply his sincere belief that producers in Hollywood were making films with Latin characters who were commonly stereotyped as lazy bandits. His work in the early years of the development of motion pictures, television, and commercials gave him a wonderful platform to make positive improvements in casting and entertainment job opportunities.

He made appearances as the Master of Ceremonies for various charities and community efforts to raise funding and awareness of disasters, as in the 1985 Mexico City earthquake. Ricardo recorded several radio and television pleas for assistance for the recovery. He was credited as having been the spark for over $8 million in donations from his efforts."

In an interview with Martha Bonds for *Starlog* magazine in 1983, Judson Scott recalled of the *Star Trek II* shoot, "For three months, I enjoyed getting up in the morning and going to work, mostly due to the director, Nicholas Meyer, and Ricardo Montalban."[9] Born in Azusa, California in 1952, Scott studied acting at California State University, the Actor's Studio of Los Angeles, and the Julliard School. When he landed the role of Khan's de facto lieutenant, Joachim, Scott was no stranger to science fiction, with a starring role in television series *The Phoenix*. Scott became close with Montalban on set and during rehearsals at the veteran actor's home, developing an enduring friendship. He returned to the world of *Star Trek* twice, playing Sobi in the *Star Trek: The Next Generation* season one episode "Symbiosis," with *Star Trek II* colleague Merritt Butrick. He also played Romulan Commander Rekar in *Star Trek: Voyager*'s "Message in a Bottle."

Credit-watchers may note that Scott's name is not listed among the other actors. The reason? A mistake. According to Scott, his agent tried to negotiate a higher billing for the actor, but instead waived

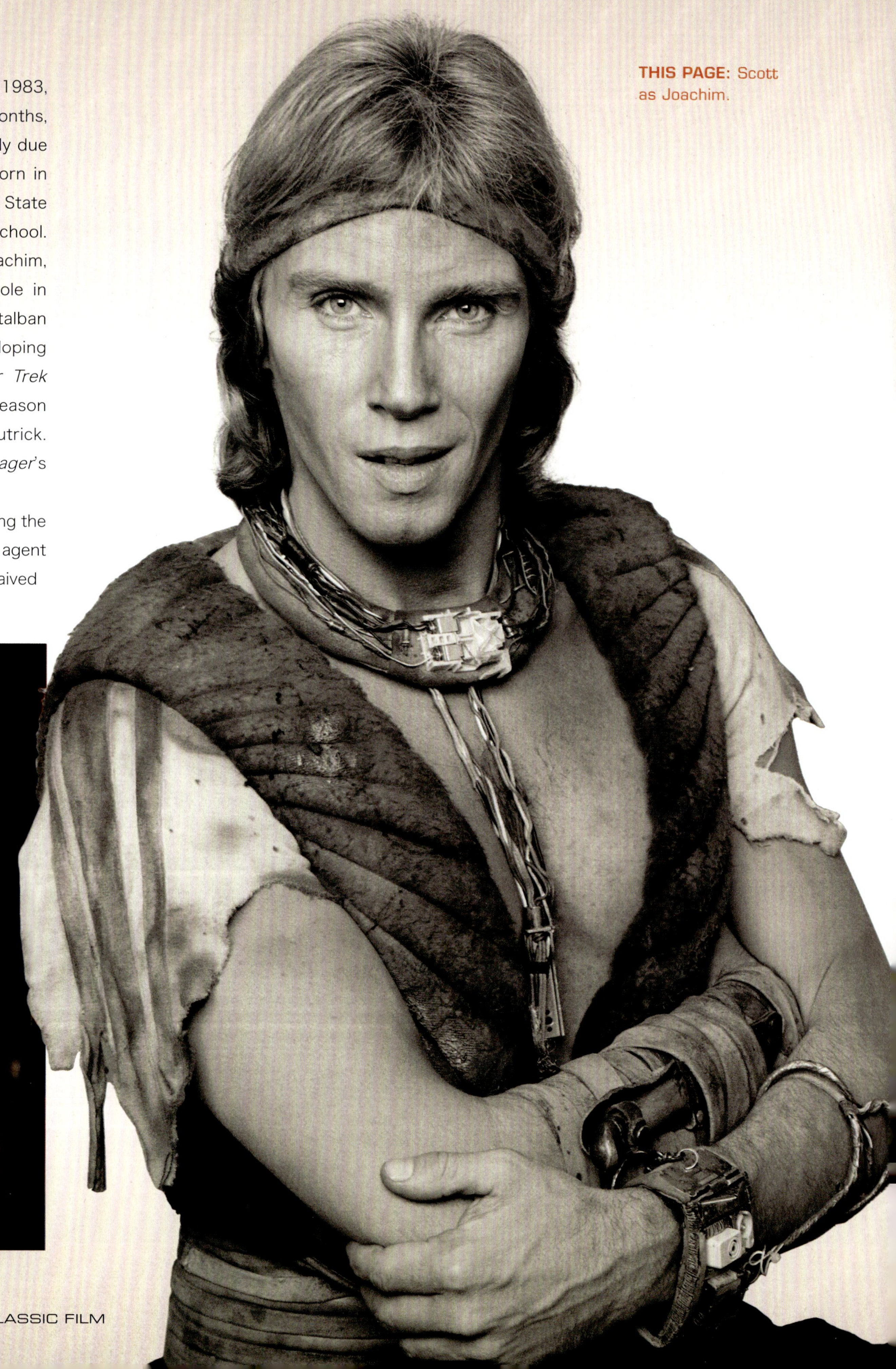

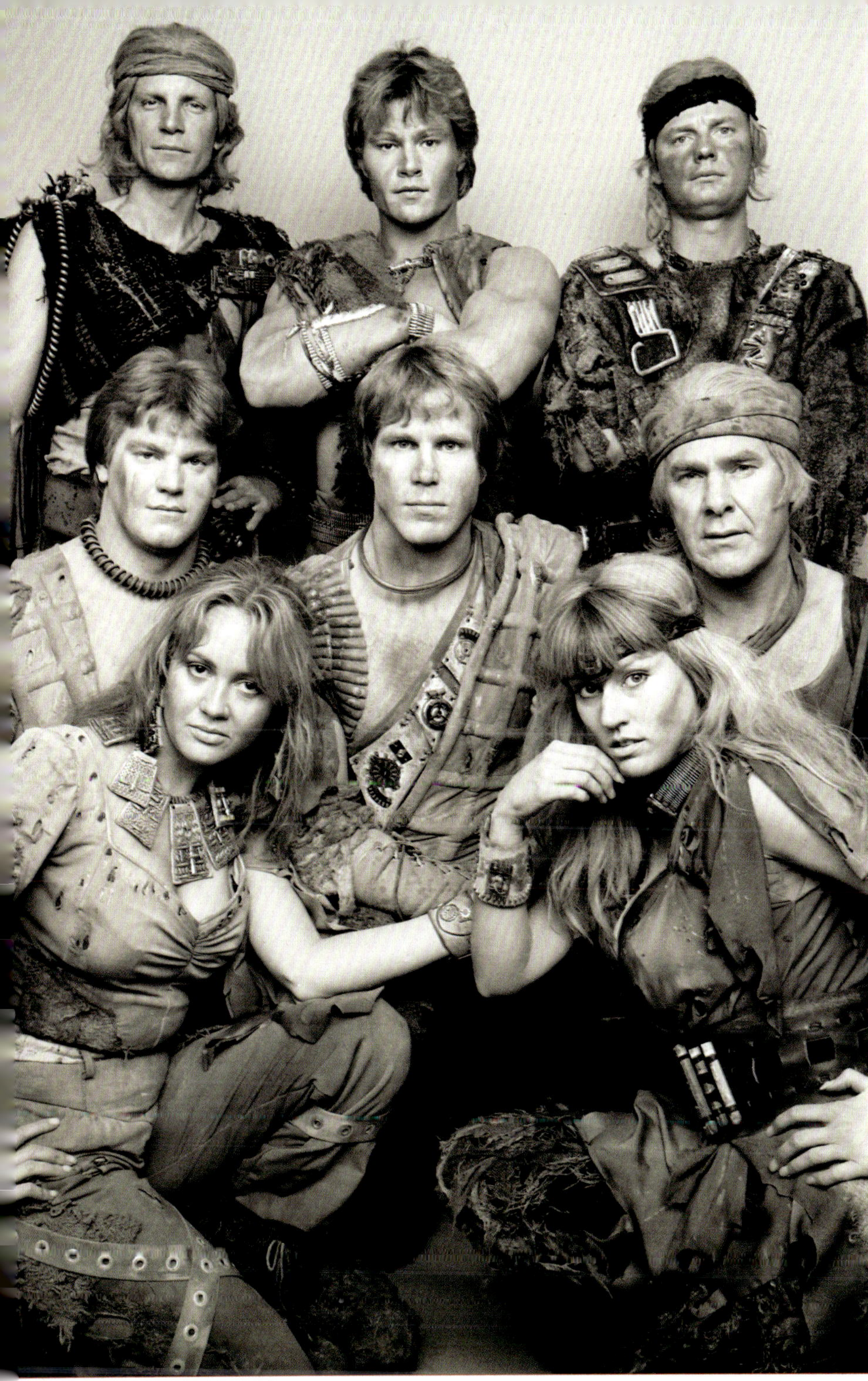

the billing when negotiations did not work out. Scott thought that the agreement had been to place his name at the end of the credits, not waive his name entirely from the film.[10]

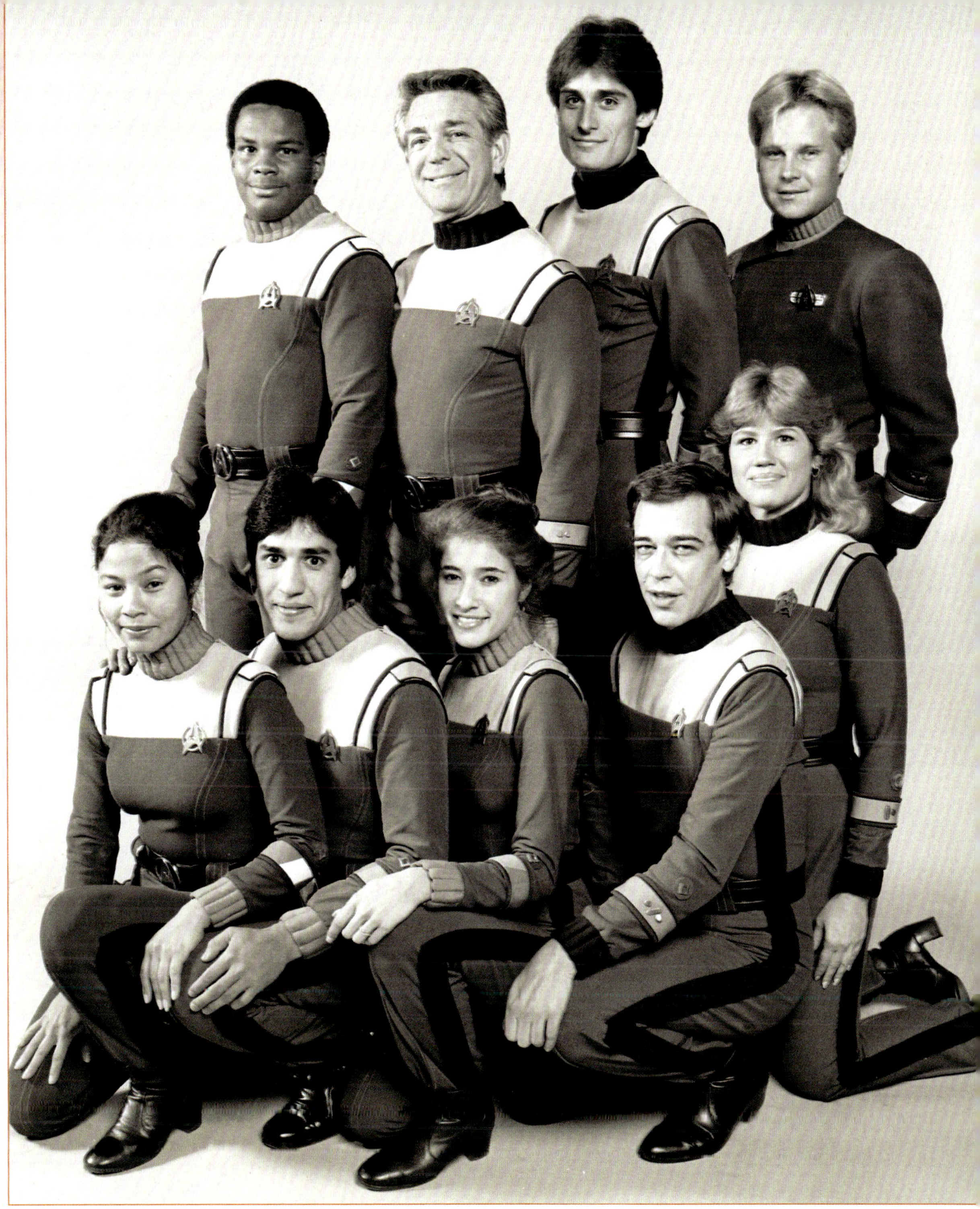

As an adjunct to the dominant theme of aging that runs throughout *Star Trek II*, Kirk, Spock, Carol, and Khan each have young people for who they are responsible. Kirk is reintroduced to David; Spock is mentor to the *Enterprise* cadets, most especially Saavik; Carol has her son David and her team of scientists to lead; and Khan has his followers. One of the most prominent of those followers is the *Reliant* Navigator, played by Laura Banks.

Although *Star Trek II* was Banks' first film role, she had already been acting for several years in plays at the University of Kansas, where she studied art and theater, and had performed at the famed Comedy Store in Los Angeles. "I was a follower of *Drama-Logue*, which is your backstage-of-New York City… employee rag for actors, where you would look at the classifieds and see what's up, and I

IS JOACHIM KHAN'S SON?

By design, *Star Trek II* does not answer every question the audience may have. Why does Khan wear a single glove throughout the film? How does Khan recognize Chekov when Walter Koenig's character was not yet part of the *Enterprise* crew when the episode "Space Seed" premiered? Perhaps the most fascinating question has to do with the relationship between Khan and Joachim. The special attention that Khan gives to Joachim, and the fact that Joachim alone appears to be able to challenge Khan's decisions, make many wonder if there is a familial relationship.

There are facts that support the conjecture that they are father and son. When rehearsing at Montalban's home, Scott and Montalban thought of and practiced their scenes as father and son. In a 1983 *Starlog* interview with Martha Bonds, when asked, Scott replied, "He was my Daddy!"[14] While only fifteen years have passed from the original episode and Joachim appears more than fifteen years old, perhaps genetically engineered humans mature faster. Or Joachim could be Khan's son, but not with Marla. The audience did not see all seventy-two of Khan's followers aboard the *Botany Bay* during "Space Seed." There could have been children, and Joachim could have been one of them, explaining why most of Khan's surviving followers appear to be mostly in their twenties and thirties.

Then again, maybe not. Continuing his *Moby Dick* homage, Meyer thought of Joachim as the first mate Starbuck to Montalban's Captain Ahab, although he consistently cautions that the director or writer's interpretation is no more valid than that of the audience. The name Joachim is similar to Joaquin, Khan's lieutenant in "Space Seed" played by Mark Tobin, and it is as likely he is Joaquin's son as Khan's, thus providing an alternative explanation for Khan and Joachim's special relationship. The September 16, 1981 and January 18, 1982 versions of the script specifically identify Joachim as "Khan's Lieutenant. He is the largest and brightest of Khan's group." There is no mention of him as Khan's son.

saw a post for literally what were my measurements—my height, just uncannily, five-foot eleven inches measurements. It was from Central Casting. I immediately called and said, 'Yeah, this is me.' So they said, 'Alright. Get down here.' So that's how I found it."[11]

It was the strength of Banks' emotional reaction in the scene where Khan relates his people's misfortune to Terrell and Chekov that led Meyer to select her for the *Reliant* sequences as Navigator. Banks reminisces, "I knew when the camera was rolling and when they were shooting. I was acting as if I had a principal role and responding and things. I really believe now that's why I kept getting moved forward to where Nick put me."[12] While on set, Banks learned as much as possible about acting from the iconic Montalban. "He took the time to answer every one of my questions."[13] Banks would use what she learned on her next endeavors, which included reuniting with William Shatner on an episode of *T.J. Hooker*, starring in Roger Corman executive produced film *Wheels of Fire*, and continuing to write and perform comedy.

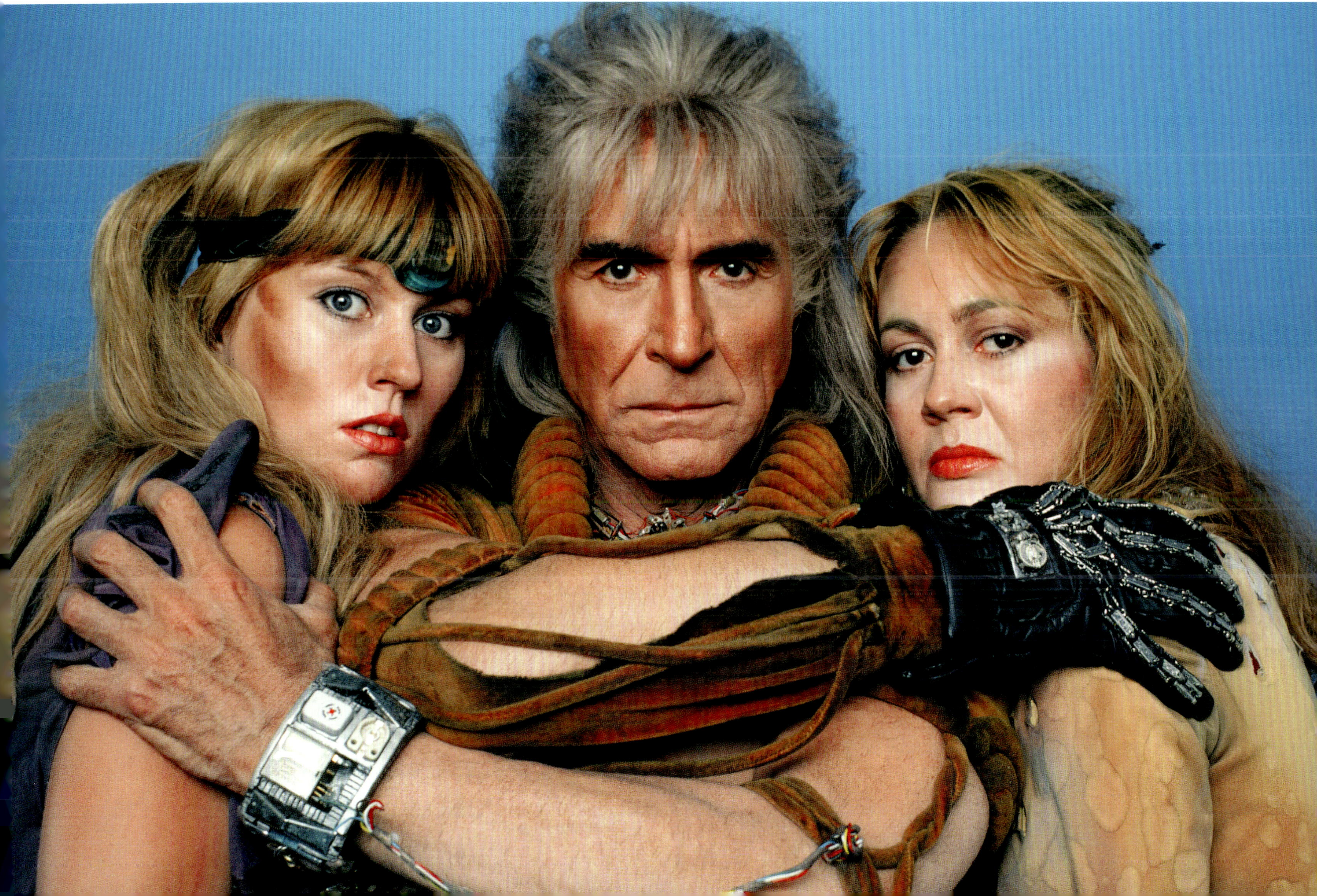

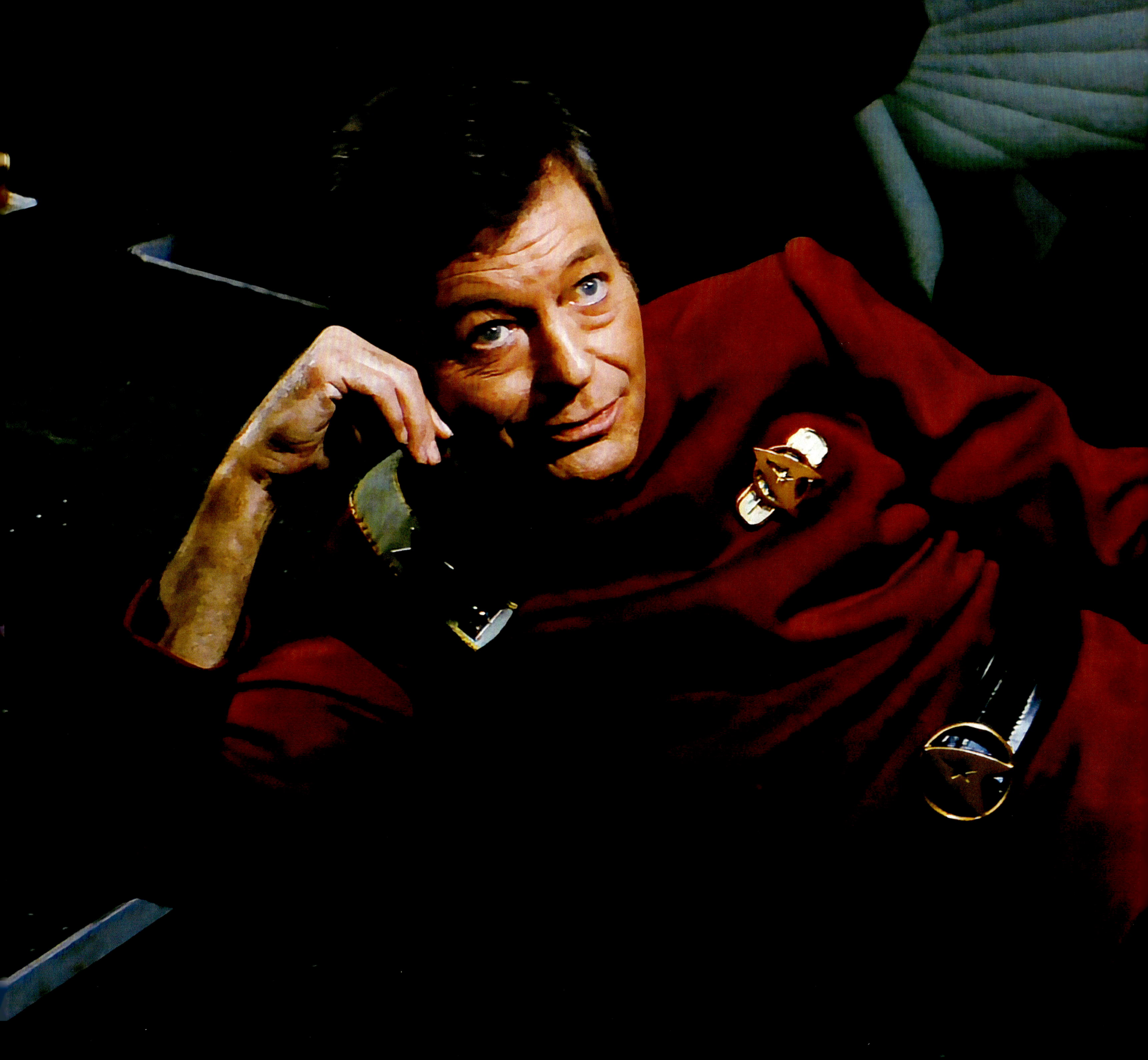

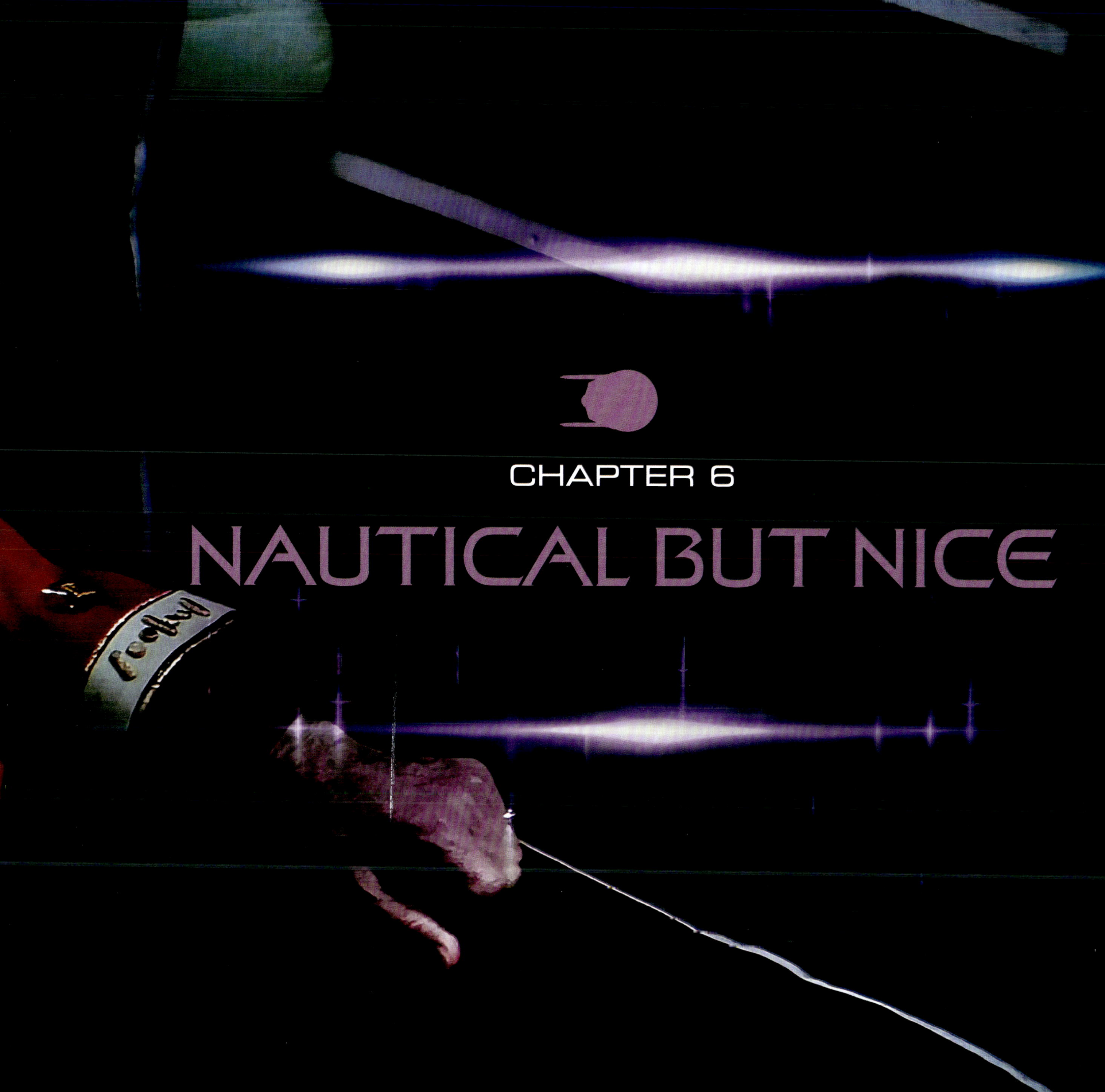

CHAPTER 6
NAUTICAL BUT NICE

ROBERT FLETCHER AND COSTUME DESIGN

It is a rare occasion which permits an artist to revisit past designs and make improvements. Such would be the fortune of costume designer Robert Fletcher, who would return to *Star Trek II* with an eye towards correcting what he considered some of his follies while designing costumes for *Star Trek: The Motion Picture*. There are many fans of the *Motion Picture* costumes. Fletcher was not among them. Of those who wanted something fresh, Fletcher said, "I don't blame them. I didn't like [the uniforms] much myself!"[1]

Director Nicholas Meyer and Fletcher had a shared understanding that costumes serve as a shorthand for audiences, revealing character and story details through visuals such as color, texture, and details. Fletcher's goal was to "bring out the personalities of the characters in their clothes."[2]

On a film with a limited budget, ambitions must usually be measured against economic realities. It is here that producer Robert Sallin brought his years of experience to bear. In concert with Fletcher, Sallin conducted tests to determine which colors the *Motion Picture* Starfleet uniforms could be dyed for reuse by the cadet characters in *Star Trek II*. With alterations to colors and ornamentation, the expensive *Motion Picture* costumes would amortize time and costs. The fabric took best to blue-gray, gold, and dark red. It would be the dark red or maroon that would win approval, influencing Fletcher to create the new Starfleet officer costumes that would be featured in six *Star Trek* movies and episodes of the various television shows.

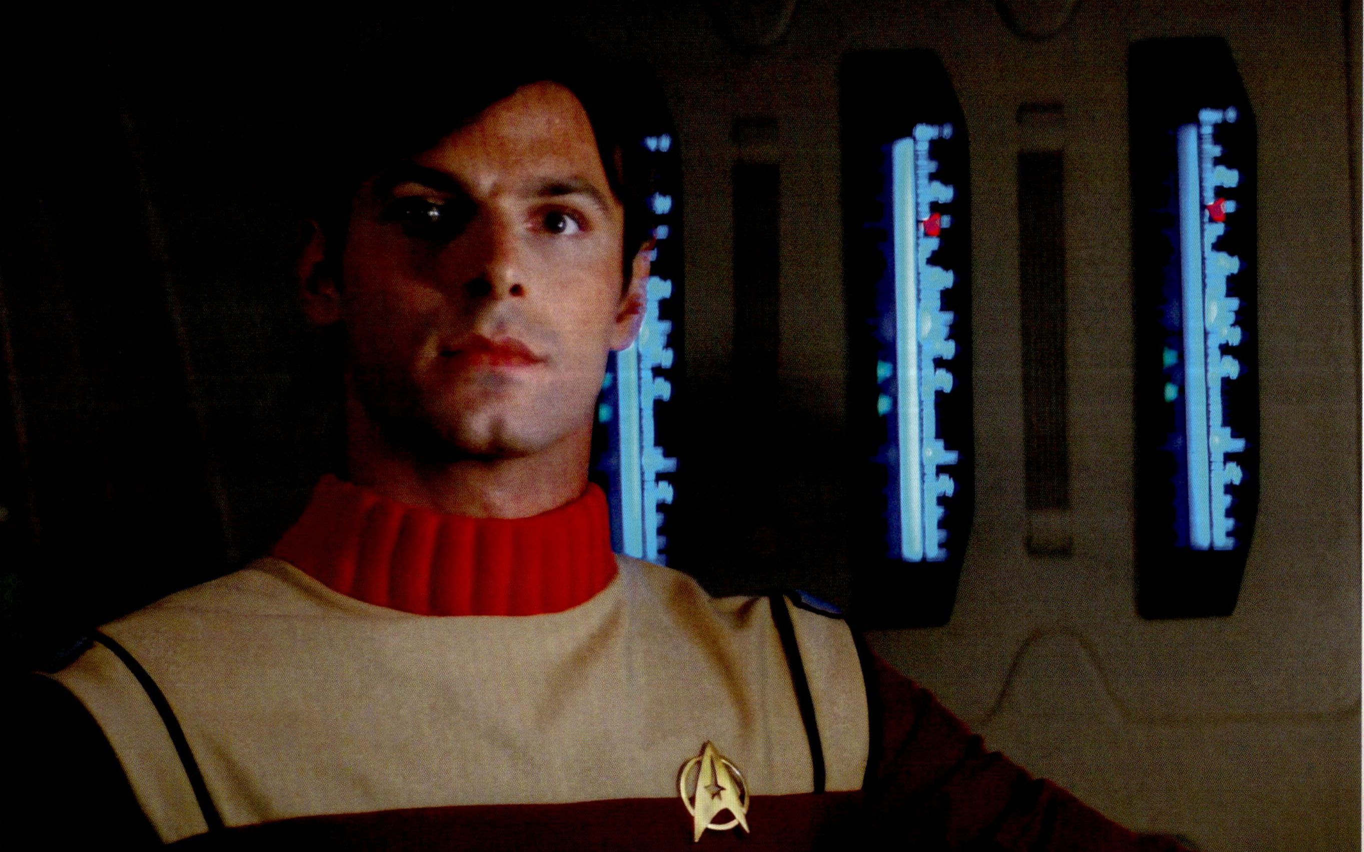

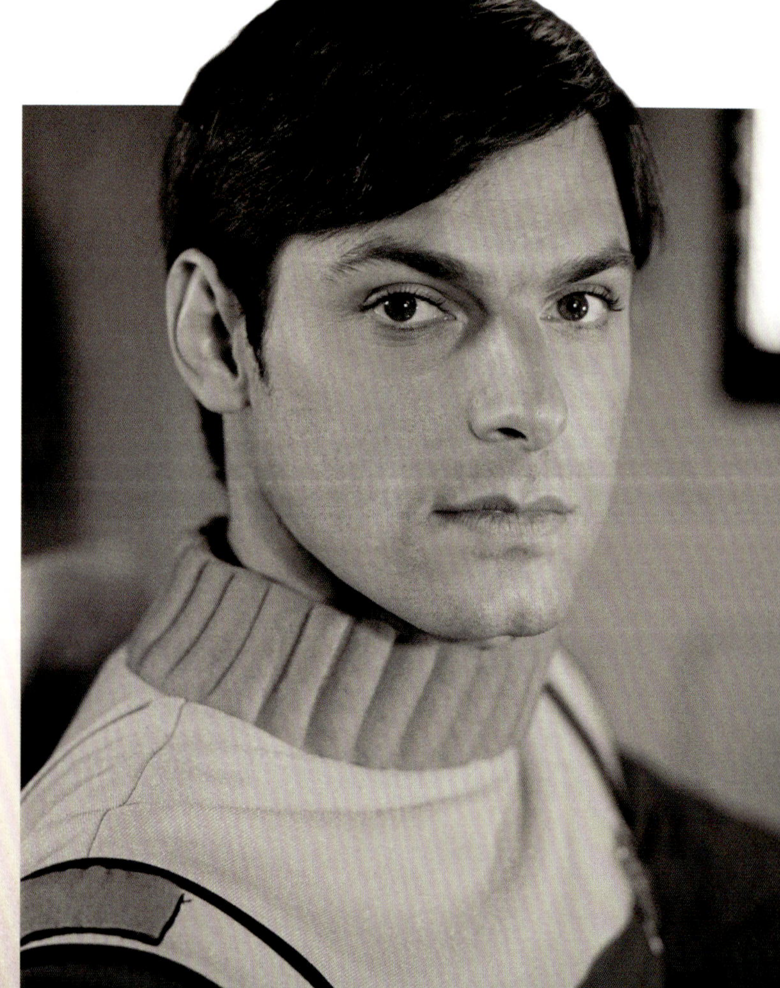

ROBERT FLETCHER

Considering the impressive contributions he made to many *Star Trek* films, it is perhaps no coincidence that Robert Fletcher was born about forty miles from the future birthplace of James T. Kirk. Born on August 23, 1922, in Cedar Rapids, Iowa, Fletcher had started his entertainment career on the front stage as an actor before transitioning to set and costume designs for operas and the theater. A three-time Tony Award nominated costume designer, Fletcher worked with Orson Welles on his 1956 production of *King Lear*, designed costumes for Katherine Hepburn for the play *The Tempest*, and created the original costumes for *How to Succeed in Business Without Really Trying*. It was Fletcher's reputation for operatic creativity that inspired director Robert Wise to ask Fletcher to create the *Star Trek: The Motion Picture* costumes, the first Hollywood film for the costume designer.

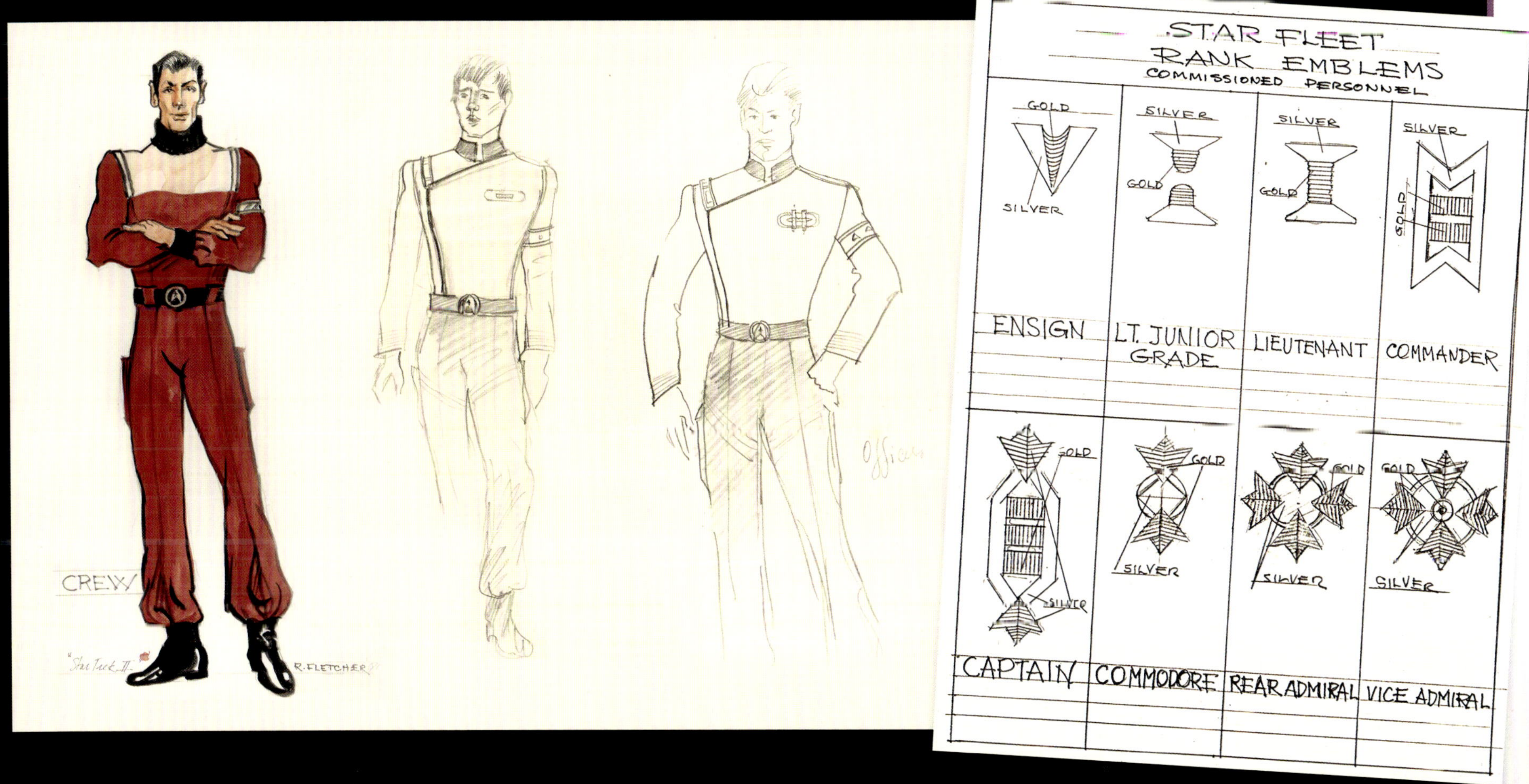

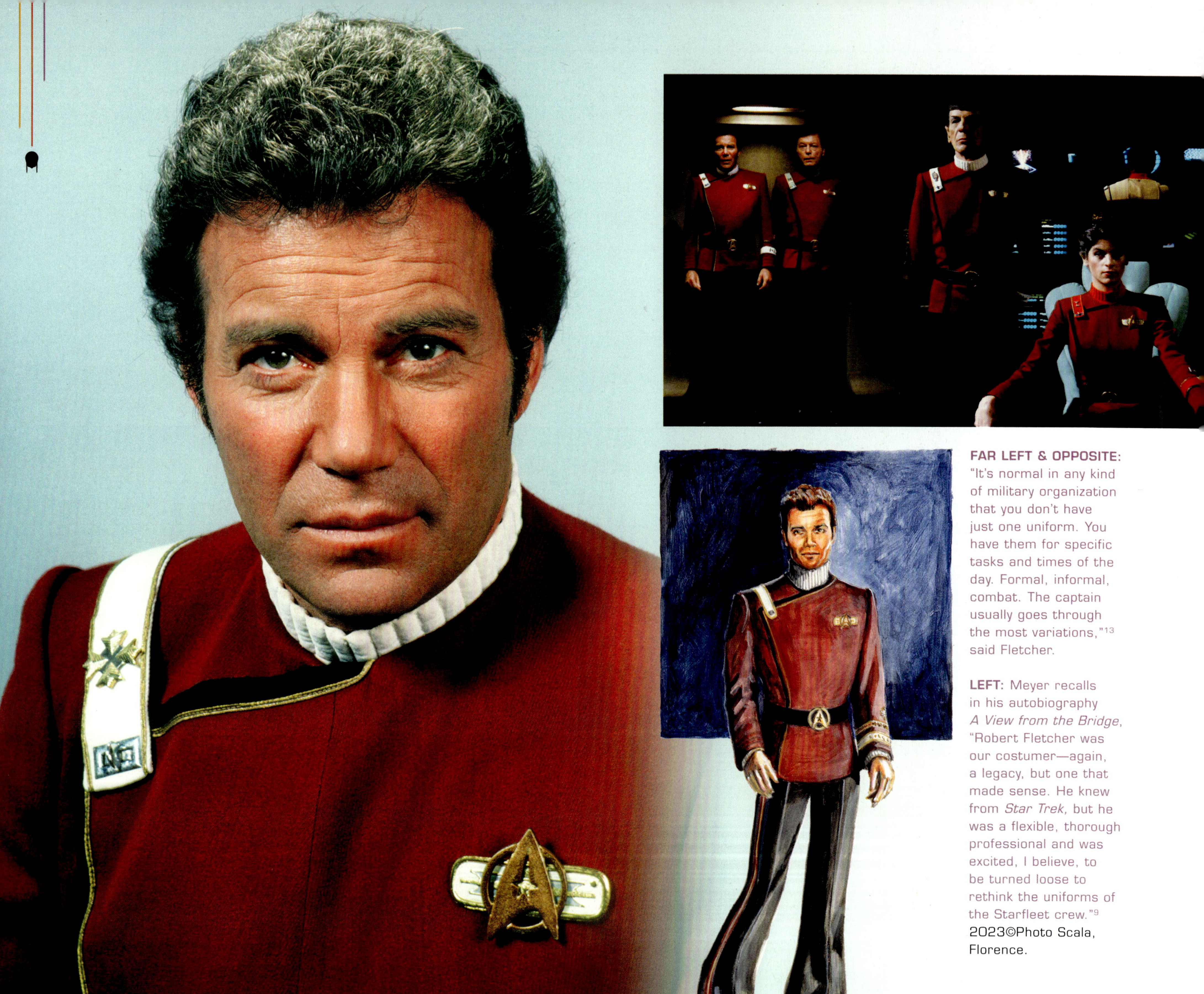

FAR LEFT & OPPOSITE: "It's normal in any kind of military organization that you don't have just one uniform. You have them for specific tasks and times of the day. Formal, informal, combat. The captain usually goes through the most variations,"[13] said Fletcher.

LEFT: Meyer recalls in his autobiography *A View from the Bridge*, "Robert Fletcher was our costumer—again, a legacy, but one that made sense. He knew from *Star Trek*, but he was a flexible, thorough professional and was excited, I believe, to be turned loose to rethink the uniforms of the Starfleet crew."[9]
2023©Photo Scala, Florence.

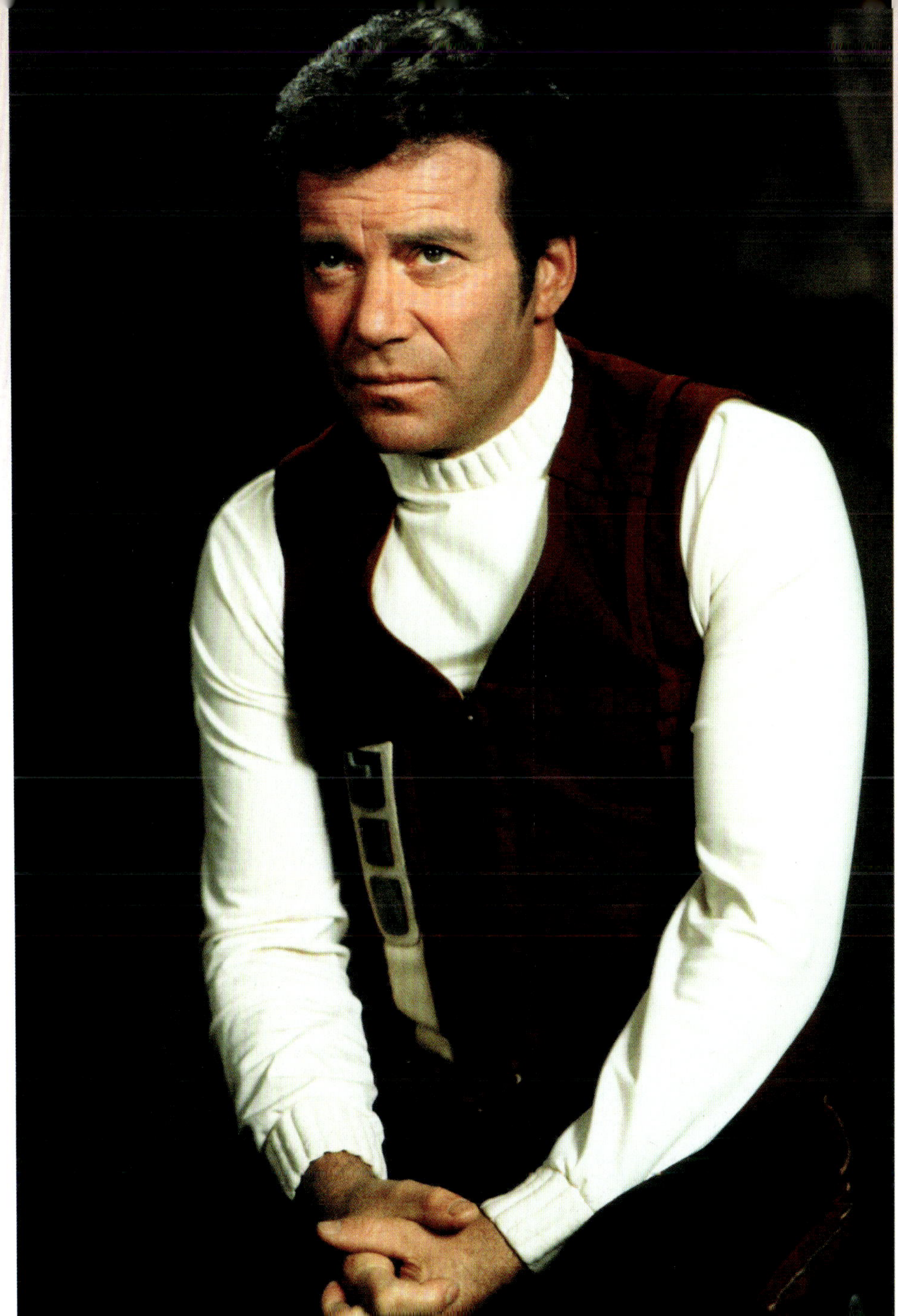 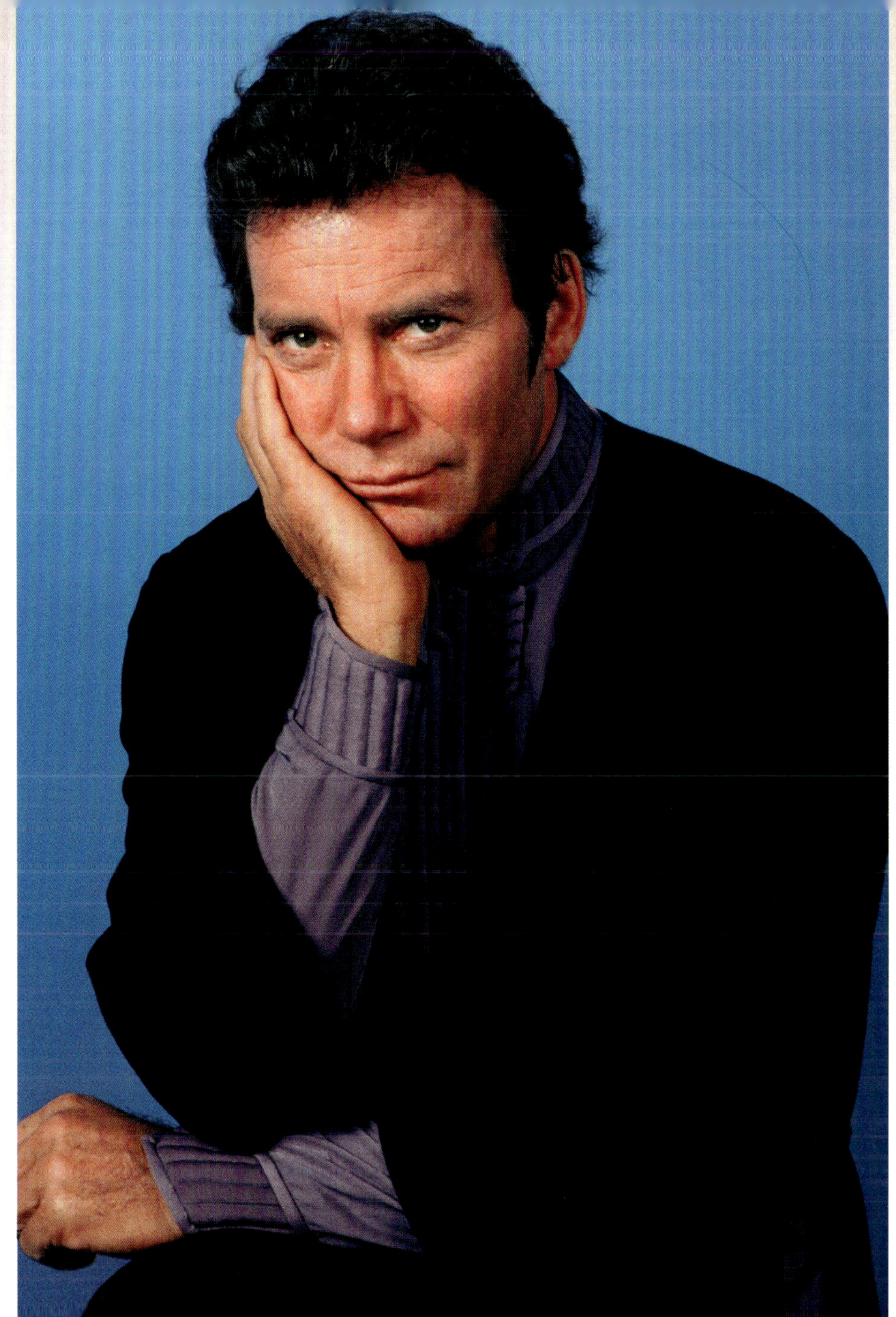

Cosplayers now call the *Star Trek II* Starfleet uniform the "Monster Maroon," which is appropriate, because color choice is essential to costumes serving the narrative of the film. Fletcher believed that the colors of *Star Trek* costumes should be "corrupt." meaning not-quite-pure colors. "The uniform jackets aren't quite red. Kirk's civilian shirt, in the scenes in his place in San Francisco, is a sort of dusty teal blue. Spock's Vulcan robe isn't a true black. Everything is an 'ish' color. Maroonish red. Brownish green. Purplish black. They're not colors you see today, so in a subtle way, they indicate another time."[3]

The new costume designs, with brimming ornamentations and corrupted colors, were designed to not only serve the story, but purposely differentiate the sequel from its more muted predecessor.

By varying the colors of the matching rank insignia shoulder strap and the trapunto vertical quilted undershirt by starship department, Fletcher was able to add even more vibrancy to the visual appeal of *Star Trek II*. "There was a kind of complicated arrangement of divisions and ranks expressed by the braid on the sleeves. I made that up. I organized it and produced a little instruction booklet about it for the wardrobe department and anyone else who was interested."[4]

For the bridge crew and the Starfleet uniforms, the costumes were a take on—as Meyer's wife would joke—a "nautical, but nice" style. Meyer knew he wanted to add a more military dimension to the costumes. "I'd really like to stretch the nautical analogy. I said it should be like Captain Horatio Hornblower in outer space."[5]

In addition to the directive to make the costumes more nautical, Fletcher was also asked by Meyer to find inspiration from the classic 1937 film *The Prisoner of Zenda*. The high collar and jacket flaps that adorned Ernest Dryden's *Zenda* designs would inspire many elements of the new Starfleet uniforms. The jacket flap opening frames the face with its contrasting bold colors and also could be used to add character. Like the loosening of a suit tie after a taxing day, Kirk and company could loosen their formal uniforms during moments of casualness or reflection.

Limited by the availability of real-world textiles while designing futuristic elements, Fletcher relied on his creativity. Metal chains were stitched into the Starfleet jackets, outlining the perimeter of the open flap. These chains give the illusion of a means of closure while simultaneously hiding the little black snaps that are the true source of fastening the flap to the jacket. "I put those in there because being in the twenty-third century one can presume some mysterious new means of closing,"[6] Fletcher explained.

 Budget limitations played a role in costume design as much as any other area of production. Meyer spoke to that concern, "Our budget was so tight and it hadn't improved by *Star Trek VI* either, it actually may have gotten worse, that I couldn't have pockets on their pants. And I really wanted pockets, because an actor sometimes needs something to do with his hands. Couldn't afford the pockets."[10]

 The fan-monikered "Monster Maroon" in its final form as worn by Koenig, Takei and Nichols.

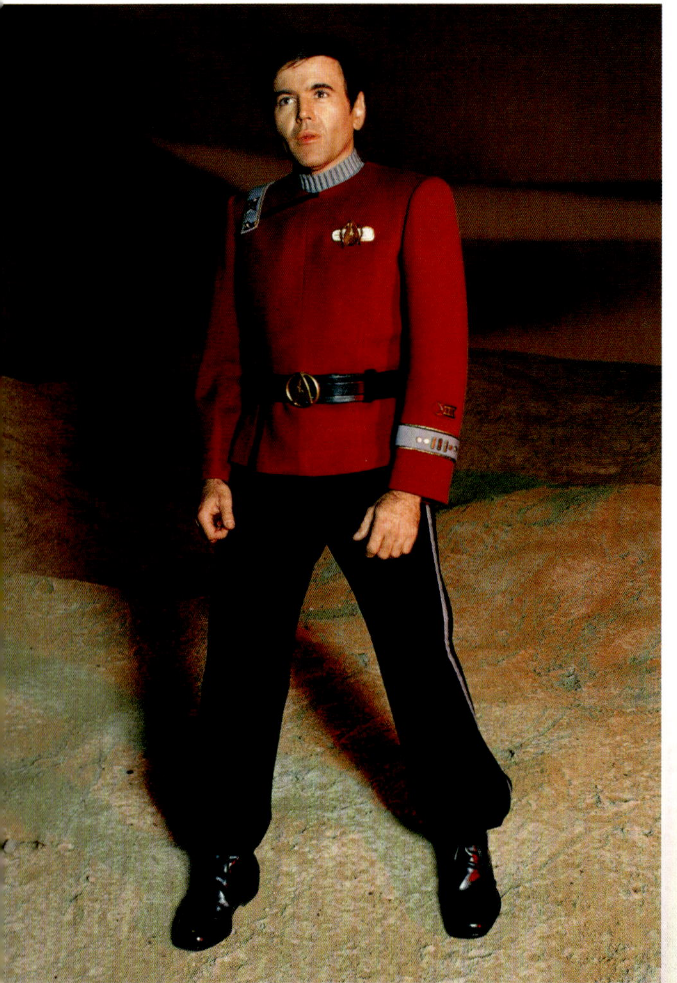

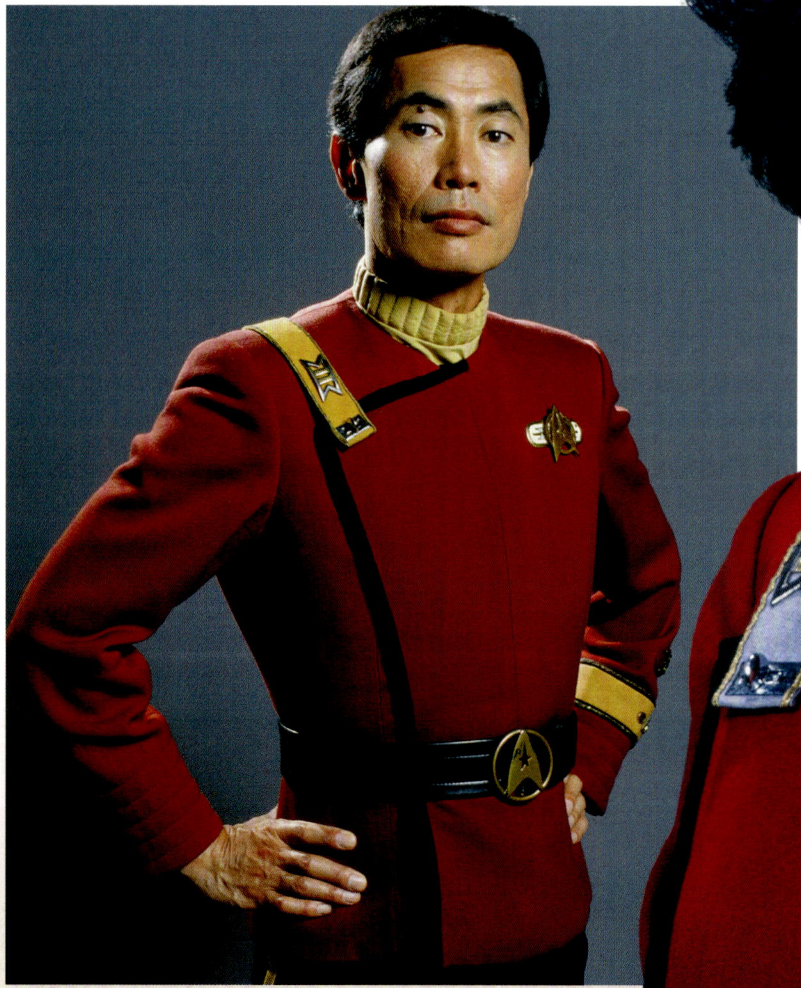

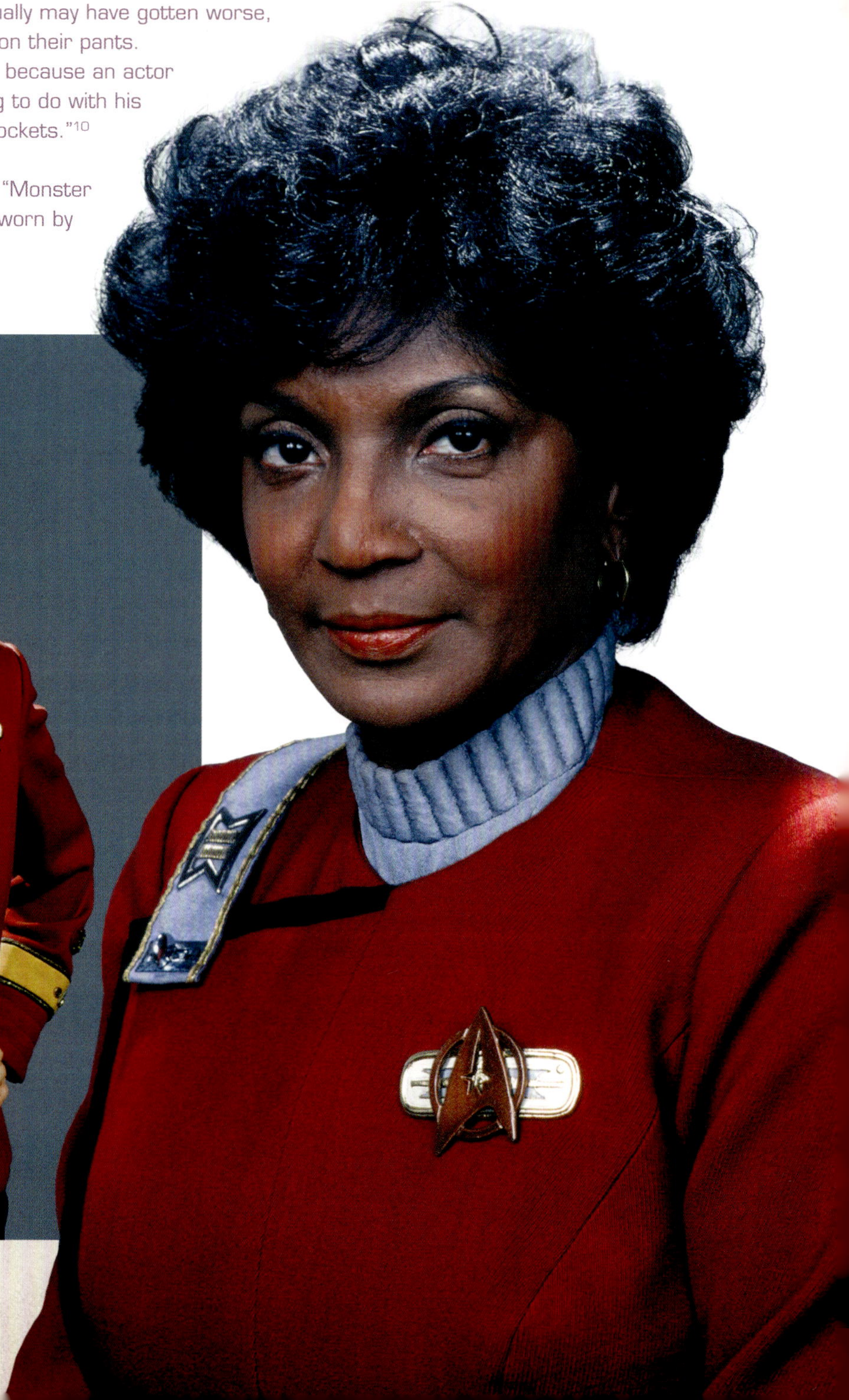

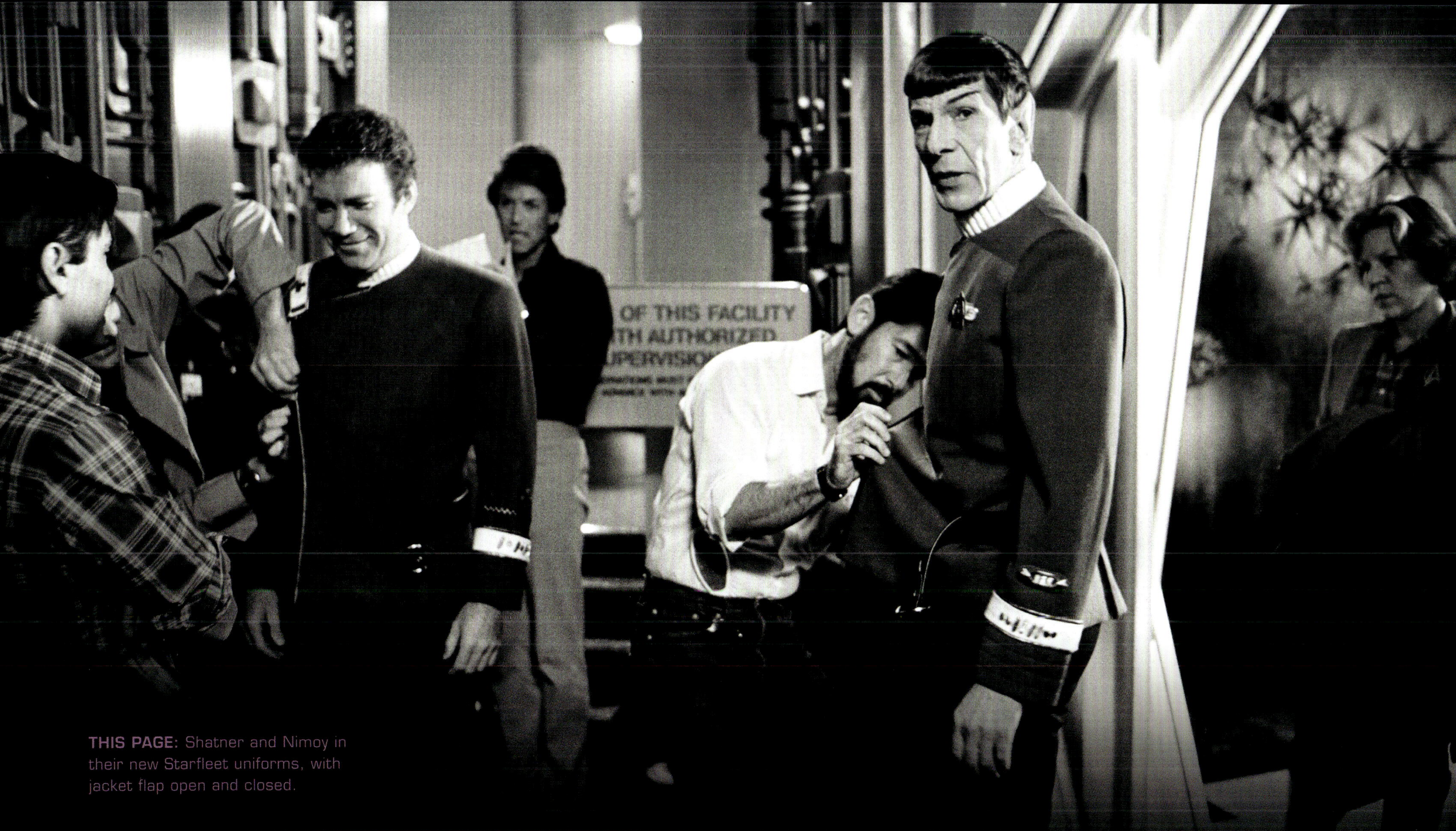

THIS PAGE: Shatner and Nimoy in their new Starfleet uniforms, with jacket flap open and closed.

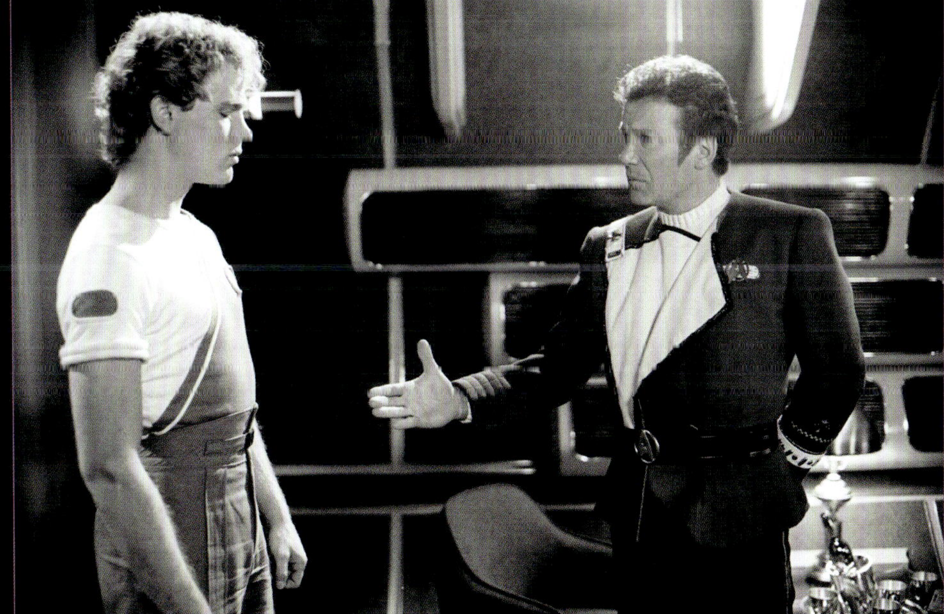

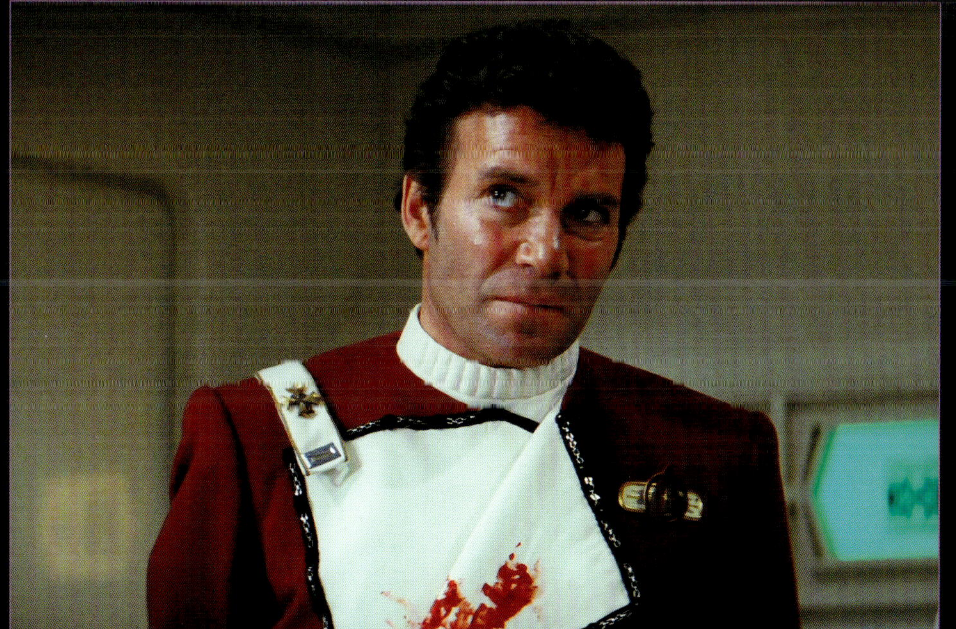

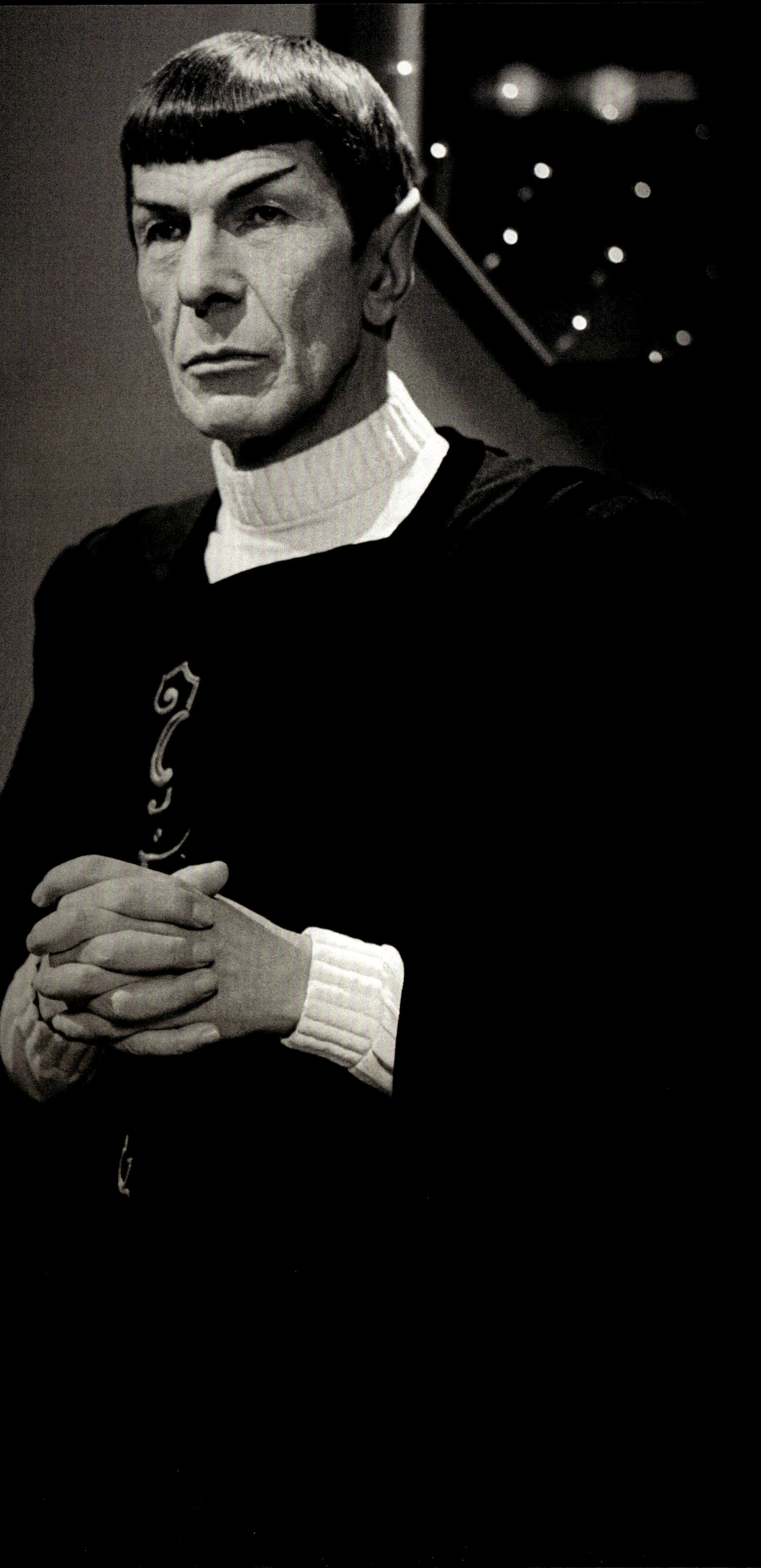

Fletcher reused Spock's costume from *Star Trek: The Motion Picture* to save money and provide a visual continuity of character. "People always ask me what the writings on the front of Spock's black velvet at-home costume symbolized. I have to explain the language I invented to decorate those things, and I can't! All I can say is it's very much akin to Chinese; it's non-syllabic, and the various shapes contain an entire thought and you don't use them to make words."[7]

Similarly, the space suits worn by Chekov and Terrell were a modified reuse of the space suits from *Star Trek: The Motion Picture*, which had originally cost $15,000 to $20,000. Sallin and the *Star Trek II* creatives knew the value of economic recycling, demonstrated by their reuse of the *Motion Picture* models, sets, visual effect sequences, and costumes.

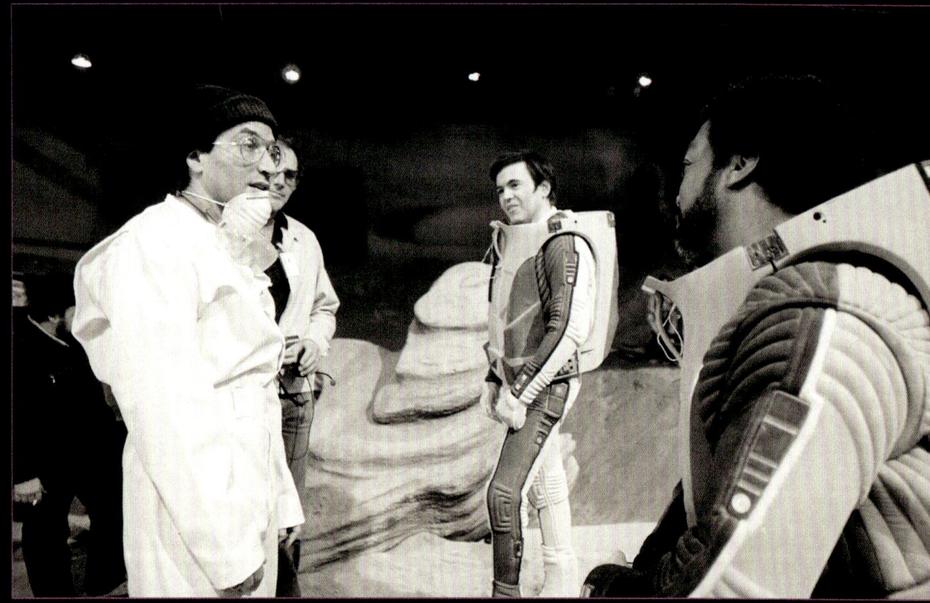

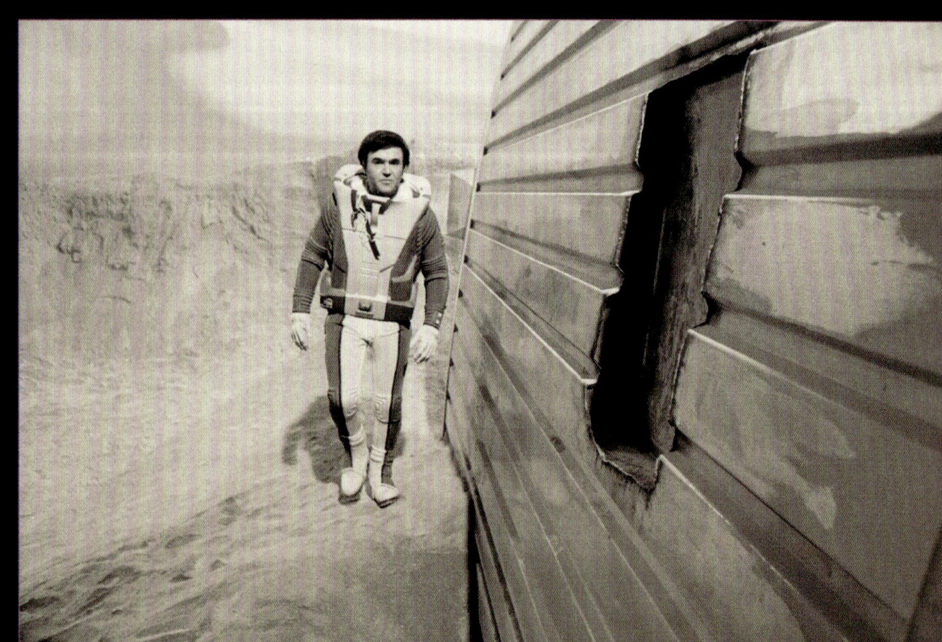

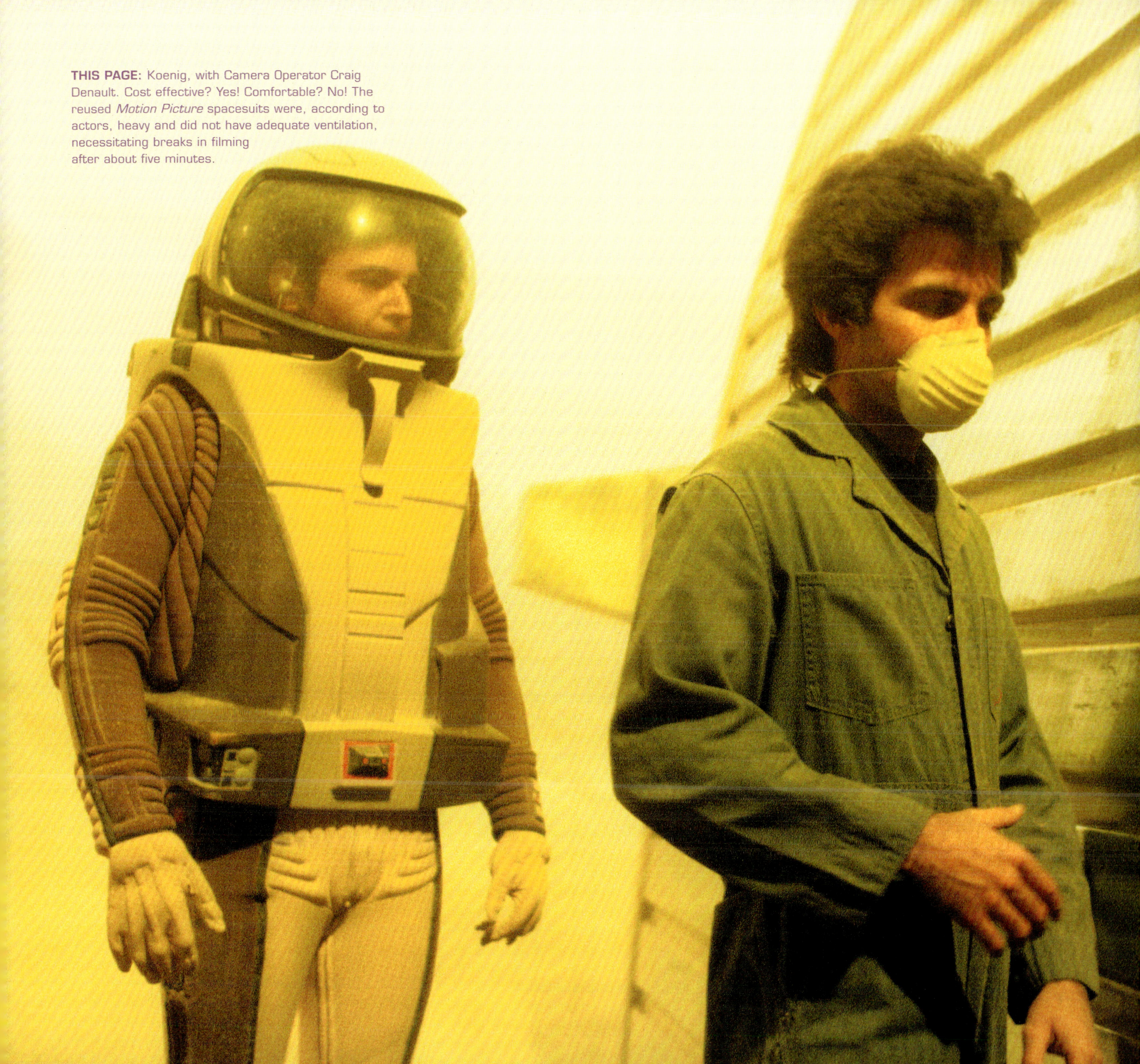

THIS PAGE: Koenig, with Camera Operator Craig
Denault. Cost effective? Yes! Comfortable? No! The
reused *Motion Picture* spacesuits were, according to
actors, heavy and did not have adequate ventilation,
necessitating breaks in filming
after about five minutes.

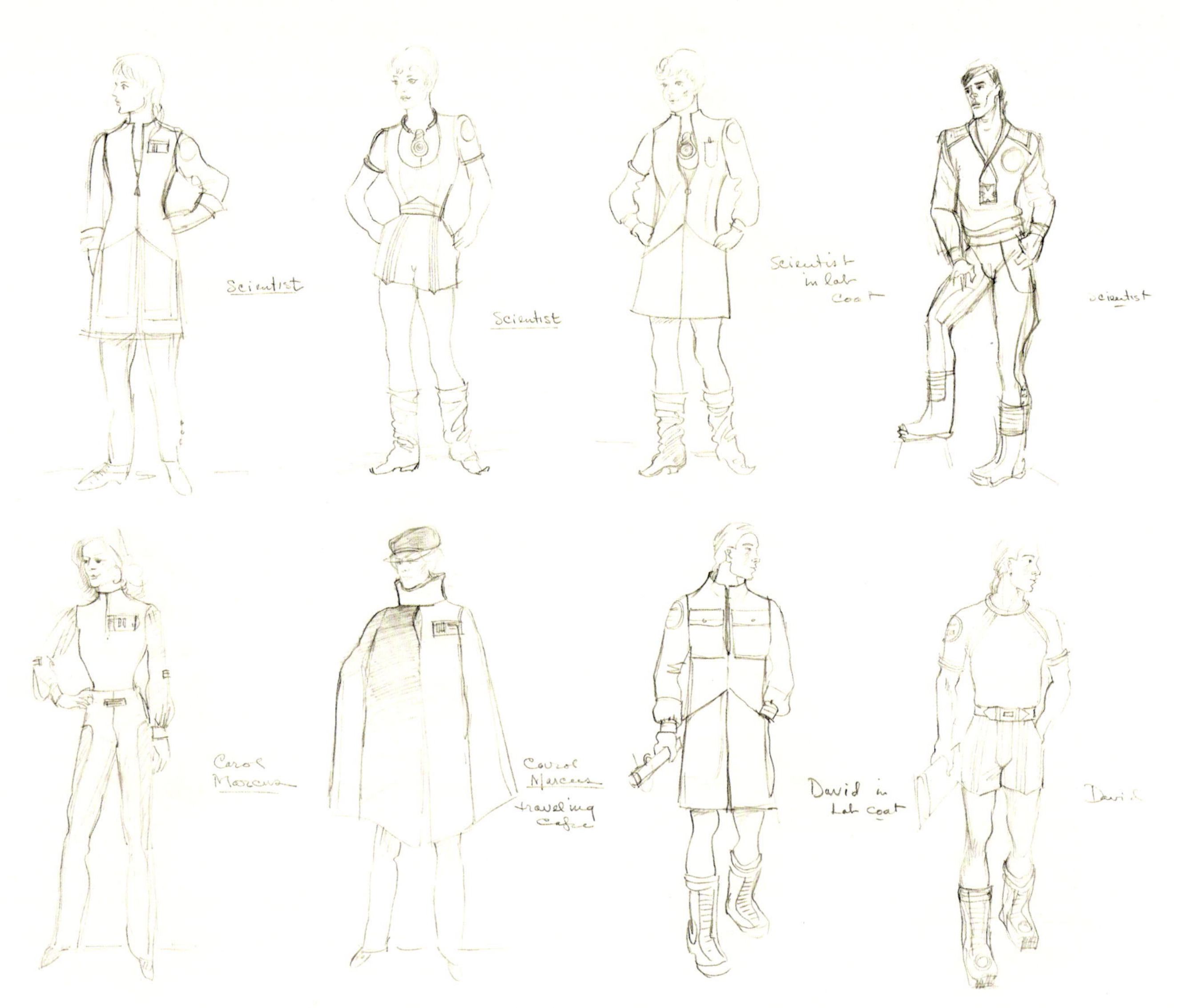

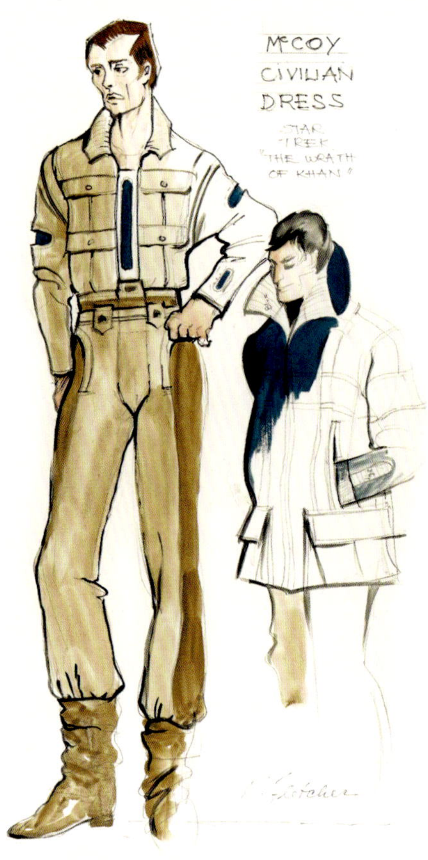

LEFT & BELOW LEFT: Fletcher's costume designs for the scientists, including David and Carol.

ABOVE & BELOW: Fletcher's costume design for McCoy's "civilian dress."

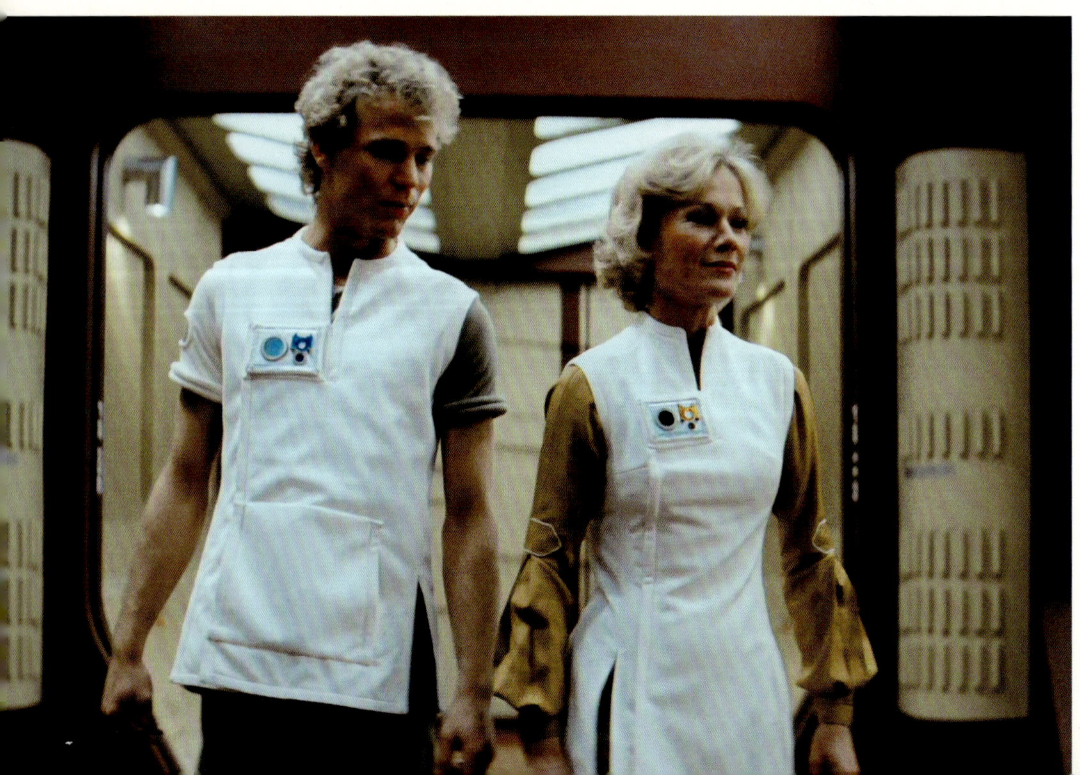

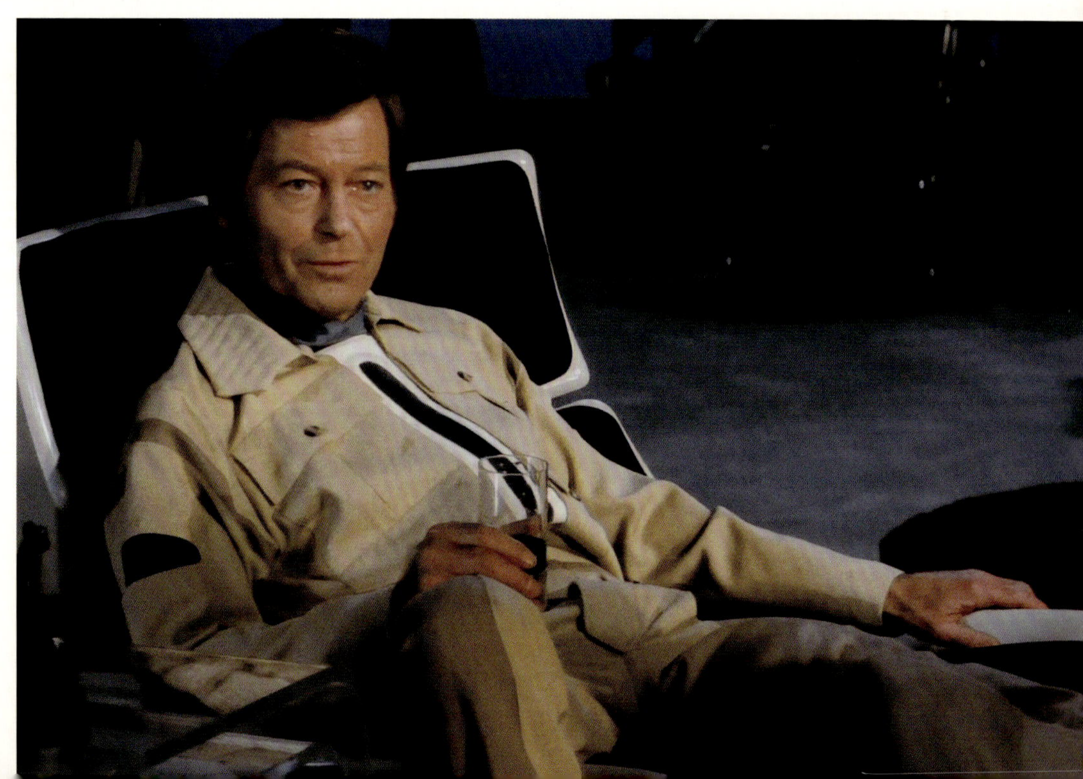

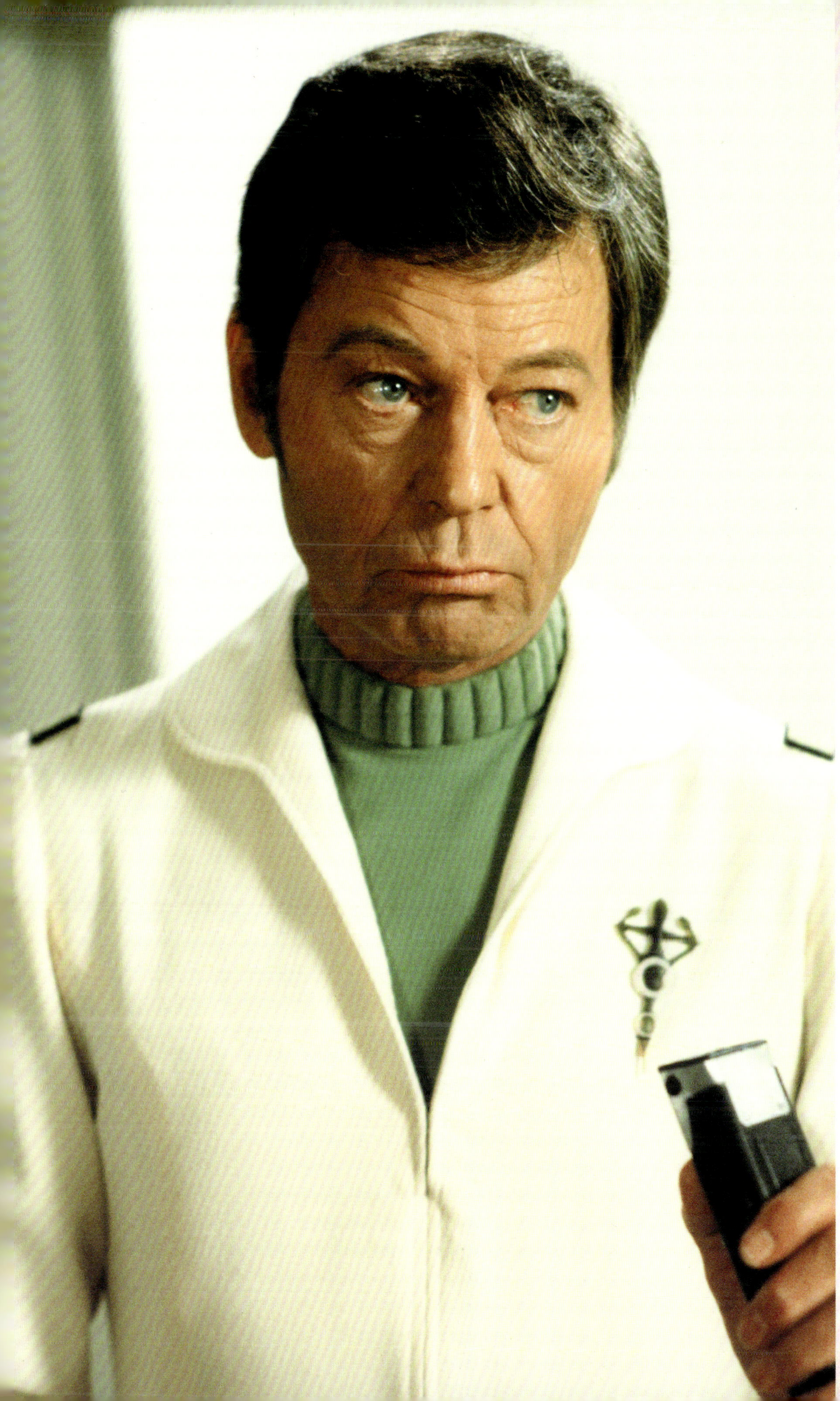

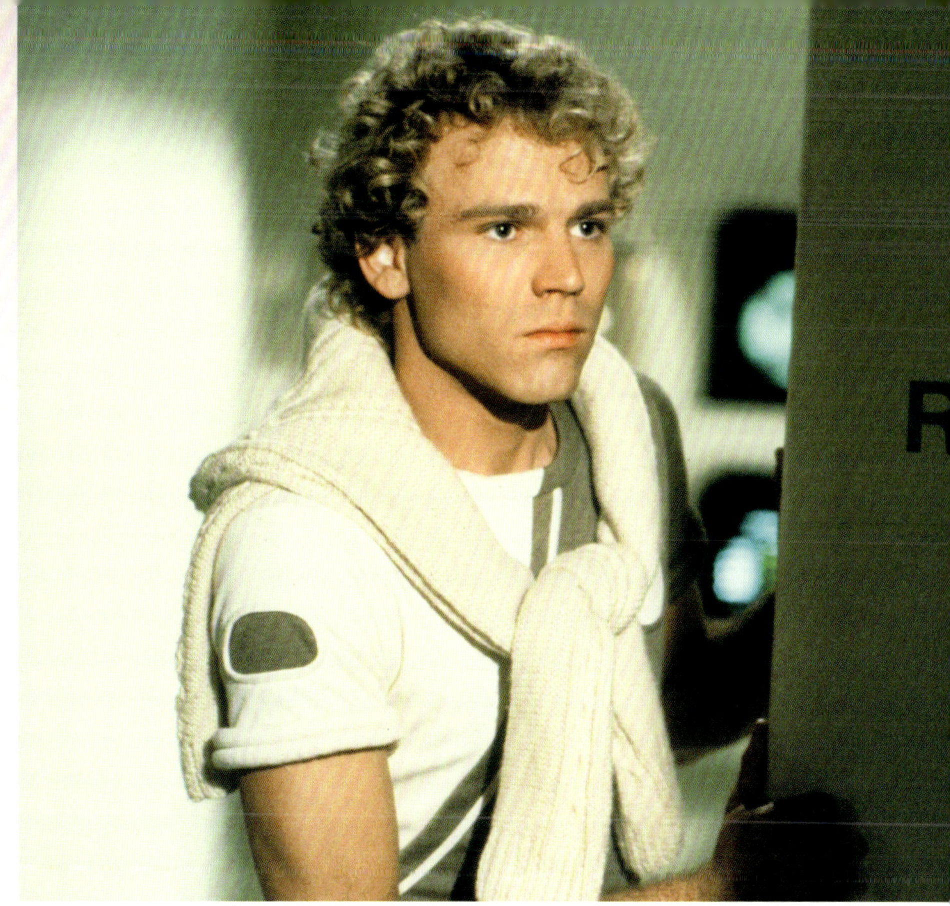

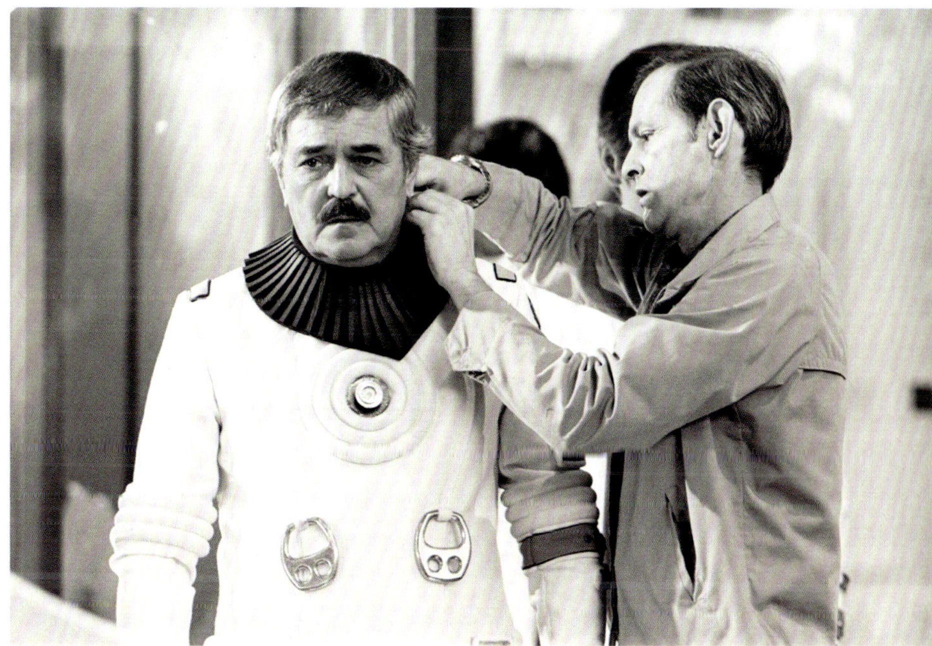

LEFT & ABOVE: Reuse and adaptation of *Motion Picture* uniforms were not limited to the spacesuits or Cadet costumes. *Star Trek: The Motion Picture* engineering and medical costumes were tweaked, adding the trapunto undershirt to Doctor McCoy's uniform.

TOP: David's penchant for wearing his sweater around his neck, a popular fashion trend during the 1980s, gave the character a provinciality that supports his allegiance to science.

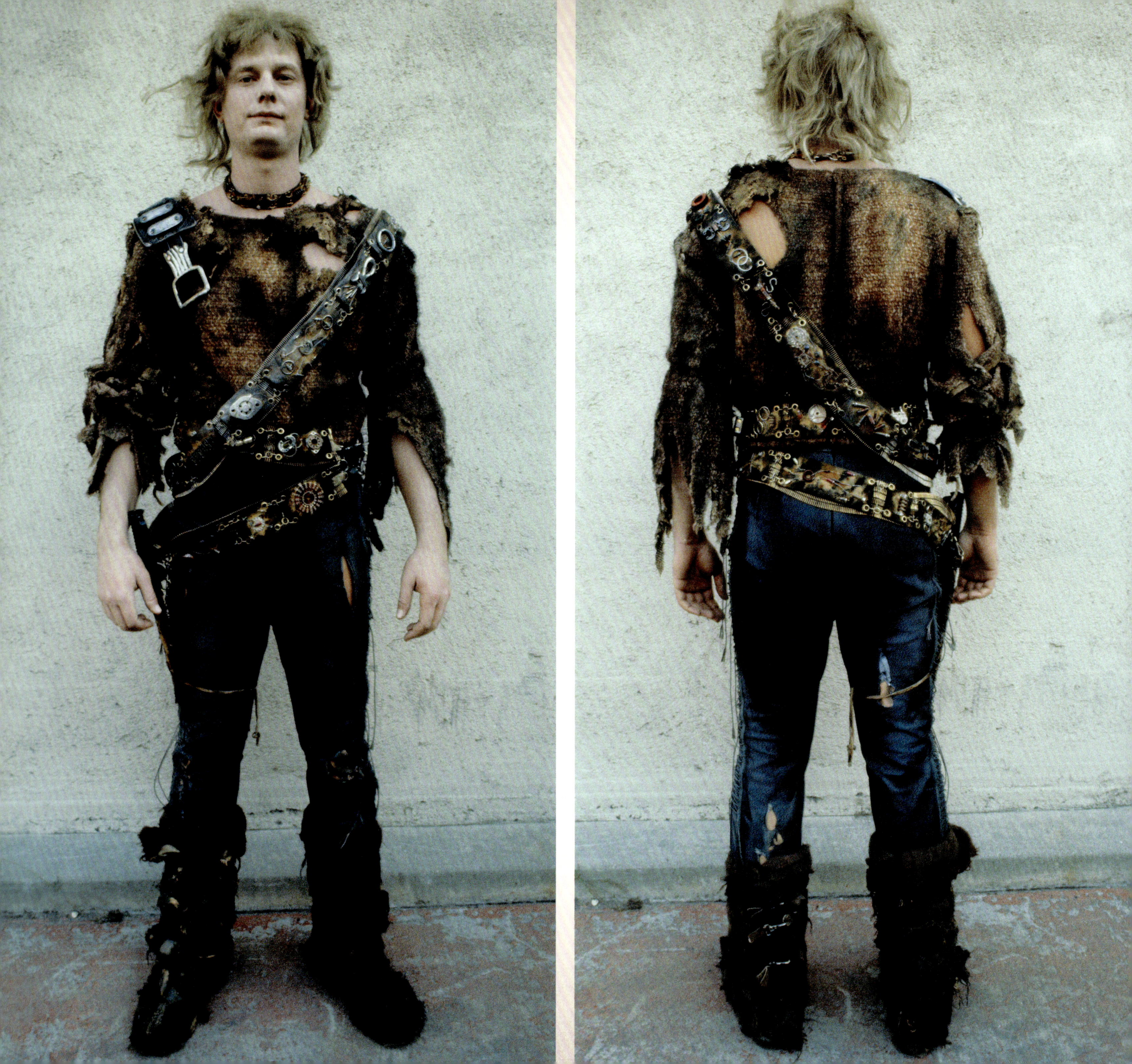

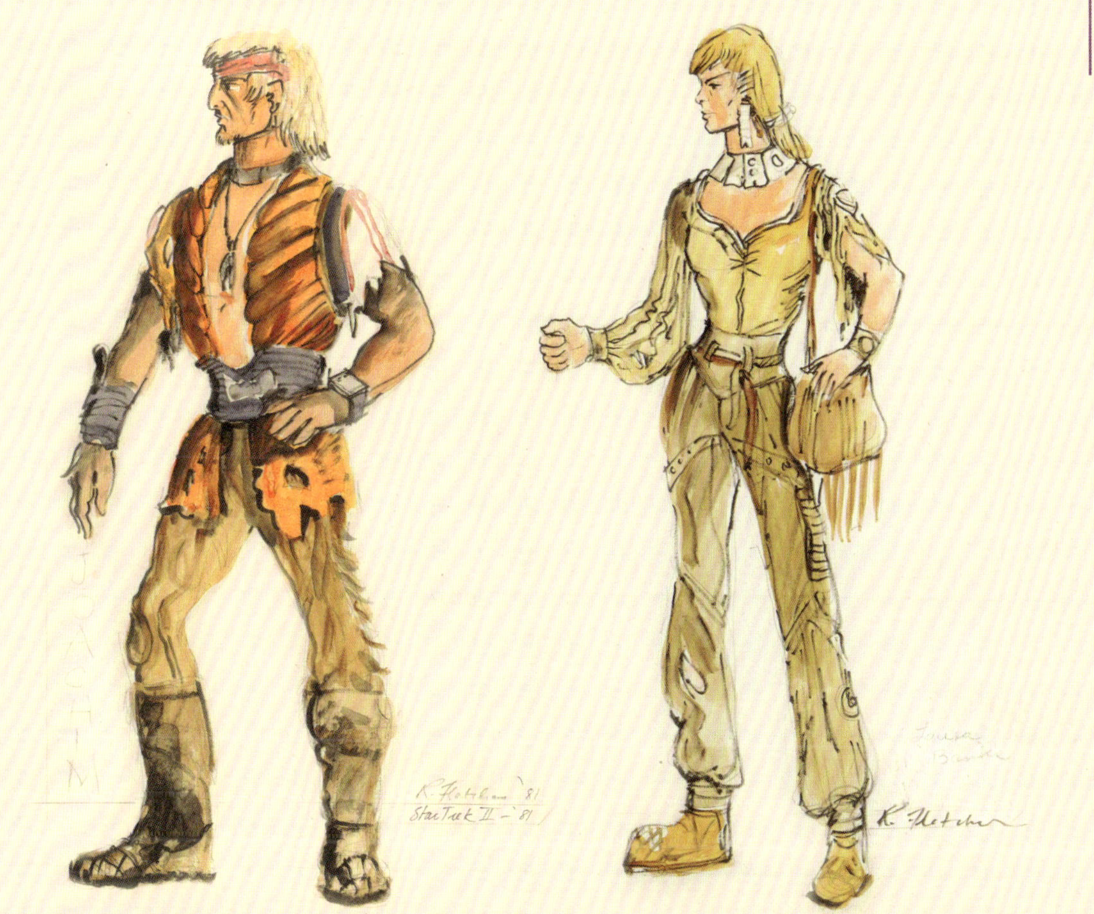

For his inspiration when designing the costumes for Khan and his followers, Fletcher turned to his own school days. Before the theater became his vocation, Fletcher had considered becoming an archeologist and he put his affection for the discipline to good use by envisioning the survivors of Ceti Alpha V as a kind of "Hell's Angels in space." Eking out a harsh existence on a barren planet, they had to fashion protective clothing and face coverings to survive, using the precious few materials available to them. Fletcher reasoned, "My intention with Khan was to express the fact that they had been marooned on that planet with no technical infrastructure, so they had to cannibalize from the spaceship whatever they used and wore. Therefore I tried to make it look as if they had dressed themselves out of pieces of upholstery and electrical equipment that composed the ship."[8]

FAR RIGHT: The original Robert Fletcher design for the *Reliant* navigator played by Laura Banks, who remembers that her costume was going to originally be worn by actress Lana Clarkson. "I went right to wardrobe and I fit like a glove into these clothes and it was Lana Clarkson's. Her and I had gone on a lot of film auditions together."[11]
Heritage Auctions, HA.com

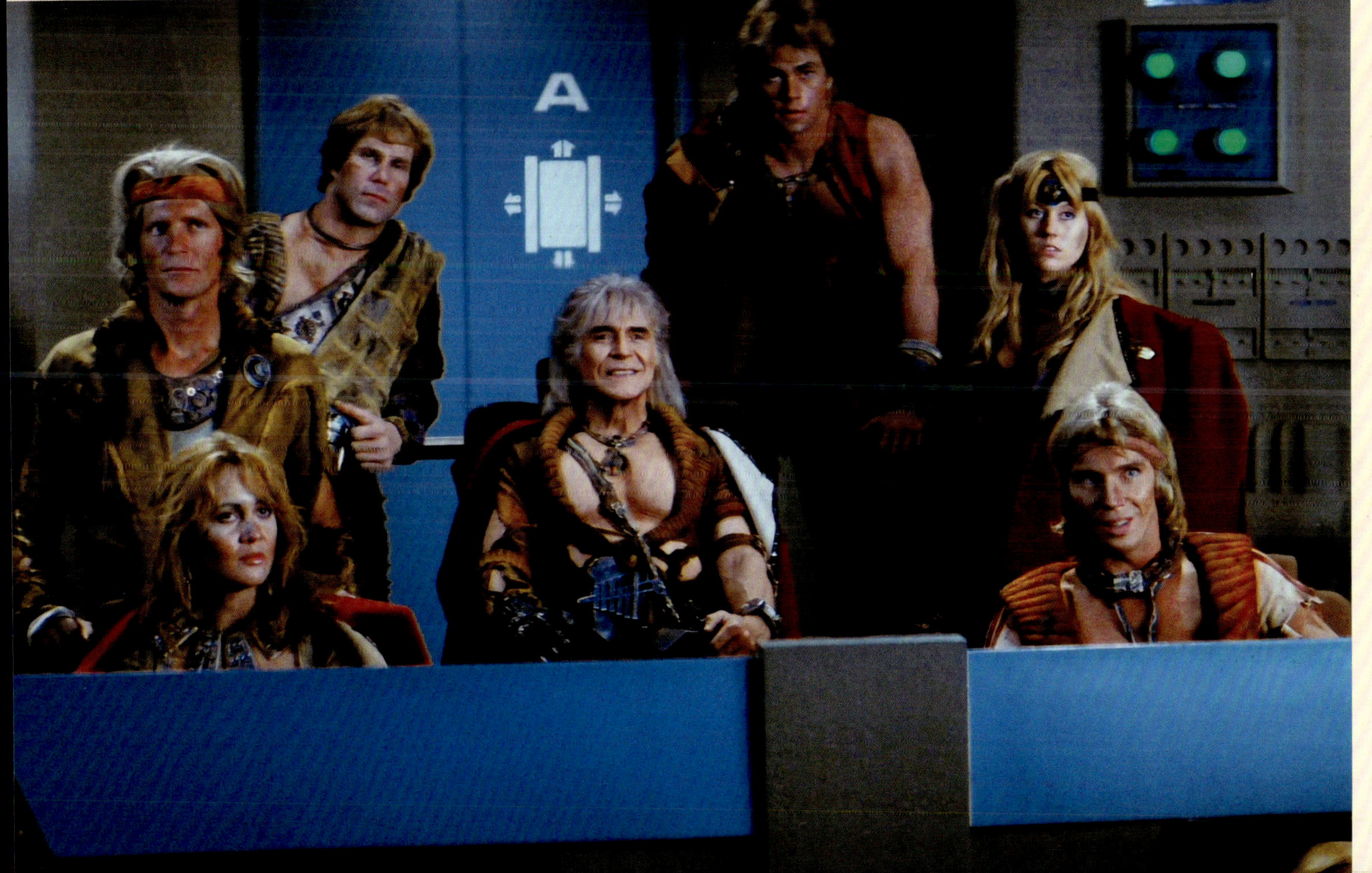

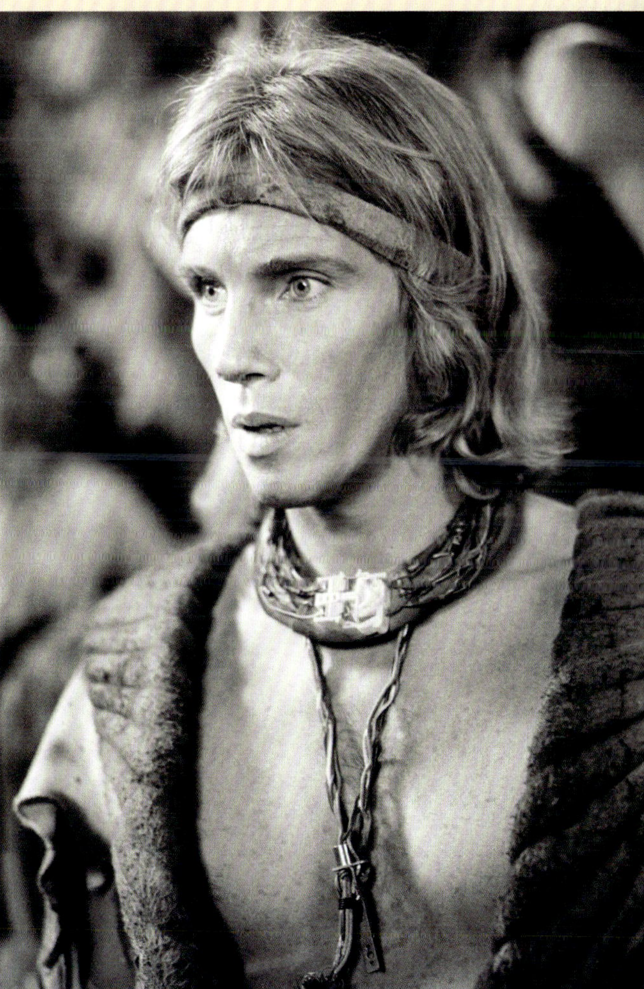

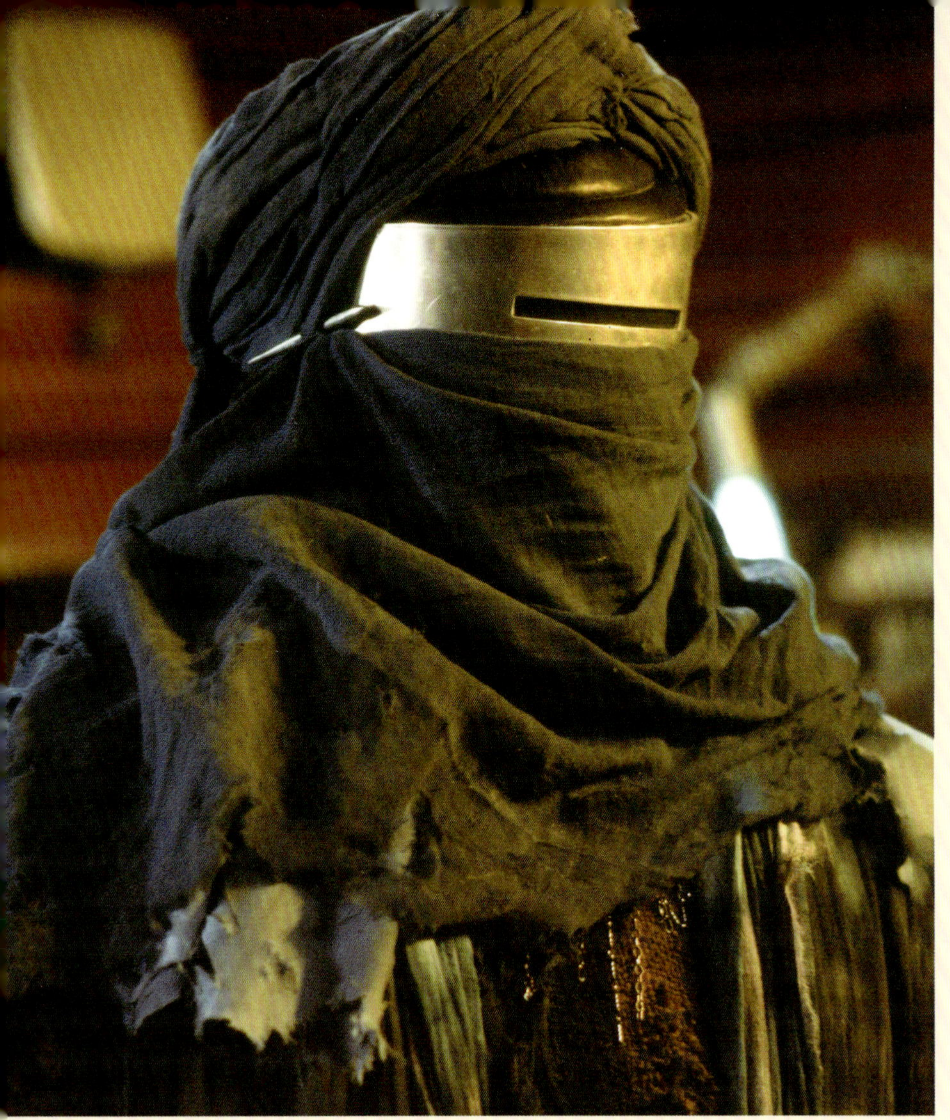

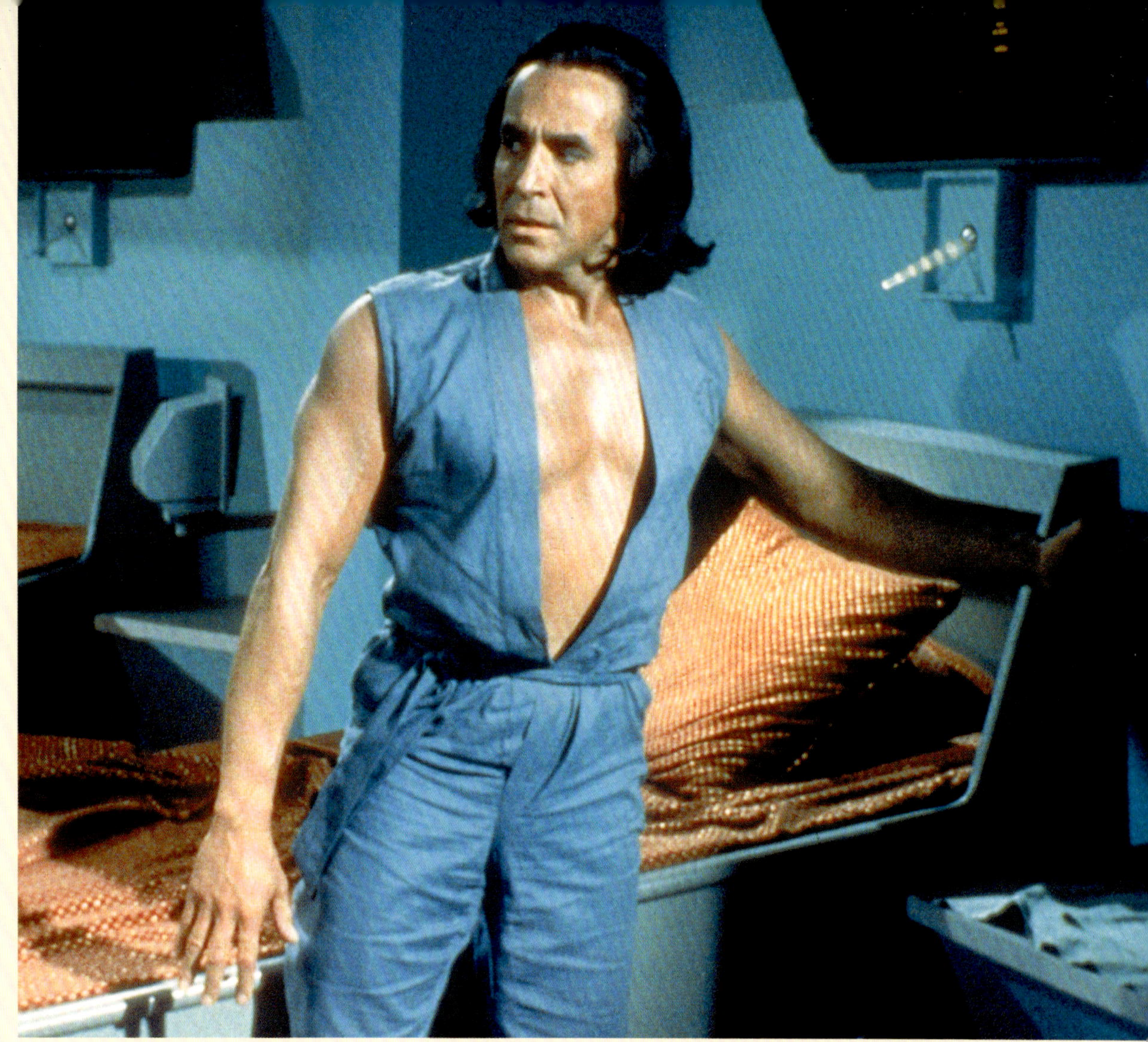

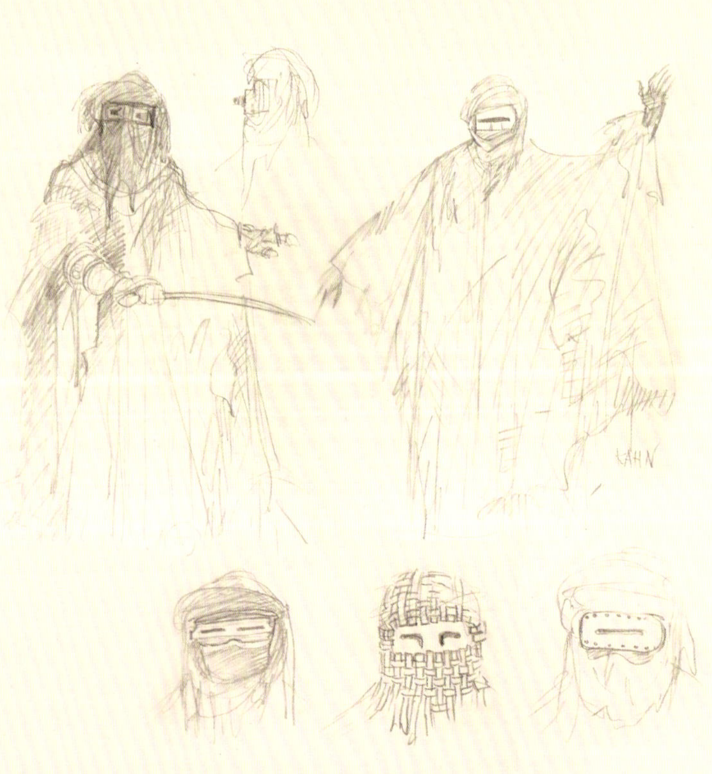

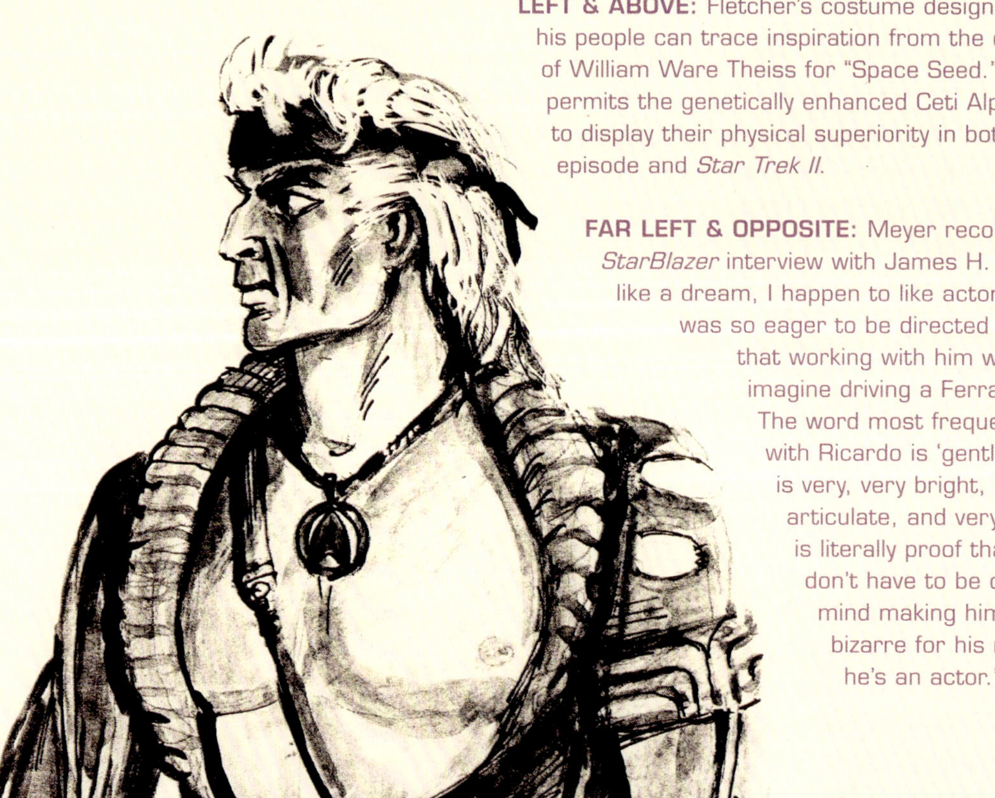

LEFT & ABOVE: Fletcher's costume designs for Khan and his people can trace inspiration from the original costumes of William Ware Theiss for "Space Seed." Bare skin permits the genetically enhanced Ceti Alpa V survivors to display their physical superiority in both the original episode and *Star Trek II*.

FAR LEFT & OPPOSITE: Meyer recollected in a 1982 *StarBlazer* interview with James H. Burns, "It was like a dream, I happen to like actors, but Ricardo was so eager to be directed and responsive, that working with him was what I imagine driving a Ferrari would be like. The word most frequently associated with Ricardo is 'gentleman.' He is very, very bright, incredibly articulate, and very funny. Ricardo is literally proof that good manners don't have to be dull. He didn't mind making himself look a bit bizarre for his role, because he's an actor."[12]

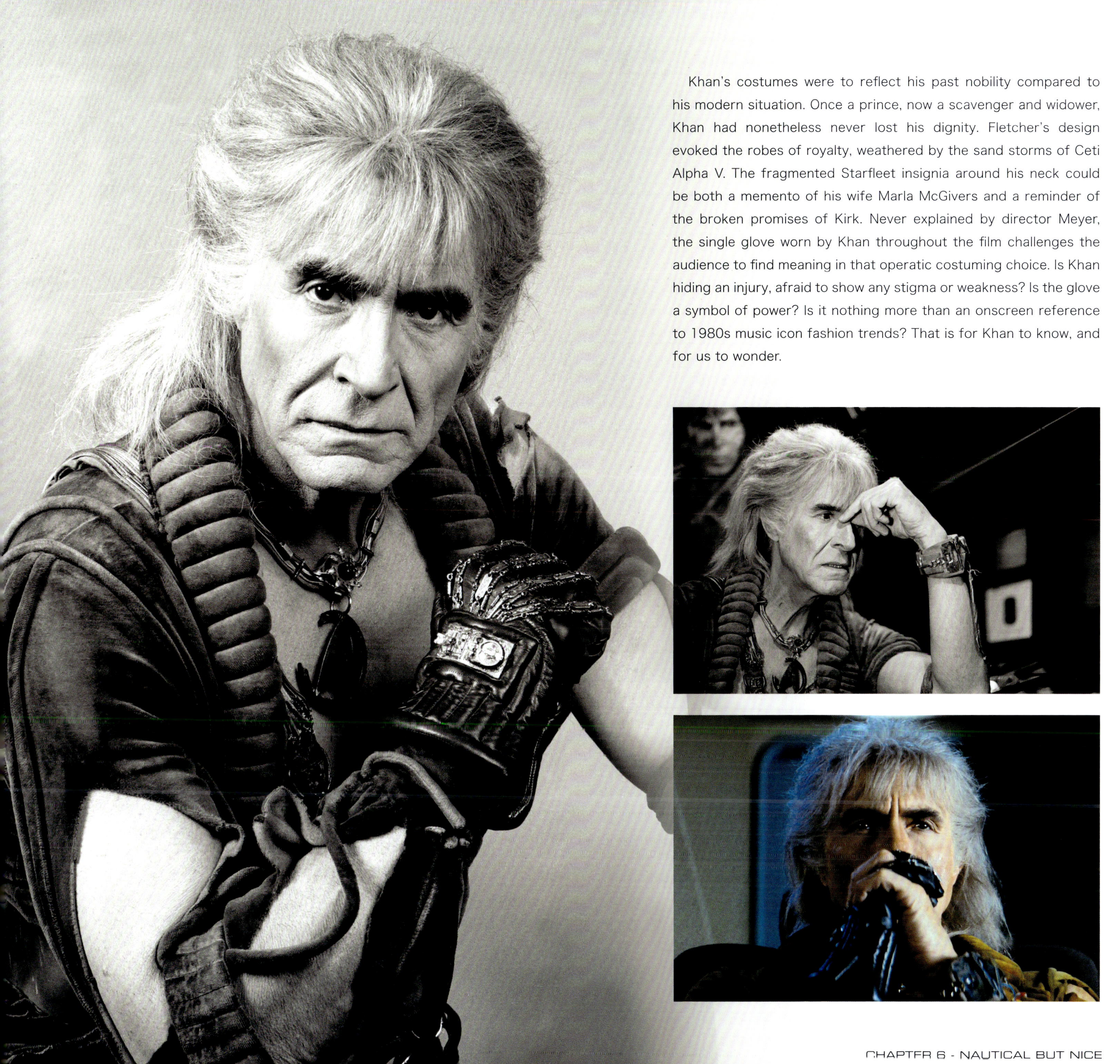

Khan's costumes were to reflect his past nobility compared to his modern situation. Once a prince, now a scavenger and widower, Khan had nonetheless never lost his dignity. Fletcher's design evoked the robes of royalty, weathered by the sand storms of Ceti Alpha V. The fragmented Starfleet insignia around his neck could be both a memento of his wife Marla McGivers and a reminder of the broken promises of Kirk. Never explained by director Meyer, the single glove worn by Khan throughout the film challenges the audience to find meaning in that operatic costuming choice. Is Khan hiding an injury, afraid to show any stigma or weakness? Is the glove a symbol of power? Is it nothing more than an onscreen reference to 1980s music icon fashion trends? That is for Khan to know, and for us to wonder.

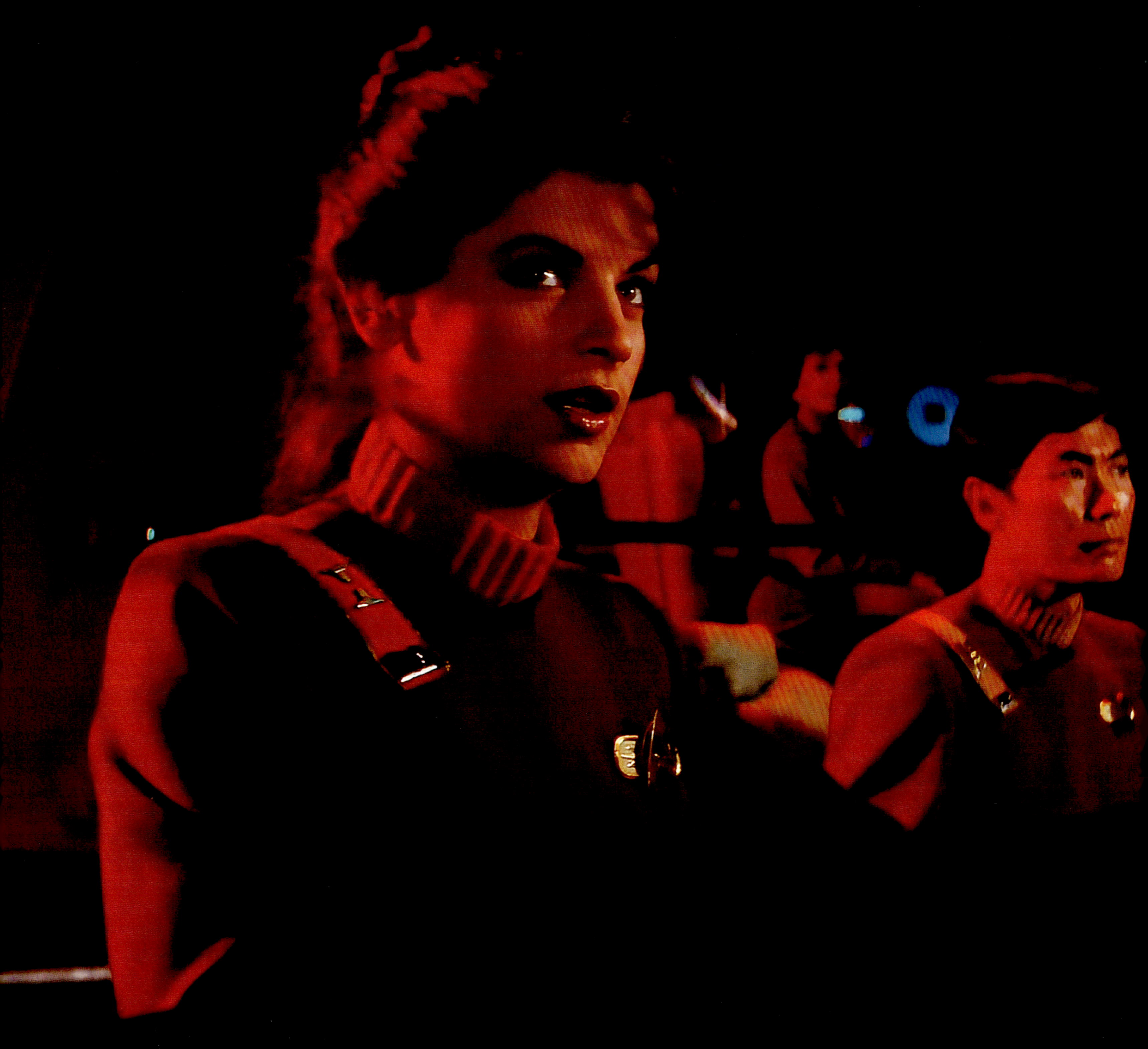

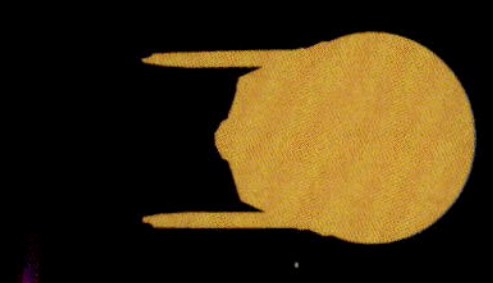

WHY THINGS WORK ON A STARSHIP

THE ART DEPARTMENT

O n June 26, 1966, Gene Roddenberry wrote the first of two syndicated newspaper articles with the goal of introducing viewers to his new *Star Trek* show that would be premiering a few months later. They are fascinating reads, because they reveal his early perspectives on what would be an iconic creation before a single episode had been shown. One of the minefields he details was the challenge of producing a show set in the future, imagining and designing how that future would look. "For example," Roddenberry wrote, "In our huge starship of the future, what will a bed look like? What kind of fabrics? What about a simple thing like sheets? Obviously things are going to get different... but *how* different? Suddenly we on the production staff find ourselves trying to out-think the hundreds of designers across the country already working in established million-dollar bedding industries."[1]

That design "minefield" was foremost on the mind of production designer Joseph Jennings as he began work on *Star Trek II*. Speaking to Henry Coleman during a 2002 Television Academy Foundation interview, Jennings, more than thirty-five years after Roddenberry's articles, revealed he faced much the same problem: "Science fiction is always a challenge, because you're taking materials of today and you're making them look like something nobody's ever heard of, if you're lucky and if you're clever and if it works."[2]

There were few in Hollywood with as many years of design association with *Star Trek* as Jennings. During the second season of *Star Trek*, Jennings served as an assistant to Walter M. Jefferies, the art director and production designer on the original series. It is here Jennings would be first introduced to Roddenberry's futuristic aesthetic. It was also around this time that Jennings would meet Michael Minor, his frequent collaborator and protégée. Jennings returned to *Star Trek* as the art director on the *Star Trek: Phase II* television show, which would eventually morph into *Star Trek: The Motion Picture*. Jennings and Minor would be part of the group that designed the refit *U.S.S. Enterprise*.

For *Star Trek II*, Jennings would get a promotion to production designer, responsible for the visual qualities of the movie. Everything from starship to environment designs were the responsibility of Jennings and those on his team. Two of those on Jennings' team that would contribute immeasurably to the film were art director Michael Minor and graphic designer Carole Lee Cole.

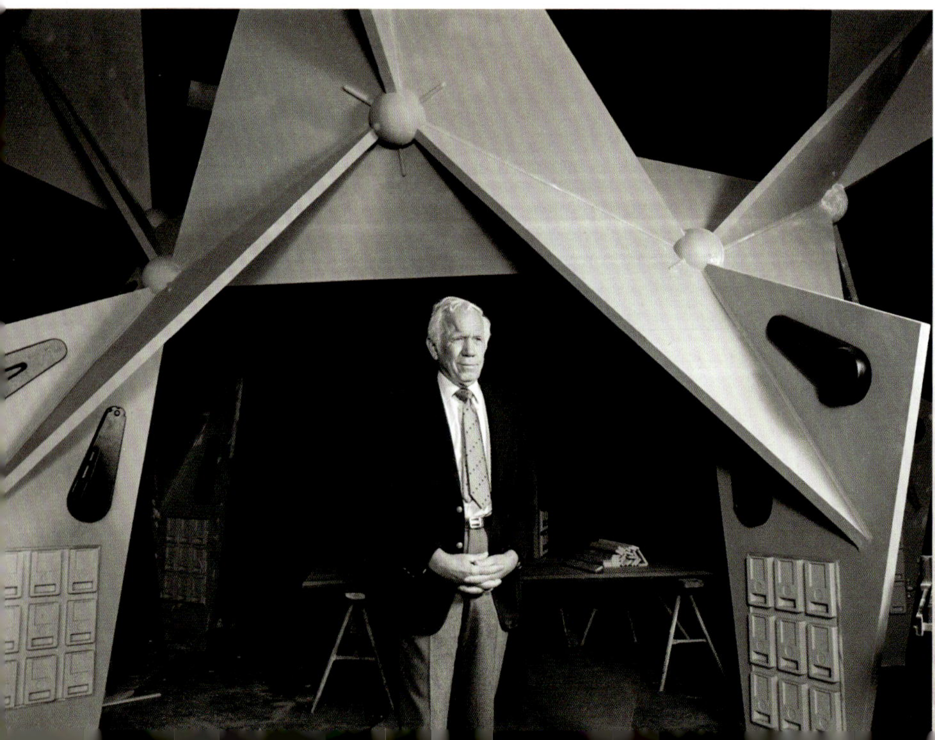

BELOW LEFT: Jennings stands outside the interior of the Regula I laboratory set, which also amalgamated some of the Klingon set from *Star Trek: The Motion Picture*.

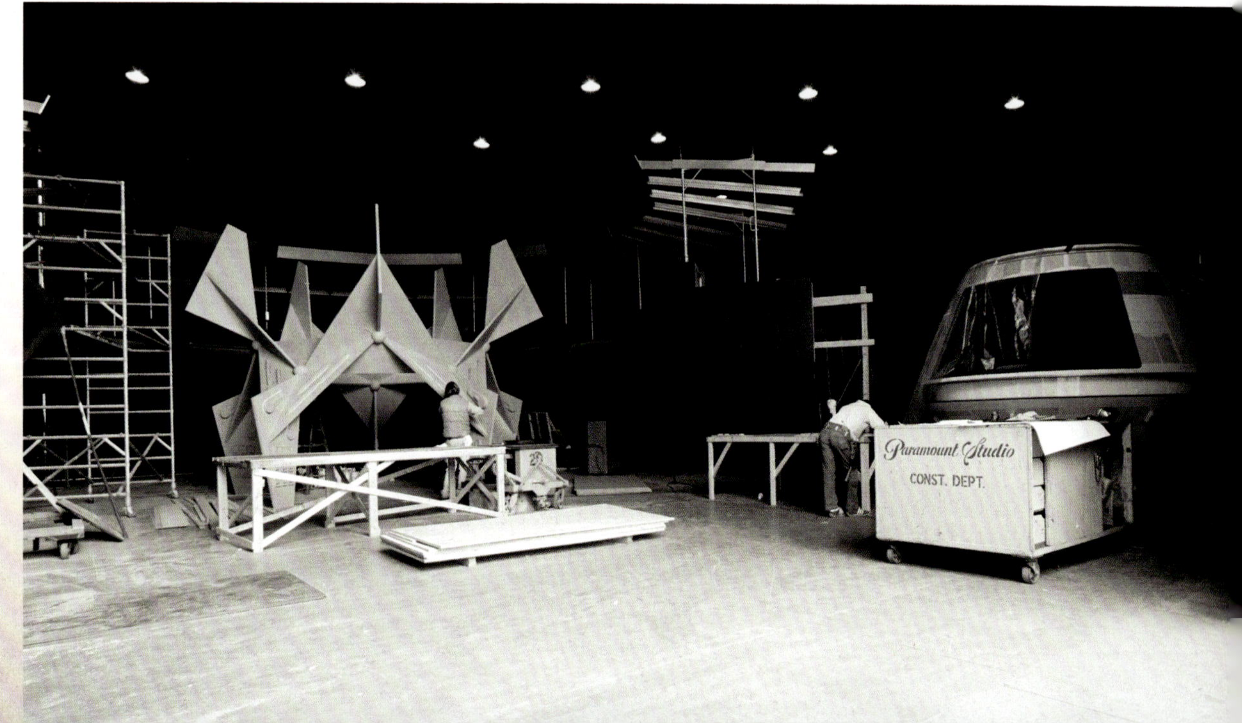

BELOW: Parked near the Regula I laboratory set while under construction is the shuttle Kirk and company use on their approach to *Enterprise*.

⟁ JOSEPH RALEIGH JENNINGS

Born in Jonesboro, Arkansas, in 1921, Joe Jennings was the son of a structural steel engineer and spent his formative years in the San Fernando Valley. He had originally planned on a career as an actor, although he admitted he discovered he was a "lousy actor"[10] after performances in high school plays. After taking some courses at the Los Angeles City College, Jennings joined the United States military, fighting in World War II. After the war, Jennings would go east and earn a Master's degree in theater arts on the G.I. Bill. He worked at local children's theaters designing and constructing sets. Film and television art department experiences followed, working on *My Fair Lady* and *Gunsmoke*. He would share an Academy Award® nomination for Best Production Direction for *Star Trek: The Motion Picture*, and be nominated twice for Emmy Awards for Outstanding Art Direction for his contributions to *Roots* and *Shogun*.

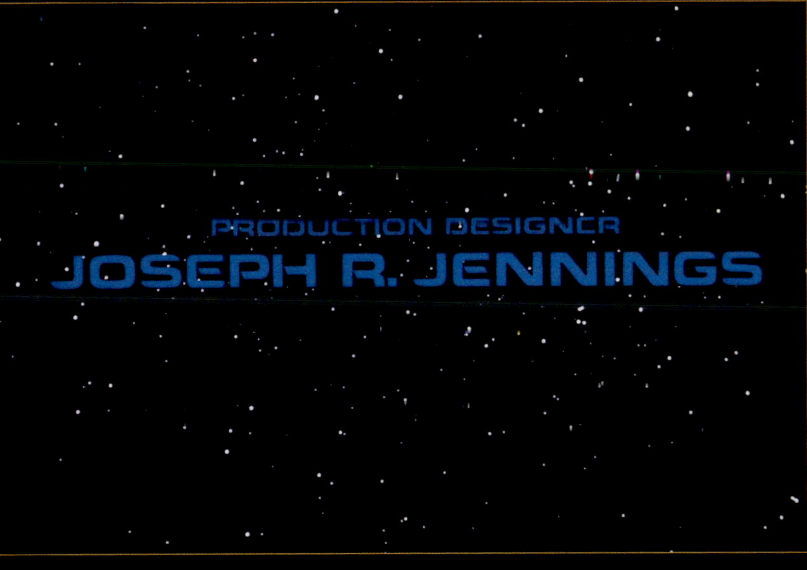

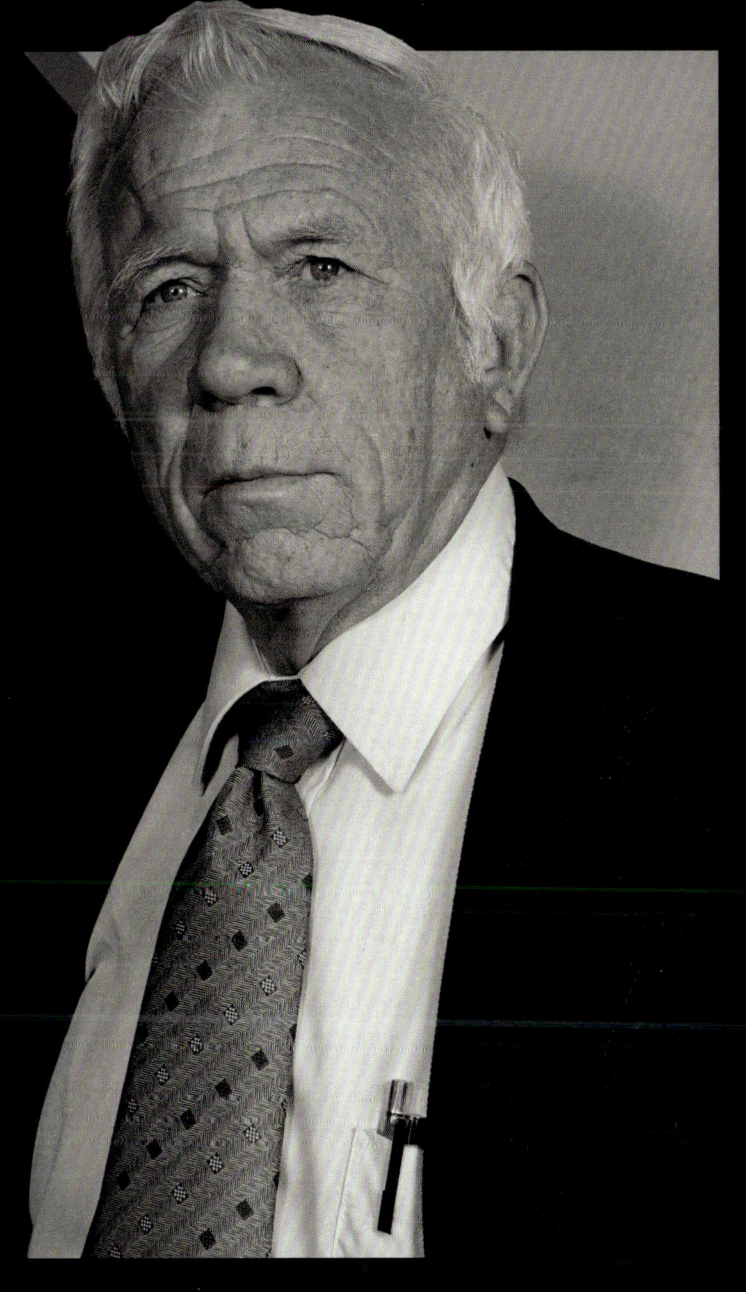

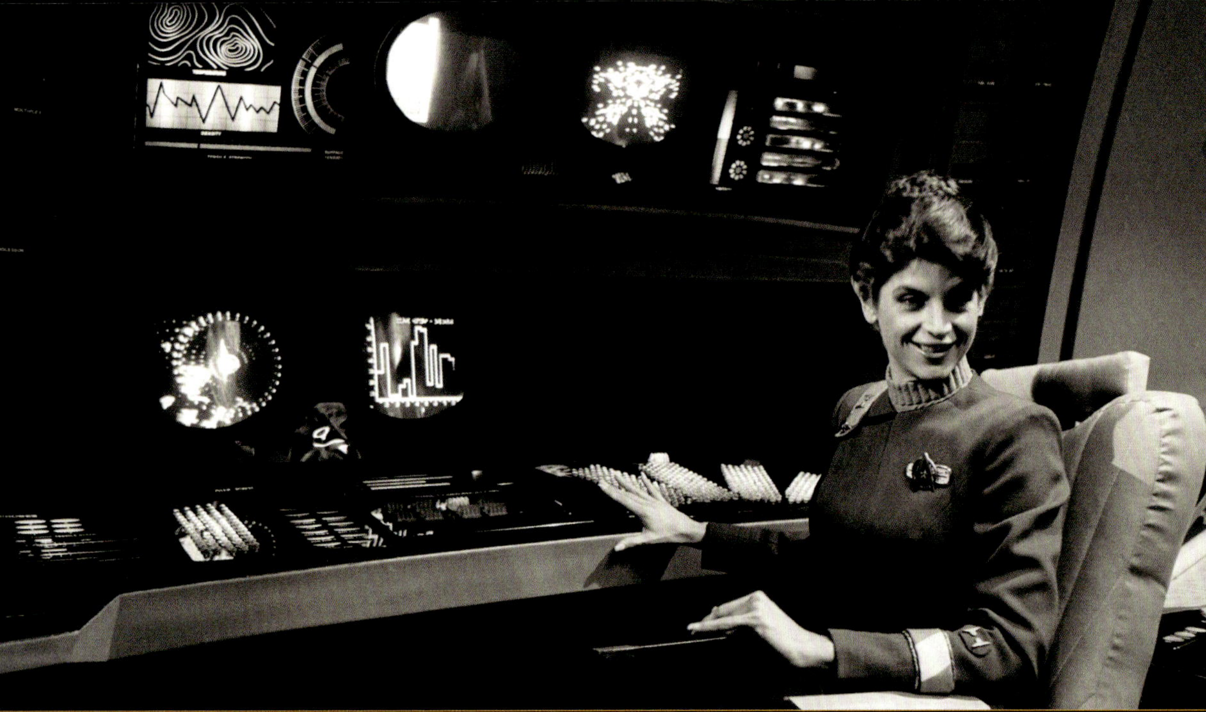

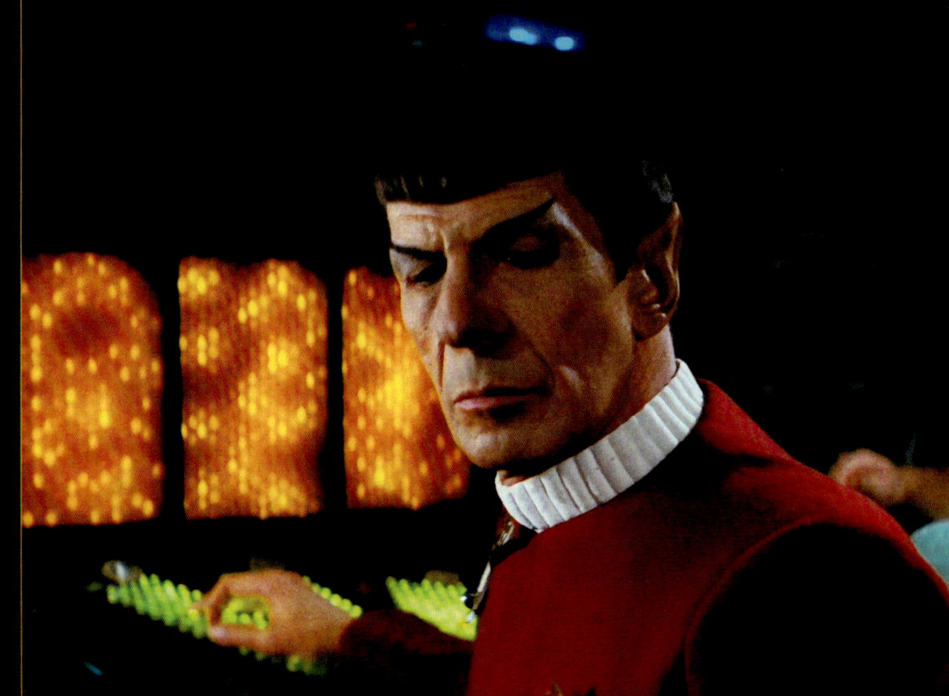

Minor described his collaborative relationship with boss Jennings on *Star Trek II* in a 1984 interview with James Van Hise for the magazine *Enterprise Incidents*: "I worked as art director underneath Joe, although we really functioned as two art directors, but he had the clout of production designer, which is a bestowed title that means you can ask a little more for your services."[3] In addition to administrative responsibilities of budgeting money and daily work schedules, as art director, Minor had creative design responsibilities such as storyboarding and coordinated with other supervisors on the film, including special effect departments and construction supervisors.

Together, Jennings, Minor, and Cole endeavored to meet the vision of director Nicholas Meyer, producer Robert Sallin, and executive producer Harve Bennett. But Jennings felt an obligation to Roddenberry, too. "A dictum that Gene first put out back when we started the series: all the technology had to look like everyday stuff. No matter how fantastic, it had to look like a screwdriver. It had to be used like a screwdriver. For science fiction, you establish a framework. You establish the rules. Now you got to be honest in those rules. You can't just do anything you want to because its science fiction. Otherwise, it doesn't become particularly believable."[4]

"I noticed from the TV series they were never looking at their consoles," Cole reminisced. "They were always looking to the camera and saying very serious lines, but somehow working this equipment, and I thought, 'How can they do that without ever looking at their instruments?' I remembered [when] I was a little kid—Oh, it's so horrible!—I used to wake up my parents early in the morning playing my accordion. The "Good Morning Waltz!" Lucky I lived to adulthood, when I think about it! But I remembered I never had to look at my left hand playing the accordion and that's because there was one key that had a little indentation in it, the middle C key. So, on Spock's console, I made like a triple accordion or quadruple, four panels of accordion buttons. I told the special effects guy, 'Now make one red button or indented button in the middle, where that middle C key would be, so you can get your position of where you are and then he can talk and look wherever he wants.'"[5]

The monitors that provide information necessary to Starfleet personnel also provided many headaches during the production of *Star Trek: The Motion Picture*. Anyone who has ever filmed their TV or computer knows that if the camera that is used to film is out of sync in terms of frames-per-second ratio to the monitor being filmed, a flickering effect occurs. This is why film had been used on the *Motion Picture* monitors. If a retake was necessary, the crew and actors would have to wait until the film-loop returned to the same location, wasting precious time. Technical advisor Todd Grodnick and video engineers Ed Moscowitz and Jim Padget used processes that solved both problems on *Star Trek II*. The monitor films used on *Star Trek: The Motion Picture* were transferred to video tape, which both improved the vibrancy of the colors and permitted easier rewinding during retakes. To avoid the flickering effect that video tape has when recorded by film, the team locked the video tape into the same light/dark phase of the Panavision camera. Cole was happy with the result, "We now have very clear video systems all over the bridge and in the medical lab."[6]

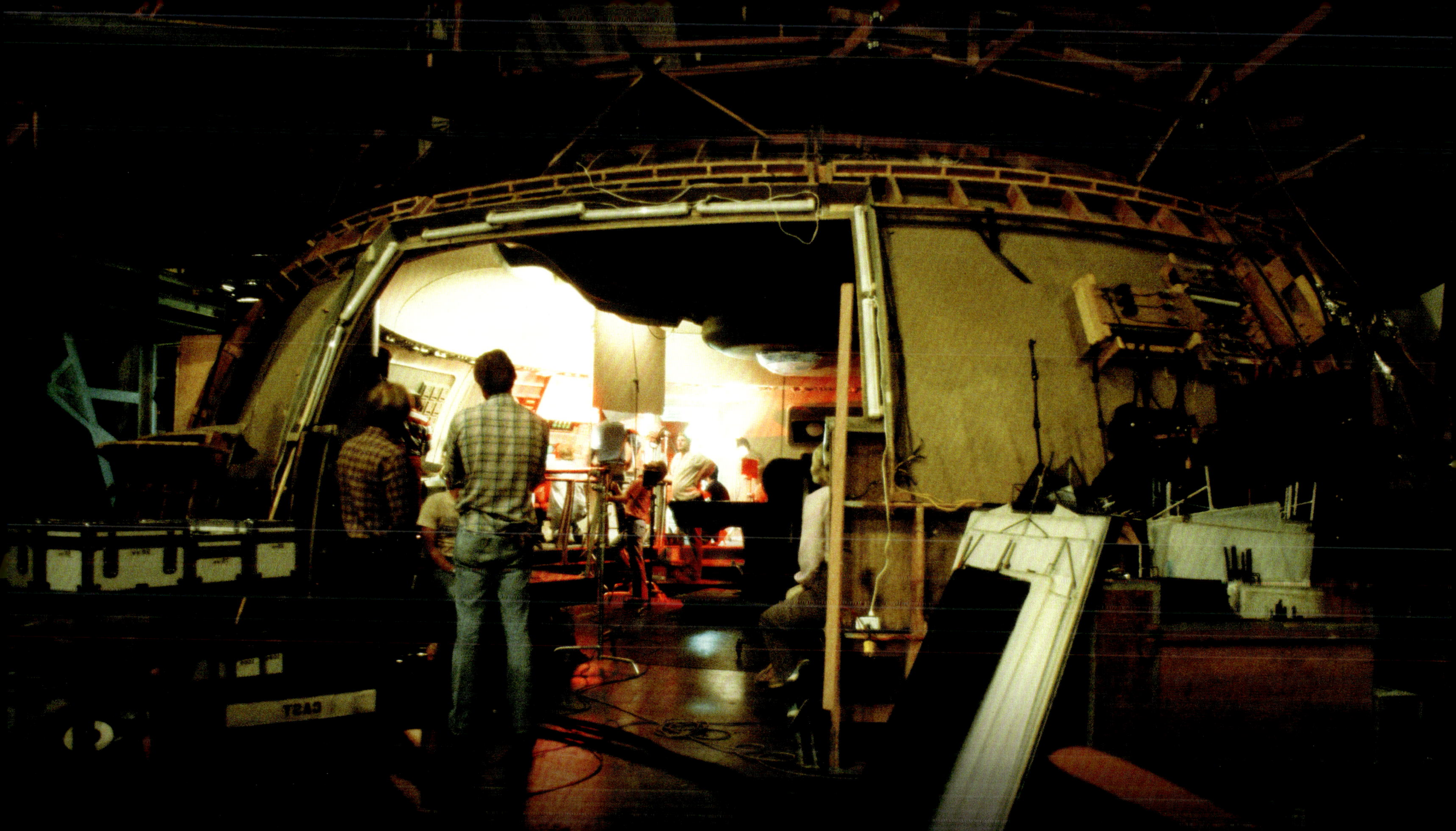

To achieve the effect of an encapsulated bridge, the *U.S.S. Enterprise* and *U.S.S. Reliant* bridge set was constructed on Stage 9 of the Paramount Lot inside a shell with movable walls to permit, supposedly, more efficient filming. However, in practice it was sometimes a no-win scenario. Meyer recalls, "One of the things that made me crazy making this film was working on that bridge set where the coverage had to be 360 degrees. That was just crazy. Before you were going to turn around and go in another direction, you really wanted to cover everything, even if it included specific camera moves that involved one direction before they started rolling out these pie slices of the set and turning everything around for hours."[7]

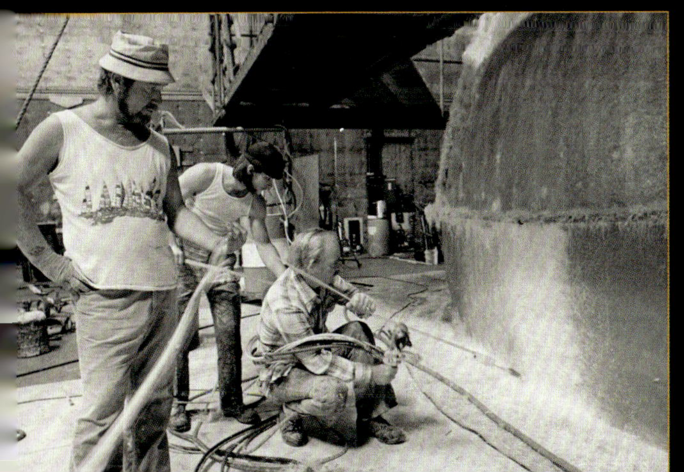

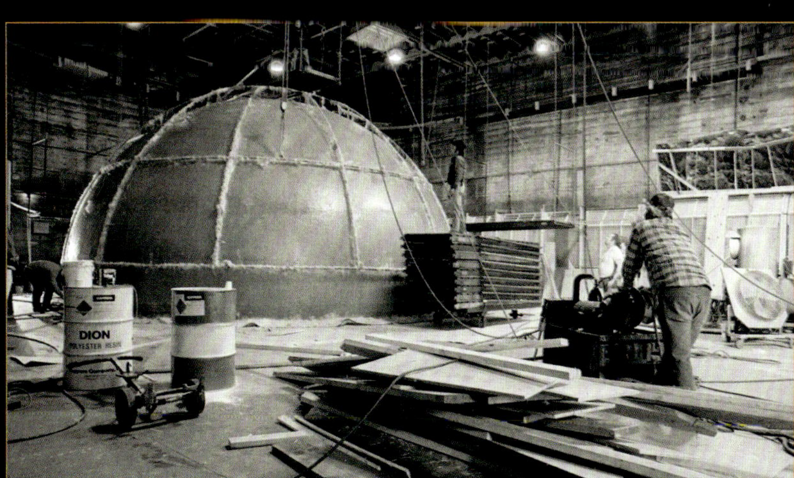

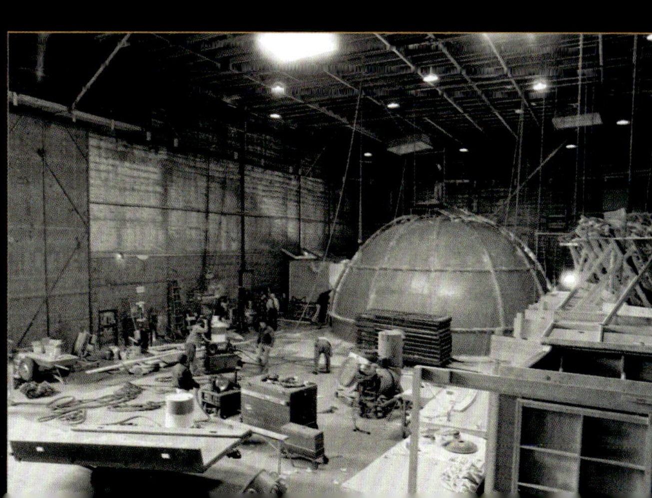

MICHAEL MINOR

As with Jennings, Michael Minor's connection to *Star Trek* originated during the TV series era. The son of a theater manager, Minor had developed a love of the arts at a young age. He had a special affinity for astronomical art and began producing his own. A meeting with Walter M. Jefferies and Gene Roddenberry led to the purchase of his art for use on the *U.S.S. Enterprise* set as decorations, including planetary landscape paintings seen behind the *Enterprise* crew as they dine with Dr. Miranda Jones and Larry Marvick in the episode "Is There in Truth No Beauty?" and in Kirk's

quarters in "The Tholian Web." More *Star Trek* followed. It was Minor who created the Melkotian for "Spectre of the Gun" and who designed and developed an economically feasible way to create the Tholian Web. After the show's cancellation, Minor would work creating commercials during the 1970s along with future ILM supervisor Ken Ralston. Moving on to movies, Minor was in the art department for Disney and on George Lucas's original *Star Wars*. Minor returned to *Star Trek* for *Phase II* and *Star Trek: The Motion Picture* as a conceptual artist and production illustrator. Minor died in 1987 at age forty-six.

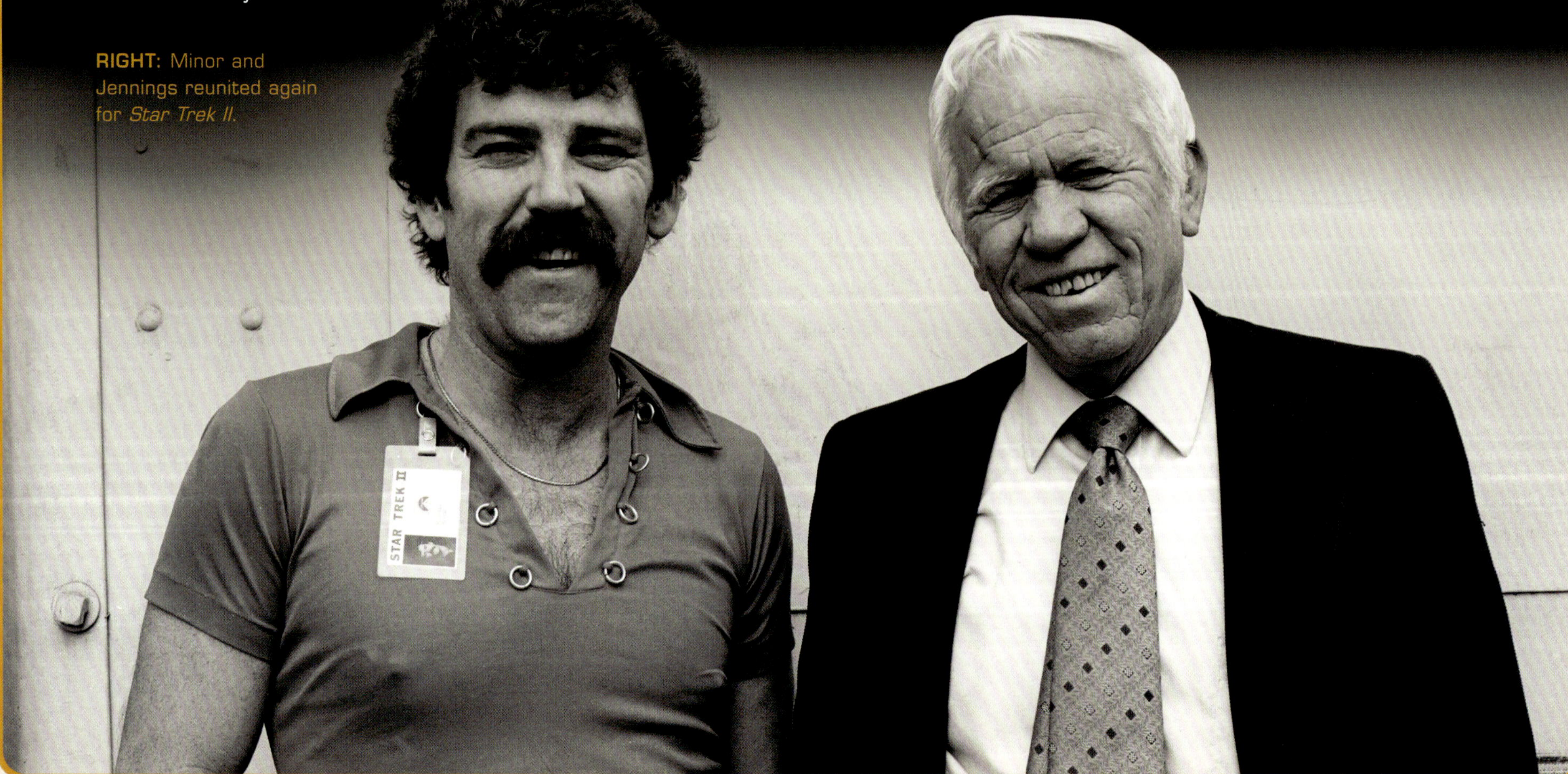

RIGHT: Minor and Jennings reunited again for *Star Trek II.*

⬟ CAROLE LEE COLE

Carole Lee Cole was another *Star Trek: The Motion Picture* alumna. Cole started both her Hollywood career and relationship with *Star Trek* in 1977 when she was asked by Jennings to join the art department of *Phase II*. With Cole, *Star Trek* was getting the real deal. A graduate of the University of California, Los Angeles, Cole had helped design real space technologies. Among her contributions working for companies such as Rockwell International was wiring the on-board computers used during the Apollo missions. Cole designed the refit *Enterprise* bridge controls and Federation signage among other responsibilities on *Star Trek: The Motion Picture* and *Star Trek II*. Because of her creative talents and real-world experience, Cole was part illustrator, part consultant.

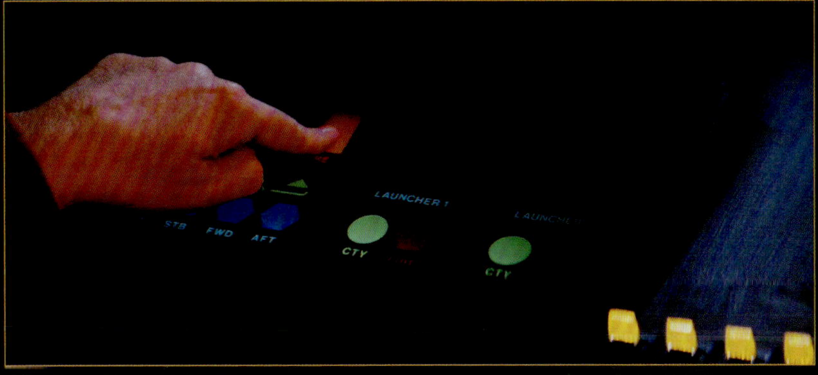

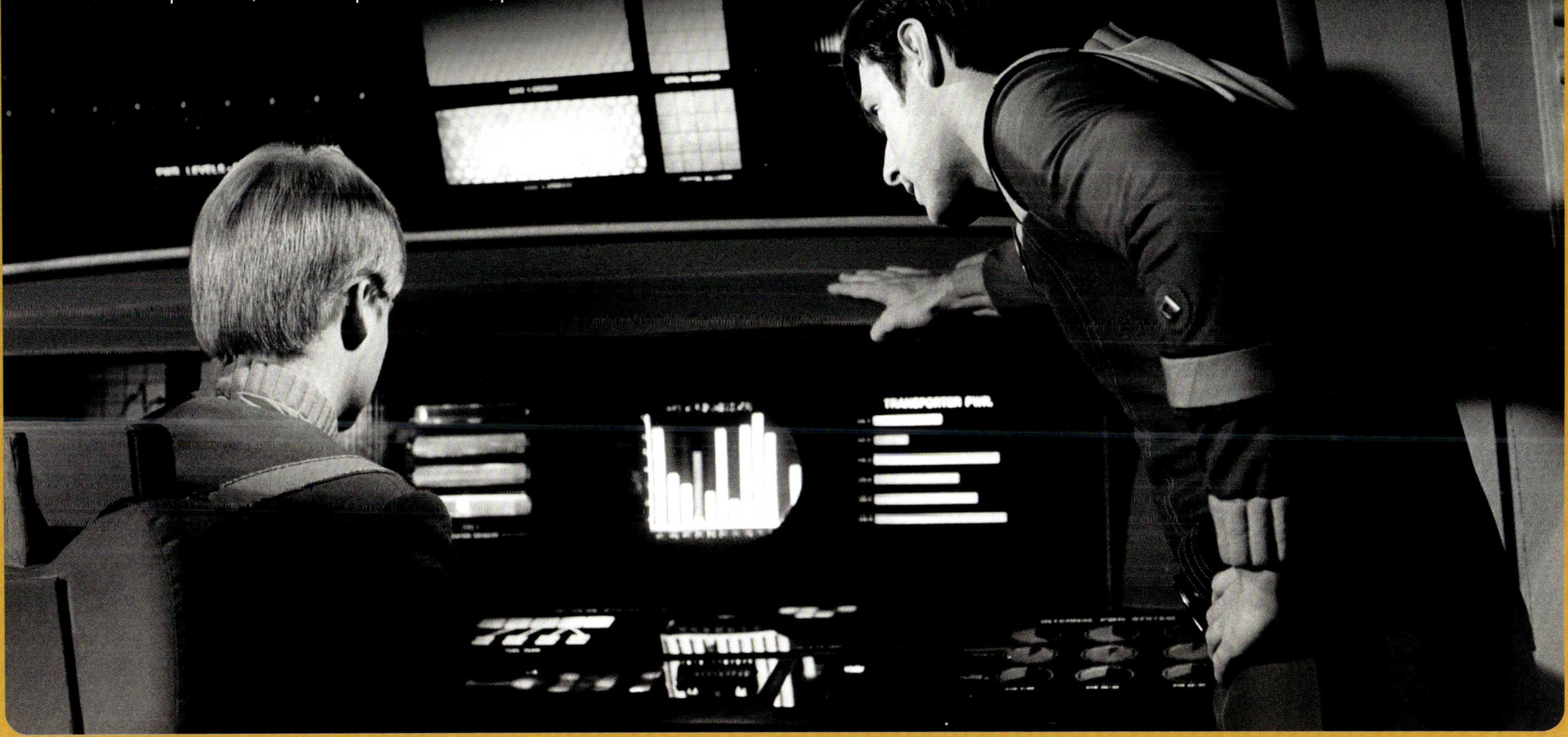

To provide an interesting, yet inexpensive texture to Starfleet walls, Jennings was inspired by the papier-mâché packaging materials used to protect fluorescent bulbs. Bennett joked that as *Star Trek II* gathered as much of the packaging materials as possible from every production at the entire Paramount lot, they gained the reputation of being scavengers. "The conventionalists in motion pictures looked at us like the desert scavengers. You know, the guys who were having some kind of scavenger hunt on their lot and, 'We don't do it this way. We take weeks to build these.' And we said, 'No, we don't need that. We just need it to look right.'"[8]

While Meyer wanted the *Enterprise* to have the claustrophobic feeling of a submarine and set corridors were shrunk to help realize that, the engine room was another reality. The engine room set on Stage 9, a reuse from *Star Trek: The Motion Picture*, was designed to be impressive and convey a massive length. By virtue of classic Hollywood sleight of hand, including warping perspectives by placing shorter actors and extras farther in the set near a painted set extension, the necessary illusion was achieved.

Meyer's favorite set was the docking bay and torpedo room on Stage 5. The torpedo room gave the director movement as weapons were loaded and gratings were lifted. It would also save the production money, being a redress of the Klingon bridge from *Star Trek: The Motion Picture*, and be the scene of Spock's funeral.

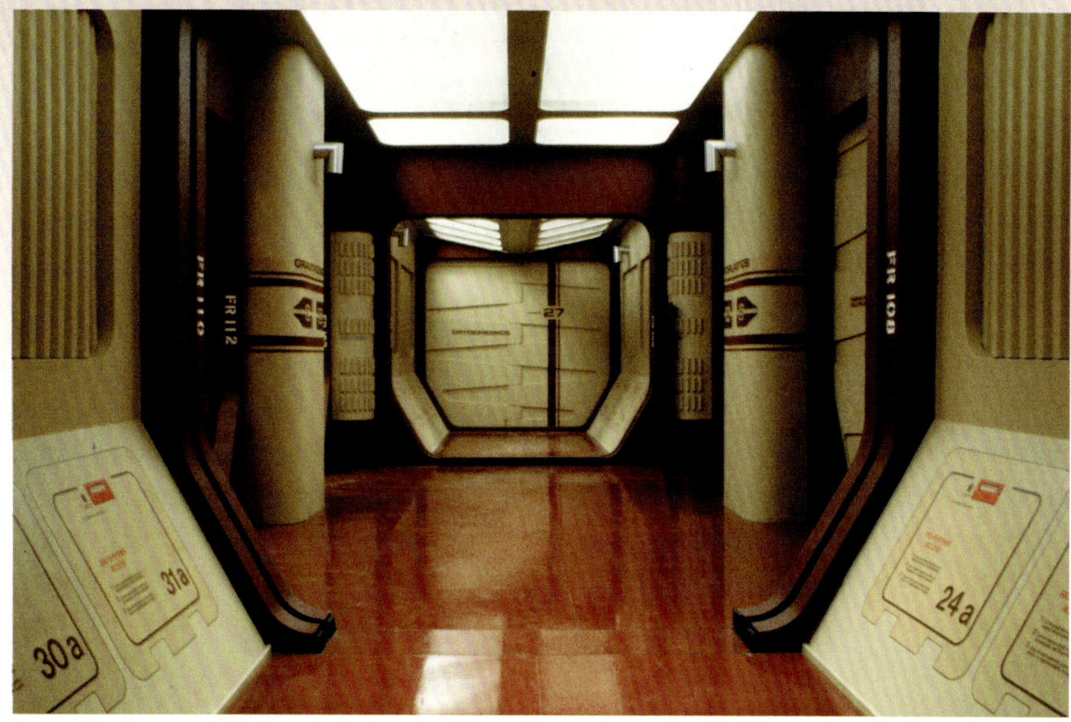

ABOVE: Jennings explained that the Starfleet walls papier-mâché material was put "all together in a sheet, so that you had these ridges, and we made a plastic mold out of it and cast it in fiberglass and then we turned it over and cast the other side. That's a skin that's still being used to this day."[12]

BELOW: The torpedo room and the engine room set.

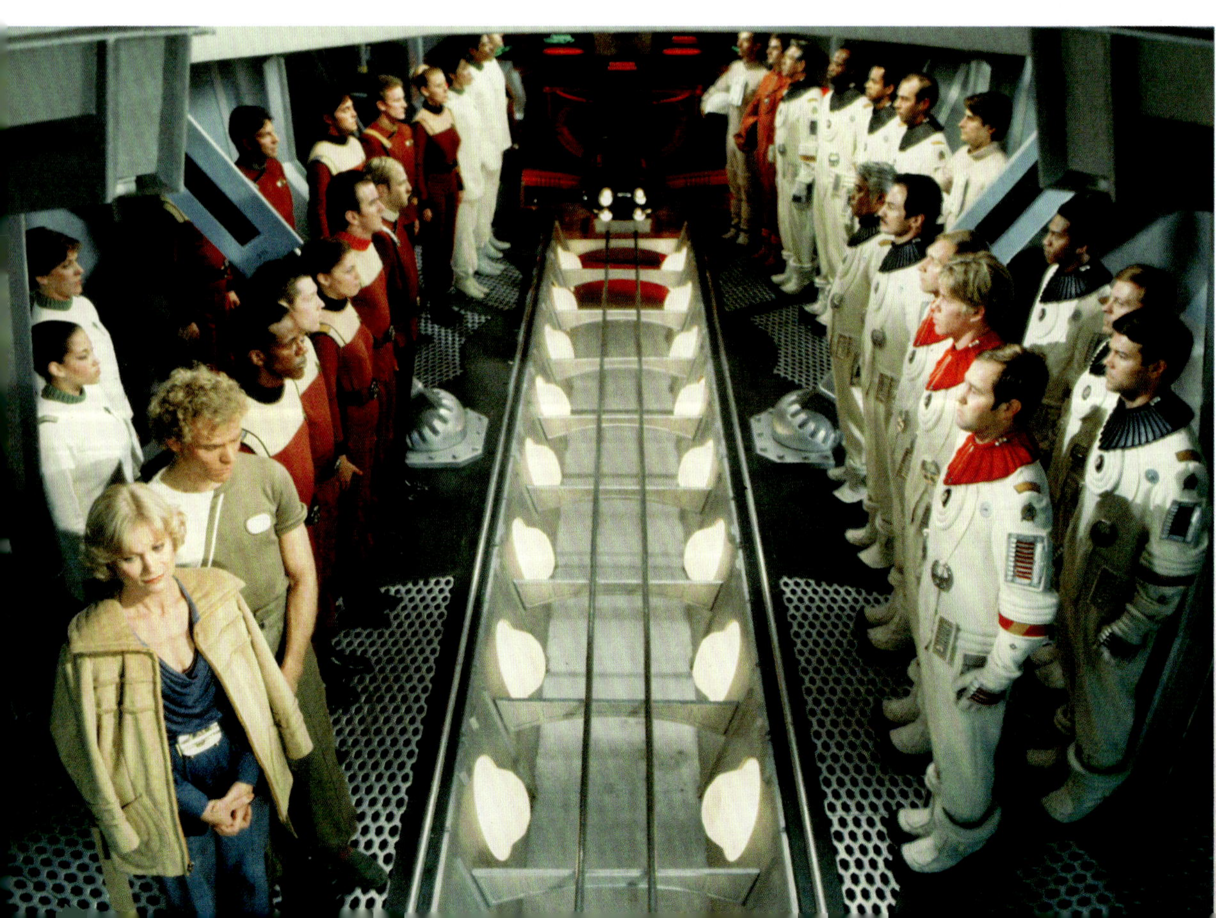

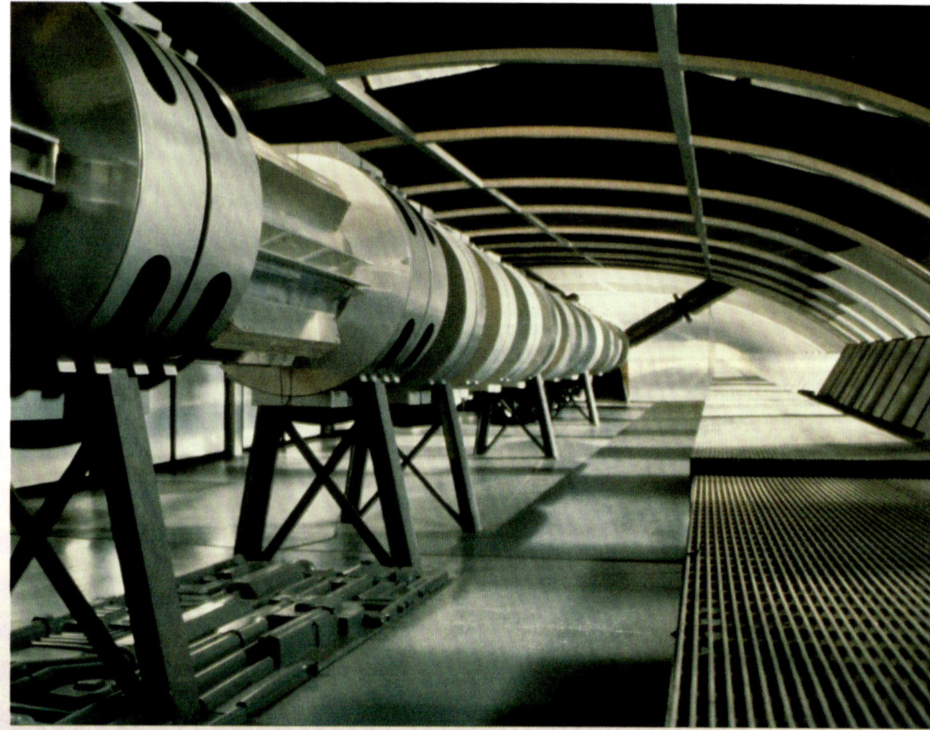

A PICTURE IS WORTH A THOUSAND NAMES

A picture that demonstrates the obvious affection and camaraderie that existed between William Shatner and Leonard Nimoy, but is also a fun Easter egg. Never meant to really be seen clearly by audiences, the names featured on the sign behind the pair are in-joke tributes to real behind the scenes artists. Alongside nods to Jennings, Minor, and Cole herself, a few of the highlights of the signage designed by Cole include: Vice Admiral D. Gluck (set designer Daniel Gluck), Captain D. Maltese (set designer Daniel Maltese), Captain M. Becker (special effects artist Martin Becker), Captain C. Graffeo (set decorator Charles Graffeo), Lieutenant Commander J. Longo (property master Joseph Longo), Vice Admiral G. Rescher (cinematographer Gayne Rescher), Commander D. Arakelian (assistant to producers Deborah Arakelian), Captain R. Fletcher (costume designer Robert Fletcher), Captain A. Henry (wardrobe supervisor Agnes Henry), Commander D. Wise (first assistant director Doug Wise), Commander J. Wong (Nicholas Meyer's assistant Janna Wong Healy).

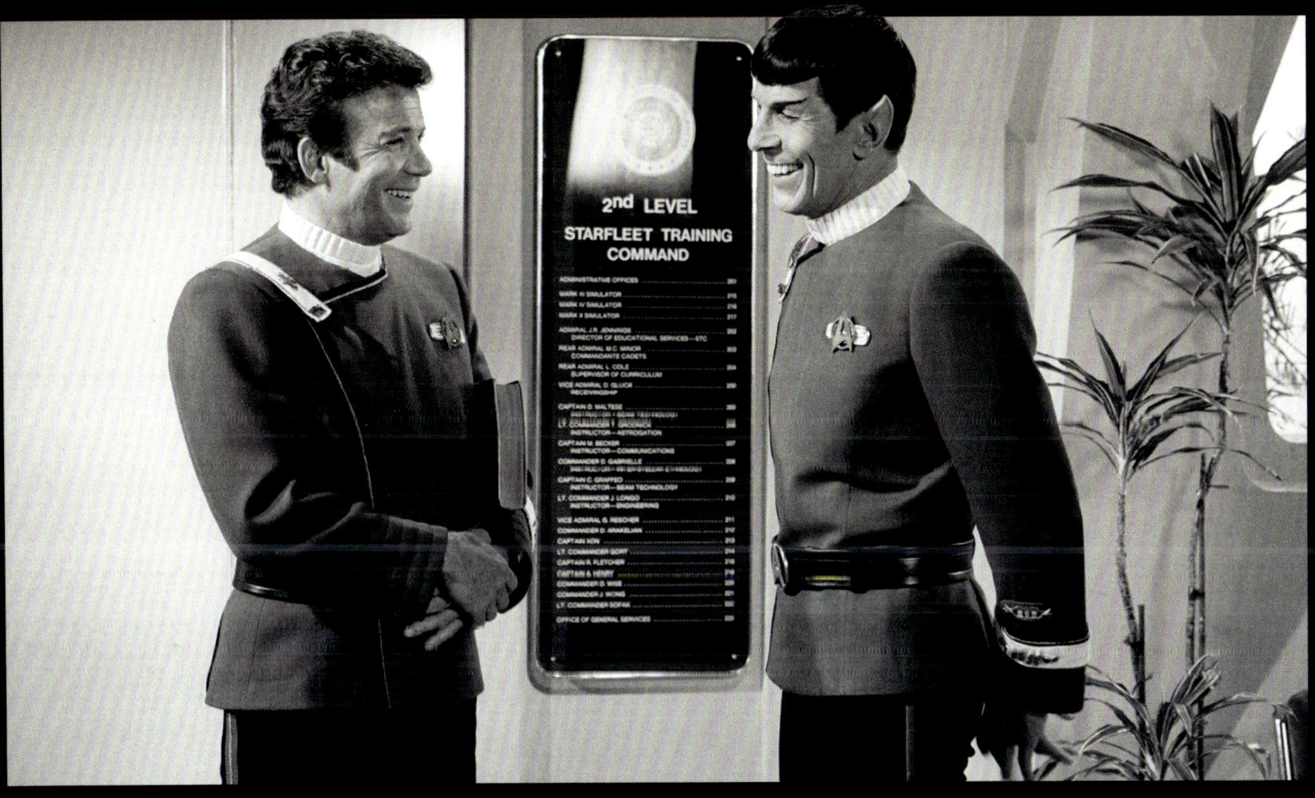

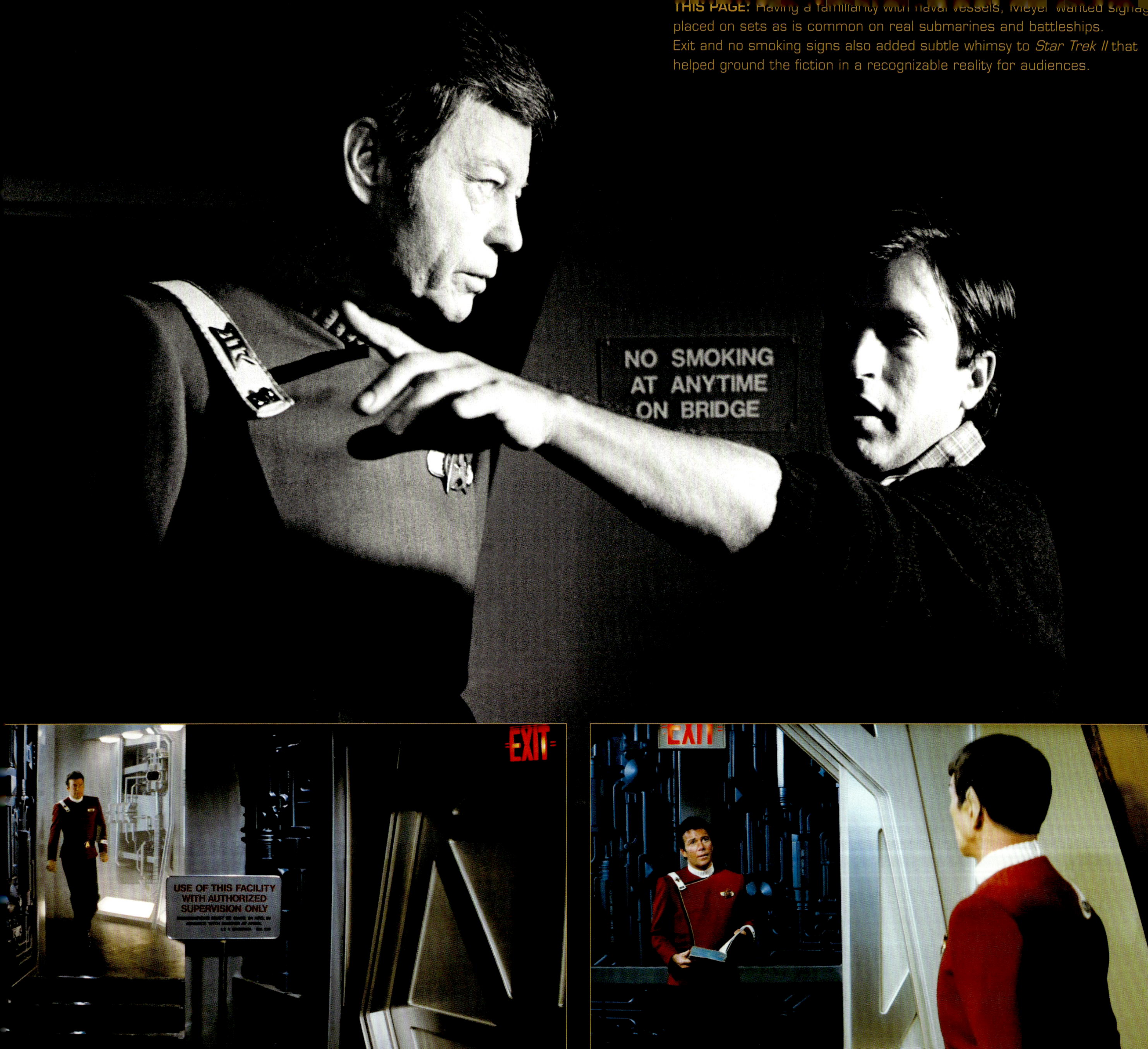
NO SMOKING
AT ANYTIME
ON BRIDGE
EXIT
USE OF THIS FACILITY
WITH AUTHORIZED
SUPERVISION ONLY
EXIT

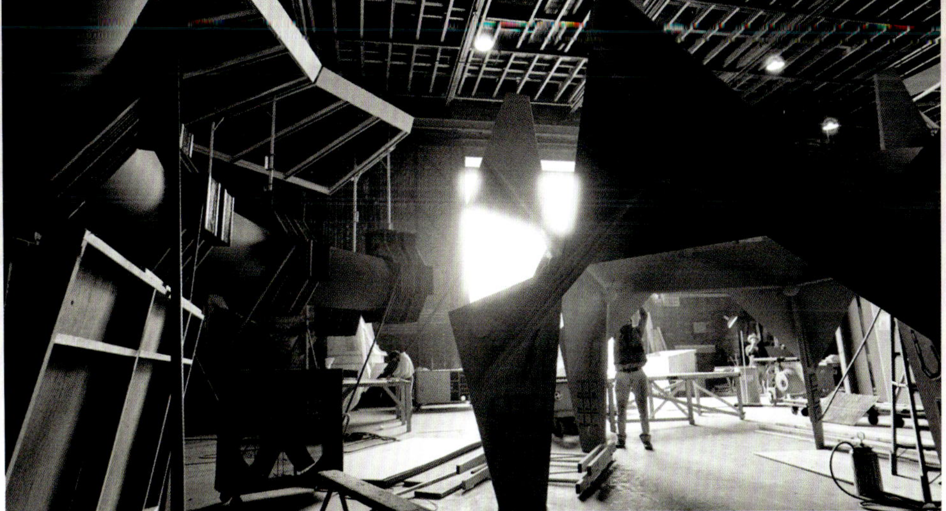

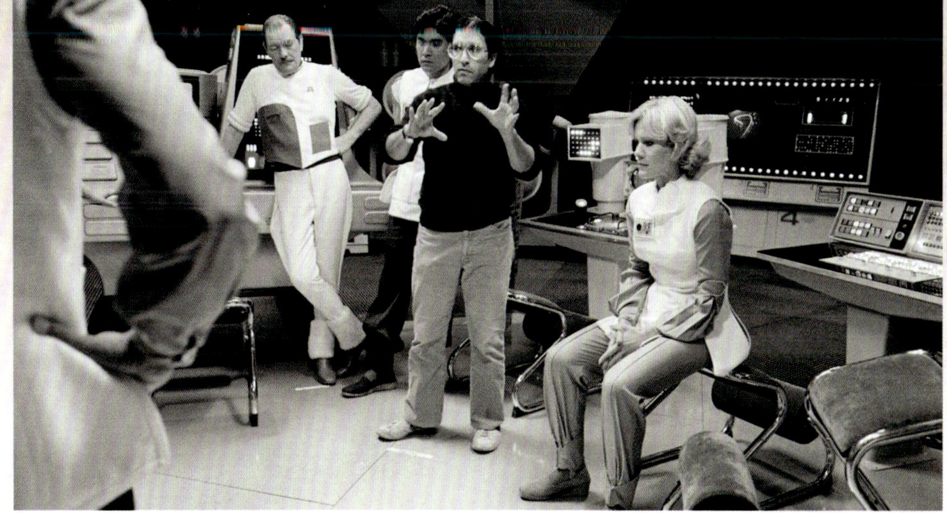

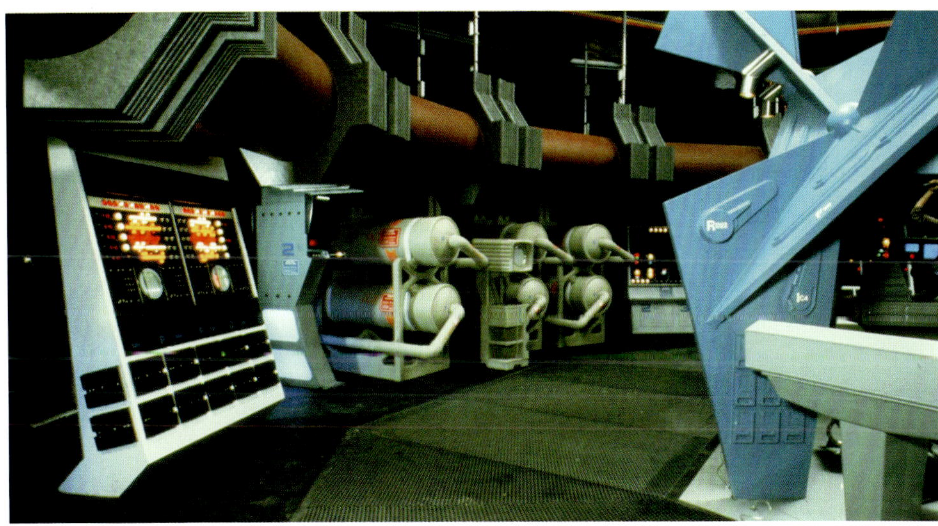

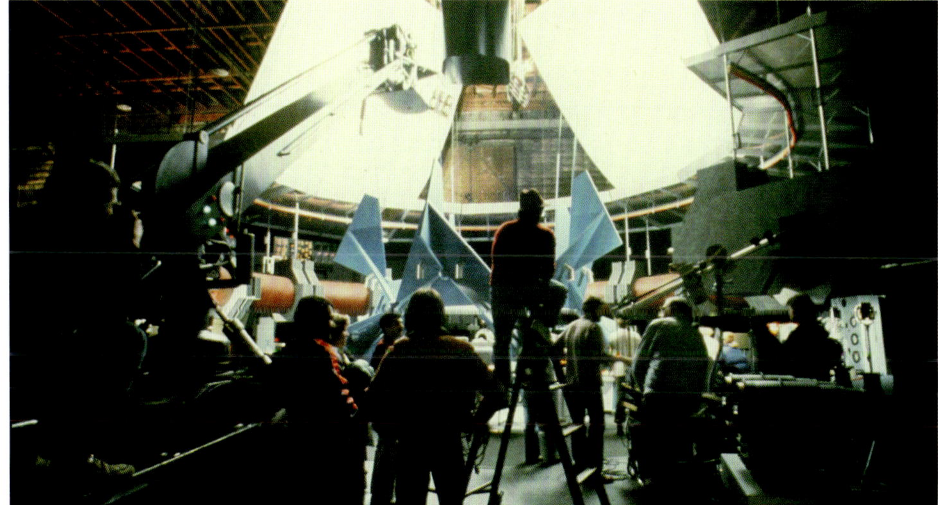

THIS PAGE: The central and ornate scaffolding constructed as part of the computer lab of Regula I served both an aesthetic and budgetary purpose. The triangular lines and texture add a dimension of richness to the set. Because of its shape, the scaffolding breaks up and hides the areas of negative space behind the characters, a budget-saving device reused in the Starfleet briefing room sequence in *Star Trek VI: The Undiscovered Country.*

TOP RIGHT: Meyer directing Bibi Besch on the completed Regula I set.

RIGHT: The use of consoles, computers, and futuristic equipment provides animation and also serves to sell the Regula I set as a scientific research laboratory.

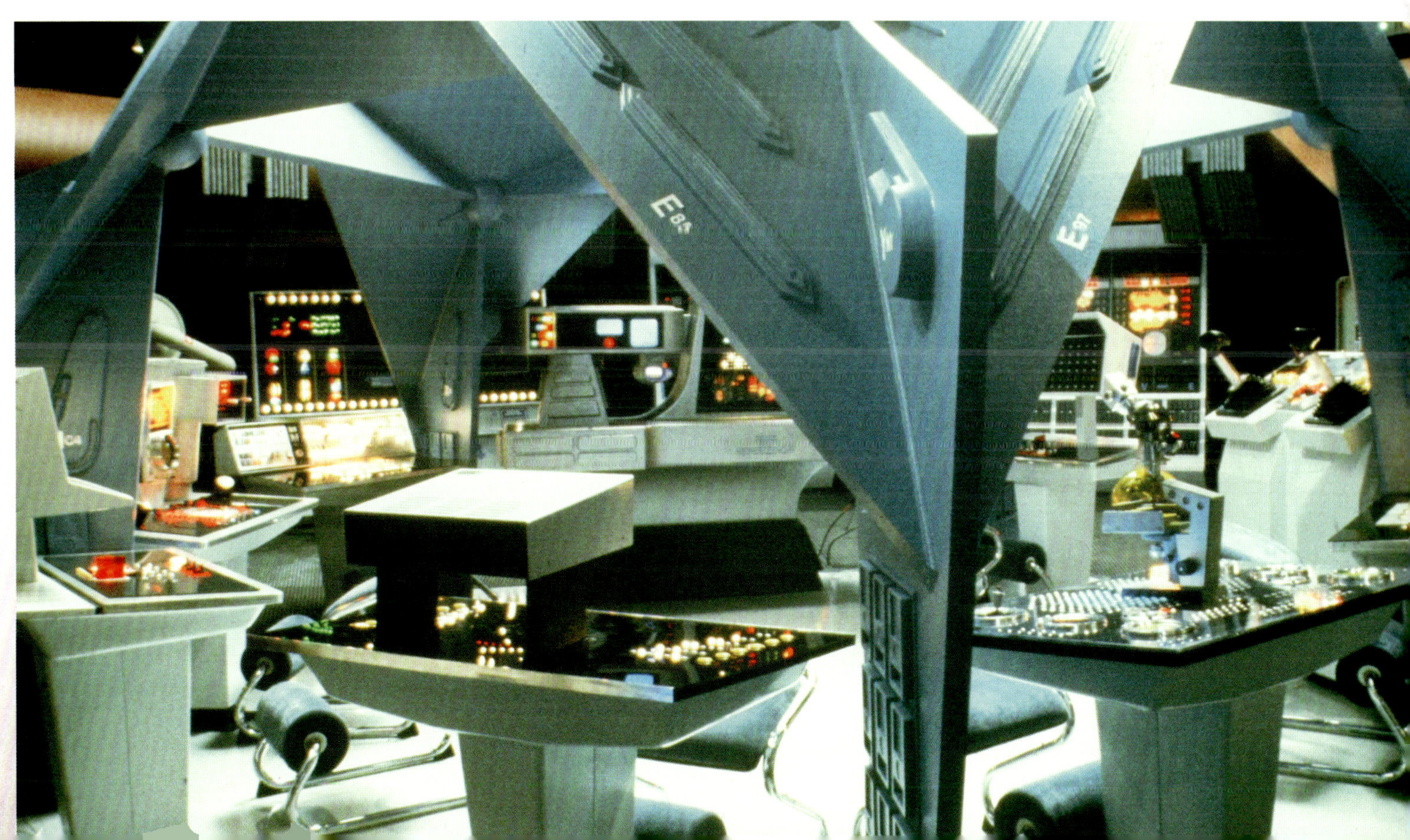

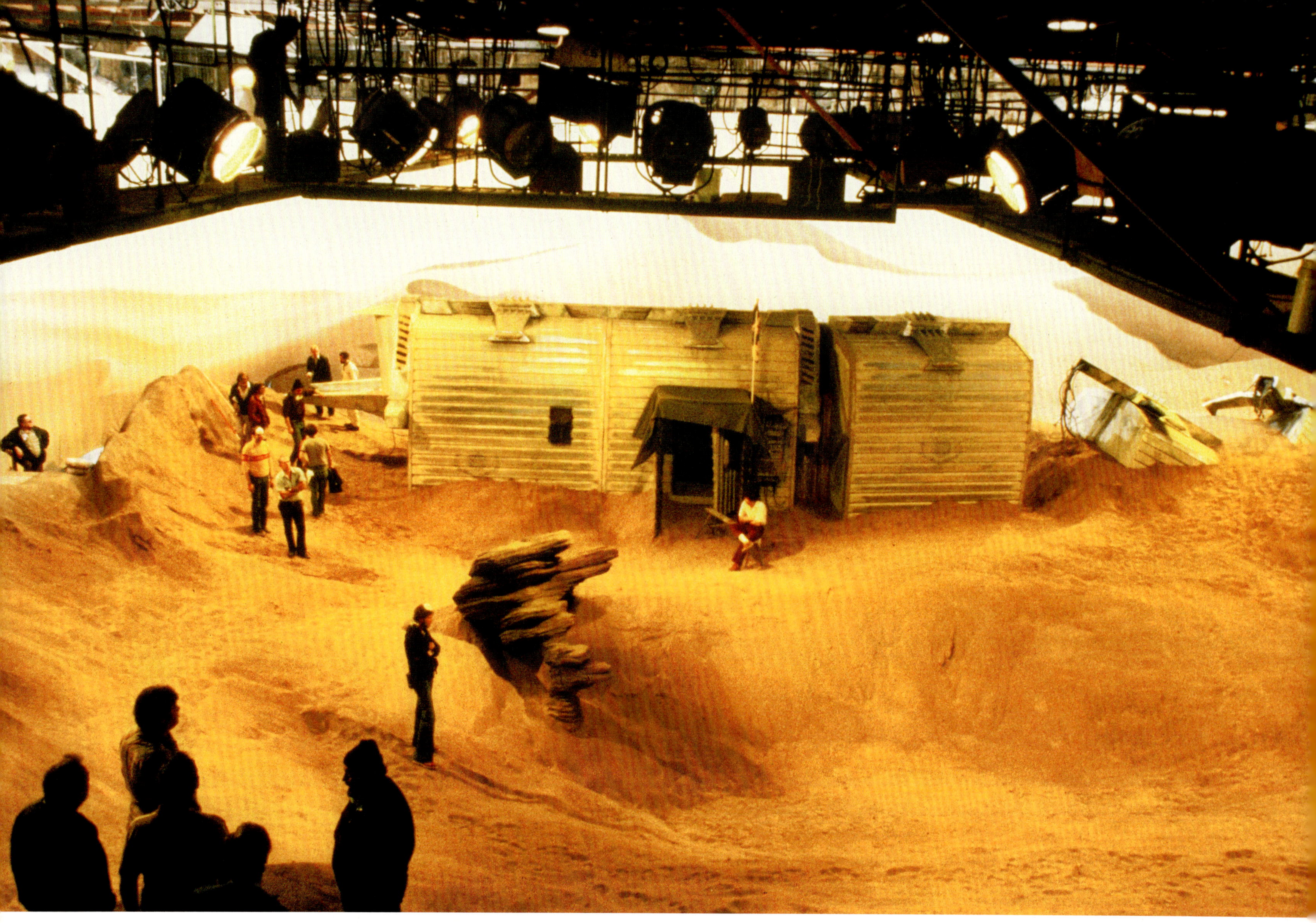

The digital or rear-projected LED screens that dominate modern set designs were not available to the creatives of *Star Trek II*, so the harsh, sand-swept world of Ceti Alpha V had to be a practical environment. First laying wood lattices to mimic uneven ground, the crew then used a smaller amount of Fuller's earth (a common type of clay material used by Hollywood) sand to simulate imposing mounds of sand on the surface of Ceti Alpha V. Special effects supervisor Robert "Bob" Dawson was responsible for securing as many Ritter fans as possible to create the planet's sand storms. Each fan can produce winds as much as forty miles per hour in about three seconds, making them especially valuable and exceptionally loud. The finished Ceti Alpha V set would feature not only the unforgiving terrain, but a fully realized cargo container that was shelter to Khan's people.

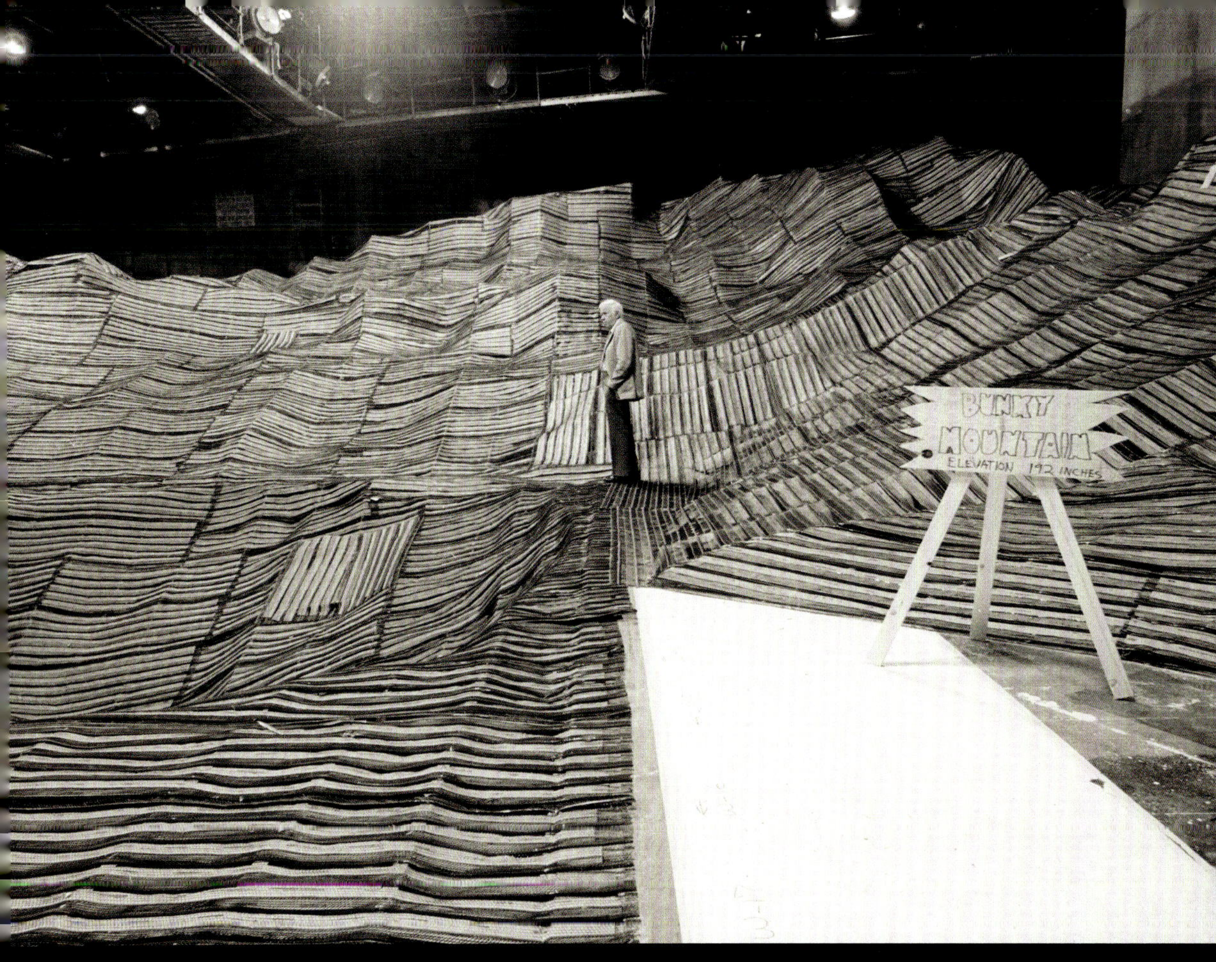

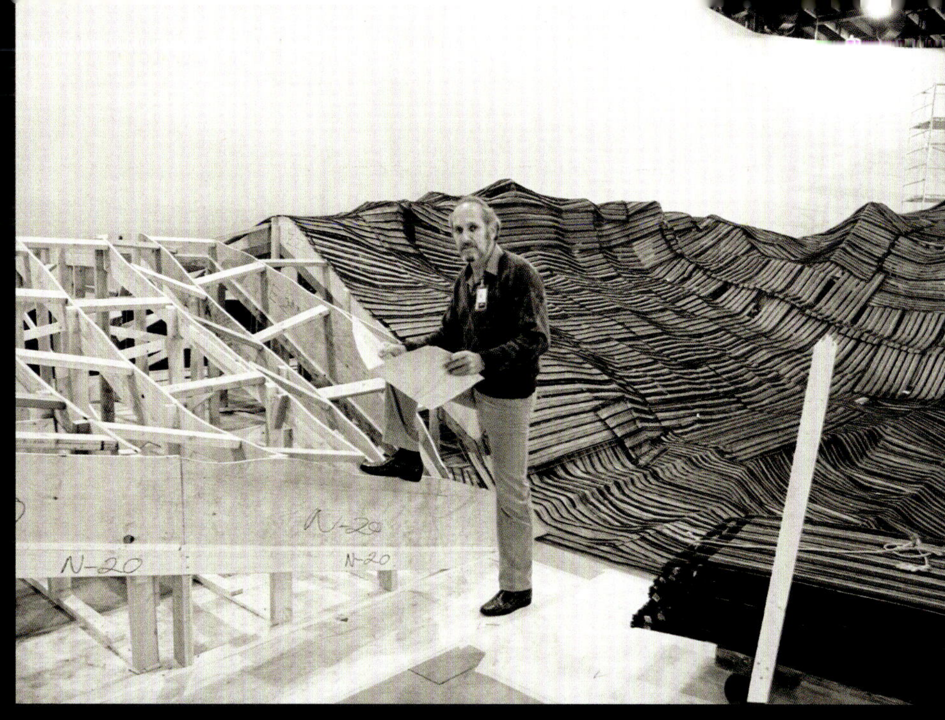

LEFT: Here, Jennings stands on the Stage 8 Ceti Alpha V set, with a whimsical sign created by the construction team naming the set.

BELOW: A demanding and laborious effort, Fuller's earth was required by the truck load, delivered to Stage 8 on the Paramount lot to create the surface of Ceti Alpha V.

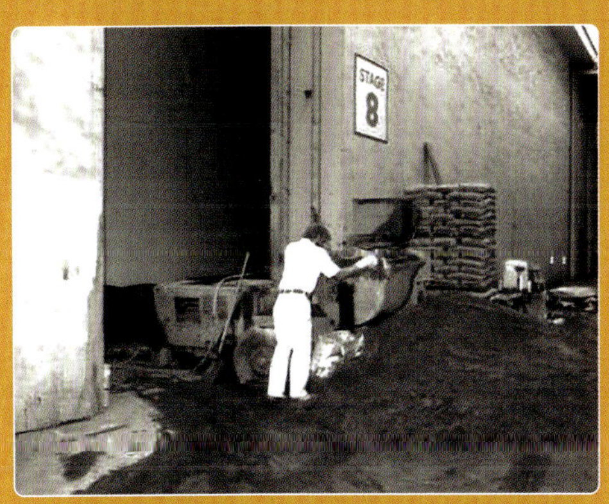
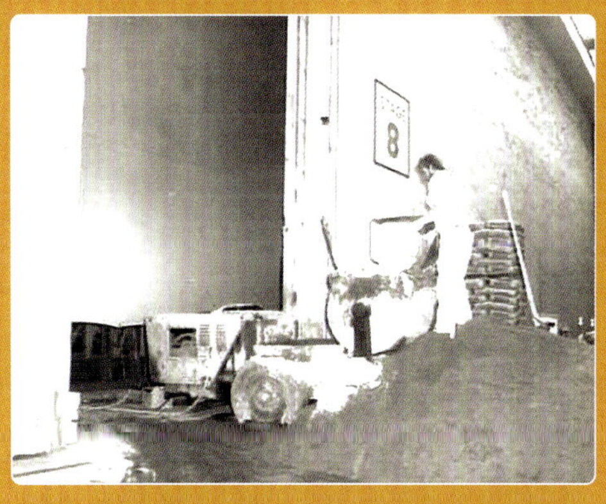
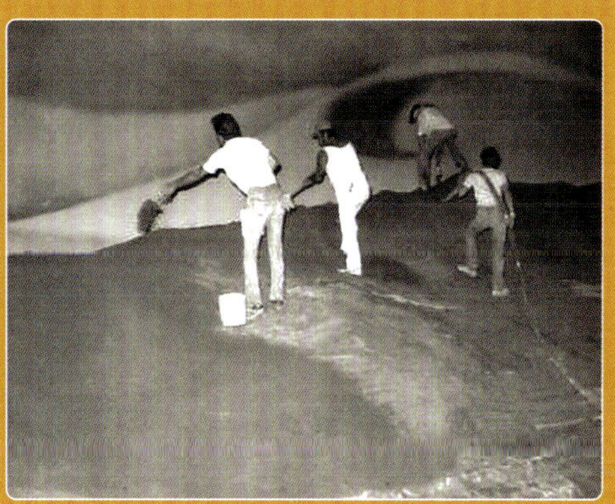
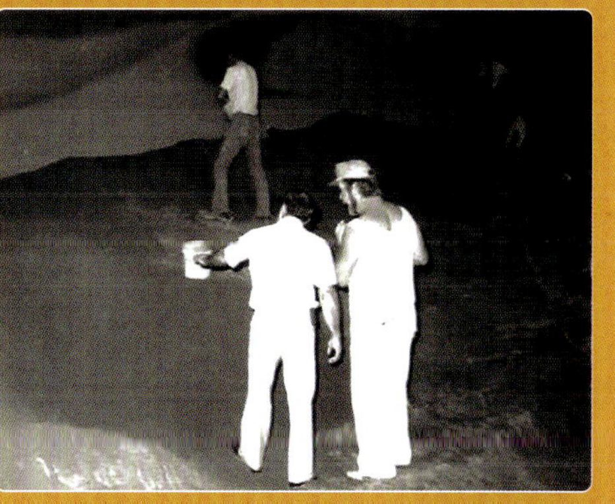
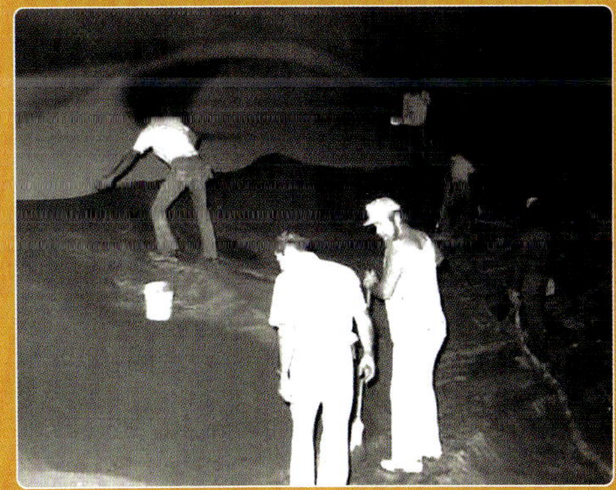
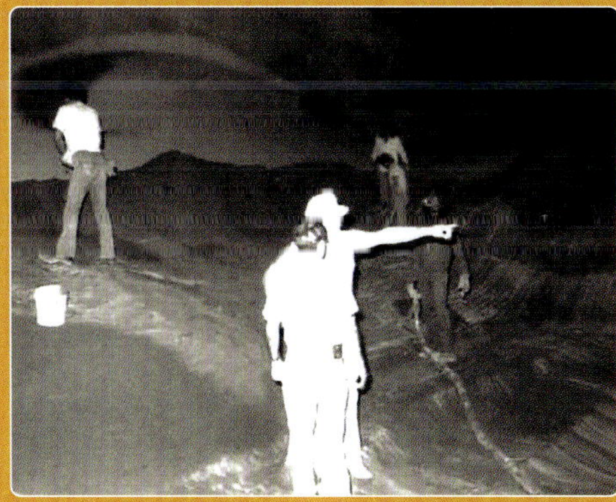
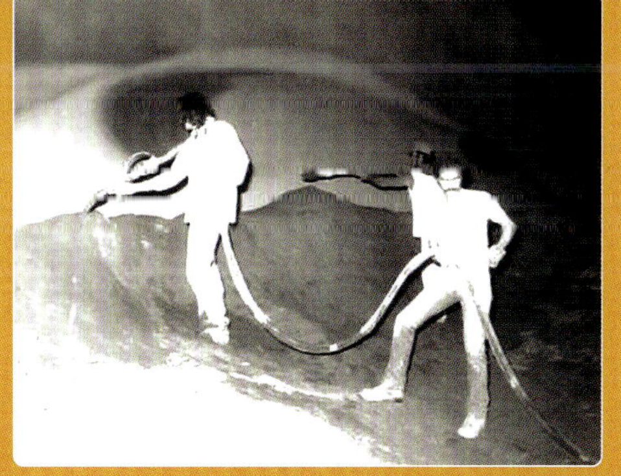
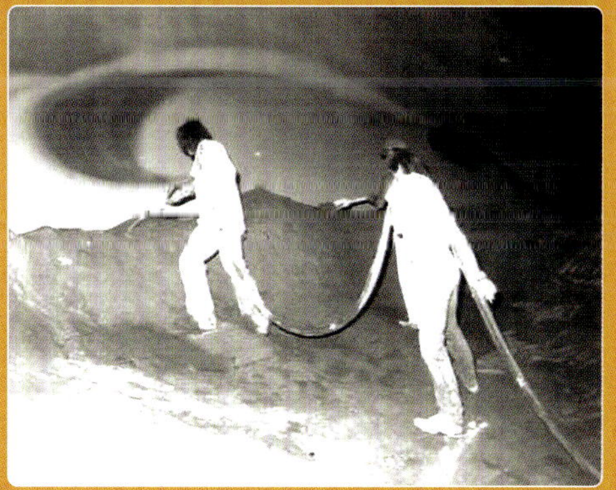

BELOW & RIGHT: Sand got everywhere, requiring protective gear for people and equipment. Meyer with goggles, mask, and coveralls worn by the crew, including first assistant camera Catherine Coulson and director of photography Gayne Rescher operating a plastic-covered camera. The cast, including Paul Winfield (with Meyer), did not have quite the same protection.

BOTTOM: Although a fan of *Star Trek*, Winfield was understandably not a fan of the Ceti Alpha V set. "Oh, that was awful. They put us in spacesuits, which kept the dust and sand out, but no air came in either; they clamp you in and that's it, and you can't see through the mask after a while. We had to climb up these mountains of sand, and I got very claustrophobic."[11]

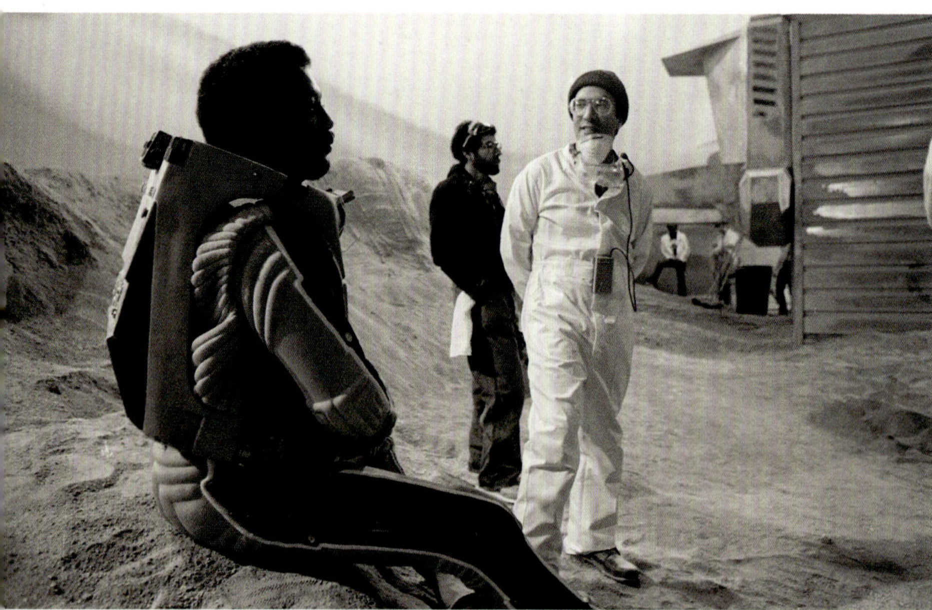

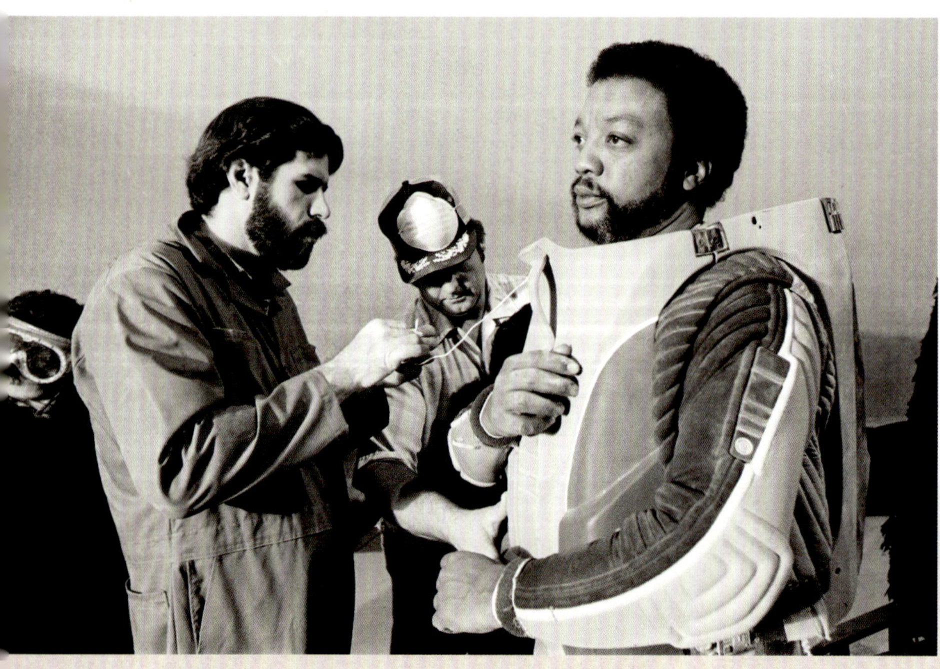

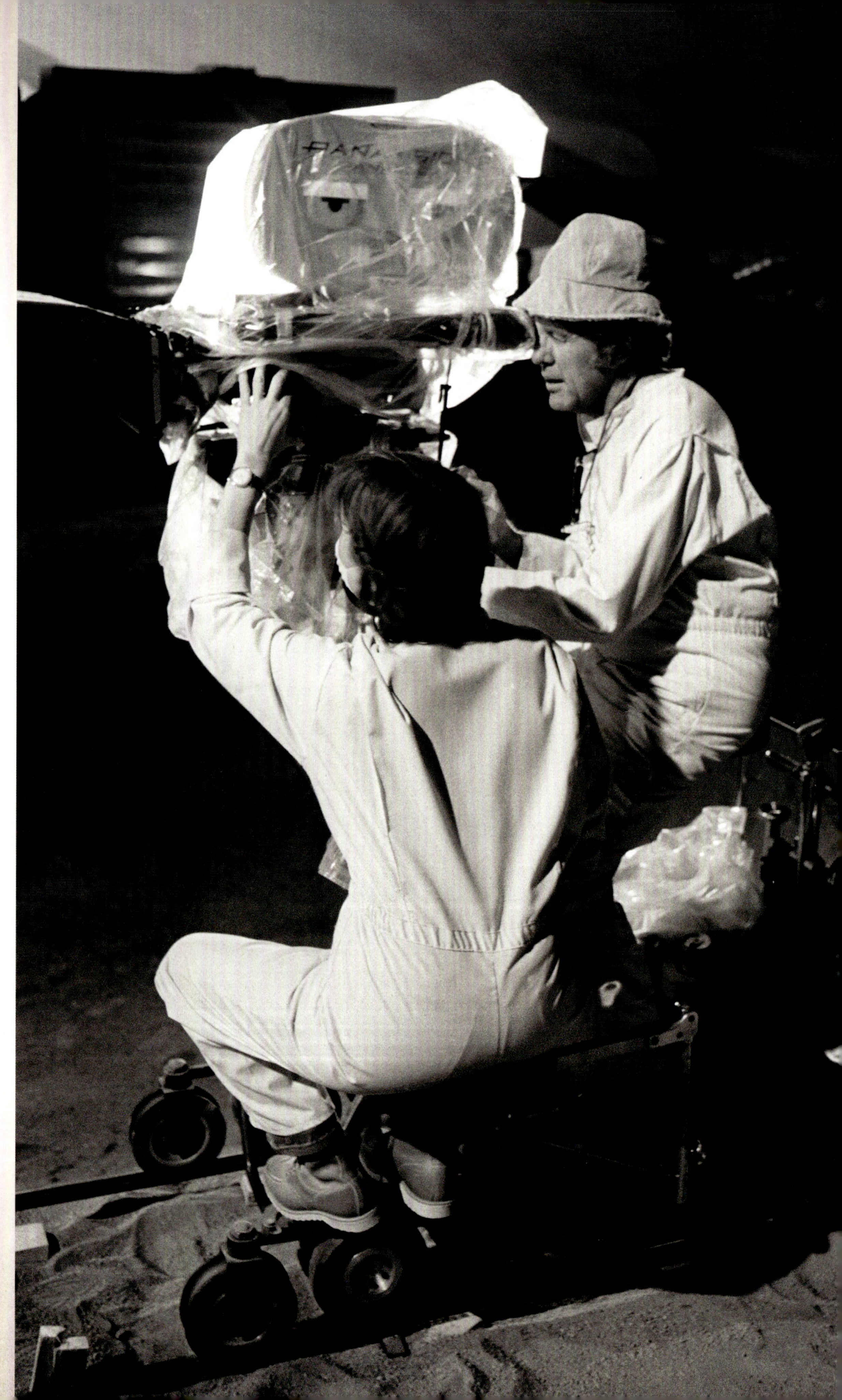

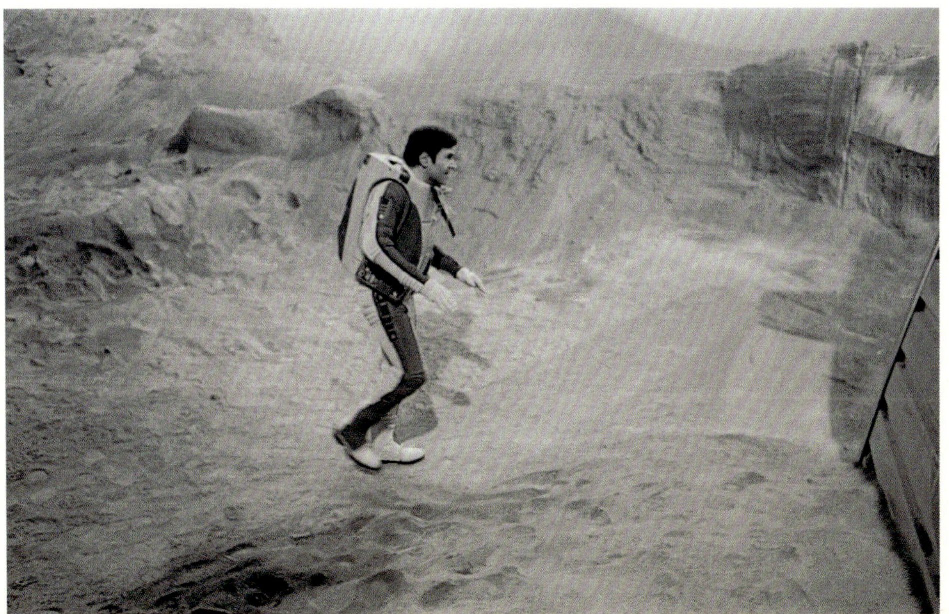

ABOVE: Koenig rehearses on the finished set. Underneath the surface of Ceti Alpha V lies not Ceti eels in reality, but rather wood.

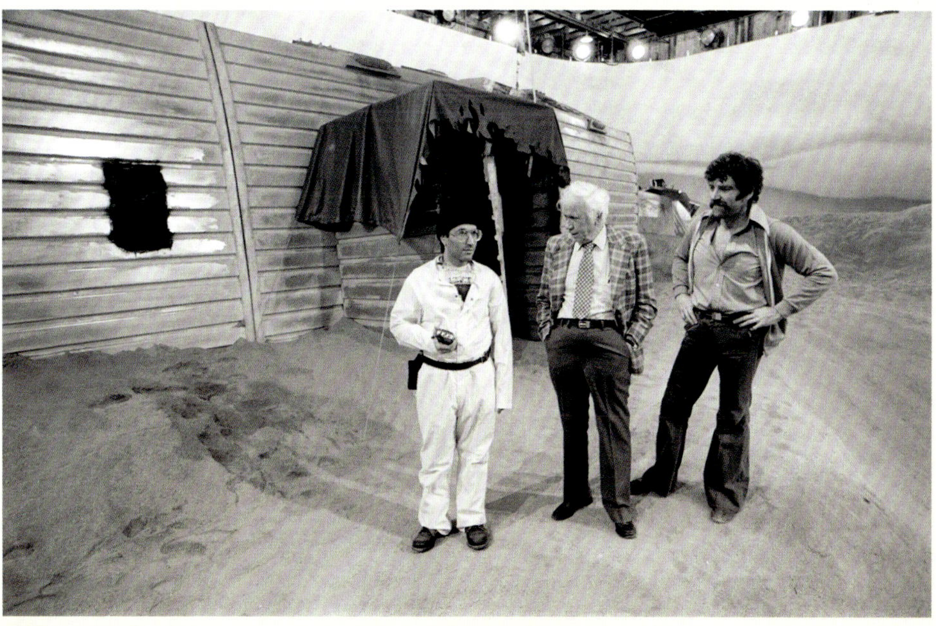

ABOVE: Production designers and art directors bring to reality the vision of their directors. Here, Meyer, Jennings, and Minor on the practical set they collaborated to create.

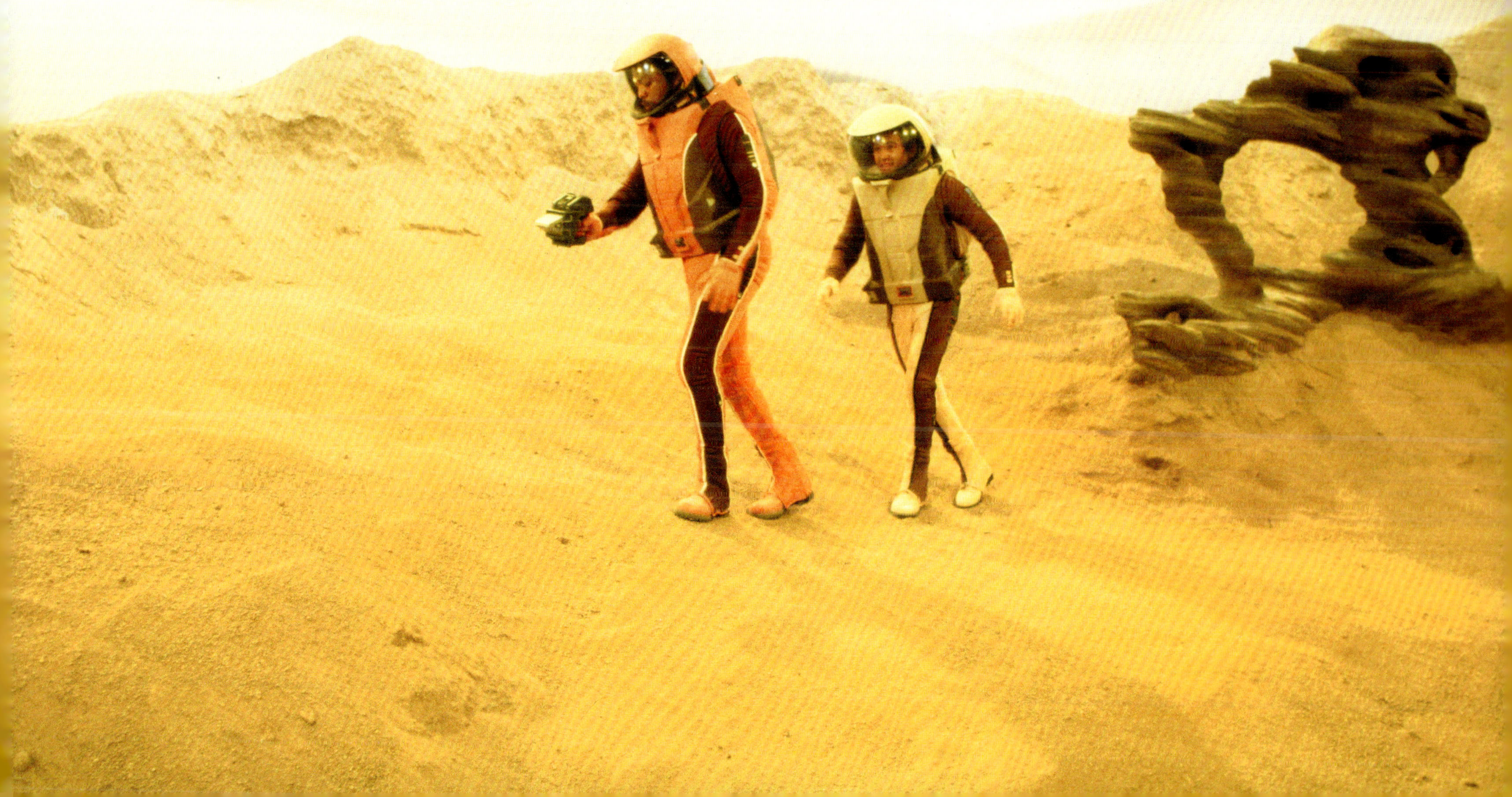

Star Trek II provides audiences with the first ever look at the private apartment of James T. Kirk. The use of antiques as decoration was an idea suggested by Sallin and brought to fruition by Jennings, who selected the items that adorn Kirk's walls and shelves. The original design of Kirk's apartment by Minor included a staircase and two floors, but $40,000 was saved by making the apartment one level. A few weeks before, Kirk's apartment was the location of the Ceti Alpha V set.

BELOW: More antiques than meets the eye. Careful observation reveals that Kirk must collect antique computers, because on his desk near his window is a Commodore PET, first introduced in 1977. The reality is that the computer was chosen because to audiences of 1982, most of whom did not have home computers, the device looked futuristic.

BOTTOM: Barely seen on screen, the intricate design of Kirk's fireplace demonstrates the care and craft that artists working on the film had. Time, budget, and technology may have been limited, but the imagination and creativity of those working on *Star Trek II* was not.

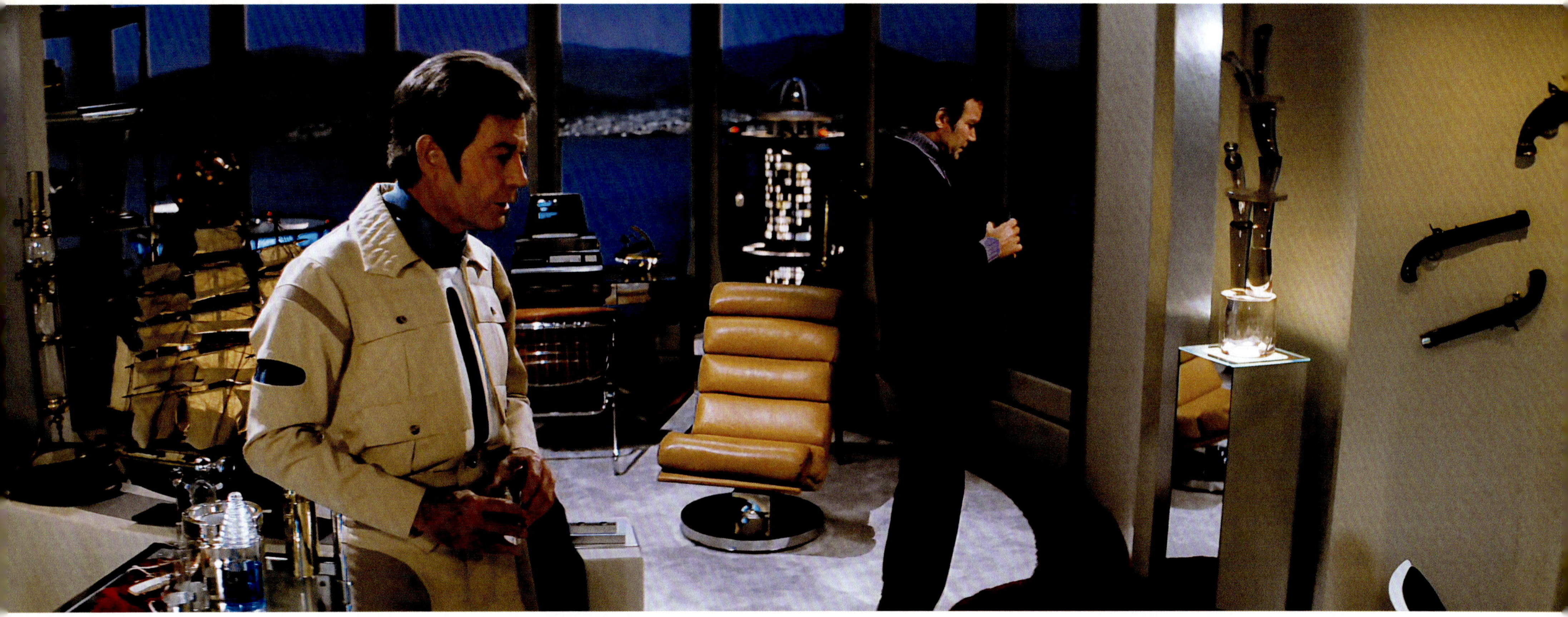

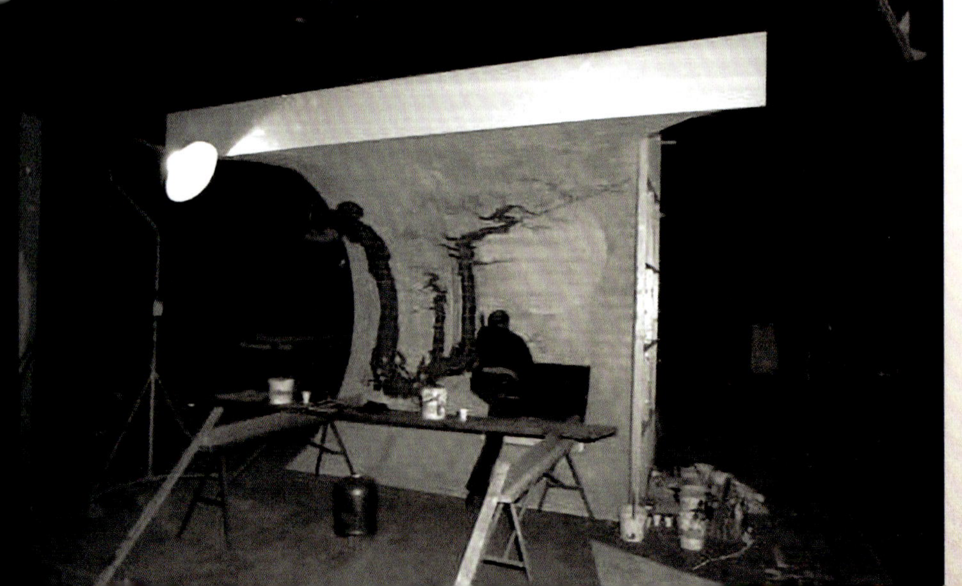

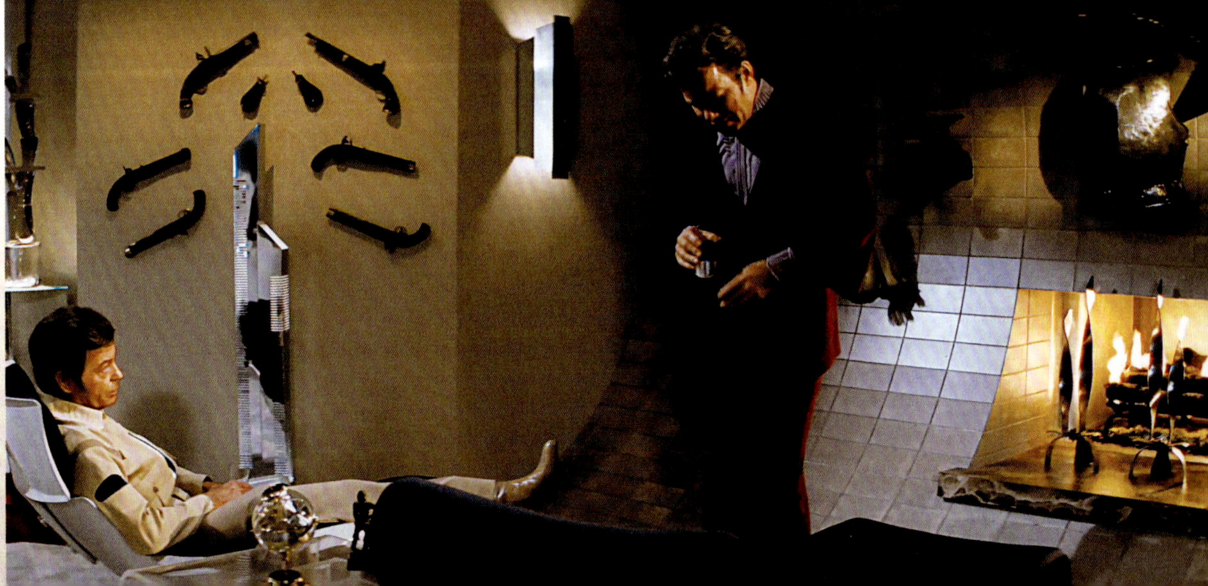

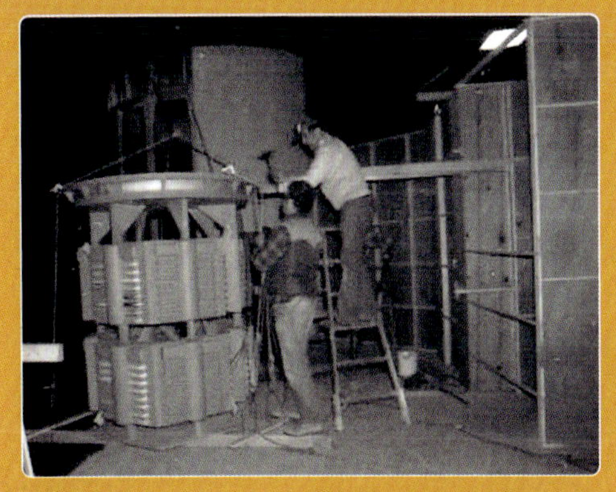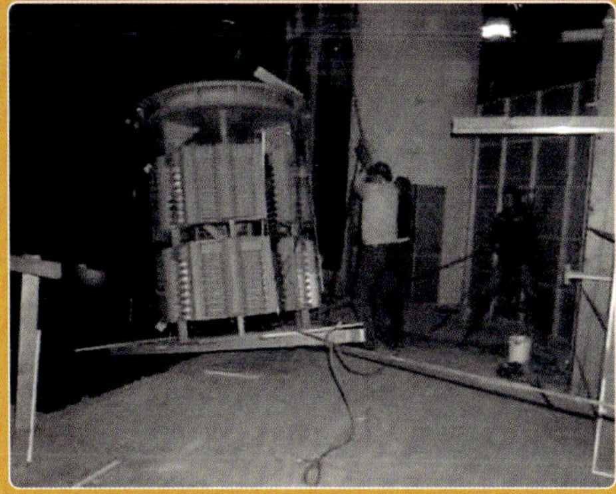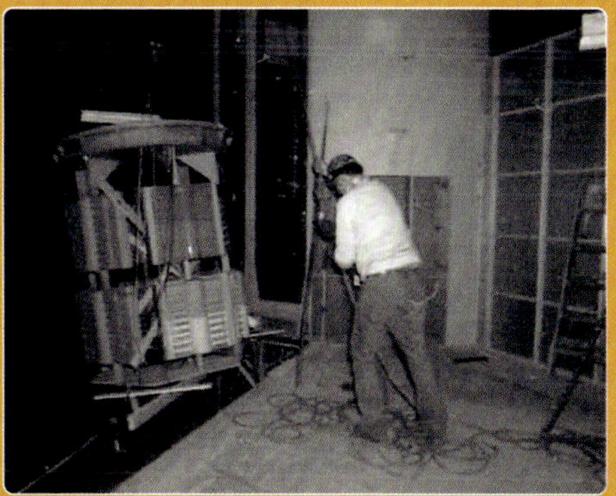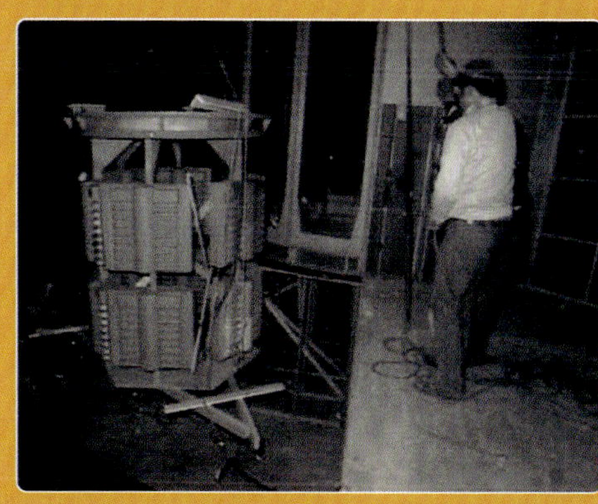

ABOVE & LEFT: To compensate for the loss of a second floor, the windows to Kirk's apartment were made more interesting. Minor revealed, "I felt happy that I could at least get two miniature buildings thrown out against the backdrop. They're just a throw-away, but the elevator is going up and down past him in that opening sequence in the apartment at night."[13] The view of San Francisco from Kirk's apartment is the same used in the 1974 film *The Towering Inferno* (by Matthew Yuricich, who also created matte paintings of San Francisco, Starfleet docking bay, and the *U.S.S. Enterprise* hull for *Star Trek: The Motion Picture*). The production paid 20th Century Fox for a small section of the painting and then enlarged the image to give the illusion that Kirk lived right near the water. The trench between the painting and the set helped create the illusion that Kirk's apartment was not far from the San Francisco bridge.

BELOW: Minor and Jennings wanted to give Kirk's *Enterprise* quarters more personality that was not too afield from his antique-inspired San Francisco apartment. Adding carpeting and roll-top desk-inspired cabinets helped sell the idea.

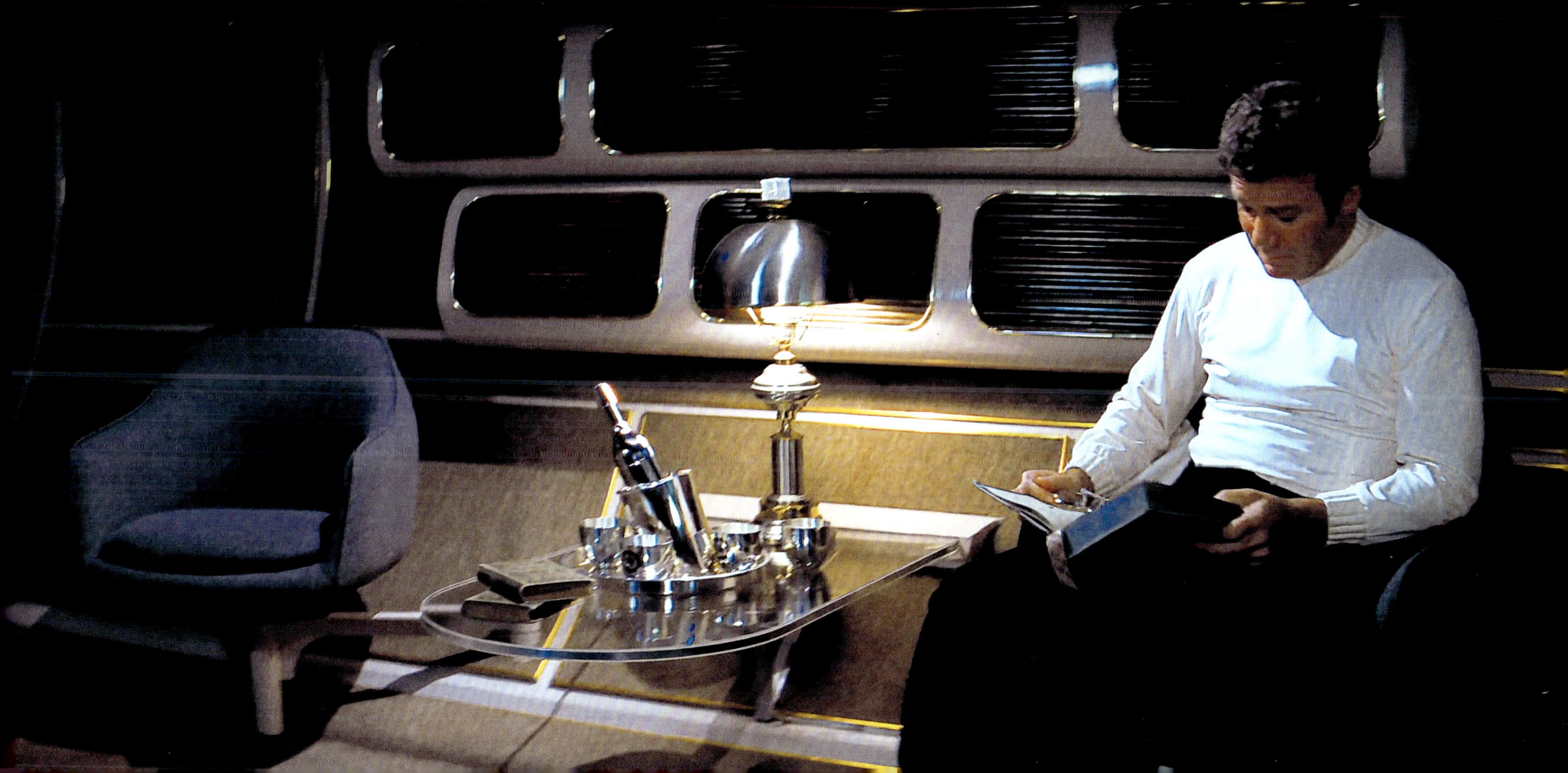

DELETED SCENE: MCCOY, EYE DOCTOR

Despite being filmed, a scene where McCoy teaches Kirk about eyeglasses was deleted from the theatrical version of the film and never restored for subsequent editions.

Right before McCoy chastises Kirk about treating his birthday like a funeral, he shows Kirk how to use his gift.

It is a small moment preserved in this collection of images (below), but the eyeglasses are an important symbol in *Star Trek II*. While open to interpretation, the glasses can be seen as a physical manifestation of

```
                    BONES (continuing)
          Slide them down your nose. Now look at
          me over the top. And you read printed
          matter through the bottom.


                    KIRK (reacts):
          Amazing! I don't know what to say—

                    BONES
          Say thank you.


                    KIRK
          Thank you.
```

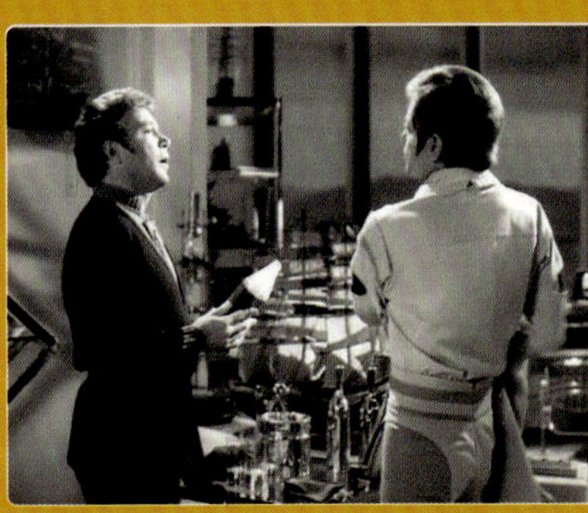
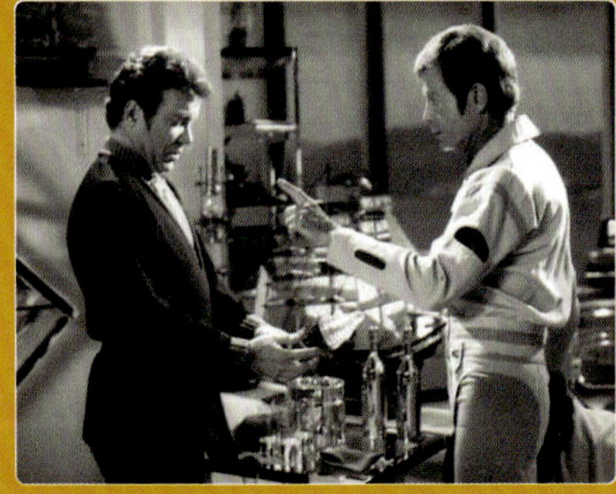
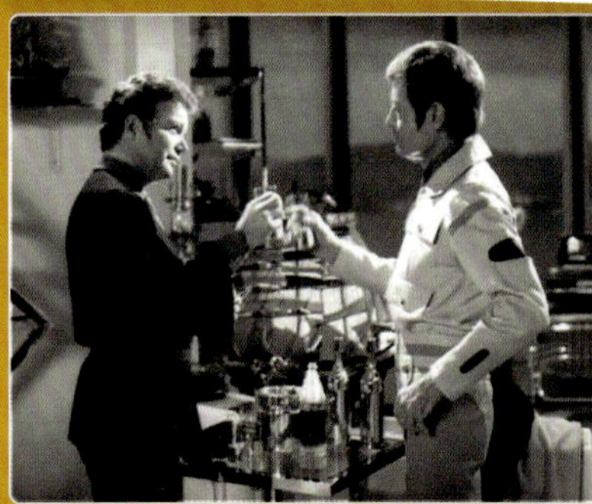
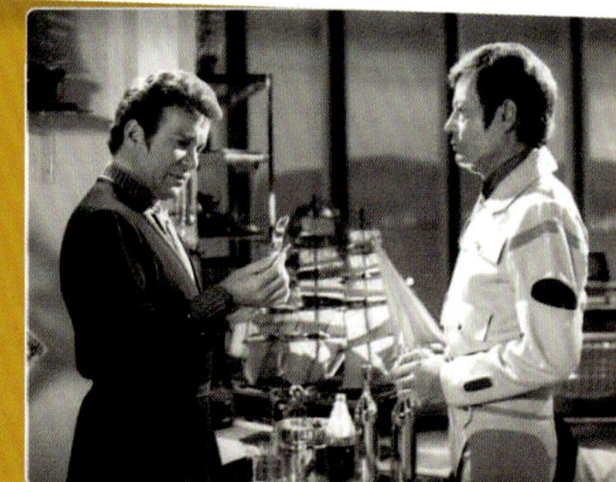
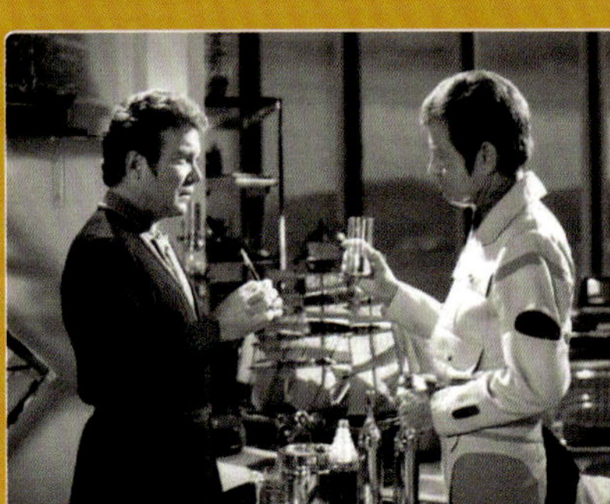
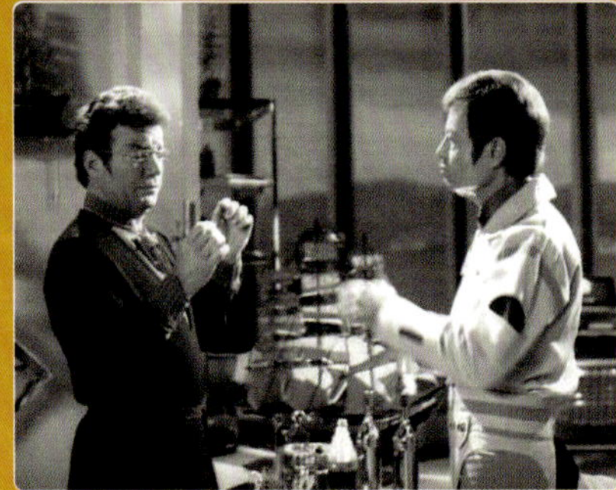
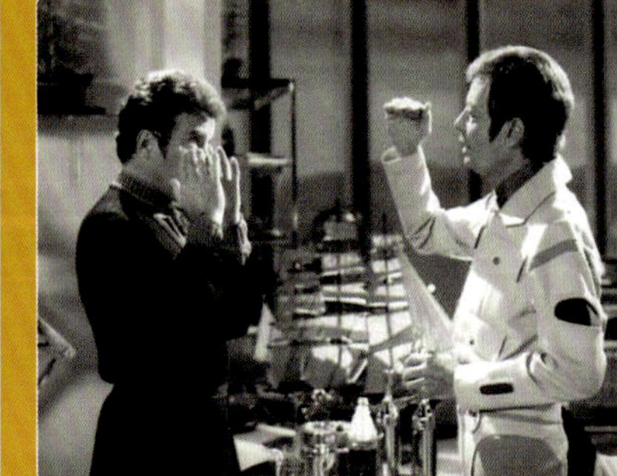
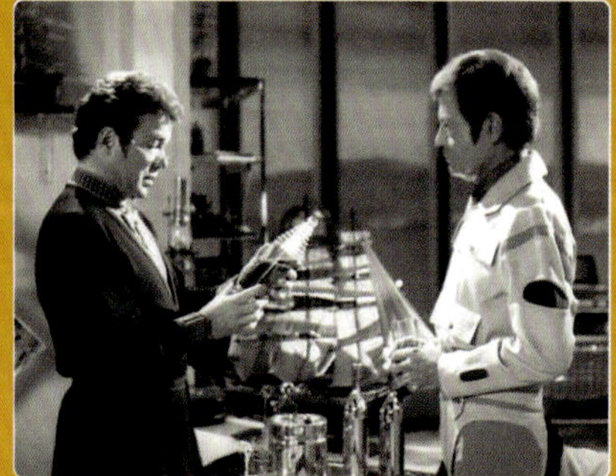

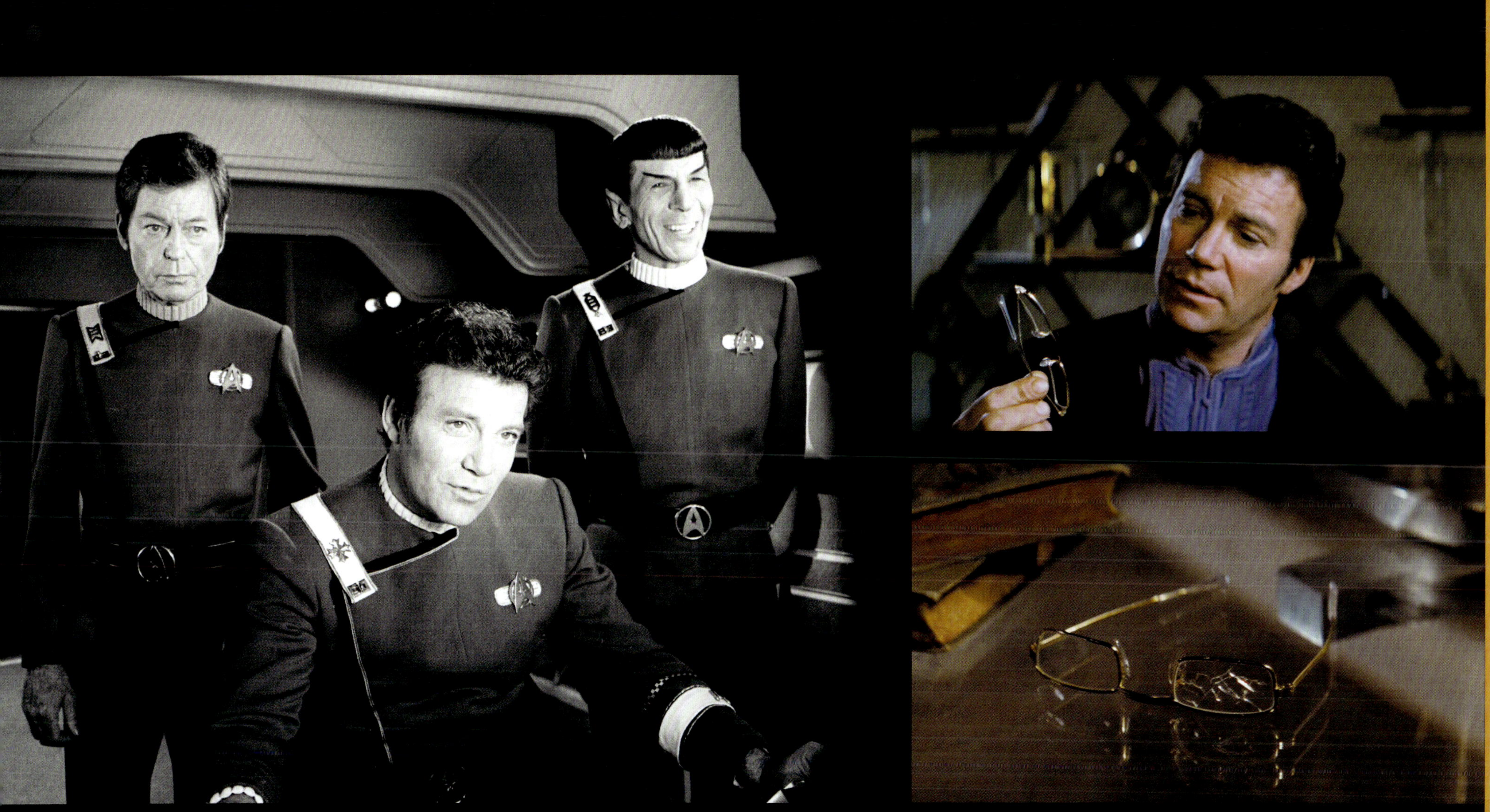

the relationship between McCoy, Kirk, and Spock. For his birthday, Kirk is given a book by Spock; he is given information. But Kirk needs McCoy's gift of the eyeglasses to clearly see that information.

The scene where the trio debate the merits and demerits of the Genesis device on board the *Enterprise* is a classic example of how the logic of Spock is tempered by the empathy of McCoy, with the ethos of Kirk having to make decisions and achieve a balance. At the end of the film, when Spock has died, the eyeglasses are broken and Kirk can no longer access the information he once did. The trio, too, has been broken.

The scene was praised by Roddenberry in his September 30, 1981 script comments, writing, "good scene, and I love it when our people can be human like this." However, Roddenberry had a concern about Kirk not knowing what eyeglasses were. "He is, after all, a very educated man and I suspect he would have seen and read enough of the twentieth and other centuries to have an idea of what they are, although he certainly can be unsure about how they are attached, how well the magnification works, and so on."

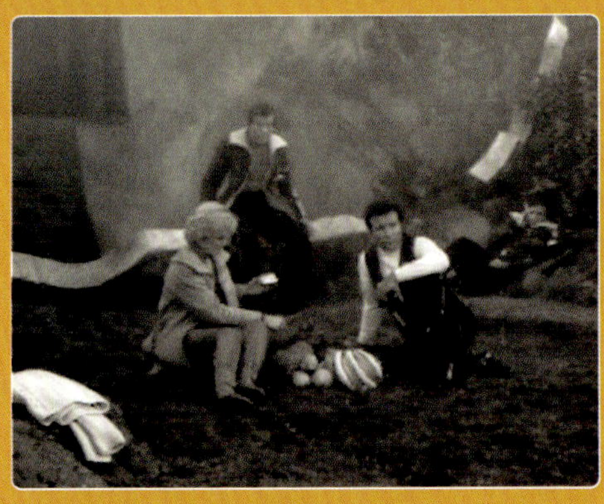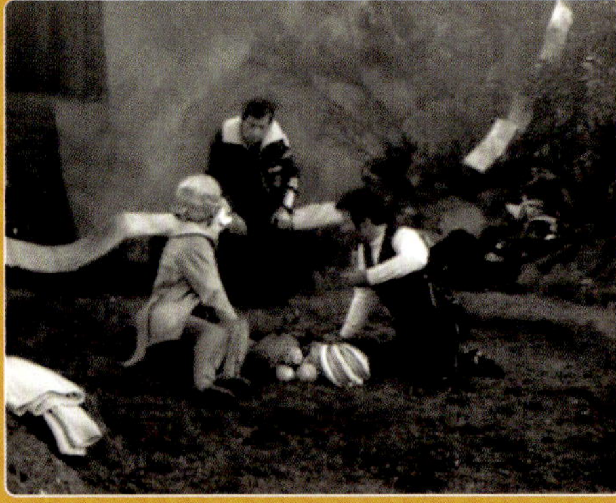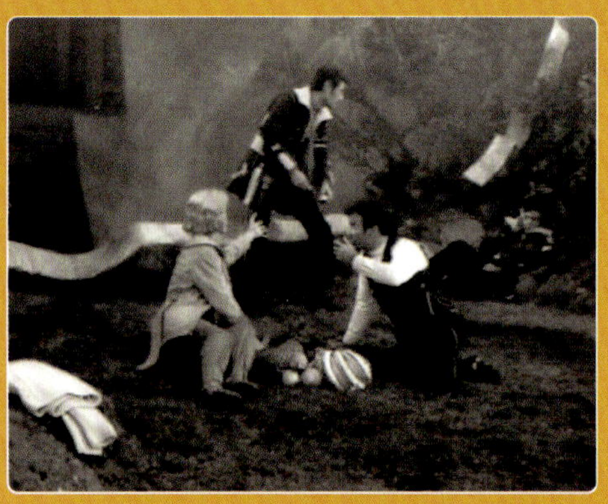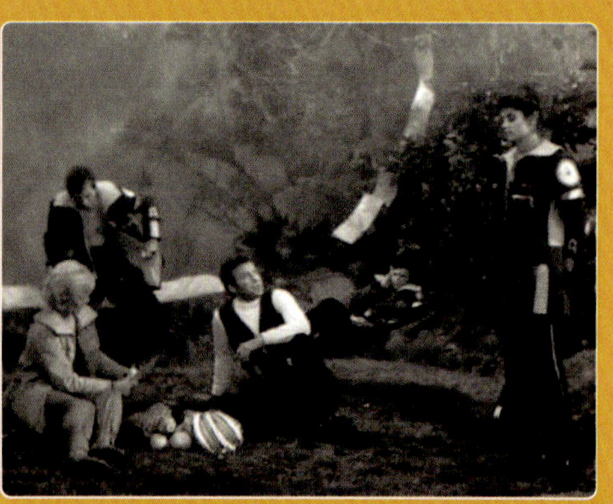

Known as the Eden Cave while filming, the Genesis Cave set was less grand than originally envisioned, having been scaled back—like Kirk's apartment—for budgetary reasons. "We were planning, for instance, to build a real Eden Cave, with a huge waterfall sixty feet high," Minor explained. "It was going to fill up Stage 15 at Paramount, which has a huge tank in it. We were planning to build all of the cliff faces, and we couldn't do it. So we cut back from the scale of things to doing the bubble effect in a fifty-by-fifty area and the rest [was] accomplished through a fairly successful matte painting done by ILM."[9]

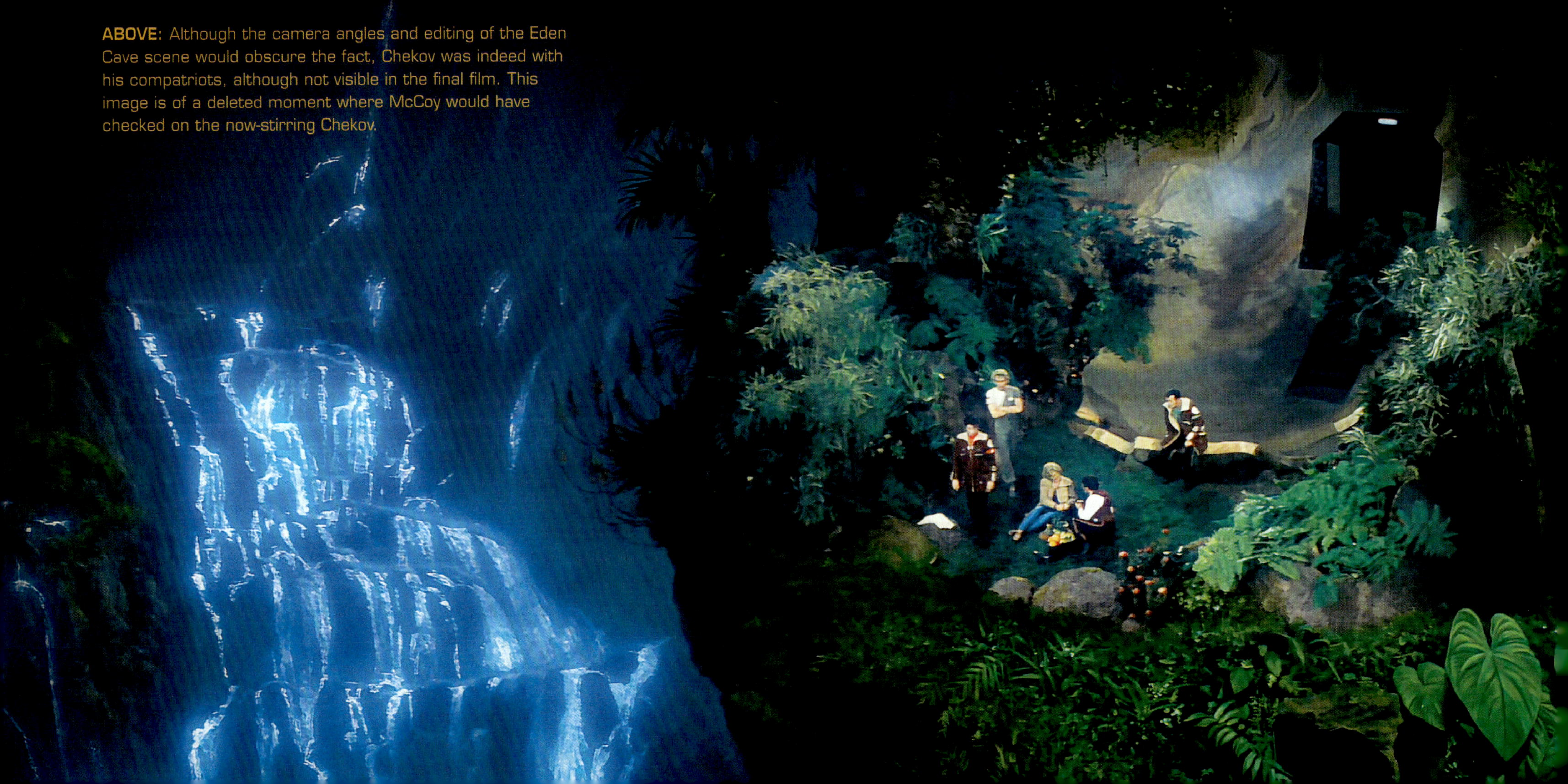

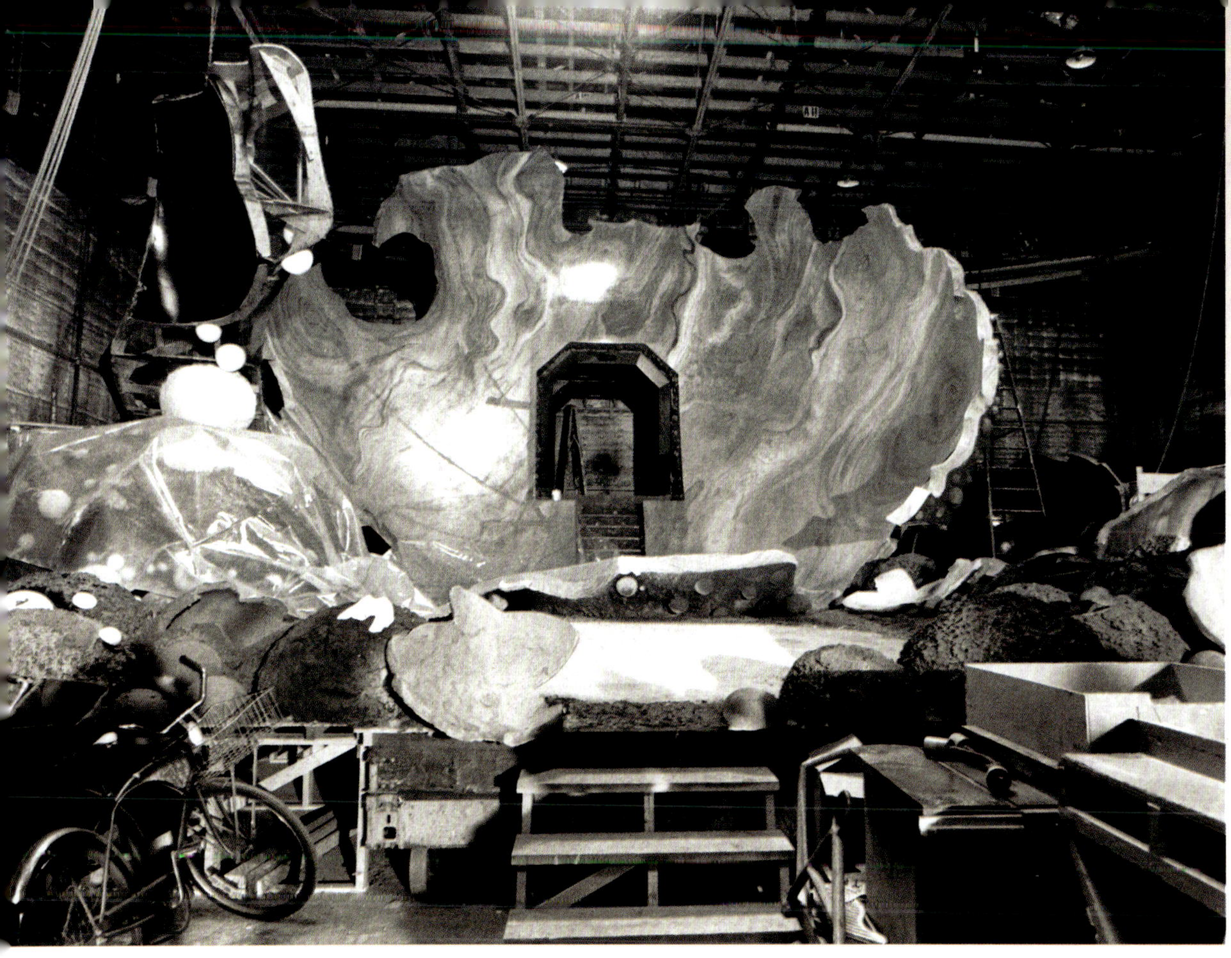

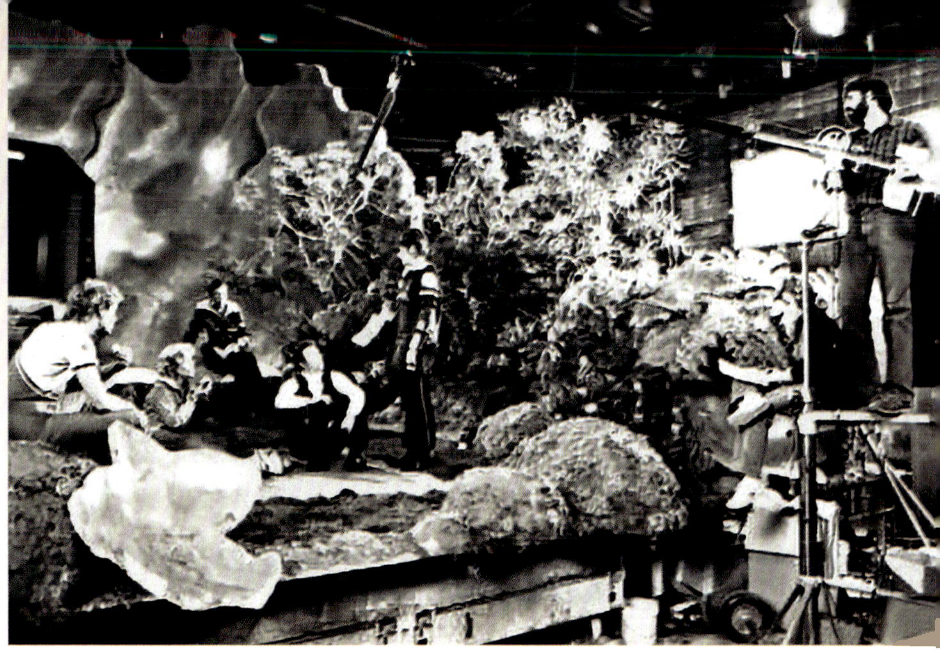

LEFT & ABOVE: Referred to as the Eden Cave while filming, but known as the Genesis Cave to fans, this set was the result of a reduction in budget of about $300,000.

BELOW: Filming on the scaled-down Eden Cave set did not diminish the emotional effectiveness of the scene, with Kirk demonstrating a character-defining trait that gives hope to the audience: he doesn't believe in no-win scenarios.

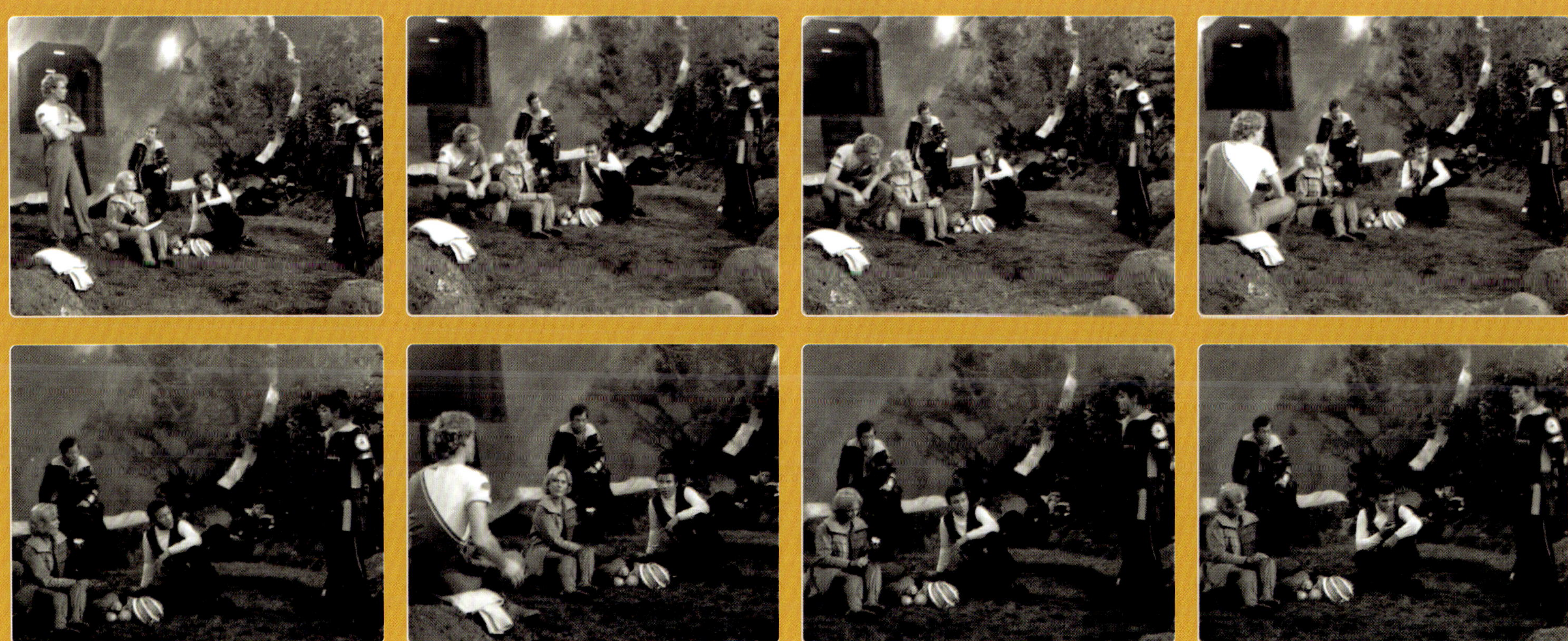

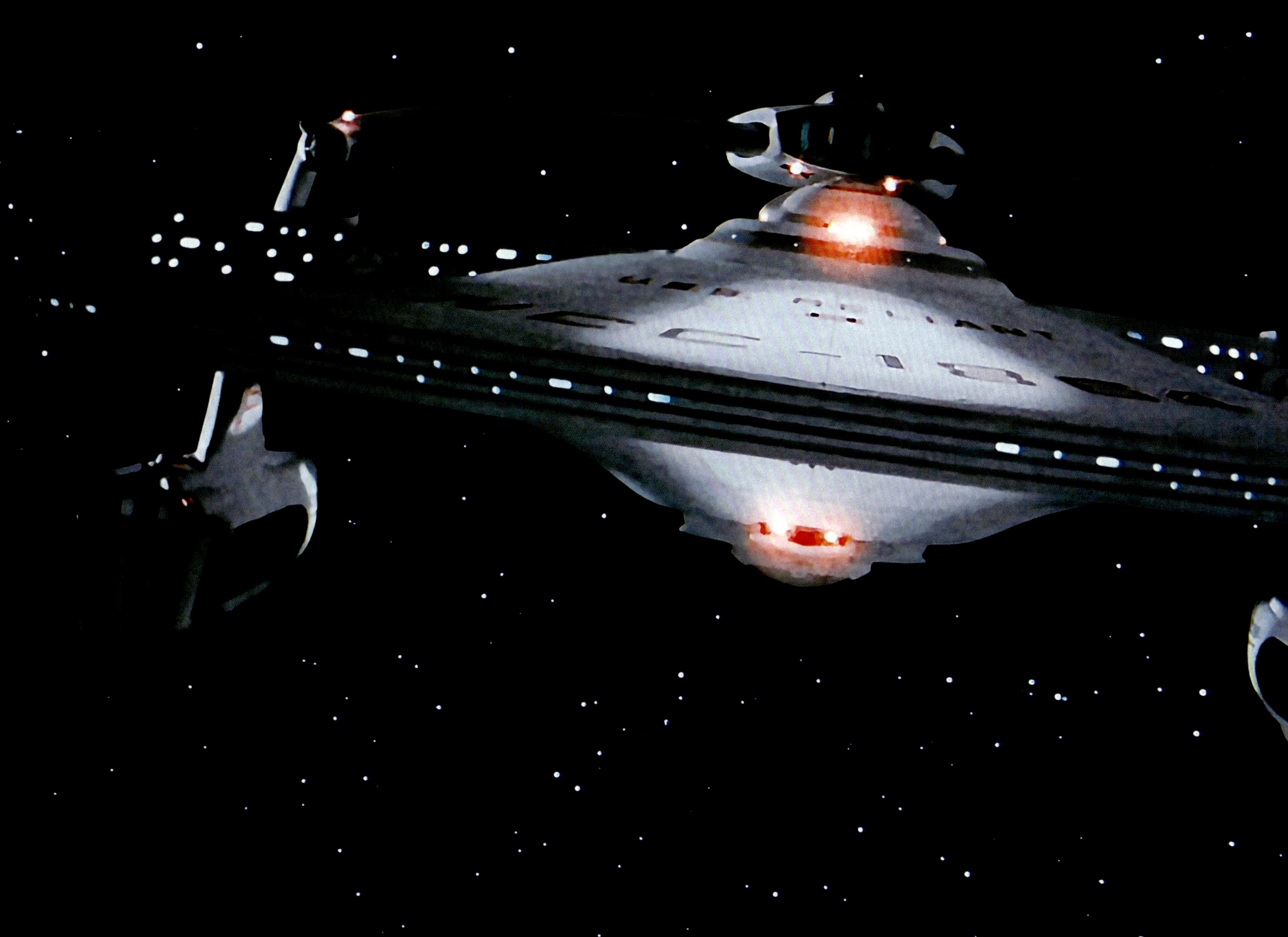

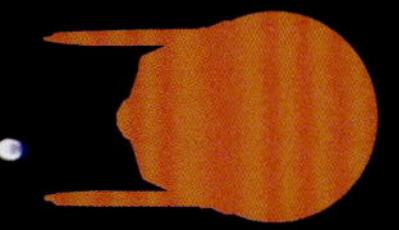

ONE BIG HAPPY FLEET

INDUSTRIAL LIGHT & MAGIC

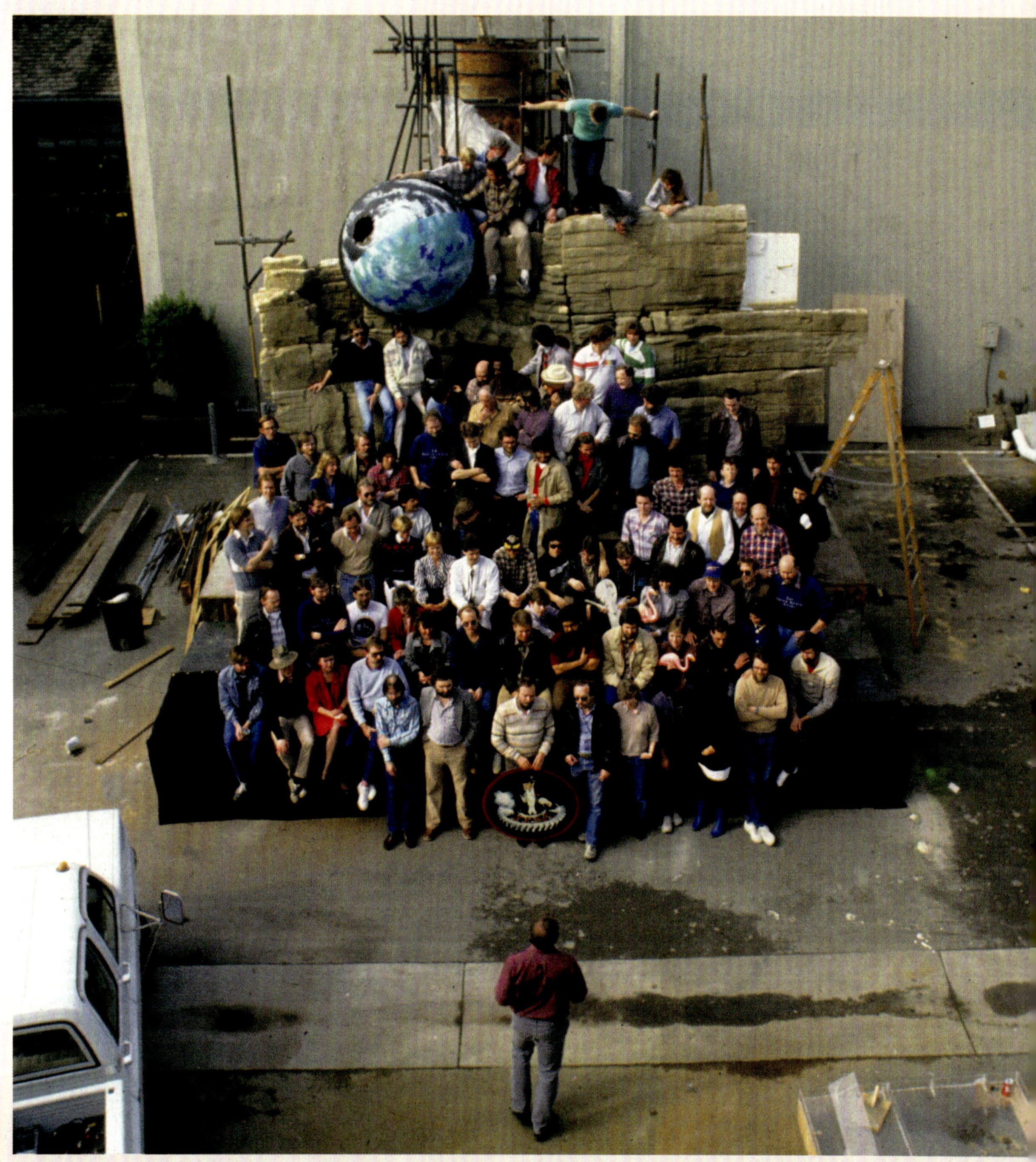

ABOVE: Using Smith's metaphor, the ILM band assembled for another gig in this photograph.
© Industrial Light & Magic

While producer Robert Sallin contributed to every aspect of *Star Trek II*, it is reasonable to suggest that the most important of those contributions were in the areas of pre-planning as well as shepherding the visual effects (VFX) and acting as a liaison with Industrial Light & Magic (ILM). Early production problems creating VFX had nearly ruined *Star Trek: The Motion Picture*, until visual effects pioneer Douglas Trumbull and his team had saved the day. The creatives of *Star Trek II* were not about to make that same mistake. With his background as a commercial director and producer, Sallin had the experience to help the film through this possible minefield, as television commercials were frequently a proving ground for new filming techniques and effects.

Both because Sallin knew the time- and money-saving value of preparation and because the original idea was to have different special effects companies working on different effects, he wanted a detailed plan outlining those effects. Sallin asked art director Michael Minor to produce storyboards, in addition to his own, that would be of immeasurable value to director Nicholas Meyer on set and to ILM when creating visual effects later. With ever-changing scripts and writers, the storyboards became that much more important. Though it was a challenge for Minor to keep apace of the malleable pre-production, putting an estimated four-hundred hours, beginning June 1981, into getting storyboards ready to help producers get bids from effects companies. The visuals helped the companies give better estimates.

The shepherding of the effects would prove to be an area of conflict between Sallin and Meyer. There had reportedly been some commentary by Meyer during production about exactly how effective he thought the organization of the special effects work had been, which Sallin responded to while speaking to Kay Anderson of *Cinefantastique*: "Nick did not supervise the creation of the effects storyboards, and Nick did not supervise the execution of the shots… I resent Meyer saying about the effects, 'We didn't know what we were doing'… *He* might not have known what he was doing, but we knew exactly what we were doing… If there had been any confusion we could not have come in so close to budget."[1]

STORYBOARD OCT 16 1981
REVISED DEC 2 8 1981

DESCRIPTION: Reverse on ENTERPRISE as Torpedo approaches...

NOTES: RELIANT in B.G. *Does Have Nebula*

SHOT # / SEQUENCE: **NEBULA BATTLE — 177

ELEMENTS:	STAGE	ANIMATION	ILM PLATE	MATTE DEPT.	NON-ILM
Enterprise	X		X E&S		
Stars		X			
Photon Torp.	X				
Nebula Cloud				X	
PTG Nebula/Stars		X			
Reliant (Small)					
TOTAL:					

FRM COUNT | PAGE # 1 of 3

STORYBOARD OCT 16 1981
REVISED MAR - 2 1982

DESCRIPTION: KIRK & BONES in front of ENTERPRISE VIEWSCREEN watching new planet.

NOTES:

SHOT # / SEQUENCE: **FINAL GENESIS — 247A

ELEMENTS:	STAGE	ANIMATION	ILM PLATE	MATTE DEPT.	NON-ILM
Viewscreen: LA Plate			X		
			X from 247		
Rastar Overlay					
Planet "Genesis"	X				
Sun	X		X from 247		
E&S Stars					
TOTAL:					

FRM COUNT | PAGE #

As always, budget was a major concern. As the bids were considered, the reality was that ILM, the Lucasfilm special effects company, was the best choice. Rather than a no-win scenario, it was a win-win. From ILM's perspective, they were interested in the project partly because *Star Trek II* would be the second non-George Lucas produced/directed film the company would work on, alerting the industry that ILM was open for more diversified business. From the perspective of the *Star Trek II* production team, ILM offered everything that was needed under one company. Both Meyer and Minor used the metaphor that ILM was the Rolls-Royce of special effects companies. Sallin agreed. "They were incredible. The most professional, the most delightful, the most responsive; I couldn't say enough good things about the whole crew."[2]

ILM was formed during June 1975 to create the effects needed for the first *Star Wars* movie. By 1981, they led the industry as pioneers, with resources not found in most other special effects companies. A model shop, creature shop, carpentry shop, machine shop, the computer graphics research team, electronics, rotoscoping, animation, and optical printing were all services available at ILM. ILM's Alvy Ray Smith wrote in *American Cinematographer*, "I like to think of the group as an off-line rock group. We work very tightly together on our individual instruments for months, and only later do we face the music. The point is that all members of the team are creative contributors and a project requires all of them.

A drummer is absolutely necessary, but a fantastic drummer cannot carry a piece alone."[3] The *Star Trek II* production's only concern was that ILM was located in San Rafael, near San Francisco, while Paramount was situated in Los Angeles. While not unusual, the time crunch made it an extra challenge. To solve that problem, Bennett explained, "Producer Bob Sallin was the liaison between Hollywood and the ILM base of operations in Northern California."[4]

With time limitations the most daunting concern, the decision was made to have two special visual effects supervisors instead of the traditional one. Ken Ralston would be responsible for the Ceti eels and the *Reliant* versus *Enterprise* battle scenes. Jim Veilleux would supervise starfields, matte paintings, the Carol Marcus Project Genesis proposal sequence, and the creation of the genesis planet. Sallin's plan was effective, enabling effects sequences to be delivered even as Meyer was filming with the actors, something rare during the days of practical effects.

As Smith had observed, visual effects require collaboration, and the design of the *U.S.S. Reliant* and the Mutara Nebula battle scene were a perfect example of that. "I had the most fun I've ever had working with Nick on this show because he had all the right instincts," recalled production designer Joseph Jennings. "He wanted a dogfight between two space ships. 'No, I'm sorry. That's a violation of your frame of reference, because we know that the distances involved there are astronomical. The speeds are incredible. The time frame is all wrong.' But Nick was right. What *Star Trek* really wanted was a dogfight between two space ships. So this is where Mike Minor and I came up with the idea: Let's stage the final confrontation in

a nebula and how we can see *Enterprise* come up behind the other ship and pow! And they can play hide and seek through this nebula. And I think it was quite successful. But this is what I say: Let's be honest within our framework."[5]

What the narrative required, then, was a ship and a nebula to confront the crew of the *U.S.S. Enterprise*. Enter the *Reliant*, originally storyboarded as a Constitution class, nearly identical in appearance to the *Enterprise*, which would have permitted the use of the same model and saved the production money. However, it became clear that audiences would have had quite the challenge figuring out which ship to root for if both were the same design. So Jennings and Minor produced a new design for the *Reliant*, with illustrations by Minor and graphic designer Carole Lee Cole.

Originally, the nacelles of the *Reliant* were positioned the same as the *Enterprise*, above the hull. However, an inadvertent turn of the blueprints created the distinctive look of the *Miranda*-class ship. Cole recalled, "They had done this nice little rough sketch of what this *Reliant* ship would look like and we sent it off to Israel, where Harve Bennett was making a movie about the life of Golda Meier. He took the envelope and pulled it out, and he pulled it out upside down and looked at this ship we had designed and he said, 'Well, okay.' So he signed off on the bottom, 'This looks fine to me.' And he sent it back. We got the package back and opened [it] and he had signed it upside down. So we spent about a half hour debating if we would send it back and say, 'Please turn this the

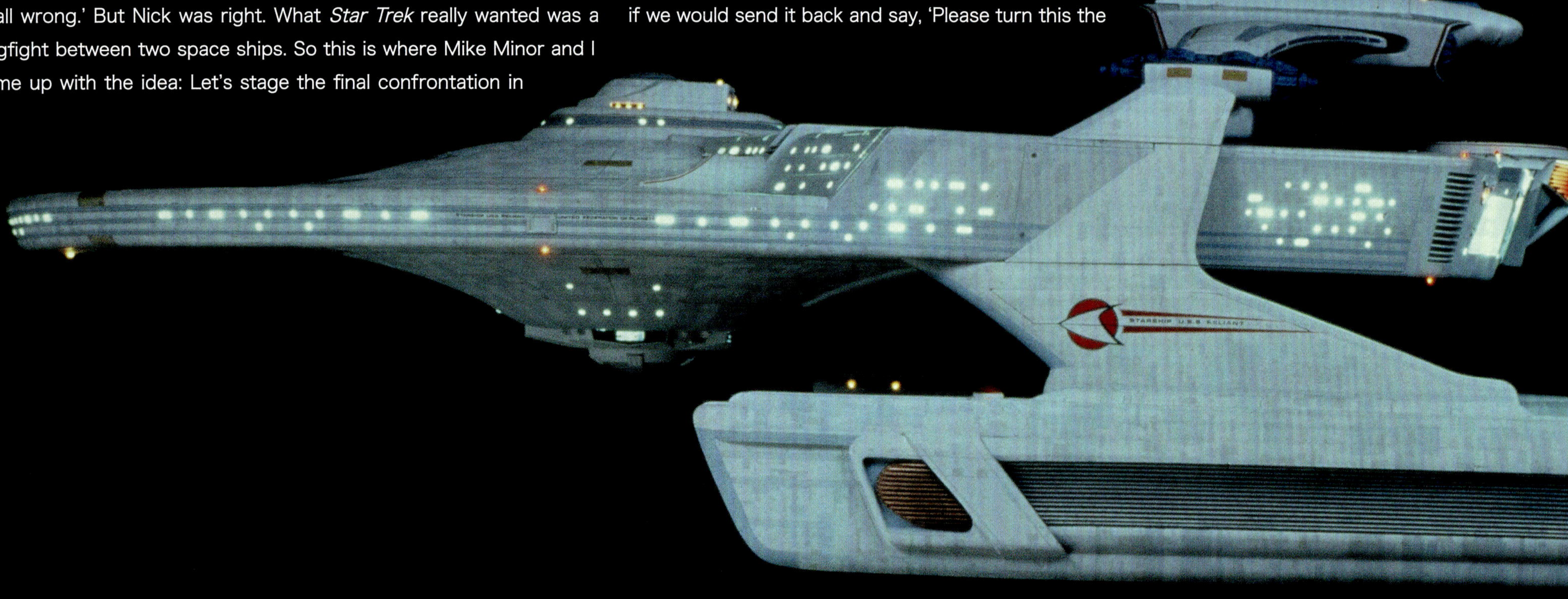

BELOW: The *Reliant*.

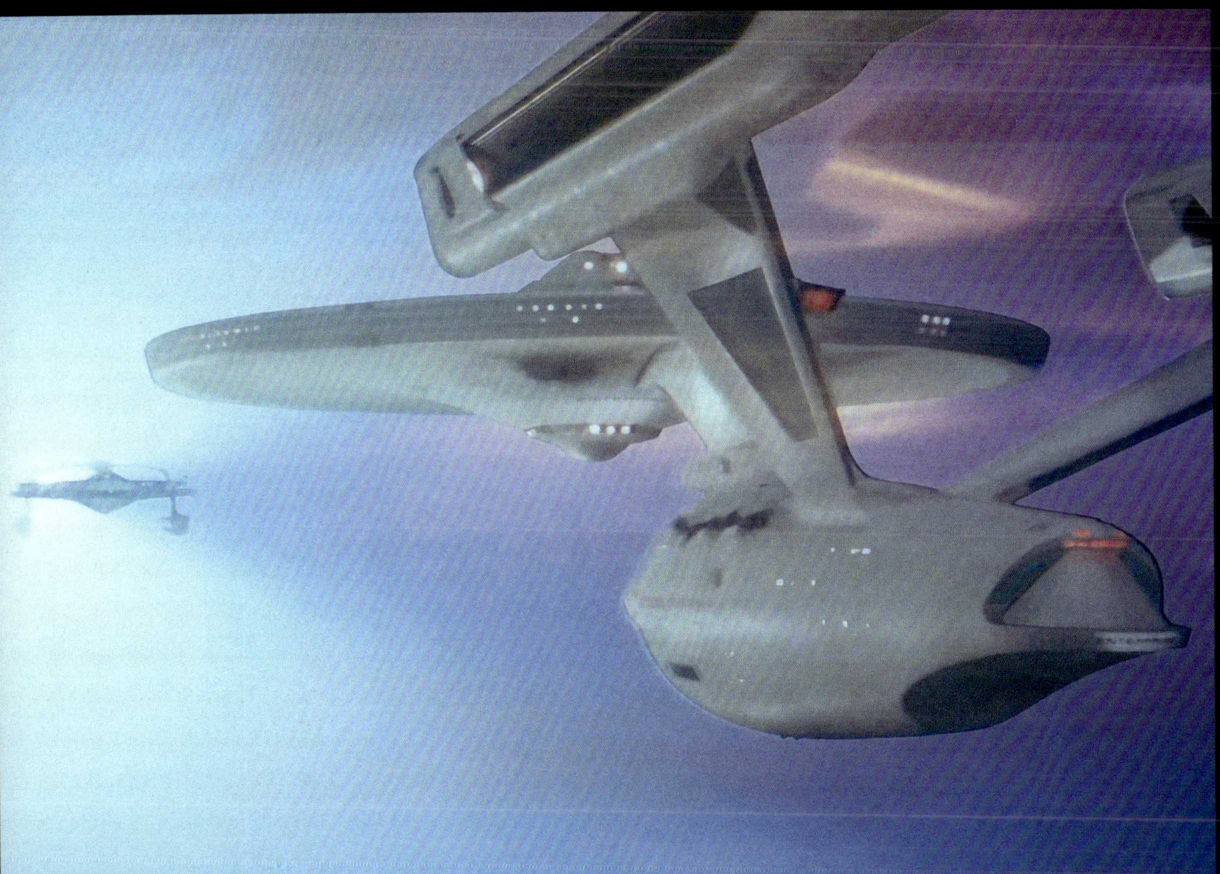

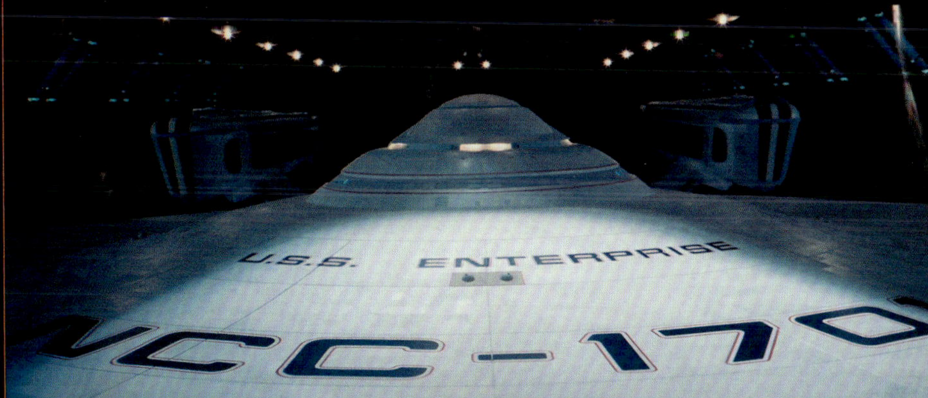

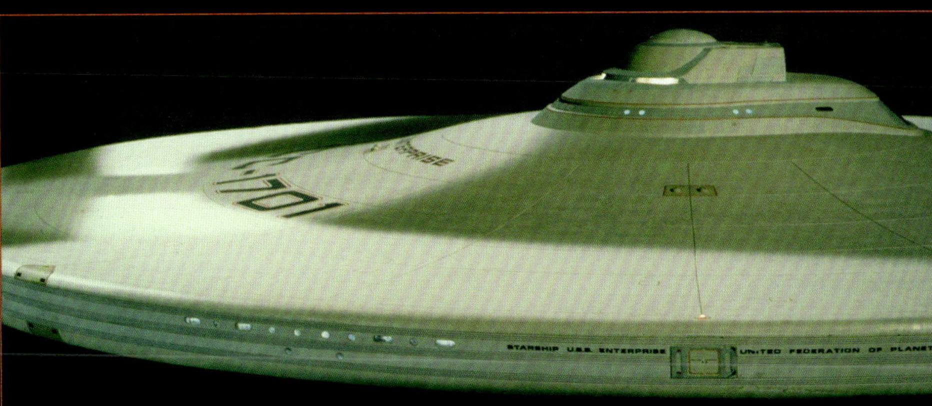

right-side up,' and finally Joe Jennings and Mike Minor said, 'You know, I don't think there's time to send it back to Israel and get it back here. Lee, why don't you see what you can do. Just take this upside down and make a ship out of it.' Turned out rather well. We made it work."[6]

Constructing the model would be the responsibility of ILM modelmakers under the supervision of Steve Gawley. Though working from the plans supplied by Jennings, the modelmakers still made some adjustments. "The one thing that was a little bit different on the drawings was that they had come up with a totally new color scheme for the graphics, thinking that would make it look different. They were done in like a yellow and green checkerboard," modelmaker Bill George revealed. "When I got them in, I said, 'This can't happen.' So I showed them to Ken Ralston. His take on it was, 'Let's put on the Federation graphics we've seen before and see what they say.' Thankfully, the producers were happy with that."[7]

The ILM model makers were guided by Minor and his design philosophy, which Jennings explained: "We kept the saucer. All right, that puts it in the same Navy. It's the same technology, different ship. You look at a Navy ship, you look at a destroyer, you look at a cruiser, you know they're American vessels and belong to the same navy, because they look alike in a lot of ways." ILM made two *Reliant* models, a smaller model of 17 x 10 x 4 inches and a larger studio model of 63 x 37 inches, during four months of 1981. The larger model would be modified and reused for subsequent movies and television programs. Some of its appearances were as the *U.S.S. Saratoga* (*Star Trek: Deep Space Nine*), *U.S.S. Lantree*, and *U.S.S. Bozeman* (*Star Trek: The Next Generation*).

The *U.S.S. Enterprise* model was a reuse of the one built by Magicam, Inc. for *Star Trek: The Motion Picture*. Supervising modelmaker Steve Gawley recalled, "I believe it was a 4 or 5 foot diameter dish, and I think the overall length was maybe 10 feet plus. Our biggest fear was dropping it. It took maybe eight or nine people to move it, and you could only hold on to the center area; you couldn't hold on to the engines."[8] In addition to its size, another challenge was the paint, because the bluescreens were reflected on the hull. By using a chalk dust and dulling spray, visual effects cameraman Scott Farrar was able to film the model more effectively. The *Enterprise* also needed new rewiring, done by Marty Brenneis and his model electronics team.

ABOVE LEFT: The *Reliant* confronts the *Enterprise*.

ABOVE: The *Enterprise*.

✪ KEN RALSTON

During the 1970s, Ken Ralston got his start working on advertising campaigns and television commercials. After helping make two hundred commercials, Ralston had gained experience with everything from stop motion to model creation, from optical compositing to animation. In 1976, Ralston was hired as one of the first employees of ILM, working on the original *Star Wars* film as a miniature and optical effects assistant camera operator. *Star Trek II* was the first film for which Ralston was a visual effects supervisor, a role he continued to play on many subsequent films, including *Star Trek III: The Search for Spock* (1984), *Cocoon* (1985), *Back to the Future* (1985) and its sequels, *Star Trek IV: The Voyage Home* (1986), *Who Framed Roger Rabbit* (1988), and *Forrest Gump* (1994). A fan of creature work, he is the inventor of the design of the Ceti eel (see Chapter 9) and worked the puppet of Kruge's pet and the macro microbes on the genesis planet of *Star Trek III*. Ralston would win five Academy Awards® for his pioneering work.

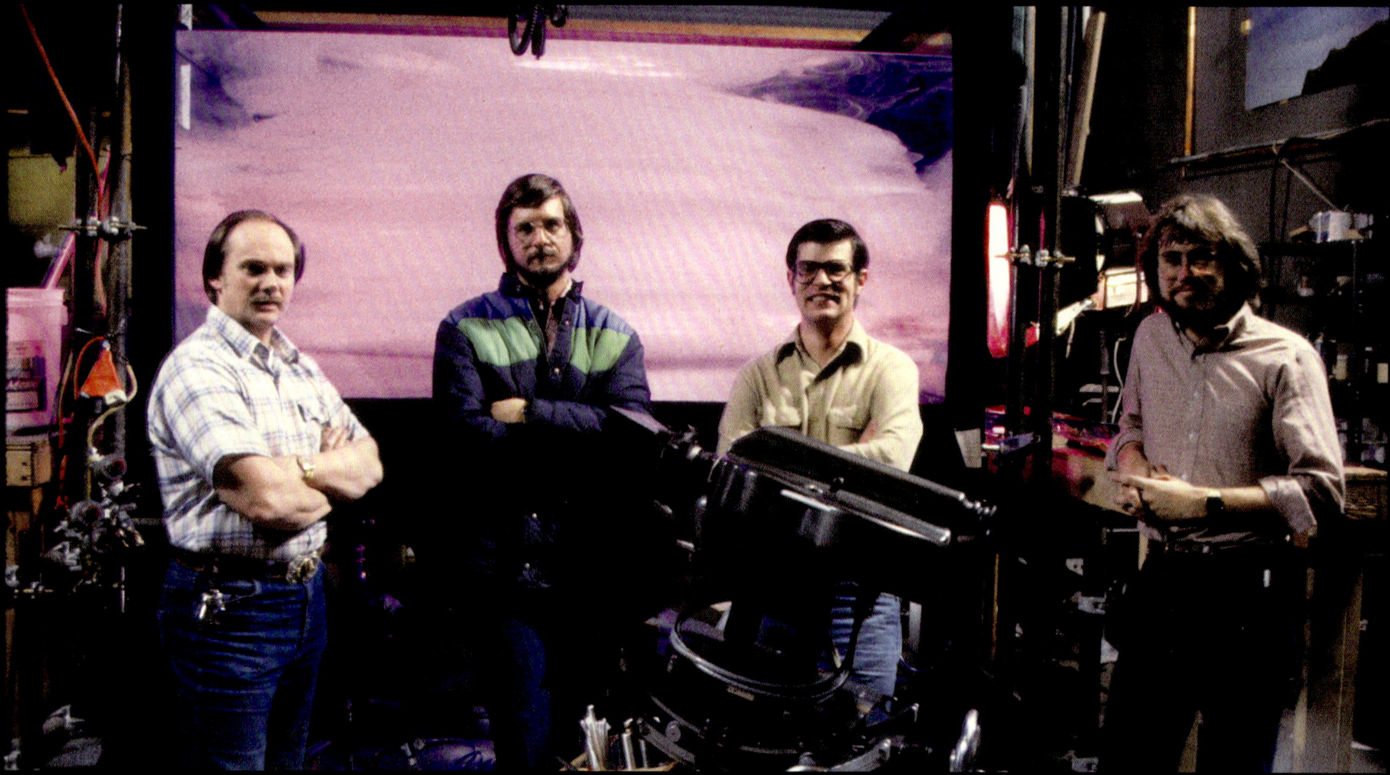

© Industrial Light & Magic

LEFT: Ralston, second from left, with effects cameraman Don Dow and assistant camera operators Selweyn Eddy III and Mike Owens in front of the tank that was used to create the Mutara Nebula.

⬟ JIM VEILLEUX

Despite Jim Veilleux being a real nuclear scientist, having earned a degree in nuclear physics from the Massachusetts Institute of Technology, his career would reflect his passion for cinema and photography. After earning a Master's degree in cinematography from the University of Southern California and time in the United States Army serving during the Vietnam War, Veilleux began a career as a camera operator and special effects artist working on television and educational films. His reputation for smart and creative innovations was one reason he was considered to help produce effects for *Star Trek Phase II* during 1977, the television series that eventually morphed to be *Star Trek: The Motion Picture*. Veilleux would join ILM during its production of visual effects for *Star Wars: The Empire Strikes Back*. During the 1980s, his interest turned to computers and programming, something that would affect the making of *Star Trek II*, which is considered among the first films to ever use computer-generated image effects. Veilleux passed at age sixty-nine in 2013.

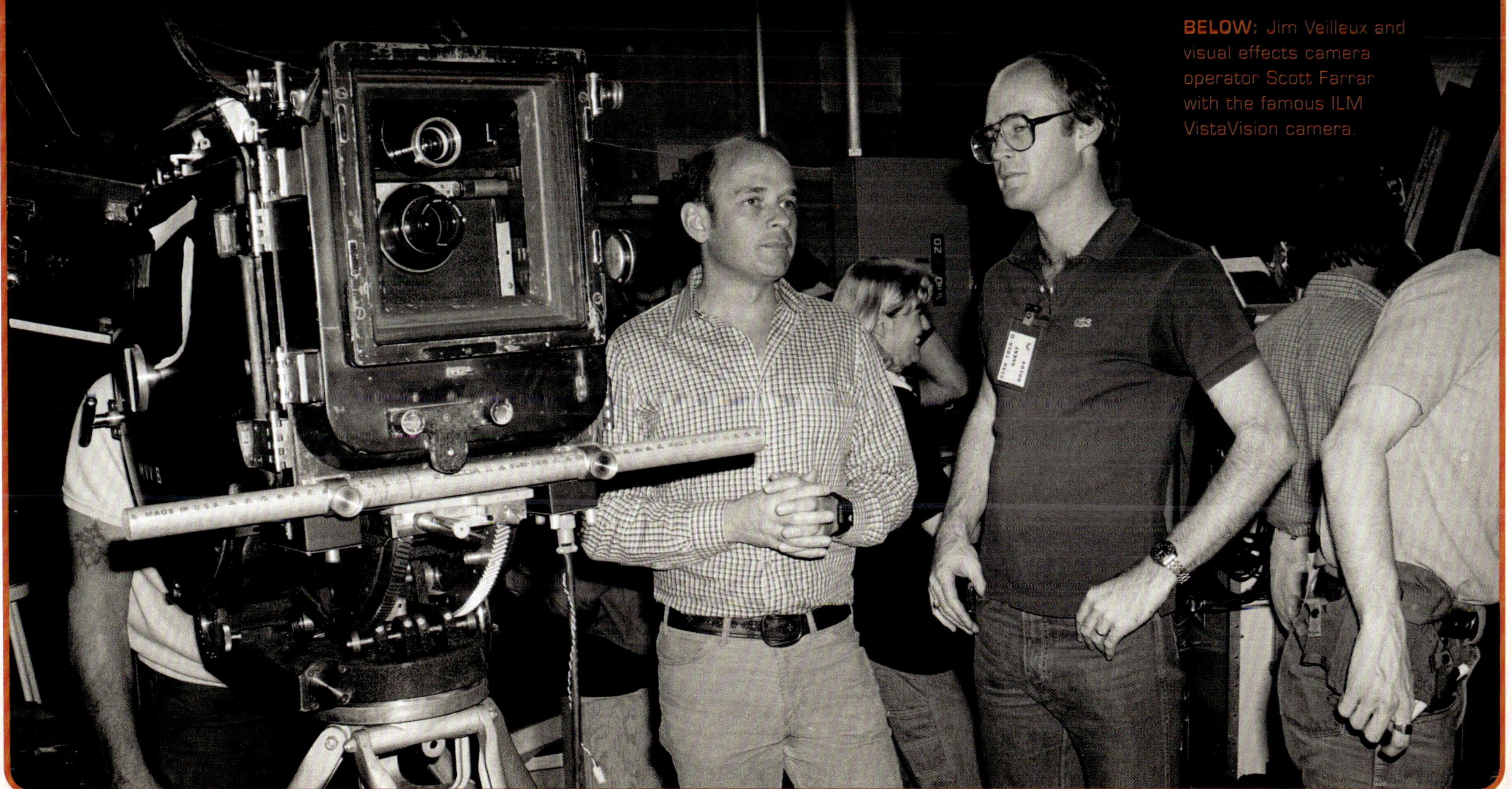

BELOW: Jim Veilleux and visual effects camera operator Scott Farrar with the famous ILM VistaVision camera.

The first step in the creation of the nebula where the "dog fight" between the *Reliant* and the *Enterprise* would occur was both researching what real nebulas looked like and generating ideas for how to create a simulated version. Ralston's solution was to create and film a cloud tank. "It was probably 5 or 6 feet deep by 8 to 10 feet wide. I used this weird concoction of some kind of [liquid] rubber material mixed with white cartoon paint. It took a lot of care. If I remember this right, you'd put in a layer of salt water, lay a plastic sheet on the top of it, and then you'd put in a layer of just regular water. You would very gently remove the plastic, and the salt would keep an inversion layer where the two met so they wouldn't mix, and that would give you some interesting ways to play with what you did with the rubber. I had these long (for lack of a better description) turkey basters, and to make it more interesting you'd start to kind of churn the layers around a little bit and create these different shapes for it."[9] Because of the unpredictable nature of the shapes, it took days to film. Ralston and his team also experimented with lighting, trying to film whenever interesting shapes and patterns formed.

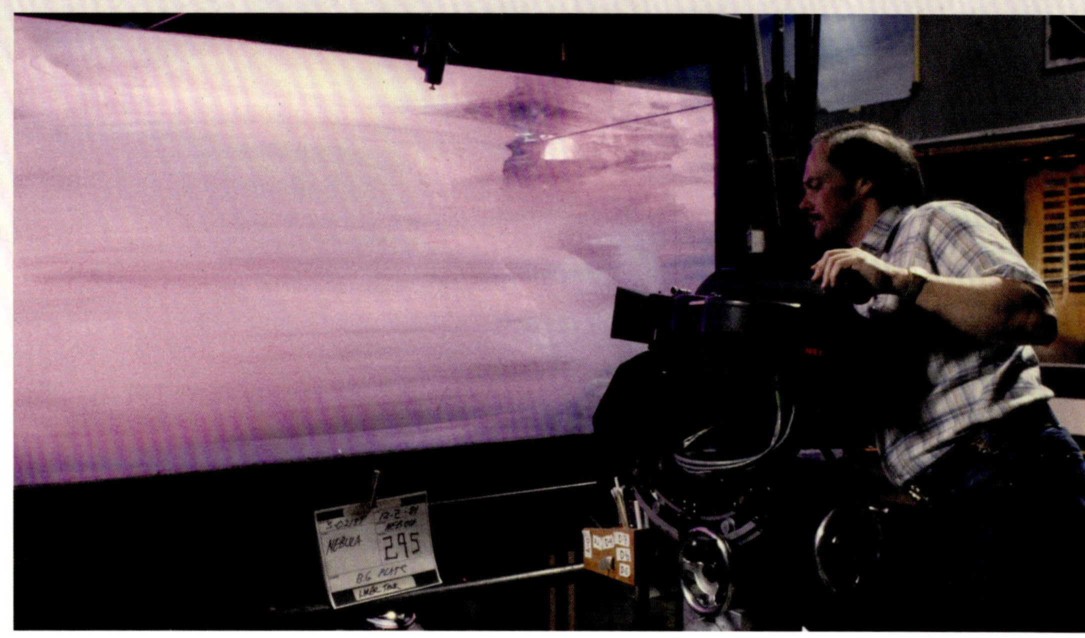

ABOVE: Dow operates the camera filming the Mutara Nebula cloud tank.
© Industrial Light & Magic

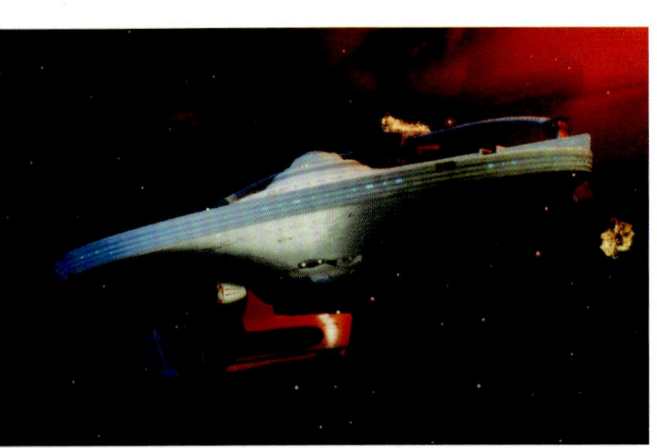

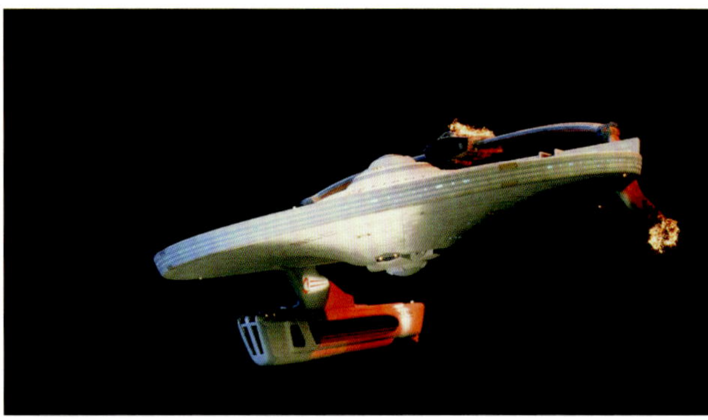

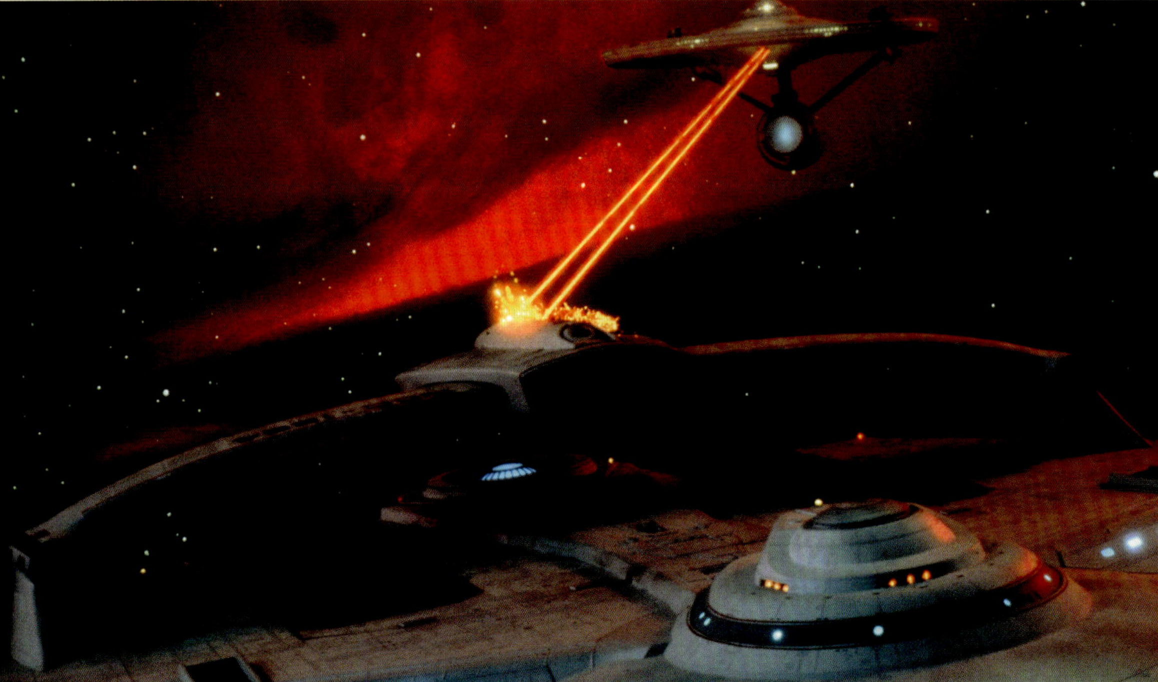

An important element of the Mutara Nebula battle were the phasers and photon torpedoes, created by animation supervisor Samuel Comstock and his team, Kim Knowlton, Scott Caple, Jim Keefer, Kathryn Lenihan, Jay Davis, and Judy Elkins. Elkins explained the process of animating phasers and photon torpedoes: "We used animation stands. We had some that were called lockdowns, so they did not move. This overhead camera was for the rotoscoping. And they had very large, custom cels, made by ILM. You shoot your art backlit. The animation cels were 18 or 20 field, 18 or 20 inches wide. Normal cartoon cels are 12 field, 12 inches wide, but we used 20 field at ILM, because you got a bigger image. The camera was locked down and pointed at a table that had open glass or plexiglass that could be backlit. You'd put your cel down and the camera would beam that image down, like on a slide projector, onto your workspace. Then you could trace. Since the cel was big, you were able to get more detail. With Rotoscoping, the exposed film is put into the camera and

LEFT: Elkins shares, "I remember one phaser shot that hit the *Reliant* and the engine pod caught on fire. The phaser was done on clear animation cels with black tape and paper. The fire was very simple—holes made with torn black paper for rough edges, photographed with colored filters and the optical department put them together."[17]

⊕ JUDY ELKINS

Judy Elkins first saw the 1968 film *2001: A Space Odyssey* while a junior high student and was inspired to wonder how it was that the visual effects had been achieved. She studied art and photography in college and took film-making classes teaching stop motion animation using both Super 8 and Oxberry animation cameras. After time spent as a traditional art teacher, Elkins worked in film labs, where she learned about film processing, camera lenses, film stocks, and color correcting. Films continued to inspire Elkins, notably the amazing snow battles scenes of *Star Wars: The Empire Strikes Back* that somehow, despite the white backgrounds, had achieved the amazing effect of compositing ships and Imperial walkers without obvious matte lines. Elkins observes, "The ILM optical department was very impressive. They skillfully combined elements from the other departments into final composites that looked real and natural."[15] Elkins joined ILM making rotoscoping mattes for *Raiders of the Lost Ark* (1981). She would serve as an animator on *Star Trek II* and then move to the ILM creature shop as a sculptor for *Star Wars: Return of the Jedi*. Returning to *Star Trek*, Elkins worked as a visual effects coordinator and supervisor on all seven seasons of *Star Trek: Deep Space Nine*, earning four Emmy nominations.

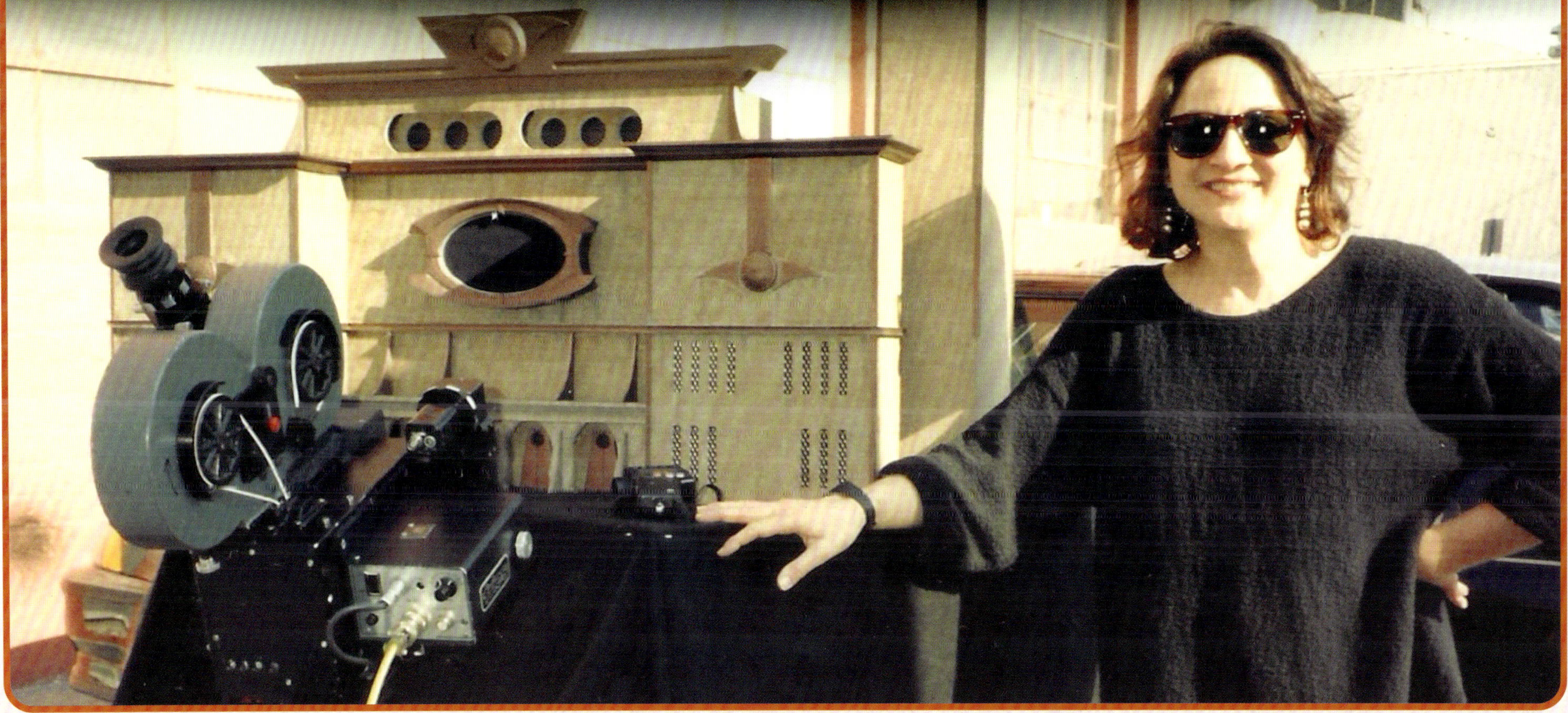

BELOW: Judy Elkins with a Cardassian building model. Elkins returned to the worlds of *Star Trek* after creating animations for *Star Trek II*. Image courtesy of Judy Elkins.

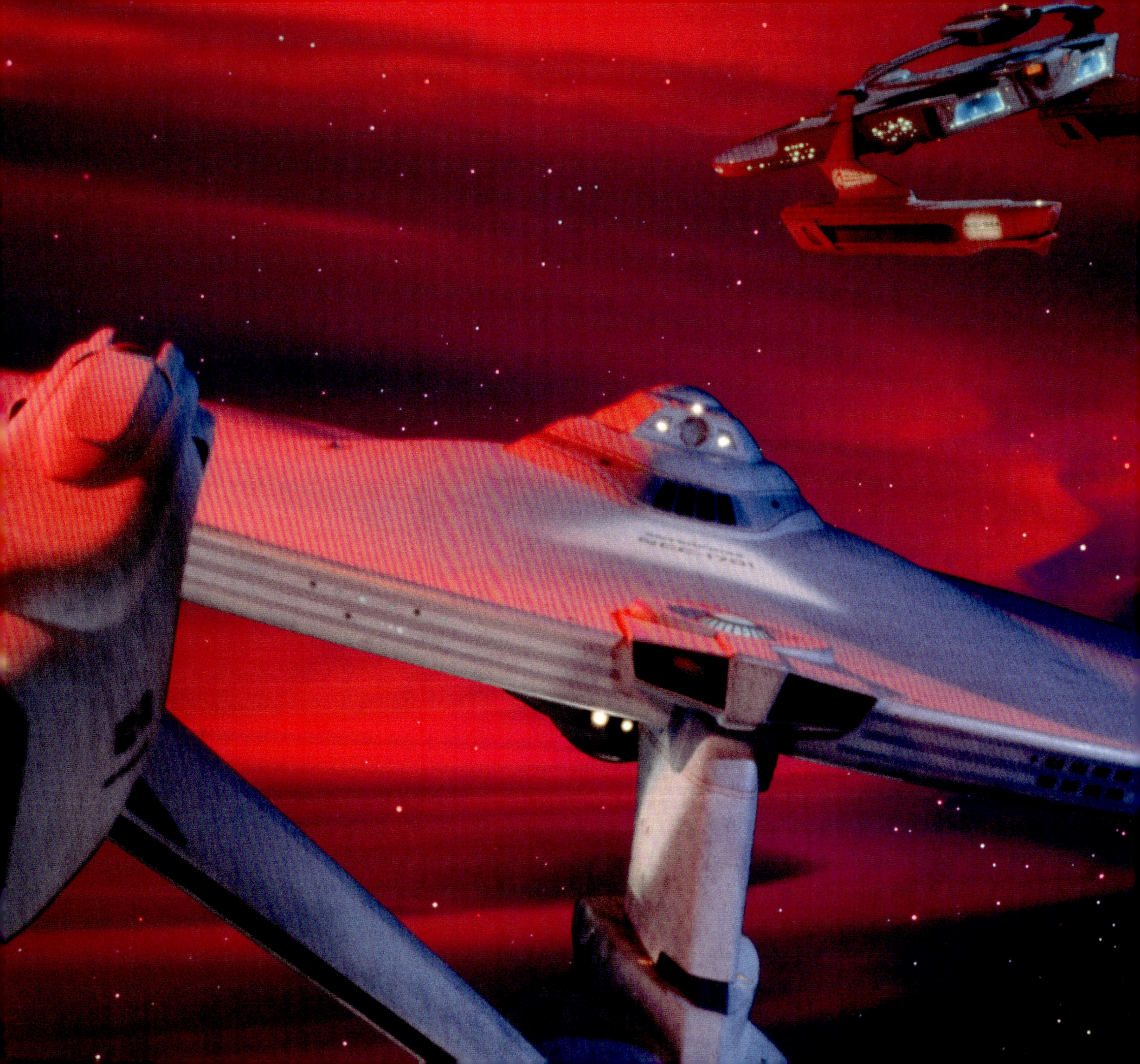

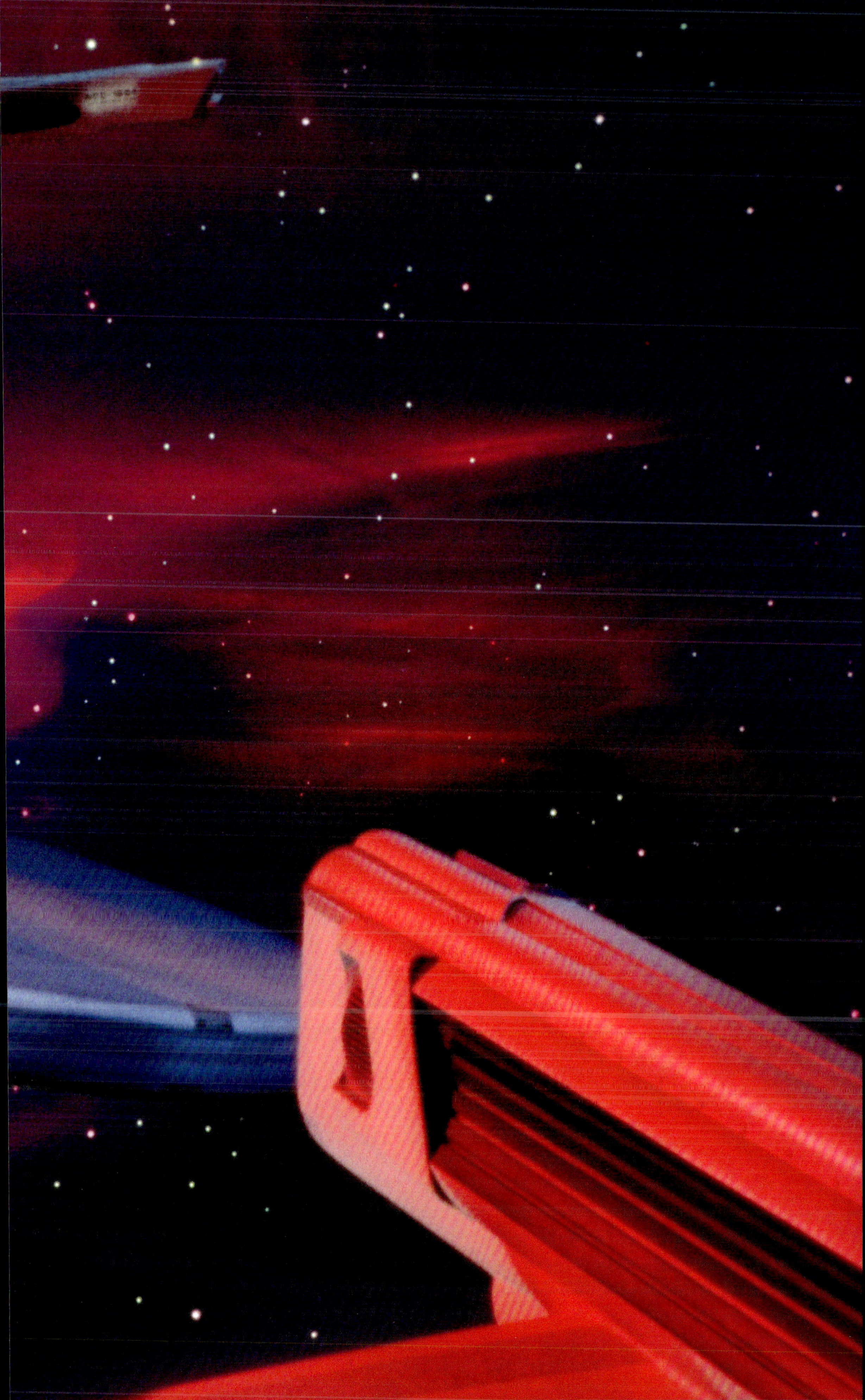

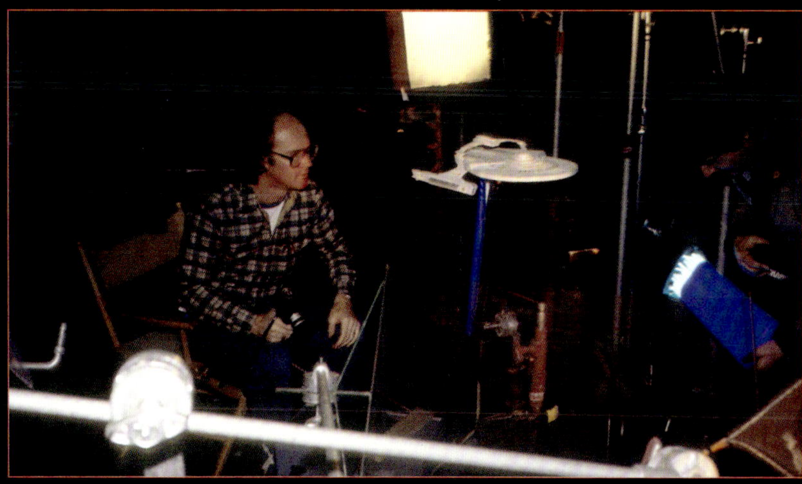

© Industrial Light & Magic

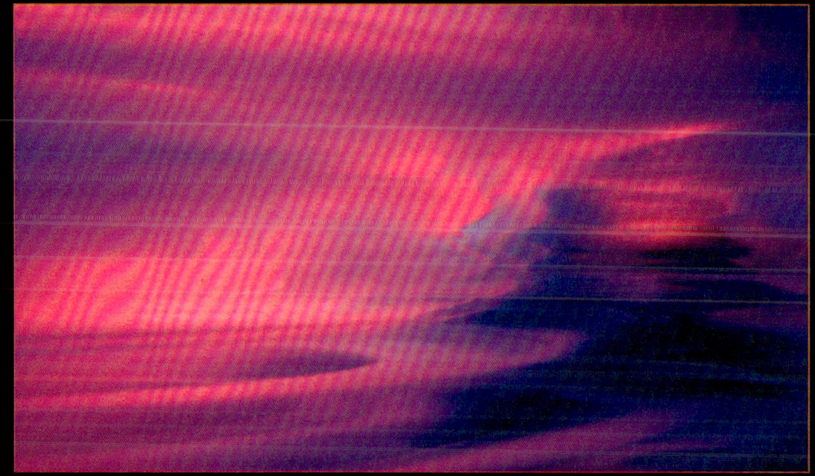

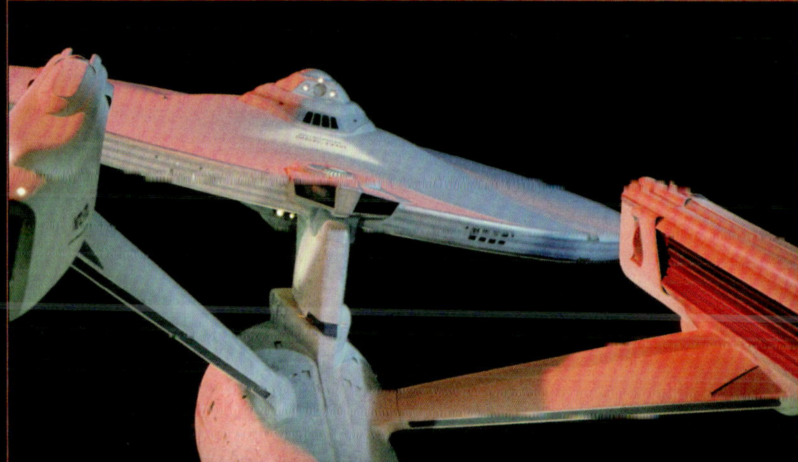

THIS SPREAD: *Reliant* hunts *Enterprise*: Farrar films the smaller model, with its under hull mounting arm colored the same as the bluescreen background (top); the Mutara Nebula generated in the cloud tank (above middle); the *Enterprise* model with the bluescreen removed (above); the composited shot as it appears in the film (left).

projected onto paper or an animation cel. A prism is inserted next to the camera movement to direct a bright light source from the camera to the paper. For the phasers, they would start with a large acetate cel and create a clear window with black tape and special black paper to create the path the phaser would follow. Rotoscoping was used to plot the position and movement of the phasers. The artwork was then created to follow the path of movement."[10]

Hesitant to damage the expensive studio model, the painful moment when the *Reliant* phasers surgically open the side of the *Enterprise* was done using clever chicanery. A wax replica of one section of the *Enterprise* was created, large enough to provide detail, yet cheap enough to damage as needed (right). Ralston used stop-motion photography and air-brush painting on the replica section to achieve the burning effect. Elkins explained that the team then "matched the animation to look like the phaser was raking across that."[11]

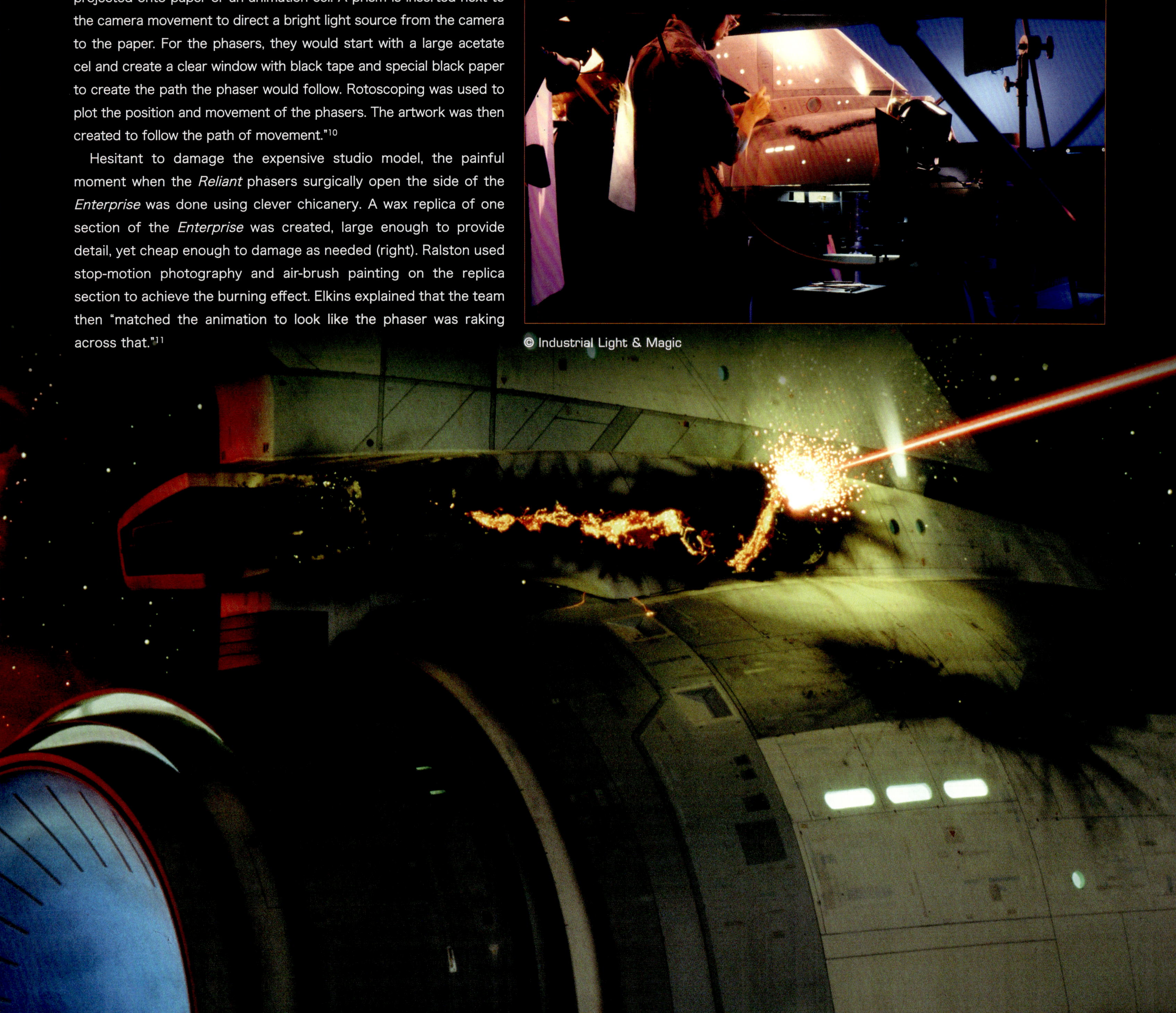

© Industrial Light & Magic

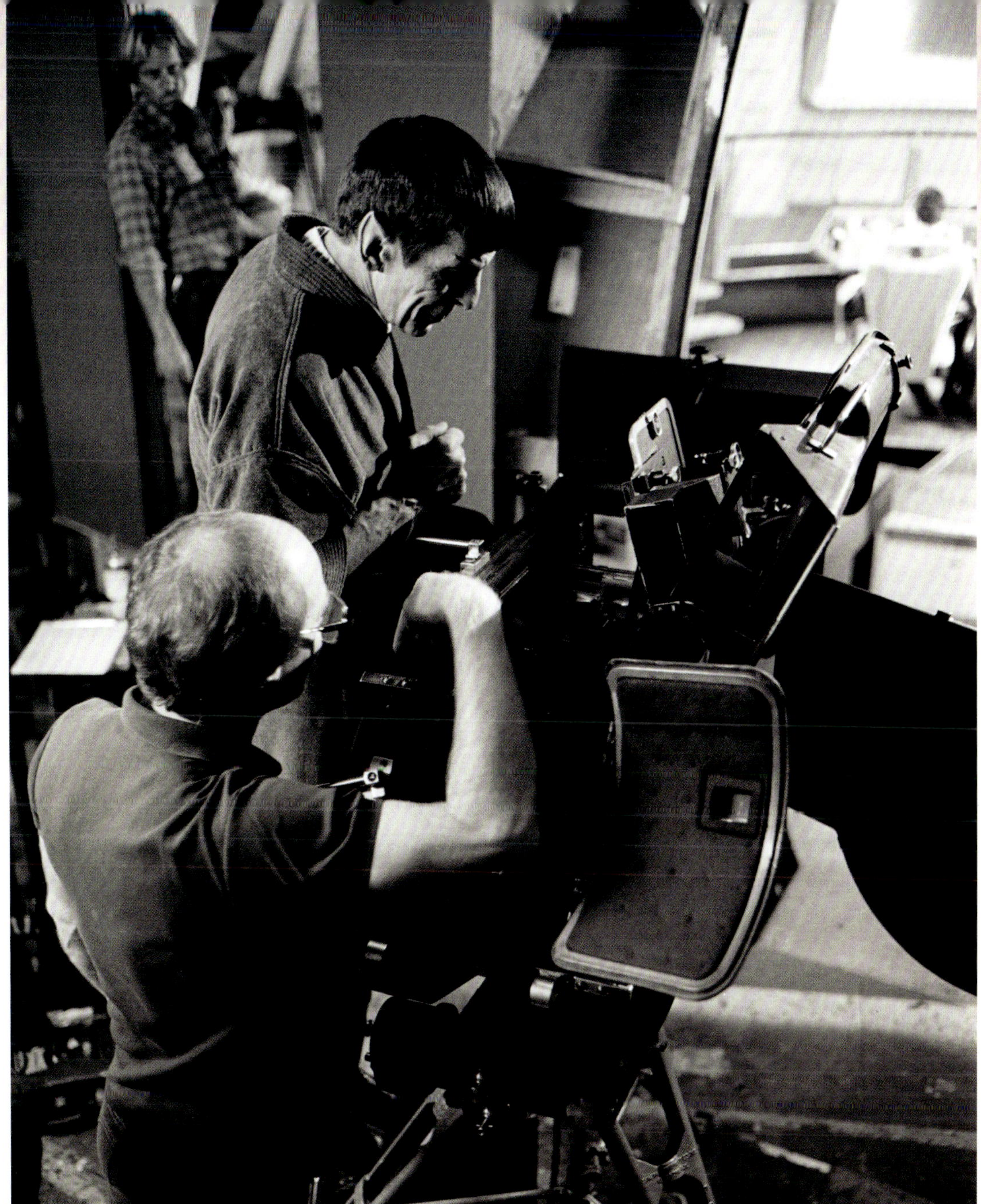

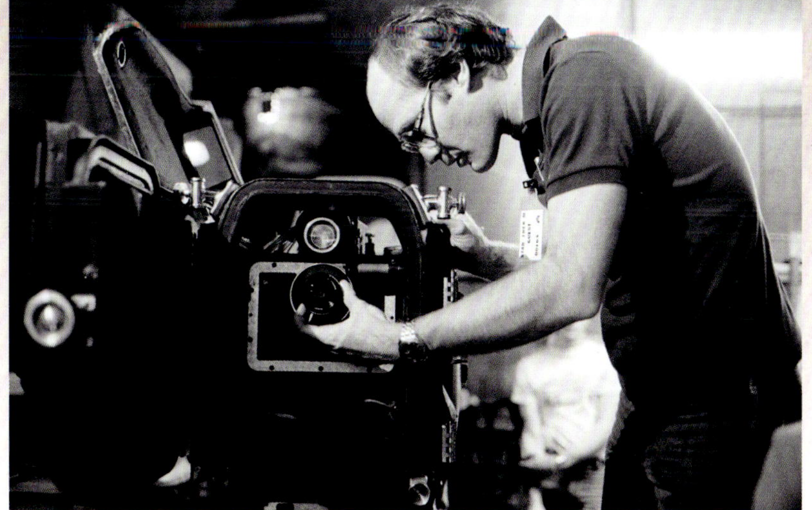

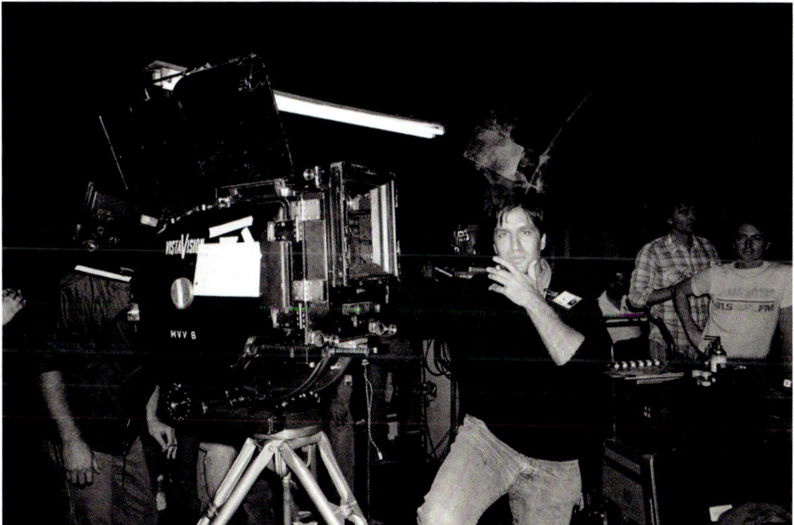

LEFT: During a break from filming on the bridge, Leonard Nimoy peaks inside the VistaVision camera on the set of *Star Trek II*. A unique feature of the ILM VistaVision was the orientation of the 35mm film negative horizontally, which benefited filmmakers during the pioneering steps into widescreen formats during the 1950s. Nimoy would direct *Star Trek III: The Search for Spock* and *Star Trek IV: The Voyage Home*.

TOP: Farrar prepares for filming with the VistaVision.

During scenes involving the crew looking at the viewscreen while they are visible and moving in frame or when requiring background plates for compositing, a special camera was used, flown in by ILM to the Paramount sets, the VistaVision. Invented by Paramount Pictures in 1954, although other cameras had subsequently come to take the bulky camera's place on movie sets, special effects artists during the 1970s, especially those working on *Star Wars*, would begin using adapted versions of the VistaVision. This was because the larger negative the camera produced permitted more effective optical compositing and the weight of the camera produced a more stable image. The specific VistaVision camera used on *Star Trek II* had seen its fair share of Hollywood history. Meyer remembers, "It was the camera they used for *North by Northwest* and *The Ten Commandments*. Those things were notched on the side, its credits were notched… The camera was flown down from ILM. I think George Lucas owned it. The reason they owned it was because you could make it so steady that if you were doing special effects shots and you didn't want any matte lines… you wouldn't get any shimmy at the edges. So every time we photographed events that were supposed to be happening on that forward viewing screen, that's when the VistaVision camera would come in."[12]

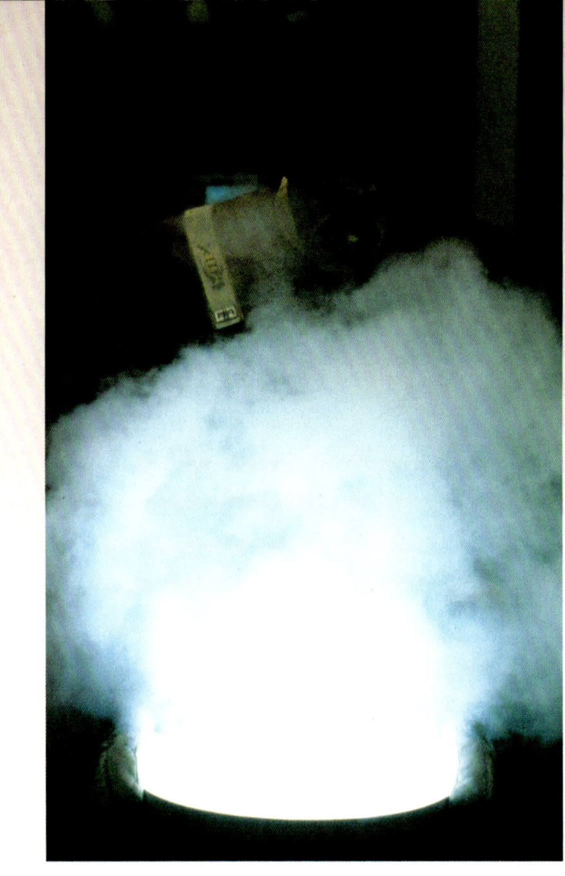

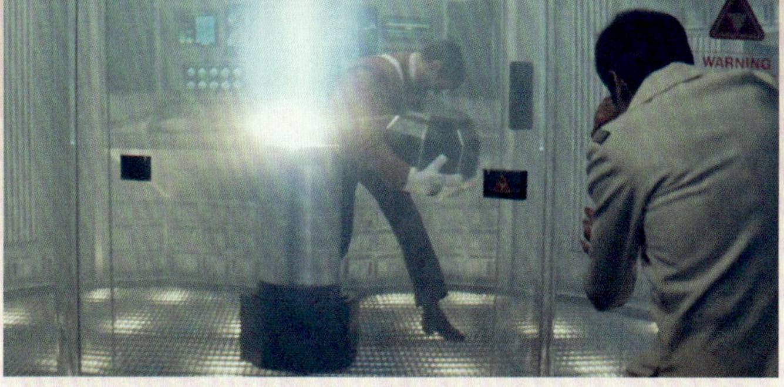

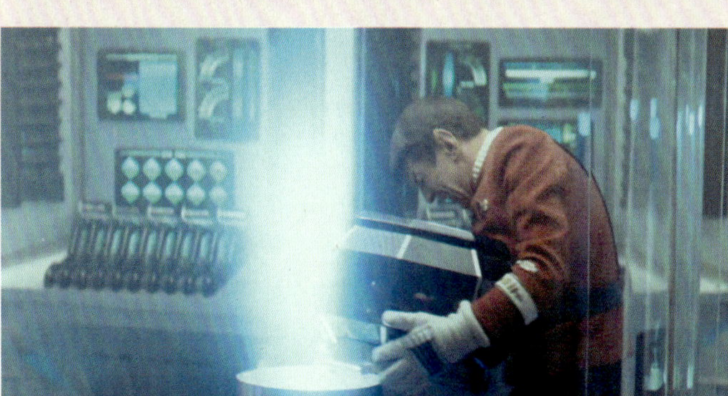

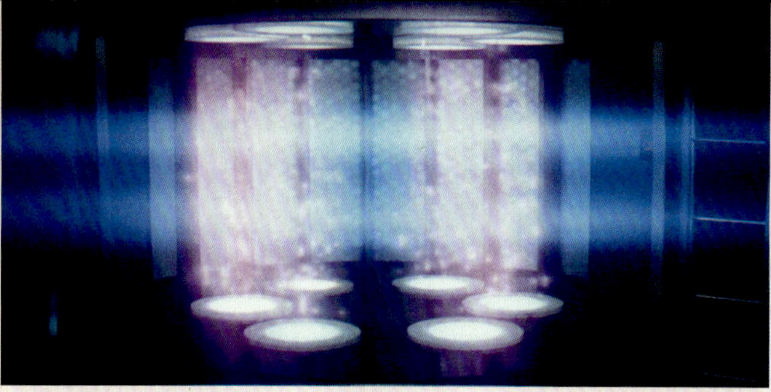

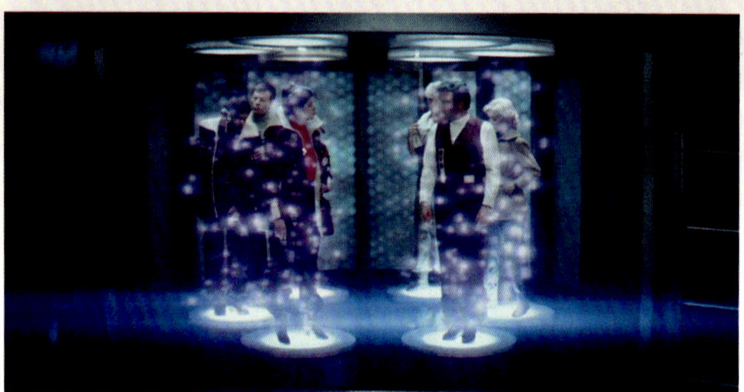

ABOVE: Some of the effects in the movie were not supplied directly by ILM. Instead, former ILM artist Peter Kuran's company Visual Concepts Engineering was contracted to produce transporter effects and augmented radiation lighting during the scene where Spock repairs the *Enterprise*. Comparing the on-set photograph of Nimoy (left) with the finished scene (above left) demonstrates how the added lighting and particle effects improve the moment.

Sometimes, time tested visual effects artistry is the better choice. To create the explosion of the *Reliant* and the Genesis Device, the team left the ILM warehouse and went to the Cow Palace in Daly City, California. The famous venue has been the location of sporting events and concerts by Liberace, The Beatles, and Elvis Presley, among many others. Stuntman Evel Knievel performed there and John F. Kennedy and Martin Luther King Jr. gave speeches at the arena. To generate the explosion effect, a high-speed camera was built by ILM with a prism that bent the image when filmed. Then, the ceiling of the Cow Palace was covered with a dark cloth to mimic space and an explosion was rigged from the rafters, so that the camera, filming upwards, would capture the effect from its perspective. This produced the illusion that the explosion occurred in zero gravity. Because the camera filmed at 2,500 frames per second, the explosion, which really lasted only 1.2 seconds, appeared to take much more time.

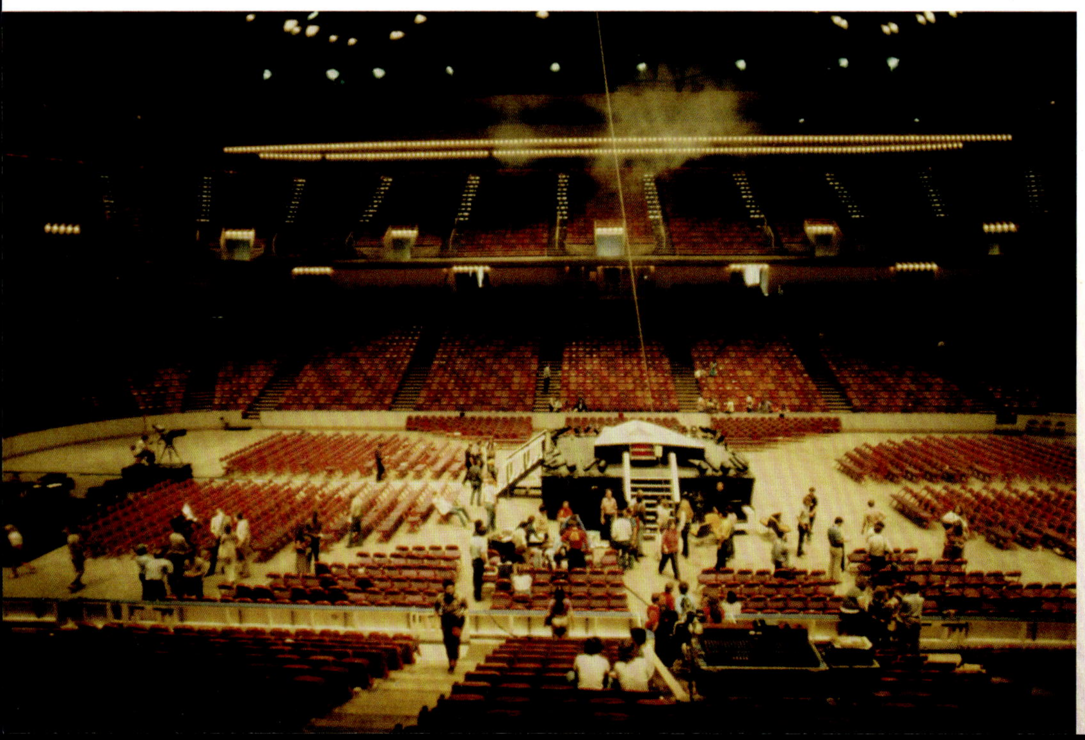

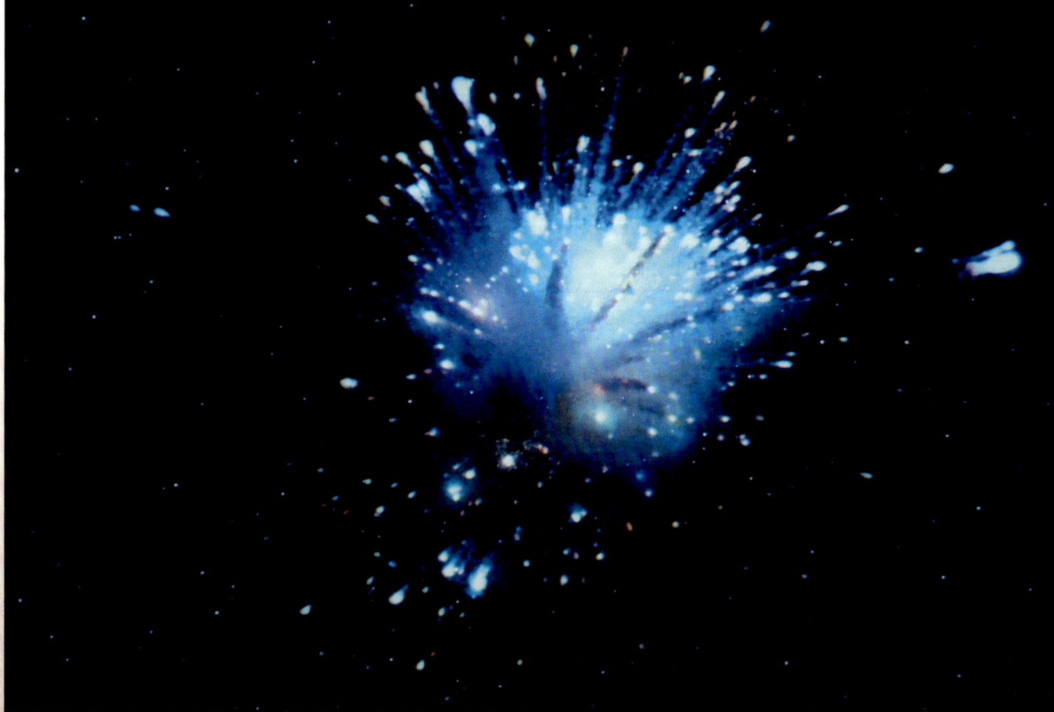

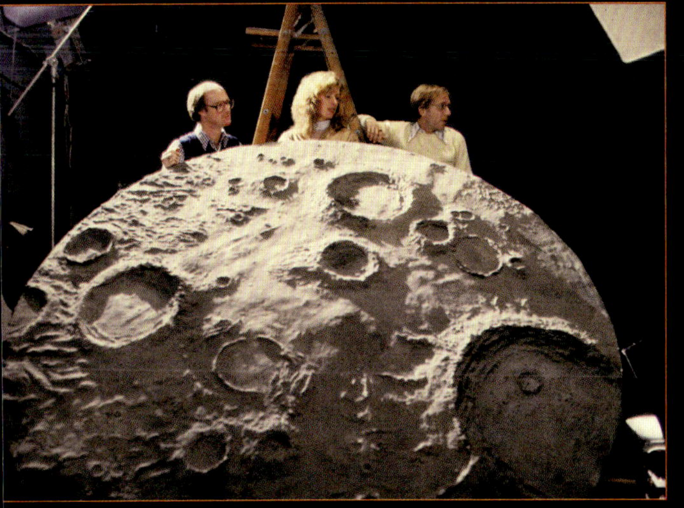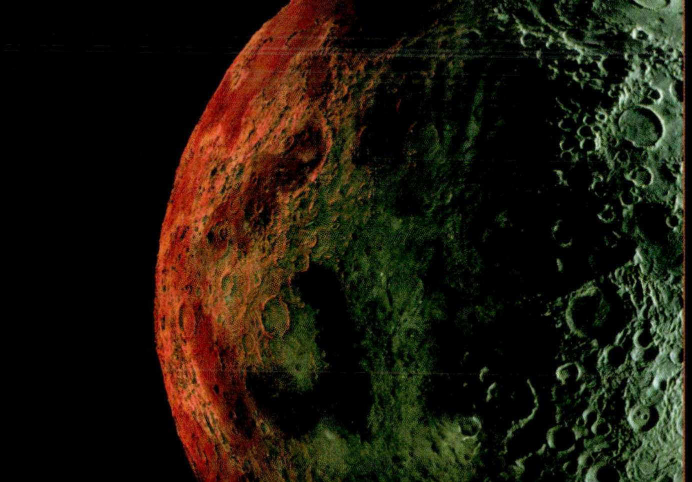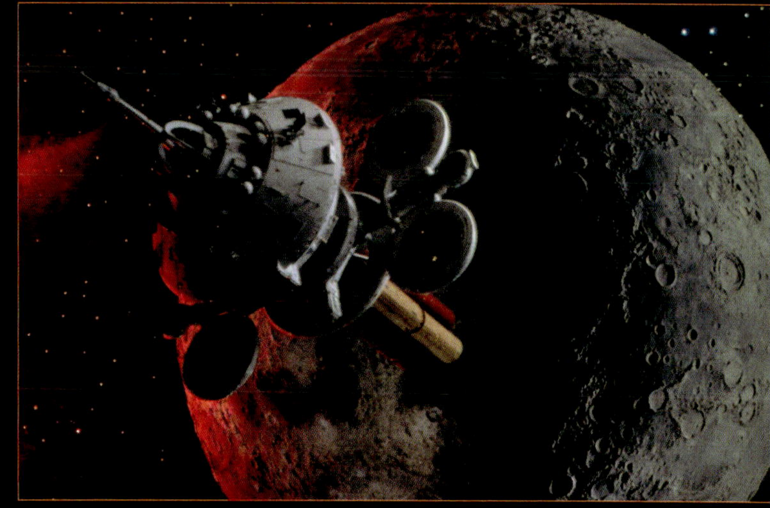

The collaboration of the *Star Trek II* production team and ILM as a solution to challenges and minefields was effective. The visual effects of *Star Trek II* were pioneering, proving the versatility of computer effects and forever changing the landscape of how movies were made. For Ralston, *Star Trek II* was important personally and professionally. "I loved it. You know, that's what I loved about ILM. If you could do a job, you had opportunities to do it. So it wasn't just, 'I'm going in to shoot spaceships and that is all I am ever going to do.' We wanted *Star Trek II* to be more like the energy and the fun of the TV series. And so that was one of our mantras during this whole process."[13]

At the time, Mike Minor summarized, "There are 150 effects shots in this film and they're all quite dramatic. We have a lot of great distance and perspective shots. You'll be awestruck when you see this floating city hit warp speed. This movie cost one third the amount of the first *Star Trek* picture but it is thirty times as exciting!"[14]

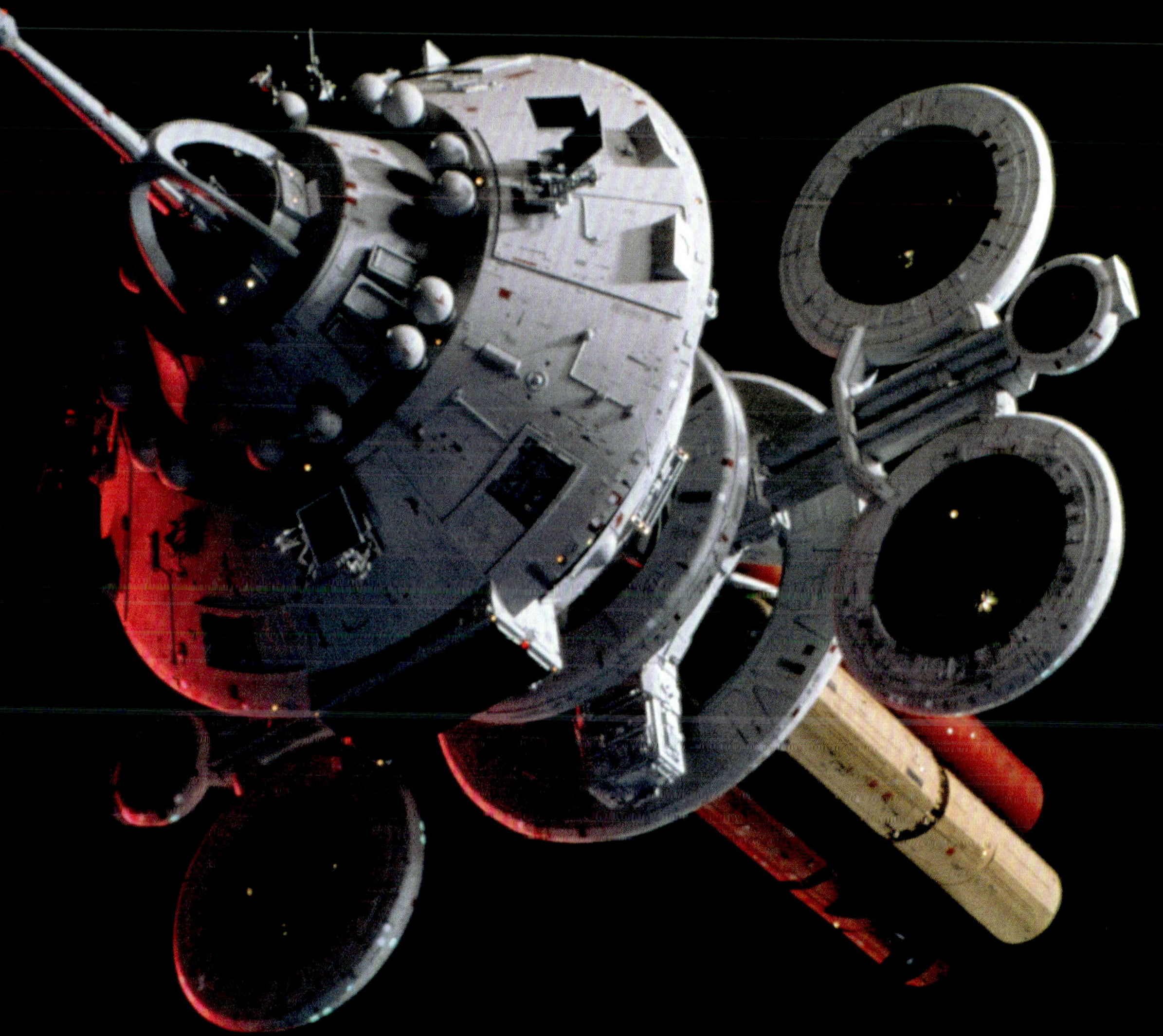

CREATING THE PROJECT GENESIS PROPOSAL SEQUENCE

1982 was a fulcrum year in visual effects artistry, when companies started seriously experimenting with computer generated effects. *Tron* was at theaters a month after *Star Trek II* and *The Last Starfighter* was starting production. The Computer Graphics Group of the Lucasfilm Computer Division, later Pixar, led by Dr. Edwin Catmull, made pioneering and significant contributions to the *Star Trek II* Project Genesis proposal scene. As originally scripted, Carol Marcus was going to demonstrate the power of Genesis by turning a rock in a zero gravity chamber into a flower, but Jim Veilleux thought the scene could be more dramatic and consulted with the Computer Graphics Group. The team used Loren Carpenter's 3D rendering program, named REYES, an acronym of Renders Everything You Ever Saw, to create a proof of concept of the *Enterprise* following a Klingon battlecruiser.

Alvy Ray Smith storyboarded and directed the sequence, which needed to be finished before March 19, 1982, giving the team only five months to produce the 67 second proposal scene.

Pat Cole rendered the retina scan of Admiral Kirk that begins the sequence. (1)

The inorganic to organic molecule sequence was rendered not by the Lucasfilm Computer Graphics Group, rather by Dr. Robert Langridge at the University of California San Francisco, a pioneer of 3D computer graphics of molecular structures. Veilleux asked Langridge for guidance, and Langridge was able to supply the production with an already generated computer model. (2)

Bill Reeves used a particle creation program to generate the fires of Genesis creation. (3)

Tom Duff created the moon sphere and crater textures. (4)

Carpenter, a former Boeing engineer, created a Mandelbrot fractal program that produced mountain landscapes for simulators and aircraft design. The technology and Carpenter's expertise was ported to ILM, who utilized his innovation to generate the mountains and atmosphere, among other elements of the demo moon. Because the mountains were generated randomly, a more natural and hence realistic environment was created as Genesis transforms the moon. The sequence was so effective that some in the audience felt their stomachs turn as if they were riding a rollercoaster. (5)

1

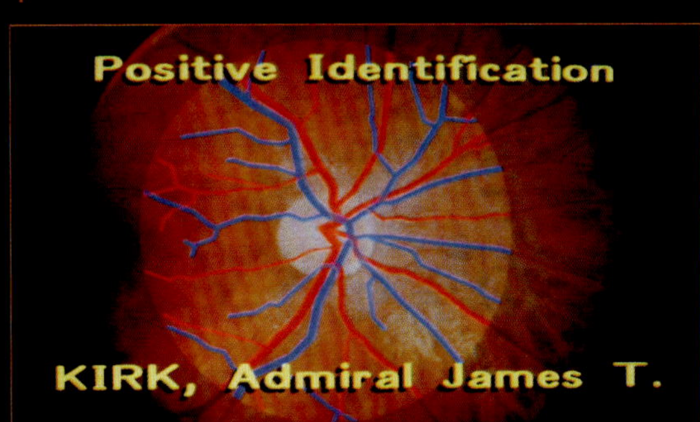

2

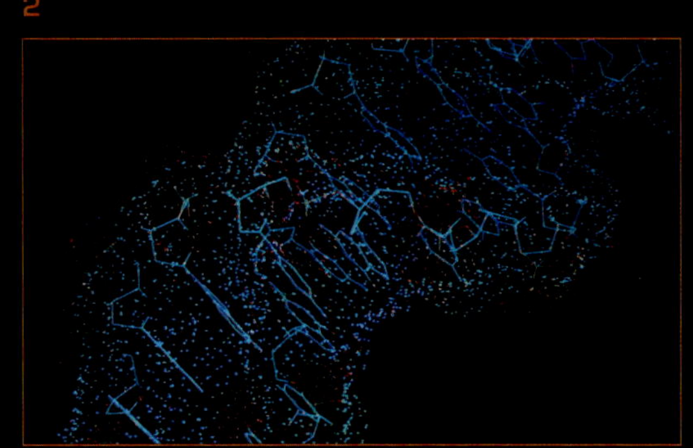

3

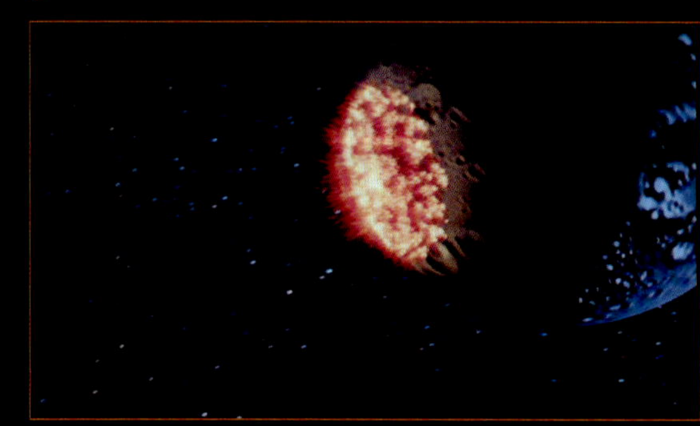

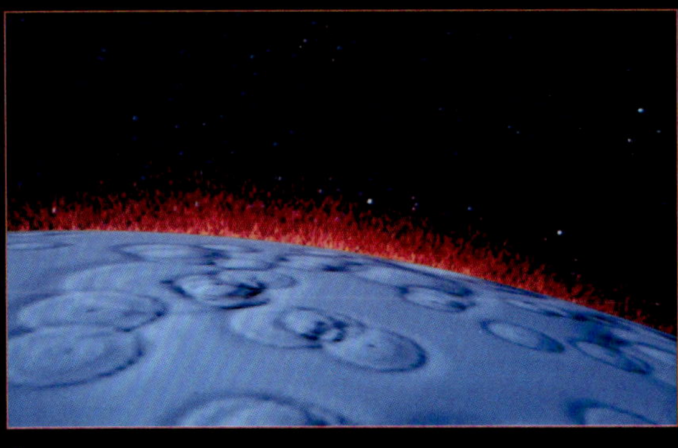

4

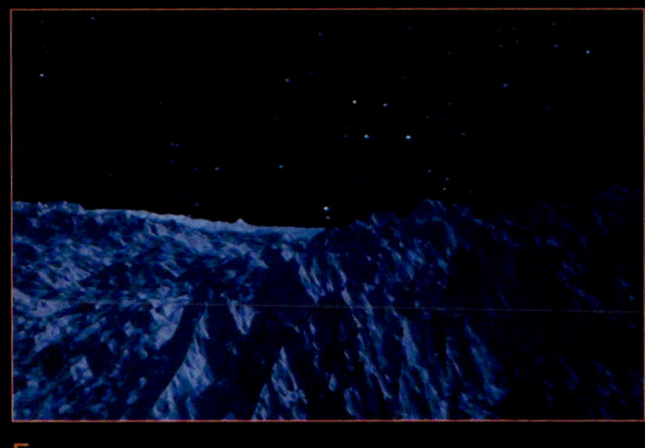

5

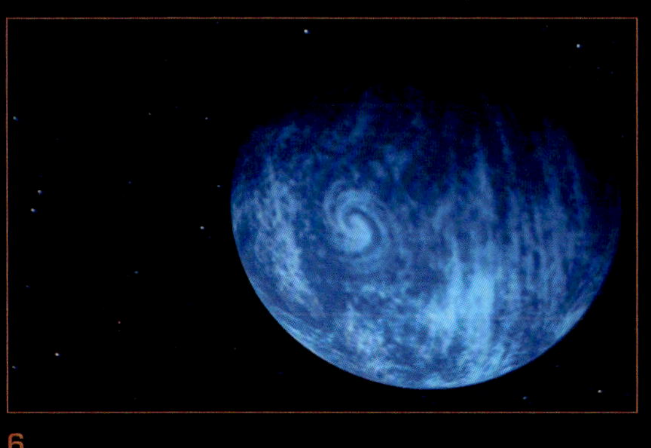

6

Chris Evans, usually a traditional matte artist, created the first digital matte painting for *Star Trek* when the transformed planet is finally seen during the demo. Thomas Porter developed one of the first paint programs and Evans used it and a light pen to produce the clouds and surface of the planet. As Evans drew with his pen, the computer recorded his art. (6)

Porter generated stars and composited the independent elements into its final form. Using a computer to composite had the benefit of no matte lines, which had historically been a problem for visual effects artists, especially when creating certain environments such as snow. To add to the realism, Catmull created motion blurring effects, randomly generated by the computer. (7)

Elkins reflected on what an important moment the Genesis proposal was for the future of visual effects: "The Genesis Project scene just blew our minds at that time. We had never seen anything like it and were amazed. That was a perfect use for computer generated effects. It would have been difficult if not impossible to do it with traditional animation or miniatures, and the look was perfect."[16] (8)

7

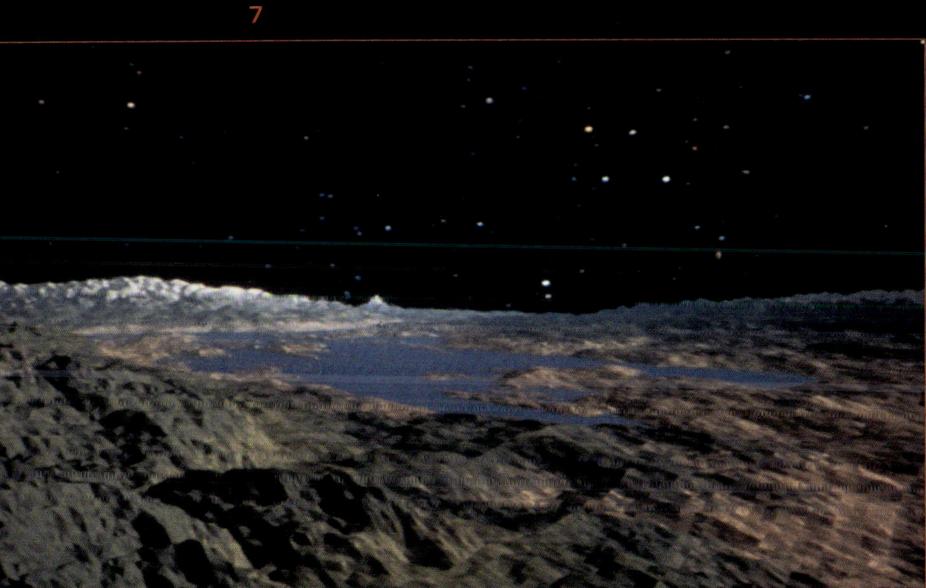

© Industrial Light & Magic

8

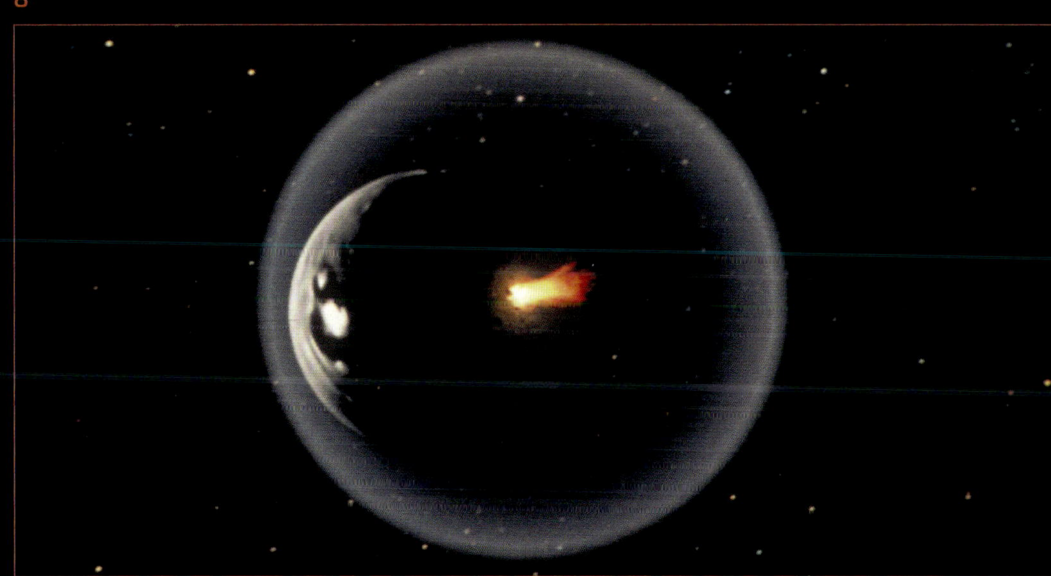

© Industrial Light & Magic

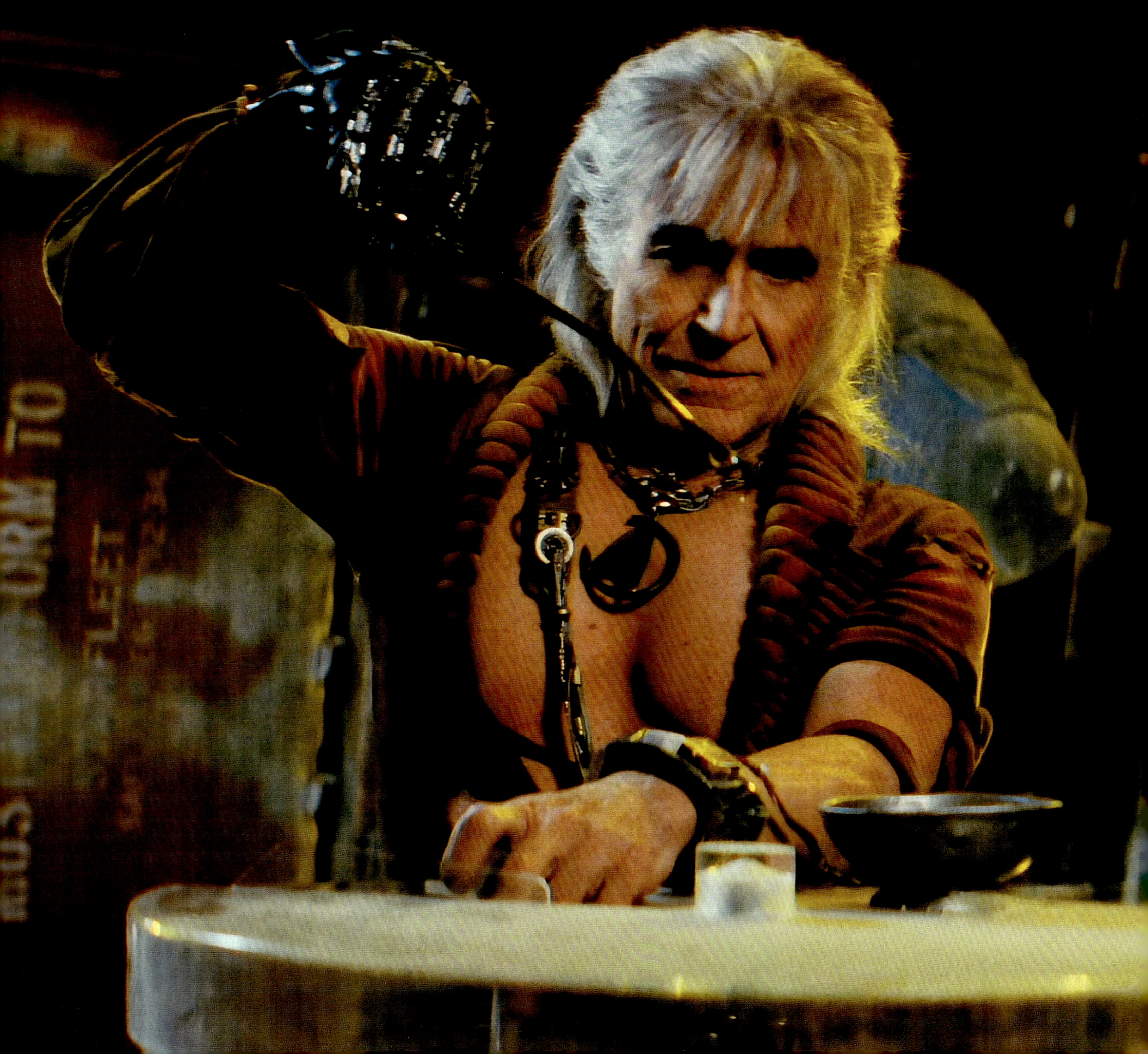

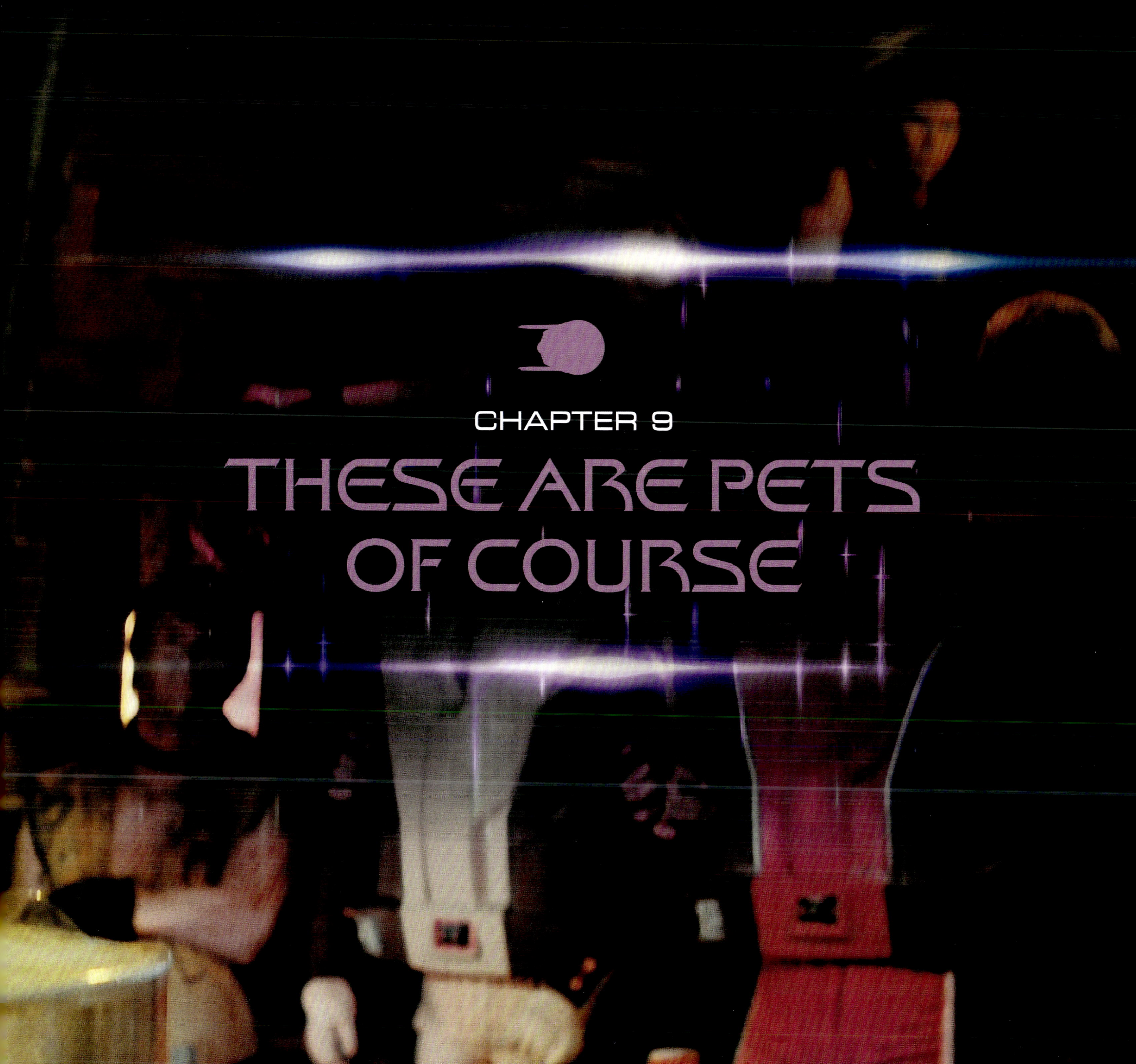

CHAPTER 9

THESE ARE PETS
OF COURSE

THE WEE BEASTIES OF CETI ALPHA

Although never named on screen, the creatures fans know as Ceti eels have a distinctive design. That, along with their ability to enter the ear, causing hosts to be susceptible to suggestion until madness and death occurs, has earned the creature an honored place among cinema's most cringe-worthy creations. The eels also serve an important story function in *Star Trek II*, permitting Khan to be a physically present threat despite him not being in the same room ever with Admiral Kirk. Via his mental control of Terrell and Chekov, Khan is able to apply pressure remotely and directly at the same time.

The eels began, however, in a very different form. Sowards saw the need for a creature that Khan and his wife Marla McGivers could use to gain control of Starfleet officers in his February 20, 1981 "The Omega System" screenplay. Much as with the final film, Khan uses creatures on Terrell and Chekov. However, they were not eels, but rather "creepy, crawling, 'Wee Beasties'… Like spiders, or crabs, only soft and slithery." The name is a nod to the poem "To a Mouse, on Turning Her Up in Her Nest With the Plough, November, 1785" by Robert Burns, about how Burns accidently destroyed a mouse's nest while farming. It is a poem about the interference of humans in nature, an apropos theme for *Star Trek II*. Unlike the eels, who burrow through the ear, the "Wee Beasties" would attach themselves to a person's back. Eighty-five percent of the creature is described as pure brain. In Sowards' script, the "Wee Beasties" control more than Terrell and Chekov, but the entire away team, including characters named Ray and William who attack Kirk and Savik as they search the desert for rebels led by Kirk's son David Wallace. After Savik saves Kirk from Terrell's attack, it would be Dr. Christine Chapel and Lieutenant Diana O'Rourke, the *Enterprise*'s new communication officer, who would discover that the "Wee Beasties" were indigenous to Ceti Alpha V and hence piece together that Khan was the real culprit.

Upon reading the script, Sallin noticed an uncanny similarity between the "Wee Beasties" and the hive-brained flying parasites that Captain Kirk and crew encounter on the Deneva colony in the episode "Operation – Annihilate!" Sallin reveals, "I said, 'Wait a minute, guys, that's "Operation – Annihilate!" That's straight out of the television show; everybody's seen that. There's no drama in that.' They kind of looked at me and said, 'Well, great then. You go figure it out.' So the

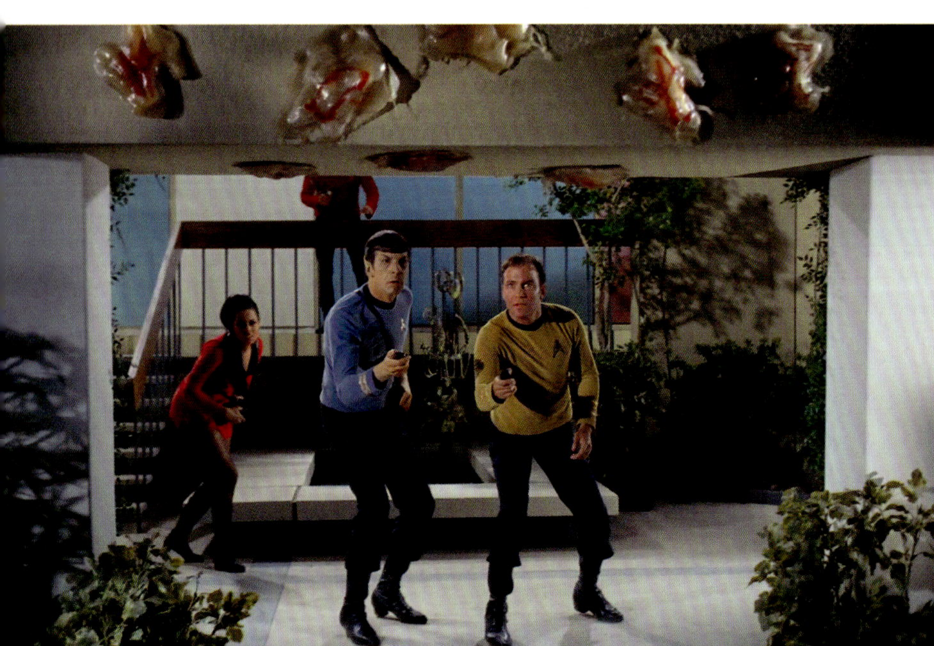

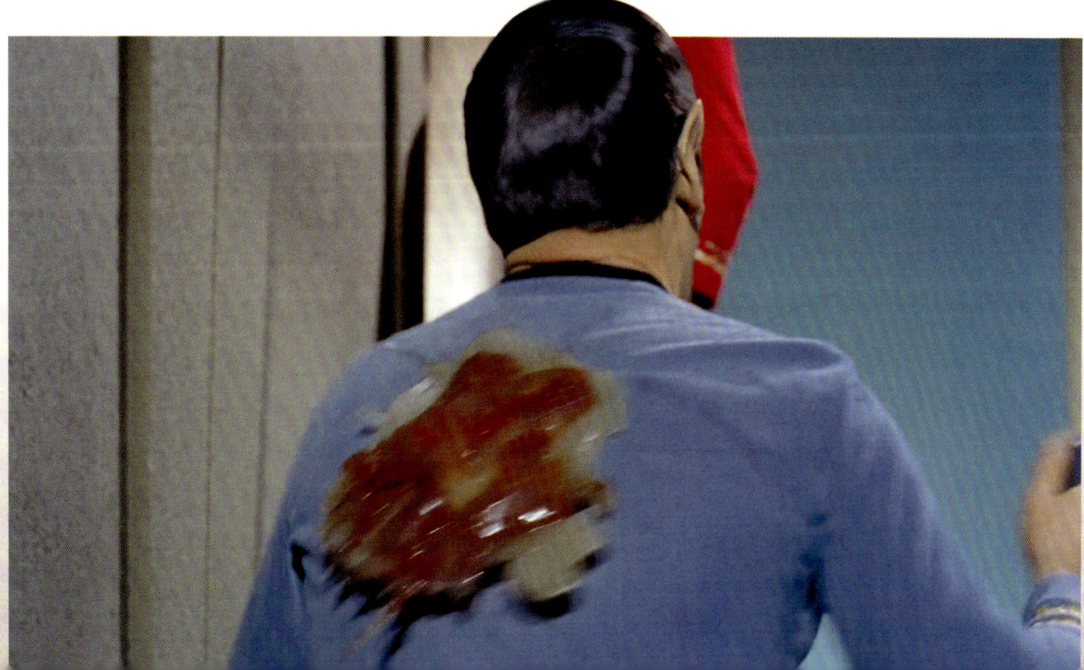

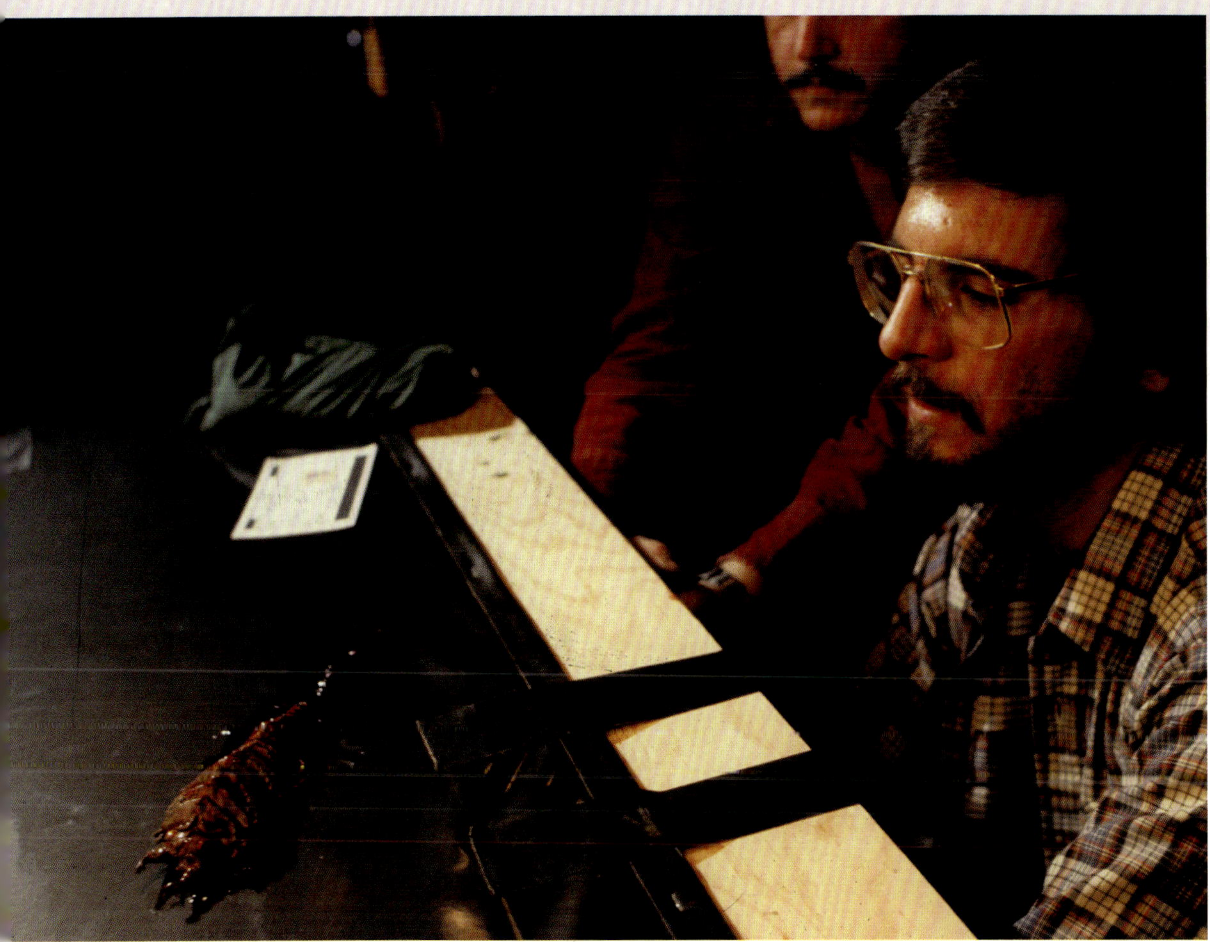

© Industrial Light & Magic

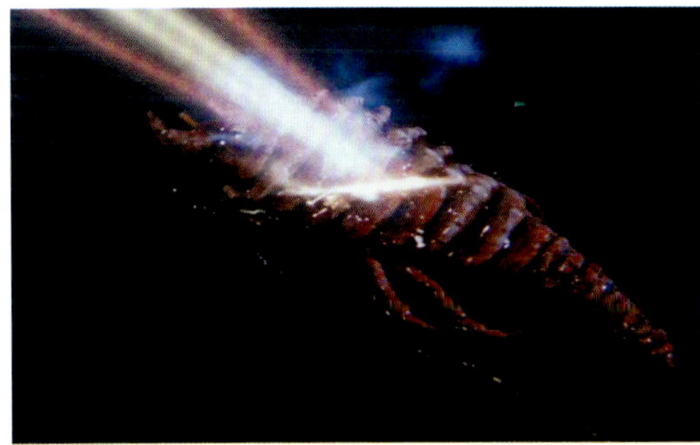

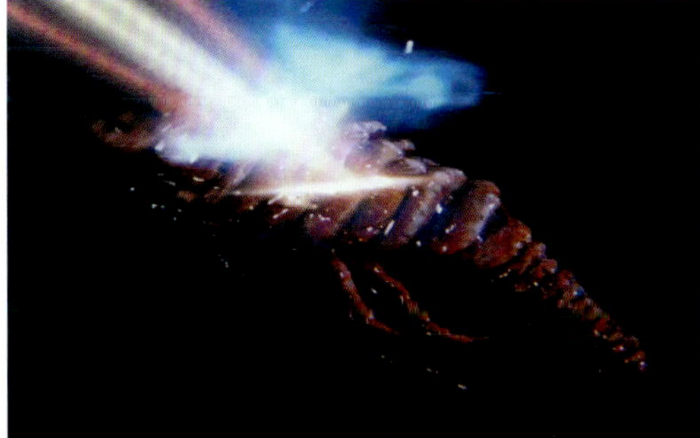

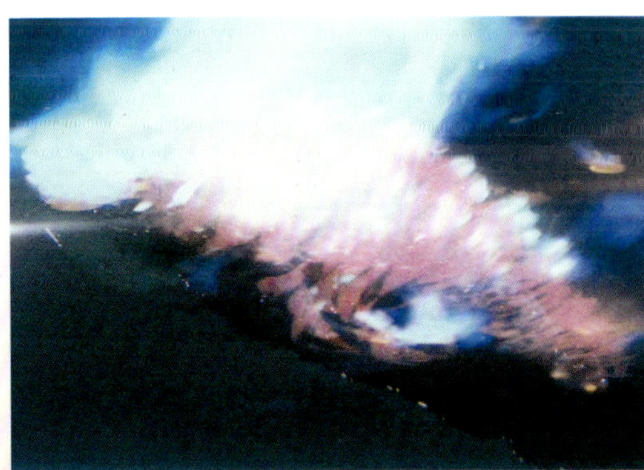

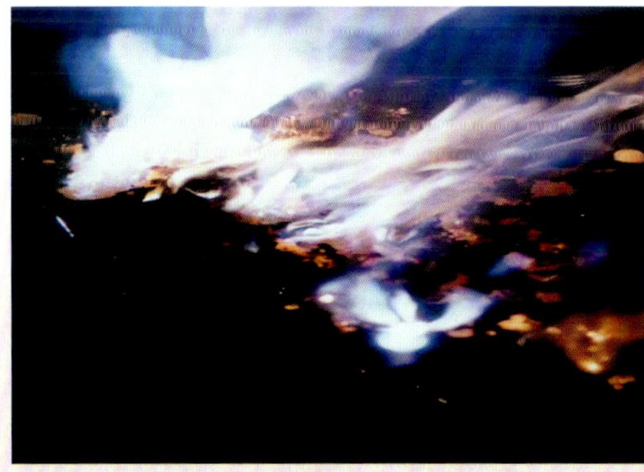

next day I woke up and went out to get my morning paper, and there on my walkway was a slug. I look at it and thought, 'Perfect. I hate these things. Everybody hates these things. What if…'"[1]

By the next draft of the script dated April 10, 1981, Sowards had changed the "Wee Beasties" to the more familiar eels. In this version, it would be McCoy and O'Rourke who solve the mystery of the creature's origins. During their investigation, more details about the eel would be revealed. The eel's scientific name was Ungulus Cetus Tex, a silicon-based life form which communicates using radio energy.

Meyer's September 16, 1981 version of the script describes the eels as "ghastly items, wriggling" and posits they function by wrapping themselves around the cortex of the brain, "rendering the victim extremely susceptible to suggestion. Later, of course, as they grow, follows madness, paralysis— and death." Khan would describe, then, in some detail that, "There is some pain at first, I am told, and then the effects are quite benign—until the end. That was what I learned from watching my wife—and the poor wretch we were out burying today when you so unexpectedly dropped in to visit Napoleon on St. Helena." This additional detail explained why Khan and his entire group of followers had left their shelter en masse.

Creating the "ghastly items, wriggling" would be the responsibility of ILM special effects supervisor Ken Ralston and his team. Ralston enjoyed the challenge, observing, "Ray Harryhausen is my hero, and this was a perfect opportunity for me to do something different."[2] Ralston wanted the eel to be alien but also recognizable to audiences, so they would have an emotional reaction to the creature. To achieve the needed effect, a mother eel puppet was crafted, approximately 14 inches in length, with Ralston making the most of what was available. "For the shell, since I wasn't really into using topline materials, I just used car Bondo. I did each one of the hard shell segments separately and then glued those on the rubber thing. Those plates are what they pulled the little baby eels out of with the forceps. Then, I painted it."[3]

Nearly a dozen different design possibilities were created, including a maquette study model, and shown to Sallin for approval. Ralston details his process: "The way I usually would work is I would do drawings, mainly for myself, trying to find something I thought was interesting. If I thought there was a cool design, then—you know, everyone does this trick—I would do a sculpture of it, making it all detailed and everything, trying to sell it. That would be the one I would show."[4] Of the final effect, Sallin said, "It was an amazing device that Ken Ralston built. When you see it on the screen you believe it. Every time we show that scene, someone goes, 'Urrgh.'"[5] In fact, the design was unique enough that the studio was granted a United States Patent on October 4, 1984.

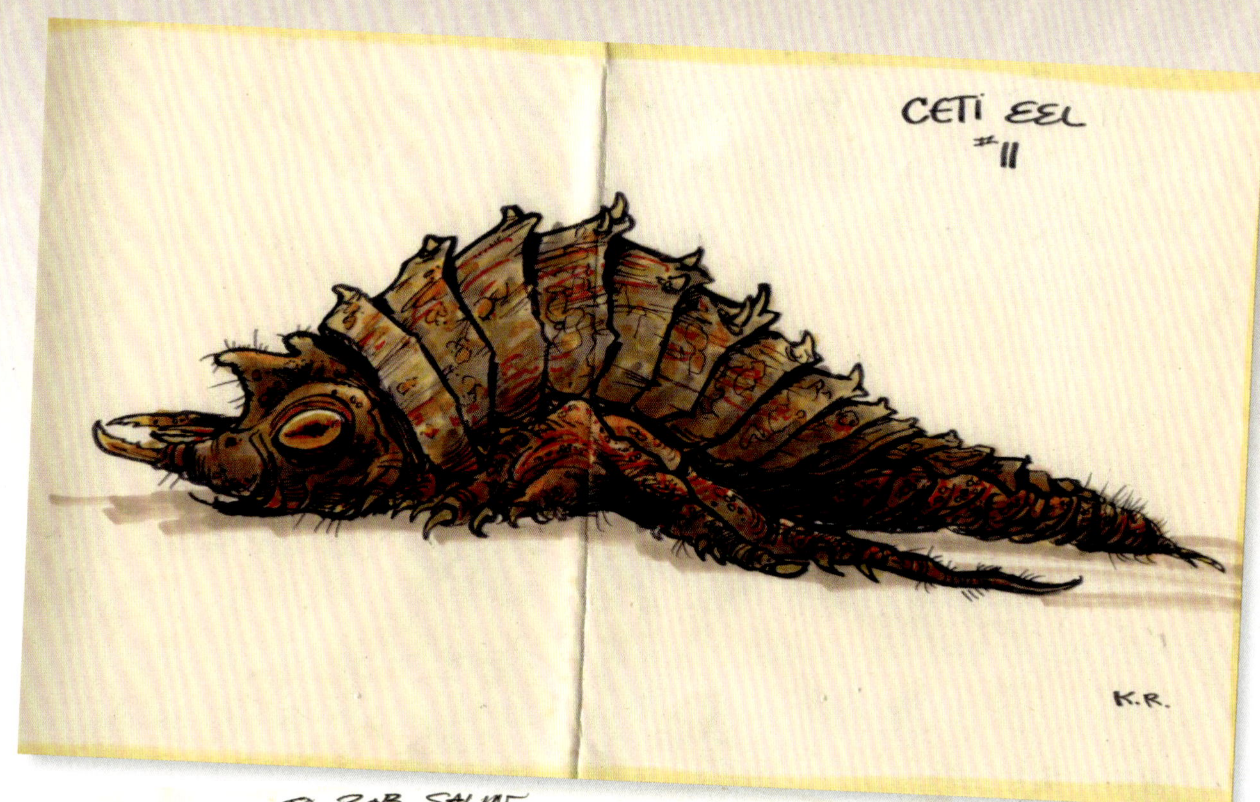

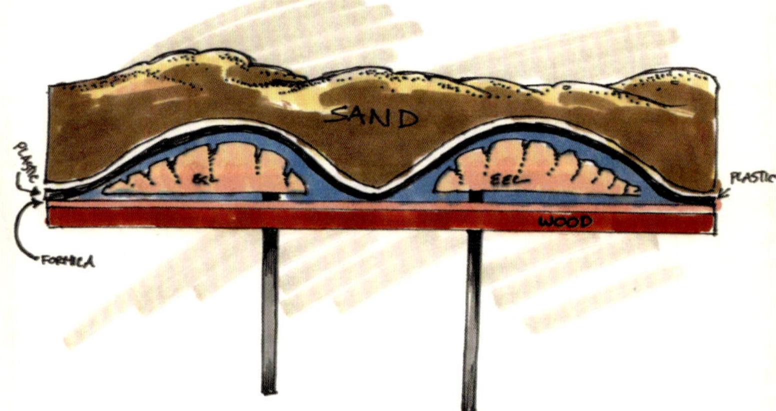

—WOOD BASE SHOULD HAVE FORMICA SURFACE— ALSO WITH THE SLOTS CUT IN IT— EELS ARE PLACED IN —RODS THRU SLOTS— A TOUGH PLASTIC SHEET IS PLACED OVER THEM [EDGES GLUED TO TANK BASE] AND SAND LAYED OVER IT ALL * PLASTIC SHOULD BE PAINTED TO MATCH SAND TO PREVENT ANY OF IT SHOWING THRU SAND.

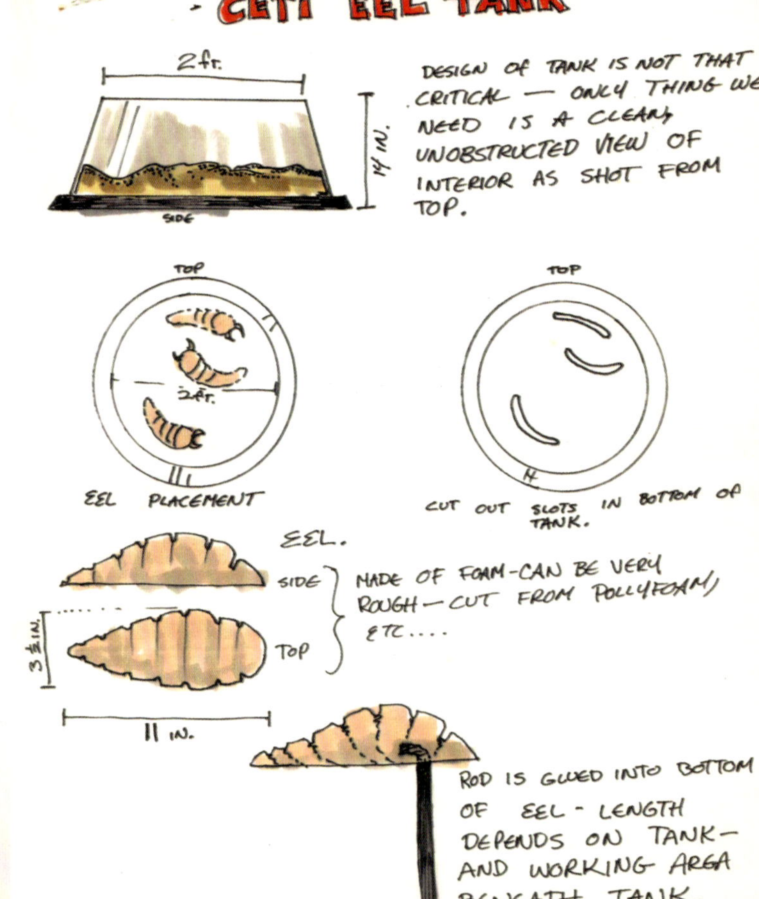

THIS PAGE: The movement of the puppet was accomplished by connecting two rods fore and aft that could be hidden underneath the sand in its tank. This meant that Ralston and his team not only had to design and create the eels, but their tank also.

☆ GENE RODDENBERRY

Gene Roddenberry took his executive consultant role on *Star Trek II* seriously, making comments and suggestions as various versions of the scripts were produced. His memos served as a reminder of the various elements he felt made *Star Trek* resonate with fans. Following some memos about what Roddenberry considered less important concerns, which included suggestions about jargon, he crafted a seven-page single-spaced memo dated September 30, 1981 headed "SCRIPT COMMENTS — Items Considered Important." He begins the memo by praising the script version created by Nicholas Meyer earlier that month: "First, let me say again how pleased I am with the number and quality of script improvements. As I looked over the rather long memo sent you on the other script I was struck with the amount of work that had been done to attend to the items criticized."

Roddenberry writes both with the authority of a creator and the experience of a producer. He knew that the production of any entertainment as sophisticated as *Star Trek* required compromise. "Also, I freely admit that every *Star Trek* 'rule' I mention can be seen violated on television episodes. No one can make a television show comparable to producing half a SF movie every week and have it all as he and his associates want. What you can do, however, is see that your several years of episodes do add up to what you wanted—even though individual shows didn't. So, please accept it in the spirit of 'this is how we tried to do it, mea culpa.'"

Roddenberry's suggestions were always considered seriously, and sometimes followed. Those that were followed helped improve the final film.

Illustrative of Roddenberry helping the production was his argument that Kirk would never abandon Khan on such a hostile world. The scripts until then did not feature any kind of explanation as to why Ceti Alpha V was that harsh an environment. Kirk had known that Ceti Alpha V would present a challenge when he offered Khan the opportunity to tame the world in "Space Seed," but the conditions as depicted in the scripts were too unfriendly. Roddenberry offered a solution that would ultimately be accepted in the final script: "Fortunately, there may be a way out of this dilemma—it depends on our science advisor coming up with a believable natural catastrophe which could change the marginally livable planet of the television episode into this frightening place. Perhaps a near brush with a comet or asteroid?" And so, Ceti Alpha VI would explode and the orbit of Ceti Alpha V would shift, hence producing conditions unforeseeable by Kirk.

Sometimes, however, Roddenberry's objections were not taken on board, such as his thoughts about the Ceti eels. His October 2, 1981 memo has Roddenberry offering what he detailed as "FINAL SCRIPT COMMENTS." He was adamant that Kirk would not kill the Ceti eel in the Genesis Cave. "Under no circumstances would Kirk pick up a phaser and fire it at as interesting a life specimen as the Ceti eel. At worst he might STUN it for later examination." This observation of Roddenberry evokes the approach Kirk and Spock take to the flying parasites at first during "Operation – Annihilate!" However, by episode's end, when Kirk realizes the danger, Kirk does order the use of satellites to use ultraviolet light to destroy the creatures.

Although his suggestion was ignored, it reveals the passion Roddenberry had for Starfleet characters always symbolizing the best of humanity.

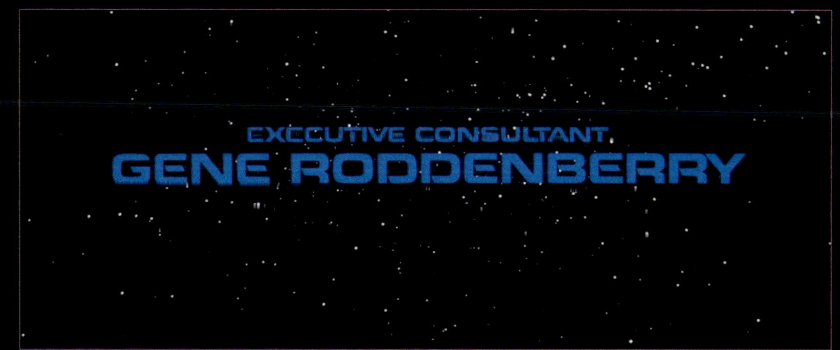

A trick of editing in the final film, on set Montalban never actually interacted with the mother Ceti eel puppets. Montalban only handled the youngling eels. The only movement in the tank on set with Montalban was some sand being disturbed, jostled by a hidden technician, creating the illusion and anticipation of something lurking beneath. For filming, two tanks were created, one for the Paramount Ceti Alpha V set, and a larger one for use at ILM, and it was at ILM that the puppets would actually be filmed. Later, sound effects and music sell the creatures as being realistic and dangerous. Ralston reflects on how the distinct puzzle pieces of production eventually create a unified whole: "I'm very happy with how it turned out, obviously. You get so tied up into the work and the shots, and I always keep trying to pull myself out of that, especially as I got more into supervising later. I keep reminding everyone the movie isn't about their one shot. It is about the whole thing. You keep thinking about that. So when you see it all put together and with the sound effects and everything, it is always so cool."[6]

The youngling eels were made of foam, appropriately from the remains of the foam used to create the mother eel. The foam permitted more flexibility. According to Ralston, "I never sculpted anything; I just took a piece of foam—I think it was probably left over from the big eel—and cut it out with fingernail scissors! I made basically a hunk of rubber in a slug form with the smallest little rubber connections between each little segment so it would hold together. It was so simple."[7]

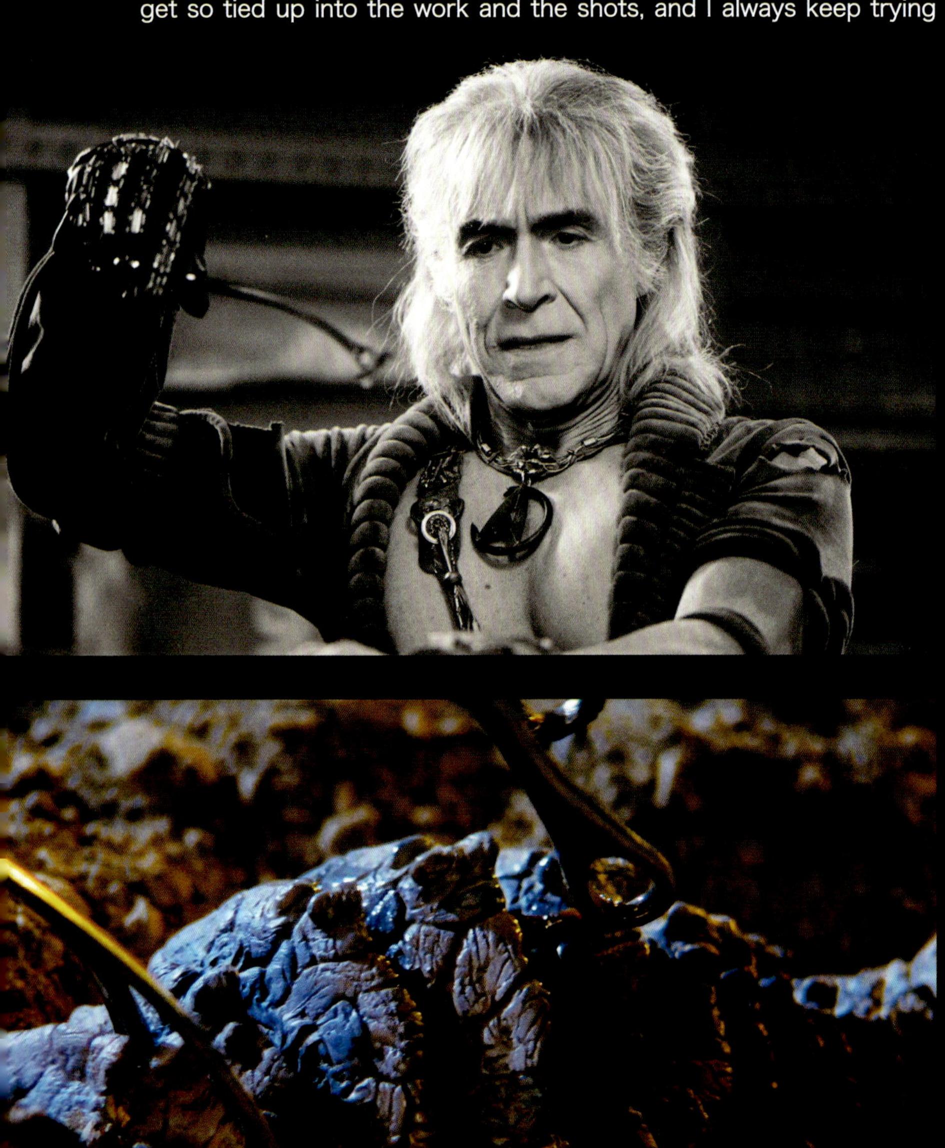

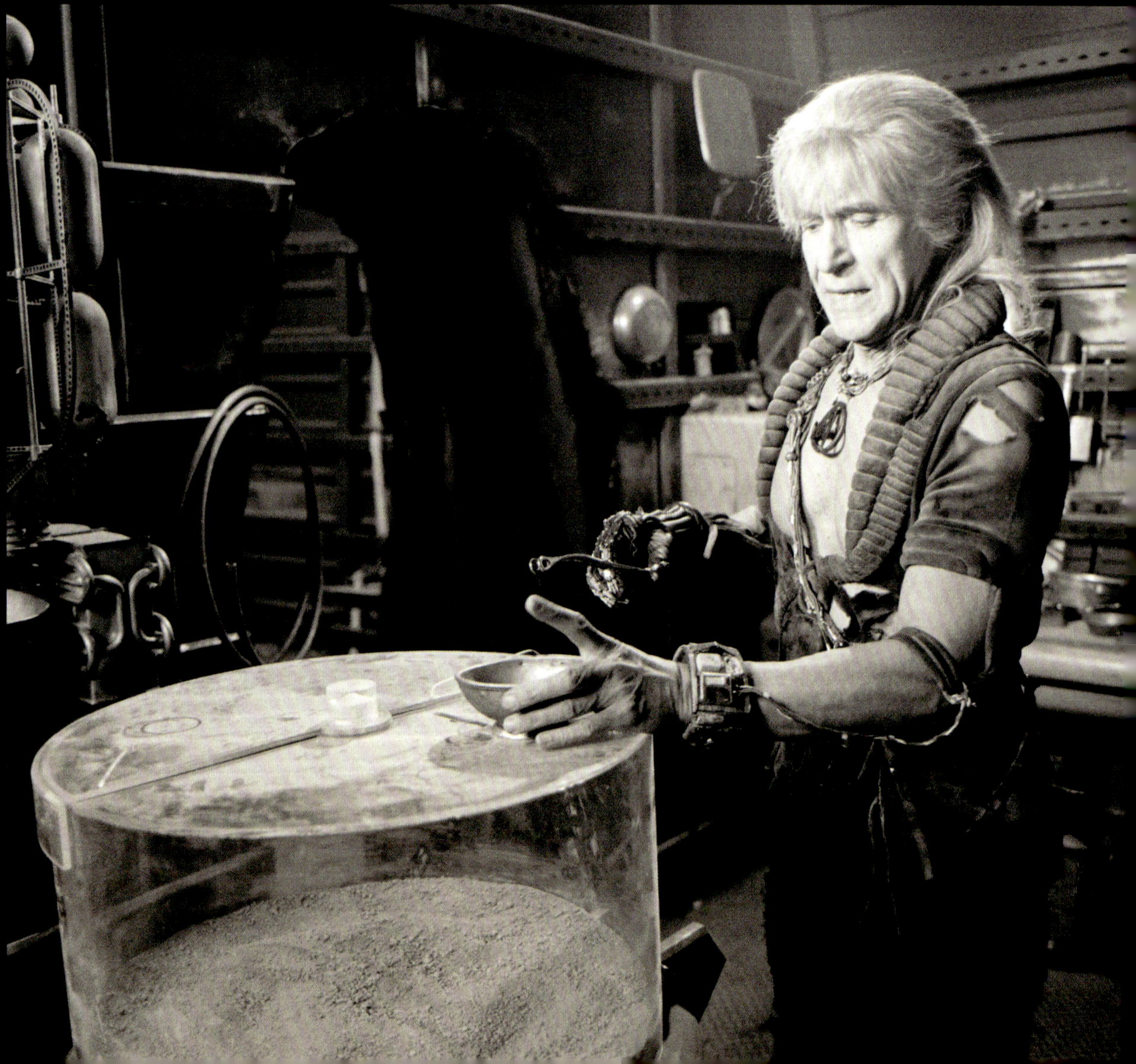

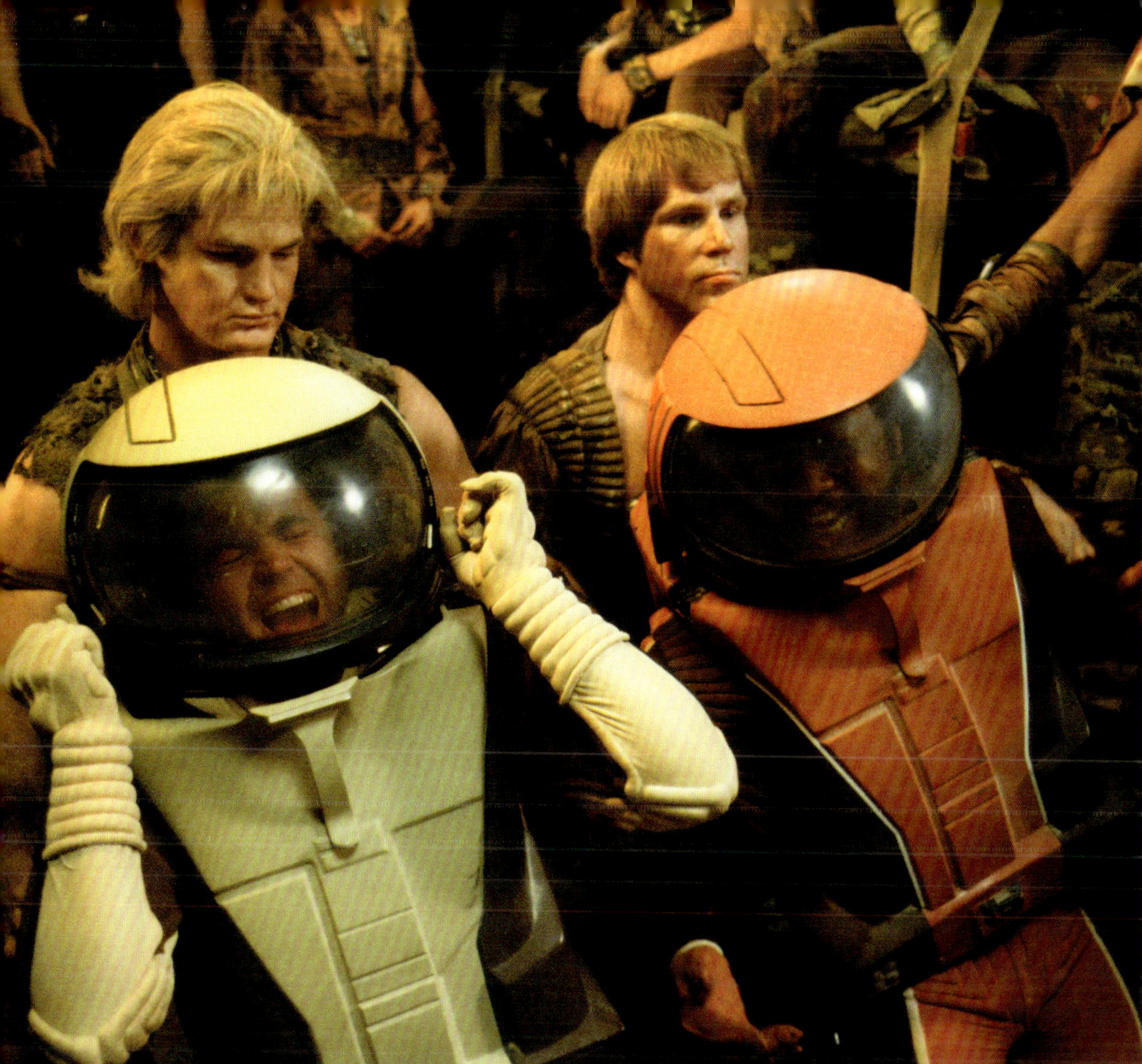

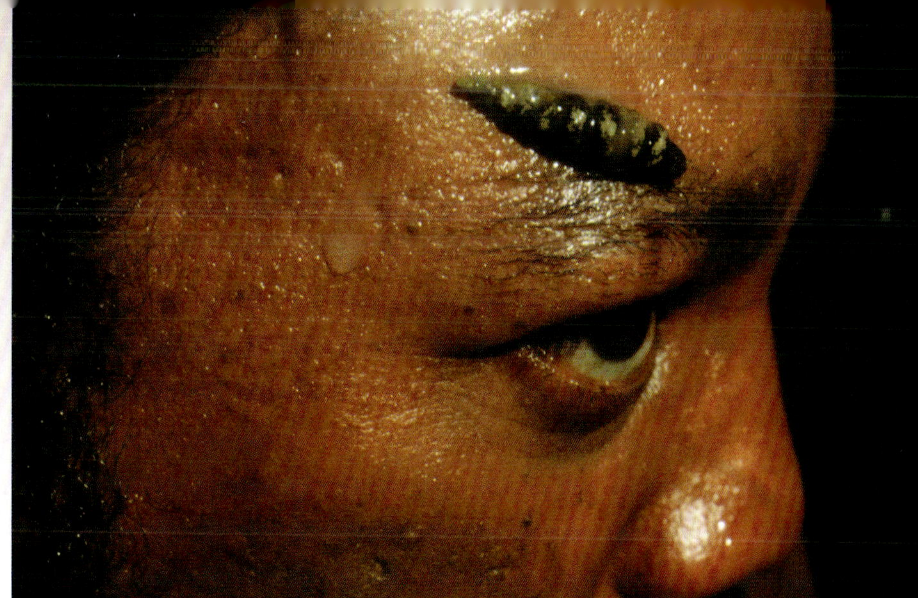

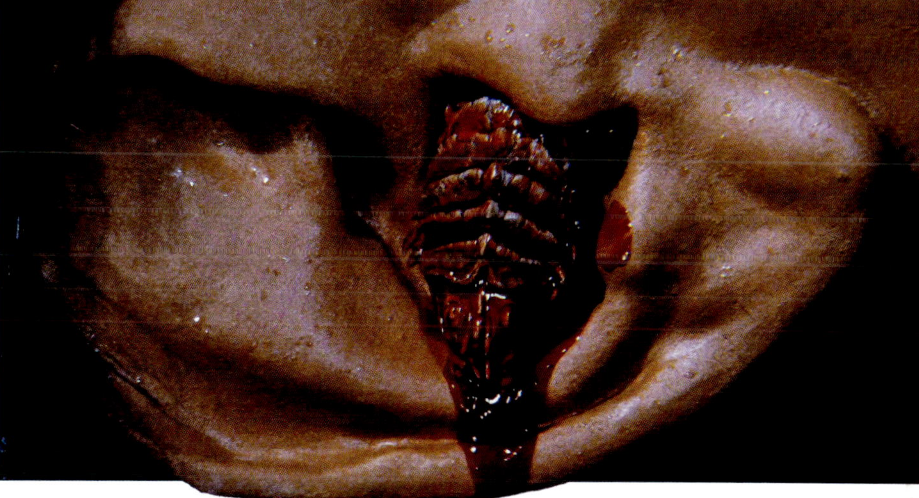

While the reaction of Terrell and Chekov would be filmed at Paramount Studios, actors Walter Koenig and Paul Winfield would film the eels crawling on their faces and into their ears at ILM. The foam creatures were covered with methylcellulose to create a slimy, mucky substance around the youngling eels. The muck would have an added benefit. Ralston explains, "This is where I really lucked out; in one of our tests I just laid it on a guy's face and pulled the wire. I hadn't planned it, but the method acted almost like a slight glue, so the front of the eel would move forward and then, just when the tension got a little too much, the back end in that muck would catch up to it, so it looked like it was inching along."[8]

"My biggest joy is finding the simplest solutions that work really well,"[9] Ralston shares.

Winfield remembered, "That was very effective. I had to fly up to Lucas's laboratory, and they actually put a thing in my ear; it was on a string that made it move, and boy, it looked real! I didn't have to act scared."[10] Koenig had a different reaction. "I loved that. Are you kidding me? They had it on a very fine filament. They had drilled a hole in the helmet that I was wearing, and then they dropped it through into the helmet. It was gooey, so it adhered to my face, and there was somebody standing above me pulling it up my cheek."[11]

Ralston used the 14 inch mother eel puppet to create the scene where an eel exits Chekov's ear. Koenig remembered the filming of the effect while at ILM: "I went up to Marin County, to George Lucas's place. They had created a sculpture of my ear, which was larger, and a mold of my ear, which was obviously the same size. They recreated the flooring where I had fallen down on a table. I lay on that and they had somebody underneath, and now, instead of drawing it up my face, they stuffed it into my ear and they pulled it out. For the sculpture with the far larger orifice they used a hand puppet." At one point, someone made a giant Q-tip, and as a joke, left it in the model ear.

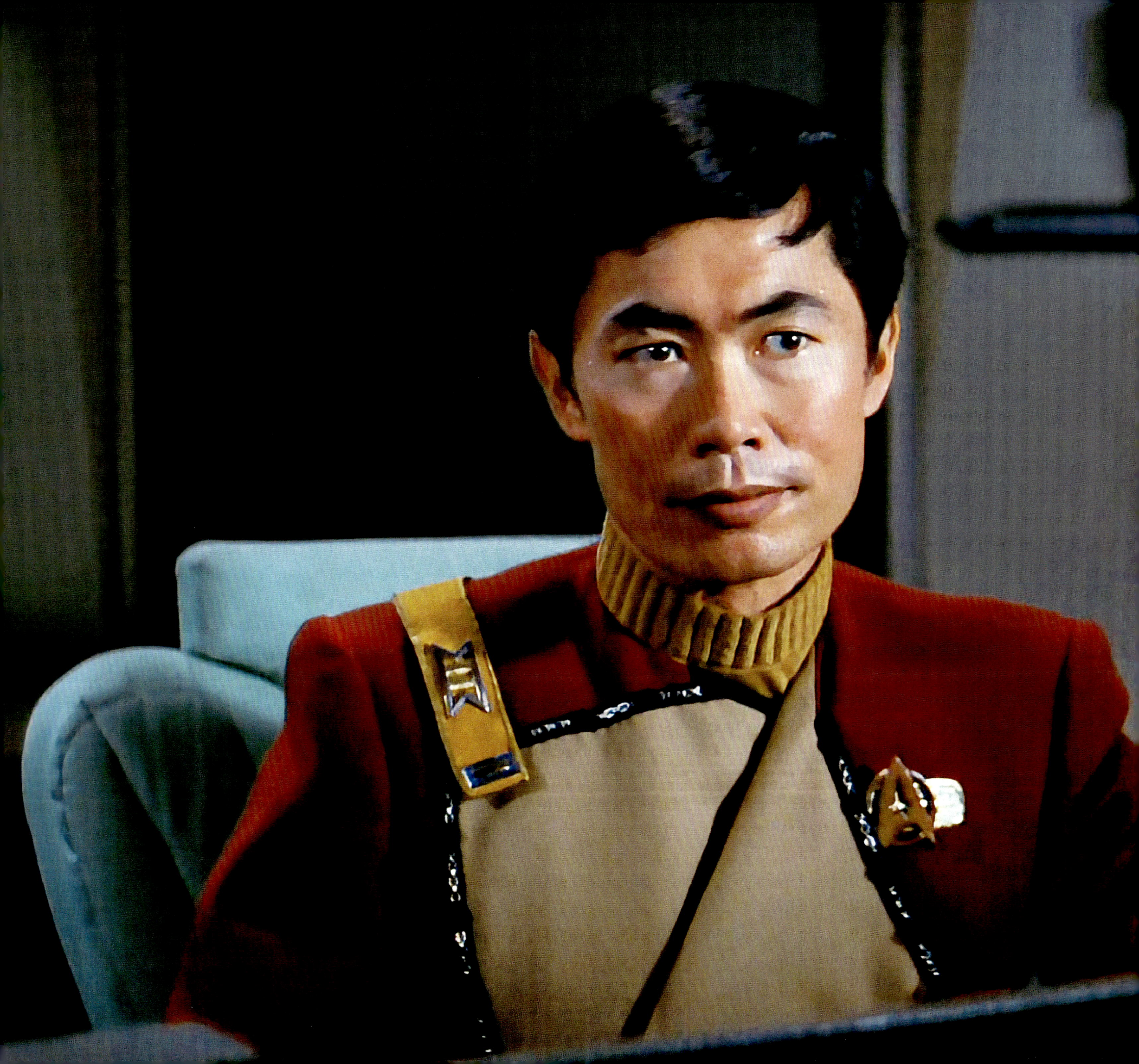

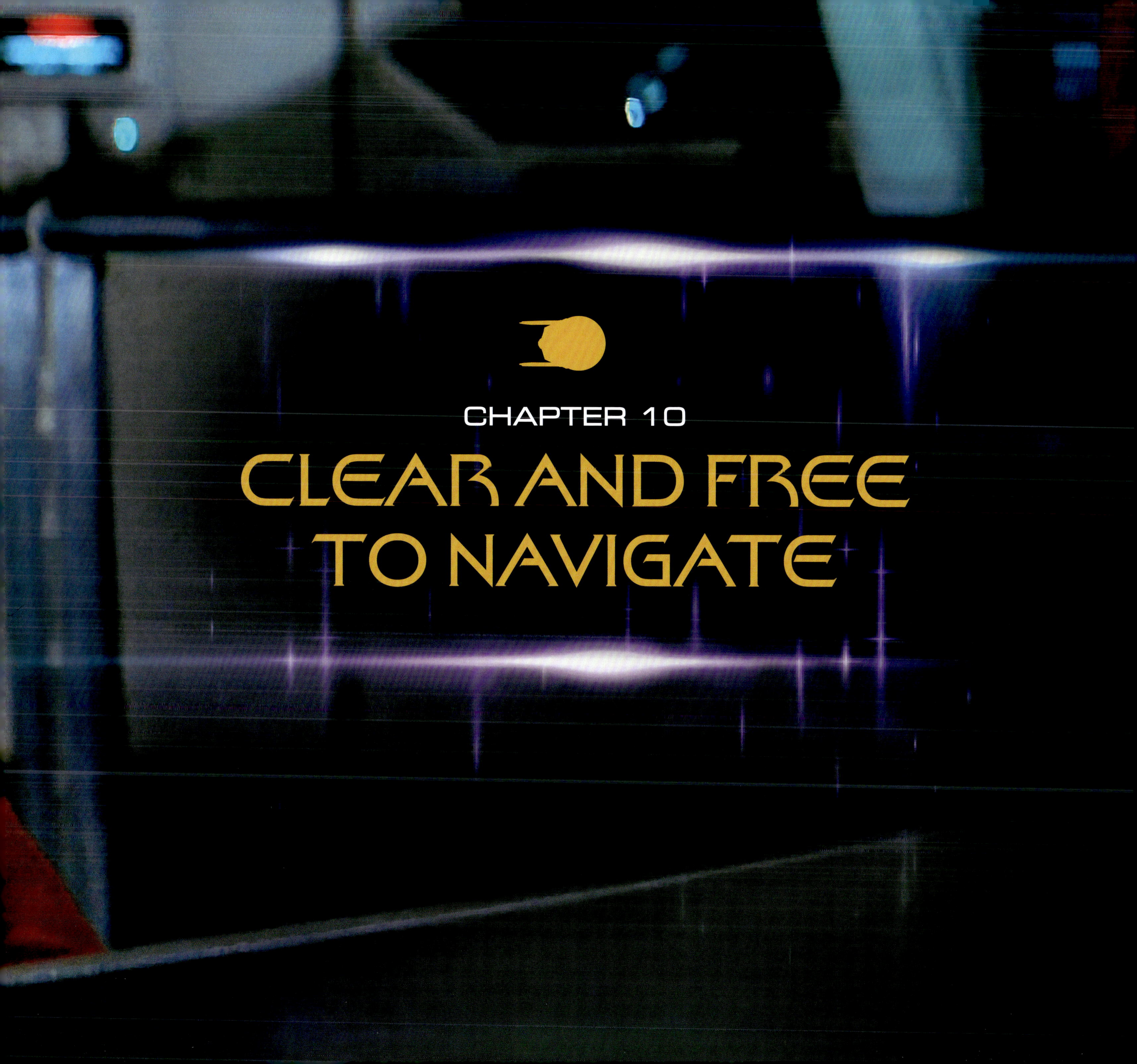
CHAPTER 10
CLEAR AND FREE
TO NAVIGATE

THE CAMERA DEPARTMENT

"Cinema is the most beautiful fraud in the world," extoled French New Wave film pioneer Jean-Luc Godard via the characters of his 1963 short *Le Grand Escroc*. One of the many interpretations of Godard's thesis is that to make their fictional worlds believable, filmmakers employ ruses, wiles, and subterfuge—including special effects and stunt work. In other words, filmmakers are part illusionists. Perhaps that is why the word artistic is only a few letters removed from the word artifice. That is not to say that artists do not strive to reveal truths. It is to say they sometimes need magic and cinematic chicanery to get it done. Certainly the cinematographer chosen for *Star Trek II* would have to be someone who could pull some rabbits out of the proverbial hat.

"Gayne Rescher was recommended to me as the cinematographer by Robert Sallin," director Nicholas Meyer recalls. "Gayne Rescher was one of the cinematographers on one of the greatest American movies, *A Face in the Crowd*. When I learned that… This is the only business where you get to shake hands with your dreams. He was a wonderfully sweet guy. He also shot *The Day After* for me, so we obviously had a very cordial relationship. He was a very emotional man. He was a very sensitive guy, which made two of us."[1] Joining Rescher in the camera department would be first assistant camera Catherine Coulson and camera operator Craig Denault.

Speaking about the importance of preparation, Meyer revealed, "Another condition that helped me prepare for the film so quickly was that for two hours a day during the six weeks prior to shooting, Gayne Rescher, cinematographer, and I walked over the set of the *Enterprise* mapping out every shot."[2]

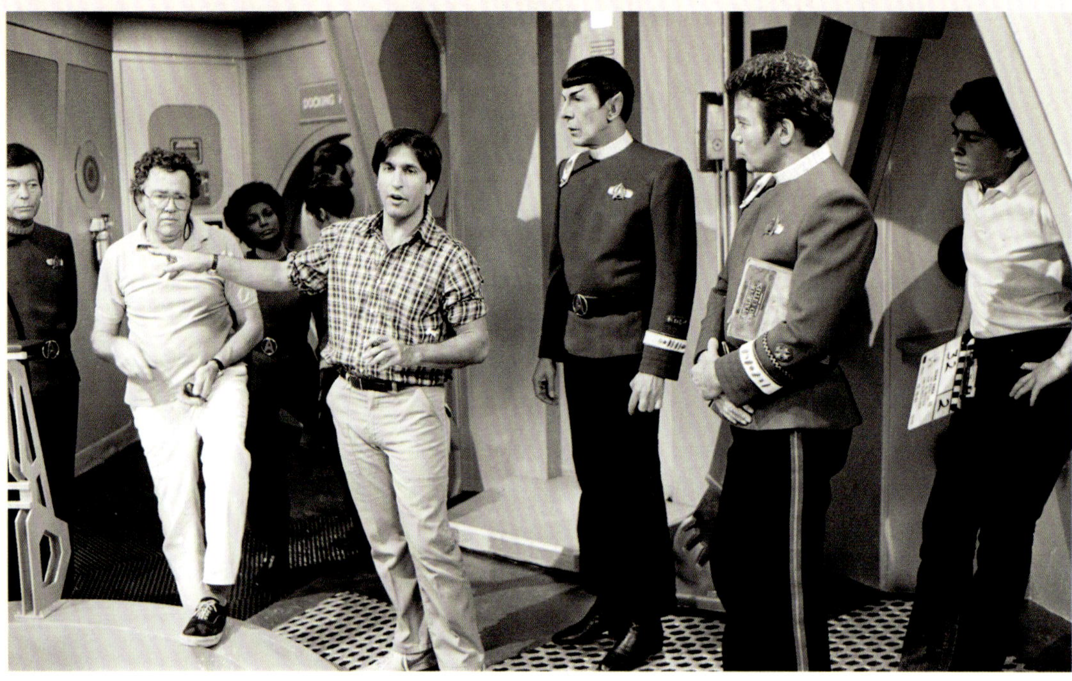

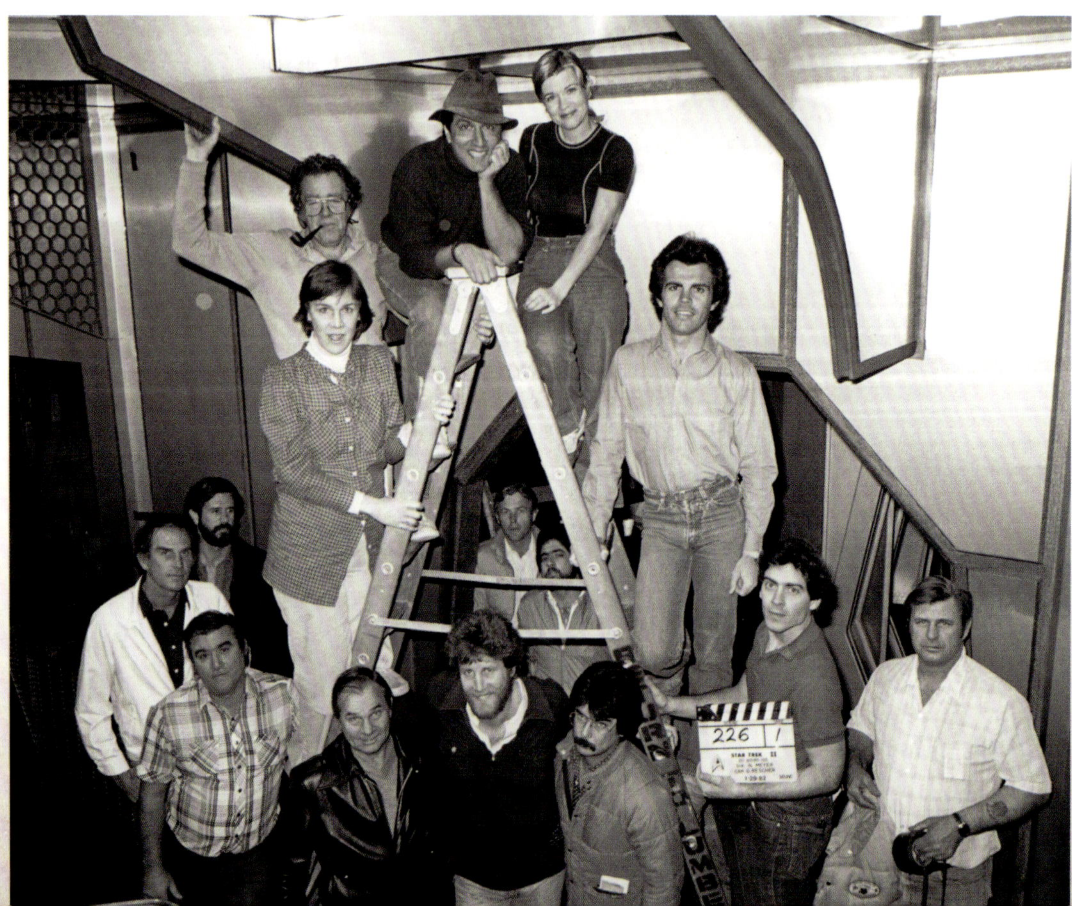

RIGHT: A ladder of creativity (from left to right, starting with the lowest rung): Coulson, Rescher, Meyer, script supervisor Mary Jane Ferguson, and Denault gather with members of the camera department. First assistant director Douglas E. Wise is in the center of the ladder on the bottom. Wise is the nephew of *Star Trek: The Motion Picture* director Robert Wise and worked on five *Star Trek* films.

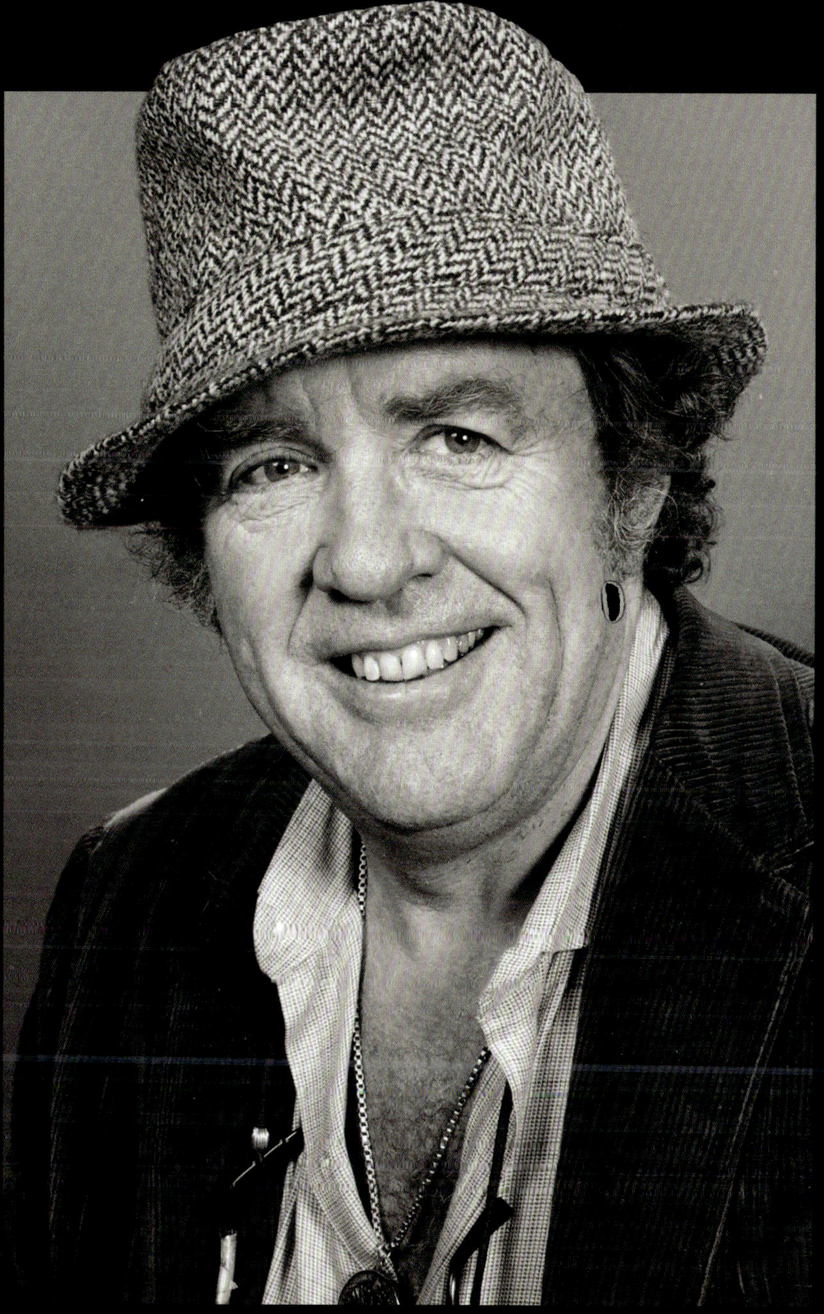 GAYNE RESCHER

Jay Gayne Rescher was born in New York in 1924. Rescher was part of a creative Hollywood family. Mother Jean Tolley was a silent screen actor and father Jay was a famed cinematographer. Rescher would enter the arts community after serving as a pilot during World War II (as did Gene Roddenberry). He was educated at the American Theater School, first as an actor, and then as a photographer and cinematographer. Rescher brought with him to *Star Trek II* both TV and film experience—something of an important plus being that *Star Trek* was continuing to find its way as a film series after starting on TV. Considered an expert at lighting, Rescher's career began in film with his first movie, *A Face in the Crowd* (1957) directed by Elia Kazan. By the late 1970s Rescher had moved to working exclusively in television—*Star Trek II* being the notable exception—and from 1980 until 1991 he earned an amazing eight Emmy nominations, winning three awards. Rescher died in 2008 at age eighty-three.

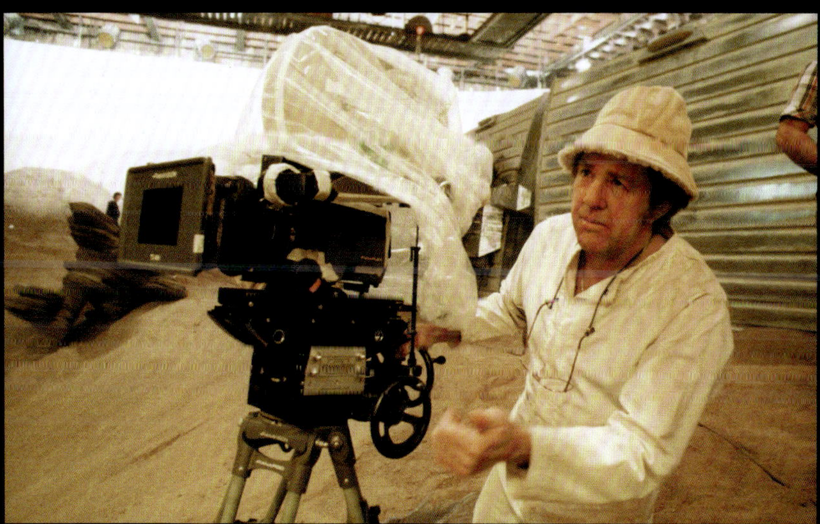

CATHERINE COULSON

Born in Illinois in 1943, Catherine E. Coulson, like Rescher, had a creative family. Her mother was a ballet dancer and her father a media producer and executive. The Coulsons moved to Southern California, where Coulson graduated with a Master of Fine Arts degree from San Francisco State University. Known as a proverbial jack-of-all-trades, symbolized by belonging to several creative unions at the same time, the diversely skilled Coulson was a pioneer of cinema. She was a stage and screen actor, most famous for her role as The Log Lady in David Lynch's *Twin Peaks* and for her work in the Oregon Shakespeare Festival. She was a producer and director, and shared a nearly forty-five-year collaboration with Lynch. Coulson died in 2015 at age seventy-one.

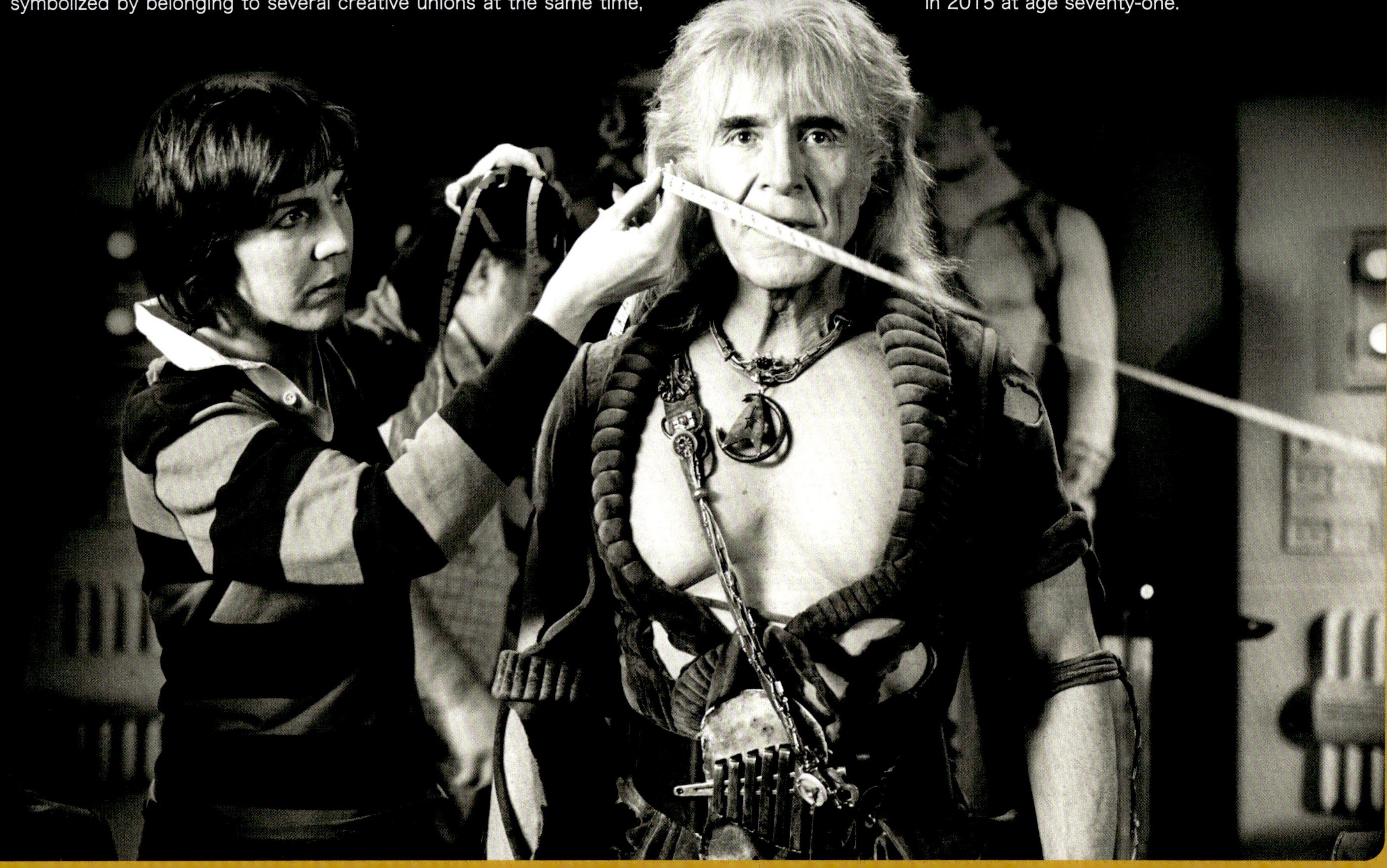

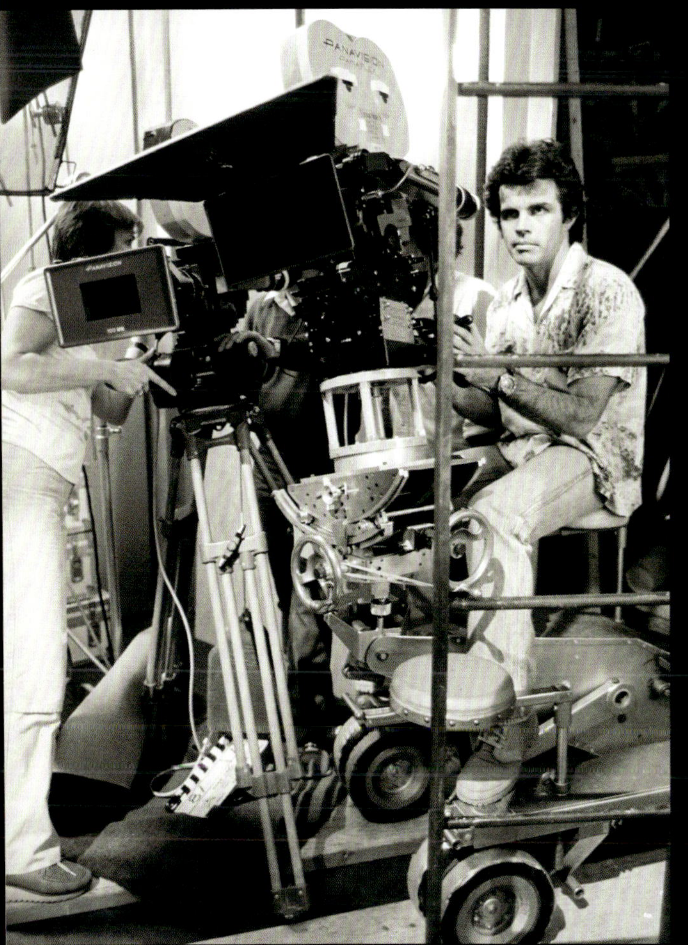

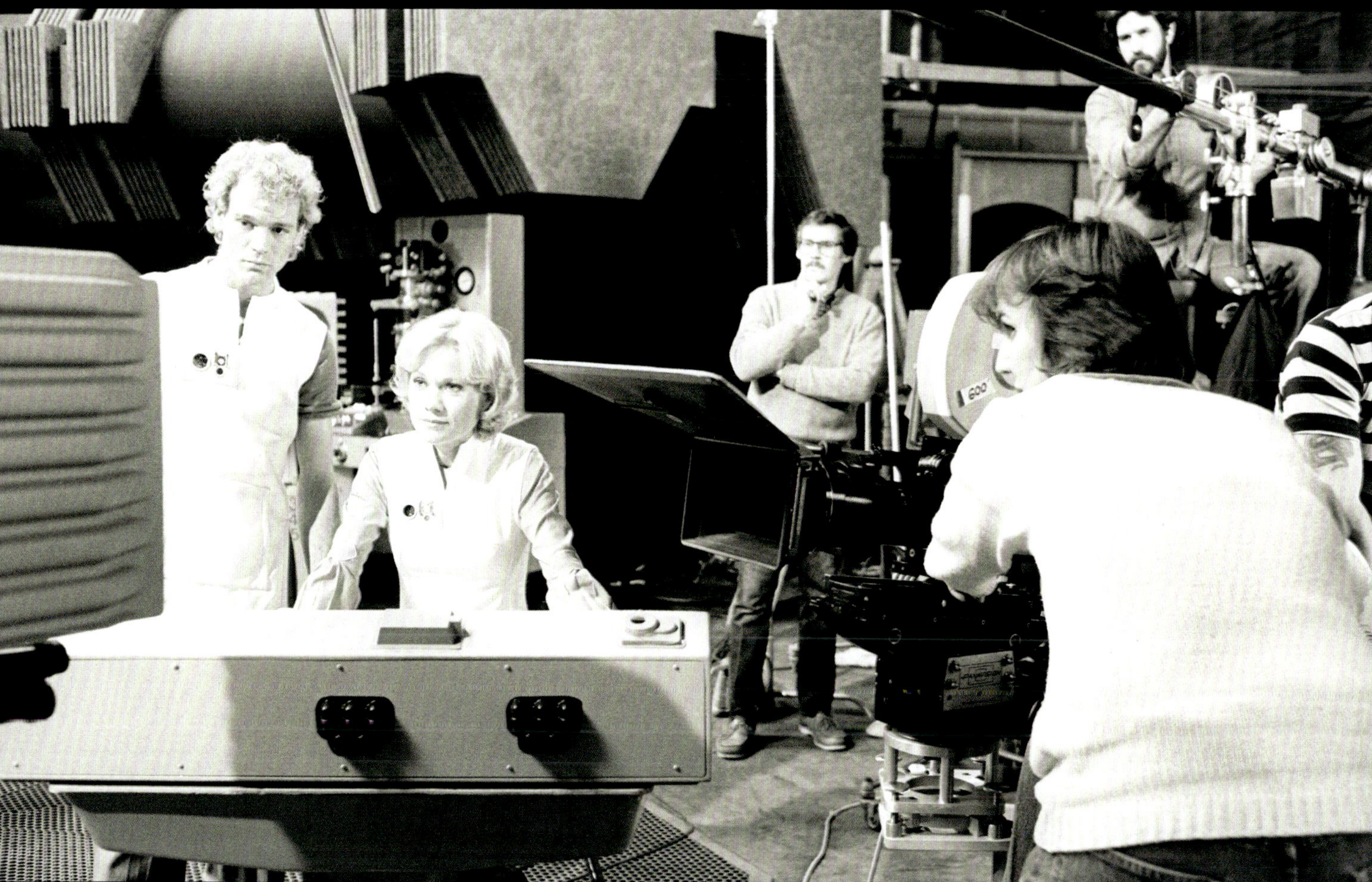

In what is largely believed to be a first for women working on major Hollywood studio productions, Coulson was a pioneer with her role as first assistant camera for *Star Trek II*. To capture the stunts and practical effects, there were at times multiple cameras that Coulson was responsible for coordinating. Having a crew that worked creatively and collaboratively was important to the success of *Star Trek II*. Meyer believes that, as director, "Whatever happens inside the frame is up to you. Ultimately, you're going to get the blame or the praise for what you compose. So I look at the shot before we start and I go, 'Yes,' and when everybody says they're ready, I always say, 'Take the picture.'"[3]

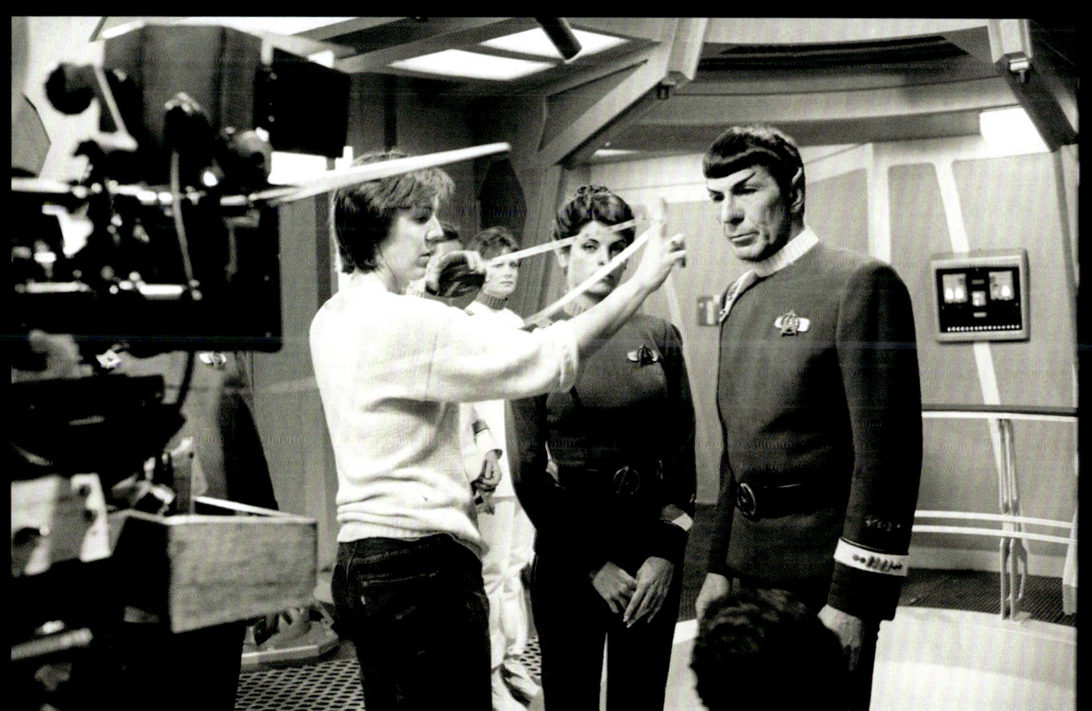

Rescher's cinematography along with Denault's creative camera movements made for a submarine vibe as requested by Meyer: "I knew what I wanted. It is claustrophobic and close-ups and things like that. Gayne took my ideas and ran with them."[4]

An estimated sixty-five percent of *Star Trek II* takes place on the same set. The *Reliant* is the *Enterprise*, and vice versa. Further, the film goes back and forth between those sets, one right after the other. When Khan is revealed as the one behind the attack on the *Enterprise*, Admiral Kirk is actually staring at his own bridge on the view screen behind his nemesis, and so is the audience. A good example of Godard's thesis and the collaboration that exists between art department and the camera department, slight alterations of everything from set decorations to lighting to camera movement helped sell the illusion that there are two bridges when there is only one.

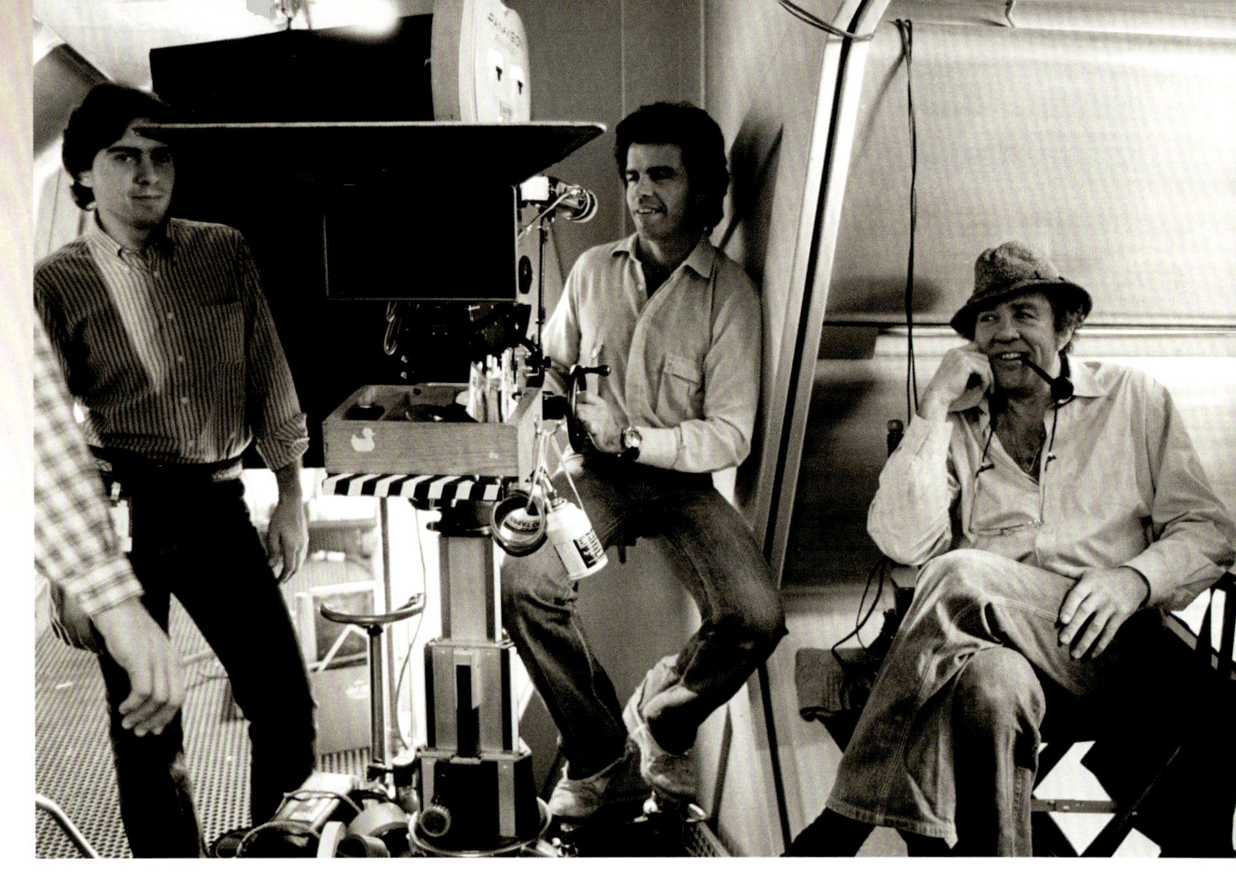

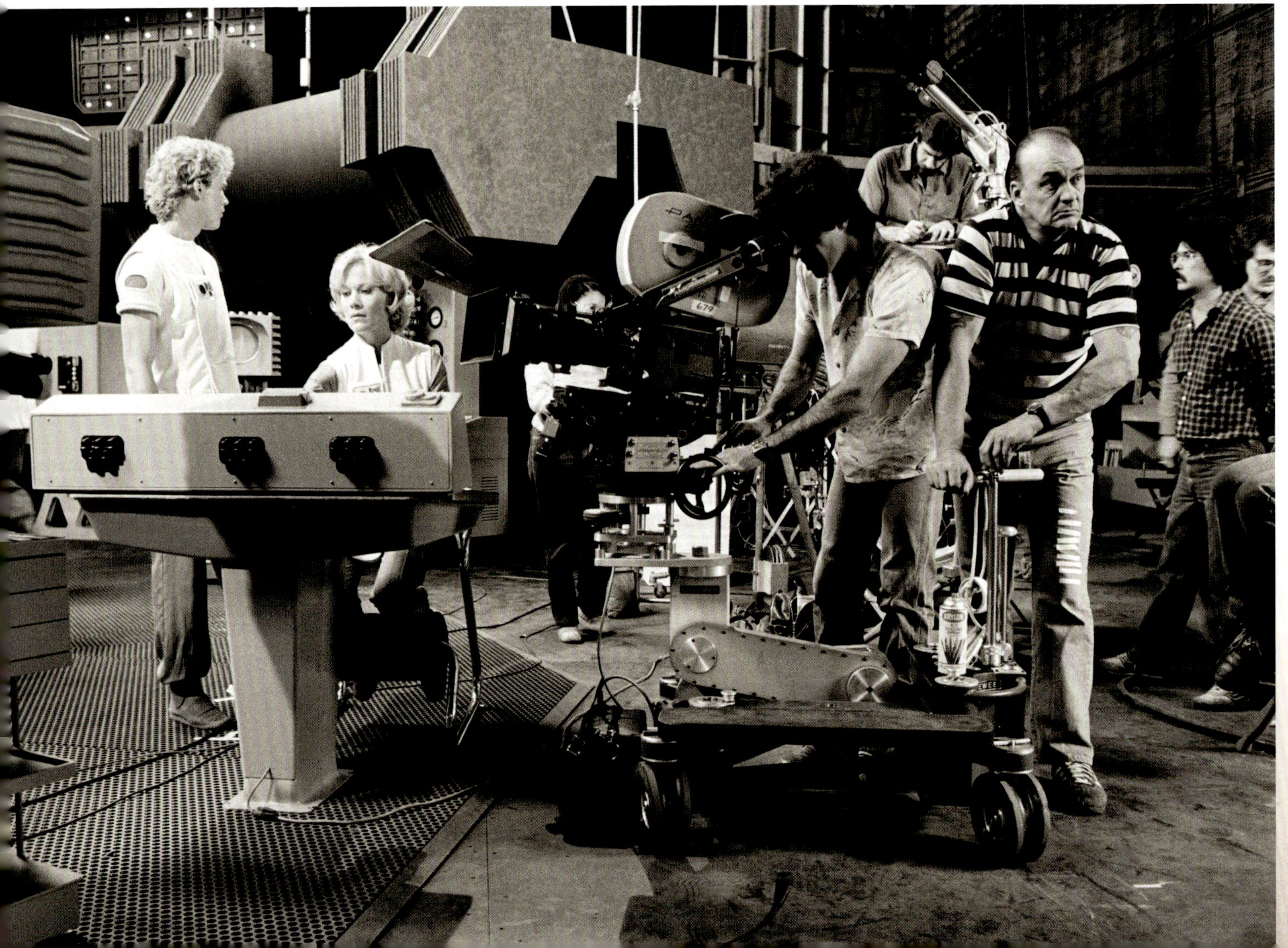

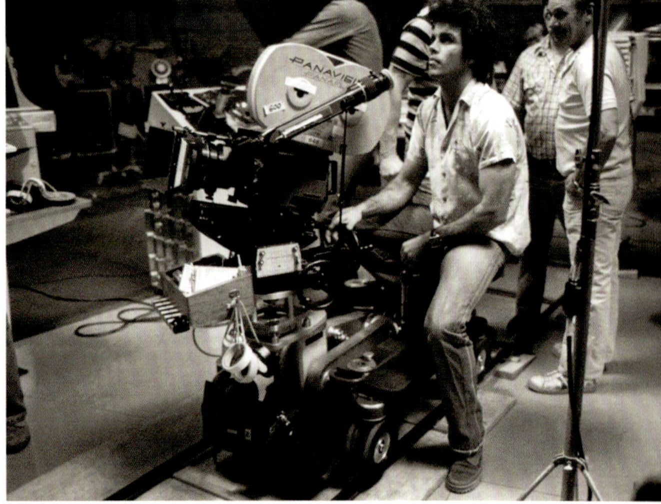

ABOVE: Denault readies the camera for filming on the Regula I lab set. Beneath him are dolly tracks that permit the camera operator and, if needed, focus puller, to glide the camera in or out for a particular shot. Specially skilled grips, known as dolly grips, play an important role moving the camera cart by hand, protecting the camera operator and the camera, and ensuring a smooth ride to a predetermined mark, so that a shot can be completed as envisioned. Don Whipple was the dolly grip on *Star Trek II*.

⬡ CRAIG DENAULT

Native to Los Angeles, Craig Denault was born in 1946. He would serve as camera operator for both films and television, as well as occasionally a cinematographer and director. Denault was so adept at his work that he became a role model and mentor to many camera operators first learning the craft. According to Daniel Gold, the 2015 Society of Camera Operators Lifetime Achievement Award Camera Operator, writing in *Camera Operator*, "Craig was a natural. He made operating a camera look easy and he always looked great doing it."[7]

Prior to *Star Trek II*, Denault was first assistant camera on the Peter Sellers classic *Being There* (1979), among many other films. He went on to be the camera operator on such popular films as *The Right Stuff* (1983), *The Natural* (1984), *Purple Rain* (1984), *Stand by Me* (1986), *The Karate Kid, Part II* (1986), and *The Next Karate Kid* (1994). Denault died in 1994 at age forty-seven.

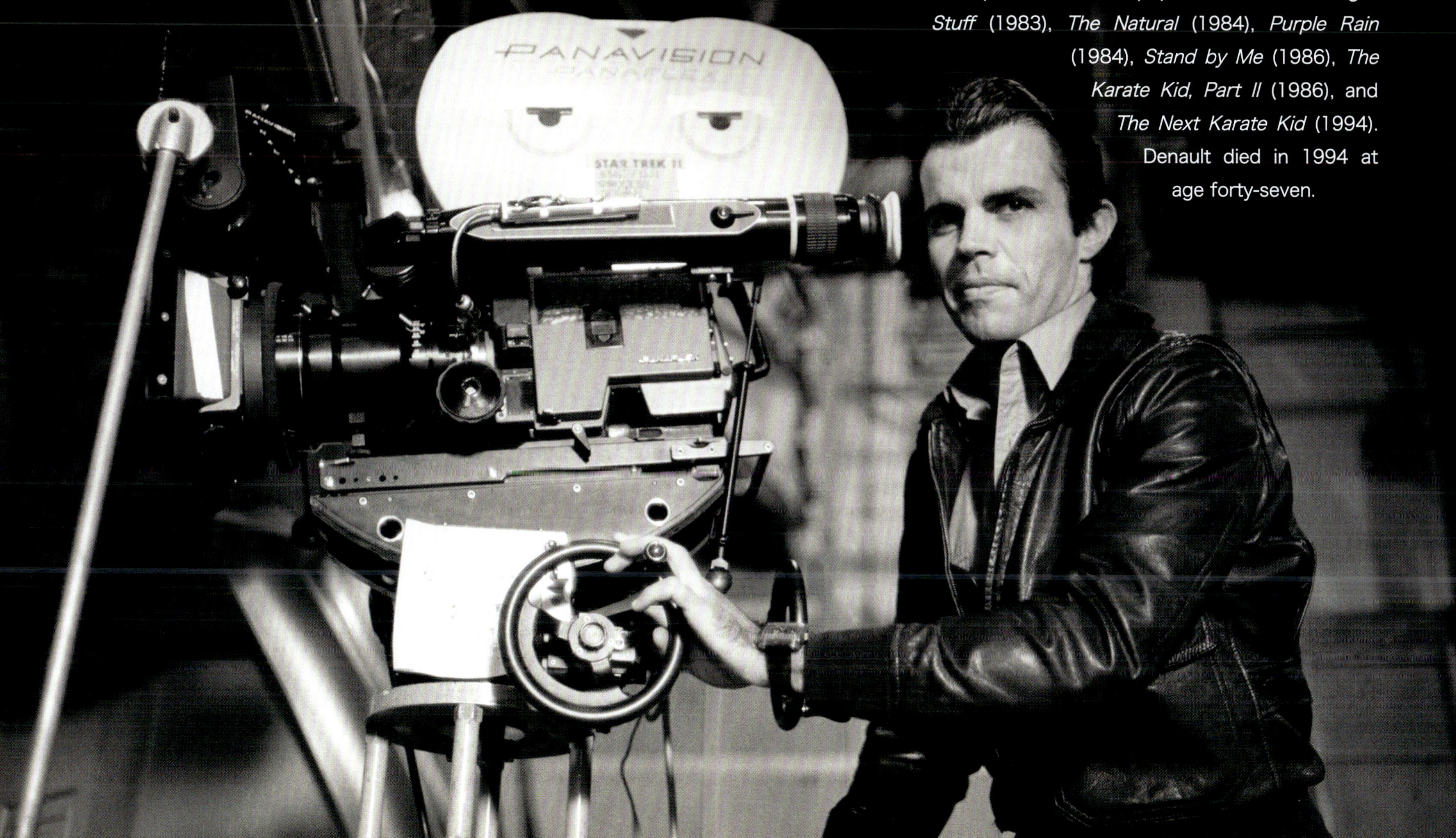

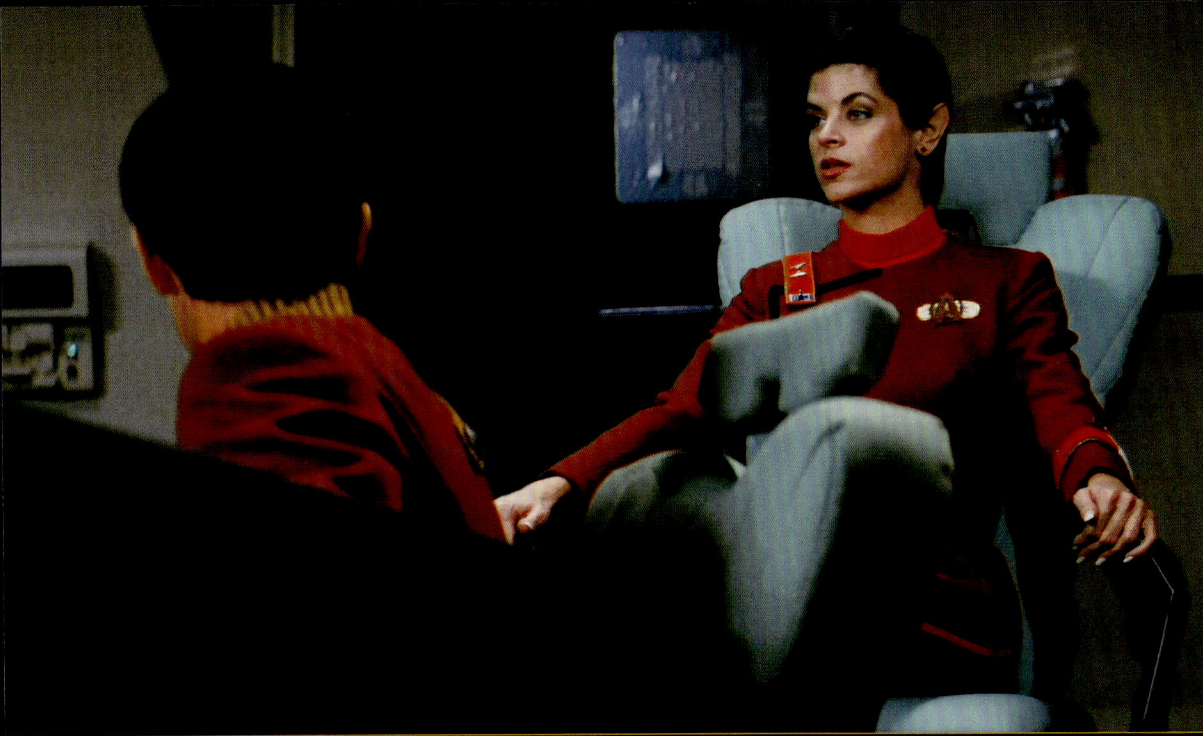

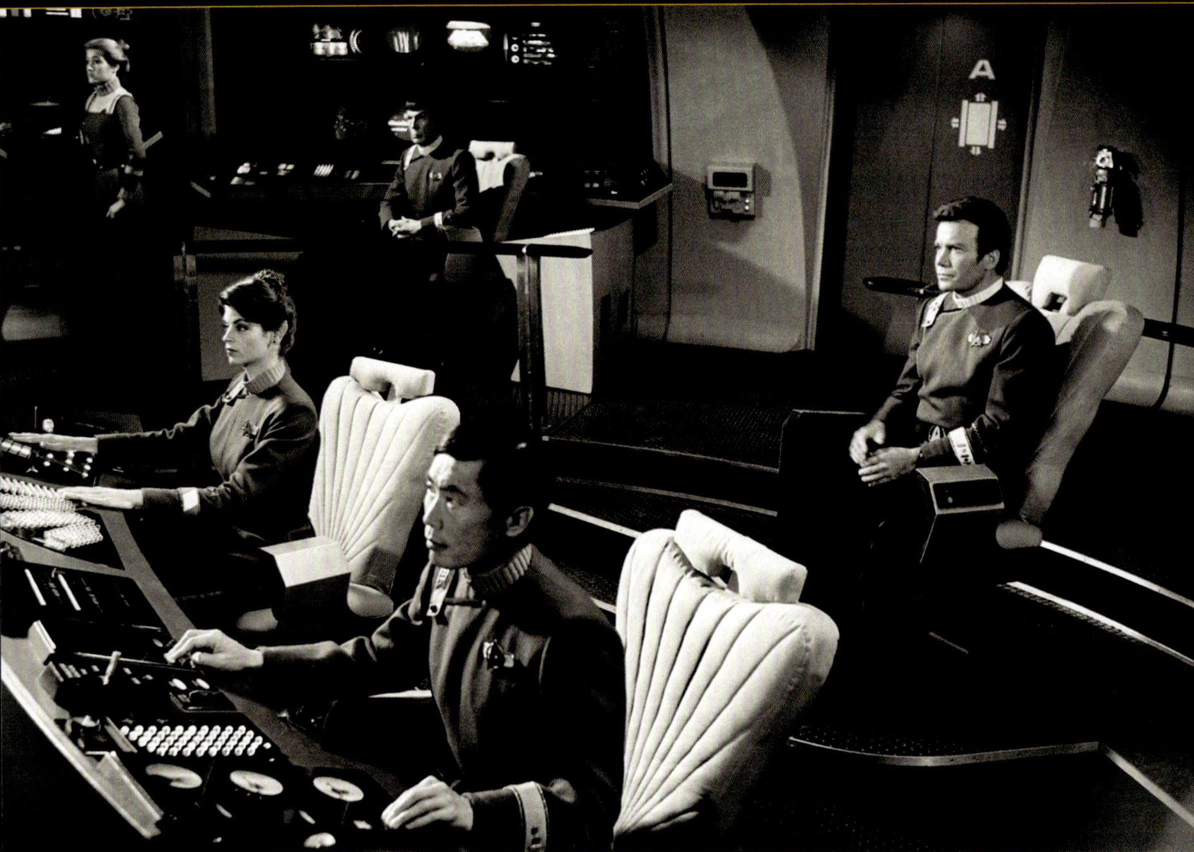

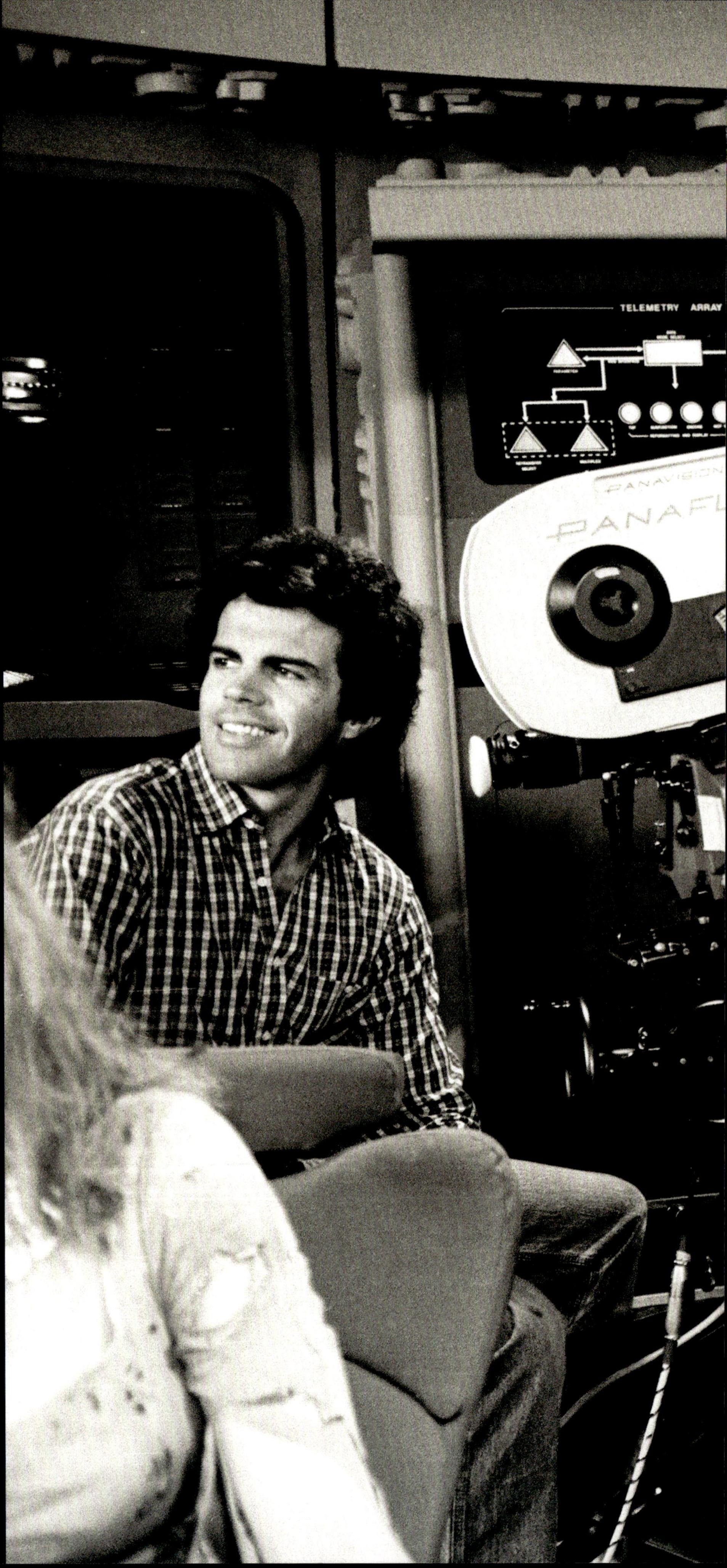

THIS SPREAD: Same bridge, different day.

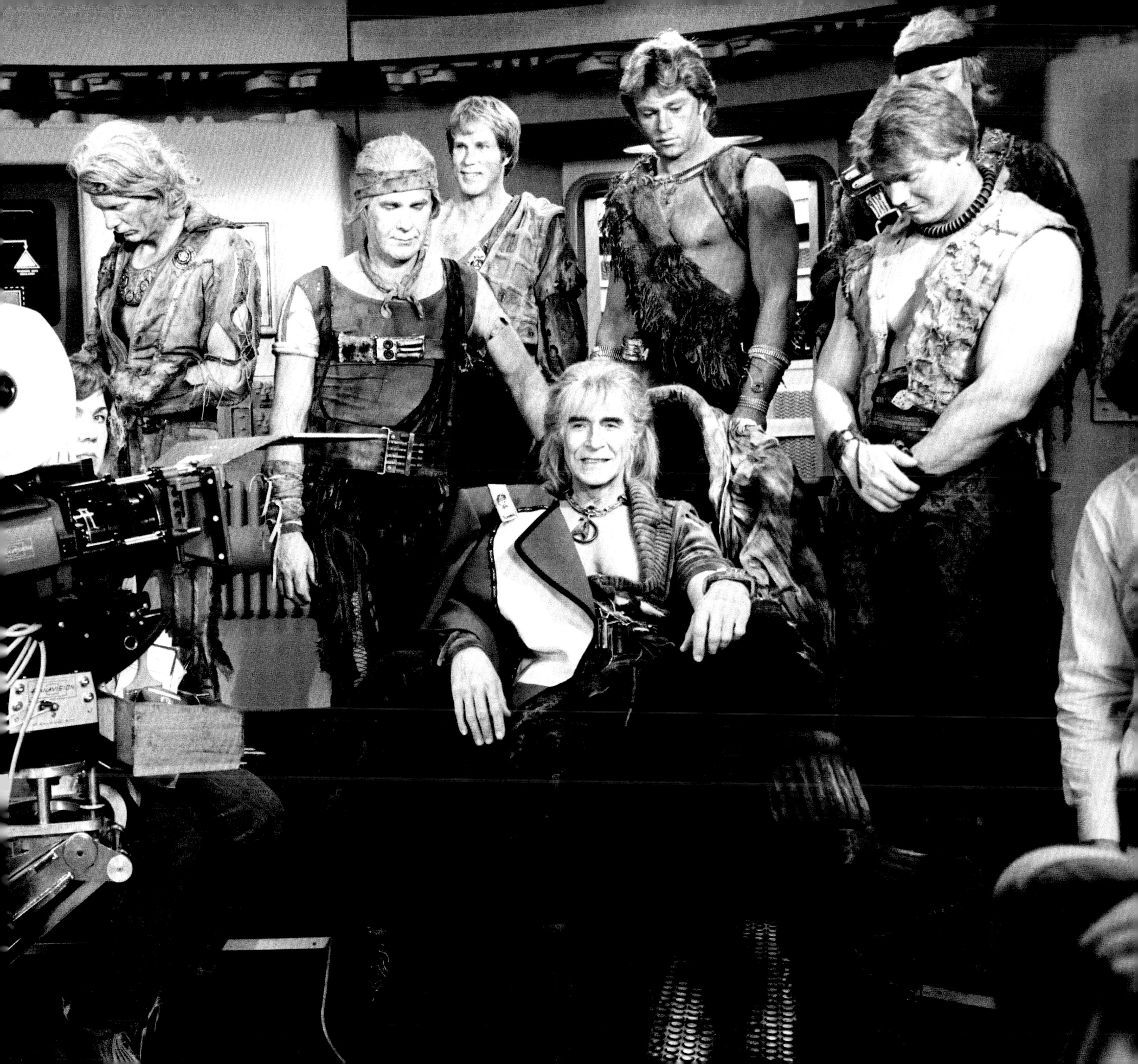

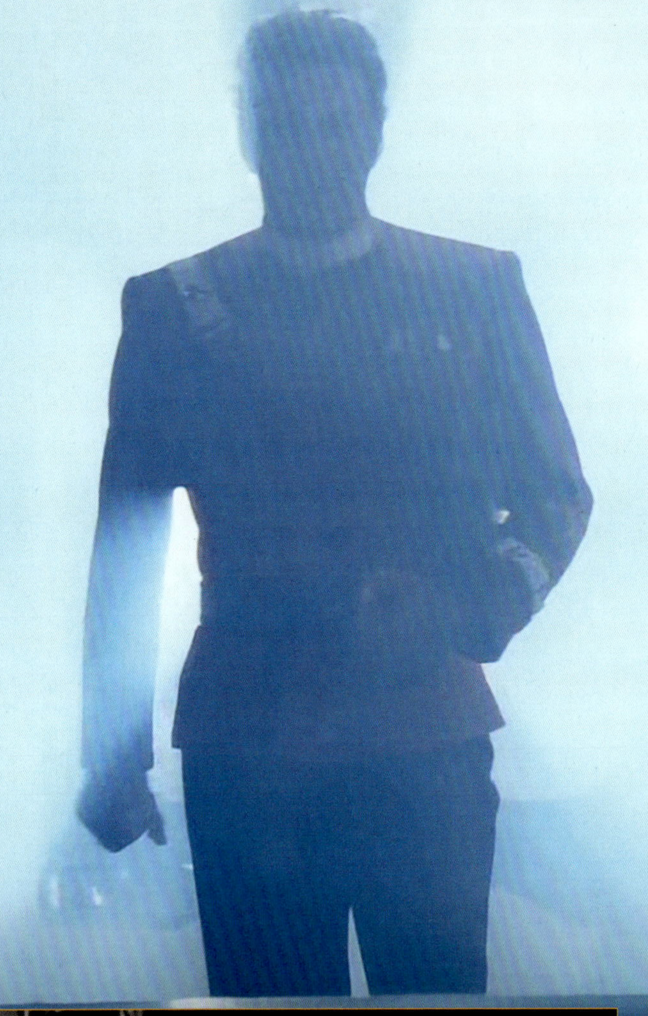

The lightweight and versatile Panasonic Panaflex camera was popular among many *Star Trek* productions, used on many of the television programs and films. One of its benefits was the ability to film in tight spaces and corners, something of a must on the bridge. Rescher helped innovate a lighting system to make it easier to light and film on the challenging bridge set. Another example of cinematic magic, Rescher was able to light and film the bridge *molto largo*, making it appear bigger than it actually was as a practical set.

Drawing on his years of experience, it was Sallin who envisioned one of *Star Trek II*'s most memorable shots, brought to realization by Rescher: the backlight, halo-effect entrance of Admiral Kirk. It was an example of how the director and producer were able to cooperate for the good of the production, although their relationship was sometimes strained. Sallin recalled for the Brian Volk-Weiss directed docu-series *The Center Seat: 55 Years of Star Trek*: "Nick didn't know me and I think he was protective and hesitant and afraid that I would somehow impinge on his world or something. And Nick was resistant. I couldn't put my arm around Nick and say, 'Nick, listen to me, you're in trouble. Now, I'm going to help you. Let me see if I can do that.' His attitude was always keeping me at a distance."[5] The two, however, were eventually able to establish a working collaboration as evidenced by Meyer's acceptance of Sallin's suggestion about how best to introduce Kirk.

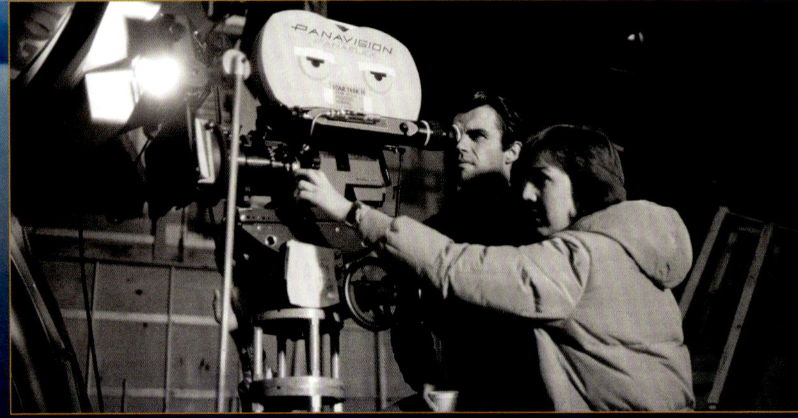

ABOVE: Denault and Coulson operate the Panavision Panaflex, the primary cameras for *Star Trek II*. The film negative was 35mm Fuji A 250T 8518.

RIGHT: Rescher, pictured behind Meyer as they ride a camera crane. Meyer is dressed in a three-piece suit here because he would be driving directly from the set after the day's work to attend a performance of the New York City Opera during their annual three-week visit to Los Angeles.

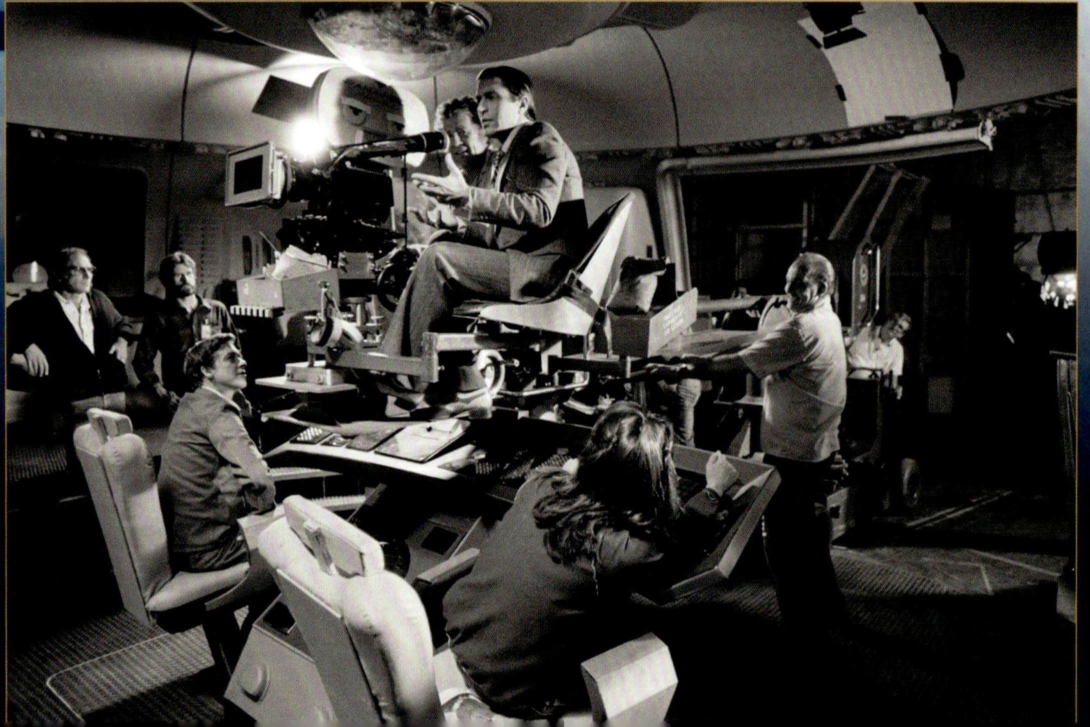

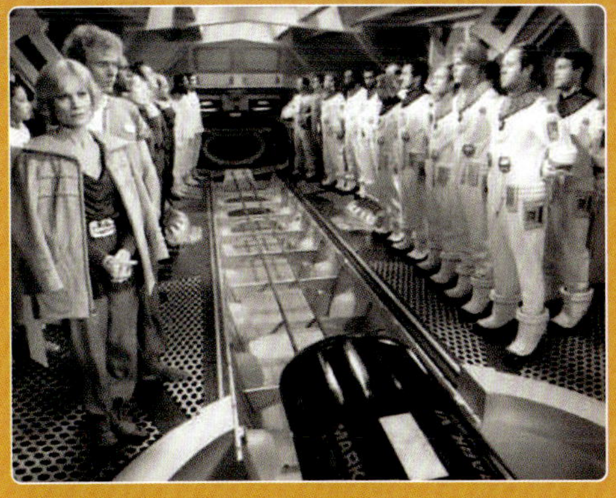
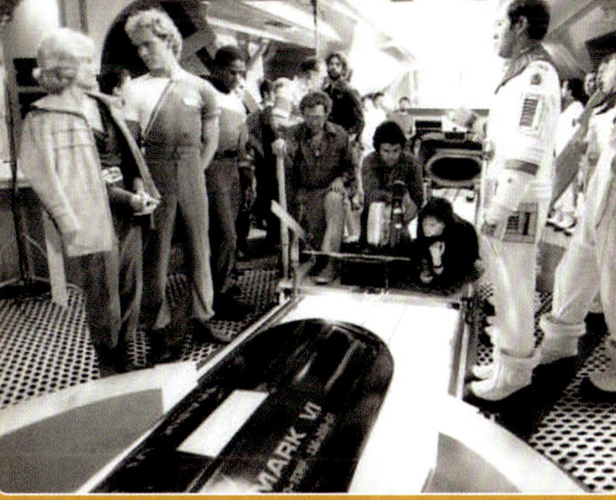
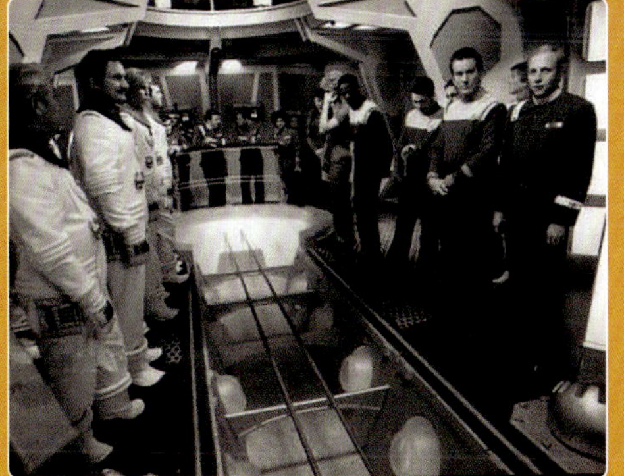
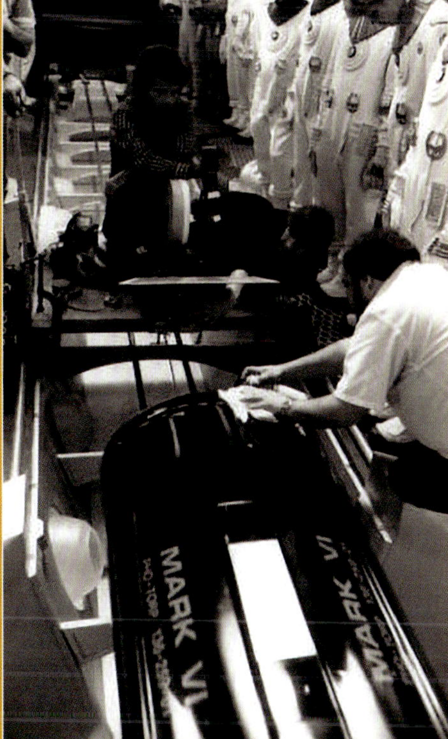
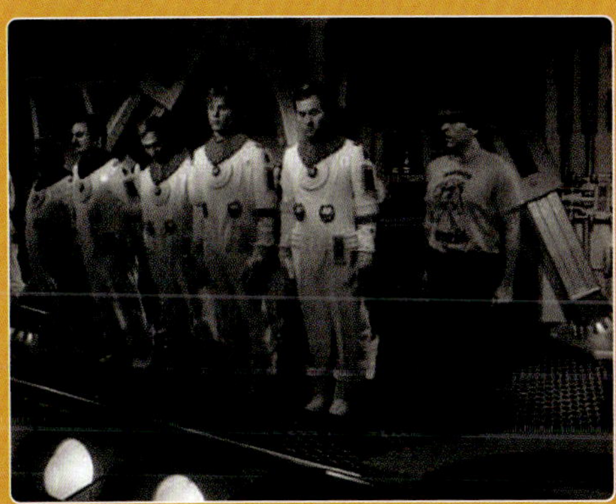
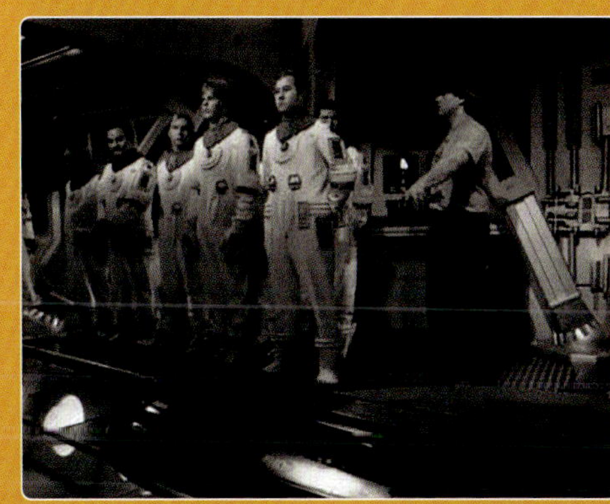
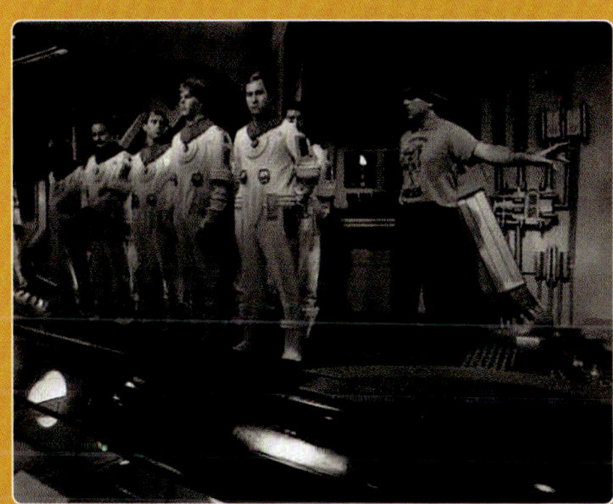

Torpedoes and the torpedo bay play an important role in both the action of *Star Trek II* and the emotion. The torpedoes help defend the ship during battle scenes and a torpedo serves as Spock's coffin after his sacrifice. "This was my favorite set, the torpedo bay," Meyer shares. "Absolutely. It's my favorite shot in the movie, the ripping up of the gratings. I got a chance to cut loose. This was the equivalent of running out the guns."[6] By filming the funeral scene from nearly the same eye-level as the torpedo, the camera becomes a substitute for Spock, seeing what he would see if alive, and adding to the sorrow of his wake. It also, again, served to make the set appear larger.

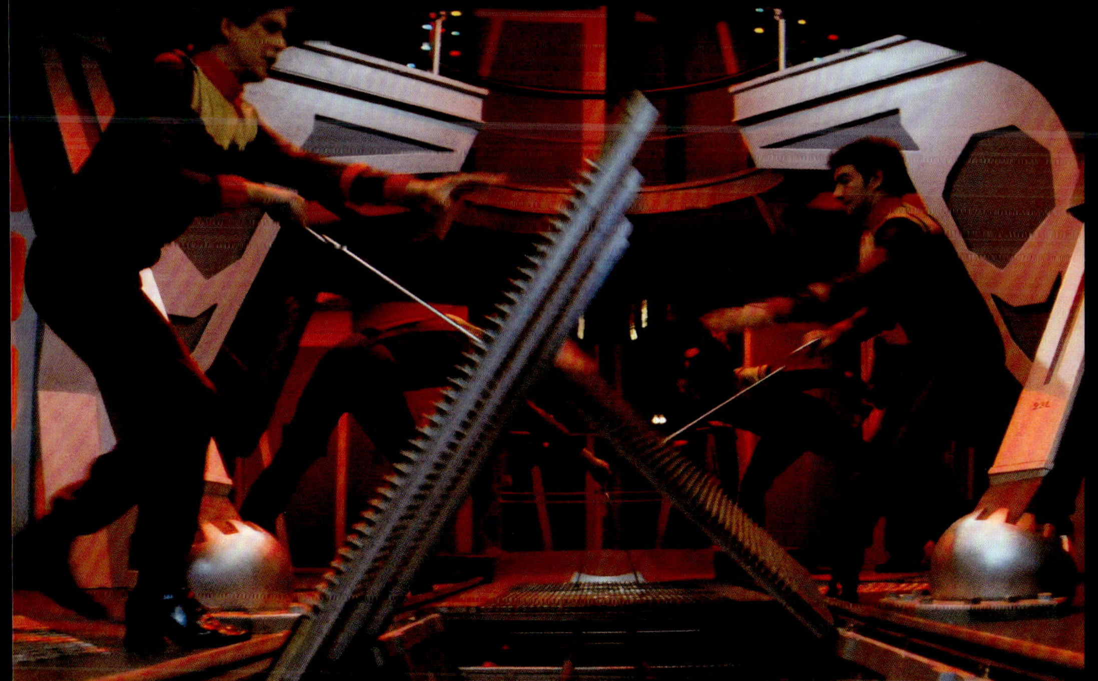
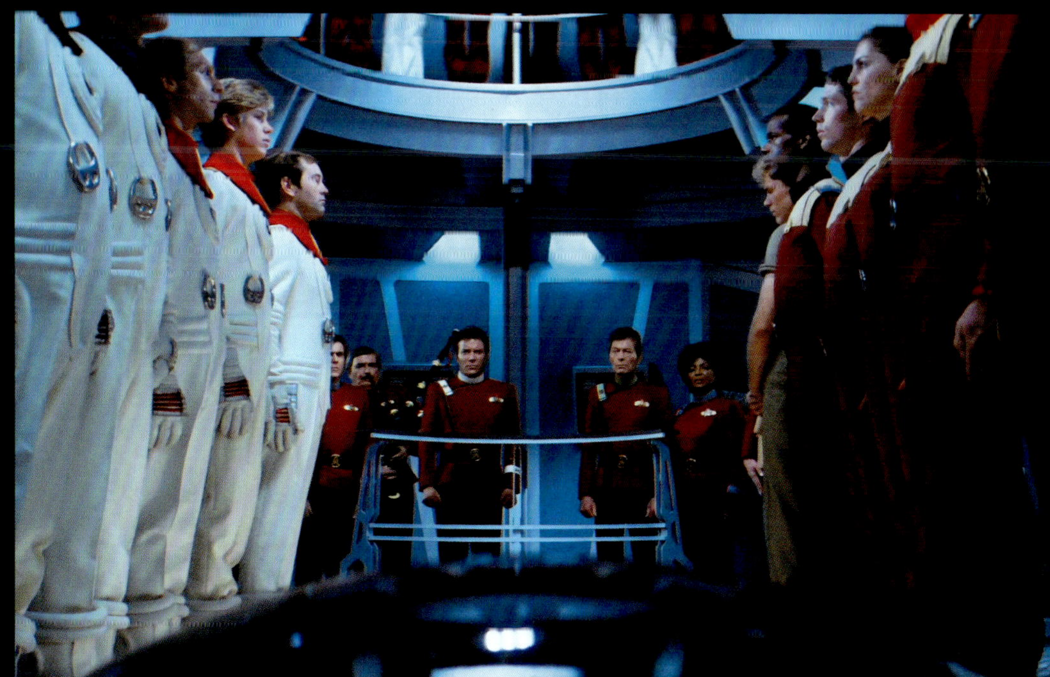

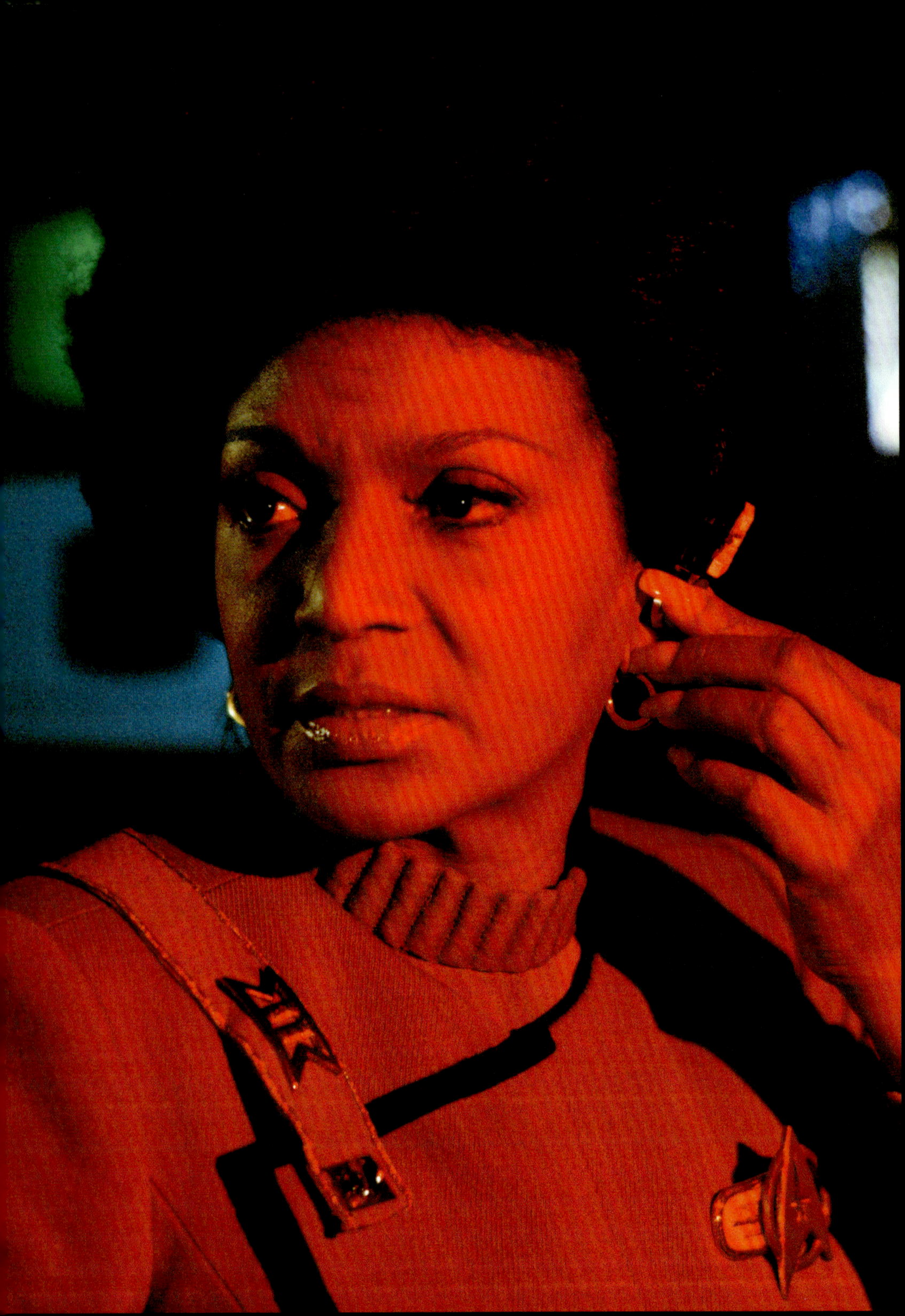

ABOVE: Rescher's choice to bathe the *Enterprise* crew in red light
added to the danger and claustrophobic emotion of the scene. The
performance by Nichelle Nichols, especially Uhura's urgent request
for confirmation that Kirk would consider surrendering, adds to the
moment. The audience is prospectively having the same reaction
as Uhura, disbelief that Kirk might actually lose.

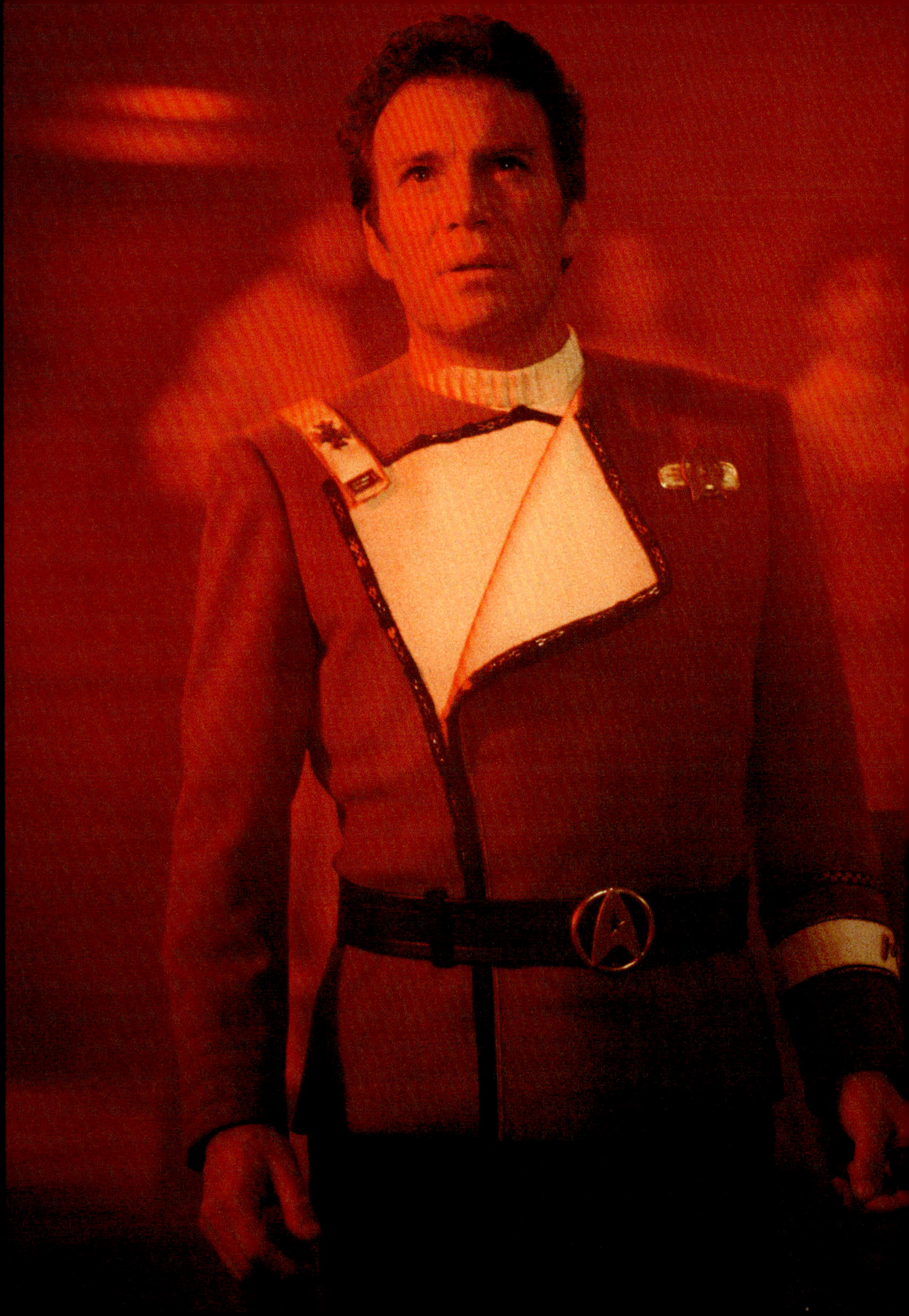

ABOVE: The costume designs of Robert Fletcher, the acting of William Shatner, and the
cinematography of Rescher complement each other to produce an effective moment.
Rescher's red lighting is a visual cue to audiences that the *Enterprise* itself is wounded,
hitching at reduced power and damaged by Khan's surprise attack. By having Admiral
Kirk have his jacket flap open—the *Star Trek* equivalent of a loosened suit tie—the stress
of the scene is reinforced. The splash of white color from Kirk's flap contrasts with
Rescher's monotone lighting. Shatner sells the scene with a performance that educes
both Kirk's understandable astonishment at the reveal that Khan is behind the attack,

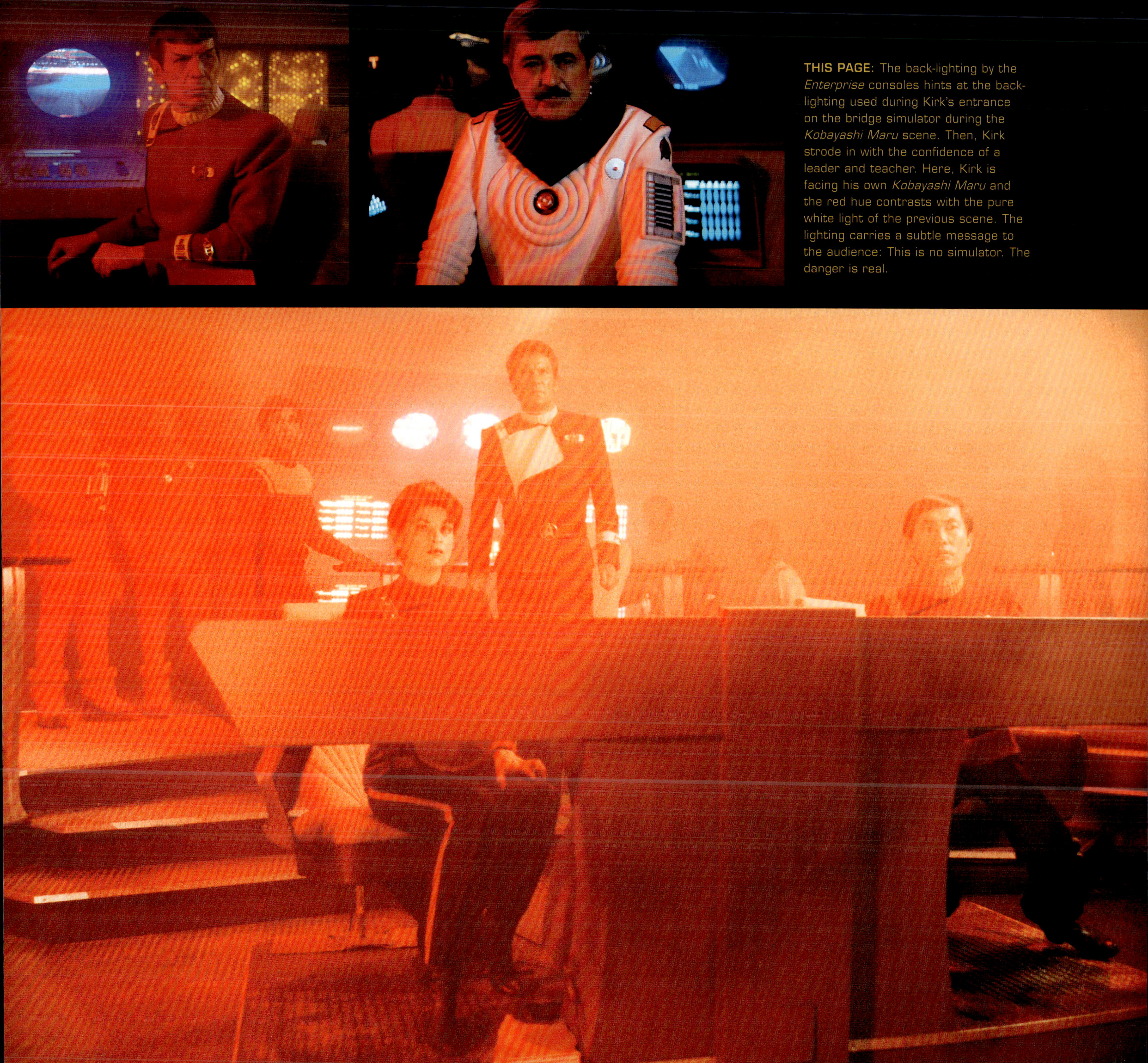

THIS PAGE: The back-lighting by the *Enterprise* consoles hints at the back-lighting used during Kirk's entrance on the bridge simulator during the *Kobayashi Maru* scene. Then, Kirk strode in with the confidence of a leader and teacher. Here, Kirk is facing his own *Kobayashi Maru* and the red hue contrasts with the pure white light of the previous scene. The lighting carries a subtle message to the audience: This is no simulator. The danger is real.

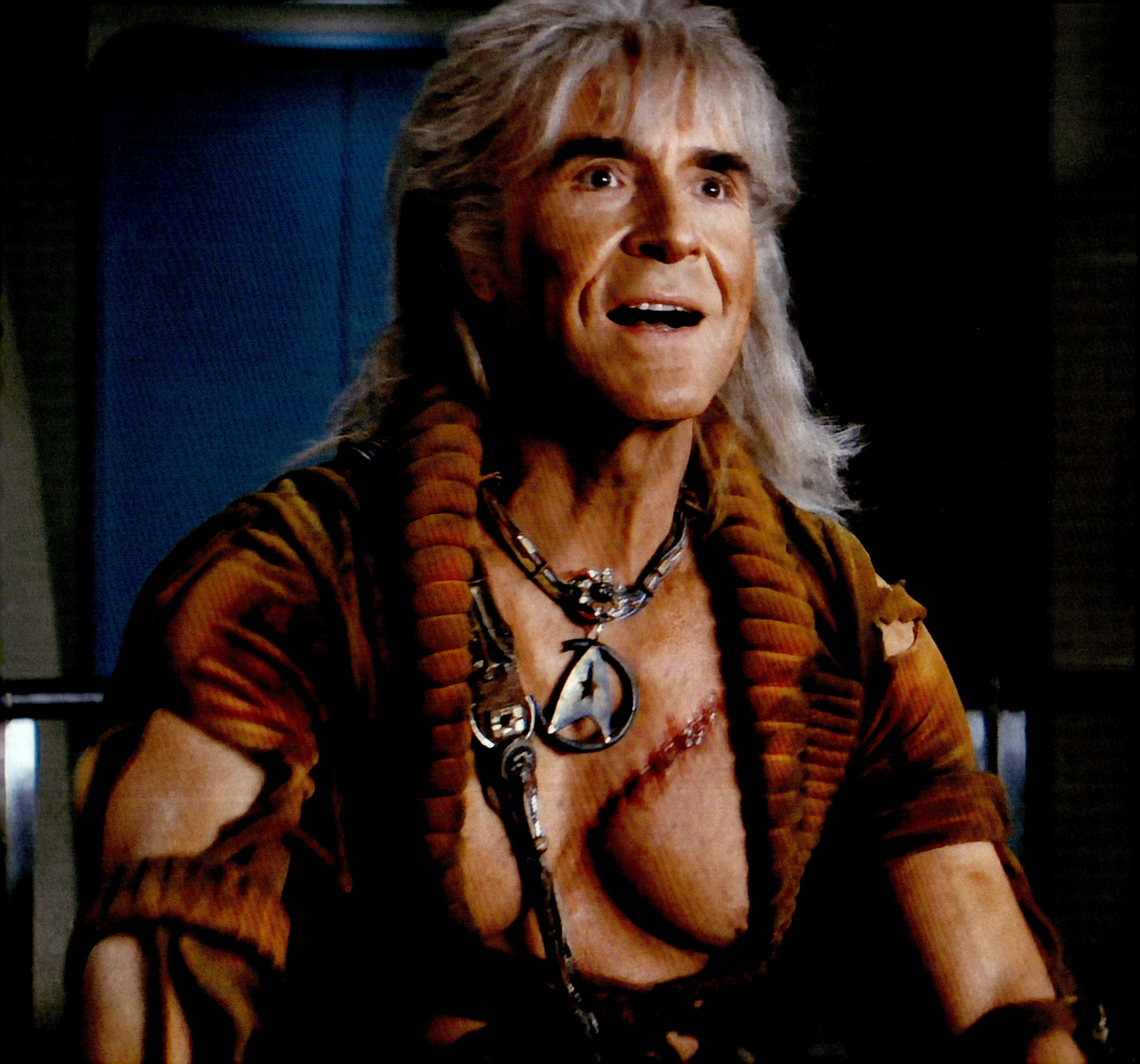

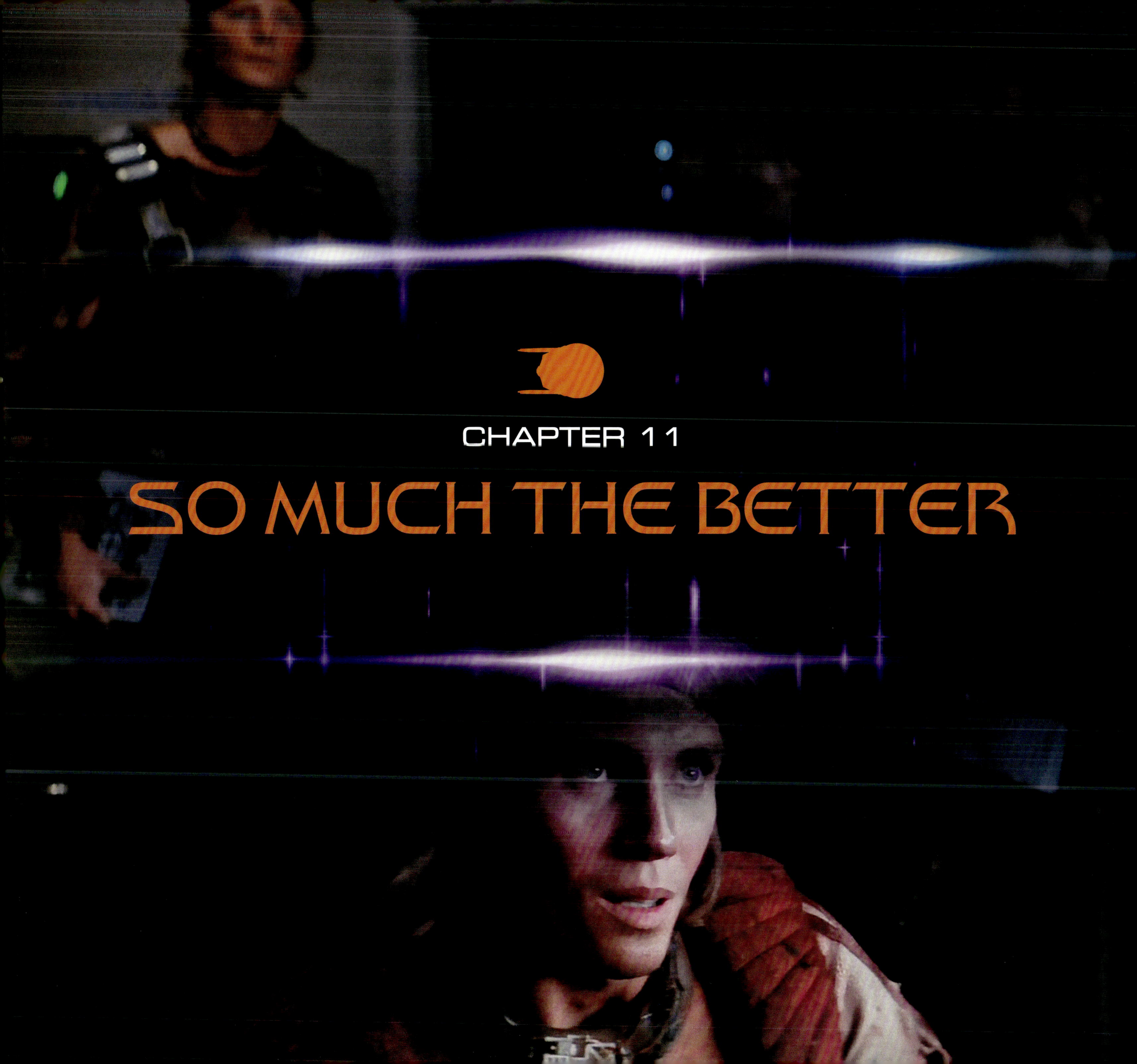

CHAPTER 11
SO MUCH THE BETTER

WERNER KEPPLER AND THE MAKEUP DEPARTMENT

The letter received at the *Star Trek II* production office during pre-production from Fred Phillips presented another challenge to be overcome. Phillips, the makeup artist who had been with *Star Trek* from its pilot episode "The Cage" through *Star Trek: The Motion Picture*, had written the letter with his regrets, declining the invitation to work on *Star Trek II*. Deteriorating eyesight and flagging depth-perception meant that his formally reliable eyes and steady hands could no longer create, nor apply, the iconic makeup and prostheses he pioneered. The original Klingon makeup, and its reinvention for *Star Trek: The Motion Picture*, had been some of Phillips' many contributions.

Even more, Leonard Nimoy credited Phillips with making the Spock makeup workable, knowing that if the application or proportions of the ears were wrong, first impressions of Spock could have been elfish and laughable. Nimoy believed that without the makeup work of Phillips, "the Spock character could have been a comic disaster from the start."[1] Simply, Phillips was irreplaceable, yet he would need to be replaced.

The choice of a new makeup team was an essential one. Because there are less alien characters in *Star Trek II* than *Star Trek: The Motion Picture*, it is easy to presume that the makeup work was concomitantly lighter. However, the sequel's increased action meant that not only did actors require makeup and hair styling, so too did their stunt performers, effectively doubling the work. Many characters sustain injuries and radiation burns during the skirmishes between the *Reliant* and the *Enterprise*. The team would need to create more makeup than meets the eye. Chosen for the task were veteran makeup artists Werner Keppler and James L. McCoy, and hairstylist Dione Taylor.

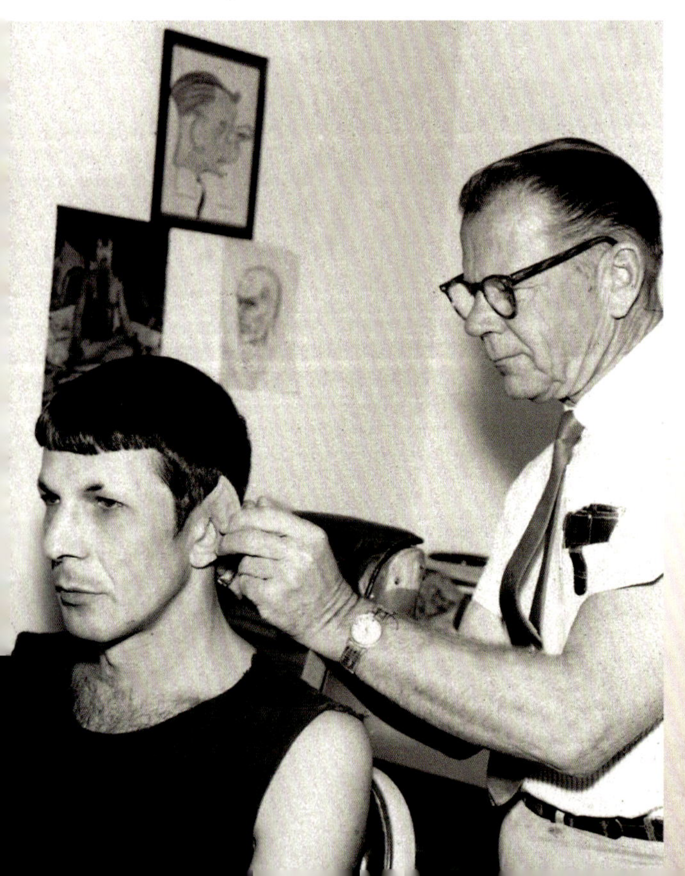

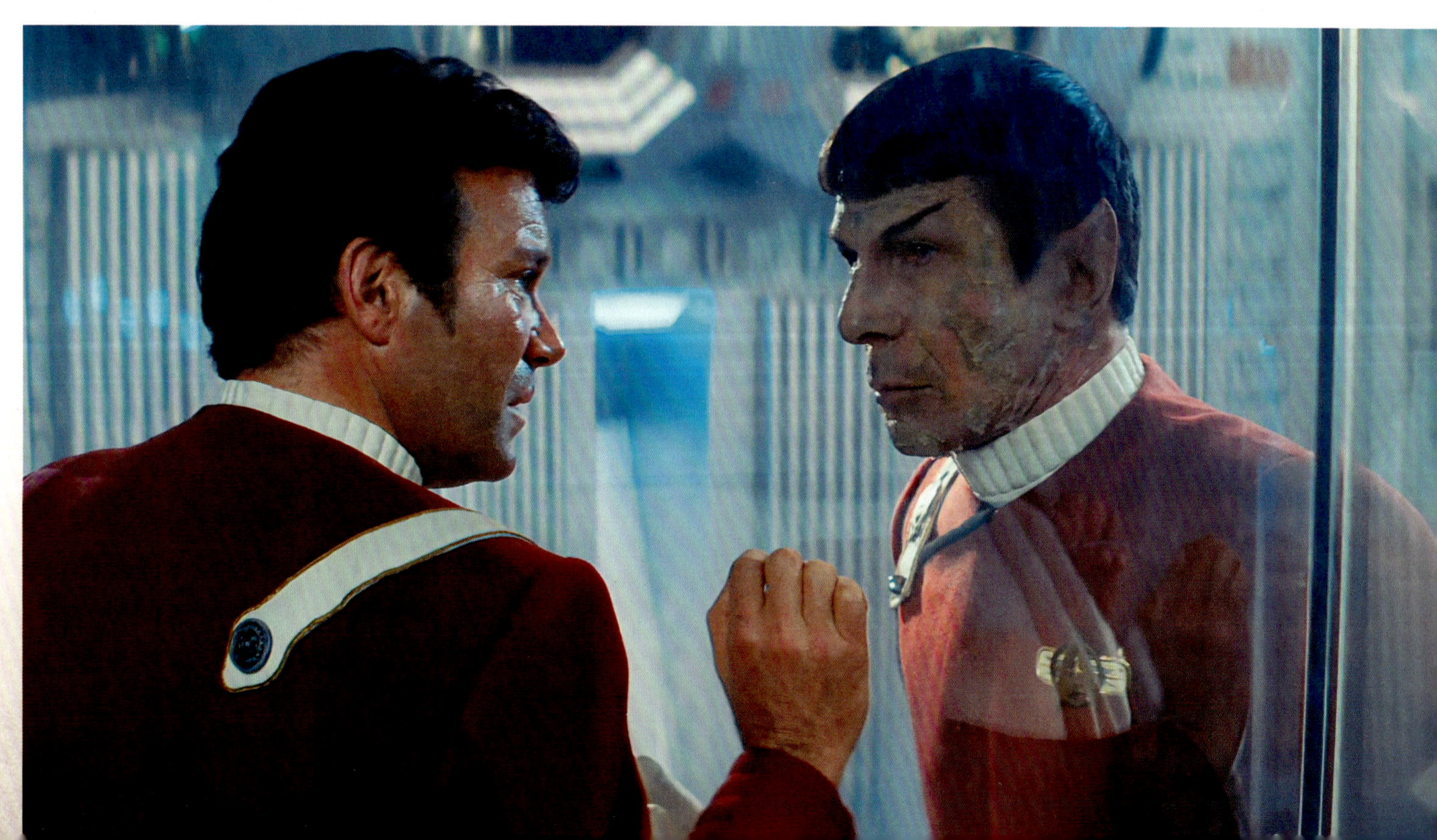

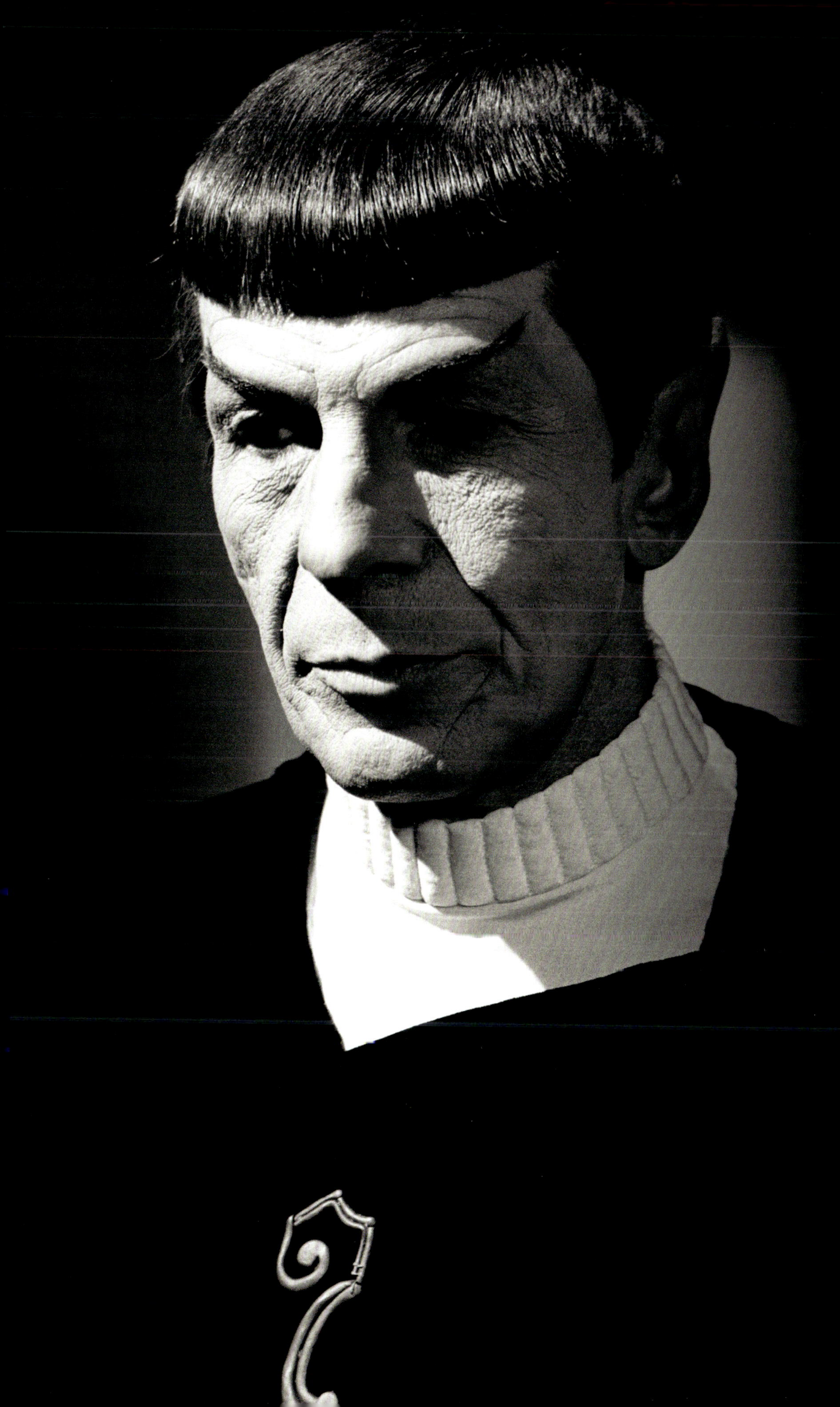

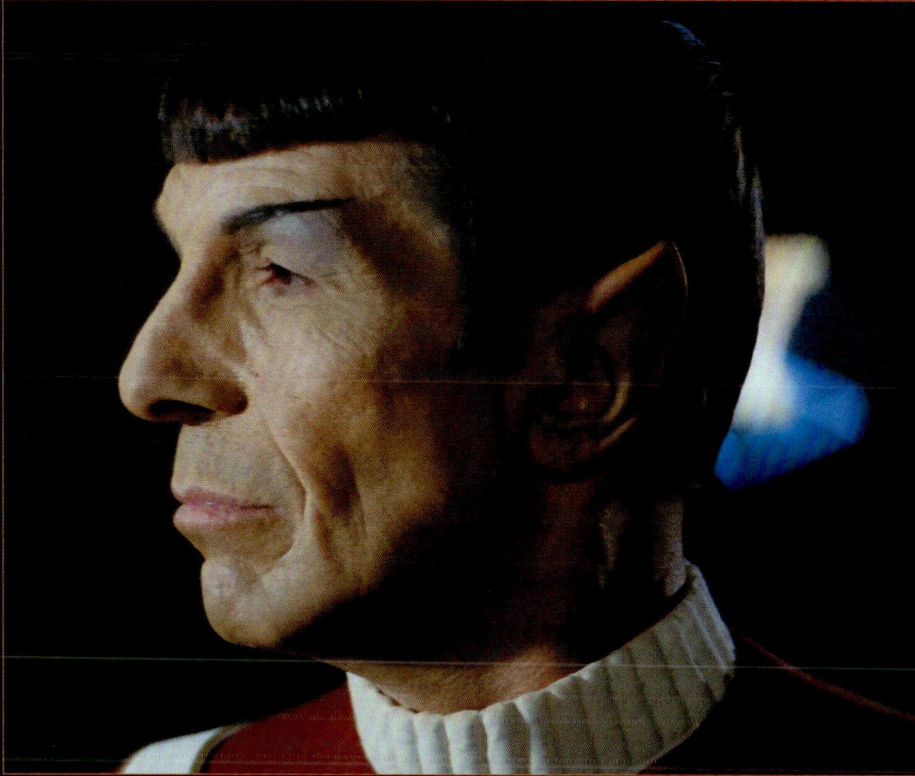

Keppler shared with Kay Anderson of *Cinefantastique* in 1982 that, "I suppose the ears were my biggest perpetual headache."[2] As with many of the *Star Trek II* production obstacles, that headache was the result of a time crunch. "Leonard Nimoy was in China making the *Marco Polo* mini-series right up to a few days before his part in this movie began; so I couldn't take the impressions of his ears from which to make the Spock ear-tips. Nimoy came in on a Friday afternoon, and as soon as he got in from the airport, practically, I took the impressions; I had to have a set of ears ready to use on Monday morning."[3]

Once behind schedule-wise, Keppler found himself in a perpetual cycle of catch-up. Each set of Spock ears could be applied and used only once because of fragility, so a new pair had to be made each evening using the single mold that existed. When production wrapped for the day, Keppler would go home and bake a new pair of ears in his kitchen oven. If there were any problems, such as bubbles or tearing, the whole process had to begin again. Keppler, only half-jokingly, revealed that many nights he did not get much sleep and that, "My wife wants her oven back at least every other night!"[4]

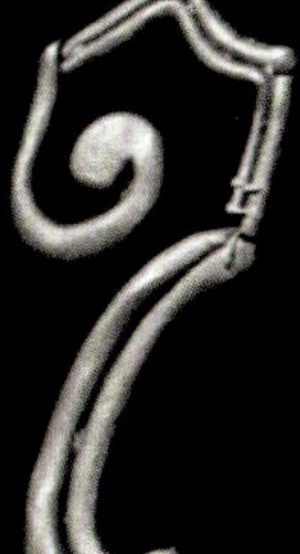

WERNER KEPPLER

Born in Germany on May 24, 1929, Werner Alfons Karl Keppler showed an interest in makeup design from an early age, working for five years as an apprentice in the opera houses and theaters of his native Hannover. After emigrating to the United States in 1955, Keppler became an instructor at a school owned by the legendary makeup artist Percival Westmore (uncle of the *Star Trek: The Next Generation*–era makeup virtuoso Michael Westmore). So close were the Keppler and Westmore families that Perc's wife, Ola, acted as a witness on Keppler's behalf when he applied for citizenship.

Working as an instructor during the 1950s and 1960s had given Keppler the time to hone his craft. He began an impressive Hollywood career of his own, working on the original *Planet of the Apes* films as part of John Chambers' team and on Steven Spielberg's *Jaws* (1975), where he gained a reputation as a jack-of-all-trades.

BELOW: Keppler (right) keeps an eye on his work on set.

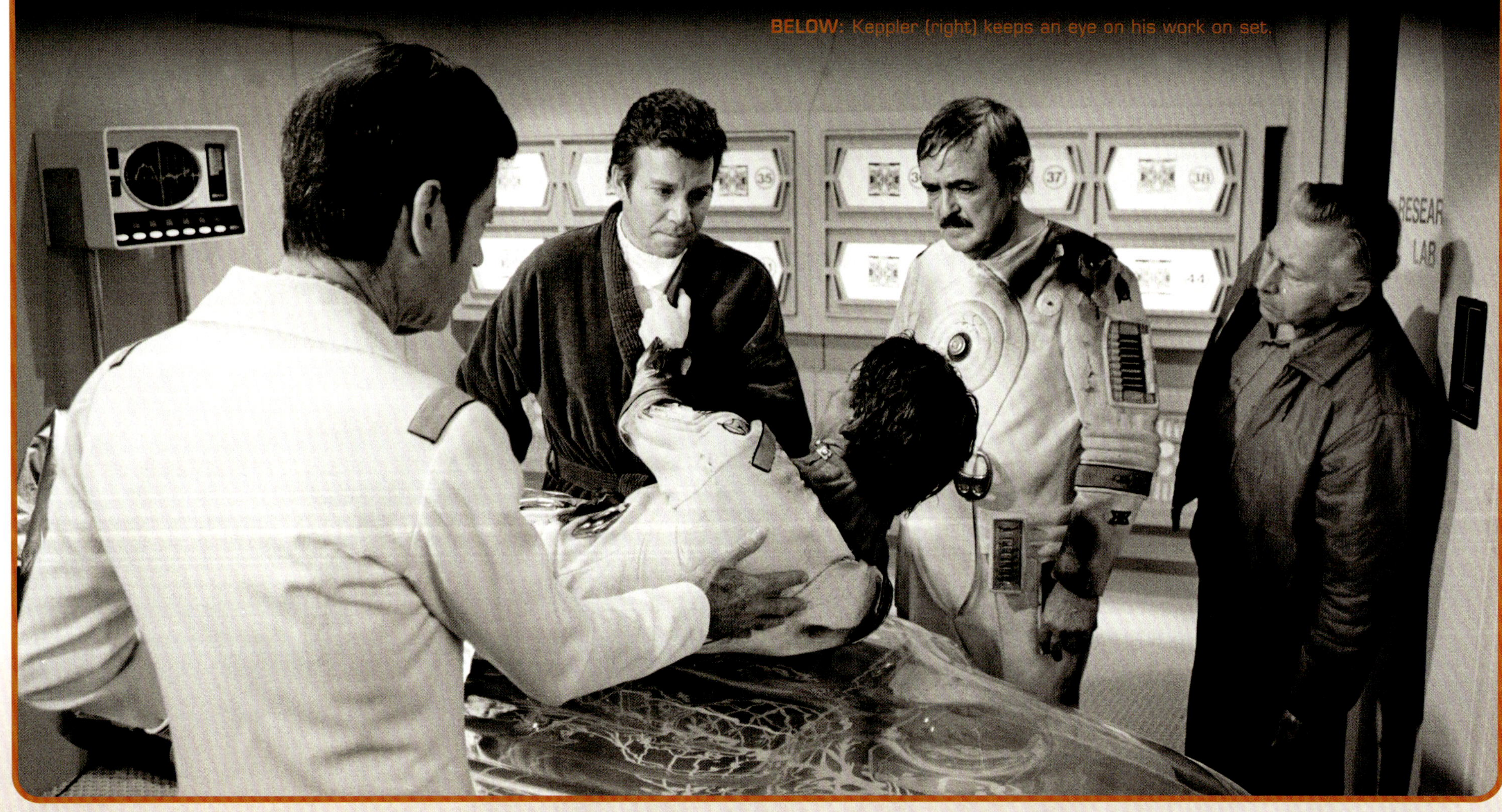

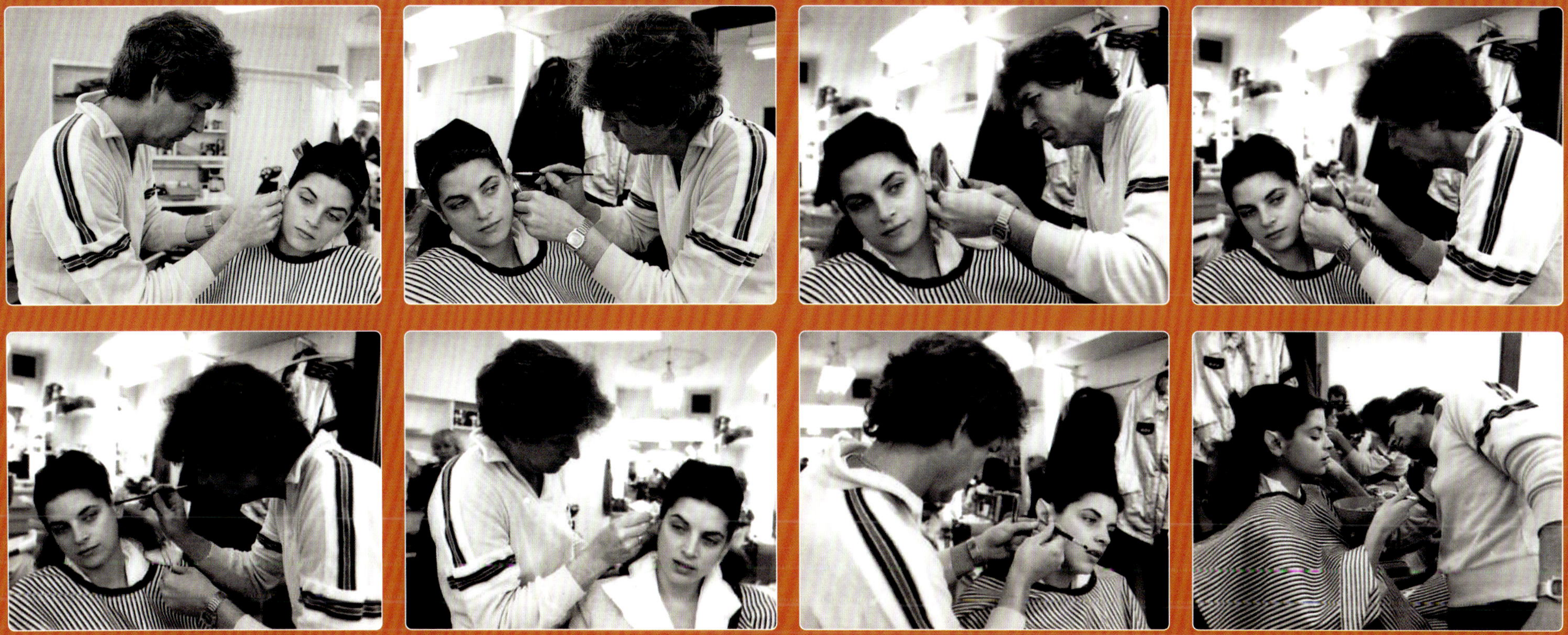

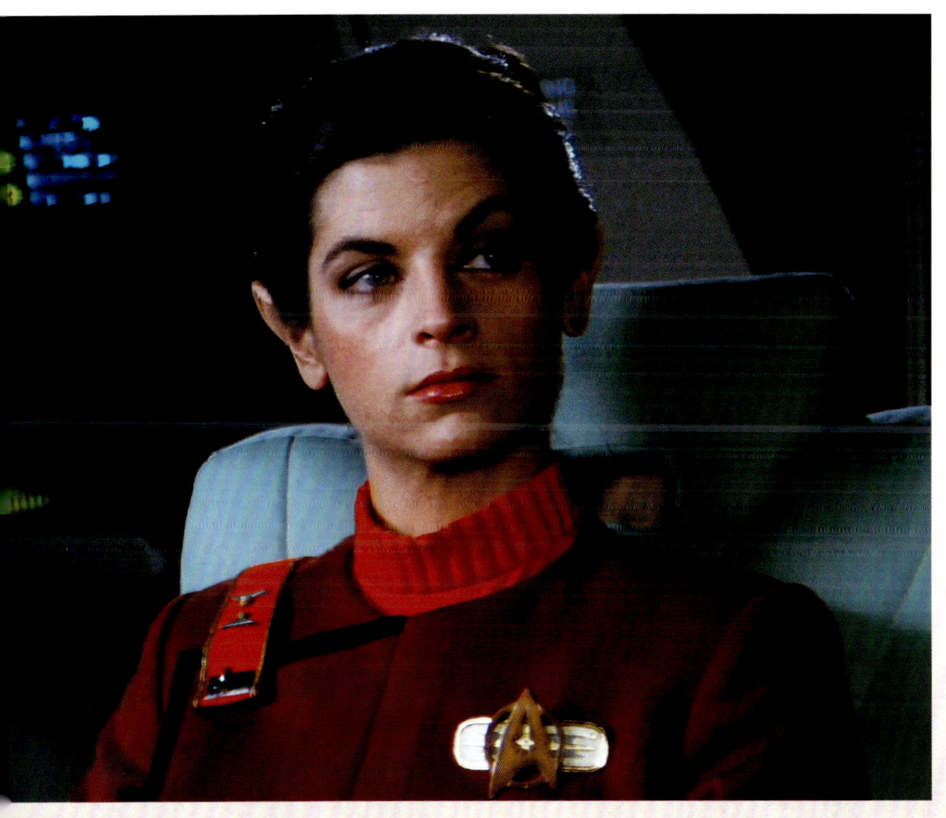

Luckily, there was more time for the creation of Saavik's makeup. Alley's maquillage was primarily the responsibility of James L. McCoy, a veteran artist with a decade's worth of experience and an Emmy nomination for Outstanding Achievement in Makeup. An additional benefit was that, unlike Spock, Saavik's makeup design was somewhat more streamlined due to the decision to avoid the upswept eyebrows traditional to Vulcans. The thinking was that upswept eyebrows would distract from Alley's face. Plus, Alley had a natural ability to make her eyebrows perform like a Vulcan. Alley recalled, "People my whole life teased me, because when I'm talking and I don't really pay attention to what I'm doing, my eyebrow goes up. Right? So even just my friends would go, 'Oh, god, your eyebrow goes up like Spock.'"[6]

Alley was a fan of the Saavik makeup and especially the Vulcan ears, joking, "They actually look better than my own. They look more natural. I should have been born a Vulcan!"[6] Director Nicholas Meyer recalls that Alley was so enthusiastic about—or should it be *fascinated* by—her ear prostheses that she would wear them home after filming.

Time crunches inspired Keppler and McCoy to innovate a new kind of burn makeup composition and application for *Star Trek II*. Ricardo Montalban, Nimoy, and Ike Eisenmann, who plays cadet Peter Preston, wore and bore the brunt of that burn and radiation makeup. Preston's brave actions result in burns across his entire body. If traditional makeup techniques, relying on latex appliances, had been used, Eisenmann would have had to sit for four or five hours each day of filming. Something the production could ill afford. Employing their own bit of *Kobayashi Maru* original thinking, Keppler and McCoy innovated a technique using food-grade gelatin. "They used this new experimental stuff that was gelatin-based," Eisenmann described. "It had not been used before, and it had a very specific look. It was used on all of us, including Ricardo Montalban and the other supporting cast members that got burned, hurt or injured."[7] Once applied to the actor's skin using a spatula, the gelatin could be shaded to give the illusion of damaged skin. "The advantage of this material is its flexibility," explained Keppler. "It moves with the actor's skin and muscles."[8] Equally advantageous, the technique took what could have been an onerous makeup time and significantly reduced it. For their efforts and innovations, Keppler and McCoy would be nominated for a Saturn Award.

Though the makeup was a time saver, it proved far from comfortable. Eisenmann remembers, "One aspect of this product that they used was that it had this tendency to shrink slowly over the course of many, many hours. And I had it applied to me on the entire side of my torso, on half of my face, my neck, my shoulder. But by the time I was in that for six, eight, or nine hours, I felt like I was in this shrink wrap, and it started to just drive me crazy… Taking it off took practically as long as it took to put on. I had to get in a hot shower, and it took about 40, 45 minutes to wash all of this stuff off.[9]

BELOW LEFT: Peter Preston symbolized the impetuousness and the potential of the *Enterprise* cadets. His call-out of Kirk during a scene originally deleted from the theatrical version was balanced by his bravery and sacrifice.

BELOW & BOTTOM LEFT: Keppler forwent traditional makeup adhesive for a kitchen pot and spatula to use his innovative food-grade gelatin technique on Eisenmann.

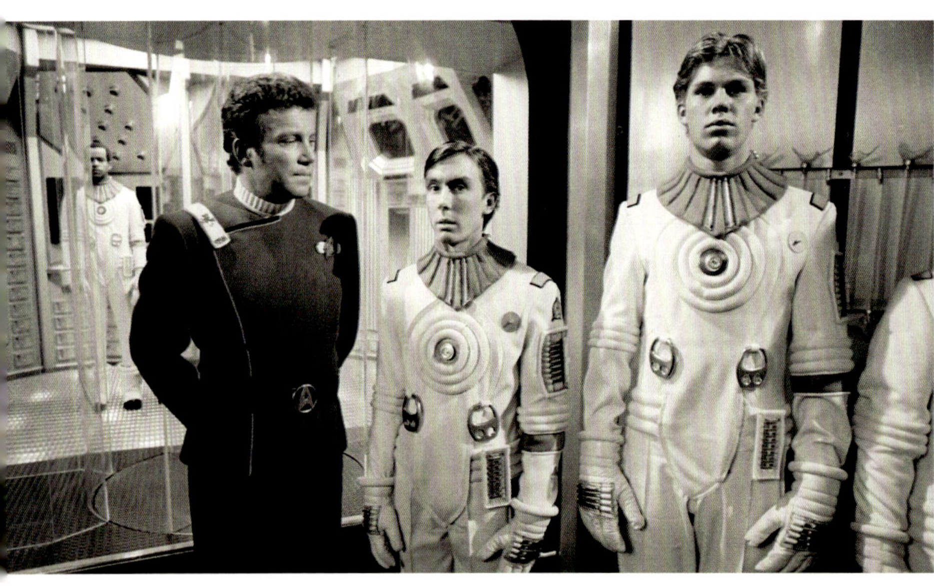

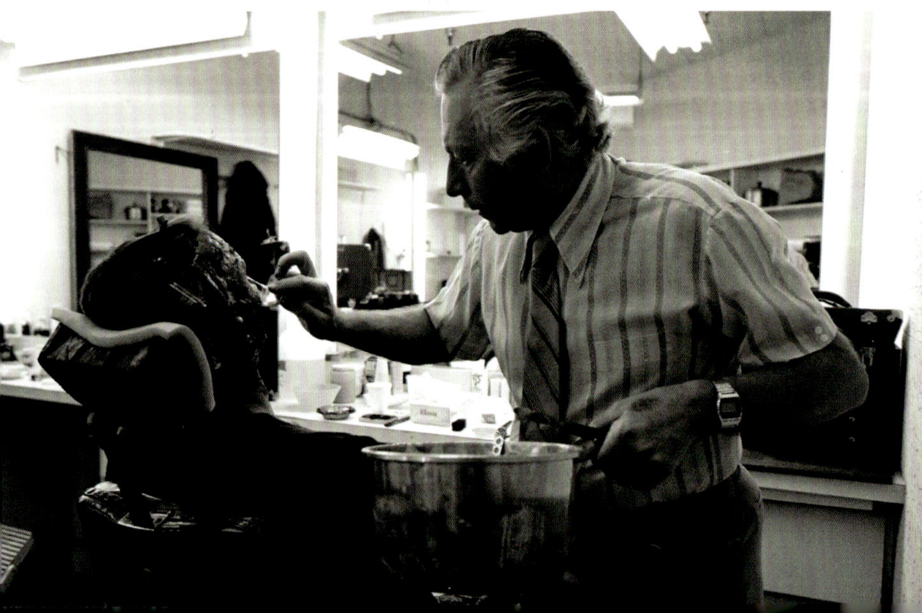

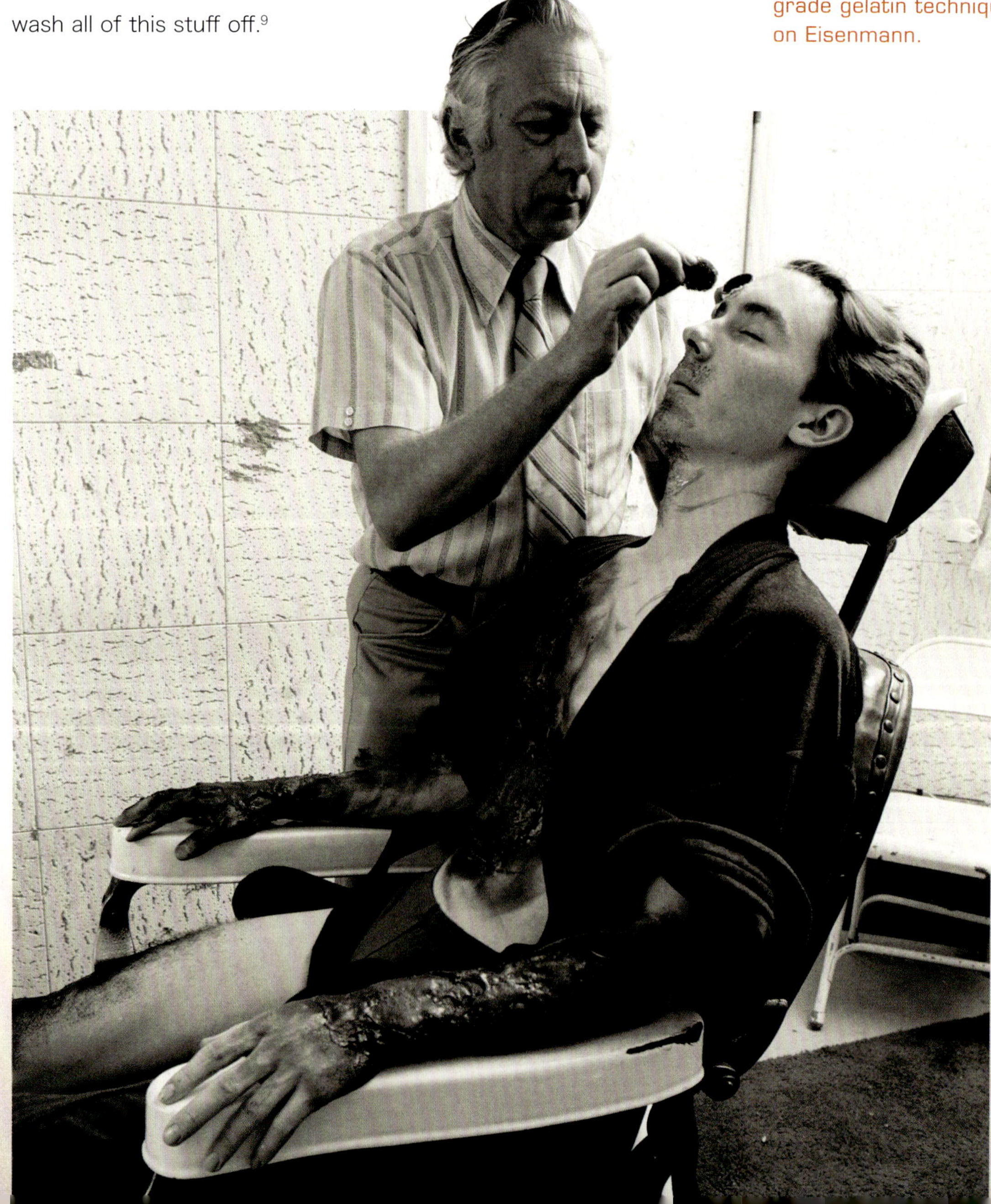

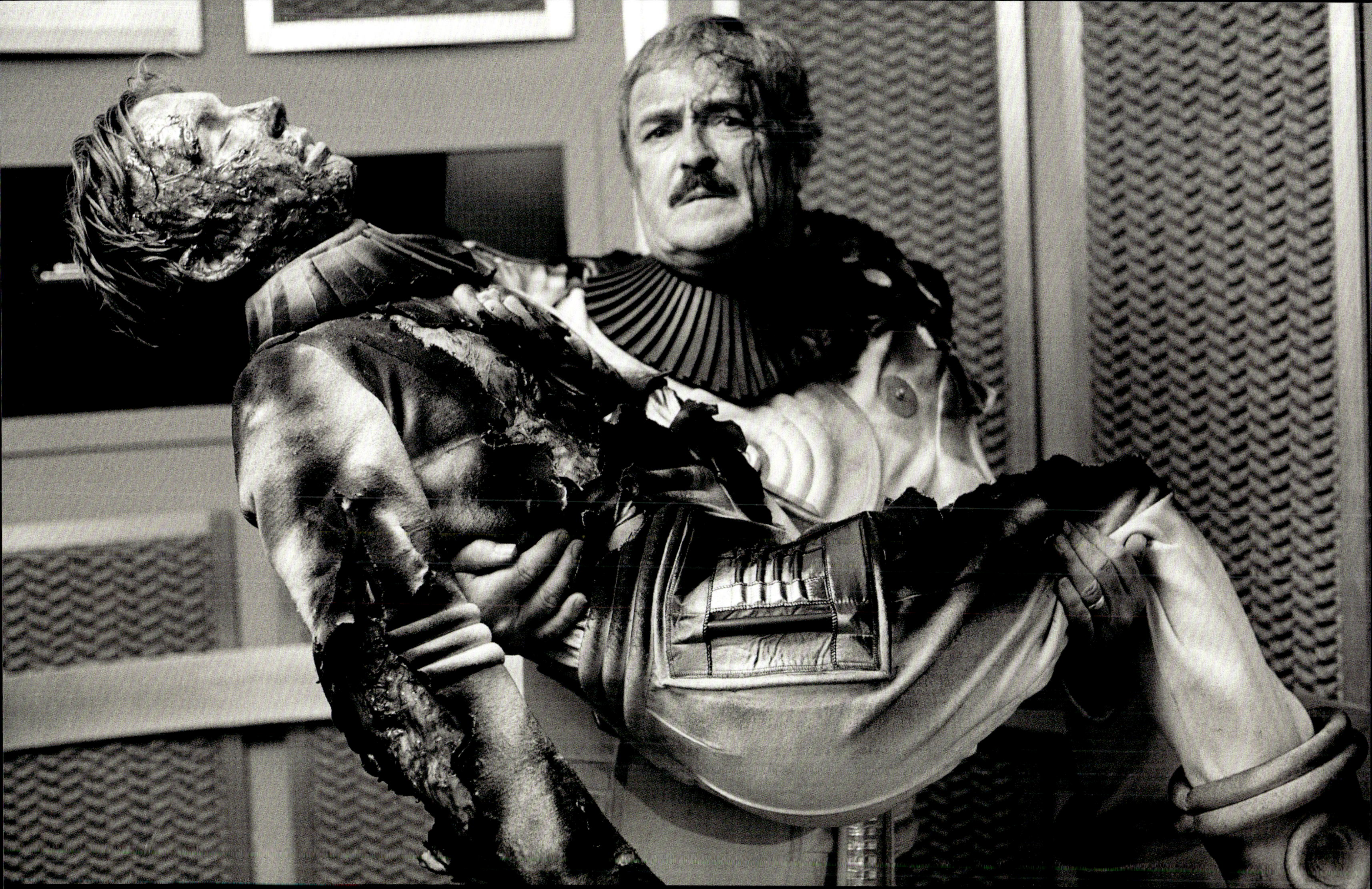

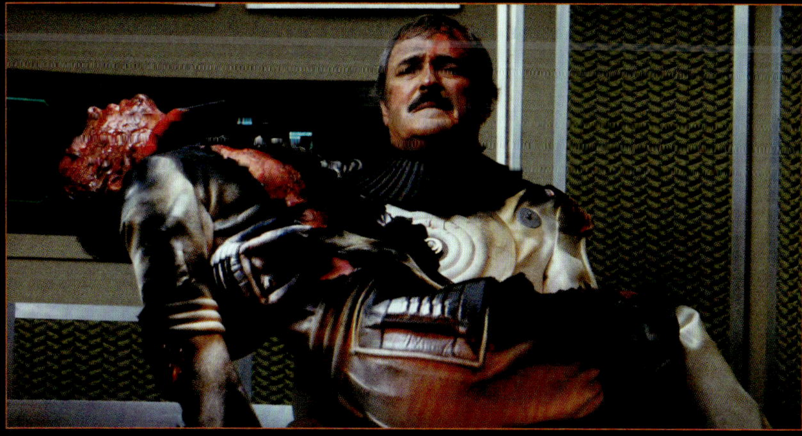

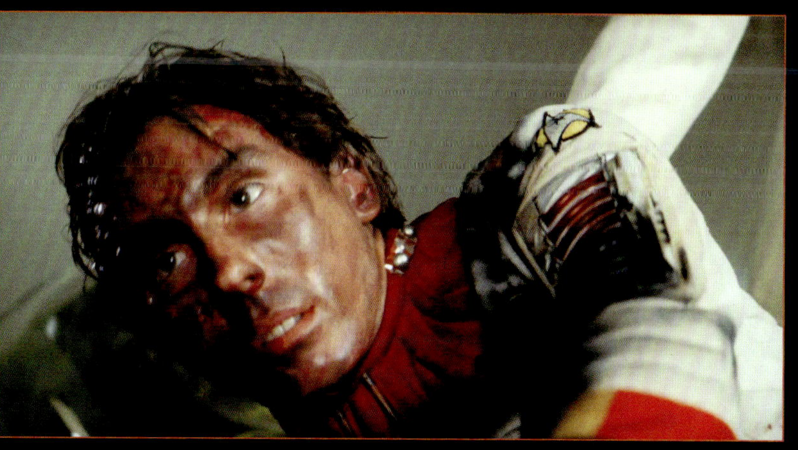

THIS PAGE: Injuries suffered as a result of Khan's vengeance comprised the bulk of the special makeup necessary. Here, Eisenmann and James Doohan's completed makeup designs help convince the audience of the severity of the danger posed by Khan.

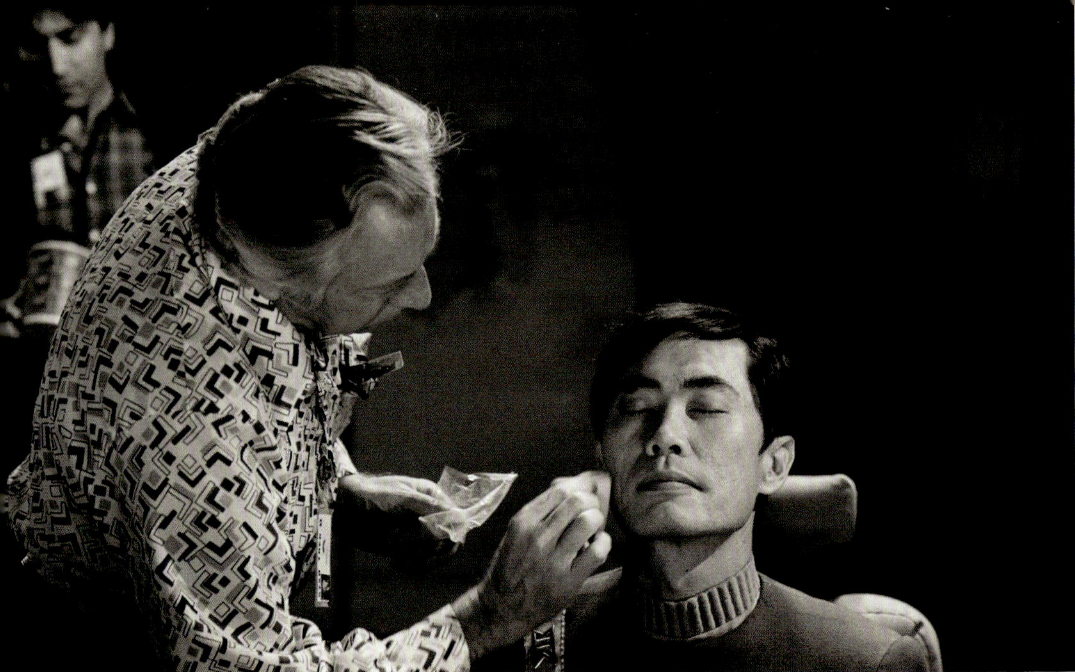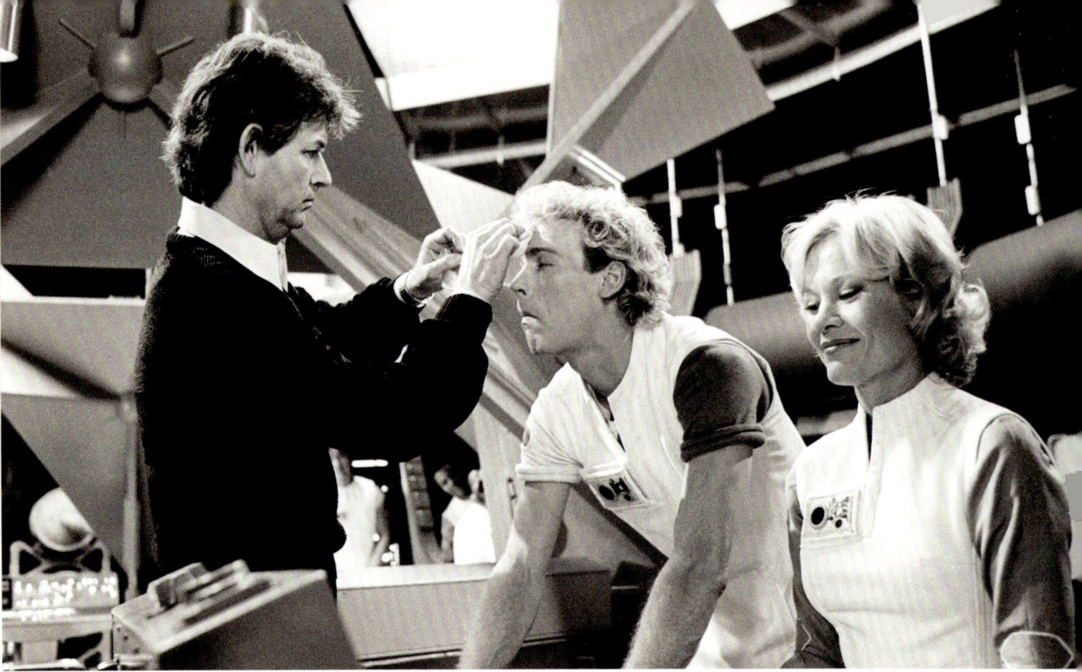

In addition to specialty makeup like Vulcan ears, Keppler and his team were also needed on set for frequent touchups, because makeup can be affected by movements of the actors, such as during the fight scene between Kirk and David, or because of lights and environmental conditions.

The scene with Saavik and Kirk in the turbolift, with McCoy joining, shows how makeup and hairstyling can be used to inform characterizations. The scene serves to remind the audience of the familiar relationship that exists between Kirk and McCoy, while at the same time hinting that perhaps Saavik is more than she seems. Alley reflected, "She's being groomed for Starfleet and she is Spock's protégé. But, she has this side of her that is a bit passionate… You know, her dress and everything is very military and she's very much into Starfleet, I mean that's her whole life, but she does have this side of her which is slightly flirtatious."[10] Hairstyles are a visual shorthand, alerting the audience that while Saavik may live by regulations, perhaps she is learning—literally and figuratively—to let her hair down. At Spock's funeral and at the end of the film, where a deleted scene would have strongly hinted of a burgeoning romantic relationship between Saavik and David, Saavik's hair is again more casual.

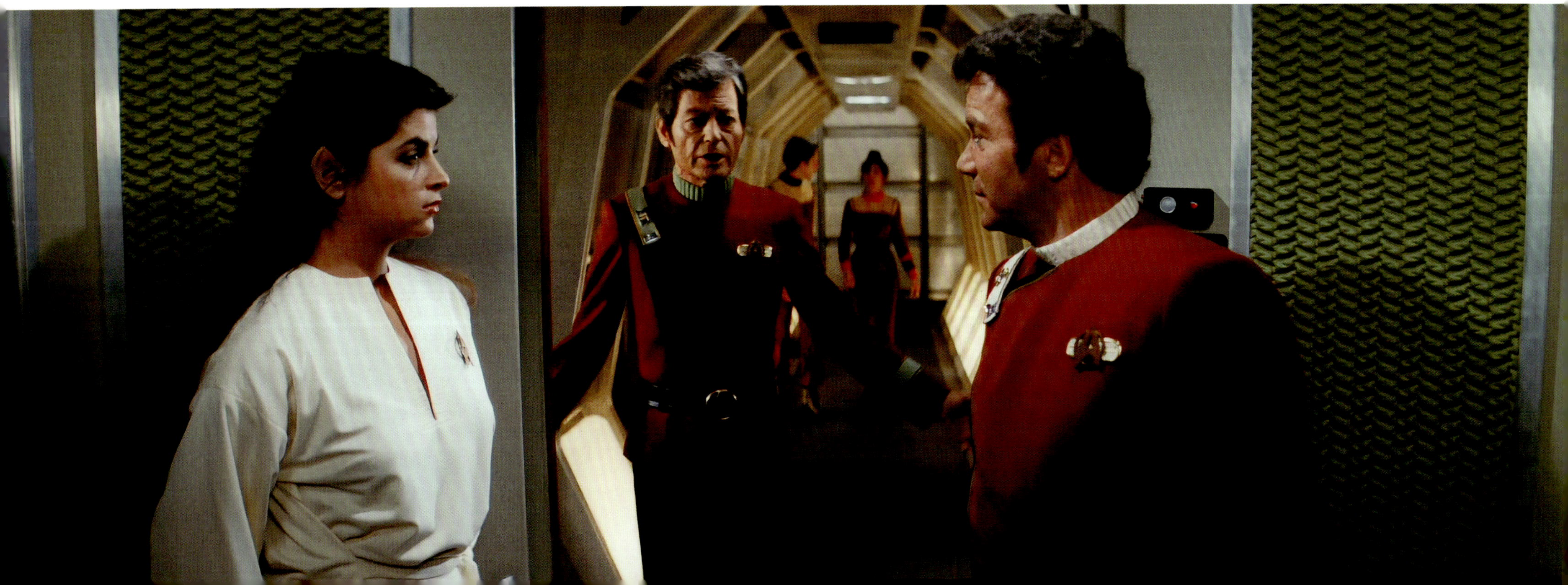

Conveying character through hairstyling was the responsibility of Emmy-nominated hairstylist Taylor, who had previously worked with Meyer on his film *Time After Time* (1979). As with many of the behind-the-scenes artist of *Star Trek II*, Taylor would need to balance using traditional *Star Trek* tropes, such as the Starfleet pointy sideburns, with original elements and styles as demanded by the story, like Saavik's regulation hairstyle.

BELOW LEFT: Unused hair style for Carol Marcus.

BELOW RIGHT: Occasionally actors took makeup and hair matters into their own hands.

BOTTOM RIGHT: Keppler and DeForest Kelley. The hairstyle of Dr. McCoy would remain relatively unchanged during the years. In 1965, Gene Roddenberry asked Kelley to get a haircut reminiscent of President John F. Kennedy, thinking that a change of coiffure might convince reluctant studio executives to approve casting Kelley as the good country doctor despite his Hollywood heritage of playing villains. "It was expensive," recalled Kelley in 1967. "It cost me $35, but I had confidence in Roddenberry."[13] Kelley landed the role and the lucky haircut stayed.

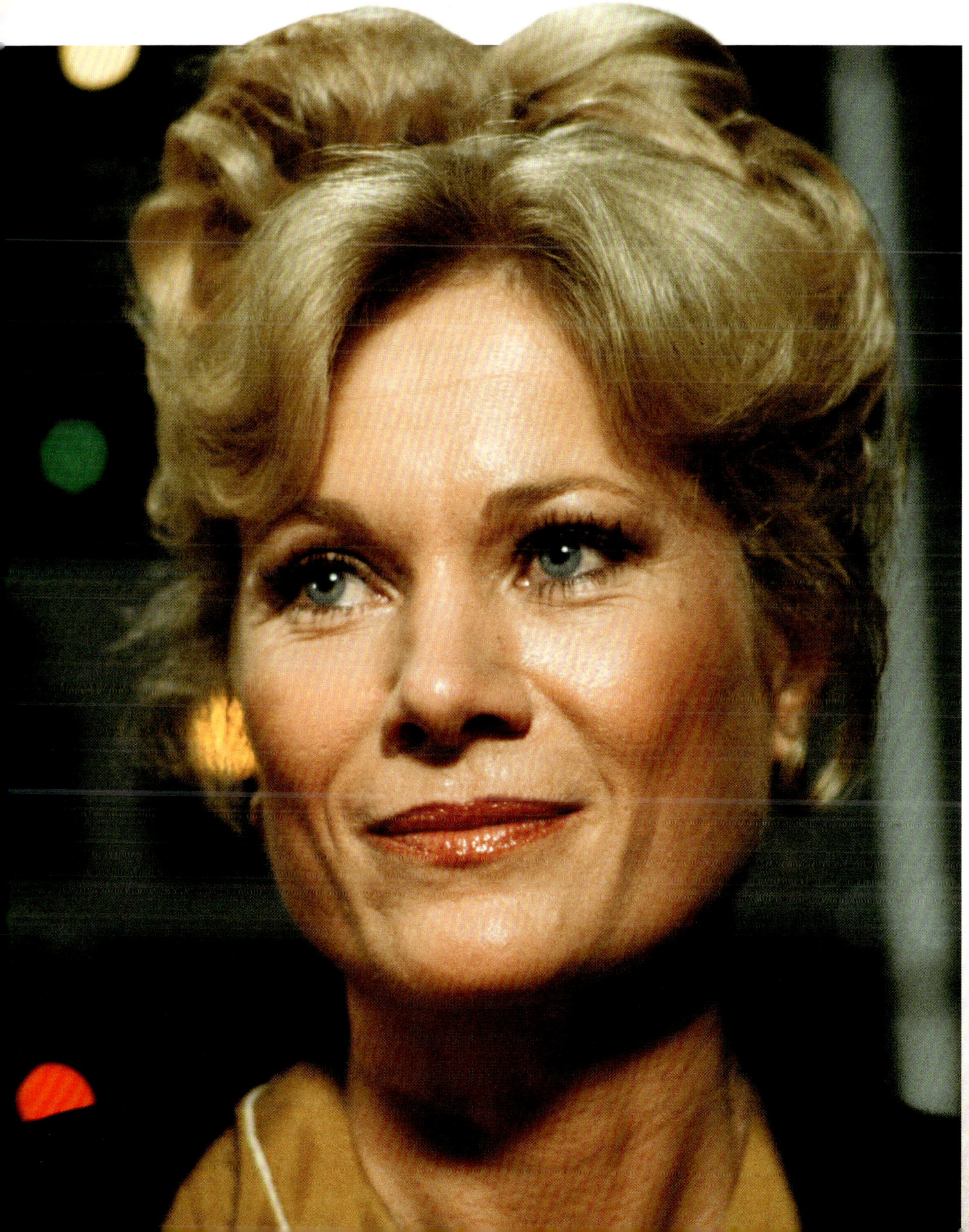

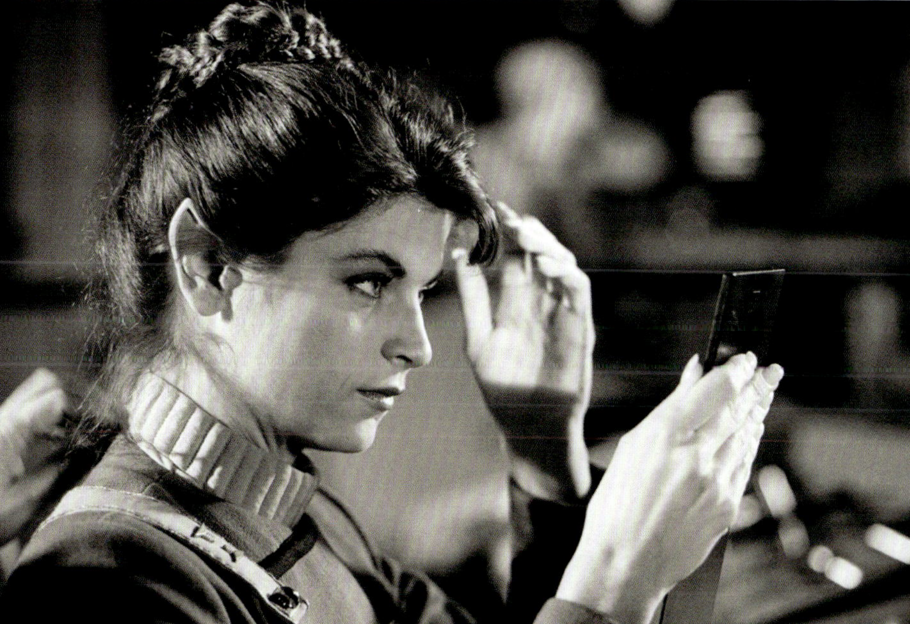

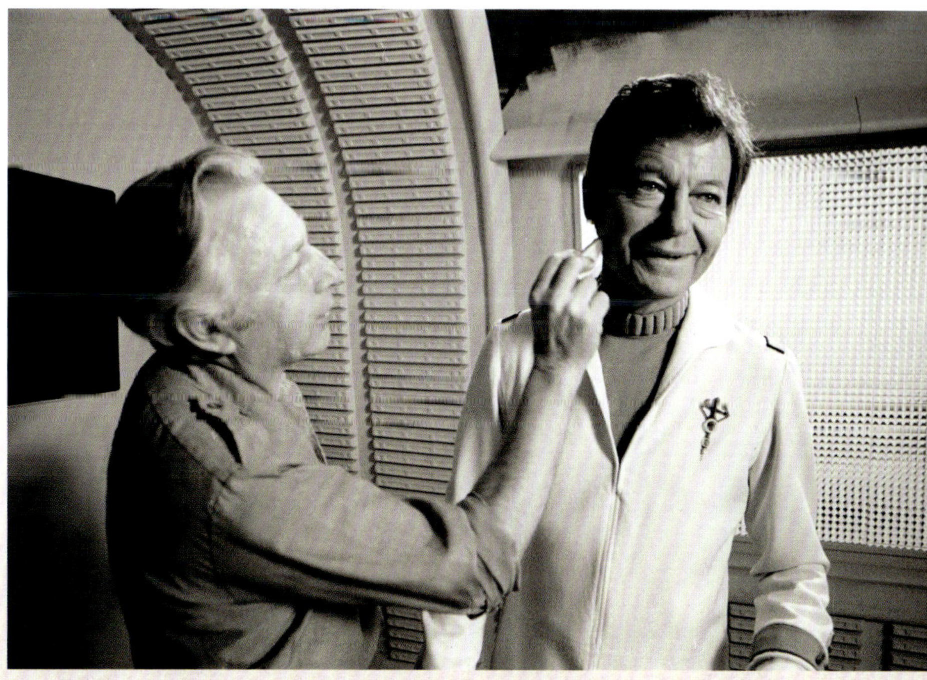

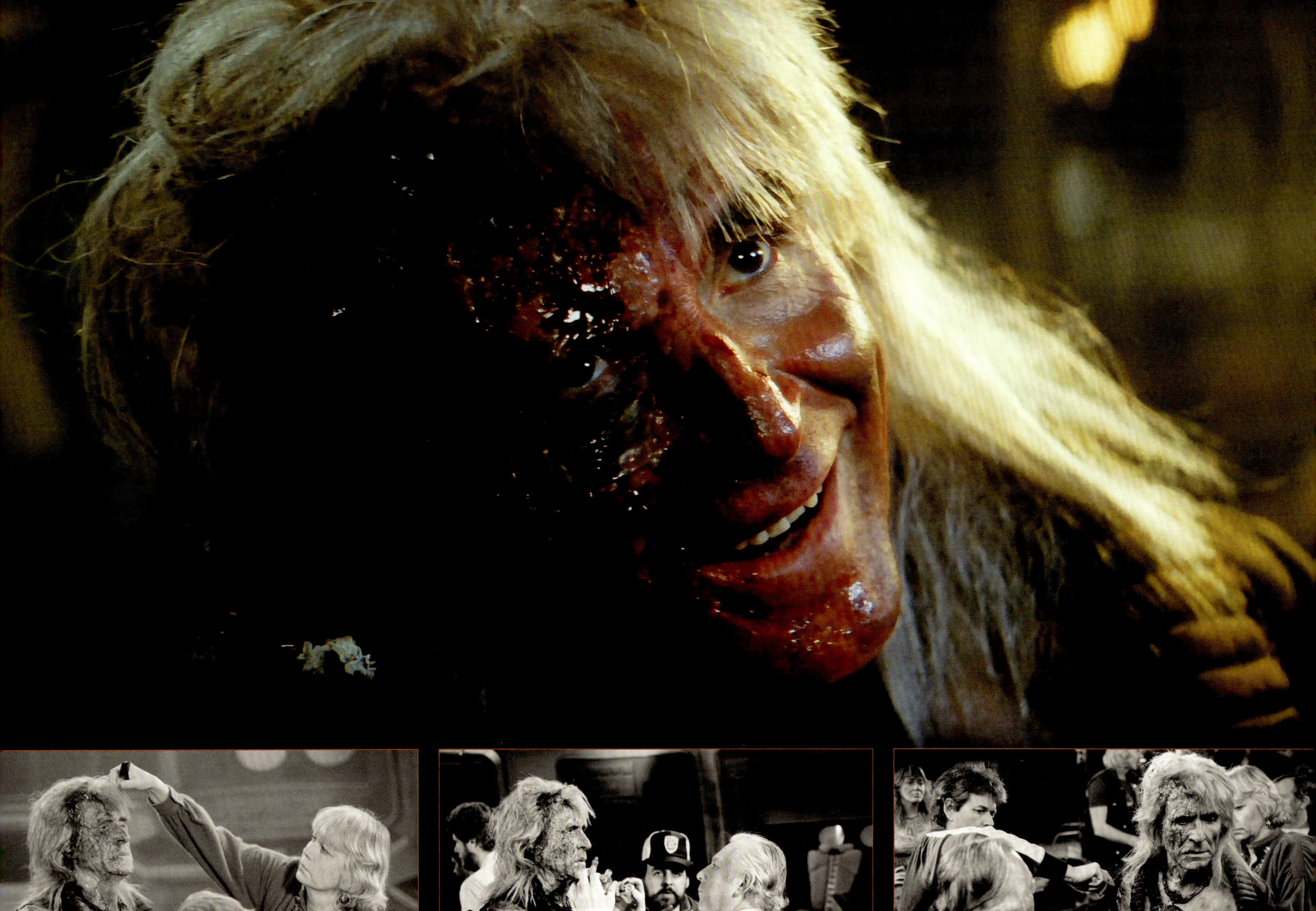

ABOVE: Taylor adjusts the styling and placement of Khan's wig. Meyer recalls, "Ricardo's hair was definitely Dionne's creation and we used it again in *Volunteers*."[14]

ABOVE: As Khan's obsession grows, so does the consequences to him and his people. Here Keppler is touching up the gelatin burn makeup he pioneered.

ABOVE: The makeup team assembled, McCoy, Keppler, and Taylor, collaborating to produce the effects of the wrath of Khan.

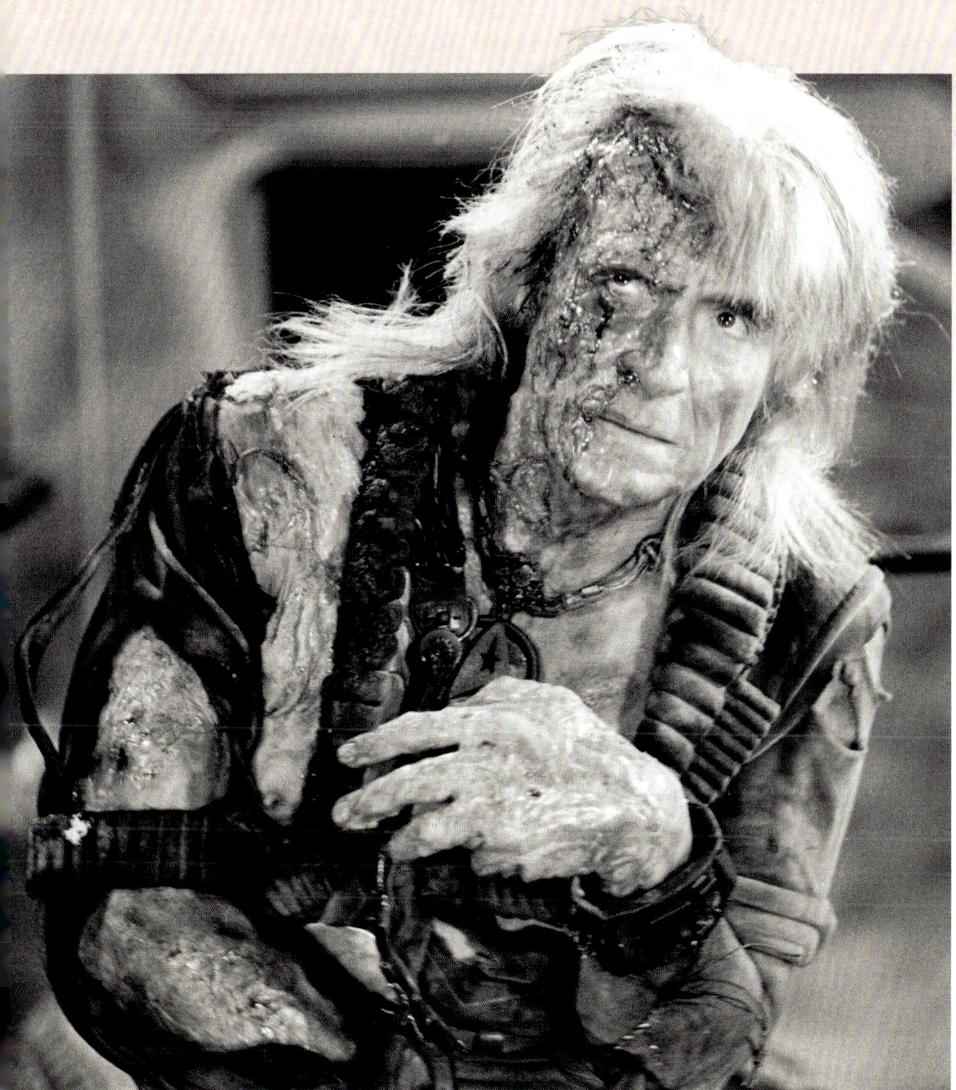

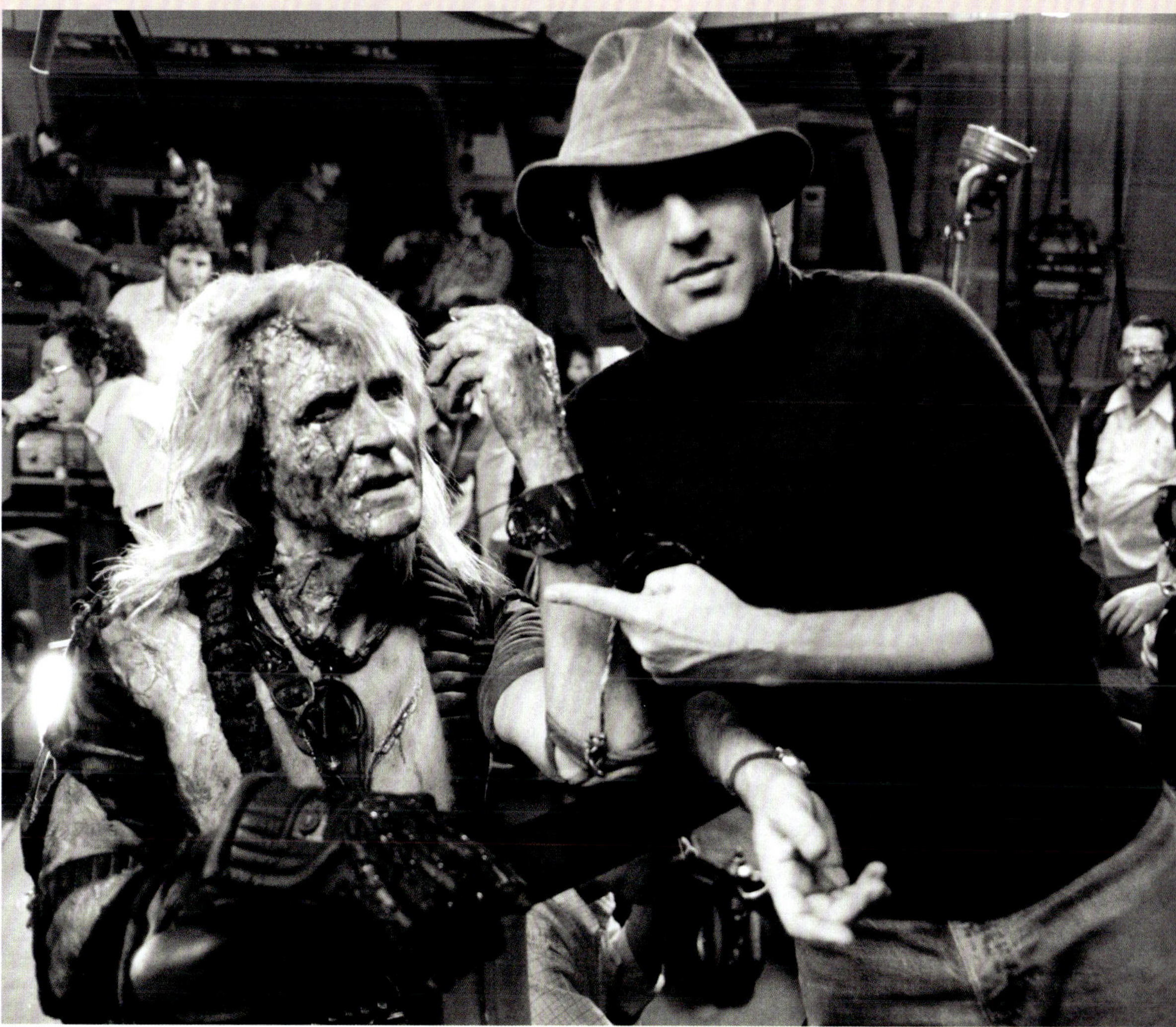

One of the unsung responsibilities of film hairstylists is to maintain wig and hair continuity so that a scene filmed hours or days apart has the same look. Otherwise, audiences can be taken out of the film if there are noticeable changes in hair color, length or styling. Actor Laura Banks spoke to this as she detailed what the transformation into one of Khan's followers was like. "They took photographs of all the characters and then the hairstylist and makeup artist work from these photographs to recreate the exact same image they had on the first day. So whatever they came up with on the first day is what they continually have to recreate."[11]

The visuals surrounding Khan and his followers were to be constant reminders of survival despite the harshest of environments. This motif extended to the hair as first sketched by costume designer Robert Fletcher and brought to fruition by Taylor. Khan's hair would look like a lion's mane, symbolizing a once proud king brought low.

The wig worn by Montalban was maintained and prepared each day by Taylor, while Keppler would make any necessary changes to the wigs as the story progressed. When Khan is wounded after the attack by the *Enterprise*, his whole visage, including his hair, needed to be affected by the devastating effects. A damaged arm, a face half burnt, and hair to match. To get that effect, and because the wigs were made of a material that would not burn but would singe slightly, Keppler used a candle to get the desired effect while Montalban was still wearing the wig.

Montalban praised these design elements, using the hair, makeup, and costumes the makeup team and Fletcher collaborated on to inform how he played the role. "With the passage of time and the conditions in which they were living, not only his clothes but his hair was sort of ill-kept and not really sharp. But there was a certain amount of elegance left. You know what I mean? Without overdoing it. There was still a little bit of the prince in him."[12]

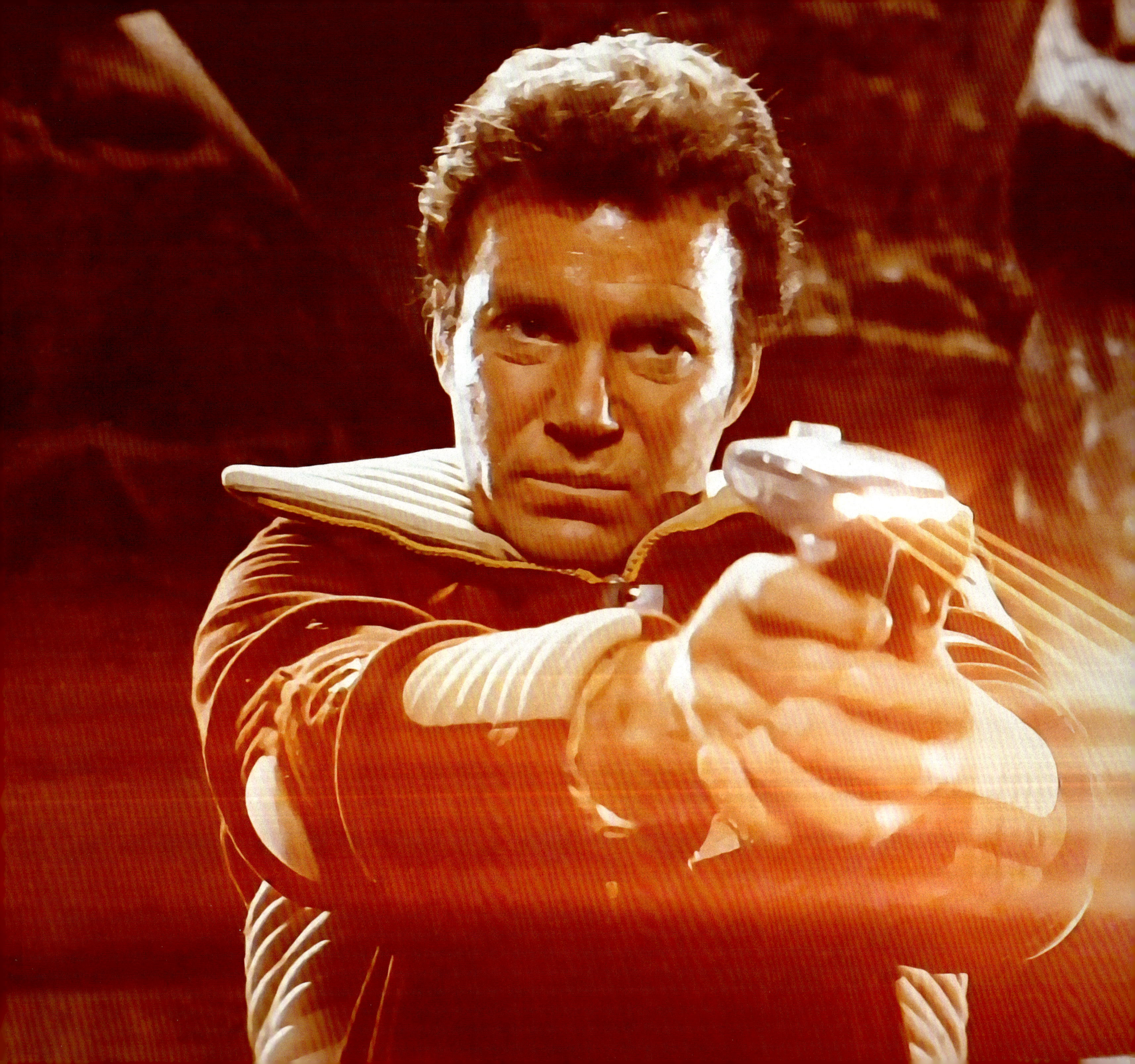

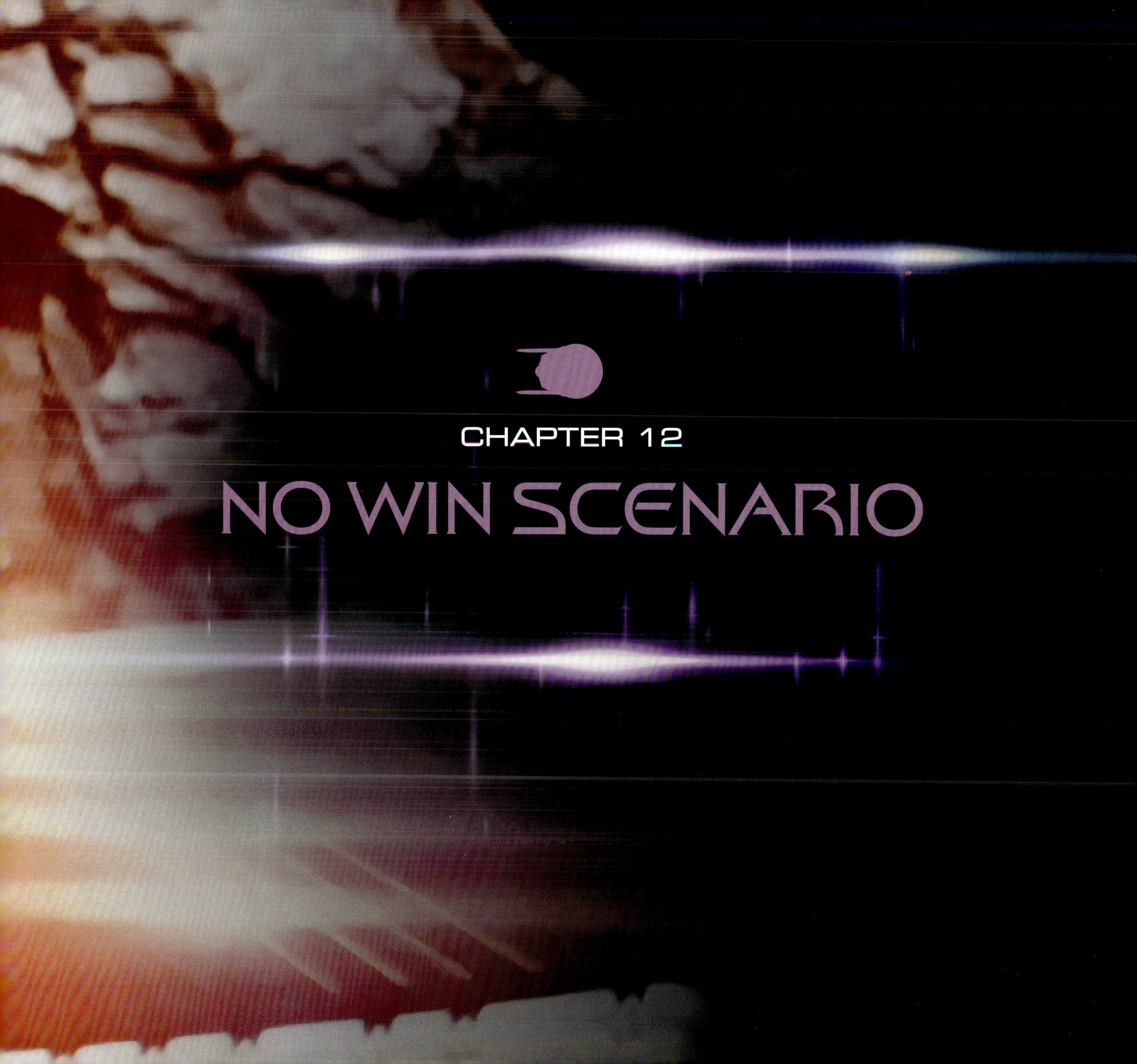

CHAPTER 12
NO WIN SCENARIO

THE STUNT PERFORMERS

The Hollywood stunt community shares similarities with the fictional Starfleet. Both groups depend on teamwork, strategic planning, and most especially, a concern for the safety of colleagues. More, both stunt performers and Starfleet are families, where trust is an important element.

The stunt team on *Star Trek II* were tasked with a daunting mission, that of safely completing the stunts in the amped sequel. The Starfleet captain of that team was Bill Couch Sr., brought on by the producers as stunt coordinator because of his extensive experience, including previous work on *Star Trek: The Motion Picture*, where he was a stunt performer, specifically doubling for William Shatner. Like costume designer Robert Fletcher and production designer Joseph R. Jennings, Couch was selected in part because his experience could help the production avoid costly mistakes and snares.

Couch explained his role as a stunt coordinator: "I'll take the script home and, page by page, go over the stunts. Then I'll put calls out to stunt men to make sure I get the right person for the job. I attend the production meeting and present a stunt budget and give it to the production manager."[1] Additional to the administrative element of his work, Couch would also direct stunts, working with actors, stunt performers, and the director to ensure both safe and spectacular stunts. Safety was always Couch's priority, not only necessary for successfully completing a film's action scenes, but for achieving that result without injury to those Couch was responsible for as coordinator.

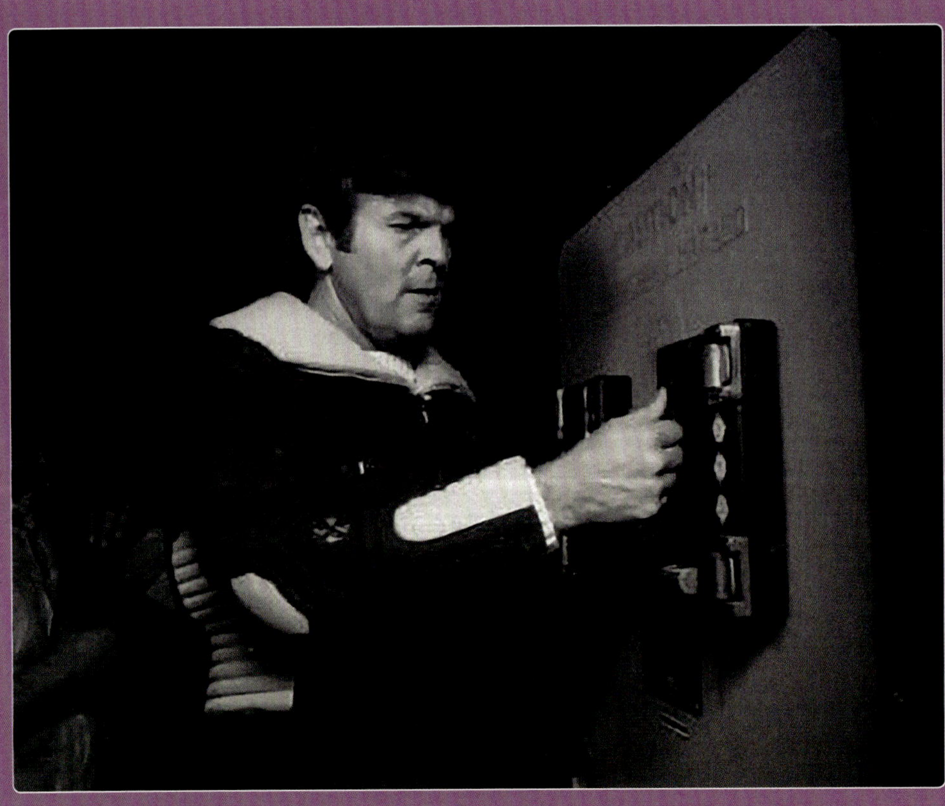
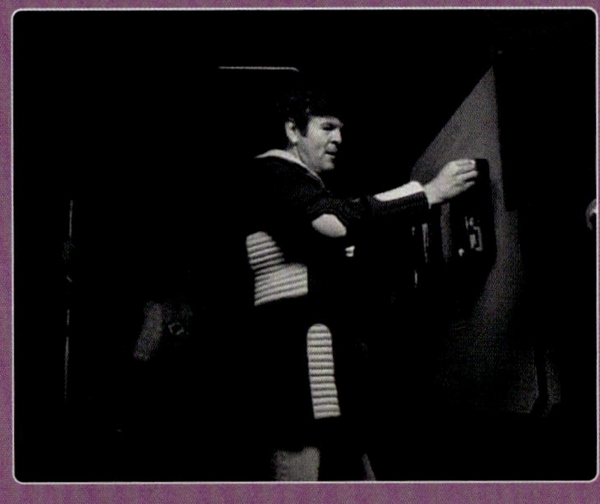
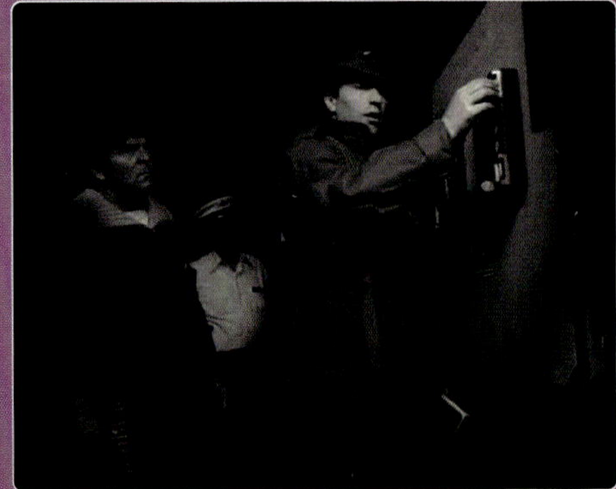
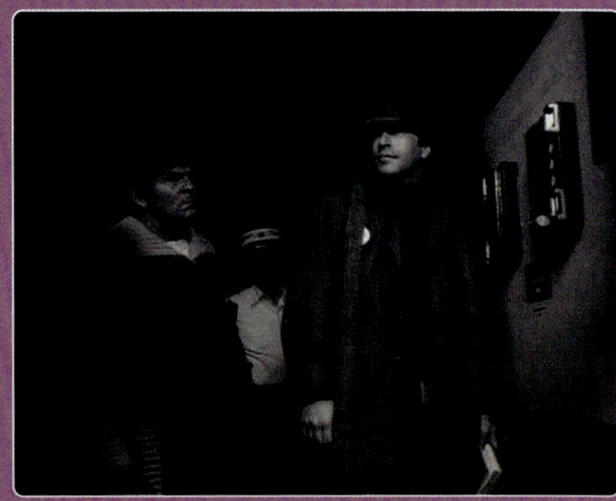
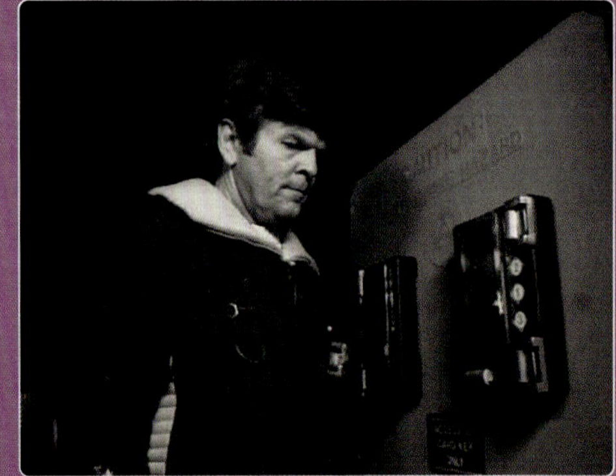

BILL COUCH SR.

Born in 1926 in Asheville, North Carolina, William "Bill" J. Couch was the youngest of five children born to railroad timekeeper Waverly Couch and Grace Sanders. Speaking to journalist Tula Andonaras during a 1989 interview, Couch revealed, "When we graduated high school, of course everyone thought of going into the service. I joined the Air Force and spent two years in Japan during the occupation. When I got out, I really wasn't sure what I wanted to do, so my brother and I joined the circus."[7] Couch's older brother Chuck would be his life-long stunt partner. Considered two of the best wire men in the entertainment industry, Couch and his brother would parlay their aerial act, customarily done without nets or safety devices, into a career in Hollywood as stunt players, actors, and eventually, stunt coordinators. Couch worked on films such as *The Love Bug* (1968), *Logan's Run* (1976), and *The Blues Brothers* (1980), in addition to television programs such as the 1974 TV version of *Planet of the Apes*. In 1967, Chuck played Khan during stunt sequences in "Space Seed." Fifteen years later, Couch would earn the mantel from his brother and perform stunts as Khan during *Star Trek II*. Couch passed away in 1999 at age seventy-two.

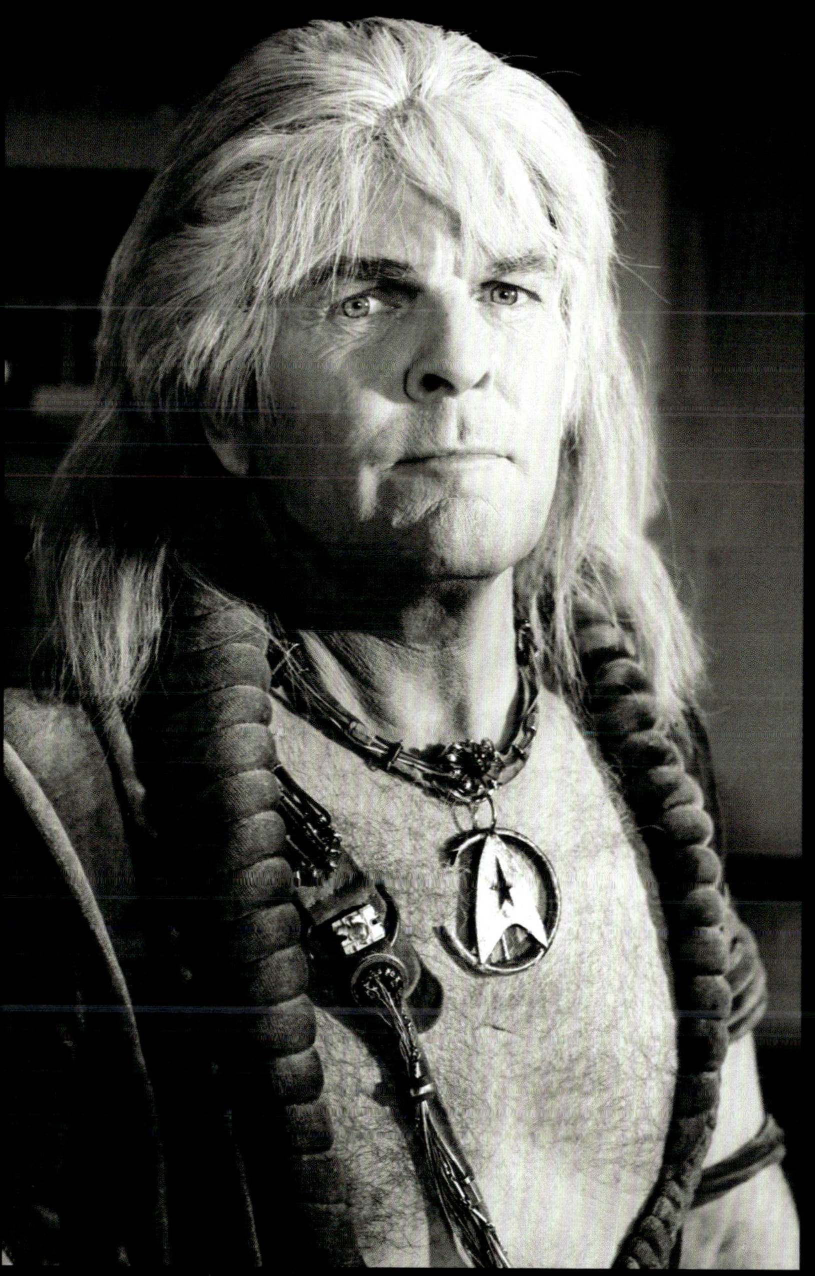

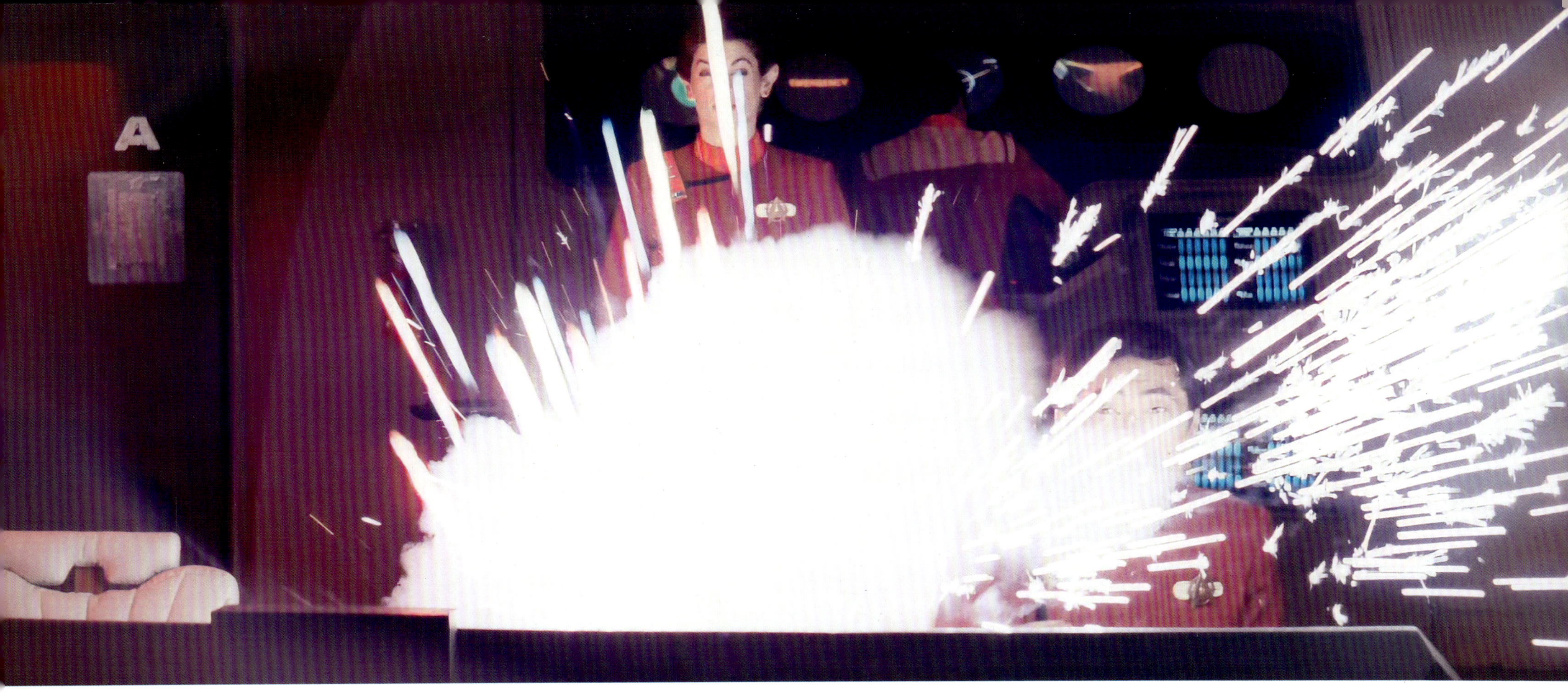

ABOVE: Takei about to perform his own stunt.

One of the (uncredited) cadet actors and stunt players on *Star Trek II* was Todd Bryant. Bryant may be familiar to *Star Trek* movie fans, as he would go on to play the Klingon antagonist Klaa in *Star Trek V: The Final Frontier*, the Klingon translator in *Star Trek VI: The Undiscovered Country*, and was Ron Perlman's stunt double as the Viceroy in *Star Trek: Nemesis*. Bryant enthused of his *Star Trek II* experience, "I had never been on sets like that before; it's just amazing. You put yourself in this fantasy mode and imagine you're walking through a real spaceship. It was the thrill of my life at that time."[2]

When he got the role as Klaa, Bryant kept the fact that he had already appeared as a cadet in *Star Trek II* a secret. He told Kris Gilpin of *Starlog* magazine, "I haven't told Bill yet [about *Star Trek II*]. He has been so busy. As far as I know, he still doesn't know. I didn't tell anybody. I didn't want them to identify me with that film; it might have affected my getting the part of Klaa."[3] Bryant did joke that it is interesting contemplating that, "Young Captain Klaa was standing at Spock's funeral."[4]

Steve Blalock was another stunt performer on Bill Couch Sr.'s team, perhaps most notably sometimes doubling for Spock. Like Bryant, after *Star Trek II*, Blalock continued to work on *Star Trek*, in both movies—*Star Trek III: The Search for Spock*, *Star Trek: Insurrection*—and TV series— *Star Trek: The Next Generation*, *Star Trek: Voyager*, *Star Trek: Enterprise*. He was part of the stunt team that won a Screen Actors Guild Award for Outstanding Performance by a Stunt Ensemble for the 2009 *Star Trek* Kelvin universe film.

Sometimes actors are permitted to do their own stunts, particularly if the risk is minimal and the actor's face will be clearly visible in the shot. George Takei fondly recalled his own experiences performing stunts on the movie for Dan Madsen in the January 1983 issue of the *Star Trek II: The Movie Fan Club* newsletter: "It was good fun! I enjoyed it frankly. Some of the stunts I did myself and I enjoy the action, the active parts of movie making. That first scene where the explosion goes off right at the console and I go flying off and died, I did that myself. I could feel the blast of heat as it went off… There was a very loud explosive sound there, but it's all choreographed and actually I'm leaping up and away just before the explosion goes off. The director is counting down: 3, 2, 1, bang. And you know, once he says '1' then I go and then the bang happens, so that, although I feel the blast of air there, my body is already flying by that time. Because of the placement of the camera it seems as though I'm being blasted out by the force of the explosion."[5]

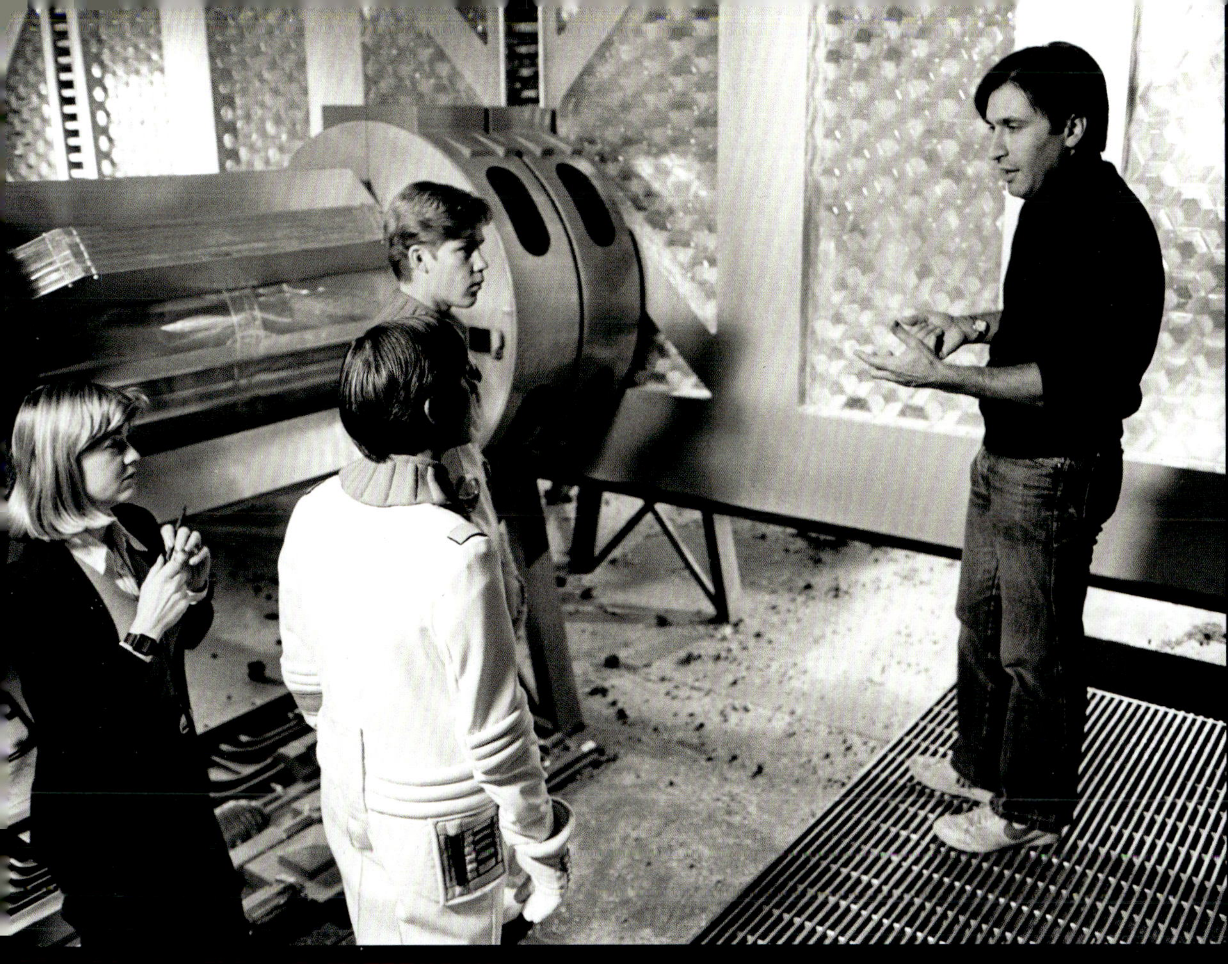

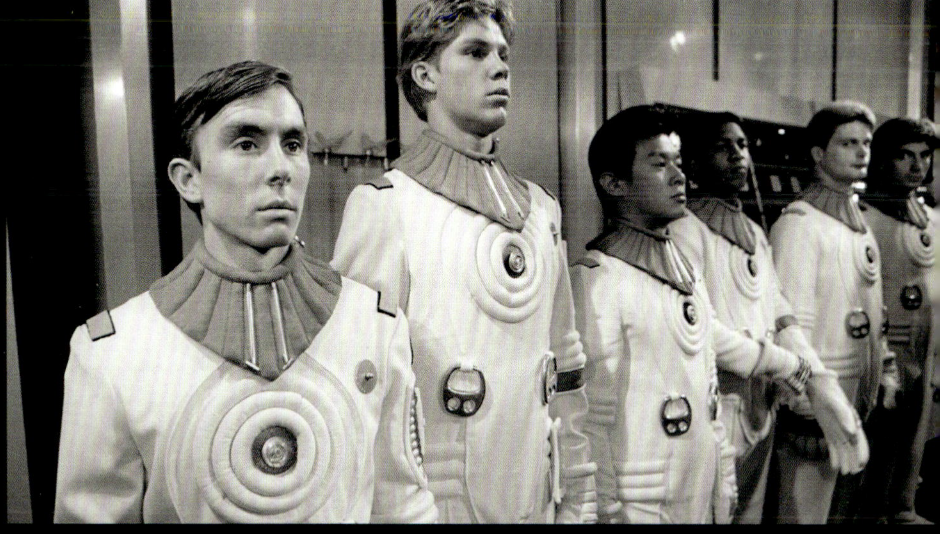

LEFT: Ferguson observes as Ike Eisenmann (Preston) and Bryant get direction from Meyer about the upcoming stunt sequence where Preston tries to rescue Bryant's cadet during the first attack on the *Enterprise*. The scene was filmed December 14, 1981. There was some controversy about the cadets panicking. However, Meyer felt that the cadets are exactly that, cadets. They are human and humans panic, especially when they do not have experience.

ABOVE: Todd Bryant (second from left) as a Starfleet cadet.

BELOW: I am not Spock? Steve Blalock, ready to double for Leonard Nimoy.

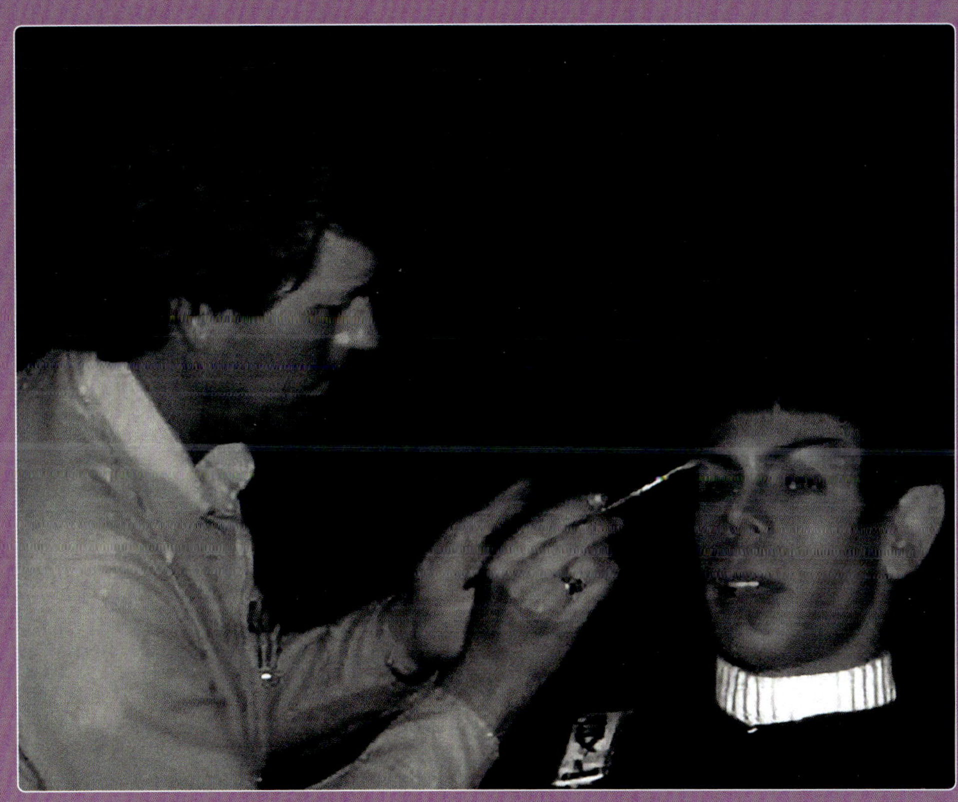

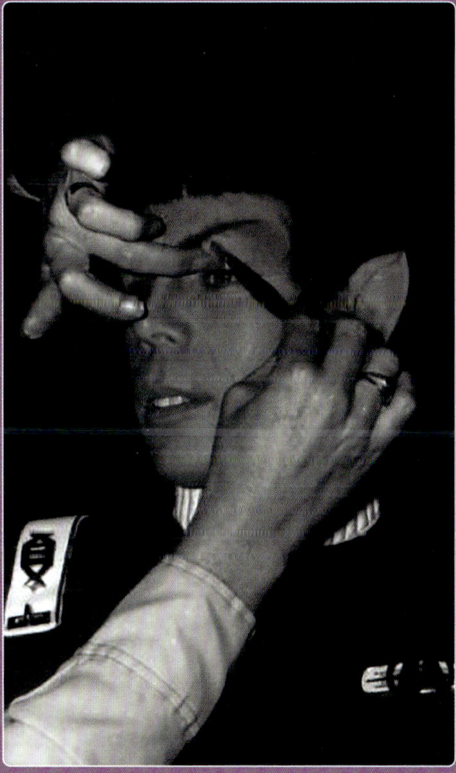

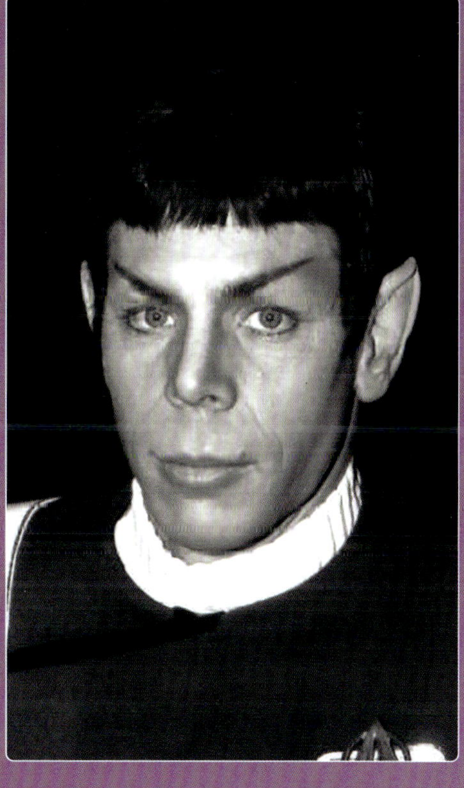

A TALE OF TWO FIGHTS

The *Star Trek II* theatrical poster features action scenes directly from the movie, and a few images that are not. The image of Khan in his protective gear never appears in the film, having been taken on set before the sandstorm was generated. Another image that never appears in the film is David hovering above his father during their fight in the Genesis Cave. A more extensive fight between Kirk and David was filmed, but an alternative, smaller-scale scrap was substituted for the final version of the movie.

The January 18, 1982 script describes the more elaborate scene as originally envisioned: "They walk by a group of crates. It all happens fast: David leaps out and tackles Kirk, throwing him to the ground and landing atop him, a knife at his throat. At the same time, Bones and Saavik reach for their phasers, but Jedda, already armed, steps out. He has them covered and helpless."

David, who believes that Kirk is responsible for the death of his Regula I lab colleagues, threatens, "You're the sonavabitch who committed mass murder up there." The dialogue would have given more details about what occurred during the escape. "We were still there, you dumb bastard! We

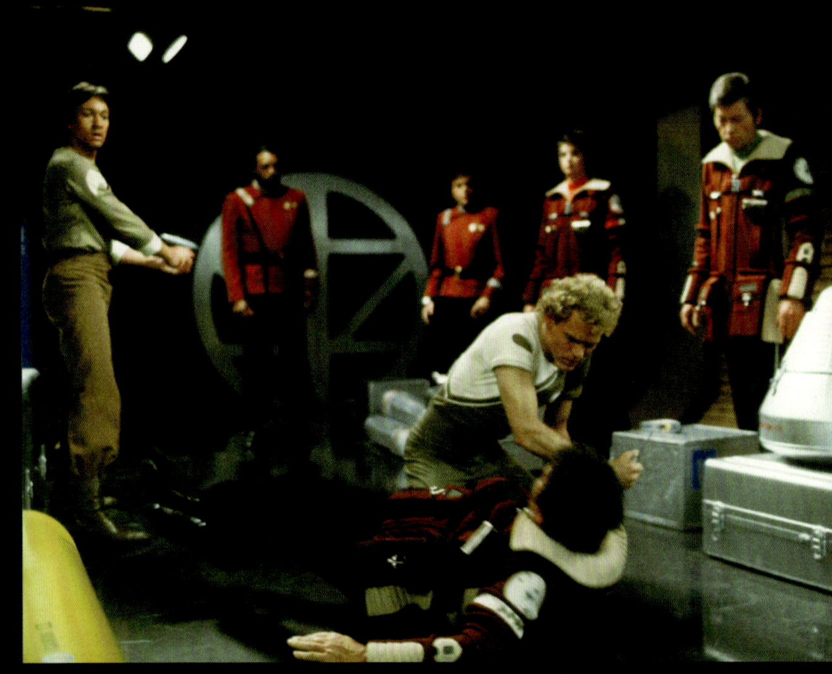

BELOW: Shatner and Merritt Butrick block the fight maneuvers with the guidance of Couch. Note the protective elbow pads Shatner is wearing.

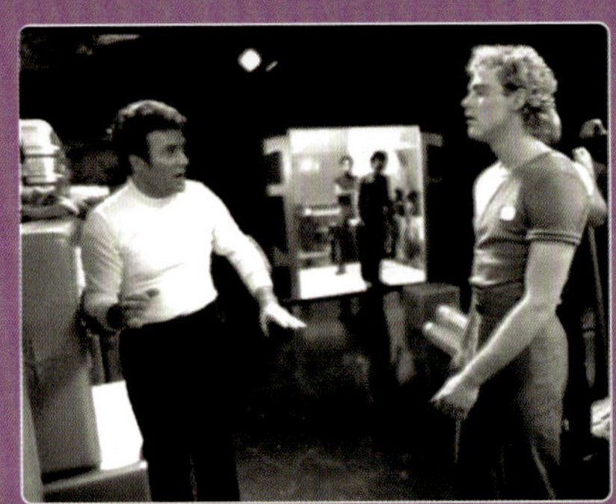
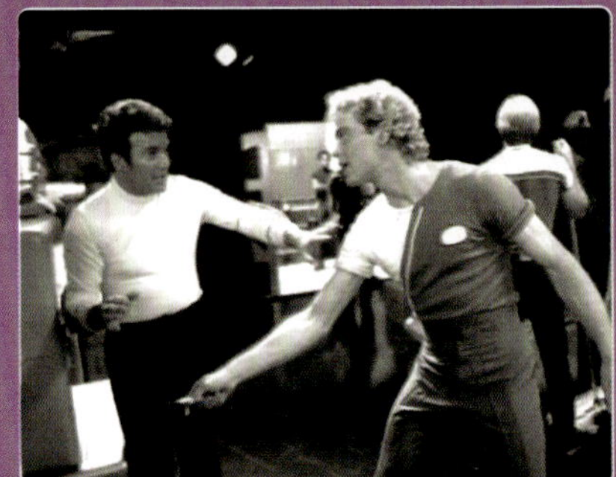
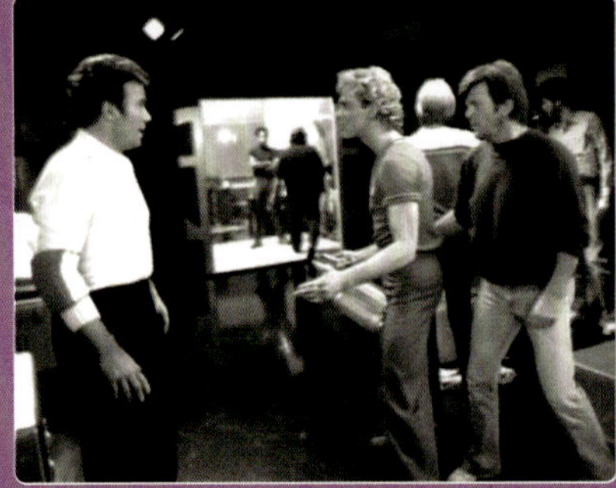
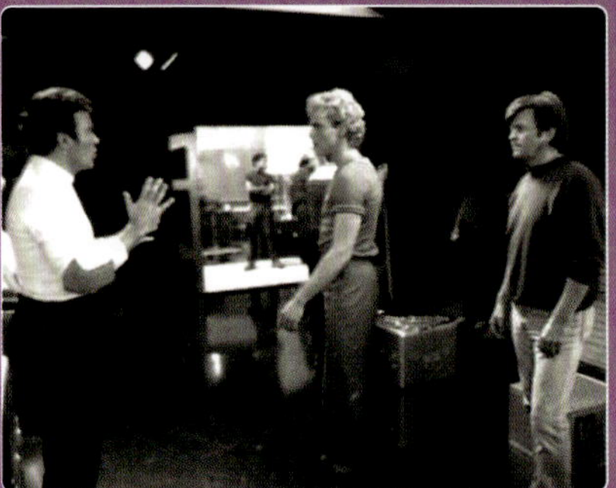

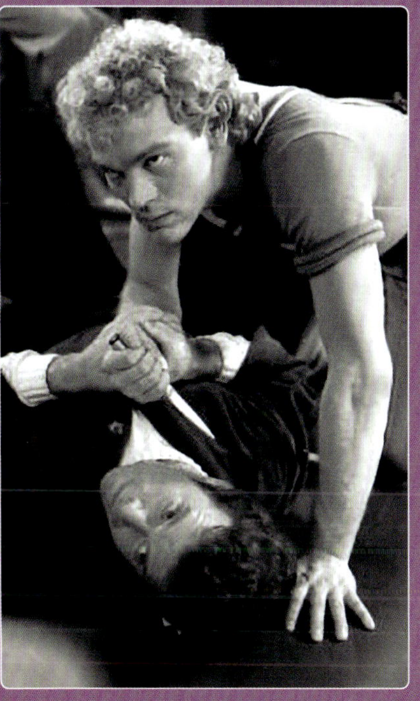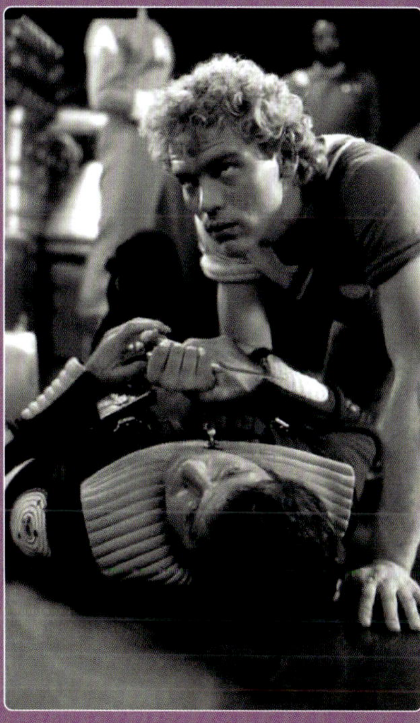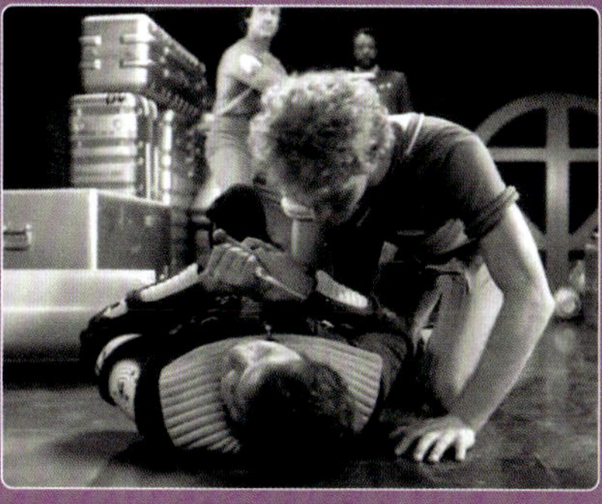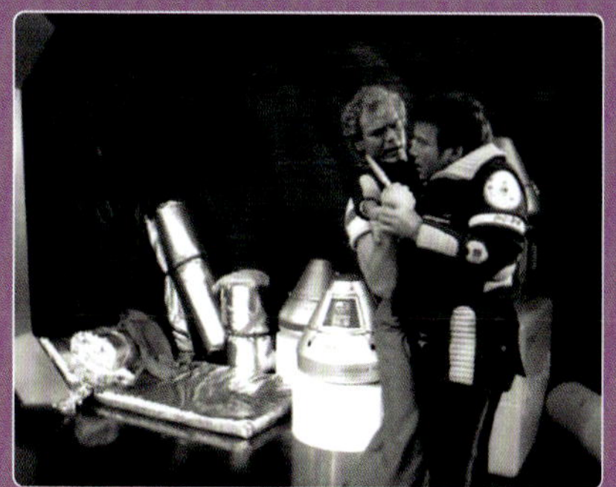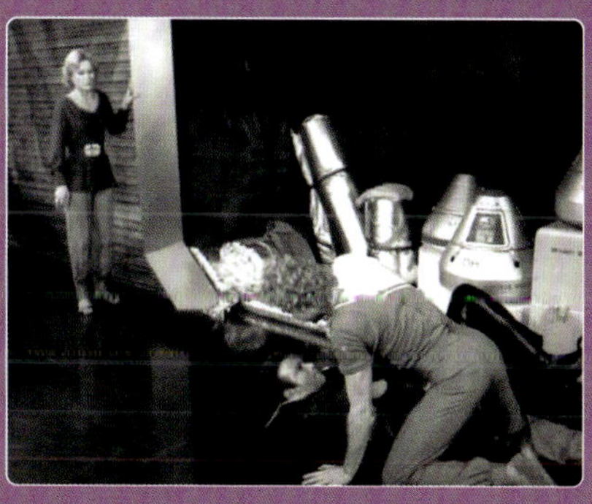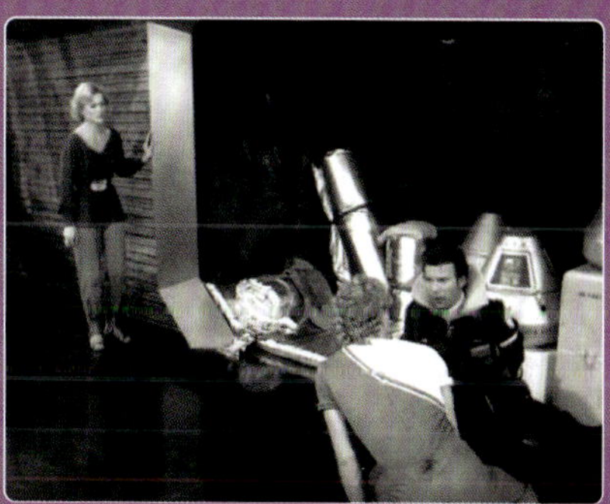

could hear the screams all the way to the transporter room." Gene Roddenberry, in his script comments, would object to David's use of profanities and it would be curtailed as the scene was reworked.

Despite David pinning Kirk and brandishing his weapon, Kirk is calm. He asks, "Where's Dr. Marcus?" When David reveals he is Dr. Marcus, Carol appears. He warns his mother, "Go back, I'm going to kill him." It is here that Carol reveals a secret that surprises David, Kirk, and the audience. "You do that and you'll have murdered your father." This version of the script clearly reveals that Kirk did not know he had a son and David does not believe it at first, because he believed his father was a professor.

Later in the Eden Cave, David comes to terms with the situation. In a cute moment, David asks Saavik what she is looking at. She responds, "The Admiral's son." David replies, "Don't you believe it." To which Saavik says, "Oh, I believe it."

ABOVE: Filmed January 18 and 19, 1982, the originally planned fight scene partially evokes the myth of Oedipus. The shorter version of the fight was filmed during March 1982 retakes.

ABOVE RIGHT: During the original version of the fight, Carol would have revealed to David and Kirk their relationship, which ended the more bitter contest. In the film, the fight never gets to the moment where Kirk is pinned on the ground. Instead, Kirk is able to dodge David's attacks and win before Carol appears.

To lend believability to the scene where Khan lifts Chekov as a demonstration of his genetically enhanced strength, it was imperative that both Ricardo Montalban and Walter Koenig's faces be shown to audiences. The effect was achieved with wires, which would be painted out of the scene later by ILM artists where visible. Koenig recalled the wire harness that created the illusion was "somewhat uncomfortable."[6]

BELOW: Meyer demonstrates Khan's display of strength.

BOTTOM: Montalban, Koenig and Winfield shooting the scene.

RIGHT: Koenig having fun, despite the discomfort.

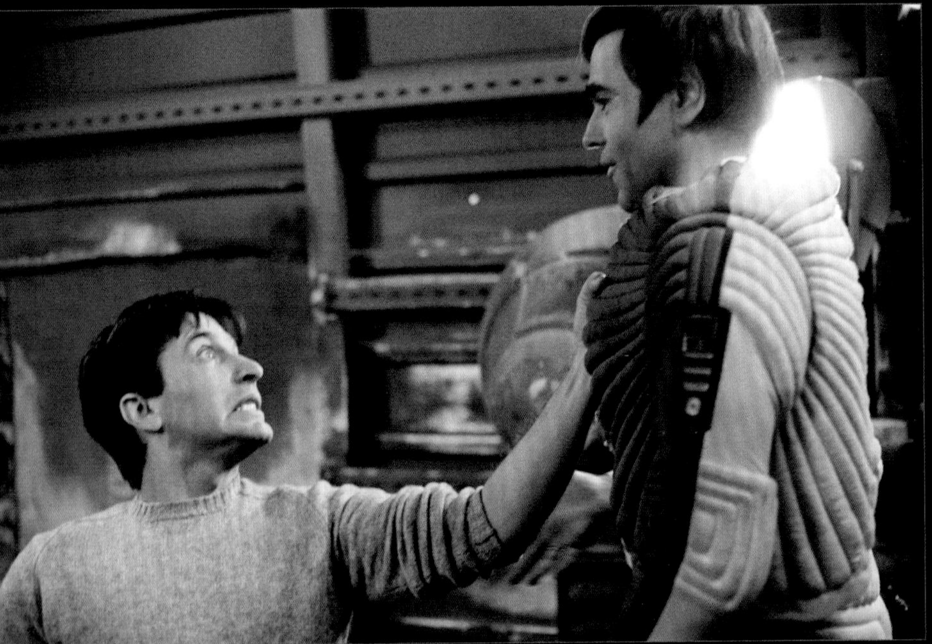

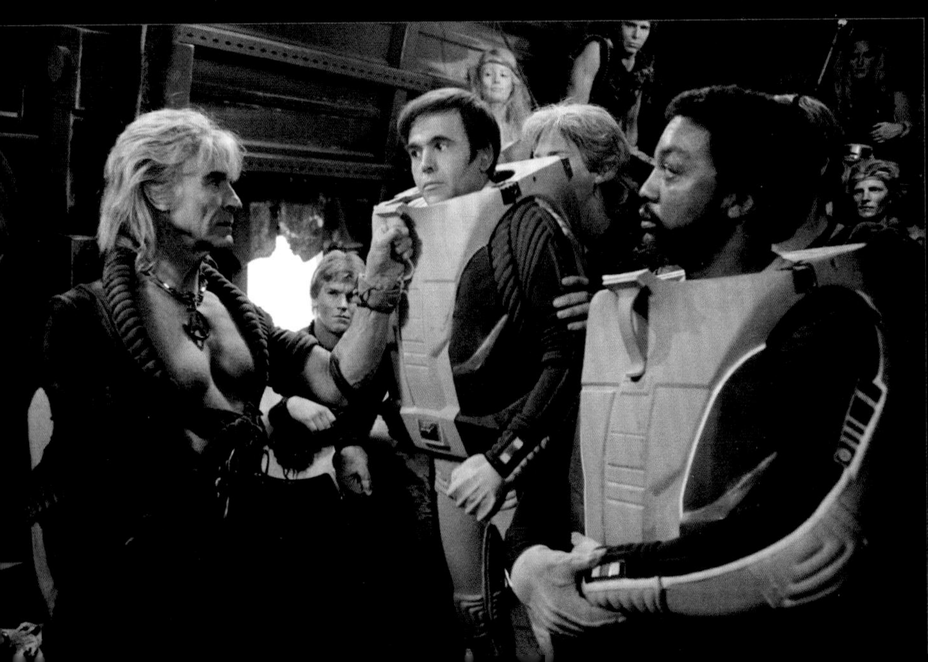

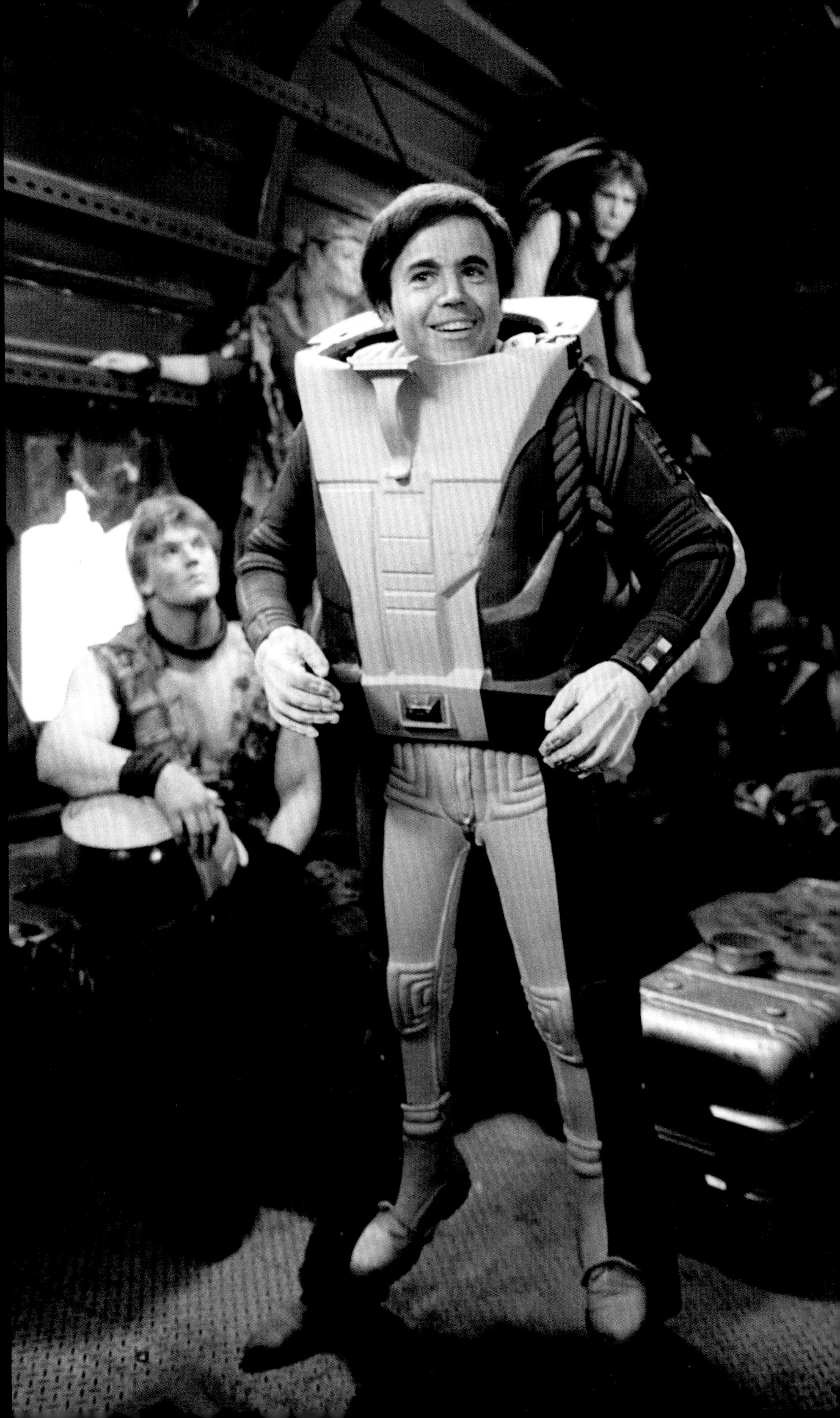

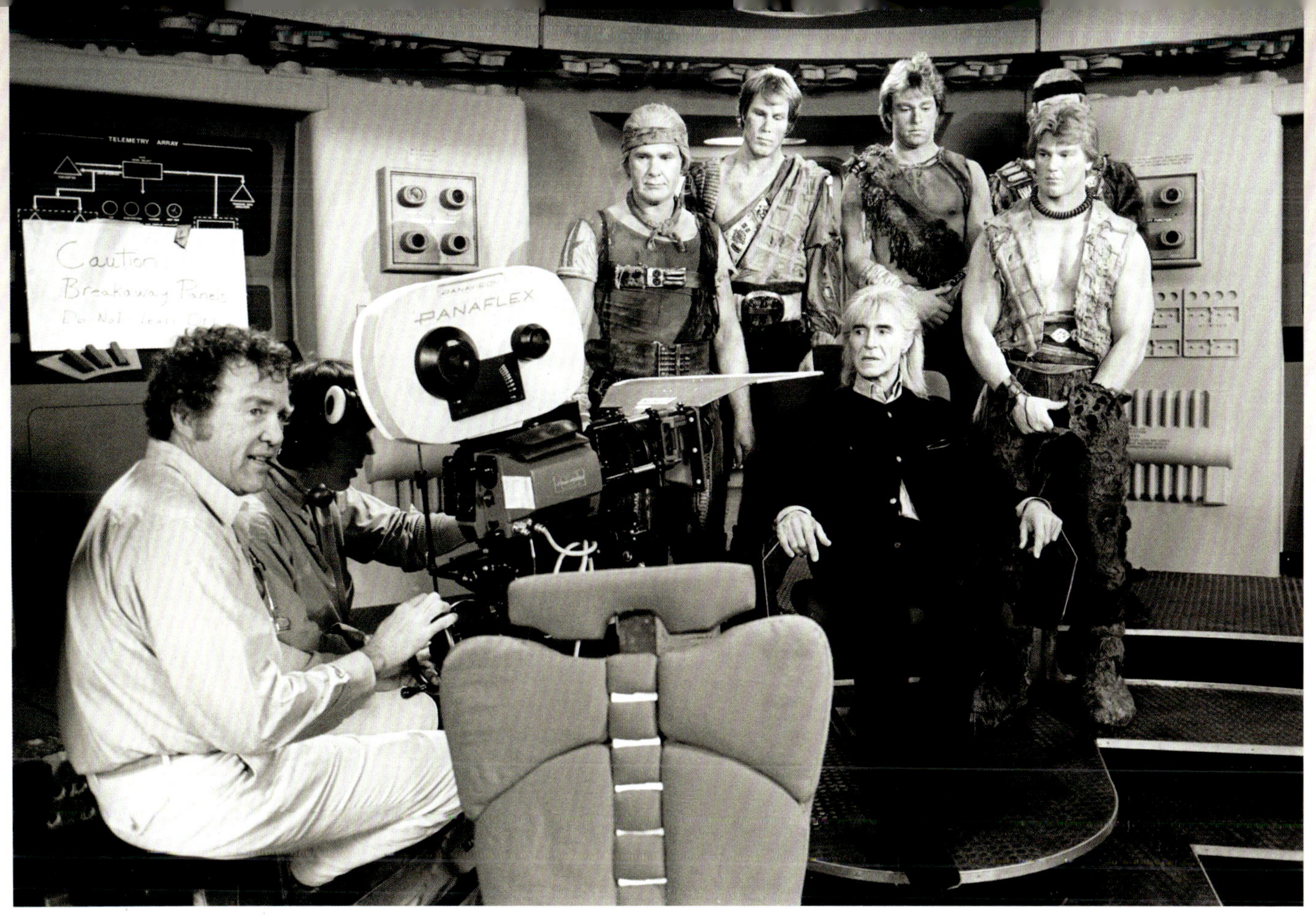

LEFT: The increased action in *Star Trek II* meant diligence to safety concerns. Note the sign behind Rescher and first assistant camera Coulson during camera blocking on the bridge set warning about break away panels and instructing actors and crew not to lean on them for safety reasons.

BELOW: *Star Trek II* had everything from laughs to scares. The scripts are clear that one of those from the lab who sacrifices themselves to buy time for Carol, David, and Jedda to escape with Genesis is the galley chef, hence the costume worn by stunt performer Eddy Donno. Here, Donno, who would return to perform stunts on *Star Trek III: The Search for Spock* and *Star Trek: First Contact*, is suspended through sheer human power, including that of stunt coordinator Couch.

BOTTOM: In the film, Kirk helps McCoy lower the bodies of Khan's victims. Once the scene was filmed. it was Shatner who helped stunt performers to safety.

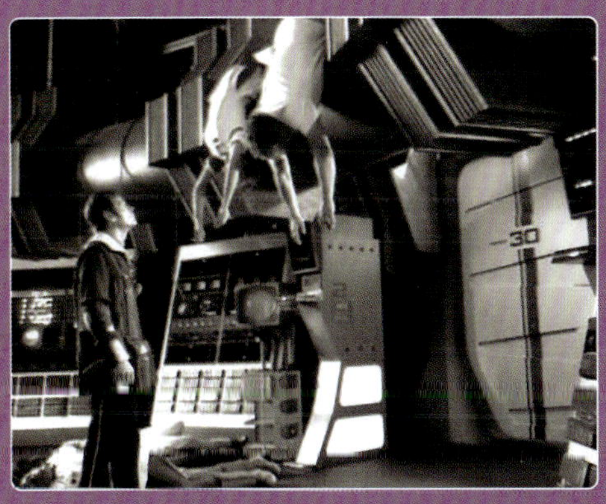
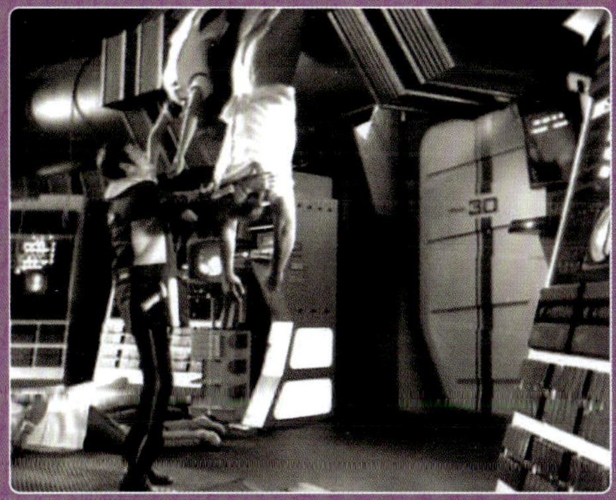
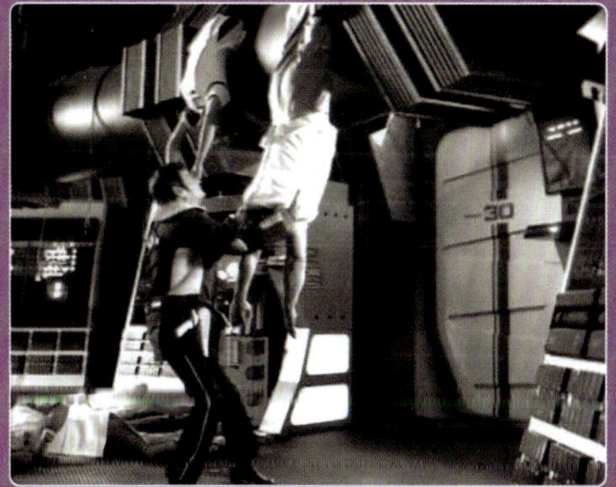
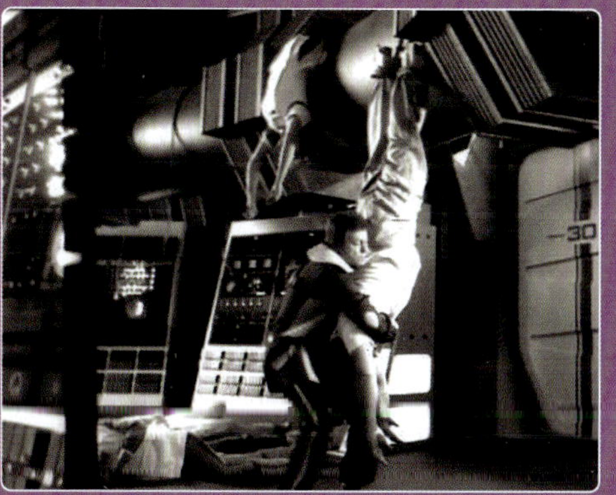
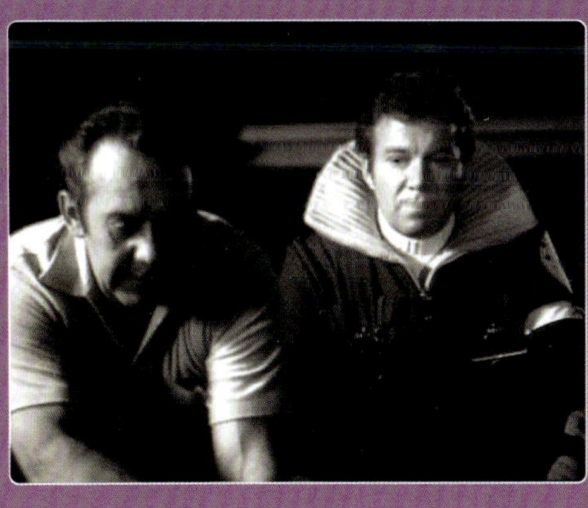
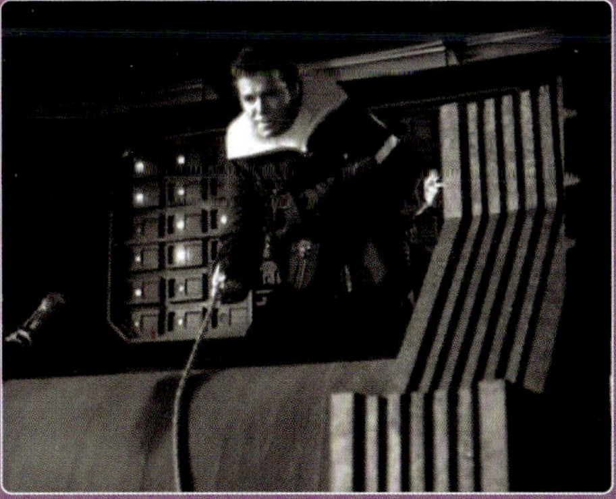
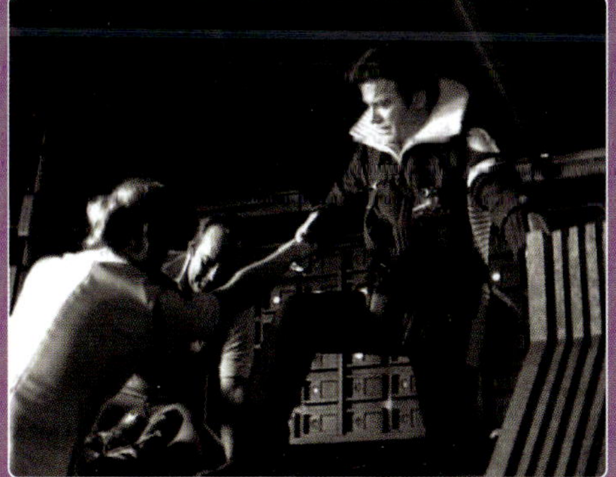
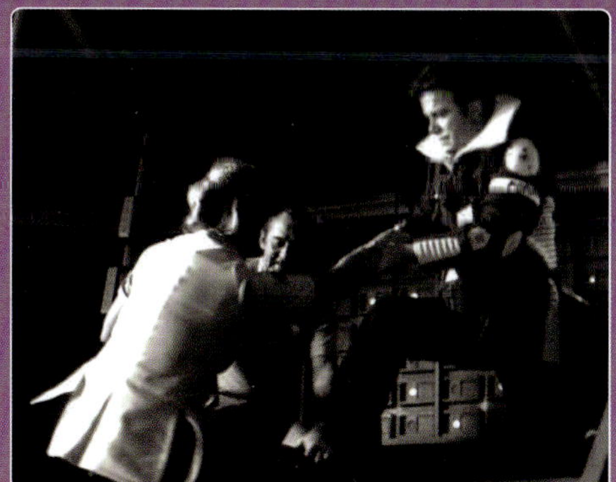

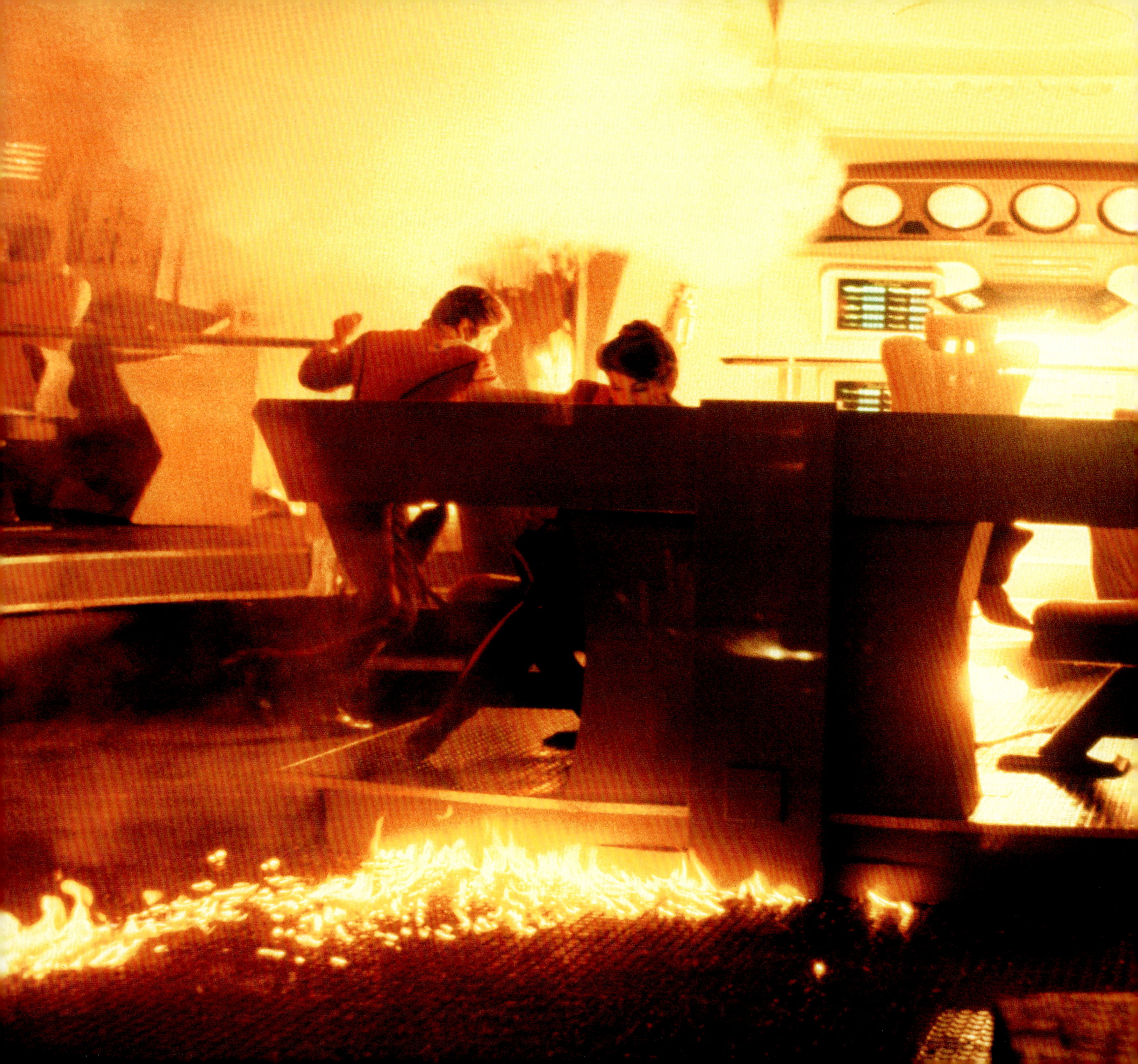

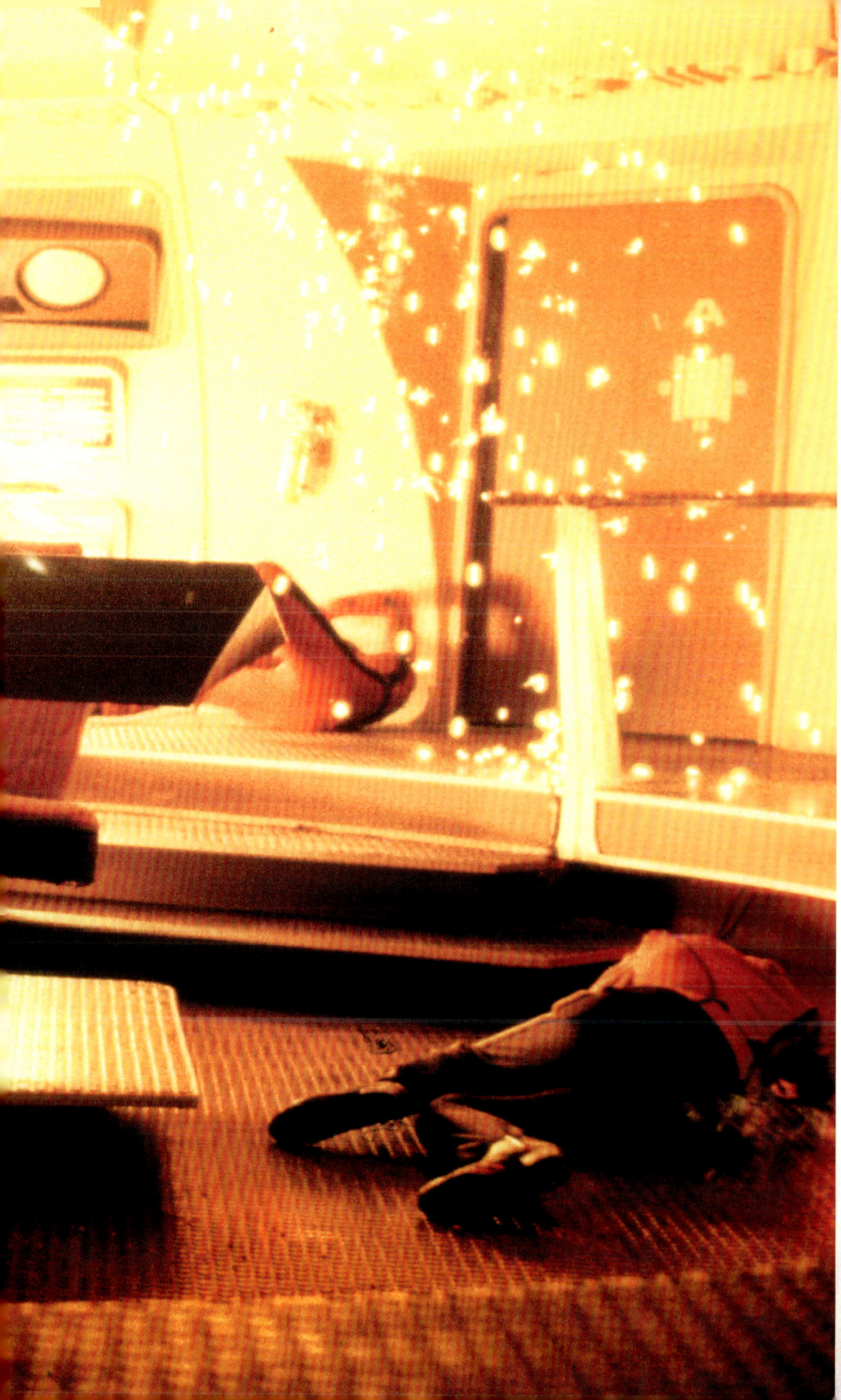

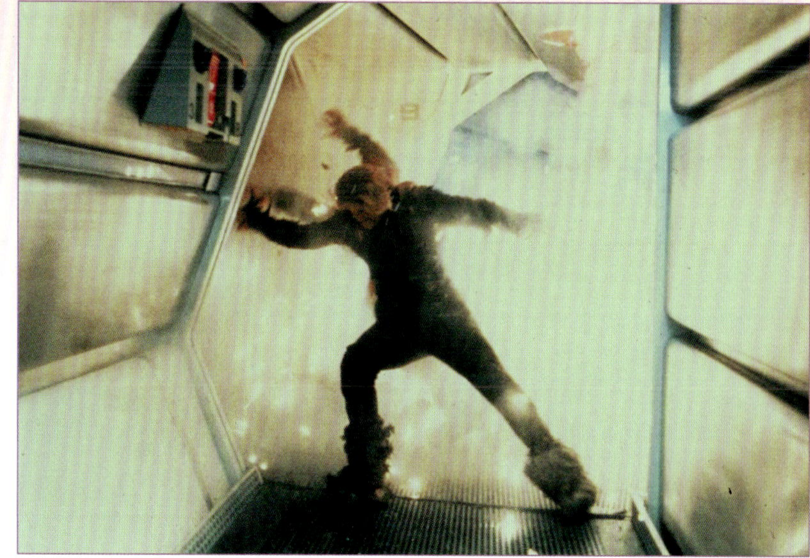

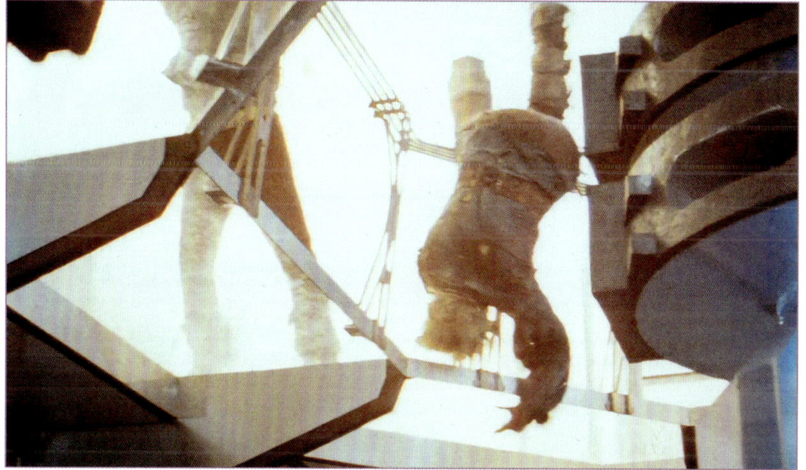

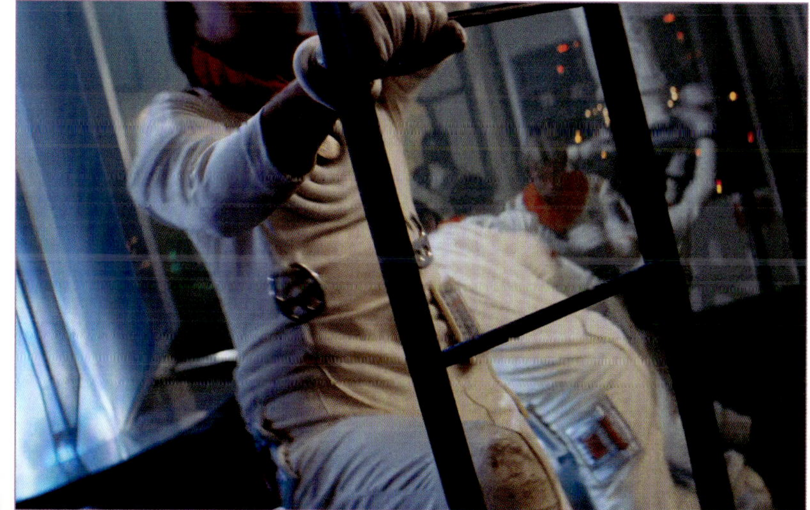

THIS SPREAD: Some of the stunt work featured in the film.

MANO A MANO

One of the most famed aspects of *Star Trek II* is that, despite the fact that the hero and villain are never in the same room together face-to-face, the script cleverly finds ways for them to interact, whether using Ceti eel-controlled proxies or via viewscreens and communicators. Because of production schedules, most especially the need to share the same set, converting between the *Reliant* and *Enterprise* bridges, Shatner and Montalban never worked with each other. Instead, the lines of the other actor were usually read by script supervisor Mary Jane Ferguson, making the amazing, emotional performances of Shatner and Montalban even more impressive. However, every version of the scripts—excepting Samuel A. Peeples' Khan-less edition and Nicholas Meyer's last versions—had Kirk and Khan fighting hand-to-hand, including Meyer's September 16, 1981 version.

What is interesting while reading the script pages detailing the fight is that it shows how good writers are also good editors. The September 16 version of the fight is ultimately unnecessary as originally scripted, with the scene ending in exactly the same place as the filmed version does without the battle. Khan does not gain anything by the fight, and neither does Kirk. Instead, the film delivers a more emotionally satisfying experience without the physical fight. There is a verbal game of chess between Kirk, trapped inside the Gamma Regula I planetoid, and Khan, speaking remotely from the *Reliant*. No fisticuffs are needed to create a compelling scene because of the directing, the acting, the music by James Horner, the editing by William P. Dornisch, the tight camera work by Gayne Rescher, and the ILM special effects.

Of course, because the scene was reworked and replaced by the verbal battle, audiences also got one of cinema's most iconic gifts: the famed Admiral Kirk "Khaaannn!" moment.

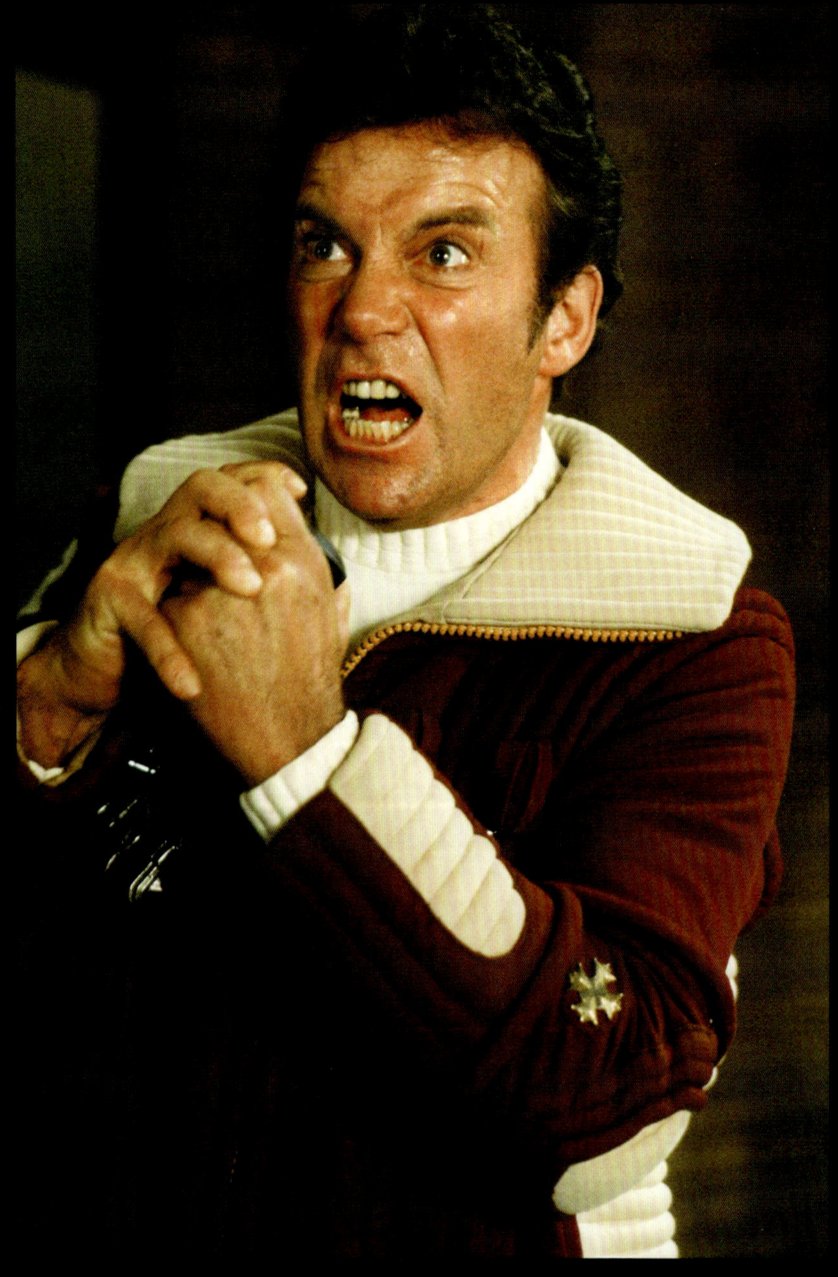

144 CONTINUED:

                    KHAN'S VOICE
          You challenge me.

                    KIRK
                  (swallows)
          Winner take Genesis.

                    KHAN
          Winner take all.

                    KIRK
                  (gulp)
          Winner take all.

145 ANGLE ON KAHN

                    KHAN
          As the challenged party, the
          choice of weapons is mine.

146 ANGLE ON KIRK

                    KIRK
                  (breathless)
          Naturally.

     Silence. . .

                    KIRK
                  (continuing)
          Are you coming or are you
          a coward as well as a murderer?

147 ANGLE ON KHAN

     flushing - -

                    KHAN
          What are the coordinates?

148 KIRK

     hands the transmitter to Spock, who eyes him,
     then starts giving the coordinates - -

                    KHAN
                  (punching
                  them down)
          Finish repairs.

                                        (CONTINUED)

---

148 CONTINUED:

                    JOACHIM
          Sir, I beg you. . .

     Khan stares frostily at him.

                    KHAN
          I am losing time.

     He starts off the bridge - -

149 INT. EDEN CAVE

     The group watches expectantly - -

                    SPOCK
          You remember how strong he is - -

                    KIRK
          I remember. . .

                    CAROL
          Jim, couldn't we try to lose
          ourselves in the - -

                    KIRK
          He's the only hope we've got.

     Even as he speaks, Khan and TWO SECONDS MATERIALIZE
     on the platform - He looks around, sees Kirk,
     blanches, then recovers. He holds a package.

                    KHAN
          Where is the device?

                    KIRK
          Behind you, in the tunnel.

     Khan starts to turn - -

                    KIRK
                  (continuing)Are you ready?

     Khan turns back; long silence as he ascends to the
     upper platform - -

                    KHAN
          I was ready a long time ago,
          Admiral. I've been ready for
          eons.

     He unfurls his package: two odd-looking pieces of
     metal --

---

149 CONTINUED:

                    KIRK
          What are these?

     Khan smiles grimly - -

                    KHAN
          My choice of weapons. They
          were called swords. You are
          unfamiliar with the idea? A
          pity. In a way it demonstrates
          the degeneracy of your age.
          You push buttons. In the
          twentieth century we yet
          believed in the value of things
          accomplished by hand.

     He pulls out a sword. Uncertainly, Kirk takes his as
     Carol watches in horror - -

                    CAROL
          Jim, this is slaughter - -
          it's barbaric. . .

                    KHAN
          My seconds will see to it
          that no one interferes with
          our quarrel.

                    KIRK
                  (hefts the
                  thing)
          No one's going to interfere.

                    KHAN
          No?

     He swipes through the air: the fight is on.

     From the first, Kirk is completely outclassed; he
     fights better than we might expect, learning how the
     weapon works as Khan backs him all over the place - -
     off the ledge of the first precipice and onto the
     lower platform. Khan follows feverishly, like a tiger
     going in for the kill. The Seconds cover the group
     with Phasers.

     (NB: This fight has yet to be staged but it's gonna
     be a humdinger, folks.)

     At the finish, as Bones, Spock, Carol and David watch,
     appalled, Khan has Kirk down, bloodied and exhausted.
     He stands triumphantly over him - - Kirk's weapon
     smashed to hits - - as he prepares to thrust home.

                                        (CONTINUED)

---

149 CONTINUED (2):

                    KHAN
          Revenge is the best revenge,
          wouldn't you say?

     Kirk can only heave and wait for the end - -

                    KHAN
          The encoder. Where is it?

                    KIRK
          You'll have to kill me.

                    KHAN
          Oh, I. shall. But what if I
          kill one of them, first - -
          slowly? The woman?

     Kirk cannot answer. Khan studies him - -

                    KHAN
                  (continuing)
          There is no encoder. That
          was simply a ruse to entice
          me here.

     The others stiffen. Khan smiles, readies his sword
     again. Kirk cloes [sic] his eyes. Khan watches, thinking;
     he lowers his sword, still ready, and sits - -

                    KHAN
          But if I kill you. I put you
          out of your misery. And I
          wish to prolong your suffering - -
          as you prolonged mine - - and my
          wife's.

     He looks around at the Eden Cave - -

                    KHAN
                  (continuing)
          I shall leave you. As you
          left me. Poetic justice.
          Marooned for eternity; to
          start your own Botany Bay
          Colony. You'll have more
          to live on than you left us.

     He rises - -

                    KHAN
                  (continuing)
          But you'll never leave. And
          no one will ever know where
          you are. You're buried alive - -
          in the middle of a dead planet.

                                        (CONTINUED)

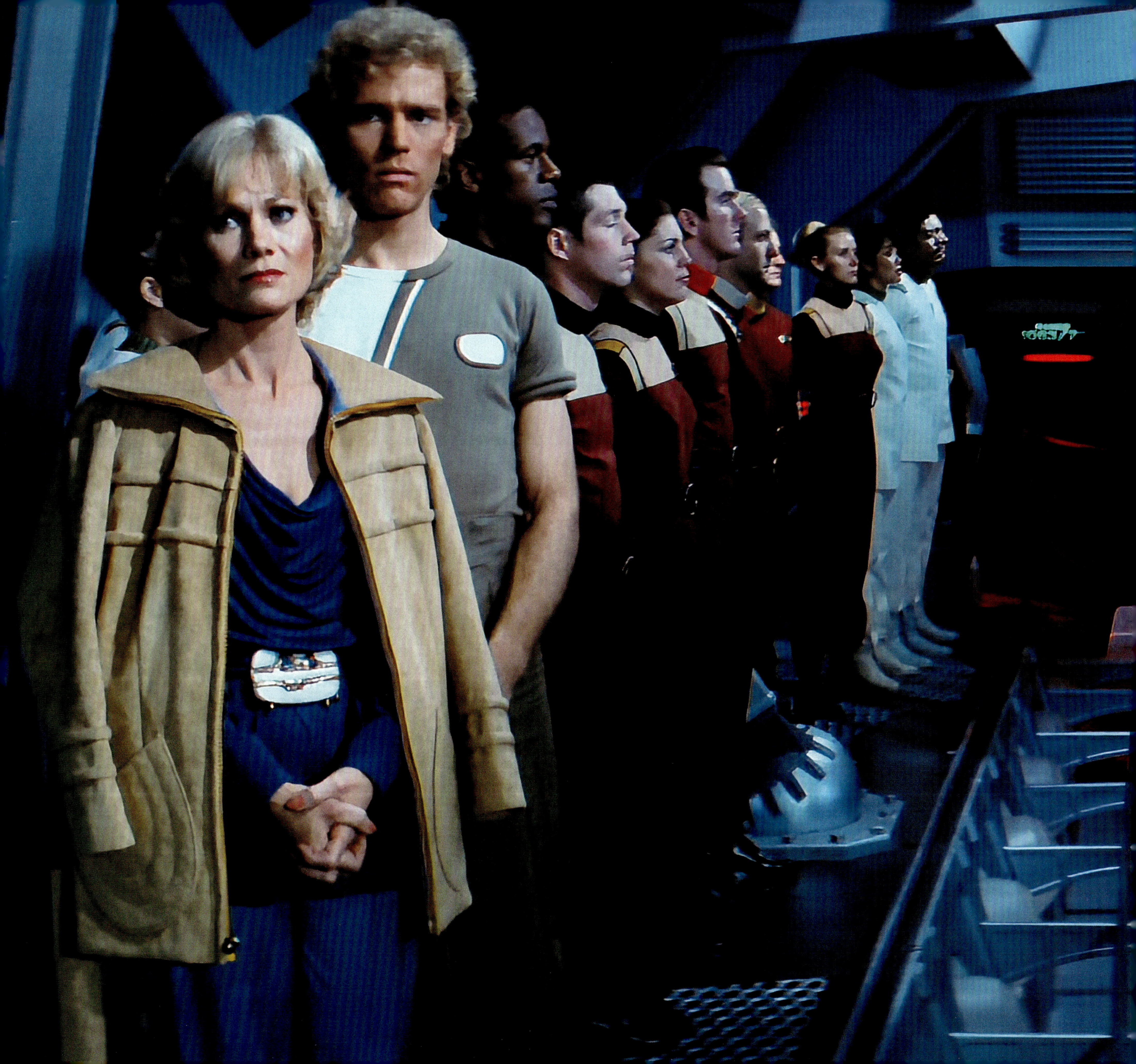

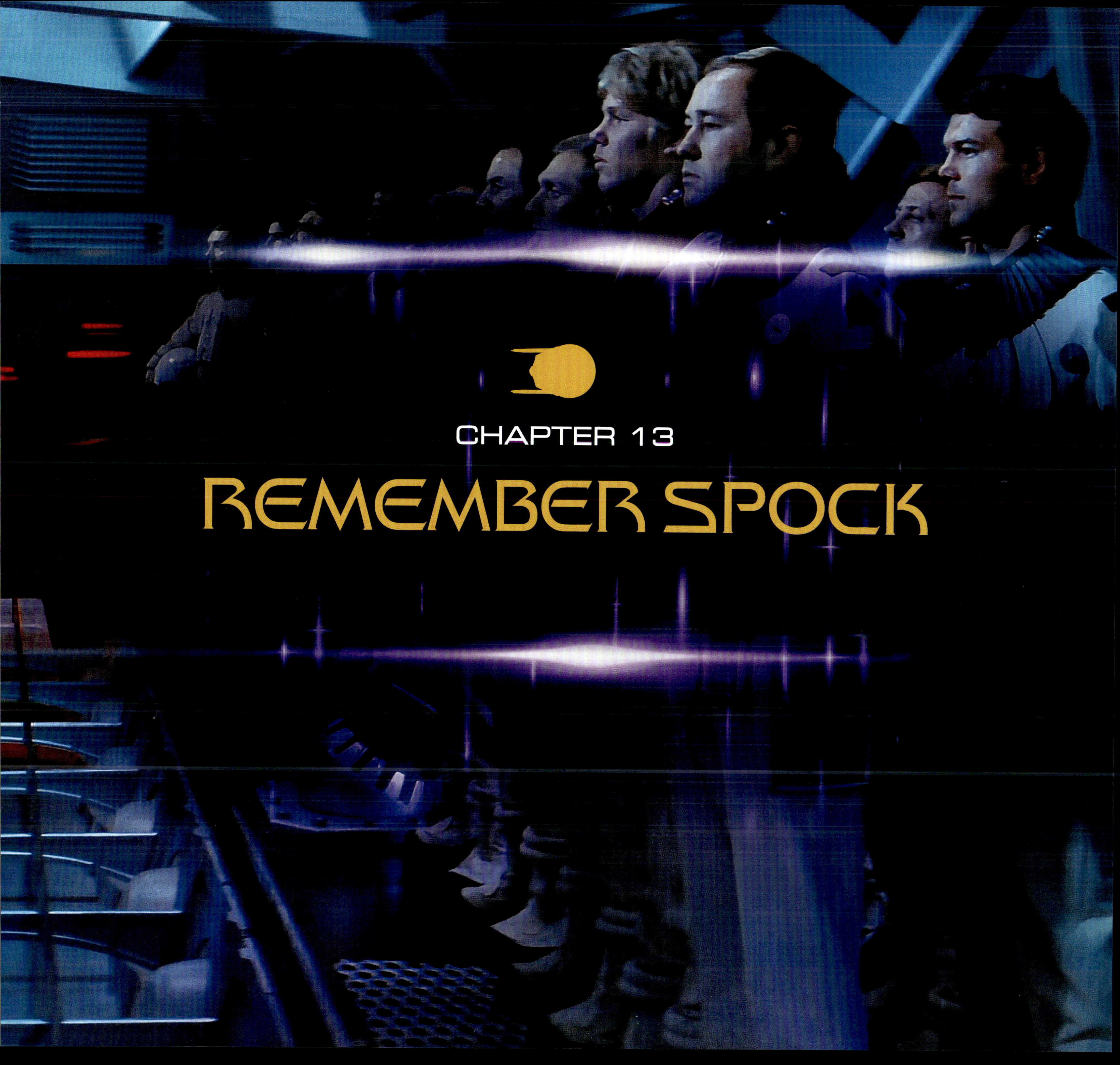

CHAPTER 13
REMEMBER SPOCK

SPOCK'S DEATH

"**H**ow'd you like to have a great death scene?"[1] Executive producer Harve Bennett had asked the question of Leonard Nimoy at the actor's house. They were reuniting with a series of meetings to discuss *Star Trek II*, having previously worked together on the 1973 television movie *The Alpha Caper*. Nimoy was reticent about returning as Spock, partially as a result of his experiences on the previous film. Nimoy shared in his biography *I Am Spock*, "Did I want to be involved? Let's just say I didn't want to be passed over, ignored, left out. I guess I wanted the decision to be mine."[2]

Contrary to common belief, there was no contractual requirement by Nimoy that Spock must die in the film. Bennett told Ed Naha of *Starlog* in 1982, "Most of the articles in print stated that Leonard agreed to do this film only if the character of Spock be killed off. He did not do this picture for that reason. He did the role of Mr. Spock because he wanted to be part of *Star Trek II: The Wrath of Khan*. Period. Seriously, the story changed half a dozen times from the point that Leonard said 'Yes' to the point where we started shooting. It would have been impossible for him to make that kind of deal."[3]

The death of Spock had been a creative solution to the problem of how to give Nimoy the certainty he needed that the character would serve a purpose organic to the narrative. Nimoy agreed to return, with the additional enticement of a "pay or play" commitment to appear in two more productions, one of which was the 1982 television movie *A Woman Called Golda* executive produced by Bennett. (Nimoy would earn an Emmy nomination for Outstanding Supporting Actor in a Limited Series or Special for the role of Morris Meyerson.) About his decision, Nimoy wrote, "Did I want to see Spock killed? No. But I couldn't help being intrigued by the idea; after all, if this was indeed going to be the one last squeeze of the cow, the final *Star Trek* effort, then it would make sense to go out gloriously."[4]

With Nimoy on board and with director Nicholas Meyer delivering his third draft of the script on September 29, 1981, the creatives began planning for the pending first day of filming to begin the second week of November. However, they could not plan comfortably, as yet another minefield would need to be navigated.

On October 18, 1981, while Nimoy was in China filming his role of Achmet in the mini-series *Marco Polo*, the article "Does Mr. Spock Die In the Next Episode Of 'Star Trek' Saga?" appeared in *The Wall Street Journal* by award winning journalist and editor Stephen J. Sansweet. *Star Wars* fans know Sansweet as the chairman and president of the non-profit museum Rancho Obi-Wan, the Guinness World Record museum that has the largest collection of *Star Wars* memorabilia. The article detailed growing protests about the death of Spock that had been leaked to fan groups, including a quarter-page ad being taken out in *Variety* claiming that Paramount would lose $28 million in sales and box office revenues if Spock died. The article included comments by Gene Roddenberry and a description of the conclusion of *Star Trek II* that was almost exactly what would be filmed.[5] A few weeks later, the article would be reprinted in local papers like *The Charlotte Observer* and *The Minneapolis Star* and featured in the international editions of *The Wall Street Journal*.

One of the international editions was published in China, where, rather than be upset by the revelation, Nimoy was touched that fans cared that much and enjoyed the economic study the fans had conducted. "I loved it! The tentacles of the Vulcan's proposed demise were reaching halfway around the globe. I had the best laugh of my entire China stay."[6] Soon, however, the situation became more serious, as threats were made against creatives and their families.

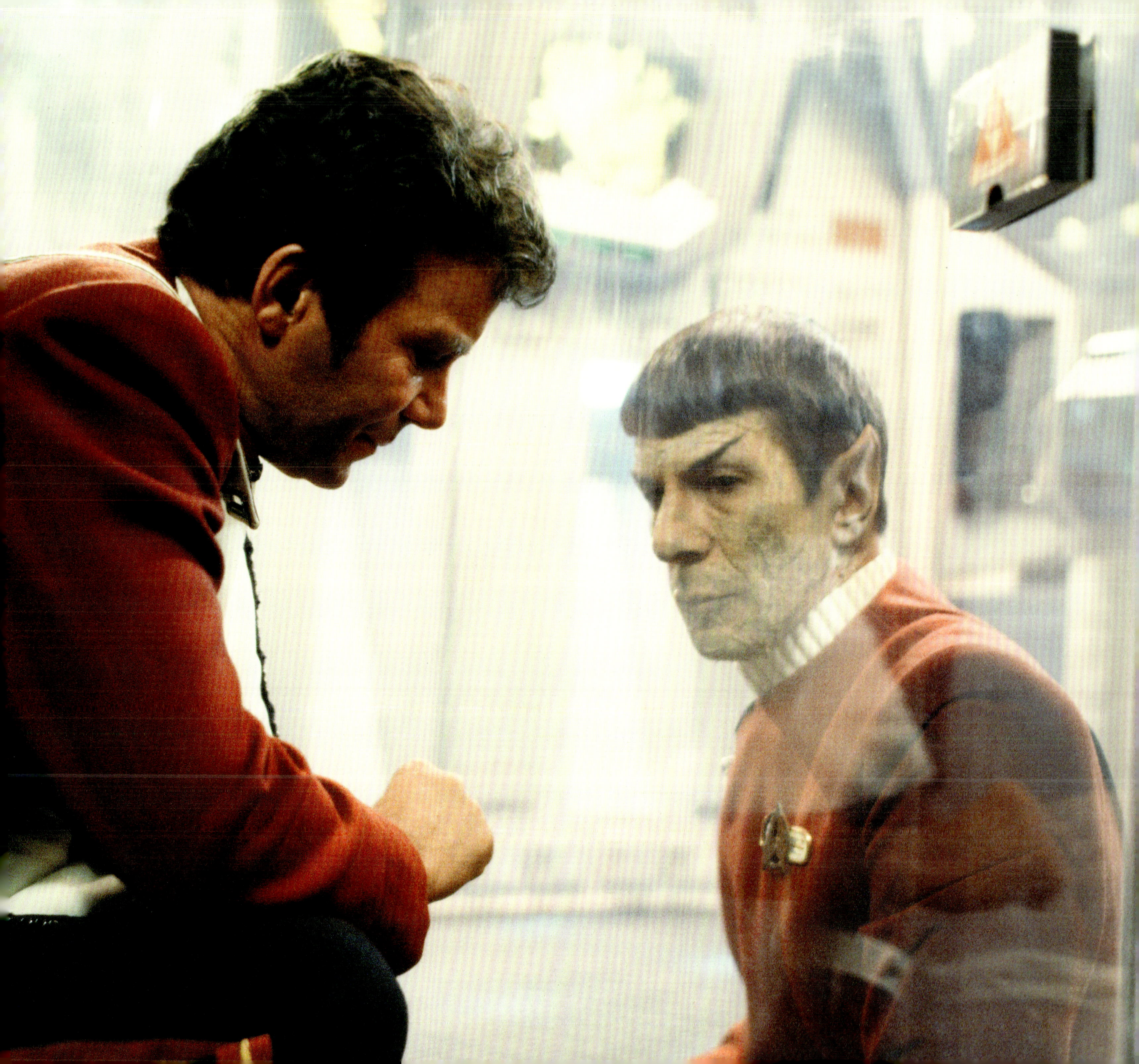

SPOCK'S UNDISCOVERED COUNTRY

The first document that features Spock's sacrifice for his crew was the January 30, 1981 final revised outline by Bennett and Sowards.

"One of the Warp Engines, which supplies power for the Phasers and the Shields, has been badly damaged. The Engine Compartment is flooded with deadly radiation. Spock turns the Con over to Kirk, and goes below to stop the runaway Warp Engine. Scotty tries to keep Spock out of the Engine room, but Spock IS the Captain, he sends Scotty back to his Console, goes into the Engine Compartment, and with the Manual Override begins to operate the ship's Shields and Armament… and giving it power to maneuver."

"Kirk hurries below to congratulate Spock on their victory, and finds Spock has been badly burned by high levels of Radiation… and Kirk arrives in time for a short scene with Spock before Spock dies in Kirk's arms. Two people who have spent years of their lives together, in discussion, talk, conversation, argument and debate… and at this moment, there is that feeling that something important has been left unsaid."[11]

Every iteration of the script afterwards had a variation of the scene, with each of the revisions evolving closer to the final version as scripted by Meyer.

"STAR TREK:The Omega System"   44

CLOSE ANGLE – KIRK AND SPOCK

Spock seems to be dazed as they sit him on the floor, and starts to keel over… Kirk catches him, supporting him for a moment.

                    KIRK
          Spock?
                    SPOCK
          Hello, Jim. . . .

He puts his hand up, and Kirk takes it. Spock holds onto that hand like it's life itself.

                    SPOCK
          How's the ship?
                    KIRK
          The ship's fine. . . We drove them off. . .
          How are you?
                    SPOCK
          I'll be all right in a few minutes. . .
          I'm just tired.
                    KIRK
          Why don't you rest?
                    SPOCK
          No. . . There'll be plenty of time to
          rest. . . later. . . .

Spock looks at Kirk, his mind working.

                    SPOCK
          There was something I wanted to tell
          you. . .
                    (He searches through his
                    mind, but it's gone)
          I can't remember. . . I guess it wasn't
          important. . . .
                    (puzzled)
          Funny. . . I thought it was important at
          the time. . . .

McCoy and Chapel arrive, and kneel down beside them. Chapel holds the small pocket diagnostic machine near Spock, and McCoy looks him over.

                    SPOCK
          Have you come to practice your black
          arts on me, Doctor?

"STAR TREK:The Omega System"   45

                    McCOY
          Tis easier to be a critic than a craftsman,
          Mr. Spock.

Spock smiles… Then chuckles at the remark…. McCoy and Kirk exchange a puzzled look. I don't think either one of them ever heard this man laugh.

                    CHAPEL
                    (softly, reading the machine)
          Good Lord!

Sha hands it to McCoy, who reads the numbers…. then looks up at Spock, shocked.

                    KIRK
          Bones. . . ?
                    McCOY
          He's gone, Jim. . . .

ANGLE – KIRK

In the f.g. we can see the two hands still clasped, as Kirk turns quickly to look at Spock. We see the fingers of Spock's hand relax and loosen their grip. Kirk clasps the hand tightly. . . His voice a choke, almost inaudible whisper.

                    KIRK
          Spock? . . . Spock? . . . .

Gradually Kirk relaxes his hand, and Spock's hand slips out of his grasp… and the CAMERA HOLDS for a long moment on Kirk's stricken expression.

INT. FORWARD TORPEDO ROOM

The Crew of the Enterprise is assembled in neat ranks on either side of a long cylindrical metal tube, resting on a set of tracks leading to an open metal door. The Forward Torpedo Tubes. A flag of the Federation is draped across the Tube… Kirk stands at one end… looking down. After a moment, he looks up and begins to speak.

                    KIRK
          (I DON'T KNOW WHAT HE SAYS YET. . .)
                    (WE'LL COME BACK TO THIS)
          Unto almighty God we commend the soul
          of our brother departed, and we commit
          his body to the deep. . . .

Kirk nods to the Pall Bearers.

"STAR TREK:The Omega System"
                                                                    46

ANGLE – THE METAL COFFIN

It is pushed forward into the tube. The door is closed, and Kirk nods to Sulu, who is standing by the Console. Sulu lowers his hand and presses the button.

EXT. THE ENTERPRISE

As the Metal tube is FIRED from the torpedo tube, and off into space.

64.
94

94 CONTINUED

Scotty holds up a hand to stop him, then looks off toward the flashing RED LIGHT over the control room. Kirk turns and sees Spock on the other side of clear plastic door, still bathed in the Blue Light, standing just inside the control room. Kirk steps forward to open the door and go in to help. . .

95

95 ANGLE - FAVORING SPOCK

He sees Kirk start to open the door, and shakes his head.

               SPOCK
No, Jim. . . Don't open the door.

               KIRK
Spock!

Kirk starts to open the door anyway, but Scotty puts a hand on his arm.

               SCOTTY
You can't open that door, sir. You'll flood this whole compartment with radiation.

               KIRK
But he'll die!

There is a look between Kirk and Scotty. . .

               SCOTTY
               (gently)
He's been in there too long.

Kirk looks at Scotty for a moment, as that sinks in, then he turns back to Spock. . . on the other side of the door.

               KIRK
Spock. . .

               SPOCK
I've been thinking about what you said, Jim, and I don't entirely disagree with your conclusion. . . It's the method by which you arrive at that conclusion.

               KIRK
What conclusion, Spock?

(CONTINUED)

65.
95

95 CONTINUED:

               SPOCK
The Kobayashi Maru. . . A Captain's primary consideration is the safety of his ship and crew. In which case, retreat is the answer. . . but the primary duty of the ship and crew is to protect and serve the citizens of the Federation. And in that case. . . In that case. . .

Spock sways and Kirk starts to reach for him, but his hands encounter the plastic door. Spock sinks to his knees.

               KIRK
Spock. . . ?

Spock takes a beat to collect himself and continues in his cool manner.

               SPOCK
Some lives must be sacrificed in order to save other. . . It is a matter of logically ordering one's priorities. . .
               (stressing the word)
Logic. . . Jim. Logic. . . Without logic, the Universe is a sprawling, chaotic, inexplicable mess. . . and life as we live it, moment to moment, seems to be random, and yet. . .

Spock pauses. . . shakes his head to clear it, and leans against the door to support himself. . .

               SPOCK
               (continuing)
Looking back. . . It is amazingly ordered. Almost as if it were ordained. Predestined. All neatly organized. . . with a beginning. . . a middle. . . and an end. . .

Spock puts his hand against the door to support himself. . . and Kirk puts his hand on the outer side of the door.

               SPOCK
               (continuing)
All. . . very logical. . .

(CONTINUED)

110.

STAR TREK II - Rev. 11/6/81

236 CONTINUED: 236

               SPOCK
Or the one.

He props a hand on the glass to support himself. Kirk's hand reflexively goes to match Spock's on the other side of the glass - -

               SPOCK
               (continuing)
I never took the Kobayashi Maru test - - until now. What do you think of my solution?

               KIRK
Spock. . . !

               SPOCK
I have been - - and always will be - - your friend. . .Live. Long. And. Prosper.

Spock falls. Bones and Scotty react.

               KIRK
No. . . !

               SAAVIK'S VOICE
               (intercom)
Admiral, you've got to see this! There's new life   a whole new world, a Genesis world - - !

But Kirk is past hearing or caring. He is huddled up against the glass, destroyed. Bones looks on, helpless.

DISSOLVE TO:

237 EXT. SPACE 237

A spectacular Look at Carol's planet being born!

238 OMITTED 238

239 CAMERA PULLS BACK TO REVEAL 239

the Ship's Company in full dress uniforms assembled for ship's burial service. Over the PULLBACK, we HEAR:

(CONTINUED)

STAR TREK II - Rev. 10/19/81

109.

235 INT. ENTERPRISE ENGINE ROOM 235

Kirk emerges to encounter Scotty and Bones. Their looks tell him. He sees the flashing light over the Reactor Room. He dashes for the control panel. Bones grabs him.

               SCOTTY
No, sir! You'll flood the whole compartment. . . !

               KIRK
He'll die - - !

               BONES
               (also holds him)
He's dead already, Jim.

Kirk's eyes bulge.

               KIRK
Oh, God.

236 ANGLE AT REACTOR ROOM GLASS ROOR 236

With stunned understanding, Kirk stumbles to the door, sees Spock on his knees, hands blackened, face cracked with radiation lines and scars.

Spock shakes his head. With a feeble hand he reaches the intercom button: filtered communication.

               KIRK
Spock!

               SPOCK
The ship - - out of danger?

               KIRK
Yes - -

Spock is satisfied; he fights for breath - -

               SPOCK
Don't grieve, Admiral - - it's logical: the good of the many outweighs - - -

He almost keels over. Kirk has tears streaming down his face - -

               KIRK
. . . the good of the few. . .

(CONTINUED)

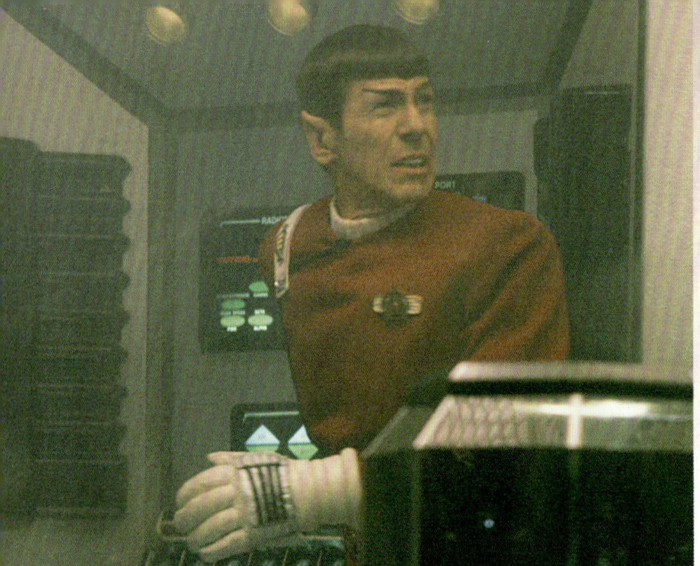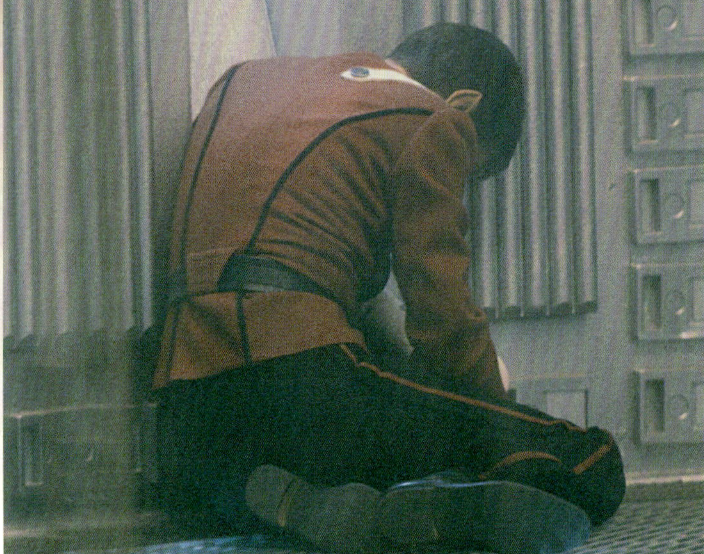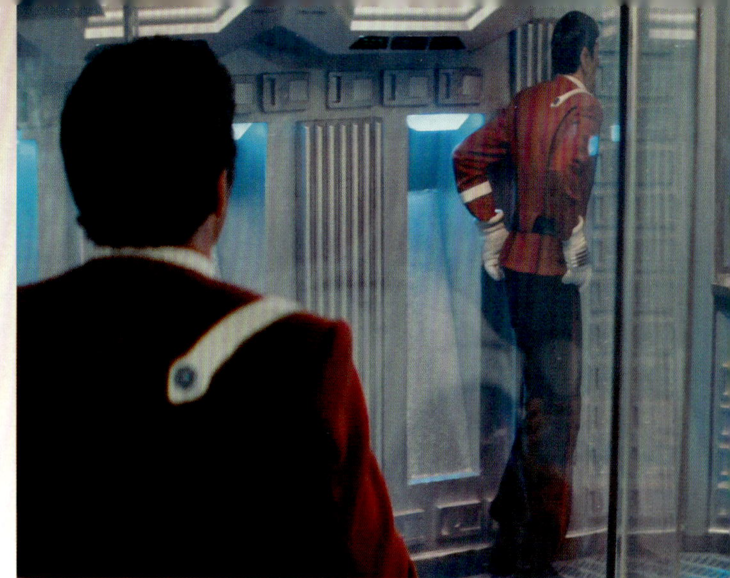

Two additional problems loomed. First, the good will of fans is essential to the success of any production, especially *Star Trek*. Second, script secrecy had been paramount. Solving the first problem would be the result of how emotional and meaningful Spock's sacrifice was as determined by audience reaction. Solving the second problem required a bit of rewriting on Meyer's part.

Although the *Kobayashi Maru* had been part of the scripts since the versions by Jack B. Sowards, the Meyer scripts did not originally have Spock on the simulator with his cadets during the test. The September 16, 1981 script has Spock revealing that he did not want his presence to inhibit his crew. An idea was devised, however, to add Spock to the scene, trusting that his fake demise, along with Uhura, McCoy, and Sulu, during the simulation would inspire the audience to forget about the rumors and proverbial grapevine. Meyer recalls that the idea to add Spock to the *Kobayashi Maru* scene early in the film came to him while he and Bennett were in one of Paramount's small screening rooms. As the two discussed the leak, Meyer, joking and thinking out loud, mostly to himself, mentioned that they should have Spock die in the first part of the movie. Bennett replied, "That is genius!"[7] Spock's addition to the opening scene would also make for a symbolic and emotional bookend, as the Vulcan ultimately faces his own *Kobayashi Maru* scenario.

The death scene was scheduled to be filmed December 15 and 16, 1981. "The closer I came to the day Spock was scheduled to die," Nimoy wrote, "the more a sense of ominous foreboding settled over me. The effect caught me totally by surprise; I suppose I could argue that I took each day's work as it came—but when the day finally came, it rocked me."[8] Despite the emotional nature of the demands on Nimoy and William Shatner especially, the actors were able to complete the sequences in a minimum number of takes. Although one take had to

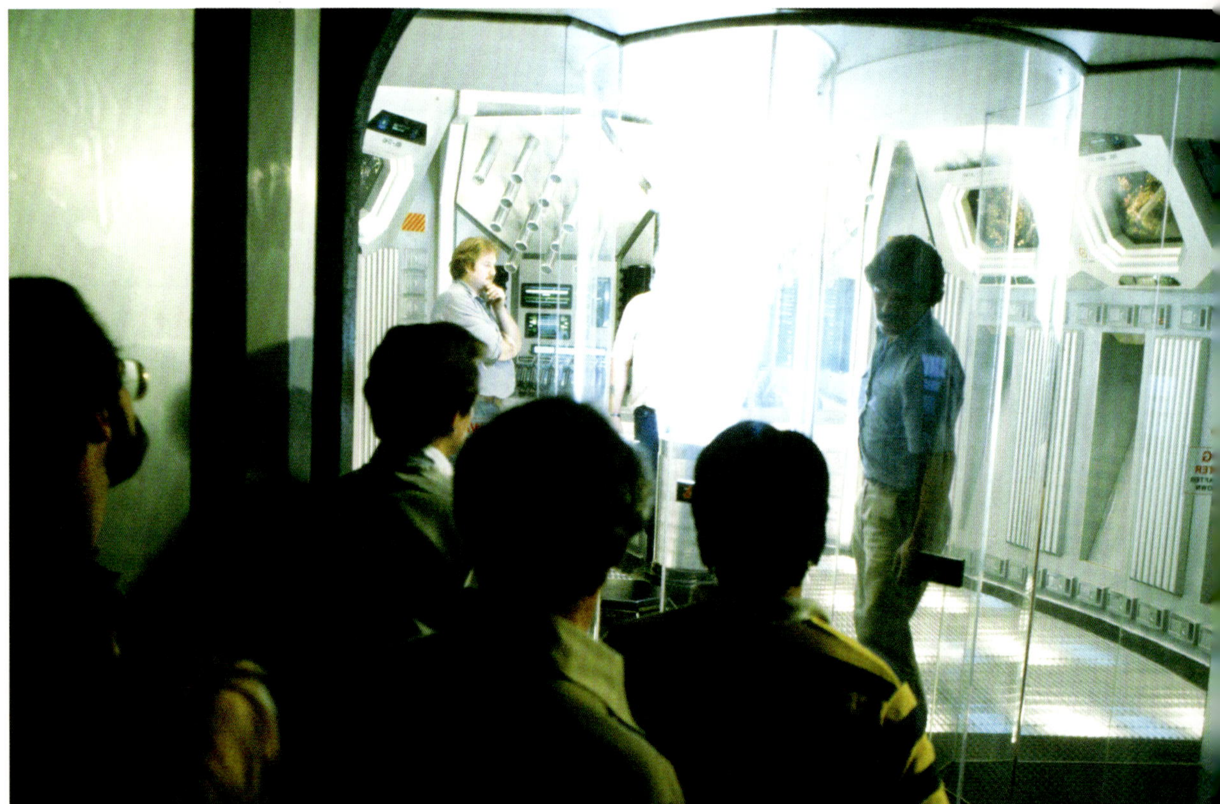

TOP: "Whenever we sat down," Nimoy wrote in his autobiography, *I Am Spock*, "the jackets hiked up, giving the feeling that the collar was riding up around our necks. So we actors all developed the habit of taking hold of the bottom and pulling down whenever we stood up. This quick movement would have a significant effect in my final scene in the film."[16]
"I gave a slight downward tug on my jacket, which had, as usual, crept up on me. I was quite conscious of doing it, but hoped it would appear to be in character, because despite the physical agony, Spock would have wanted to make a proper and dignified appearance when presenting himself to his captain for the last time."[17]

ABOVE: Only approximately thirty people were on set at the time that Spock's sacrifice was filmed, both out of concerns for secrecy and respect for the actors.

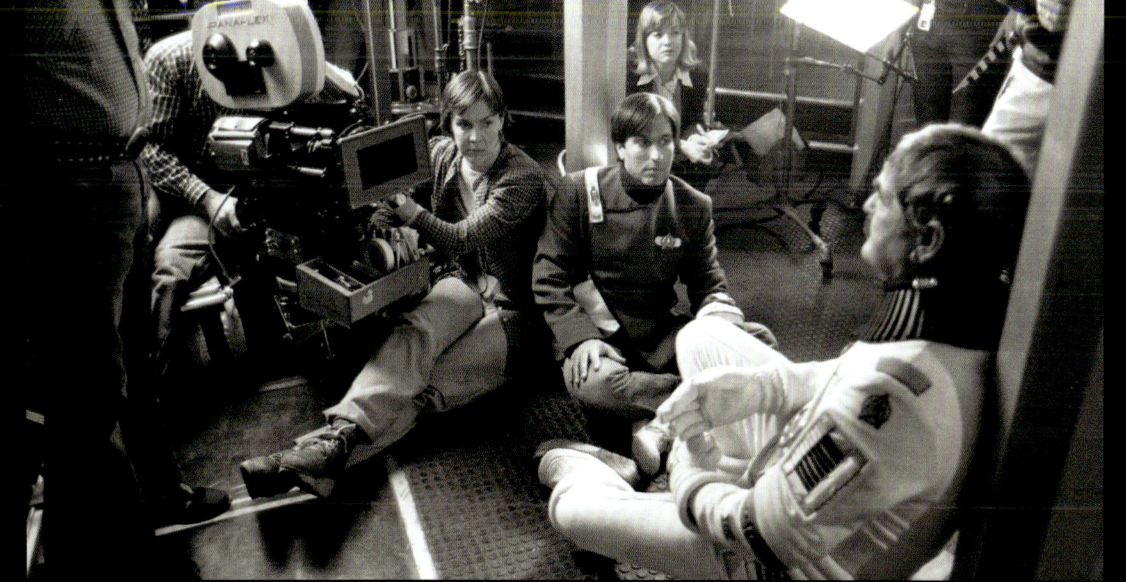

LEFT: Meyer, wearing a Starfleet jacket, not because of some secret cameo, but rather because it was cold on the set that day.

BELOW: Nichols, reflecting on Spock's death: "Every time I see it, I'm caught between being a fan and being Uhura and not the pragmatic Nichelle Nichols that says life goes on and we have to do without him. When I heard that Spock might come back, I was delighted because my concern is not for Leonard Nimoy because he's doing so much more. Once again, the thrust of my feelings towards *Star Trek* are the fans and their concerns. It's a family and he's a symbol that means certain things to people. He's a sign of hope and strength and intelligence and advancement and that's what life must be about."[18]

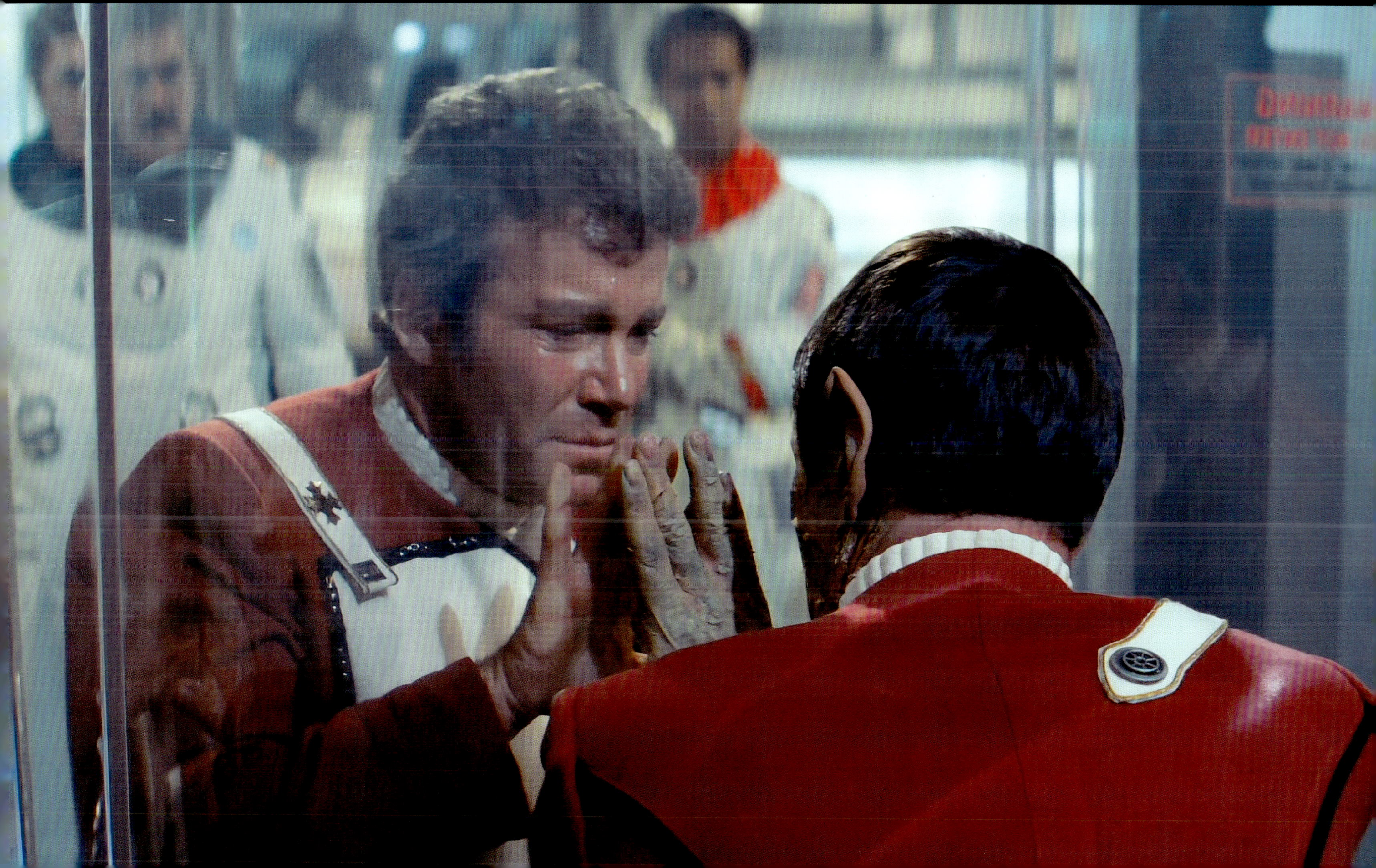

RIGHT: Takei shared, "You know, I guess
for all of us who have been with the series
and gotten to know Spock and be fond
of the character it really was a deeply
affecting sequence, particularly the funeral
sequence... the funeral sequence was
absolutely devastating."[19]

BELOW: Meyer: "When we filmed Spock's
death and when we filmed the funeral,
everybody there was crying, so I guess
it was very emotional. The cameraman
was crying, the crew were crying, the
actors were crying. I was surprised and I
got choked up and I thought this is really
interesting. I had never watched, as I say,
Star Trek, and the first movie didn't do
anything for me so it was very shocking in a
way to discover how affected I was by this.
I was really surprised when I turned around
and I saw the cameraman, Gayne Rescher,
with tears streaming down his face."[20]

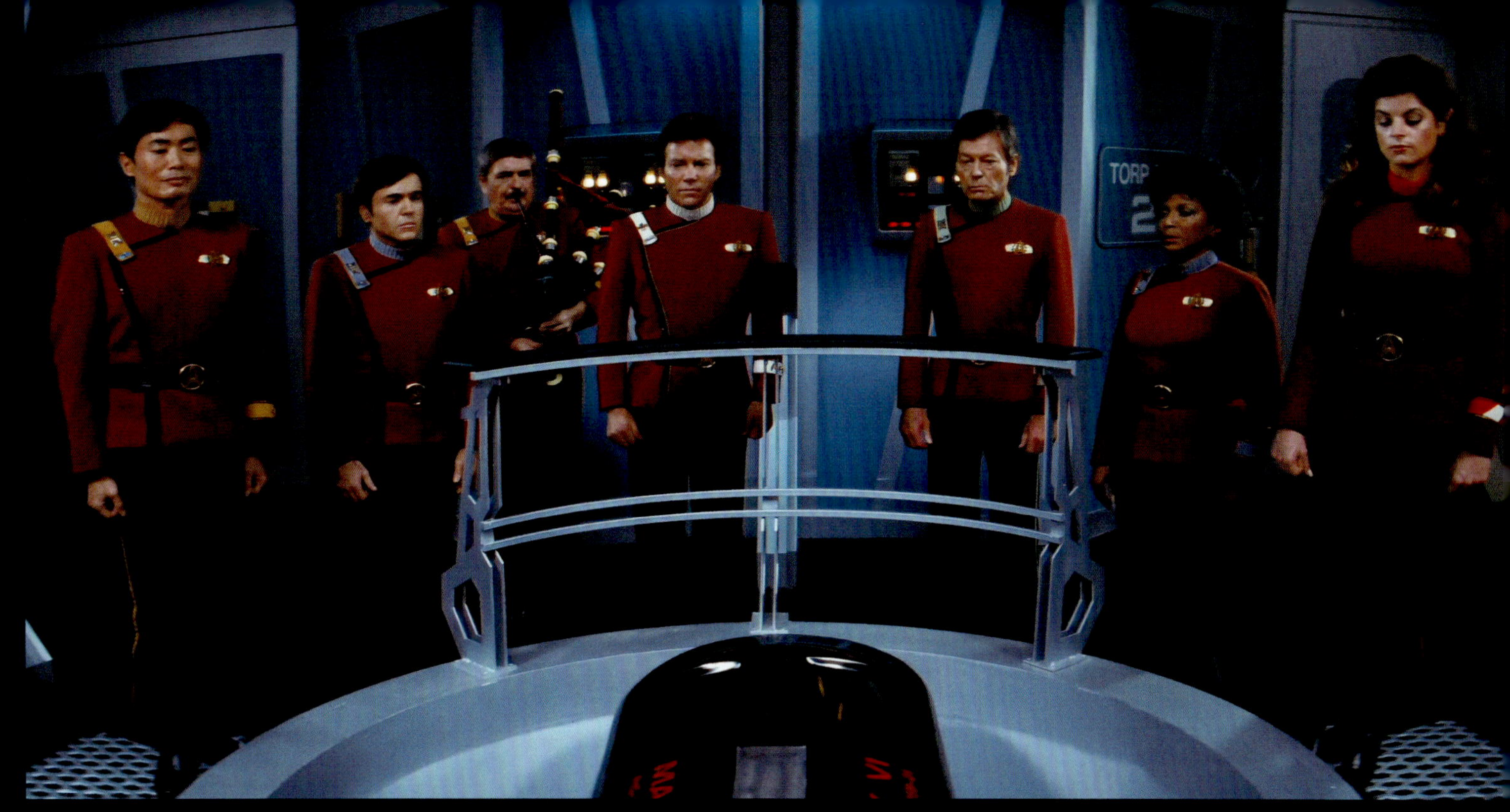

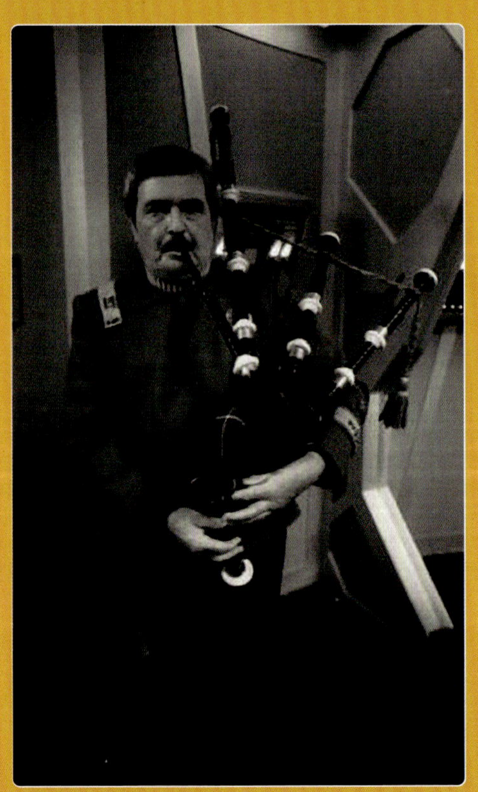

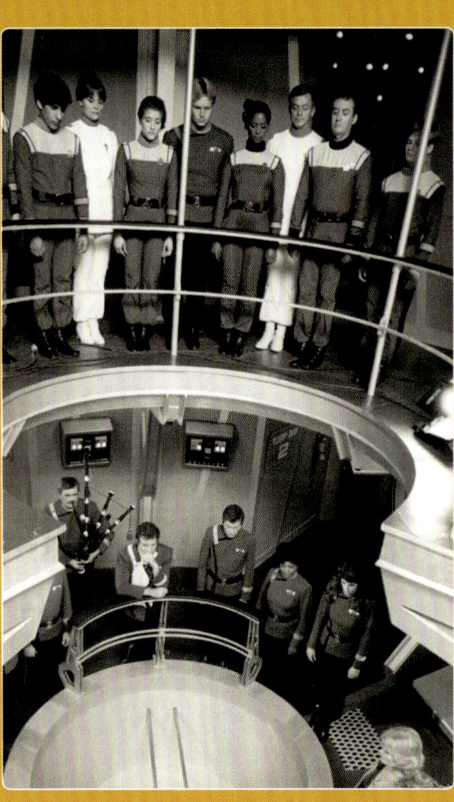

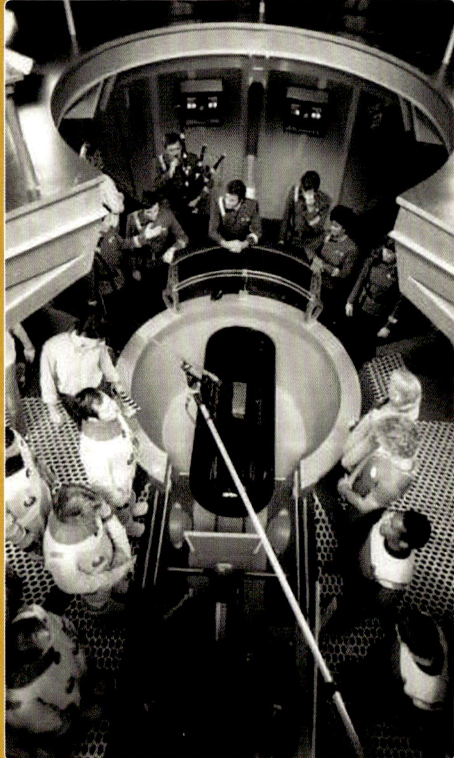

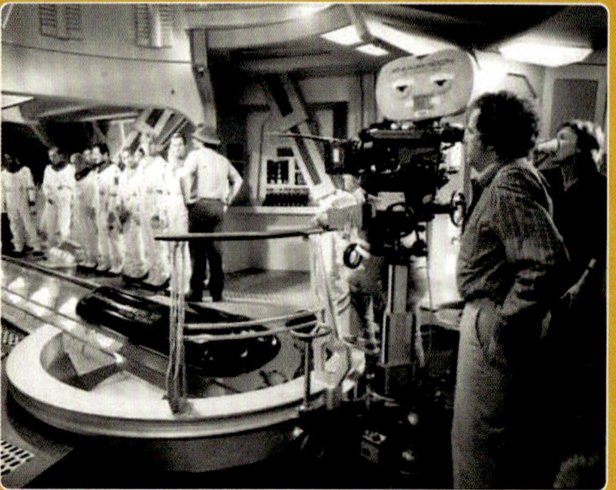

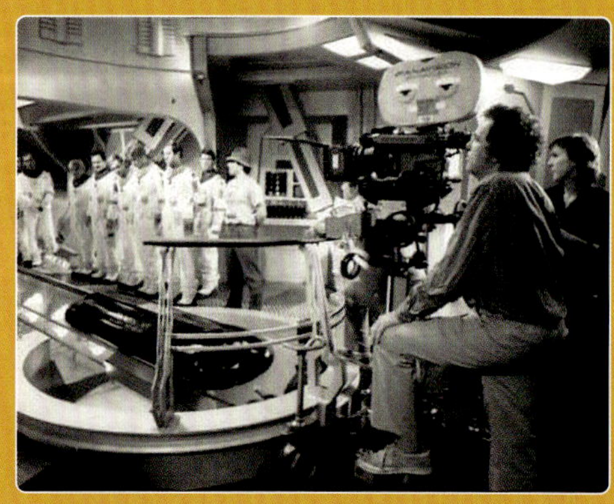

be redone because film had not been loaded in the camera. As movies are usually shot out of order, Nimoy had other scenes to film after Spock's death. Two days after filming Spock and Kirk saying goodbye, the characters would be saying hello, as the scenes of Kirk boarding the *Enterprise* for inspection were filmed on December 18 and 21.

The problem was that the scene was too effective. "We previewed it, and I will never forget," Harve Bennett notes. "The audience filed out in silence, streaming tears, and I felt like I'd been part of an assassination. I felt guilty."[9] Conversations began about how to make the ending more hopeful and yet preserve the dignity of Spock's sacrifice. One of those who objected was Meyer. "Pick your battles, I learned—and this is the battle I picked. I did not want the death of Spock to end in a betrayal of the audience's emotional investment in that moment. In this I had no hesitation in believing that I was in the right. I fought the proposed idea of hinting at Spock's resurrection every way I knew how. I argued against it. I stalled. I lied. I refused to cooperate, trying to let the clock run out against the moment when it was time to cut negative or miss our release date… I even came up with what I thought was an elegant compromise… I proposed letting Spock's sepulchral voice read these lines at the end of our film. The audience wouldn't know how he came to be saying them—was it his ghost speaking?—but they would get the idea of Spock's own 'ongoingness.'"[10]

The decision was made, however, and a coda showing Spock's casket safely on the genesis planet, and not burned in its emerging atmosphere, was added without Meyer's participation. The sequence was created, storyboarded, and filmed by special visual effects supervisor Ken Ralston, producer Robert Sallin, and the ILM team at San Francisco's Golden Gate Park. With James Horner's music, William Dornisch's editing, and Spock's narration complimenting the scene, the moment brought to the film's conclusion the needed amount of ambiguous hope.

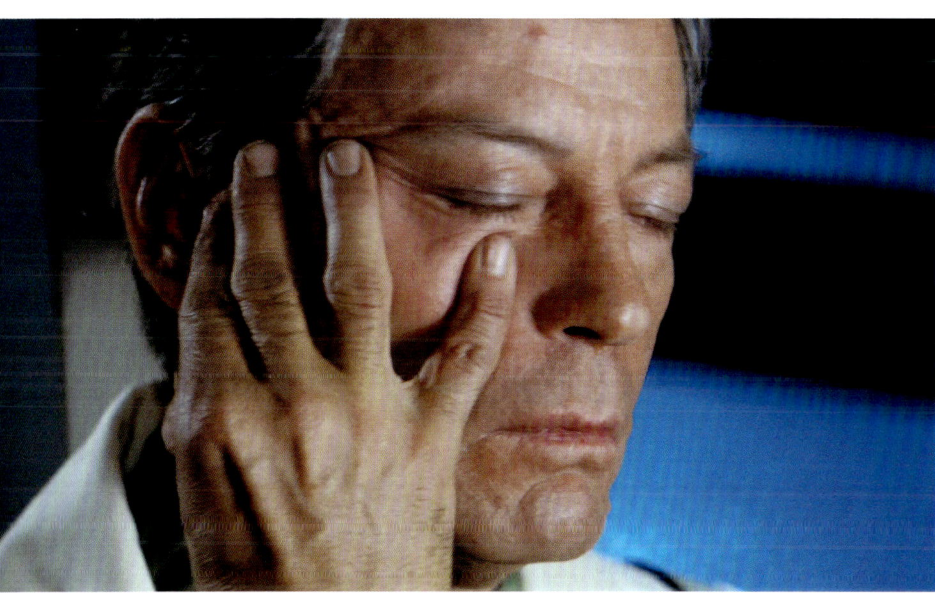

ABOVE: As originally scripted, there was no "Remember" mind-meld. On the day of filming, Bennett asked Nimoy if there was anything that could be added to the scene to make it ambiguous, a kind of vagueness to it that could leave possibilities for future films. It was Bennett who thought of the mind-meld and Nimoy who thought of having Spock say, "Remember." Nimoy remembered, "De[Forest Kelley] and I rehearsed the scene until we were ready for the cameras. I admit, I didn't really want to be finished with this scene—because I knew which one would be coming next."[15]

RIGHT: The *Star Trek II* "Remember" scene is an inversion of the emotional scene from the third season episode of the original *Star Trek*, "Requiem for Methuselah," where Spock helps an exhausted Kirk forget his love Rayna. Spock mind-melds with Kirk while he sleeps, saying, "Forget."

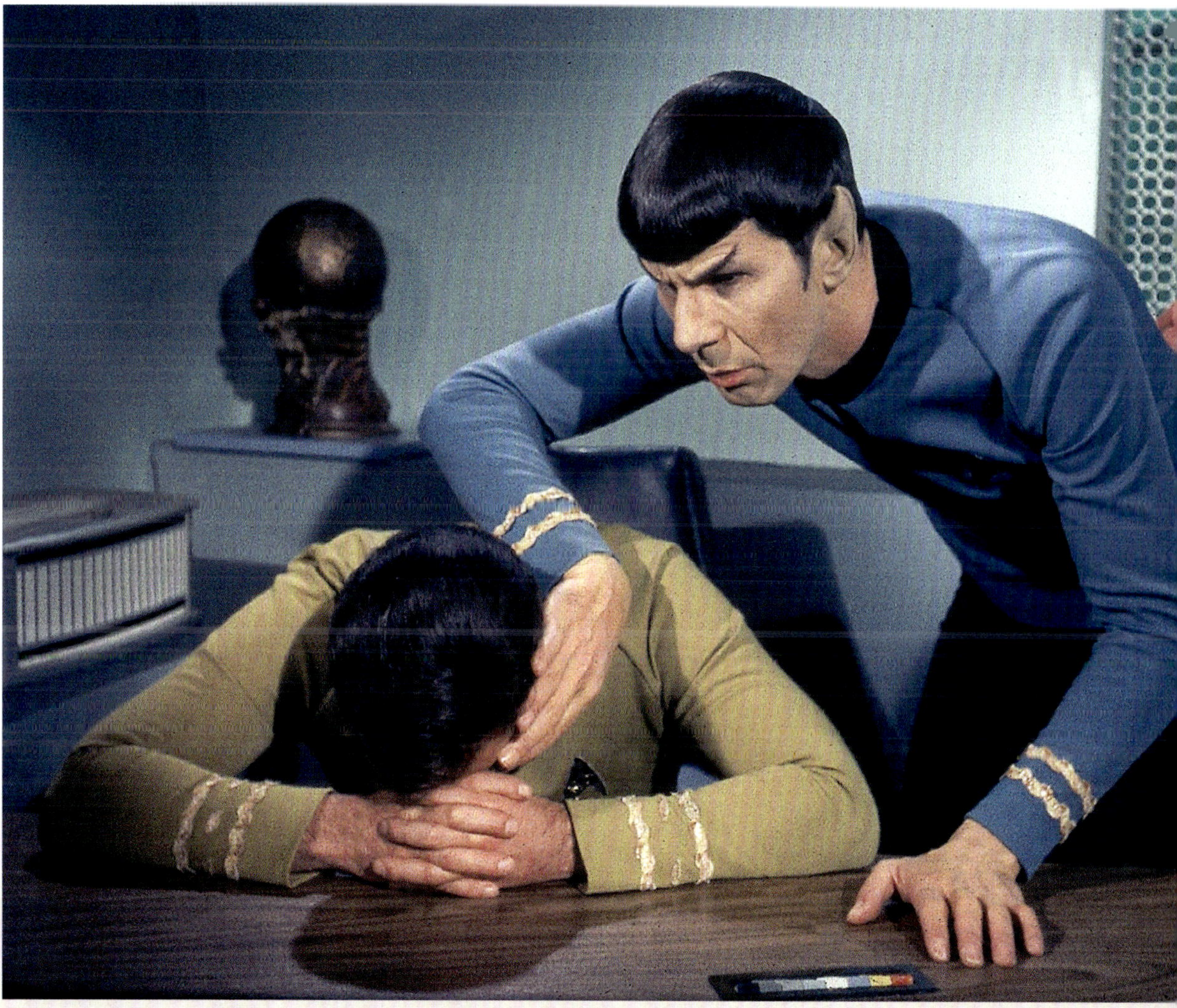

A DAUGHTER REMEMBERS: JULIE NIMOY ON HER FATHER, LEONARD

During the late 1970s, Leonard Nimoy's daughter, Julie, was exploring the idea of a career working behind-the-scenes in the television and film industry. To learn more about the possibilities, and to get a chance to work with her father on what was thought to be his last turn as Spock, Julie accepted a position as a production assistant on *Star Trek II*. The experience would give her a unique perspective during the making of the film.

Each day, she would drive with her father to the studio, sometimes driving, sometimes as a passenger with her father driving. Julie recalls, "Driving times would vary depending on the call sheet. Sometimes we would have to leave at 5:00am for makeup—which ended up being a very 'quiet drive' as we both were pretty tired! Other days, he'd be chatting the whole time with me about how the day went and what I learned. Of course, it always made me feel really good when he told me that the crew said I was doing a good job. If it was a heavy shooting day or something he was very excited about, this would give me a pretty good idea of how he'd be feeling on the drive home."

Julie shared, "Dad was very serious about studying his lines every evening and immersing himself in the character so he'd be prepared for the next scenes he'd be shooting. Since I was old enough to see him working on a set, I have always observed how passionate, dedicated, and serious he was as an actor. I saw how important it was to him to really delve into the character's psyche and know the individual inside

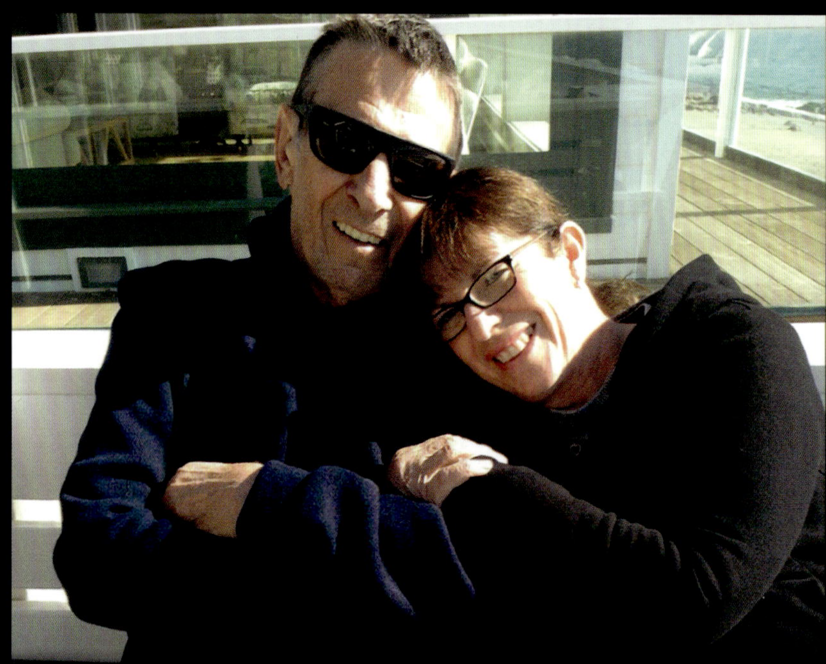

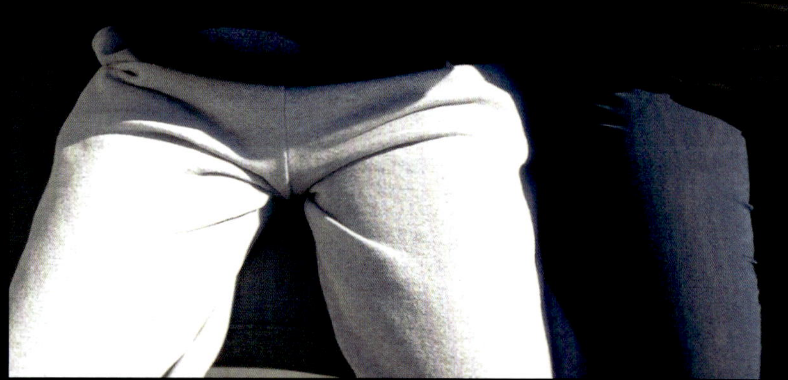

and out. He felt very comfortable playing Mr. Spock. He knew his 'alter ego' almost as well as he knew himself."

December 15 and 16 were days that would forever remain in Julie's memory. "I have very vivid memories of 'that day'—the day of Spock's death scene. When I got to my dad's house, he was more quiet than usual. I knew this would not be a typical day for him. He had briefly talked to me prior about Spock's character dying, and that he was trying to get used to the reality that it would be the 'end' of Spock. I could see he was sad and I asked him if he was okay. He said he was, but he needed time to reflect, and so we spent most of the car ride in silence. Spock's death scene created a lot of emotion for everyone on the set, which included the cast and crew alike. My dad spent most of his time in his trailer and I left him alone so that he could focus and be ready for the scene. When it came time to shoot, my dad walked onto the set and everyone was eerily quiet. We all watched as Spock and Kirk played out the scene. It was very emotional for everyone. I believe I even saw some tears—I know that my eyes welled up. After the scene was shot, my dad walked off the stage towards the doors as everyone was clapping for him. Personally, I felt sad for not only the character, Spock, but for my dad, because he was so connected to Mr. Spock and I could feel his loss. I knew it was hard for him to accept the fact that the *Star Trek* movies would continue to go forward without his beloved character."[13]

Leonard's passing on February 27, 2015, due to chronic obstructive pulmonary disease, would result in a world-wide outpouring of affection for him and his family. In 2014, Nimoy had announced that he had COPD, spending the next year trying to share with others the dangers of smoking. Julie and her husband, documentary film maker David Knight, produced *Remembering Leonard Nimoy*, about Leonard's battle with COPD. Even after his passing, Leonard continues to inspire.

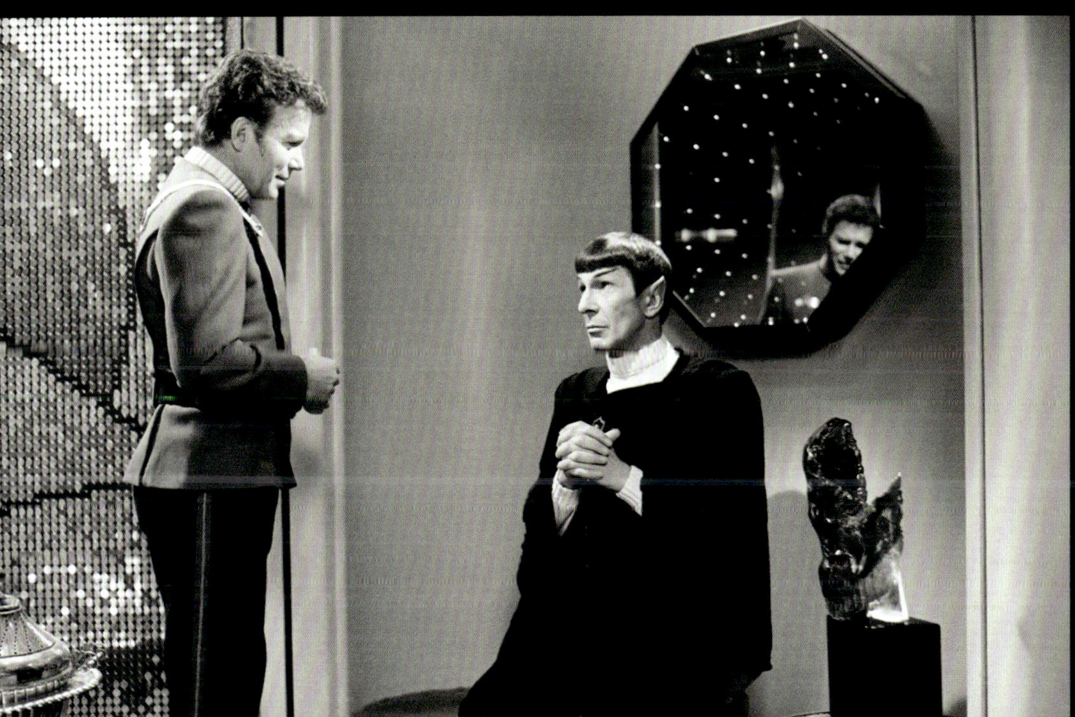

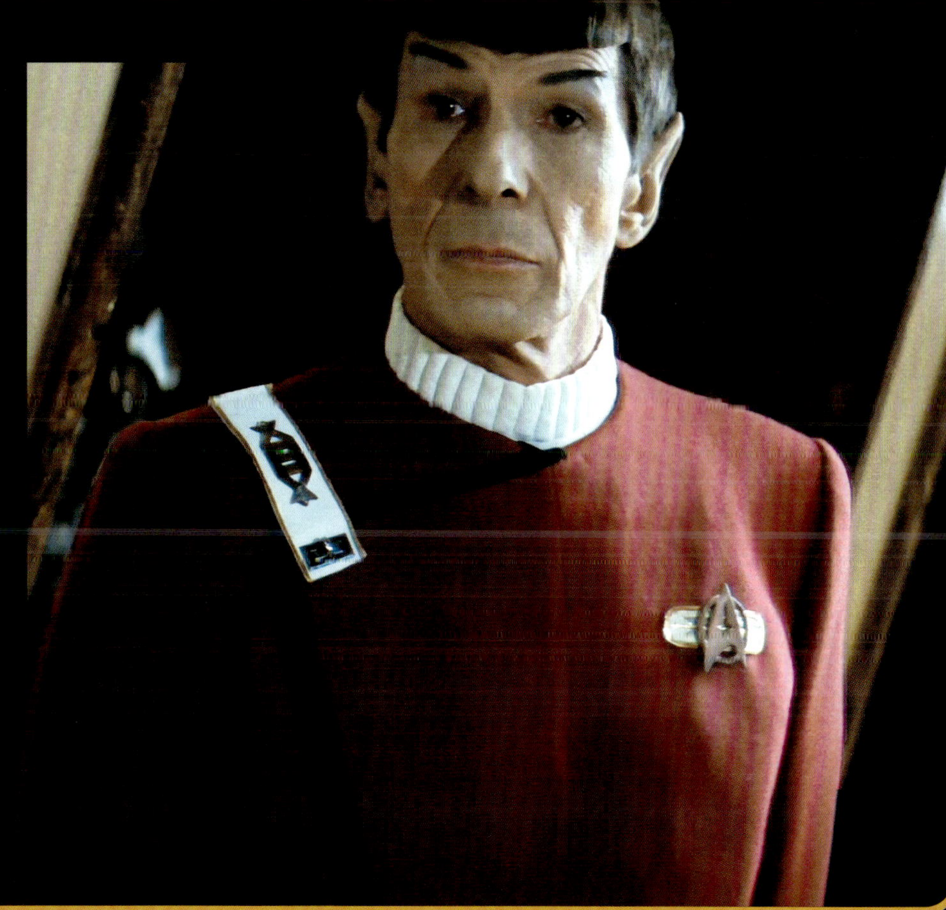

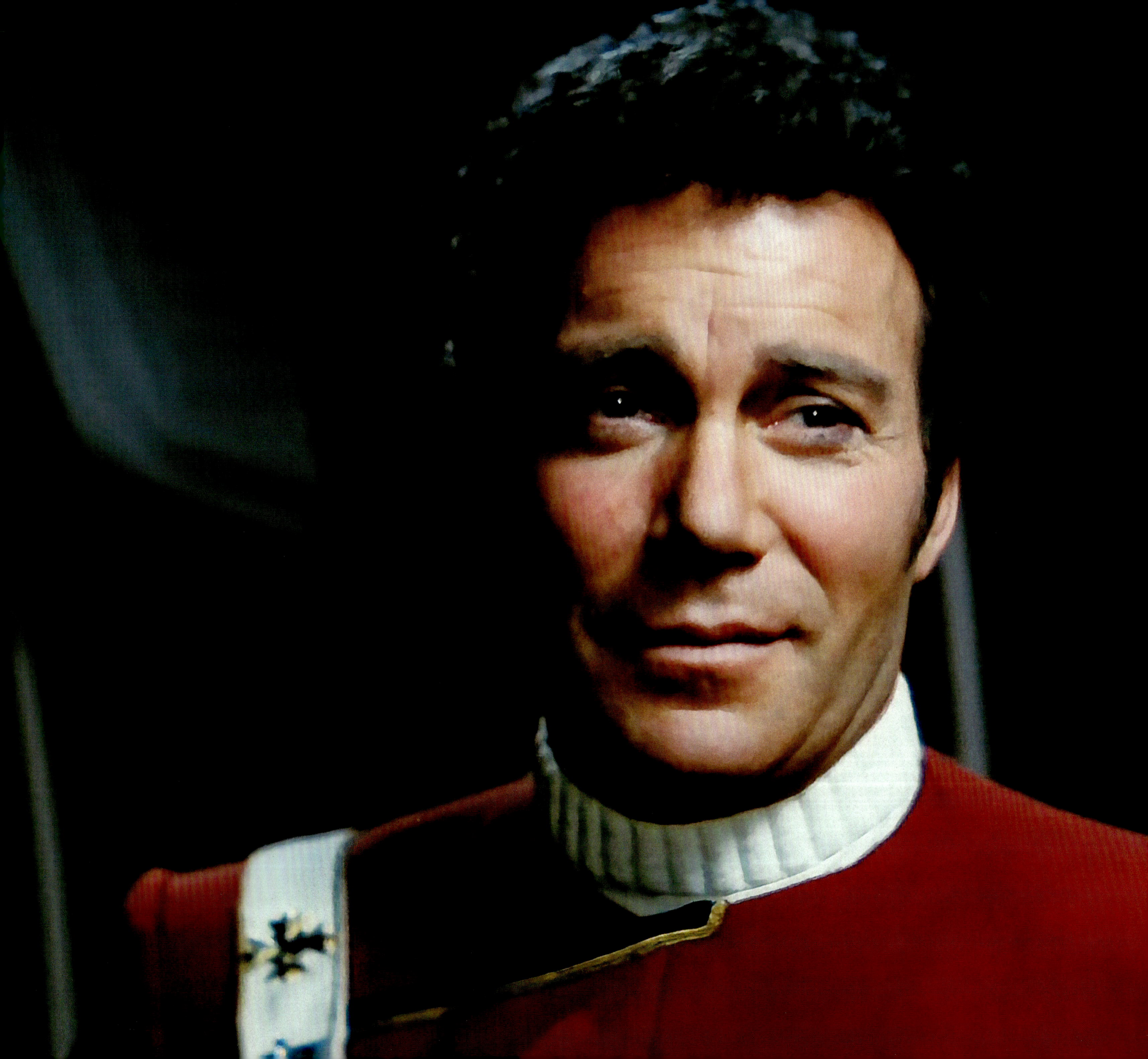

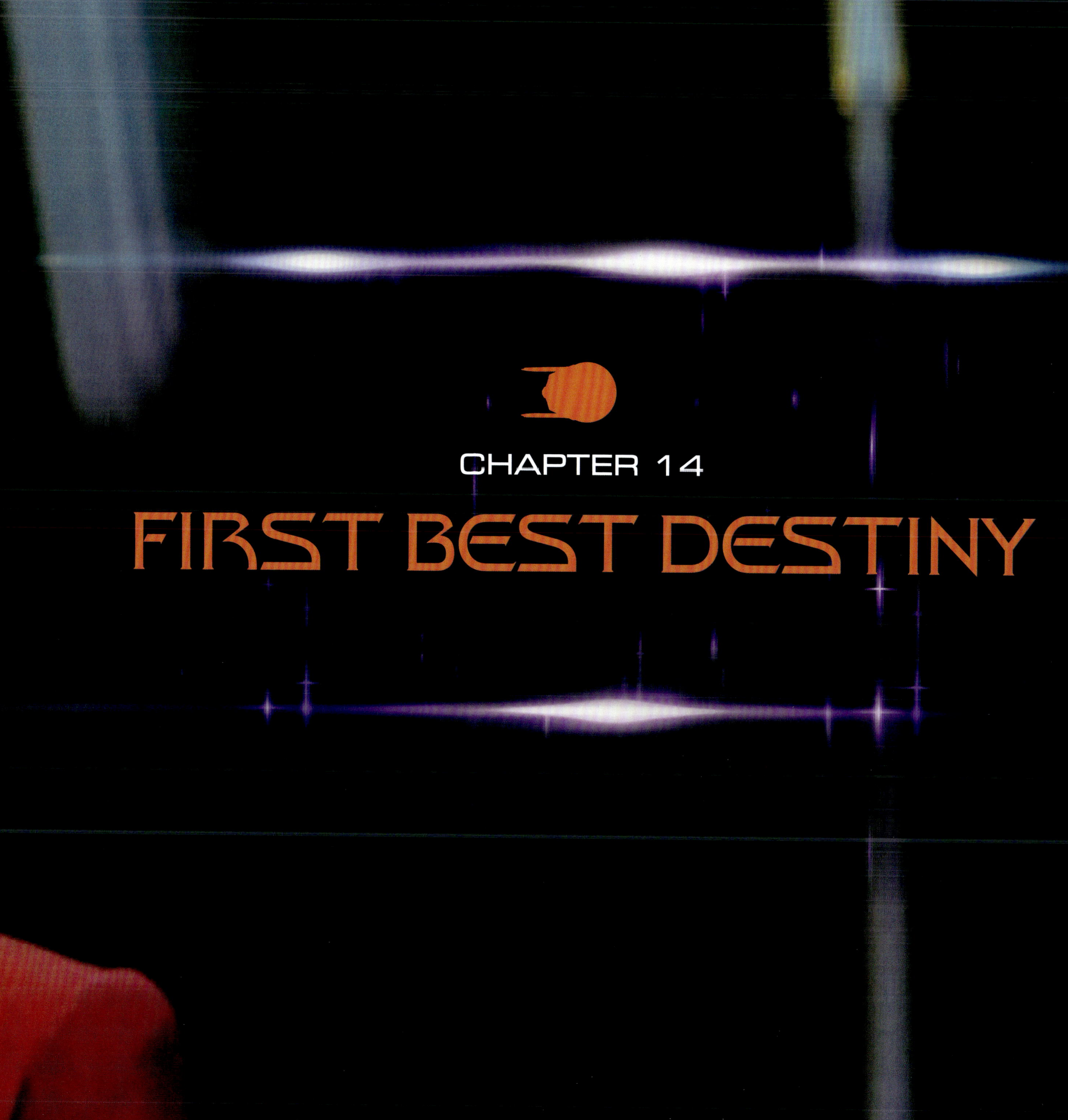

CHAPTER 14
FIRST BEST DESTINY

THE REACTION TO *KHAN*

With the completion of principal photography on January 18, 1982, and a looming June 4 premiere, the proverbial clock was ticking on *Star Trek II* post-production. Several minefields would materialize, requiring the same kind of creative thinking to resolve problems, before facing the biggest minefield of all—audience reaction.

One minefield was the varied conflicts that were occurring between Paramount executives and the film's principal creatives. One of the most important battles was about the naming of the film. During pre-production, the film had been known by many working titles: *War of the Generations*, *The Omega System*, *The Genesis Project*, and *The New Star Trek*. During filming, the movie subtitle was *The Undiscovered Country*, a reference by director Nicholas Meyer to William Shakespeare's *Hamlet*, Act 3, Scene I: "The undiscovered country from whose bourn no traveler returns…"

The Bard had inspired *Star Trek* titles before, and Meyer's reference to the "undiscovered country" was thematically appropriate considering Spock's sacrifice, yet it was not favored by Paramount executives, who wanted a less symbolic moniker. During March 1982, the name was changed to *Star Trek: The Vengeance of Khan* without notifying Meyer or executive producer Harve Bennett.

The duo were not enthusiastic, to say the least, inspiring communications—sometimes diplomatic, sometimes not—between them and Frank Mancuso, President of the Paramount distribution division, Chairman and Chief Executive Officer Barry Diller, and Chief Operations Officer Michael Eisner. In a March 3, 1982 memo to Mancuso, Meyer objected in the strongest terms, believing the name change to be "an undignified label for our story." Put simply, Meyer felt the name was stupid. Additionally, there was concern that *Vengeance of Khan* was imitative of *Revenge of the Jedi*, which was at that time to be the title of the next *Star Wars* film. Meyer called executives out on changing the name without consulting those principally responsible for making the film and for Mancuso making the decision without having read the script or having seen the film yet.[1] By March 10, Bennett and Meyer had been asked to submit their own suggestions if *Vengeance of Khan* was not to their liking. The list included one rejected appellation that would be used

three films later, *Star Trek: The Final Frontier*, the 1989 sequel directed by William Shatner. When *The Wrath of Khan* was chosen as a replacement, it meant *Undiscovered Country* would have to wait almost a decade before it became used as a *Star Trek* film title.

With the name controversy resolved, albeit not to everyone's satisfaction, post-production continued apace. Looping (or dubbing) with the actors took place on March 23-26, and then again on March 29-30 at the historic Raleigh Studios, across the street from Paramount, where Charlie Chaplin and Mary Pickford had filmed sixty years before. Looping requires actors to re-record their lines, usually while watching video of the scene. The newly recorded lines would give supervising sound editors Cecelia Hall and George Watters II cleaner, clearer or alternative recordings to add to the sound mix. March 23 would also see the filming of retakes and a few new moments, including the shorter fight scene between Kirk and David, and a new Kirk line: "As your teacher, Mr. Spock, is fond of saying, I like to think there are always possibilities." Another new scene filmed on March 23 was a close-up on Dr. McCoy as Spock voices, "Remember."

Meyer and Hall—who would go on to be the first woman ever nominated (alongside Watters) for an Academy Award® for Best Sound Effects Editing on another Paramount film, *Top Gun*—were discussing sound effect choices when inspiration struck the director. He knew he wanted the sound of the *Enterprise* engines to be omnipresent, thudding softer or louder as a consequence of which part of the ship the characters were in, and remaining silent when there was damage to

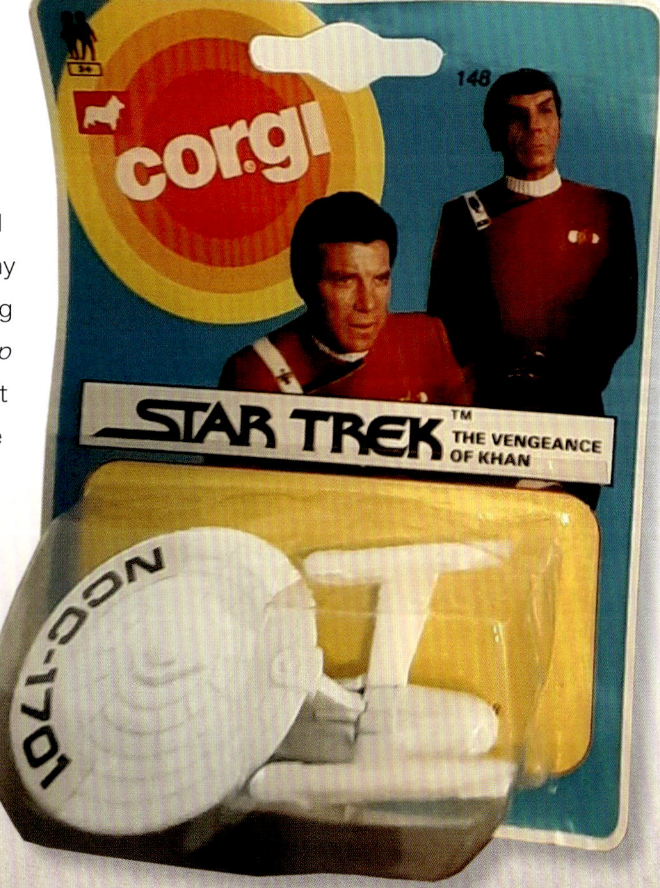

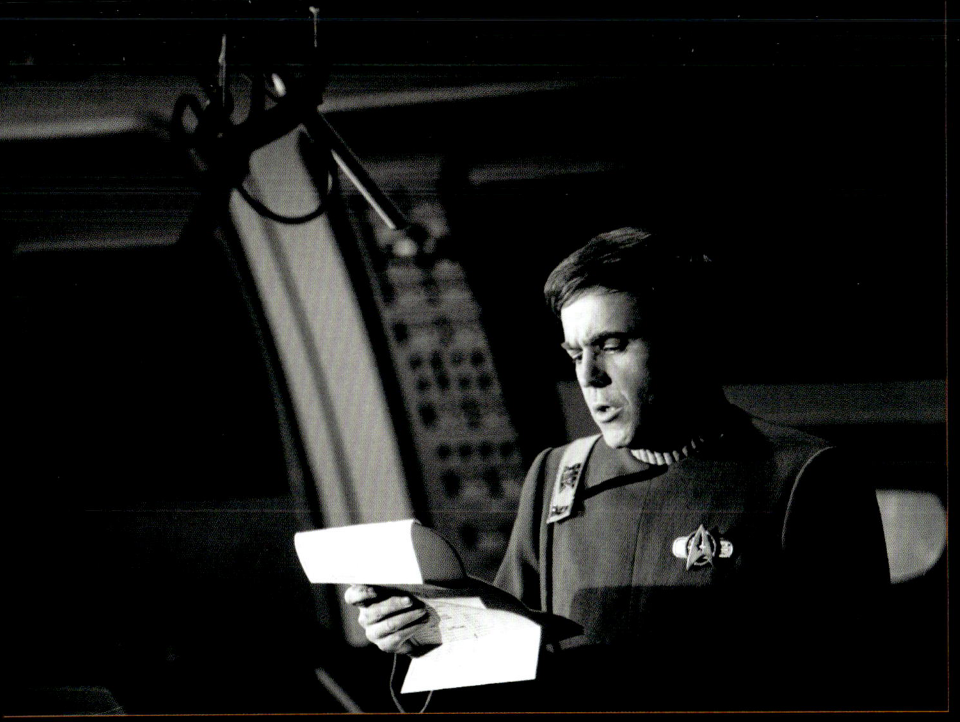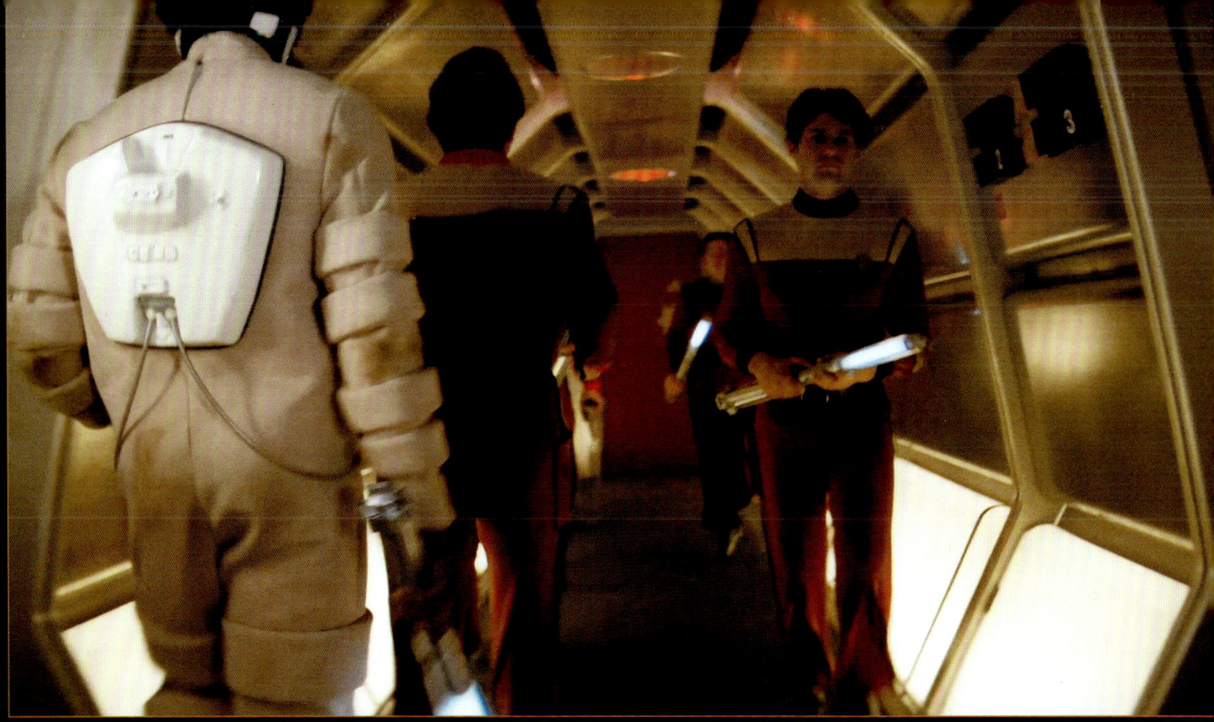

them. As the two spoke, Meyer heard a nearby air conditioning unit and said to Hall, "That's the sound I want!" It was recorded and became the basis for the heartbeat of the *Enterprise.* There was also an experiment with an idea of Meyer's to have no sound of the ship with exterior shots to add realism, but the absence of sound made the ships feel and look like only models. The sound effects by Hall and Watters helped sell the artifice that these were real working starships.[2] Hall and Watters would win the Academy Award® for their sound effects editing of *The Hunt for Red October* a few years later.

Music scoring at The Burbank Studios began on April 12, with a few additional dates added April 30 and May 3 to accommodate the recording of "Amazing Grace," edits that were made to the Genesis Cave and battle in the Mutara Nebula sequences, and the new coda with Spock's casket on the Genesis planet.

The score was scheduled for a four-day session. Budgetary limitations would not permit the return of Jerry Goldsmith, who scored the first film. Meyer and producer Robert Sallin were impressed by a tape of a young composer named James Horner. Horner had observed Goldsmith while the maestro recorded the *Star Trek: The Motion Picture* score a few years before he would be handed the baton. Horner thought that the most important element of *Star Trek* was the relationships, telling Sophie Monks Kaufman in a 2015 interview for the Little White Lies website, "What has to be brought to the surface more in the storytelling is the deep affection that occurs between these two characters, Spock and Kirk, and that's really what I focused on."[3] Meyer recalls that, "The music was to be nautical from the get-go. James Horner and I had several discussions

before a note was written, especially featuring talk of Debussy's 'La Mer,' followed by sessions at my place where we'd sit at the piano while James played themes and we discussed cues."[4] Horner peppered uses of Alexander Courage's original fanfare throughout the film.

The score was recorded on what was then a pioneering technology, a 3M-designed digital system. Atlantic Records made a vinyl LP available to fans. Readers of credits may note that Meyer's sister, Constance Meyer, a violinist and teacher, performs on the soundtrack. Constance contributed to many film scores, from *Pocahontas* and *Back to the Future Part II* to *Star Trek VI: The Undiscovered Country.*

After nearly two years of development, and minefields having to do with scripting, budgeting, and technology, among others, *Star Trek II: The Wrath of Khan* premiered on Friday, June 4, 1982 at 1,621 theaters in the United States. The film would eventually open in nearly twenty other nations, distributed by Cinema International Corporation.

Nearly two years after Bennett's initial meeting with Chairman of Gulf and Western Industries, Inc. Charles G. Bluhdorn, *Star Trek II* faced its greatest minefield: the uncertainty of how fans would react. The film faced tough summer rivalry, with *Rocky III*, *E.T. The Extraterrestrial*, and *Raiders of the Lost Ark* only a few weeks in either direction sharing theater space. Despite the competition, the movie would become the 8th highest grossing film in a year with more than 130 movies released. More than that, by Monday, June 7, *Star Trek II* had the biggest box-office three-day opening in film history, earning $14,347,221.

For fans, the hours in line waiting for the film were spent in fellowship, from playing trivia games to cosplaying (before that term had been

A NOVEL MINEFIELD

During the era before home video and streaming, novelizations were one of the few alternatives for fans wishing to relive their favorite movies without going to theaters. The novelization of *Star Trek II: The Wrath of Khan* by Vonda N. McIntyre was published by Pocket Books, a subsidiary of Simon and Schuster. By June 27, 1982, the book was the sixth bestselling mass market paperback of the week.[3] The novel was translated into numerous languages, including Thai, German, and French. McIntyre, a biologist who was a Nebula Award winner and the third woman ever to earn a Hugo Award for Best Novel, had previously authored the *Star Trek* original novel *The Entropy Effect*, credited for giving Sulu his first name, Hikaru. Because McIntyre was working from scripts that changed during production and post-production, there are some fascinating differences between the novel and the film. The Khan Baby, edited from the film, is featured during the Botany Bay scene. Preston is confirmed as Scotty's nephew, a fact missing from the original theatrical edition of the movie. McIntyre also added details about the Regula I lab scientists and a mentoring relationship between Saavik and Preston. There is no "Remember" scene in the novel.

Yet, the novel almost never came to be. That particular minefield was the result of needing to balance the secret of Spock's sacrifice with the need to publish the novelization before or at least on the same day as the film's theater premiere to maximize profits. It was estimated in production memos that if a novelization was not sold at the time of the film's premiere, it could earn less than one fifteenth of its anticipated sales.

During December 1981, discussions began to determine how or if a novelization could even be produced. One proposal was to sell the book without a final chapter. Fans could buy the book and then return to stores to obtain the final chapter after the film had been in theaters. Another proposal was to release the book with multiple endings, including the real ending. Fans would not know which ending was the honest-to-goodness conclusion. The third proposal got the approval of Paramount executives. The book would be written, but the last chapter would be withheld from printing until the last possible moment. The publisher could then add the last chapter to the book and get the novelization to bookstores on the same day as the film's premiere. This "go day and date" approach made it possible to best preserve the secret and yet get fans the novel when interest was at its highest.

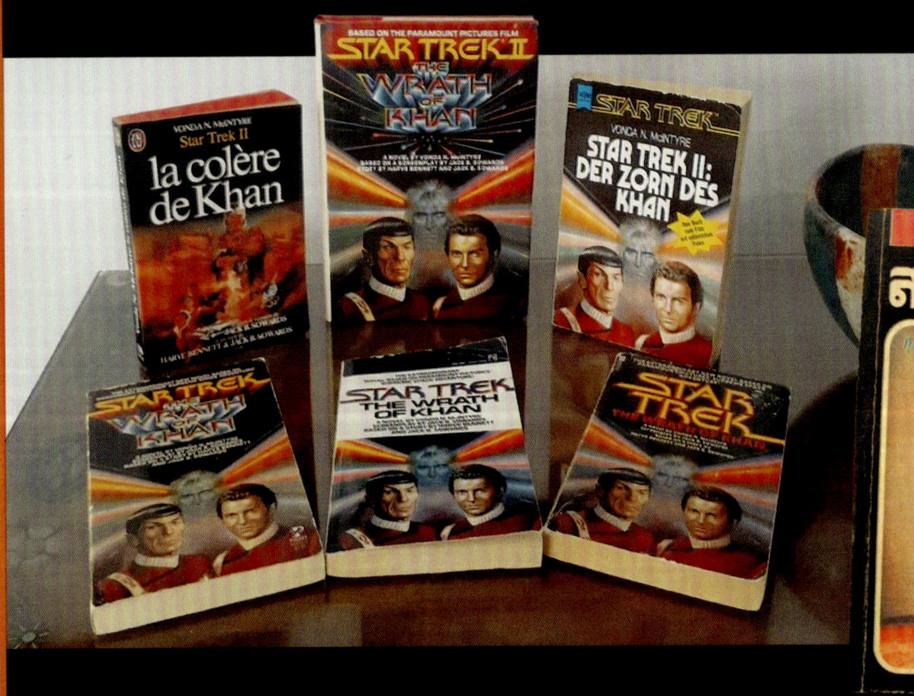

coined for dressing as favorite characters). They not only chatted beforehand, but it was common after the screening for people to stay in theater lobbies or outside with newly made friends discussing and debating the film, although not so loudly as to spoil it for the group waiting in line to see the next showing.

Bennett, traditionally a television creative, enjoyed the new experience of being able to witness audience reaction to his film. "To be able to sit in a theatre and hear your audience react is just wonderful. You're not able to do that with television, because your audience is at home. That's been the gift of *Star Trek* to me."[5] Meyer would see the film on opening night with his parents, siblings, and then-girlfriend at a theater in Times Square, waiting up in anticipation of reviews. The success of the film secured the assurance of another sequel and proved that *Star Trek* had a future. Bennett had been asked to save *Star Trek*, and together with the actors and behind-the-scenes artists and technicians, they did exactly that.

Fan and critic praise was winningly positive and occasionally fulsome. Roger Ebert of the *Sun-Times* wrote in his review words that must have been sweet for those who had worked diligently to bring back to fans a more familiar version of *Star Trek*. Ebert's words stand forty years later as a tribute to all those, still with us or now gone, who side-stepped every minefield with creativity and imagination to produce a science fiction classic:

"The peculiar thing about Spock is that, being half human and half Vulcan and therefore possessing about half the usual quota of human emotions, he consistently, if dispassionately, behaves as if he possessed very heroic human emotions indeed. He makes a choice in "Star Trek II" that would be made only by a hero, a fool, or a Vulcan. And when he makes his decision, the movie rises to one of its best scenes, because the "Star Trek" stories have always been best when they centered around their characters. Although I liked the special effects in the first movie, they were probably not the point; fans of the TV series wanted to see their favorite characters again, and "Trek II" understood that desire and acted on it."[6]

Bennett's favorite review, however, was that of Janet Maslin of *The New York Times*, which began: "NOW this is more like it…"[7]

Evidence of the lasting effect of *The Wrath of Khan* was the announcement by Meyer himself on September 8, 2022, at *Star Trek* Day, that he would be returning to script a new Khan-centric adventure, this time as an audio experience. *Star Trek: Khan: Ceti Alpha V* will be a scripted podcast prequel outlining the years of exile endured by Khan and his followers as they struggled to build a new world. Executive producer Alex Kurtzman said, "Nick made the definitive *Trek* movie when he made *Wrath*, and we've all been standing in its shadow since. Forty years have offered him a lot of perspective on these extraordinary characters and the way they've impacted generations of fans. Now he's come up with something as surprising, gripping and emotional as the original, and it's a real honor to be able to let him tell the next chapter in this story exactly the way he wants to."[9] As with much of *Star Trek II*'s legacy, the new story will be pioneering: the first scripted podcast in *Star Trek* history. And so the adventure continues…

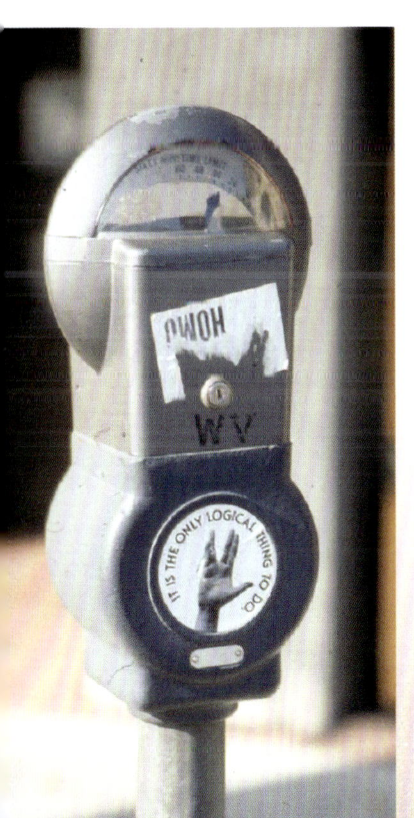

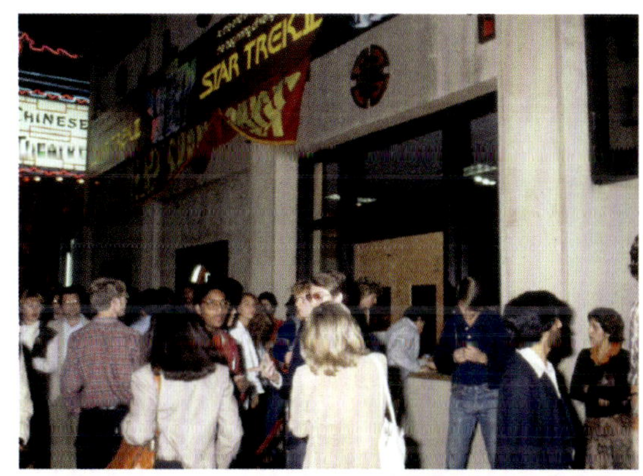

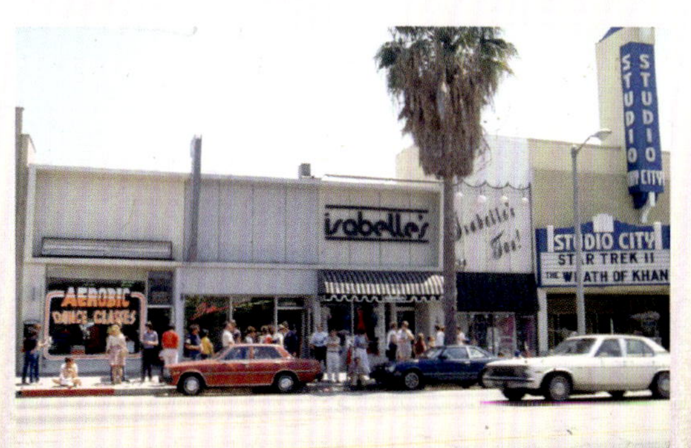

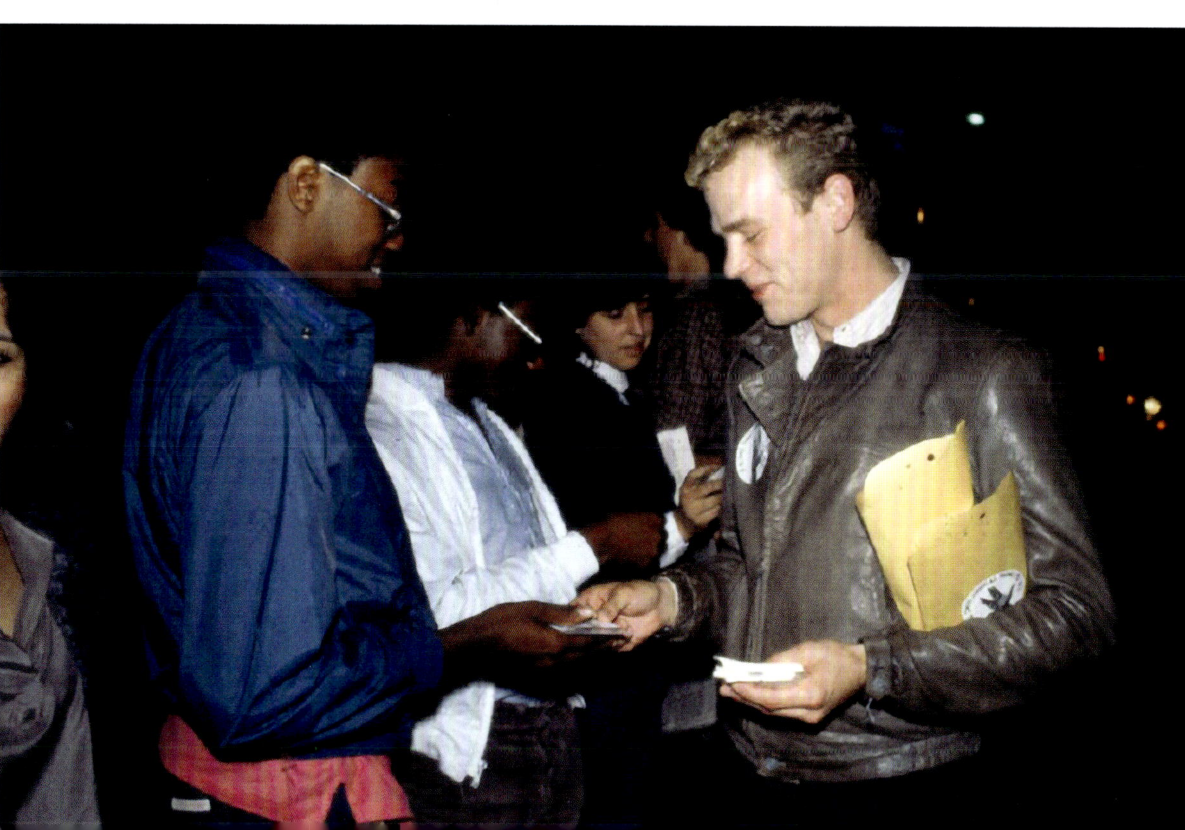

KHAN-LLECTIBLES

Despite *Star Trek II* being an unqualified success, there was less memorabilia to collect for the sequel, mostly because of trepidations about the somewhat disappointing sales of *Star Trek: The Motion Picture* merchandise. That is not to say that there was nothing on store shelves. There was the soundtrack, the novelization, tie-in books, mugs, keychains, buttons, pendants, magazines, posters, ViewMasters, an Armitron video game watch, 5 by 7 inch trading cards from Fantasy Trading Card Company, cards from Monty Gum, role-playing miniatures, and ships from Corgi, to name a few. However, proper action figures would have to wait until Playmates Toys Limited sold a Khan and Saavik figure and even more, and until the film's twenty-fifth anniversary for Diamond Select Toys to produce an entire line of figures for *Star Trek II*. It would be 2009 when the comic book adaption was available from IDW Publishing. Then there was the story of the VHS tape.

During the late 1970s and early 1980s, VHS, Betamax, and CED players were becoming increasingly common. However, due to the cost of the actual tapes, most people could not afford to purchase their own copies and thus rented films on VHS or Betamax. A single blank tape was $20 or more during the 1970s, and a tape with a movie on it was usually $80 and up. To rent a film at a video store usually required a deposit commensurate with the cost of a film, or at least the placement of a credit card on file, due to the high costs of the tapes. Many stores only allowed the rental of one or two tapes at a time. Paramount ran a unique experiment during the summer of 1982 in an effort to determine if there might be interest by consumers in purchasing films on VHS and Betamax to own. Such an experiment would require two things: offering TV shows or films directly to consumers that would be popular enough to entice people to buy them, and a lower price tag. Enter "Space Seed" and *Star Trek II: The Wrath of Khan*.

Along with a select group of titles such as *Raiders of the Lost Ark*, Paramount's home video production group, named Paramount Gateway, made "Space Seed" available during June 1982. With *Star Trek II* as the

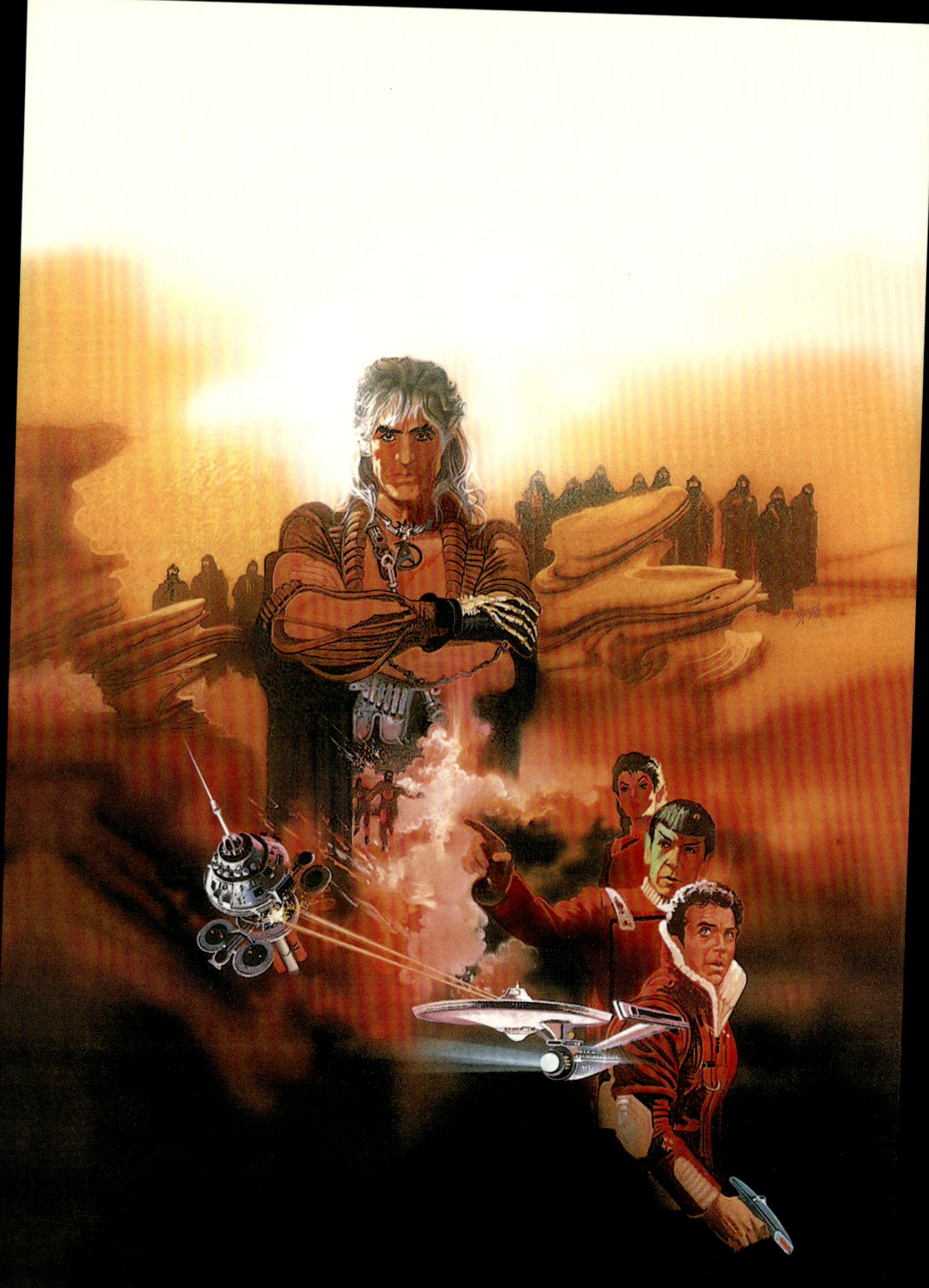

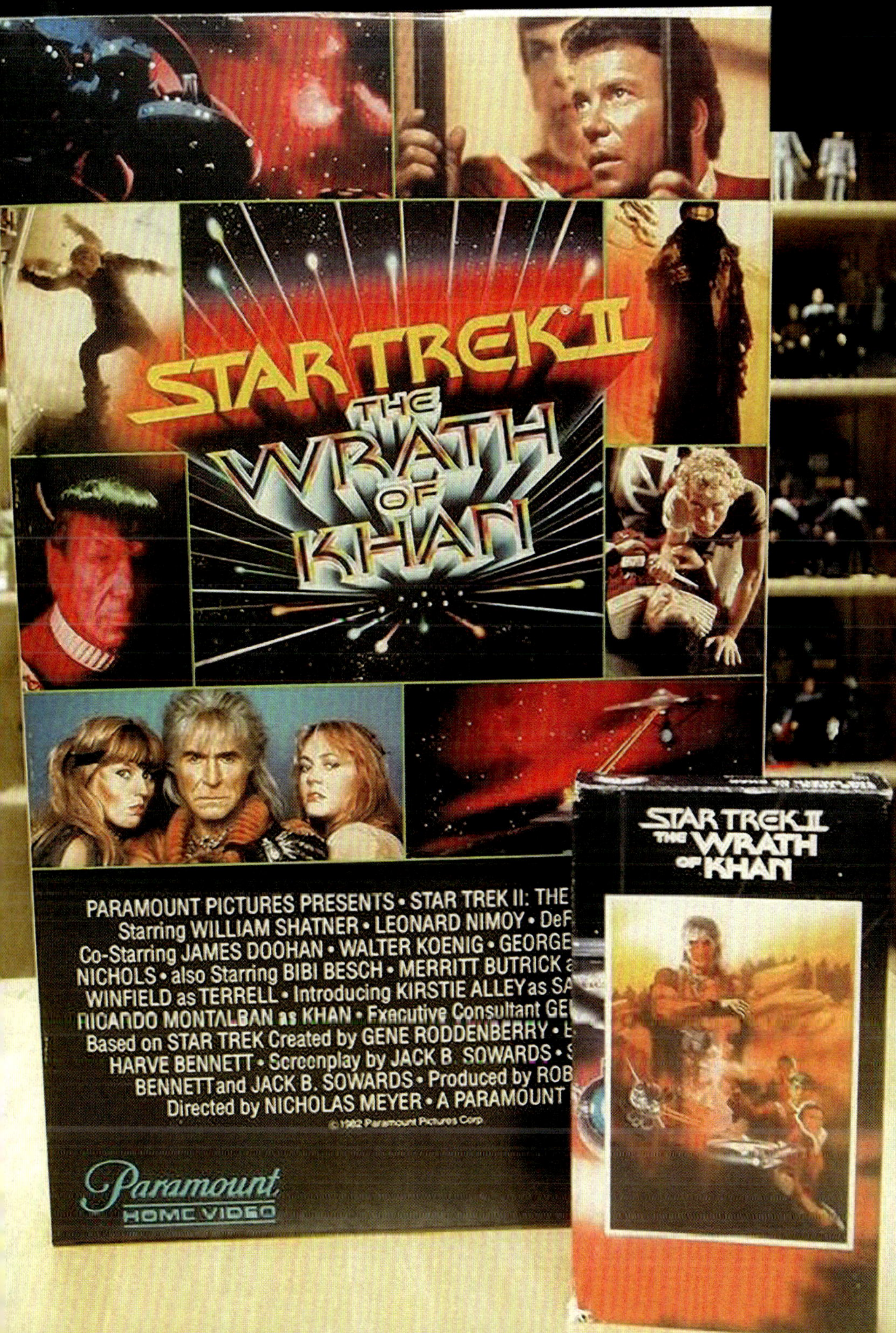

biggest opening box office weekend in cinema history earlier that month, "Space Seed" seemed an appropriate episode to test the interest in what would become known as the "sell through" market. When "Space Seed" was released on VHS that June, it earned the distinction of being the first *Star Trek* episode ever released on video tape designed specifically for the home ownership market rather than rental. The question: Would fans be willing to spend $29.95 for the *Star Trek* episode that inspired the film?

The answer was an unqualified yes.

A check of Billboard's "Videocassette Top 40" shows that "Space Seed" stayed on the list of bestselling tapes nearly every week from the summer until the end of the year, and into 1983, bolstered again by the release of *Star Trek II* on home video. Some versions of the tapes had a bonus film trailer, while others did not.

Indeed, lightning struck again when *Star Trek II* was made available to the home market at $39.95, a saving of about $40 compared to the then-available *Star Wars* films and the previously available *Star Trek: The Motion Picture*. There was an extensive advertising campaign, complemented by a Paramount-sponsored retailer contest through which store owners assembled creative displays.

By 1983, *Star Trek II* was the bestselling videocassette ever at that time. Expectations of sixty-thousand sales were more than doubled in actual sales. This success was important because *Star Trek* played an important role in popularizing the idea of home video libraries. "Space Seed" gave Paramount the confidence to eventually offer every original series episode for purchase, a precursor to today's DVD, Blu-ray, and streaming collections. *Raiders of the Lost Ark* and *Star Trek II* demonstrated that movie fans would buy their favorite films to watch again and again whenever they wished, the beginnings of the on-demand experience common today.

APPENDIX: FOOTNOTES

CHAPTER 1

1. McWhirter, Norris. *Guinness Book of World Records 1985 Special Book Fair Edition*. NY: Bantam Books, 1985. Pg. 238.
2. Malcolm, Derek. "Arts Guardian." *The Guardian*. 20 Dec. 1979. Pg. 9.
3. Sources: Bennett, Harve. *Star Trek Communicator*. Number 150. June July 2004. Pg. 47. Shatner, William, with Chris Kreski. *Star Trek Movie Memories*. NY: HarperCollins Publishers, 1994. Pg. 100-102. *Television Academy Foundation*. Harve Bennett Interview by Stephen J. Abramson. 13 Feb. 2008.
4. Madsen, Dan. *Star Trek: The Official Fan Club Magazine*. Number 50. June July 1986. Pg. 7.
5. Asherman, Allan. *The Making of Star Trek II: The Wrath of Khan*. NY: Pocket Books, 1982. Pg. 78.
6. *Television Academy Foundation*. Harve Bennett Interview by Stephen J. Abramson. 13 Feb. 2008.
7. *Ibid*.
8. Spelling, Ian. "Interview with Harve Bennett." *StarTrek.com*. 2010 Aug. 23.
9. *Television Academy Foundation*. Harve Bennett Interview by Stephen J. Abramson. 13 Feb. 2008.
10. Madsen, Dan. "Harve Bennett." *Star Trek: The Official Fan Club Magazine*. Number 55. April May 1987. Pg. 4.
11. Asherman, Allan. *The Making of Star Trek II: The Wrath of Khan*. NY: Pocket Books, 1982. Pg. 81.

CHAPTER 2

1. Bennett, Harve. *Star Trek Communicator*. No. 150. Pg. 47.
2. Pascale, Anthony. "Interview: Nicholas Meyer on Roddenberry, Shatner, And The Unsung Hero of *Star Trek II*." Trekmovie.com. 1 Sep. 2017.
3. Goldberg, Lee. "Jack B. Sowards: The Man Who Killed Mr. Spock." *Starlog*. No. 67. Pg. 25.

CHAPTER 3

1. Meyer, Nicholas. Personal interview. 22 Sep. 2021.
2. *Ibid*.
3. *Ibid*.
4. *Ibid*.
5. *Ibid*.
6. *Ibid*.
7. Madsen, Dan. "Exclusive Interview: Nichelle Nichols." *The Official Star Trek II: The Movie Fan Club*. April 1983. Issue 37.
8. *Ibid*.
9. Adamo, Susan, editor and compiler. "Log Entries: *Star Trek* Back on TV Track." *Starlog*. May 1981. Issue 46. Pg. 9.
10. "Nicholas Meyer Directs '*Star Trek II* For Par; TV For US; Screen O'Seas," *Weekly Variety*. 9 Sep. 1981, Pg 4.
11. Burns, James H. "The Man Who Saved *Star Trek*: Nicholas Meyer." *StarBlazer*. 1982. Pg. 53.
12. Meyer, Nicholas. Personal Interview. 22 Sep. 2021.

CHAPTER 4

1. Meyer, Nicholas. *The View From the Bridge*. NY: Viking Press, 2009. Pg. 86. © Nicholas Meyer 2009.
2. Spelling, Ian. "Catching Up with Kirstie Alley." *StarTrek.com*. 15 Aug. 2016.
3. Madsen, Dan. "Interview With Bibi Besch." *Star Trek II: The Movie Fan Club*. No. 29. August 1982.
4. *Ibid*.
5. Madsen, Dan, and John S. Davis. "Merritt Butrick." *Star Trek: The Official Fan Club*. No. 49 April/May 1986. Pg. 15.
6. *Ibid*.
7. *Ibid*. Pg. 16.
8. "Interview: Paul Winfield." *Star Trek: The Magazine*. Vol. 3. No. 5. Pg. 91.
9. "Interview: Nicholas Meyer." *Star Trek: The Magazine*. Vol. 3. No. 5. Pg. 17.

CHAPTER 5

1. Montalban, Ricardo, with Bob Thomas. *Reflections: A Life in Two Worlds*. Garden City: Doubleday & Company, Inc., 1980.
2. Madsen, Dan. "Exclusive Interview: Ricardo Montalban." *The Official Star Trek II The Movie Fan Club Magazine*. No. 41. Pg. 2.
3. *Ibid*. Pg. 3.
4. Maslin, Janet. "New "*Star Trek*" Full of Gadgets and Fun." *The New York Times*. 4 June 1982. Section C. Page 12.
5. Interview. September 6, 2021.
6. Meyer, Nicholas. *The View From the Bridge*. NY: Viking, 2009. Pg. 107. © Nicholas Meyer 2009.
7. "Interview: Robert Fletcher." *Star Trek: The Magazine*. Vol. 3. No. 5. Pg. 95.
8. *Ibid*. Pg. 147.
9. Bonds, Martha. "Judson Scott: A Phoenix Rises from the Ashes." *Starlog*. No. 71. Pg. 15.
10. *Ibid*.
11. Interview. 6 September 2021.
12. *Ibid*.
13. Madsen, Dan. "Exclusive Interview: Laura Banks." *Star Trek II: The Movie Fan Club*. No. 33.
14. Bonds, Martha. "Judson Scott: A Phoenix Rises from the Ashes." *Starlog*. No. 71. Pg. 15.

CHAPTER 6

1. Interview: Robert Fletcher." *Star Trek: The Magazine*. Vol. 3. No. 5. Pg. 95.
2. Anderson, Kay. "*Star Trek: The Wrath of Khan*. How the TV series became a hit movie, at last." *Cinefantastique*. Volume 12. No. 5. No

13. Meyer, Nicholas. *The View from the Bridge: Memories of Star Trek and a Life in Hollywood*. NY: Viking Press, 2009. Pg. 99. © Nicholas Meyer 2009.
14. *Ibid*.

6. Pg. 56.
3. *Ibid*. Pg. 57.
4. "Interview: Robert Fletcher." *Star Trek: The Magazine*. Vol. 3. No. 5. Pg. 93.
5. Asherman, Allan. *The Making of Star Trek II: The Wrath of Khan*. NY: Pocket Books, 1982. Pg. 105.
6. Asherman, Allan. *The Star Trek Interview Book*. NY: Pocket Books, 1988. Pg. 259.
7. "Interview: Robert Fletcher." *Star Trek: The Magazine*. Vol. 3. No. 5. Pg. 95.
8. "Interview: Robert Fletcher." *Star Trek: The Magazine*. Vol. 3. No. 5. Pg. 95.
9. Meyer, Nicholas. *A View from the Bridge*. London: Penguin Publishers, 2010. Pg. 95. © Nicholas Meyer 2010.
10. Meyer, Nicholas. Personal interview. 22 Sep. 2021.
11. Banks, Laura. Personal interview. 6 Sep. 2021.
12. Burns, James H. "The Man Who Saved *Star Trek*: Nicholas Meyer." *StarBlazer*. 1982. Pg. 54.
13. "Interview: Robert Fletcher." *Star Trek: The Magazine*. Vol. 3. No. 5. Pg. 94.

CHAPTER 7

1. Roddenberry, Eugene. "*Star Trek*-TV's Newest-Part I." *TV Week* Guest Columnist. Syndicated. 26 June 1966.
2. Coleman, Henry, interviewer. "Joseph Jennings, Production Designer." *The Interviews*. Conducted 17 October 2002. *Television Academy Foundation*. https://interviews.televisionacademy.com/interviews/joseph-jennings
3. Van Hise, James. "Mike Minor: *Star Trek* Through the Years." *Enterprise Incidents*. No. 14. 1984 February. Pg. 50.
4. Rance, Mark, with Jennifer Peterson, producers. "Designing *Khan*." *Star Trek II: The Wrath of Khan*. DVD Bonus Feature.
5. *Ibid*.
6. *Star Trek: The Wrath of Khan Official Movie Magazine*. Starlog Press, Inc. 1982. Pg. 41.
7. Nicholas Meyer. Personal interview. 22 Sept. 2021.
8. Rance, Mark, with Jennifer Peterson, producers. "Designing *Khan*." *Star Trek II: The Wrath of Khan*. DVD Bonus Feature.
9. Van Hise, James. "Mike Minor: *Star Trek* Through the Years." *Enterprise Incidents*. No. 14. 1984 February. Pg. 51.
10. *Ibid*.
11. "Interview: Paul Winfield." *Star Trek: The Magazine*. Vol. 3. No. 5. Pg. 91.
12. *Ibid*.
13. Van Hise, James. "Mike Minor: *Star Trek* Through the Years." *Enterprise Incidents*. No. 14. 1984 February. Pg. 51.

CHAPTER 8

1. Anderson, Kay. "*Star Trek: The Wrath of Khan*: How the TV series became a hit movie, at last." *Cinefantastique*. Volume 12. Nos. 5 & 6. (July & August 1982) Pg. 73

2. "ILM: Visual Effects." *Star Trek: The Magazine*. September 2002. Pg. 19.

3. Smith, Alvy Ray. "Special Effects for *Star Trek II*: The Genesis Demo: Instant Evolution with Computer Graphics." American Cinematographer. October 1982. Pg. 1050.

4. *Star Trek: The Wrath of Khan Official Movie Magazine*. Starlog Press, Inc. 1982. Pg. 53.

5. Rance, Mark, with Jennifer Peterson, producers. "Designing Khan." *Star Trek II: The Wrath of Khan*. DVD Bonus Feature.

6. *Ibid.*

7. "ILM: Visual Effects." *Star Trek: The Magazine*. September 2002.

8.

9. "ILM: Visual Effects." *Star Trek: The Magazine*. Sept. 2002. Pg. 24.

10. *Ibid.*

11. *Ibid.*

12. Meyer, Nicholas. Personal interview. 22 Sep. 2021.

13. Ralston, Kenneth. Personal interview. 1 Nov. 2021.

14. *Star Trek: The Wrath of Khan Official Movie Magazine*. Starlog Press, Inc. 1982. Pg. 53.

15. Elkins Judy. Personal interview. 12 Aug. 2021.

16. Elkins, Judy. Personal interview. 12 Aug. 2021.

17. *Ibid.*

CHAPTER 9

1. "Interview: Robert Sallin" *Star Trek: The Magazine*. Vol. 3. No. 5. Pg. 47.

2. "Ceti Eels" *Star Trek: The Magazine*. Vol. 3. No. 5. Pg. 27.

3. *Ibid.*

4. Ralston, Kenneth. Personal interview. 5 Nov. 2021.

5. Anderson, Kay. "*Star Trek: The Wrath of Khan*: How the TV series became a hit movie, at last." *Cinefantastique*. Volume 12. No. 5. No 6. Pg. 63.

6. Ralston, Kenneth. Personal interview. 5 Nov. 2021.

7. "Ceti Eels" *Star Trek: The Magazine*. Vol. 3. No. 5. Pg. 30.

8. "Ceti Eels" *Star Trek: The Magazine*. Vol. 3. No. 5. Pg. 30.

9. Ralston, Kenneth. Personal interview. 5 Nov. 2021.

10. "Interview: Paul Winfield" *Star Trek: The Magazine*. Vol. 3. No. 5. Pg 91.

11. "Interview: Walter Koenig." *Star Trek: The Magazine*. Vol. 3. No. 5. Pg. 57.

CHAPTER 10

1. Meyer, Nicholas. Personal interview. 22 Sept. 2021.

2. Burns, James H. "The Man Who Saved *Star Trek*: Nicholas Meyer." StarBlazer. 1982. Pg. 53.

3. Meyer, Nicholas. Personal interview. 22 Sep. 2021.

4. Meyer, Nicholas. Personal interview. 22 Sep. 2021.

5. *The Center Seat: 55 Years of Star Trek*. The Nacelle Company. Dir. Brian Volk-Weiss. 2021.

6. Meyer, Nicholas. Personal interview. 22 Sep. 2021. -

7. Gold, Daniel, SOC. "Establishing Shot." *Camera Operator*. Spring 2015. Pg. 10.

CHAPTER 11

1. Nimoy, Leonard. *I Am Spock*. NY: Hyperion, 1995. Pg. 28.

2. Anderson, Kay. "*Star Trek: The Wrath of Khan*: How the TV series became a hit movie, at last." *Cinefantastique*. Volume 12. No. 5. No 6. Pg. 64.

3. *Ibid.*

4. *Ibid.* Pg. 65.

5. Spelling, Ian. "Catching Up With Kirstie Alley." *StarTrek.com*. 15 August 2016.

6. Madsen, Dan. "Kirstie Alley." *Star Trek The Official Fan Club*. No. 50. Pg. 18.

7. Spelling, Ian. "Spelling, Ian. "Catching Up With Khan's Peter Preston, Ike Eisenmann." *StarTrek.com*.

8. Anderson, Kay. "*Star Trek: The Wrath of Khan*: How the TV series became a hit movie, at last." *Cinefantastique*. Volume 12. No. 5. No 6. Pg. 65.

9. Spelling, Ian. "Spelling, Ian. "Catching Up With Khan's Peter Preston, Ike Eisenmann." *StarTrek.com*.

10. Madsen, Dan. "Kirstie Alley." *Star Trek The Official Fan Club*. No. 50. Pg. 18.

11. Madsen, Dan. "Laura Banks. *Star Trek II: The Movie Fan Club*. #33. Pgs. 5-6.

12. Davis, John S. "Ricardo Montalban." *Star Trek: The Official Fan Club*. #71. Pg. 8.

13. "Haircut Proves Lucky for DeForest Kelly." 1967 Aug. 7. *The Herald Journal*. Pg. 13.

14. Meyer, Nicholas. Personal interview. 22 Sep. 2021.

CHAPTER 12

1. Andonaras, Tula. "Asheville Native is Movie Stunt man." *Asheville Citizen Times*. 6 January 1989. Pg. 44.

2. *Ibid.*

3. Gilpin, Kris. "The Universe Beneath His Heel." *Starlog*. December 1989. No. 149. Pg. 65.

4. *Ibid.*

5. Madsen, Dan. "Exclusive Interview: George Takei." *Star Trek II: The Movie Fan Club*. January 1983. Issue 34.

6. "Interview: Walter Koenig" *Star Trek: The Magazine*. Vol. 3. No. 5. Pg. 57.

7. Andonaras, Tula. "Asheville Native is Movie Stunt man." *Asheville Citizen Times*. 6 January 1989. Pg. 44.

CHAPTER 13

1. Nimoy, Leonard. *I Am Spock*. NY: Hyperion, 1995. Pg. 180.

2. *Ibid.* Pg. 179.

3. Naha, Ed. "The Re-Making of *Star Trek*: Part II." *Starlog*. Aug. 1982. No. 61. Pg. 20.

4. Nimoy, Leonard. *I Am Spock*. NY: Hyperion, 1995. Pg. 180.

5. Stephen J. Sansweet, "Does Mr. Spock Die In the Next Episode Of 'Star Trek' Saga?" Wall Street Journal, October 9, 1981.

6. Nimoy, Leonard. *I Am Spock*. NY: Hyperion, 1995. Pg. 193.

7. Meyer, Nicholas. Email communication. 1 Feb. 2022.

8. Nimoy, Leonard. *I Am Spock*. NY: Hyperion, 1995. Pg. 205.

9. Handley, Rich. "*Star Trek II* at 20." *Star Trek Communicator*. October November 2002. Issue 140. Pg. 45.

10. Meyer, Nicholas. *The View from The Bridge*. 2009: Viking. New York. Pgs. 130-131. © Nicholas Meyer 2009.

11. *Star Trek: The Omega System*. The Story by Jack B. Sowards and Harve Bennett. Revised Final Draft revised. 30 January 1981 pgs. 6 and 7.

12. Meyer, Nicholas. Personal interview. 22 Sept. 2021.

13. Nimoy, Julie. Personal interview. 29 Aug. 2021.

14. Shatner, William, with Chris Kreski. *Star Trek Movie Memories*. NY: Harper Collins, 1994. Pg. 128.

15. Nimoy, Leonard. *I Am Spock*. NY: Hyperion, 1995. Pg.206.

16. Nimoy, Leonard. *I Am Spock*. NY: Hyperion, 1995. Pg. 198.

17. *Ibid.* Pg. 212.

18. Madsen, Dan. "Exclusive Interview: Nichelle Nichols." *The Official Star Trek II: The Movie Fan Club*. April 1983. Issue 37.

19. Madsen, Dan. "Exclusive Interview: George Takei." *Star Trek II: The Movie Fan Club*. January 1983. Issue 34.

20. Madsen, Dan. "Exclusive Interview: Nicholas Meyer." *The Official Star Trek II: The Movie Fan Club*. March 1983. Issue 36.

CHAPTER 14

1. Meyer, Nicholas. Email communication. 1 Feb. 2022.

2. Meyer, Nicholas. Email communication. 1 Feb. 2022.

3. Monks Kaufman, Sophie. "James Horner Reveals the Story Behind Five of His Classic Film Scores." *Little White Lies*. 30 Apr. 2015. https://lwlies.com/articles/james-horner-reveals-the-story-behind-five-of-his-classic-film-scores/

4. Meyer, Nicholas. Email communication. 1 Feb. 2022.

5. Madsen, Dan. "Harve Bennett Interview." *Star Trek: The Official Fan Club Magazine*. June July 1987. No. 56. Pg. 24.

6. Ebert, Roger. *Star Trek II: The Wrath of Khan* Review. June 1982. Rogerebert.com.

7. Maslin, Janet. "New '*Star Trek*' Full of Gadgets and Fun." 4 June 1982. *The New York Times*. Section C, Page 12.

8. *The New York Times*. 27 June 1982. Section 7. Page 28.

9. "2022: First Scripted Podcast *Star Trek: Khan: Ceti Alpha V* Announced." StarTrek.com. 8 September 2022.

ACKNOWLEDGMENTS

Kirk: "I don't know what to say."
McCoy: "Well, you could say thank you."

The authors are grateful to the following individuals:

Kay Anderson, for writing the singularly best making of article about *Star Trek II* in 1982.

Allan Asherman, whose original making of book gave fans the first look behind the curtain.

Laura Banks, for her time and insights.

Harve Bennett, posthumous thanks for writing to us long ago and for saving *Star Trek*.

Bruce Birmelin, for his historic photography.

Jo Boylett, for counsel and advice.

Paul Camuso, for his usual willingness to help.

Marian Cordry, for photographic resources.

Judy Elkins, for helping us understand the art of visual effects and for everything you contributed to *Star Trek*.

David Knight, for encouragement and sharing of his family resources.

Michael Kmet, for his scholarship and research.

Dan Madsen, for being THE source of *Star Trek* information for a generation.

Adam Malin, for bringing the celebrities and generations of fans together.

Ian McLean, for his time and memories.

Industrial Light & Magic, for amazing behind-the-scenes photographs.

Sean McMahon, for resources.

Nicholas Meyer, for writing and directing our favorite film and for making John's dad laugh in 1982 with your line, "Can I cook, or can't I?"

Maurice Molyneaux, for his research and concern about the facts.

Larry Nemecek, Dr. Trek for certain.

Julie Nimoy, for sharing her remembrances and experiences of Leonard.

Denise Okuda, for her inspirational journey from fan to *Star Trek* professional.

Michael Okuda, for his defining designs and helping us contact his colleagues.

Kenneth Ralston, one of the really good guys who happens to be a genius visual effects artist.

William Robinson, the designer of this book, who made our words better with his artistry and, to riff on Spock's observation, his "three" dimensional thinking.

Stephen J. Sansweet, journalist and collector, for making it cool to be a science fiction fan.

Anita Montalban-Smith, for her remembrances of Ricardo, and above everything, her courage.

Gilbert Smith, for his generosity and for continuing to preserve Anita and Ricardo's dreams.

Lydia Smith, for sharing her family memories.

Ian Spelling, for starting us out and for hours of advice.

James Tenuto, for buying John the *Star Trek II* music cassette in 1982.

Joseph Tenuto, even though he got to see *Star Trek: The Motion Picture* before John did.

John Van Citters, for his confidence and for caring about *Star Trek* so much.

Brian Volk-Weiss, our friend who documents everything *Star Trek*.

Simon Ward, for the original invitation to write this book.

DEDICATION

To all those lost to us
Who worked on *Star Trek II*
You beat the no-win scenario
Because your art lives on.

ABOUT THE AUTHORS

John Tenuto and Maria Jose Tenuto have been sociology professors for twenty-four years. John was named the 2020 Association of Community College Trustees' Central Regional Faculty Member Award winner, recognizing him as one of the top five community college educators in the nation. Maria Jose was named the 2019 Illinois Outstanding Adjunct Faculty of the Year by the Illinois Community College Trustee Association. The couple have been married for twenty-four years and have a twenty-year-old son named Nicholas Jose.

John first saw *Star Trek II: The Wrath of Khan* at the Esquire Theatre in Chicago on opening night with his late father Vincent. When John and Maria Jose were married, their wedding song was the theme to *Star Trek: Voyager*. The couple's research on *Star Trek* has been featured in *Wired* magazine, *USA Today*, *Chicago Sun-Times*, and on CBS, WGN, and the BBC. They have been featured in the Netflix TV show *The Toys That Made Us* and the History Channel's *The Center Seat: 55 Years of Star Trek* docuseries, and have been invited to speak at the Official *Star Trek* Convention, the St. Louis Science Center, and by the future birthplace of James T. Kirk, Riverside, Iowa, and the town of Vulcan, Alberta, Canada.

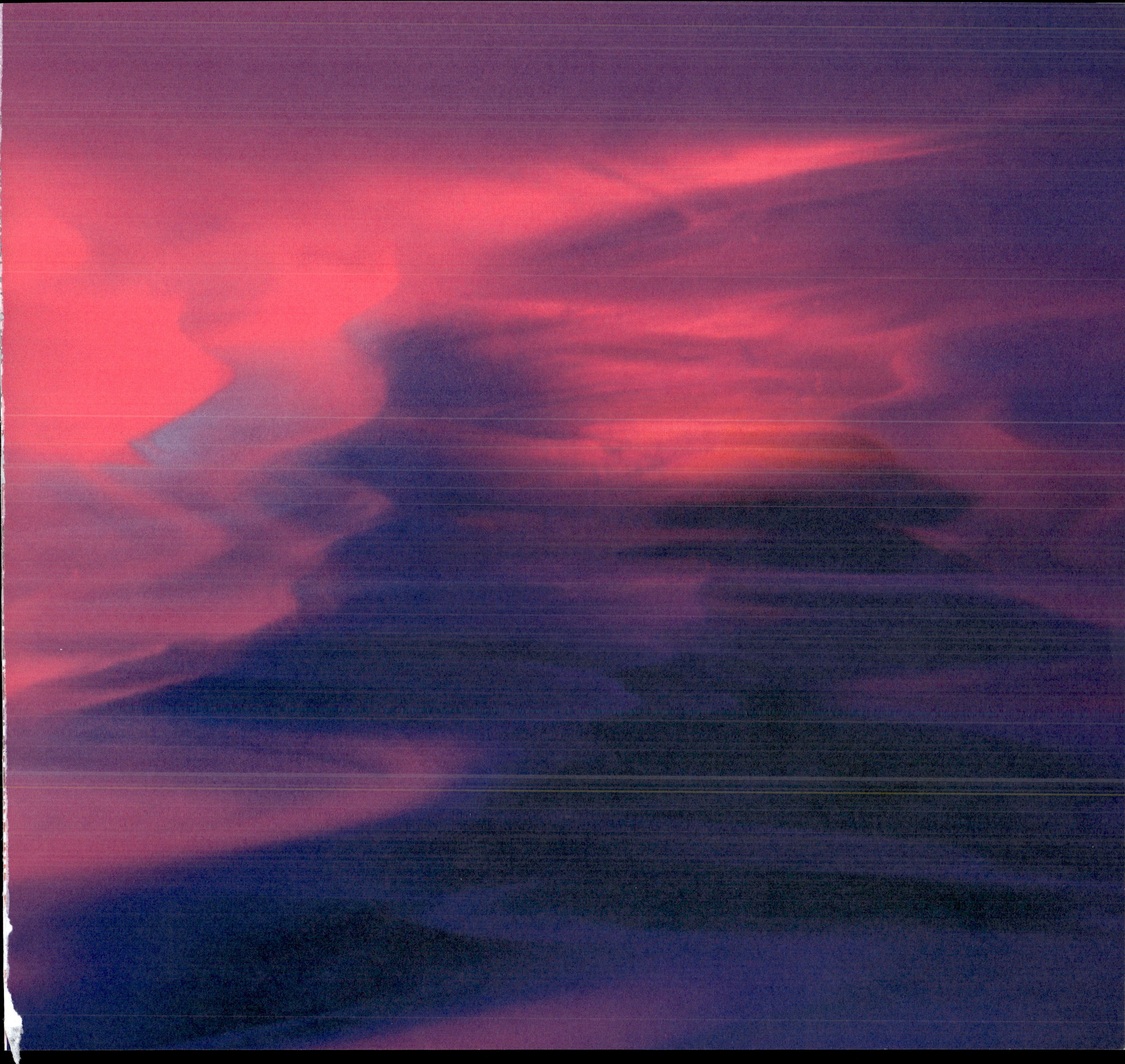

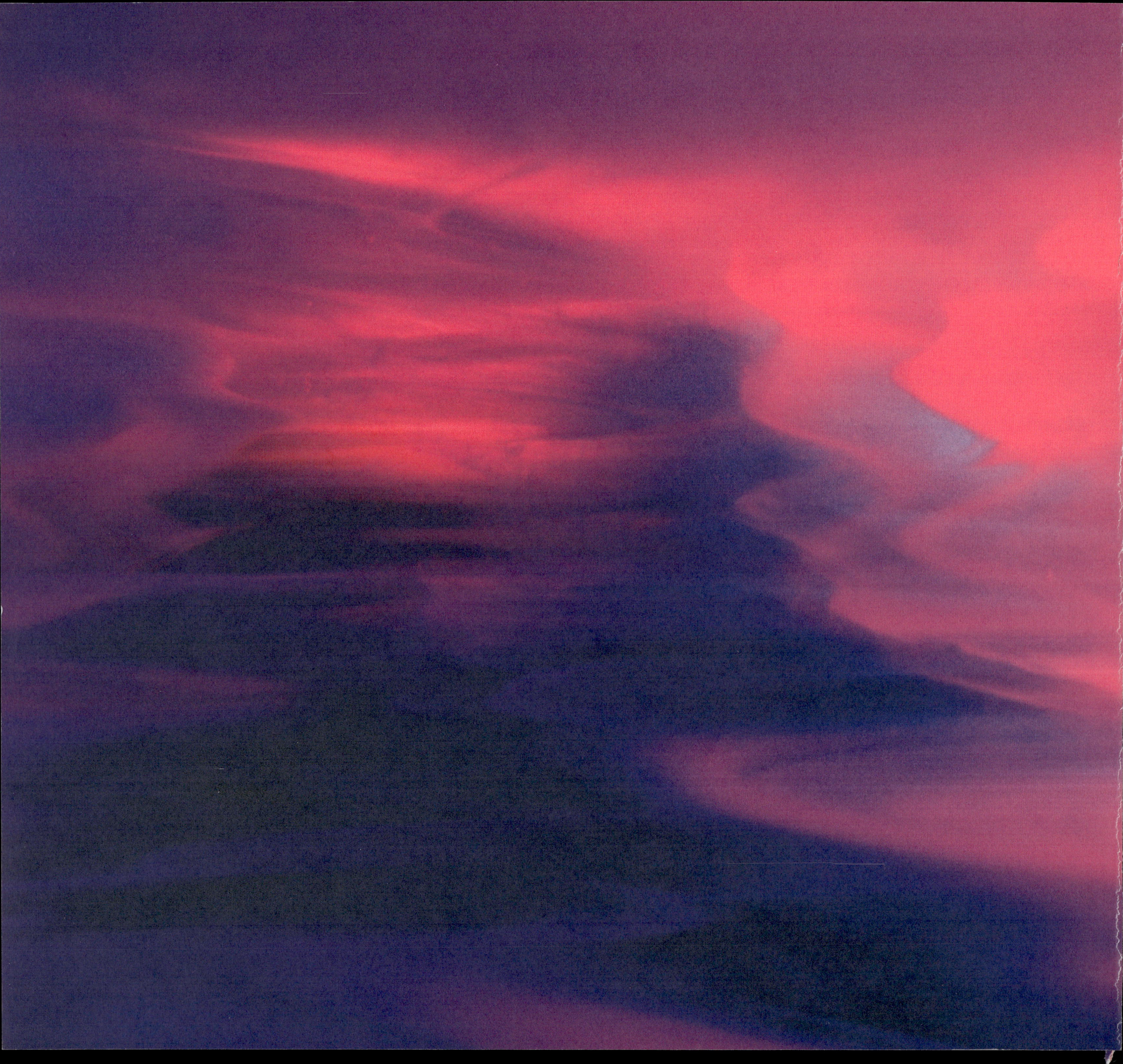